Global Perspectives
on the
Education of the Deaf
in
Selected Countries

Edited by H. William Brelje

Butte Publications, Inc.
Hillsboro, Oregon

Global Perspectives on the Education of the Deaf in Selected Countries

Edited by H. William Brelje

Acknowledgements:

Editor: Ellen Todras
Cover Illustration: Brad Henson
Design & Layout: Anita Jones

Butte Publications, Inc.
P.O. Box 1328
Hillsboro, Oregon
U.S.A.

Publisher's Cataloging-in-Publication
(Provided by Quality Books, Inc.)

Global perspectives on the education of the deaf in
   selected countries / edited by H. William Brelje.
   -- 1st ed.
    p. cm.
    ISBN: 1-884362-36-2

    1. Deaf--Education.   I. Brelje, H. William.

HV2430.G56 1999   371.91'2
                 QBI00-900066

TABLE OF CONTENTS

For my wife and for deaf and hard of hearing children around the world

ACKNOWLEDGEMENTS

I would like to express my gratitude to the many professional colleagues who suggested possible chapter authors. I would like to single out Carol Erting, the Gallaudet Center for Global Education, and several of the participants of the Deaf Way Conference who provided the names of possible chapter authors. Without the chapter authors who consented to undertake this formidable task, it would not have been possible to bring this book to fruition.

I am indebted to Sylvan Fremaux and Anna Maria Hulse for their expertise in translating chapters from the native languages of the authors into English.

A very special thank you to those who aided in manuscript preparation: Cameron Kenny, Aileen Fisher, Barbara McCormick, Valerie McCourt, Heather Andrews, Alexis Hutera, and Libby Spencer. These special people spent countless hours at a sometimes onerous task.

Finally, I want to express my love and deep appreciation to my wife Ginny, who gave me positive encouragement and support when I became discouraged and my spirits lagged. Her faith in me and her professional advice and counsel was critical in the successful completion of this project.

INTRODUCTION

The education of the deaf* has a long and distinguished history that traces its antecedents back nearly 400 years to the pioneering efforts of early Spaniards. In the 1500s and 1600s, Pedro Ponce de Leon, Manuel Ramirez de Carrion, and Juan Pablo Bonet established the first organized classes for the deaf and set the foundation for the future of the education of the deaf.

In the late 1700s in Paris, Charles Michel Abbé de L'Épée, Abbe Sicard, and others developed the first school for the deaf. It enrolled both rich and poor, and male and female, which were revolutionary ideas for the time. It also taught through signing. At about the same time in Germany, Samuel Heinicke, an army officer, and other people, opened schools and classes using the oral method, a vastly different approach to the education of the deaf. These dual approaches would eventually launch schools for those with hearing losses throughout the world. Their establishment continued the controversy concerning the best approach or method of educating the deaf, which lasted unabated for over two centuries. The ideas and methods of these early pioneers and subsequent significant events have molded the education of the deaf worldwide and contributed to current global practices, trends, and directions.

Throughout history, powerful forces with both a positive and negative impact have shaped the course of the education of the deaf worldwide. During times of war in Europe, Asia, Africa, and the Middle East, the education of deaf students often ceased to exist or was driven underground. As an outcome of some of these military conflicts, people with a hearing loss were incarcerated or executed. On the other hand, revolutions or armed conflicts in some countries led to conditions that improved educational opportunities for the people of the country, sometimes including the deaf.

Economic factors have played a pivotal role. In many underdeveloped countries with insufficient resources to provide for the basic needs of life, the education of disabled individuals, including the deaf, has assumed a low priority. Except for a few notable exceptions, the level of development of educational and vocational services for the deaf has mirrored or tracked the country's level of industrial development. In most highly industrialized countries, educational services are well established and widely available.

The general attitude of society towards the deaf often shapes politics, laws, and policies, and thus the priority assigned to the provision of educational services. People who consider deaf persons to be uneducable, developmentally delayed, or the product of the sins of their parents, passed laws and policies that led to the curtailment of common human rights, including the ownership of property, the right to marry, hold a driver's license, serve on a jury, or teach. The constitution of one country considers a deaf person to be one-half of a citizen. Restrictive laws that require a teacher of deaf students to have normal hearing ban all individuals with a hearing loss from the teaching profession.

In some societies, deaf children have been destroyed, and deaf adults reviled, neglected, or ignored. Although the ways of thinking that justify such brutality can still be found today, the trend is toward acceptance, full rights, and equal opportunities. In a few countries deaf citizens have achieved a status close to full equality.

* The term *deaf* also implies hard of hearing students.

There is a growing awareness that persons who are deaf have the same range of abilities and capabilities found in the general population. In many countries, restrictive and discriminatory laws and policies are being eliminated, replaced by laws and policies that reflect society's changing attitude.

The overall goal of the education of the deaf has changed from one that focused upon providing the deaf person with the tools needed for salvation, or for the deaf children of wealth and nobility to assume their rightful titles and maintain familial responsibilities. It has evolved into one that finally recognizes that deaf persons are capable of learning and of developing their full potential to be independent and contributing members of contemporary society.

The means by which the deaf person's full potential is to be developed has vacillated widely throughout the history of the education of the deaf. Several conflicting models of how to best educate a child with a hearing loss have developed. One method follows a medical or pathological model. The deaf person is considered to be defective, and in order to fit successfully into society needs to be made whole or as "normal" as possible. The supporters of this educational model define "normal" as using speech and hearing to express and receive communication. Only through the development of speech, speechreading, and residual hearing will the individual achieve social acceptability. Any system of communication that seems to detract from this goal of normality is discouraged or banned. The use of sign language is a prime example, since the supporters of the "oral/aural" model hypothesized that sign language would detract from and hinder the deaf child's ability to fully develop his or her mental capacities, speech, speechreading, and listening skills.

Those representing the opposing communication model view deaf people as a distinct cultural and linguistic group with its own institutions, customs, traditions, community, and language, the natural sign language of the respective country. This group stresses that people who are deaf should be proud of their heritage, language, and culture and that sign language be viewed as the "natural" language of the deaf and be the major vehicle for communication and learning. In this bilingual, bicultural approach the natural sign language of the adults of the respective country is used as a conduit for learning to read, write, and later speak the oral language of the country.

Many support a middle ground that recognizes the merits and strengths of both of the previously discussed communication models. This methodology is child-centered and has as its goal the development of all of the child's respective and expressive communication channels, including the ability to speak, read, write, listen, and sign. This child-centered approach is often referred to as the "total communication" philosophy.

These three communication models, or variations and combinations of each, have governed the history and path followed by the education of the deaf from its modest beginnings to the present day.

Great advances in hearing science and technology during the comparatively recent past, in the form of amplification systems, advances in medical practices, acoustics, computer technology, and assistive devices and cochlear implants are causing modifications in existing communication models and methods of educating the deaf and have significant implications for the future directions.

Several individuals, including Bender, Lane, and Scouten, have authored books that provide comprehensive and accurate historical accounts of the development of the education of the deaf. Yet research indicates that few articles and no books have been written that provide a comprehensive picture of the current state, trends, and directions in the education of the deaf in countries representing most areas of the globe.

For over thirty years, the editor of this text has taught a course entitled Psycho-Social and Educational Foundations of Deafness. One of the areas covered in the course content is international perspectives on the education of the deaf. Except for anecdotal accounts of individuals' personal experiences gained while visiting countries and an occasional article that looks at a particular aspect of the education of the deaf, little information of a comprehensive and quantifiable nature is available.

This text is an attempt to rectify this glaring gap in the available literature base by presenting chapters by authors from twenty-seven countries that detail the development, current state, and future directions of the education of the deaf. The difficulty encountered in locating credible sources of information in the many countries that comprise this planet has caused the development of this book to be a much more formidable task than was anticipated.

Choice of Topic Areas

Possible topic areas for the potential chapter authors were infinite in number and clearly had to be limited. After developing many lists of possible topic areas and after much consultation with colleagues in the field, it was decided that the topic areas would be limited to the following:

- A historical review of the individuals and events that shaped the course of the education of the deaf in the country
- The extent and kind of educational services for the deaf
- Parent education and guidance availability and opportunities
- Communication philosophy and methodologies followed

- The type of sign system used
- Academic performance of deaf children
- Vocational and career education/ opportunities
- Postsecondary educational opportunities for deaf individuals
- College or university programs to prepare teachers of deaf students
- Certification standards for teachers of the deaf
- Current issues in the education of the deaf
- Future directions in the education of the deaf
- Demographic data on the number of deaf children, gender, schools, classes, teachers, and so on

Not every chapter contains coverage of all of the topics listed above. Some topics are not applicable since the areas in question have not been developed, or data on the topic is not available.

Search for Authors

The search for the perfect chapter author took on the elements of a good detective story, entailing countless phone calls and correspondence, and with any and all leads explored. To find authors who held the proper credentials, background, and experience, who were knowledgeable as well as unbiased, and who had the proper resources needed, was somewhat similar to finding several needles in a haystack.

In some instances, potential authors had to be rejected for the lack of one of the requisites listed above; in other cases, authors who were accepted did not follow through. For the most part, the authors selected met all requirements and their products were superb.

Chapter Uniformity

As countries worldwide vary greatly in their level of development, chapters submitted also varied greatly. Some chapters were very polished with extensive bibliographies and were developed with the use of the latest computer technology, whereas others were handwritten on inexpensive paper and included little bibliographical information. In the countries with few published materials and authoritative resources, much of the narrative comes from the actual experiences of the authors.

Editing

An attempt was made to retain the vernacular and flavor of the English used by the authors as much as possible while staying within the accepted bounds of standard English. This was especially true of Australia, Canada, and to a lesser degree the African countries included. The use of British spellings of words was the most common difference found in these chapters. Many chapters were originally in a language other than English and required translation. In each case the chapter was translated by an individual versed in the language. After translation and editing were completed, the chapters were returned to the authors for verification of accuracy.

Alphabetical Order

After much thought and discussion with colleagues, no rational way to organize chapters representing far-flung areas of the world emerged. Without a meaningful schema to guide the progression of the chapters, it was decided to use an alphabetical order.

Final Chapter

The final chapter provides a summary of findings and perspectives in each topic area and a look at current directions and future trends in the education of the deaf in each country.

Hopefully, this volume will provide a resource for those planning to do more extensive research on any of the countries or topic areas included. It can be used as a database by countries planning educational services for deaf persons, or it can serve as a general perspective of the current state and trends in the education of the deaf and hard of hearing worldwide. It is hoped that it will provide an opportunity for countries to compare and contrast services for their deaf citizens with those in other countries.

Australia

by Catherine Rumsey

Introduction and Overview

"Australia is the world's largest island and the world's smallest continent," the writer learned many years ago in primary school. In area Australia is 7,717,000 square kilometres (2,968,000 square miles), equal to the continental United States of America excluding Alaska. Its population of 17,148,000 (September, 1990, Australian Bureau of Statistics, cited in Population Grows, 1991) is said to be the most highly urbanized of any nation. About three quarters of the population live in cities and towns, the majority of them on the eastern seaboard. Indeed in some organisations, business travel to New Zealand, another country 2,000 miles across the Tasman Sea, is classed as "local" while travel to Perth, 2,000 miles across the continent, is classed as "overseas." The inland, or outback, of Australia is sparsely settled because of its arid conditions, where heat and drought are the norm rather than the exception.

Politically, the Commonwealth of Australia consists of seven States and two Territories of unequal geographical area and population. These States and Territories almost all began as separate British colonies which gradually progressed towards self-government and finally came together as the Commonwealth of Australia in 1901. Each State and Territory is responsible for the provision of primary (elementary), secondary, and further education services to its inhabitants. The Commonwealth provides the funding for the University sector of postsecondary education.

New South Wales is the oldest and most populous State with more than one-third of the national population living there (5.83 million, Cook, 1991). Likewise, more than one-third of hearing impaired students born in Australia are born in New South Wales and are educated there. In an attempt to focus information relevant to the education of hearing impaired students in Australia, much of

the emphasis in this chapter will be on New South Wales as being representative of provisions and developments in such education.

Before 1788, Australia had been the home almost exclusively of the Aborigines, whose occupancy can be traced back at least 40,000 years. European explorers of the seventeenth century had touched Australia's shores and perhaps traders and fishermen from other countries to the north had landed and lived briefly on her northernmost coast. Captain James Cook had sailed along and charted the eastern coast in 1770 during his circumnavigation of the globe under orders from the English government. In 1788, Captain Arthur Phillip arrived as foundation Governor of the British Colony of New South Wales and took possession of the land in the name of King George of England. Australia was originally settled as a prison colony. European settlement quickly reduced the black population in three ways: 1) by means of diseases such as influenza and measles against which the ancient occupiers had no immunity; 2) by "dispersal" (often a euphemism for killing) of the Aborigines from their original sources of food gathering and shelter; and 3) by loss of life in direct clashes between the original inhabitants and the white invaders.

From the beginning of British settlement there were free settlers as well as the convicts, their gaolers, and the armed forces, but the free settlers were very much in the minority. Transportation of convicts did not cease until the 1850s. With the goldrushes of the 1850s the ethnic composition of the inhabitants began to broaden, with many immigrants from China especially. In South Australia, German Lutherans arrived to practice their religion freely, and Turks and Armenians also sought refuge. However, the greatest influx of non-English-speaking migrants arrived from Europe in the wake of World War II.

Australia's population mix has dramatically changed with the abandoning of policies excluding Asians, with the influx of refugees from Asian and South American nations, and with the arrival of people from South Pacific countries. The population now is reputed to be second only to that of Israel in the number of ethnic groups represented. Indeed, 40 percent of Australians are first- or second-generation immigrants and (in a country where English is the official language) 20 percent come from homes where no English is spoken. These percentages are much higher in urban settings as immigrants tend to congregate in those areas. For example, the writer knows of one church in Sydney where 68 different national flags hanging in the church indicate the diverse ethnicity of the congregation of some 500 people. In New South Wales government schools, 17 percent of students are from non-English-speaking backgrounds and 89 percent of these students attend schools in metropolitan Sydney (Scott Management Review, 1990).

This diverse mixture of cultures and languages has led to some particular problems in the education of hearing impaired children from non-English-speaking backgrounds, but has been advantageous in gaining recognition of Australian Sign Language as a community language.

This chapter will trace the history of the education of deaf students in Australia and describe present services. Attention will be given to parent education, communication methodologies, academic performance of deaf students, vocational and postsecondary education opportunities, preparation and certification of teachers, significant current issues, and future directions in the education of students with hearing impairments.

History

Education of deaf students began in Australia in 1860 in the space of three weeks in two state capitals 600 miles apart. In both cases the founding teacher was a deaf man who had been educated in the United Kingdom, of which the Australian states were then separate self-governing colonies.

Thomas Pattison from Edinburgh, Scotland, established the New South Wales Institution for Deaf Children in Sydney, and Frederick J. Rose from England, the Victorian School for the Deaf in Melbourne. Both these schools were influential in the development of education for deaf children and later in sustaining the deaf community throughout the country. Each began as a charitable institution and soon provided residential accommodation as well as schooling. Initial enrollments expanded to include students from rural areas, other states and territories, and from countries in the Pacific. These two institutions have developed over the ensuing 130 years in response to changing attitudes about the education of children with sensory impairments. Today they are known respectively as the Royal New South Wales Institute for Deaf and Blind Children, the North Rocks School for the Deaf, and Garfield Barwick School in Sydney, New South Wales and as the Victorian School for Deaf Children and Princess Elizabeth Junior School in Melbourne, Victoria.

As an aside, it is perhaps a nice touch that the British colonies in the Antipodes played a role in the education of deaf students in Great Britain. As a result of teaching a deaf pupil while he was in Australia in the nineteenth century, Thomas Arnold set up the first high (secondary) school for deaf students in England when he returned there.

Within forty years of the establishment of the first schools for deaf children, each of the six states of Australia had its own charitable institution for the schooling and, if necessary, residential accommodation of deaf students. Gradually, between 1913 and 1963, state education departments took responsibility for the education of students attending the institutional schools (McGree, 1963). By 1990 most of these special schools had closed as changing policies and practices had led to the education of the majority of deaf students in neighbourhood schools.

The Roman Catholic presence in the education of deaf people in Australia began in the late nineteenth century when the

Dominican Sisters at Maitland, some 150 miles north of Sydney, in 1872 sought support in teaching deaf children from their Sisters at Cabra in Ireland. In 1875, Sister Gabriel Hogan, "the most competent Sister in the Community ... herself a deaf mute, but a teacher of remarkable talent" (O'Hanlon in Dooley, 1989, p.9), arrived to begin teaching deaf students in the Roman Catholic faith (Dooley, 1989). In 1948 the Sisters opened a second, oral, school in Portsea, Victoria. Today the Dominican Sisters offer educational and family support to deaf people in a variety of settings in almost all states of Australia.

In 1922, two Christian Brothers, J. O'Farrell and Damien Allen, from the Christian Brothers School for Deaf Boys in Cabra, Ireland, established St.Gabriel's School for Deaf Boys in Sydney, New South Wales (St. Gabriel's, n.d.). Originally residential, it is now a coeducational day school providing integrated schooling through the co-operation of a wide range of neighbourhood schools. A family support programme is available from the age of diagnosis of deafness.

State government involvement in the education of students with hearing impairments began in 1872 when the parliament of South Australia passed an Act to subsidize any individual effort to teach deaf mutes. This resulted in the establishment in 1874 of Townsend House, a school for deaf and blind children in Adelaide, South Australia (Barkham, 1974).

Tasmania was the first state to make education compulsory for deaf students. In 1905 an Act was passed by the Tasmanian parliament making education compulsory for deaf and blind children from 7 to 13 years of age (McGree, 1963). In 1910 the state of Victoria required parents of deaf, blind, physically and intellectually disabled children to provide education for them (Ashman and Elkins, 1990).

State government involvement in the education of deaf children in New South Wales had its roots in the introduction of free, compulsory, and secular education, when that state passed its 1880 Public Instruction Act.

However, it was not until 1944 that the Public Instruction (Blind and Infirm Children) Amendment Act made school attendance compulsory for "blind and infirm children" (Public Instruction Act, 1944). Parents were required to ensure that their disabled children who were "not capable of being educated by the ordinary methods of instruction" regularly attended a special school "established for children suffering from the class of infirmity from which such child is suffering" if such a special school was in the district, as defined by the state, in which the child lived. It is interesting to note that in both Victoria and New South Wales, initially it was the parents and not the state upon whom the onus was placed to educate children with disabilities.

Gradually the various state governments themselves began to provide educational facilities for deaf children within the ages of compulsory schooling. Queensland in 1947 set up classes for partially hearing children in neighbourhood schools. In New South Wales, an Inquiry into the education of deaf children was begun in 1947. This coincided in that state with the arrival at school entry age of an increased number of deaf children because of the 1941 rubella epidemic. Eventually, in 1948 the New South Wales State Education Department met the increased need by setting up special day classes in eight metropolitan neighbourhood schools. The report of the 1947 Inquiry, released in 1949, formally recommended the day classes already in operation, the provision of preschool education for deaf children, and the establishment of a training course for teachers of the deaf. In the 1950s both South Australia and Western Australia set up classes for deaf and partially hearing children in neighbourhood schools. These classes were sometimes called Speech and Hearing Centres.

In 1950, at the request of all the state governments with the exception of Western Australia, and of the Commonwealth Office of Education, Professor Alexander and Dr. Irene Ewing from the University of Manchester, United Kingdom, visited each state of

Australia and reported on the education of deaf children. Following their visit, separate oral schools for deaf students, Princess Elizabeth Kindergarten (1950) and Glendonald School (1951) were established in Melbourne, Victoria. Later, in 1957, the Victorian Department of Education provided a hostel to enable country children to attend Glendonald (Rumsey, 1980). The states which had provided special day classes also by this time had developed oral day schools.

In the case of the schools originally set up by charitable institutions, state government responsibility was not completely accepted until the 1960s. The last states to do so were New South Wales in 1956 and South Australia in 1963 (McGree, 1963). Initially, such responsibility generally took the form of paying the salaries of the teachers and renting the classroom accommodation from the charities concerned. Eventually, responsibility for the curriculum and the training of teachers was assumed.

The 1940s and '50s also saw the development of small private schools. These were usually oral schools set up to provide an educational setting where children would not receive any chance influence from people using any manual method of communication. Two such day schools were the South Australian Oral School in Adelaide, South Australia, established in 1945, and Farrar School in Sydney, New South Wales, established in 1946 (Rumsey, 1980). Beginning in 1945 with a playgroup which included two hearing impaired children, a group of parents in Victoria eventually set up two schools in the early '50s in the provincial centres of Ballarat and Bendigo. They financed four scholarships for teachers to train as teachers of the deaf at the University of Manchester in the United Kingdom and sponsored nine trained teachers of the deaf from overseas to teach in their schools. They also built a residence for those children who lived beyond reasonable traveling distance from the schools. This was opened in 1958 (John, 1990). Eventually, financial constraints compelled the proprietors of most of these schools to seek government subsidies or sell their schools to the state education department.

The development of state education for hearing impaired students since the 1950s probably can best be seen by tracing the two different tracks followed by the two most populous states in Australia, New South Wales and Victoria. Both states by the mid-'50s were providing preschool parent guidance, and both states retained the schools initially established by the charitable institutions and one or two relatively small private, or formerly private, oral schools. However, they differed in their approaches to State school provision.

In New South Wales, day classes were established in both primary and secondary schools, first in Sydney and later in the larger provincial cities and towns. Contrary to the practice in some other states, New South Wales provided trained secondary teachers to staff secondary classes in both special class and special school settings. Generally, the central authority endeavoured to place more than one class for hearing impaired children in a school for two reasons: firstly, in order to provide collegial support for the teachers who often felt unsupported by their colleagues in regular education and, secondly, to provide the possibility of grouping students appropriately for instruction. Units of two or more classes also meant that the students were unlikely to have one teacher for more than two years.

In one unusual situation, one teacher remained with his class for the total five years of their secondary education. With the hard-earned support of the regular teachers, he prepared the boys in his class in all the required subjects for the final public examination. He then left the field of deaf education! He did return, after his eventual retirement, as a casual [substitute] teacher of deaf students.

The purposes of units in regular schools were to enable children to attend school in their own or a reasonably close neighbourhood and to provide opportunity for integration in the activities of the host school. Such integration was dependent upon the goodwill of the school executive and teachers and was usually the result of persistent hard work by the teacher(s) of the deaf students. In some situations some students were integrated for academic instruction, in others nonacademic activities were shared, while in still others there was no integration at all.

In New South Wales for many years the parents' wishes in the school placement of the hearing impaired child were paramount. Consequently, the day classes enrolled students across the whole range of hearing loss. Eventually, as schools were established in more and more centres in response to parent and teacher demand, the hearing impaired student population was roughly equally divided between the day classes and the two special schools. A small number of hearing impaired students were enrolled in regular classes but educational support for them was minimal beginning with one visiting teacher in 1950. By the late 1960s, three visiting teachers of the deaf provided consultancy services to the mainstreamed students and supervised all the units in a state some 700 miles square with a total population of about 2.5 million.

In the mid-1970s the increasing number of hearing impaired students in regular classes led to a rapid development of the New South Wales itinerant teacher of the deaf service. The itinerant teacher provided a consultancy service to the class teacher, a tutoring and personal support service to the deaf student and, often, educational and emotional support for the child's family, on a daily, weekly, monthly, termly, or yearly basis depending on the perceived needs of the student and the availability of the service. In 1979 there were 55 such teachers (Murphy, 1980), while 98 teachers taught in units ranging from preschool to secondary school.

By 1982 the vast majority of deaf students in New South Wales were being educated in neighbourhood schools, either in special classes or in fully mainstreamed settings (Rumsey, 1984).

In contrast, in addition to the original School for Deaf Children and Princess Elizabeth Kindergarten, the Victorian state education department in 1951 set up the Glendonald School for the Deaf, an oral day school for students who were judged to require enrollment in a special school. In 1957 residential facilities were established within walking distance of the school for students from rural areas. All other oral deaf students attended their local schools and were strongly supported by a sizeable centralised visiting teacher service which commenced in 1958. Special class placement in a regular school was available only in the private school system until the 1980s, when a small number of Ministry of Education classes were provided in regular schools.

Present Position

At present, the vast majority of hearing impaired students across all States and Territories in Australia attend state neighbourhood schools. Less than 10 percent, including those with moderately severe additional disabilities, attend special state schools. A small minority of hearing impaired students attend Catholic and independent schools where they are mainstreamed with itinerant teacher support or divide their time between the special school or class and the hearing school or class.

Total numbers of children enrolled in educational services throughout Australia are not readily available. A survey (Rumsey, 1991) of services in the State of New South Wales indicated an estimated 2100 students currently receiving support from government and non-government facilities. This enrollment ranged from age of diagnosis to approximately age 18. Not included were those students of similar age who had left school at, or after, the minimum school leaving age of 15 and were enrolled in postsecondary services, nor multiply disabled hearing impaired students enrolled in facilities for students whose primary disability was not hearing impairment and who were not receiving services from a teacher of hearing impaired students. Given that one-third of Australia's population lives in New South Wales, it is possible that the number of children receiving early intervention/preschool, primary (elementary), and secondary school services in Australia is at least 6000.

Current Concerns

Throughout Australia, state education of hearing impaired students was highly centralised from its inception, as was regular education. Indeed, the New South Wales State Education system was reportedly described by the Minister for Education as "one of the world's largest centralised education systems" (Totaro, 1990). In the late 1980s regionalization was introduced in many areas of education, including special education. In New South Wales, for example, this initially led to increased opportunities for teacher promotion as regions set up their own service delivery structures. However, some professionals and parents fear the eventual fragmentation and reduction of services in the case of low incidence disabilities such as deafness, if central support units are no longer present to provide leadership to government and regions in policy, planning, and coordination of hearing impaired student services and teacher development. A further threat is the "multiskilling" concept by which administrators and teachers without qualifications in hearing impairment will be responsible for services to deaf children. To prevent such retrograde steps occurring, local and regional lobby groups must remain vigilant. A more pressing threat to services is the continuing economic recession and the pressures upon government departments to reduce expenses by instituting economically attractive cost-cutting measures.

Incidence, Prevalence, Severity, and Etiologies of Childhood Hearing Impairment in Australia

Hearing loss in Australia is second only to musculo-skeletal problems as the most prevalent disability. Census figures indicate some seven per cent of the total population report some form of hearing disability (Project Knock Knock, 1989).

Hearing-aid-fitting figures for the school aged population are obtainable from the records of the National Acoustic Laboratories (described below), which are considered to include all children fitted with hearing aids in Australia. The information available is consistent over time and location. However, because it is based on hearing-aid-fitting numbers, it probably does not include all children with mild hearing losses, unilateral losses, or intermittent losses accompanying recurrent otitis media. Reviews of the records of children up to age 17 indicate an incidence of 2.75 children per 1000 live births fitted with hearing aids, with a mean of 813 new children of all ages fitted each year (Upfold, 1988). As early as 1967 in Victoria, the average age of diagnosis was 11.7 months (Murphy, 1980). However, the national average age of diagnosis remains at about two years of age, despite the increasing numbers of children who are diagnosed well before that.

While the mean hearing-aid-fitting rates of children with hearing loss have remained consistent over many years, the proportion of children with severe and profound losses has decreased by half since 1970. Surveys of hearing aid fitting in the 1980s indicate that only one in five (20 percent) aided children had severe or profound impairments while one in three had better ear average losses of 31dB or less (Upfold, 1988).

Another significant change in hearing-aid-fitting patterns is the increased inclusion of children with middle ear disease—not so much as a result of changes in prevalence but rather a realisation that even mild and/or fluctuating hearing impairments adversely affect language development and educational progress. In surveys covering the birth years 1953-76, middle ear disease accounted for an average of 5.7 percent of hearing aid fittings, but for birth years 1964-86 the percentage had increased to 14.8 percent. Including other pathologies, by the 1980s one in five children fitted with hearing aids had a conductive hearing loss. Previously many of these children would not have been considered candidates for hearing aid fitting (Upfold, 1988).

In etiology, two significant changes have occurred in recent times. Comparing etiological studies across the birth years 1946-77 with his most recent one, across the birth years 1964-86, Upfold (1988) noted that both haemolytic disease of the newborn (RH factor) and maternal rubella have been virtually eliminated as causes of hearing impairment. The reduction of RH factor as an etiology began as far back as the mid-1960s with the result that the proportion of hearing loss from that cause has decreased from 10 percent to 1 percent. The successful nation-wide anti-rubella vaccination of female high school students has resulted in high levels of acquired immunity in Australian females. Consequently, the incidence of hearing impairment caused by maternal rubella has fallen from 0.60 to 0.06 per thousand live births and from 27.3 percent across the years 1953-70 (NAL, Queensland, 1971 in Upfold, 1988) to 2.7 percent. In order to reduce this incidence even further, combined measles, mumps, and rubella immunisation for infants 12-18 months was introduced in 1989/90 with consequent checking of vaccination documents becoming a requirement for school entry (Hayes, 1991, Thomas, 1989).

Prematurity alone has never been a significant cause of hearing impairment in Australia. Even with the survival of increasing numbers of very small babies, the incidence of

hearing loss directly attributable to this cause has declined from a high of 5.7 percent across the years 1956-72 (Murphy, 1973 in Upfold, 1988) to 1.5 percent. Similarly, the percentage of children whose deafness was a result of meningitis has declined from 6.3 percent in the birth years 1946-58 (Green, 1962 in Upfold, 1988) to 0.6 percent (Upfold, 1988).

The two etiologies in which there has been virtually no change in incidence are the unknown and the genetic categories. Since 1946 the proportions have remained roughly the same at 42 percent and 18 percent respectively (Upfold, 1988).

National Acoustic Laboratories

The Australian National Acoustics Laboratories (NAL) has played a major part in the education of Australian hearing impaired children and youth through its programme of research and hearing-aid provision. Large numbers of deafened World War II servicemen and children born deaf as a result of the 1939 and 1941 rubella epidemics provided the impetus for the establishment of this federal agency by an act of Parliament in 1944 to study the effects of noise on humans and the use of hearing aids by hearing impaired people.

NAL's foundation director, N.E. Murray, persuasively advocated the cause of rubella deaf children, many of whom he insisted had sufficient residual hearing to benefit from hearing aids and education with hearing and speaking children. Consequently, in 1946 rubella deaf children were allowed to enroll in infants (preprimary) departments in New South Wales government schools. Such enrollment usually was limited to one child per school. The first school psychologist/counselor for deaf children, Walter Parr, was appointed to introduce the children to the schools, monitor their progress and liaise with the Laboratories. When it became obvious that many of the deaf students needed more individual support than was available at that time, it was recommended that special classes be established in neighbourhood schools. Because of the post-war teacher shortage, this recommendation was not implemented until March, 1948 (Parr, 1968).

Through its research and service departments the Laboratories have been, and continue to be, international leaders in the field of hearing-aid design and fitting. In 1990, the *First International Conference on Tactile Aids, Hearing Aids and Cochlear Implants: Improving Speech Communication for Profoundly Hearing Impaired Children and Adults* was held at the Central Laboratory. Audiologists, teachers, and researchers attended from Asia, Europe, North America, and Australasia.

As a feature of the National Health Service, the diagnosis of hearing loss, fitting and maintenance of hearing and tactile aids, and batteries are provided free to children and youth to age 21, most pensioners, and defense forces personnel. As a result of the economic climate and increasing implementation of the "user pays" principle, an annual service fee of $25.00 (Australian) was introduced in 1991. The service is available directly to eligible persons, although many are referred through medical personnel or school or community nursing centers. Hearing Centres are located in large cities and towns throughout the country, but because of the sparseness of population in the arid inland and remote areas there are numbers of hearing impaired children who live hundreds of miles from their nearest Hearing Centre.

The hearing aids provided range from tactile aids, those worn on the body, post-auricular binaural aids, and FM wireless aids. Many pediatric audiologists and schoolteachers maintain close liaison to ensure that their clients receive the maximum benefit from the most appropriate hearing or tactile aid. In metropolitan areas, laboratory staff regularly visit schools and units to check hearing aids and earmoulds.

The National Acoustics Laboratories hearing-aid programme is second in size only to that of the British National Health Service

(Brooks, 1989). In quality it is second to none (Power, 1990a).

Because almost all hearing aids fitted to children in Australia have been supplied by the National Acoustics Laboratories, a comprehensive data base has developed. From these records it has been possible to trace the Australian incidence and prevalence of childhood deafness, etiologies, and trends in age of diagnosis and fitting of aids (Upfold, 1988).

In 1990, an inquiry into the National Acoustics Laboratories initiated by the federal government recommended its virtual disbandment and the relocating of its services to private enterprise. Such was the response to this recommendation by lobby groups such as the Australian Deafness Council, the Parent Council for Deaf Education in New South Wales, and the Australian Association of Teachers of the Deaf that the recommendation was not followed. Nevertheless, that situation underlined the necessity for constant monitoring of government actions in relation to service provision to disability groups.

Cochlear Implants

A small but growing number of deaf children has now been fitted with cochlear implants. The 22-electrode device in use was developed by Dr. Graeme Clark at the Royal Eye and Ear Hospital in Melbourne, Victoria. It is marketed worldwide by the Australian company Cochlear Pty., Ltd. In 1991 Cochlear Pty., Ltd. gained the contract to supply the Japanese market (Smith, 1991), bringing to 27 the number of countries which the company supplies. After extensive clinical trials, Cochlear gained approval from the US Food and Drug Administration for the use of their system, the Mini System 22 Cochlear Implant, in adults in 1985 and for children in 1990. The children's four-year clinical trials have resulted in 100 percent of the children showing significant improvements in detection of sound while 46 percent demonstrated significant improvement in recognizing and understanding speech without contextual or visual clues. Speech production significantly improved for 76 percent of the subjects (Follent, 1991).

Of the 650 children under 18 fitted worldwide, 88 are in Australia. The lower age limit is two years, and 28 children in the two-to three-year age group have received the device (Laidlaw, personal communication, September, 1991). All candidates are screened carefully. Only those profoundly deaf children who gain no benefit from a hearing aid or vibrotactile device are accepted into the programme. Between 70-80 percent of the implantees are prelingually deaf and about 58 percent are in Total Communication educational settings. All children receive intensive auditory skills programmes. In Australia, there are approximately eight cochlear implant clinics where evaluation, programming of the device, and training take place. The various state departments of school education and independent facilities which have implantees enrolled work in close co-operation with the implant centres. The National Acoustic Laboratories provide the same support services as they do for hearing-aid users (Follent, 1991).

As in other countries, sections of the Deaf Community in Australia have vigorously voiced their opposition to the implant programme and a considerable number of teachers and other professionals have concerns about its value and implementation. However there are hearing parents of young deaf children, deaf children and adults, and teachers and professionals who support it wholeheartedly. The Cochlear Implant programme also has added stimulus to the search for and development of improved tactile aids. Both National Acoustics Laboratories personnel and Dr. Graeme Clark with his "Tickle Talker" are actively pursuing this goal.

Educational Services

Within Australia the full range of generic educational services are provided for deaf and hearing impaired students. Education is compulsory. Across the states the age of compulsory education for all children ranges from between five and six years of age to between fourteen and sixteen years of age. The school year is 200-211 days long, spread over four terms. The longest vacation is at Christmas (midsummer in the southern hemisphere) and lasts until the end of January.

Elementary and Secondary Education

The vast majority of students with hearing loss are educated in regular state schools, with a smaller number in non-state schools. Educational settings range from self-contained class, with greater or lesser integration into the regular school academic and nonacademic activities as is appropriate for the student's needs and capabilities and can be provided reasonably and satisfactorily by the school, to total integration, or mainstreaming, with itinerant teacher support ranging from one hour per day, for example, to one hour per term for monitoring purposes. Itinerant teachers provide services ranging from consultation with the regular class teacher; large or small group team teaching and individual support in the regular classroom; withdrawal of small groups of children with language or listening difficulties who will benefit from the instruction provided for the hearing impaired child; to individual withdrawal of the hearing impaired student. The delivery of service is dependent upon the hearing impaired student's and the regular teacher's needs and the way in which those needs can be met most effectively. The itinerant teacher generally has a case load of 12-18 students who may vary from early intervention to secondary level. In urban areas it is sometimes possible for an itinerant teacher to specialize at the early intervention, elementary, or secondary level. Just over 50 percent of hearing impaired students are educated in regular classes with itinerant teacher support (Power, 1990b, Rumsey, 1991).

An important development during the mid-1980s was the granting of permission by some state secondary school examination boards for deaf students undertaking public examinations to be granted extra time and to take a dictionary and/or thesaurus with them into examinations. Permission was also granted for the examination papers to be vetted by a senior educator of deaf students to advise on the appropriateness of the language of the examination for deaf students. Frequently, this has led to the rewriting of some instructions or questions, resulting in greater clarity for both hearing and deaf examinees.

Tuition fees are not charged in state elementary and secondary schools. However, the provision of extra textbooks, for example, may be difficult for some families. In some states, parent and/or service organisations have established a small number of scholarships for hearing impaired students to assist in the financial costs of their secondary education.

An interesting development in the state of Victoria is the introduction at grades 11 and 12 of a course in "Australian Sign Language and Deaf Culture". This course, which is fully accredited for the Victorian Certificate of Education, is available as a "Language Other than English Unit" to students in regular secondary schools. Teachers and students in other states who have been advocating similar courses for a number of years are hopeful that the Victorian example will be followed by other states.

During the past decade enrollments in the special state schools for deaf students have decreased. In New South Wales, for example, in 1981, 152 (9 percent) hearing impaired students in government schools were enrolled in the two schools for the deaf (Landa, 1981); in 1988, the numbers had decreased to 87 (5.7 percent) (Project Knock Knock, 1989) with

even further decreases by 1991 to approximately 55 students (Rumsey, 1991). These schools now cater mainly to students whose additional disabilities combined with their hearing loss preclude their education in regular schools at present. In South Australia, Queensland, and Tasmania, the state schools have closed and their students, teachers, and resources transferred to integrated settings. In Victoria, the special state school, Glendonald, which provided an oral programme for deaf students, closed in November, 1991. Independent schools for deaf students have either relocated to hearing schools, enrolled hearing students, or developed networks with regular schools for the extensive integration of their deaf students into hearing classes.

Residential schools for deaf students, both state and independent, are now virtually nonexistent as the extension of services resulting from population growth means that most students are now educated within daily traveling distance from their homes. Some states provide travel assistance for hearing impaired students. In New South Wales, for example, free taxi travel to and from school is provided for all hearing impaired students up to the age of ten. It is possible for children from very isolated rural areas to receive distance education through the Correspondence School or School of the Air under the tutelage of their caregiver. Alternatively, they may live with selected volunteer host families or relatives while they attend the most appropriate or most parentally desired school or class.

The decline of the schools for the deaf has been of some regret to many members of the Deaf Community who mourn the passing of the agency which often socialized deaf children into that Community and which many of them valued equally or more than their hearing family setting.

Multiply disabled hearing impaired pupils not enrolled in programmes for deaf students, are enrolled in special programmes for multiply disabled children. In most cases these children and their teachers receive the services of an itinerant teacher of hearing impaired students.

Preschool Services

In all states support services are available from diagnosis for both parents and child. Hearing aids are fitted free of charge as soon as possible by the National Acoustics Laboratories through the local Hearing Centre, and regular review appointments are scheduled. Parents are referred to the state and nonstate services from which they make their choice as to which will benefit them and their child the most.

State departments of education provide an itinerant teacher with expertise in the education of hearing impaired babies and preschool children and their caregivers at most local Hearing Centres. Some public hospitals provide a similar service using speech pathologists rather than teachers. Nongovernment agencies of a private/charitable or denominational nature provide such services in conjunction with their facilities for school-age deaf children or for babies and preschoolers only. Most independent services receive some form of government grant and engage in fundraising activities so that parents' selection of a service is not constrained by the cost of fees. All services ensure that teachers of deaf children and other personnel such as counsellors/psychologists/social workers are available as needed, either on-site or by referral.

The delivery of the educational support service may be home-based, centre-based, or both, according to the child's age, the caregiver's needs, and the finances available to the service. Playgroups are provided for younger children, and preschoolers attend local preschools or reverse integration is practised, with hearing children enrolled in the centre preschool. The Shepherd Centre and the Royal New South Wales Institute for Deaf and Blind Children are two of the agencies that provide correspondence programmes for isolated parents and young children. The Shepherd Centre organizes and funds an annual one-week residential summer school for their correspondence parents and children, and other parents and children.

Interested teachers from other programmes are welcome on a user pays basis. St. Gabriel's Family Support Centre facilities include a self-contained apartment to enable distant parents and their young children to attend the Centre and receive intensive service for a short period of time.

Postsecondary Education

Postsecondary education is available to all persons in Australia through the Universities, Colleges of Technical and Further Education (TAFE) and for nonaward courses, the Evening college system. There is only one private university in Australia. All other universities, TAFE, and Evening Colleges are federally or state-funded. Technically, hearing impaired persons can enter any of these avenues provided they meet any entry requirements applicable to all applicants. Of course, in reality, deaf people face many obstacles ranging from their inability to meet entry requirements because of poor language or general educational levels, through to the lack of support services to provide access to courses and the uninformed attitudes and expectations of service providers towards people with disabilities in general and those with communication difficulties in particular. Historically, it has been the Adult Deaf Societies that have provided postschool educational services to deaf people.

There have always been those talented deaf persons strongly supported by parents and tutors who have overcome the general lack of access and succeeded in university or college. For the vast majority of deaf persons further education was not a possibility until the late 1960s/early 1970s, when the basis of the strong network of services in the New South Wales Technical and Further Education sector was established. Trained teachers of deaf students were recruited from existing services for hearing impaired students, to become consultants for deaf students undertaking trade and literacy and numeracy certificate programmes. These consultants acted as notetakers, tutors, interpreters, academic counsellors, and providers of FM loan aids and other devices to hearing impaired students. They also served as educational consultants to the trade teachers who had deaf students enrolled in their classes. Occasionally, a trade teacher enrolled in the diploma course for teachers of the deaf to gain formal qualifications in that area. Support for such teachers from their employer was minimal, if not nonexistent, with the result that very few trade teachers were willing to undertake such courses. By the early 1980s, the consultancy network for hearing impaired students had spread right across the TAFE sector in New South Wales. In 1989, 499 students were receiving support (Project Knock Knock, 1989). Further expansion has occurred, with the employment of appropriately qualified consultants to support not only students with hearing impairments, but also those with intellectual, physical, and vision impairments.

Although increasing numbers of deaf people are seeking further education through TAFE, the states other than New South Wales provide much more limited and less developed services. Regrettably, the economic situation has placed many of these services, including those in New South Wales, under threat in the early 1990s.

The University sector has been less responsive to the needs of deaf students. Although most Universities in line with antidiscrimination legislation have instituted minimal services for students with disabilities, they receive no designated funding for them, and provisions for deaf students generally are very limited. Students usually have to seek out their own funding for notetaker or interpreter support, or rely on the good nature of their family, friends, classmates, past teachers, or other volunteers. On rare occasions FM or infrared listening devices are available. It is usually the students' responsibility to educate their lecturers as to the needs of hearing impaired students. Indeed, some of the 67 hearing impaired students enrolled in Universities in New South Wales in 1989 received publicity concerning their plight (Lewis, 1989).

There are some exceptions to the above situations: firstly, the specific courses for training teachers of deaf students where understanding of the challenges faced by deaf students and varying degrees of financial support for necessary services is available; secondly, at some universities such as the University of Technology in Sydney where, in 1991, four deaf people training as teachers of Auslan (Australian Sign Language) were provided with interpreter services in the general Associate Diploma of Adult Education subjects; and, thirdly, the Centre for Higher Education of the Deaf at Griffith University in Queensland. Begun in 1984, the programme at Griffith University is a small but ambitious attempt to provide high quality support for hearing impaired students enrolled at the University. Interpreting, notetaking, tutorial and counselling services, and technical aids are available to both undergraduate and graduate students who are enrolled under either normal or special entry categories. By 1991, 35 students had graduated from the programme and 30 were currently enrolled (Kirk, 1991). The Centre's financial support has come from Griffith University's general funds, Commonwealth Rehabilitation Services, and the community service organisation Quota Clubs International. Initially, funding was generally on an annual basis and had to be sought actively each year. In 1989 national higher education funds were provided for the subsequent three years on the condition that Griffith University agreed to then fund the programme from its regular grant. This means that this burgeoning programme still faces a precarious future (Power, 1990b).

A recent first in tertiary education was the award of a place at the National Academy of Dramatic Art to a young, profoundly deaf actor. One of 26 successful applicants of the 1325 who auditioned, the young woman also had been granted $10,000 by the Queen Elizabeth II Silver Jubilee Trust for Young

Australians to pay for an interpreter for one term. "I have applied to the Australia Council for money for the rest of the year, but who knows?" she was reported to have said (Meade, 1991).

The Gloria Marshall Scholarship is awarded annually to substantially financially assist a hearing impaired student to undertake University studies. The scholarship, underwritten by a business organisation, is a national award.

The only postsecondary provision where the vast majority of students are hearing impaired is the Adult Education Centre for Deaf and Hearing Impaired Persons in Sydney, New South Wales. Established in 1984 with the financial support of the Adult Education Board of New South Wales and the administrative support of the then Nepean College of Advanced Education, now University of Western Sydney, Nepean, it provides a broad range of nonaward courses. Indicative of the need for such a service was the fact that 400 people participated in the programme during the Centre's first year of operation (Cipollone, P., Personal communication, 22 November 1985).

Although both hard of hearing and Deaf Community organisations were instrumental in its establishment and were active on its governing council, of recent years the Centre's appeal has been mainly to deaf people. The exception has been Australian Sign Language and Signed English classes which have been well attended by hearing people with an interest or connection with deaf people. The Centre will provide classes in any subject, provided a minimum enrollment can be guaranteed. Courses may be as short as half a day or may require weekly attendance for a term. Classes are held in the evenings and at weekends depending upon nature and demand. Fees are nominal. Most courses are offered at the two locations under the Centre's control. However, the Centre also provides access for hearing impaired persons to regular classes in other colleges operating under the same Board.

The Centre was successful in gaining funds from the federal Department of Employment, Education and Training for the development and publication of a short beginner's curriculum and teaching kit for use by deaf teachers of Auslan. The Centre has also developed teaching packages to assist employers and their staff to become familiar with the needs of hearing impaired persons in the workplace. As part of the Australian Bicentennial celebrations of 1988, the Centre successfully applied for a grant to develop a signed history of the Deaf Community in New South Wales. The resulting seven hours of edited video tapes with spoken interpretation and captions provide a social history of the Deaf Community over the past eighty years under the title "Heritage in Our Hands" (1989). The courses in Deaf Studies developed and presented by deaf people have been well attended by both deaf and hearing people and have contributed much to the increased self-esteem of deaf people and the knowledge and understanding of Deaf Culture and Sign Language by both deaf and hearing persons. Similar workshops have been organised in most other states.

While there has been improvement in the postschool services for hearing impaired students, the vast majority of hearing impaired adults still have very limited access to higher education. Approximately 500 hearing impaired students leave secondary school each year, most of them with limited qualifications. Governments must cease to pay lip service to the higher educational needs of people with disabilities and provide the funds that are necessary to ensure equal access.

Summary

Educational services in Australia for hearing-impaired students are available from preschool to postsecondary level. Most services are provided within the context of regular education settings. While there is always room for improvement, the majority of services provide an appropriate to high level of educational support. However, there is a great need for enhanced services at the post-secondary level in most states.

Academic Performance of Deaf Children

Reports of large scale research on the academic performance of deaf children in Australia are not available. There does not seem to be any reason to assume that their performance in general differs from that of deaf children in other Western countries. Power (1990a) reports his own unpublished research which indicated that reading ages more than four years below their chronological ages were characteristic of 66 percent of a representative sample of hearing impaired students aged 11 years. The low levels of employment of deaf people reported under Vocational Education probably reflect among other factors poor levels of academic achievement in some cases. An examination of the records of 321 deaf persons who sought assistance from the New South Wales Department of Industrial Relations and Employment from 1986 to 1988 revealed that of the 87 percent who had left school, only 1.6 percent had their Higher School Certificate, the minimum entry requirement for application to enter university. Only 0.9 percent had university education, while 31 percent had completed training at technical and further education colleges (Project Knock Knock, 1989). It should be kept in mind that these statistics were derived from a group of people seeking assistance in gaining information and assistance in employment. Consequently, the overall picture may not be quite so bleak, especially as the number of persons approaching that instrumentality declined by almost 50 percent in the years surveyed. Conversely, the situation may be worse as reduction of staffing in many government departments has led to a lower level of service delivery, which in turn has resulted in declining numbers of clients. On a positive note, the same survey reported that 97 students with hearing impairments

were enrolled in Universities in New South Wales. However, the majority of those students were not profoundly deaf.

The above study and anecdotal reports would appear to indicate that an increasing number of deaf students appears to be entering postcompulsory education. A contributing factor may be enhanced academic performance in some individual cases. More likely factors may be the gradually increasing services for deaf students in this area, a general trend towards such education, or the reflection of population growth.

Anecdotal evidence has always been available concerning individual deaf persons who have reached high levels of academic achievement at school. Almost without exception such students have received strong parental and teacher support. A small percentage of these individuals has gone on to achieve University or College success, again, generally with the strong support of family, teachers, and counsellors. As the network of support services for hearing impaired students at secondary and tertiary levels of education increases in line with antidiscrimination and access provisions, more deaf students may reach higher levels of academic achievement.

In the meantime, statewide, if not national, surveys of academic achievement of hearing impaired students would provide basic data from which to draw some conclusions and plan more appropriate programmes.

Communication Methodologies

Educational services in Australia employ the full range of communication methods for hearing impaired people. Some centres exclusively use one method while others are more eclectic. Students entirely enrolled in mainstream classes in regular schools would almost without exception use oral/aural methods. Students enrolled in special classes for hearing impaired students but receiving some of their education in mainstream classes would frequently be supported by Signed English or oral interpreters. In some special schools and self-contained classes communication is oral, in others the method used is Total Communication. A very small number of bilingual classes, some of them pilot pro- grammes, are in operation using Australian Sign (Auslan) and English. Another very small group of services provides Cued Speech as an option.

Within the oral/aural group, oral, oral- aural, and auditory verbal approaches are used. The Garfield Barwick School, opened in 1989, and the St. Gabriel's Family Support Centre, both in New South Wales, and the Wembley Speech and Hearing Centre for Deaf Children, in Western Australia, are committed to an auditory verbal approach. A number of other schools and classes are making strong efforts to incorporate some auditory verbal techniques and principles in their teaching but do not have the support services necessary to fully implement such a programme. They would be described more appropriately as following an auditory skills development programme.

Manual support systems using finger- spelling and signing or fingerspelling alone have always been available, especially in the charitable institution/state school settings. The degree of availability has been dependent upon the prevailing philosophy of the time and the philosophy of the school administra- tors. Australian Sign has its roots in British Sign, and two-handed finger spelling is used. A small number of elderly deaf men educated in the early days of St. Gabriel's School for Deaf Boys, some of their close contacts, and their teachers use what are referred to as the "old Catholic signs" and the one-handed alphabet, both of which were brought by the Christian Brothers from Ireland.

In the 1970s, as in other countries, a marked swing towards Total Communication occurred. Within educational settings manu- ally coded English known as Signed English has been the recognized sign system since then. In many Total Communication classes

there is an emphasis on the development of auditory and speech skills.

In the late '60s and early '70s the Victorian and New South Wales Schools for the Deaf each published a dictionary of signs. These two dictionaries demonstrated the similarities and differences that had devel- oped in the sign vocabularies of the two school communities six hundred miles apart. In 1975, a nationwide committee of represen- tatives of the Deaf Community and interested hearing persons, mostly educators, was set up to develop an *Australian Sign Dictionary*. New Zealand later joined this committee so that the second edition became the *Australasian Sign Dictionary*. The purpose of the committee was to devise a dictionary of signs for use in the education of deaf children in Total Communication settings. Guiding principles for the word-based dictionary were agreed upon and a dictionary of about 3000 words was developed, using mostly the signs of the Adult Deaf Community. Where Adult Deaf signs could not be traced or were the same for more than one word, new signs were devised according to the agreed principles. In Signed English those dictionary signs are used togeth- er with fingerspelling in the word order of English.

Auslan is used informally in a few class settings where teachers have developed adequate skills. In classes where members of the Deaf Community (deaf adults or hearing relatives of deaf adults) are teacher's aides, the students are exposed to more frequent use of Auslan. "Concerned Deaf" groups whose members belong mostly to the Deaf Community have advocated the use of Auslan as the educational communication methodol- ogy for hearing impaired students. Some educators support this approach within a bilingual methodology, and a very small num- ber of classes are operating broadly within such a context. Apart from philosophical con- siderations, a limiting factor in establishing such classes is that trained teachers who are sufficiently fluent in Auslan are few and far between. In New South Wales a conference/workshop arranged jointly between "Concerned Deaf," the State Department of School Education, the Educators of the Deaf Association, and parent groups is to be held late in 1991. In 1992, a pilot bilingual programme was introduced at preschool level in one or two regular schools. This programme will be closely monitored and evaluated. The Royal New South Wales Institute for Deaf and Blind Children is establishing its own new special school to provide early bilingual education for six or seven deaf children and fifteen to sixteen hearing children including siblings of deaf children. An important development that will support these new programmes was the production of *The Auslan Dictionary* (Johnson, 1989).

The establishment of bilingual programmes is, as in other countries, the result of society's, and educators' in particular, increased knowledge of and changed attitudes towards Sign Language. In Australia there has developed since World War II the acceptance of the coexistence of many different languages and cultures within the dominant English-speaking society. In the National Language Policy (Lo Bianco, 1987) which recognizes the needs of persons with a non-English-speaking background, Auslan is accepted as a "Community Language Other than English". This has resulted in funds for teaching and interpreting services, representation of Deaf people on relevant National Committees, and the National Accreditation of interpreters on the same basis as the other recognized Community languages.

Opportunities for Vocational Education

Vocational education opportunities for deaf students originally were provided in the special schools for deaf students through the provision of trade, low-level clerical, and domestic science subjects. Sometimes these subjects were taught by deaf tradespersons. Teachers and concerned parents spent many hours building small networks of employers who would provide work experience for deaf students, and perhaps later employment. With the decline of enrollments in the special schools, the decline of trades such as boot repairing, and changes in attitude about what types of employment are appropriate for deaf persons, the special schools and the teachers and parents of deaf students in special classes or in mainstreamed settings in the last twenty years have developed close liaisons with colleges of technical and further education and with rehabilitation agencies providing short courses.

One such short course was offered by the Royal Blind Society at the beginning of 1991 as part of the Australian Traineeships Access Scheme financed by the national Department of Employment, Education and Training. This course was unusual in that it brought together young school leavers who had either hearing or visual disabilities, a mix which is often considered educationally unsound. The twelve participants spent 30 hours in a personal development programme, 30 hours on communication, 15 hours on numeracy and literacy, and 45 hours on job skills. Most of the 16-18 year olds were aiming for clerical traineeships. Previous success rates have been 80-90 per cent (Preston, 1991). Many more hearing impaired school leavers could benefit from such programmes if they were more freely available.

The Adult Deaf Societies in some states provide career workshops and camps of short duration to introduce secondary school students to a variety of occupations and to give practice in developing some general work skills and job applications. The Link programmes previously run by the New South Wales Department of Technical and Further Education provided secondary school students with a series of work experiences and information concerning careers in which they expressed interest. Regrettably, the withdrawal of funding resulted in their discontinuance. Individual teachers and schools continue to provide ongoing career planning and preparation for their students, often in conjunction with the Department of Industrial Relations and Training and/or local employers and Commonwealth Employment Service offices.

Although lists of some occupations held by deaf people in New South Wales (Cipollone, 1990) range from solicitor, architect, and university lecturer through some one hundred jobs to unskilled labourer, there is a general consensus among professionals, parents, and the Deaf Community that deaf people are frequently underemployed. This consensus has been confirmed by a study of deaf youth in Queensland which reported that 37 percent were unemployed and 30 percent had never been employed in the six years since leaving school (Hyde, 1988). This was the highest rate of chronic unemployment in the nation for any group with normal intelligence (Hyde & Power, 1990). Preliminary results from a survey of signing deaf people in most states revealed that 32 percent were employed as clerks, service workers, or labourers; 11 percent were in trades; 22 percent in home duties; fewer than one percent were employed as professionals, managers, and administrators; and 10 percent were unemployed. Statistics are not available for the broader community of hearing impaired people which, it would be reasonable to expect, would paint a more positive picture. Comparative figures for the hearing community were 40 percent employed in trades and 20 percent in professional, managerial, and administrative positions (Hyde & Power, 1990). In 1991, national unemployment figures were running at 8-9 percent. Although a number of factors are influential in the underemployment of deaf people, it is acknowledged that communication skill inadequacies, academic underachievement, and deficiencies in vocational advising and preparation are contributors to this situation. Other perceived problems are the poor interpersonal skills and lack of understanding of the requirements of the workplace by many deaf school leavers (Cipollone, 1987; Healy, 1987; Hyde, 1988). Clearly, much remains to be done to enhance the employment prospects of deaf students.

Parent Education

Each of the states and territories provides parent education and support services. Personnel involved are early childhood educators, teachers, audiologists, psychologists, counsellors, social workers, and deaf adults. Self-help groups of parents associated with schools and on a broader basis also give strong support to families. Formal services are probably most routine and plentiful for parents and families of infants and young children following diagnosis. On a less routine basis, professional support is provided for parents at significant stages within the child's or parent's life and according to need. Monthly or more or less frequent meetings associated with particular schools or classes often comprise discussion groups or relevant addresses by invited guests. Social activities allow more informal education and support to occur. Umbrella parent groups such as the Parent Council for Deaf Education in New South Wales arrange annual conferences, generally with the needs of parents in mind but often also including a day for professionals. Frequently keynote speakers with expertise in the theme of the conference are invited from overseas.

Some nongovernment facilities require parent participation in educational and fundraising activities as a condition of enrollment in the programme. Other such services are less demanding. Generally, in government settings parent participation cannot be compelled and there are always some parents who by inclination or adverse circumstances do not take advantage of the services offered. In 1968, surveyed parents were requesting more educational and support services (Rumsey, 1968, 1977). Even though such services have expanded dramatically in the intervening years, so has the population that requires them, and parents are still calling for further expansion and greater availability of services (Rumsey, in Pieterse et al, 1988).

Special correspondence services, for example from the Royal New South Wales

Institute for Deaf and Blind Children and the Shepherd Centre in Sydney, are available to parents in isolated areas and overseas and also to those parents who are unable to regularly visit the centres or receive regular home visits. Some nongovernment agencies or schools, for example, St. Gabriel's Family Support Centre in Sydney, have an apartment available for isolated parents to use for three-, four- or five-day visits during which they receive concentrated assistance. Such visits may occur annually or as frequently as four times per year.

The needs and support of siblings, grandparents, other family members, and other caregivers are acknowledged in the provision of special meetings, conferences, workshops, and social activities for these groups. The needs of non-English-speaking parents and other involved persons are met to some extent through interpreters and written materials provided in a variety of languages. The most recent development in this area was the launching in 1991 of booklets and audio-cassettes suitable for parents and families of newly diagnosed deaf children from Arabic, Turkish, Spanish, and Vietnamese language groups (Parent Council, 1991).

Education of Aborigines with Hearing Impairments

Australia has been inhabited by Aborigines for at least 40,000 years. European settlement of the continent in 1788 resulted in a dramatic reduction in the number of Aborigines and their relegation to the position of fringe dwellers in the dominant Western culture. Today, Aborigines live in rural and urban settings, often in Aboriginal communities but also scattered among the general population. They are considered to be a disadvantaged group and receive a measure of support from antidiscrimination legislation and positive discrimination programmes.

The early European settlers noted frequent middle ear infections among Aborigines (Willis, 1985). Lewis, Barry, and Stuart (1974) reported that the incidence of childhood middle ear infection leading to conductive losses was much higher in the Aboriginal than in the white population. Most recent figures suggest that up to 80 percent of Aboriginal children in the Northern Territory, Queensland, and Western Australia suffer some kind of middle ear involvement, with 25 to 50 percent of Aboriginal children attending school in the Northern Territory having an educationally significant loss, which not unusually may be as high as 55 or 60 dBHL (Nienhuys, 1990).

As prevalence studies have typically focused on Aboriginal children living in outback or country town locations, an exploratory study undertaken in an inner suburb of Australia's largest city is of interest. Greater Sydney has a population of 3.65 million (Cook, 1991). In the inner suburbs live some 2800 Aboriginal infants and schoolchildren, of whom 100 were the subjects of the exploratory study. Screening audiometry and simple otoscopic observations were performed upon the first 100 children aged four to twelve years who presented with parent consent forms for routine annual school health screening. None of the children wore hearing aids and only one was receiving any medical attention for middle ear disease at the time of testing. Otoscopic abnormalities were noted in 81 percent of the subjects and 29 percent had educationally significant hearing losses (mean hearing level across both ears at 0.5,1 and 2kHz equal to or greater than 25 dBHL). Only 4 percent of subjects had hearing losses greater than 45dB in the better ear. The statistically significant finding that a greater proportion of the 4-7 years age group had educationally significant hearing losses than did the 8-12 years group, is of particular concern because it is the younger children who are developing foundation literacy skills. Because of possible bias in their sampling technique, the researchers believed that the study was more likely to have under- rather than over-estimated the prevalence of hearing disorders in the Sydney Aboriginal child population (Nienhuys, Sherwood and Bush, 1990).

Of particular note is the fact that the pattern of early, i.e., at age three months or less (Alperstein, 1990), intermittent, often untreated, chronic otitis media and chronic fluctuating conductive hearing loss is very similar in both urban and isolated communities in different states.

The incidence of profound deafness in Central Australian Aboriginal children was reported by Urban (1977) to be 6 per 1000 compared with the 1-2 per 1000 in the European population. Urban's review of the records indicated about 25 percent of these cases were caused by maternal rubella, and about 70 percent were thought to have resulted from such illnesses as meningitis, encephalitis, and septicaemia.

The problem of Aboriginal hearing loss is medical, socio-economic, and educational. It is further compounded by the fact that services typically have been offered by the dominant white community, which has not understood Aboriginal cultural values, languages, traditions, and practices. In the heyday of the state residential schools for the deaf, severely and profoundly deaf Aboriginal children, like their white counterparts from country areas, were removed from their communities for long periods of time. The difference for the Aboriginal children was that they found themselves in an alien culture that did not prepare them for adulthood in their own community and culture. Before government-subsidized school vacation air travel was made available to children from remote areas, many Aboriginal children spent the school holidays in State welfare institutions. Indeed, one boy saw his family only once in ten years, when the manager of the station (large farm) on which the family lived and worked had him flown home for the holidays (Green, 1977).

In 1968, the Northern Territory set up its first special class for hearing impaired Aboriginal students in Alice Springs, an inland city with a large Aboriginal population. Even

so, some children were still 300 kilometres from their tribal community and living in hostel accommodation. Eventually, in 1973, a unit was opened at the Aboriginal community of Warrabri (Watter, 1977), with teachers of deaf children seeking to work with members of the community. Since that time most of the States have attempted to provide local educational services to identified hearing impaired Aboriginal children in rural and provincial areas.

In 1979, Walpiri Hand Talk (Wright) was published. This manual of signs recorded those used by the older Aboriginal women during extended periods of mourning when they were not permitted to speak. The dual purpose of the publication was to ensure that at least some record of the signs was kept, as the younger women were not fluent in them, and to provide a basis for communication with hearing impaired children of that language group. Culturally appropriate materials about ears and conductive hearing loss and its treatment, have been prepared by education, health, and Aboriginal groups in Western Australia, Northern Territory, and Queensland for use with Aboriginal and Torres Strait Islander people. Other resource materials are currently being updated and/or developed. For example, the New South Wales School Education Department has adapted the Northern Territory, Aboriginal Teachers' Manual *Healthy Ears - Hear Better* for use in New South Wales Government schools (New South Wales Department of School Education, 1991).

At present there is a much greater attempt in all States with Aboriginal populations to offer services locally in both urban and rural settings, seeking the informed cooperation of the community and wherever possible delivering the service through Aboriginal people themselves. There is, however, a long way still to go before such services meet the needs of that population. In September 1990 a national conference on Aboriginal otitis media was held in Darwin, Northern Territory. Although Australian

Deafness Council had previously held three seminars on this topic in 1979, 1981, and 1985, this was the first to combine health, audiological, educational, and Aboriginal organisations (Nienhuys, 1991). Recommendations were made with both national and state implications. The recommendations pertinent to this chapter were: the establishment of a national data base through regular frequent screening programmes to identify all Aboriginal children with conductive hearing loss; the inclusion of issues relating to conductive hearing loss in Aboriginal students in all teacher training courses and in in-service courses relating to Aboriginal education; the development of appropriate resource material in consultation with Aboriginal representatives; the preparation and distribution of educational materials to raise the awareness of classroom teachers and provide sets of strategies for coping with students with fluctuating hearing losses; seeking with understanding and empathy the co-operation of the Aboriginal community in dealing with chronic fluctuating conductive hearing loss in Aboriginal children, and in fostering the self-esteem and empowerment of Aboriginal caregivers to act in their children's interest.

In a period of economic constraint moneys may not be forthcoming to support some of the above recommendations. However, an increasing number of teachers of deaf children and associated professionals are becoming aware of the particular needs of Aboriginal hearing impaired children and are eager to develop the understanding, knowledge, and skills necessary to meet those needs.

The Training of Teachers

History

That teachers of deaf children should be trained in their profession was a concern from the beginning of the provision of educational services for deaf children in Australia. The two founders of the two original schools were themselves trained teachers and the committees which sought their successors required that those men be trained. However, the reality was that the majority of teachers were recruited from among those individuals who had some experience with people who were deaf.

Beginning in 1870, former pupils were appointed as pupil teachers at the New South Wales school, and in 1883 the first pupil teacher who was not a former pupil of the school was appointed. In 1880 and 1897 respectively, two women teachers who had trained as teachers of deaf children at Ealing College in London, United Kingdom, were brought out to Sydney. In the early 1900s an Australian woman was sent to Ealing College to train as a "teacher of articulation." Upon her return to Australia she lectured to pupil teachers in history and principles of education of the deaf (Walter, 1960). Indeed, the employment of preservice trained teachers at the New South Wales Institution preceded the employment of such teachers in regular government schools by more than thirty years (Lund, in Walter, 1960).

Because the government trained teachers of hearing students only for its own schools, independent schools continued to use pupil teachers, recruit overseas trained teachers, and employ whatever local teachers became available. Many of the untrained teachers continued their studies to become university graduates, and a number went overseas, generally to Great Britain, to obtain a qualification in teaching deaf children at their own expense. Others qualified for the Overseas Diploma of the National College of Teachers of the Deaf, United Kingdom (Walter, 1960). In 1950, a parent group which eventually became the Victorian Committee for the Promotion of Oral Education of the Deaf, awarded the first of four scholarships for teachers to study at Manchester University in the United Kingdom (John, 1990). At the same time, while the New South Wales Department of School Education supported two teachers at Manchester University, the

Victorian Department of Education supported more than fifteen teachers, two at doctoral level, over a three-year period. (Parr, 1974). In 1956, the Dominican Sisters sent two of their number to study at Manchester (Dooley, 1989).

An Australian Diploma of Education of the Deaf

In 1938 the Australian Association of Teachers of the Deaf, founded in 1935, introduced a Diploma of Education of the Deaf. A national Board of Examiners was established to set and maintain standards. Practicing teachers could obtain this Diploma by studying the syllabus and sitting written examinations, set by the Board, in the theory and practice of teaching deaf children. Practical examinations were taken in the school where the teacher taught, the Examiner being a member of the Board or its nominee. Members of the Association who were trained teachers of deaf children and who had been actively engaged in education of the deaf for at least ten years could seek the award of Fellow of the Association by submission to the Board of Examiners of an original thesis on any aspect of education of the deaf (Rumsey, 1975).

State Funded Courses for Teachers of Deaf Students

In the early 1900s the compulsory pre-service training of teachers of hearing children in government schools superseded the pupil-teacher method of teacher training. However it was not until 1954 in Melbourne, Victoria, and 1955 in Sydney, New South Wales, that government funded training for teachers of deaf children was introduced (Rumsey, 1975).

The catalyst for this development was the report of Professor Alexander and Dr. Irene Ewing of Manchester University, United Kingdom, following their visit to Australia to advise on the education of deaf children at the request of the Victorian Government. Their first recommendation was for the specific training of teachers of deaf children. The lecturers in charge of these new training courses were Australians who had gained appropriate qualifications from the Department of Audiology and Education of the Deaf at Manchester University in the United Kingdom. Consequently, the student teachers under their tutelage were exposed to a strong oral bias in the education of deaf students, and the strong British influence in the education of hearing impaired children in Australia was to continue for at least another ten years.

Entry to both courses was open only to trained teachers of hearing children. Victoria admitted both inexperienced and experienced teachers. Until 1962, New South Wales required entrants to have completed two years of successful teaching of hearing children. In New South Wales to this day the great majority of teachers entering the basic training course for teachers of deaf students continue to be experienced teachers of hearing students.

Soon after its inception, the New South Wales programme began to include secondary teachers but it was not until the late '60s and early '70s that teachers with specific training in early childhood were enrolled. Nevertheless, preschool parent guidance programmes, as they were then known, were offered by the department of education from age of diagnosis, staffed by teachers with a particular interest and competence in this area.

Increase in Courses and Teachers

Australia-wide until the mid-1970s, virtually the only special education teachers who received formal specialized training of at least one year's duration beyond their regular teacher training were teachers of deaf students. In 1974, an infusion of Commonwealth funds into special education teacher training led to the establishment of a number of courses in special education and an increase, from two to five, in the number of courses for teachers of deaf children. This resulted in two teacher education courses being available in New South Wales and one course in each of Victoria, Queensland, and South Australia. At the same time, a private foundation financed the establishment of a Deaf Studies Unit at the University of Melbourne. Commencing with a diploma course in audiology, this unit moved into teacher education in 1977 (Rumsey, 1981).

As state governments accepted responsibility for educating deaf children and training their teachers during the 1950s, there was a rapid increase both in the number of teachers and the number of teachers who also were trained as teachers of deaf children. Before 1950, 64 teachers had specialist training, 45 of them being in New South Wales. By 1979, 729 teachers were trained as teachers of deaf children, 216 of them in New South Wales. In that year, only 42 teachers of deaf children had not received specialist training, 27 of them being in Western Australia which, at that time, was some 1500 miles from the nearest training programme (Murphy, 1980). In 1991 the vast majority of teachers of deaf students had received specialist training at bachelor or postgraduate diploma level. In New South Wales, for example, at least 98 percent of the approximately 250 teachers currently employed are specifically trained to teach hearing impaired students (Rumsey, 1991).

Since the 1980s both basic and advanced courses in the education of deaf students have been available in five of the six states of the Commonwealth, at bachelor, postgraduate diploma, and master's level. Research degrees are available at master and doctoral level. Almost all programmes are offered in both full-time and part-time mode, although the preferred mode is full-time.

Accreditation

Courses are accredited nationally through a process of initial assessment before introduction, followed by five-yearly reviews. Accreditation leads to national registration of the award and federal funding for the course.

Accreditation and review committees include academics from other courses for teachers of hearing impaired students, representatives of employing authorities and professional organisations, practicing teachers, and ex-students. The Australian Association of Teachers of the Deaf has developed guidelines for the conduct and content of courses of training for teachers of hearing impaired students. One requirement is that the major organisation and conduct of the course must be carried out by academics with qualifications and experience in the education of hearing impaired students. Although adherence to these guidelines is not a condition of accreditation, only graduates of those courses approved by the Association are eligible for full membership in it.

Sponsorship

The vast majority of teachers in postgraduate diploma programmes have been fully sponsored by their relevant state governments, which also have paid them full salary while undertaking their course. In New South Wales, the government offers the same support to selected teachers studying at the master's level. From the early 1970s until 1988, tertiary education tuition throughout Australia was free. Since the reintroduction of tuition fees the state governments have paid them for teachers studying in special education courses. In some states this has led to teachers being required to sign agreements specifying mutually acceptable education regions in which they will serve for a minimum of three years on completion of their course.

Occasionally nongovernment agencies and, more rarely, TAFE sponsor a teacher who will return to the sponsoring agency on completion of the course. Similarly, those states and territories which do not operate their own training programmes sometimes sponsor a teacher from their own education system to study interstate. Otherwise, they recruit from interstate, or employ teachers qualified to teach hearing impaired students from those who already have moved from overseas or interstate.

Certification of Teachers

Certification as a teacher in Australia requires a minimum of three years teacher education at degree or diploma level. Certification as a teacher of hearing impaired students may be gained as a result of specific studies during that initial three or four years. However, for most teachers, certification is gained through post-initial training of at least one year in an accredited course at graduate diploma or master's level.

Continuing Professional Education for Teachers

Practicing teachers are able to update their knowledge and skills by participating in local, regional, and national inservice programmes and conferences on deafness and broader educational subjects. The late 1980s and early 1990s saw a well-attended proliferation of inservice activities, but the economic downturn of the late 1990s witnessed a reduction in government financial support for professional education. The Australian Association of Teachers of the Deaf has organised a national conference every three years since its inception except for the years of World War II. Of recent years this conference has expanded to include colleagues from New Zealand. In some years the Association has been able to subsidise the attendance of representatives from the developing Pacific nations. The Association publishes the *Australian Teacher of the Deaf*; the Australian Deafness Council, the *Australian Hearing and Deafness Review*; and the Audiological Society, the *Australian Journal of Audiology*. These publications together with other Australian journals in special education, general education, communication disorders, medicine, and the behavioral sciences enable teachers to be informed of ideas and research relevant to their profession. Many schools and educators also subscribe to overseas publications.

Lecture tours, workshops, and paper presentations by overseas educators and experts in allied fields, together with their own reading, study tours, and attendance at overseas conferences enable teachers to keep abreast of international developments in the education of hearing impaired students. The consistently high attendance of teachers at professional development activities, both subsidized and unsubsidised, is indicative of their generally high level of professional commitment.

Opportunities for Deaf People to Serve as Teachers of Deaf Students

The first three schools for deaf students in Australia were founded by teachers who were themselves deaf. In the schools for the deaf, both charitable (later government) and denominational, deaf teachers were employed at least until the 1960s. Always in a minority, often without teacher training and sometimes teaching nonacademic and vocational subjects, those who retired in the 1960s were not replaced by deaf teachers. The preference for the oral mode of education precluded the hiring of deaf teachers in some private and denominational schools, and when state departments of education took over the staffing of the charitable schools for deaf children they usually insisted that new teachers be persons qualified to teach in regular schools. Deaf people were precluded from gaining teacher training because of academic entry requirements to teachers' colleges and stringent health requirements that excluded people with deafness. However, some teachers who developed mild to moderate progressive hearing losses managed to retain their employment.

The Deaf Community, together with other hearing impaired people, resented the exclusion of deaf and hearing impaired persons from the teaching profession. Over a number of years they made representations to colleges and universities with established courses for teachers of deaf students for the development of special programmes to train deaf and hearing impaired teachers and teacher's aides. In most cases, the major obstacle to such provision was the small number of people for whom these courses were to be provided and the consequent economic inviability. In many cases bridging or preparatory programmes would have been necessary to bring the applicants to acceptable entry levels. Even in times when government funding was more freely available, university administrations looked askance even at the provision of auditory devices, notetakers, and oral/manual interpreters, let alone lecturing staff for very small groups of students in special courses.

Changes in attitude toward the educational use of Signed English and the need for deaf role models for deaf children, together with the passing of antidiscrimination legislation, led in the 1980s to the training of deaf teachers. This had commenced in the 1970s with the occasional acceptance into postgraduate courses for teachers of the deaf, of hearing-impaired teachers who had managed to avoid health requirements and who generally had been educated in hearing classes and completed regular teacher training. In 1984, a federally funded pilot programme to train deaf teachers was introduced at Mt. Gravatt College of Advanced Education (now Griffith University), with the tacit understanding with some employing authorities that graduates would teach in schools for deaf students. Applicants were carefully screened for academic ability, communication skills, and general suitability for teaching. Generally, they were older than the majority of entrants to preservice undergraduate programmes, having been in employment for a number of years. The Griffith University programme is described in somewhat more detail under postsecondary education.

It is now accepted by most people involved with the education of deaf students that it is the right of academically qualified deaf people to enter teacher education programmes. The level of support provided, such as tutors, notetakers, interpreters, and assistive devices, varies from university to university. There is a small but continuous number of deaf people training as teachers of deaf students.

It is also now accepted that the presence of deaf and hearing impaired teachers and other professional role models such as psychologists, counsellors, teacher's aides, clerical assistants, social welfare workers, careers advisors, and so forth, is necessary for the personal, social, and career development of deaf and hearing impaired students. Such individuals also can provide links for the students with the Deaf Community. A minority of education settings now employ deaf or hearing impaired people as teacher's aides.

Within the Technical and Further Education sector, deaf and hearing impaired people are employed as teachers and consultants, and as teachers of Signed English and Auslan. More than fifty deaf persons are employed Australia-wide as teachers of Auslan (Duffy, 1991). The Adult Education Centre for Deaf and Hearing Impaired Persons in Sydney, New South Wales, employs a number of deaf people as teachers in a wide variety of short courses ranging from Deaf Studies to driver education. The Management Council of that Centre is comprised of deaf and hearing impaired people.

Since 1991, it has been possible for deaf teachers of Australian Sign Language to gain special entry to the Latrobe University Bachelor of Education degree for teachers of community languages. While this course does not enable its graduates to be registered as teachers, it does increase their knowledge of language, linguistics, language teaching, and curriculum development.

So the wheel of opportunity for deaf people to become teachers of deaf students has come more than full cycle in just over one hundred years. From a situation of minimal teacher training, like many of their hearing counterparts of those times, deaf people have moved through exclusion from entry to teacher education courses to acceptance with necessary support in such programmes and to subsequent employment as teachers of deaf students.

Resources for Students and Teachers

During the last twenty years the number of Australian educational resources for use with hearing impaired students has increased dramatically. Already mentioned are the *Dictionary of Australasian Signs* (Victorian School for Deaf Children, 1982) and the materials for use with Aboriginal children.

Most States have produced curricula with particular relevance for deaf students, especially in the area of personal development. The *Auditory Skills Program* (Romanik, 1991) is being used widely and has been purchased by schools in other English-speaking countries. Various states have produced storybooks in both English and Signed English or Australian Sign formats. *Hands up for a Story* (1990) is an innovative literature programme for young hearing impaired children. It consists of a set of videos and support materials which present ten popular children's stories in Australian Sign, Signed English, and spoken English.

The University of New South Wales holds an annual "Science Camp" specifically for deaf and hearing impaired school students and also encourages the more able of them to participate in its vacation schools for gifted secondary school students.

Sound Waves is a professionally produced, eight-page illustrated magazine with items of particular interest to older primary and secondary school students. Initiated in 1988 (Folan), it is written mostly by deaf and hearing impaired students.

The Australian Caption Centre, a not-for-profit company established in 1983, cap-

tions television programmes, videos, and films. It provides an educational support service in the form of a club and a bimonthly four-page publication for primary children, as well as a newsletter for teachers with teaching hints on specific captioned material.

An HIV/AIDS education programme (ACON, 1989), first developed in 1989 by a Deaf person specifically for Deaf people, has received worldwide acclaim and has been purchased by organisations in a number of countries. It is also used with hearing populations who have limited reading ability in English. Updated with the latest information, it recently has been approved by the New South Wales Department of School Education for use under specified conditions with senior secondary school students.

In the past, ingenious ideas to enhance the teaching of deaf and hearing impaired students often were not published because of the relatively small purchasing clientele. Increased allocation of funds for such purposes by state departments of education and other interested bodies has led to wider dissemination of materials and ideas. With the advent of desktop publishing the scope for sharing ideas and techniques is now almost limitless.

Deafness Resources, established in 1974 by Deaf people, is a distributor for overseas publishers, acts as a clearing house for national and international materials and information, advises on assistive devices, and is the publisher of the Auslan Dictionary (Johnson, 1989).

Australian Deafness Council, an umbrella organisation with state member bodies, is an active lobby group for a number of concerns including education. Theatre of the Deaf; professional organisations of teachers, audiologists, and so on; parent groups; and various associations of deaf and hearing impaired persons all play their part in acting as resources or support groups for the education of hearing impaired students.

Conclusion

In reviewing the development of education for deaf students since 1860, Australia has much to be proud of and probably equally much to be ashamed of. In comparison with educational provisions for other disability groups, hearing impaired students have probably been better served than most. Historically, they were the first to receive services through philanthropic means, although most State Governments were tardy in accepting responsibility. In most States they also were among the first to receive services before and after the ages of compulsory schooling. Parents and other concerned people have been tireless in their efforts to improve services. Australia is a world leader in hearing-aid provision and servicing and in cochlear implants. The majority of teachers have been committed to the best possible educational development of their charges, usually according to the prevailing philosophies of their time. Teachers of deaf students were the first group of specialist teachers to receive specialist training of at least one year's duration following initial teacher education.

Certainly there have been periods of intolerance of other points of view and of paternalism towards deaf students by administrators, teachers, and even parents. Understanding Aboriginal hearing impaired students and providing appropriate services for them have been very much neglected until recently. The recognition of the linguistic and cultural rights of the Deaf Community to their language and culture is a comparatively recent development. Much work needs to be done in the area of vocational preparation and in improving the academic performance of deaf children. In most States postsecondary education at University and Technical and the Further Education level must be developed further.

Bilingual/bicultural education for deaf children, an increase in the number of deaf teachers, and perhaps a return to special school placement at high school level are possible future developments.

As the cochlear implant programme continues, more students will have had such implants. Already, many teachers have attended in-service courses to prepare them for meeting the needs of those students.

Parents, educators, deaf people, other interested professionals, and laypeople have a continuing responsibility to ensure the improvement of both state and independent education for hearing impaired students. Their commitment and vigilance are as necessary now as at any other time.

References

ACON, (1990). *AIDS, not hearing aids: HIV/AIDS education program for the deaf community.* Sydney, New South Wales, Australia: Aids Council of New South Wales Inc.

Alperstein, G. (1990, May). *Otitis Media-Risk Factors.* Paper presented at the conference on Aboriginal students with hearing impairment, Sydney, New South Wales, Australia.

Ashman, A., & Elkins, J. (1990). *Educating children with special needs.* Sydney, New South Wales, Australia: Prentice Hall.

Australian Deafness Council (NSW). (1988). *After high school.... What do I do now?* Petersham, New South Wales, Australia: Australian Deafness Council (NSW).

Barkham, L.F. (1974). *The story of Townsend House, 1874-1974.* Adelaide, South Australia, Australia: South Australian Institute for Deaf & Blind, Inc.

Brooks, D.N. (1989). *Adult aural rehabilitation.* London: Chapman & Hall.

Burnip, L. (1988). Skills required by hearing impaired post-secondary students. *Australian Teacher of the Deaf, 29,* 65-82.

Bytheway, L. (1989). How do Australian subtitles compare. *Australian Hearing & Deafness Review, 6,* 20-22.

Center for Deaf and Hearing Impaired Persons. (Producers). (1989). *Heritage in our hands.* [Videotape]. Sydney, New South Wales, Australia: Center for Deaf and Hearing Impaired Persons.

Cipollone, P. (1987). Employment. In *Seminar on the hearing impaired child K-12.* Sydney, New South Wales, Australia: Metropolitan East Region, Department of Education.

Cipollone, P. (1990, November 5). *Post School Opportunities.* Lecture presented at the University of Western Sydney, Nepean.

Cook, D. (1991, April 5). Sydney stagnates as the population goes bush. *Sydney Morning Herald.*

Directory. (1988). *Australian Teacher of the Deaf, 29,* 86-97.

Dooley, A. (1989). *To be fully alive: a monograph on Australian Dominican education of hearing impaired children.* Strathfield, New South Wales, Australia: Catholic Centre for Hearing Impaired Children.

Duffy, A. (1991, March). *Auslan Curriculum.* Paper presented at the Annual General Meeting of the Adult Center for Deaf and Hearing Impaired Persons, Sydney, New South Wales, Australia.

Folan, S. (1991, June). *Sound waves: Youth magazine.* Melbourne, Victoria, Australia.

Follent, M. (1991, Winter). Cochlear implants in children. *SHHH News, 8.* Turramurra, New South Wales, Australia.

Green, N. (1977). The education of hearing impaired aboriginal children in Western Australia. In *Deaf children: Their parents and teachers in a cross cultural setting* (pp.17-24). Darwin, Northern Territory, Australia: Northern Territory Department of Education.

Hands up for a story. (1990). Sydney, New South Wales, Australia: Department of School Education.

Hayes, K. (1991). Causes of congenital deafness - rubella. *Taralye Bulletin, 9,* 1, 3-5. Blackburn, Victoria, Australia: Advisory Council for Children with Impaired Hearing.

Healey, P. (1987). *Integration: What it means.* Sydney, New South Wales, Australia: Metropolitan East Region, Department of Education.

Hyde, M. (1988). Post-secondary needs of young hearing impaired people in Queensland. *Australian Disability Review, 1,* 21-25.

Hyde, M., & Power, D. (1990). *Preliminary report on the study on the use of Australian Sign Language.* Brisbane, Queensland, Australia: Griffith University, Division of Education.

John, N.S. (1990). Victorian committee for the promotion of oral education for the deaf. *Taralye Bulletin, 8,* 3, 22. Advisory Council for Children with Impaired Hearing, Blackburn, Victoria, Australia.

Johnson, T. (1989). *Auslan dictionary.* Sydney, New South Wales, Australia: Deafness Resources.

Kirk, S. (1991, March 20). Silent survival: When deafness cuts you off. *Sydney Morning Herald.*

Landa, P. (1981, August). *Special education in New South Wales.* Paper presented at Conference of Special Education Teachers: Ryde, New South Wales, Australia.

Lewis, A.N., Barry, M., & Stuart, J.E. (1973). Screening procedures for the identification of hearing and ear disorders in Australian Aboriginal Children. *Laryngol. Otol. 88,* 335-347.

Lewis, J. (1989, September 2). Study finds system turns a deaf ear. *Sydney Morning Herald.*

Lo Bianco, J. (1987). *National policy on languages.* Canberra, Australian Capital Territory, Australia: Australian Government Printing Services.

McGree, P. (1963). *A history of the development of education for the deaf in Australia.* Unpublished paper, Sydney, New South Wales, Australia: Sydney Teachers College.

Meade, A. (1991, April 11). The actor you wouldn't know was deaf. *Sydney Morning Herald.*

Murphy, L. (1980). Three decades of education of the deaf in Australia. *Australian Teacher of the Deaf, 21,* 5-15.

New South Wales Department of School Education. (1991). *Healthy Ears - Hear Better.* Draft manual adapted from Northern Territory Aboriginal Teachers' Manual "Healthy Ears - Hear Better". Sydney, New South Wales, Australia.

Nienhuys, T.G. (1991). Report of the National Conference on Aboriginal Otitis Media. *Australian Hearing and Deafness Review, 8,* 18-20.

Nienhuys, T.G., Sherwood, J., & Bush, J. (1990, May). *Hearing loss in a sample of central Sydney aboriginal school children.* Paper presented at the conference on Aboriginal Children with Hearing Impairment, Sydney, New South Wales, Australia.

Parent Council for Deaf Education. (1991). *Where do we go from here?* Sydney, New South Wales, Australia.

Parr, W. (1974). *A history of the course for teachers of the deaf.* Unpublished paper. Sydney, New South Wales, Australia: Sydney Teachers College.

Population grows. (1991, April 3). *Sydney Morning Herald.*

Power, D. (1990a). Hearing impairment. In A. Ashman & J. Elkins (Eds.). *Educating students with special needs.* Sydney, New South Wales, Australia: Prentice Hall.

Power, D. (1990b). *Post-compulsory education for deaf people in Australia.* Brisbane, Queensland, Australia: Griffith University.

Preston, Y. (1991, February 15). Fear of the future: Helping disabled kids cope. *Sydney Morning Herald.*

Project Knock Knock: A profile of the Deaf Community of New South Wales. (1989). Sydney, New South Wales, Australia: Deaf Society of New South Wales.

Public Instruction (Blind and Infirm Children) Amendment Act 1944, Act No. 7. (1944). Sydney, Australia: New South Wales Government Printer.

Rumsey, C.N. (1968). *A study of maternal concerns and attitudes toward young deaf children.* Unpublished bachelor's honors thesis, University of Sydney, New South Wales, Australia.

Rumsey, C.N. (1975). Directory: Provisions for professional training in fields related to deafness in Australia. *The Australian Teacher of the Deaf, 16,* 32-33.

Rumsey, C.N. (1977). Maternal concerns for young prelingually deaf children. *Australian Teacher of the Deaf, 18,* 30-40.

Rumsey, C.N. (1980). Directory of schools for hearing impaired children in Australia and New Zealand. *The Australian Teacher of the Deaf, 21,* 30-32.

Rumsey, C.N. (1981). Courses of training for professionals working with hearing impaired people and services for hearing impaired adults. *The Australian Teacher of the Deaf, 22,* 53-67.

Rumsey, C.N. (1991). [Survey of educational services for hearing impaired students in New South Wales]. Unpublished raw data.

Scott Management Review. (1990, June 25). Education, p. 19.

Smith, I.D. (1991, March 4). Australian firm has Japan by the ears. *Sydney Morning Herald.*

St. Gabriel's School for the Deaf: Golden Jubilee 1922–1972. Castle Hill, New South Wales, Australia: St. Gabriel's School for the Deaf.

Thomas, A. (1989). Combined measles, mumps, rubella immunisation : A strategy for elimination of all three diseases. *Australian Hearing & Deafness Review, 6,* 8-9.

Totaro, P. (1990, May 29). Education flexibility 'assured'. *Sydney Morning Herald.*

Upfold, L.J. (1988). Children with hearing aids in the 1980's: Etiologies and severity of impairment. *Ear and Hearing, 9,* 75-80.

Urban, A. (1977). Finding the profoundly deaf child. In *Deaf children: Their parents and teachers in a cross cultural setting* (pp. 4-12). Darwin, Northern Territory, Australia: Northern Territory Department of Education.

Victorian School for Deaf Children. (1982). *Dictionary of Australasian signs for communication with the deaf.* Victoria, Australia.

Walter, J. (1960). *The history of the New South Wales Schools for Deaf Children and for Blind Children.* 1860-1960. Unpublished thesis, Fellow of the Australian Association of Teachers of the Deaf.

Watter, E. (1977). *Opening address.* In *Deaf children: Their parents and teachers in a cross cultural setting* (pp. 1-3). Darwin, Northern Territory, Australia: Northern Territory Department of Education.

Willis, R. (Ed.). (1985). *Ear disease in Aboriginal children.* A seminar held in Perth, Western Australia, September, 1985, under the auspices of Australian Deafness Council Ltd. and the Otolaryngological Society of Australia.

Wright, C.D. (1979). *Walpiri hand talk.* Darwin, Northern Territory, Australia: Northern Territory Department of Education.

Canadian Education of Deaf and Hard of Hearing Students in the 1990s

by Mary Ann Bibby

Introduction

The education of deaf and hard of hearing people in Canada has a long and varied history. The 1990s are proving to be a time of change and improvements, due to recent changes in human rights legislation, advances in medical technology, and telecommunication. In order to understand the full impact of today's issues and concerns, it is first necessary to take a brief look at the historical development of the country itself. Canada's history has affected not only education in general, but also the specialized area of education for people with impaired hearing.

Canada is a vast country, stretching over 5,600 kilometers from east to west and 4,800 kilometers from north to south. The southern portion consists of ten large Provinces, and the northern region is divided into two territories, the Northwest Territories and the Yukon. For such a large country, the population is small, just 26.9 million people. Most live in areas of concentration to the south, close to the border with the United States. The cities and towns in each Province are often separated by densely forested areas, vast open expanses of prairie, or huge mountain ranges. Although linked by modern road, rail, and air systems, and of course by modern telecommunication systems, travel is expensive both in time and money. These geographical conditions and settlement patterns have provided Canada with exciting variety, and are also at least partially responsible for the unique educational systems that are now in existence.

Historically, Canada belonged to the Indians and Inuit. There is evidence of early linking of a Norwegian settlement but it was not until the late 1700s that large-scale immigration had established both French and English settlements. After a turbulent history these joined together in 1867 to initiate Confederation. Canada was originally ruled by Great Britain but now, although still a member of the Commonwealth of Nations, it is fully independent. The linking of Canada to other members of the Commonwealth has traditionally allowed for a fairly free exchange among very diverse cultures in areas such as education, sports, culture, and the arts. It has also provided for international exchanges among students in school and in Universities, facilitated by the use of English which is the official language of the Commonwealth (Ojile & Carver, 1987).

The recent influx of immigrants from many other countries of the world is continuing to expand the international mosaic. Canada is a country with two official languages, French and English, but Canadians pride themselves on the multicultural nature of their citizens. There is a sincere effort to support linguistic and ethnic diversity. At this time in Canada's history however, two issues are paramount: minority rights and linguistic cultural freedom. In 1982, the Canadian Charter of Rights and Freedoms became one of the most important legal documents in Canada's history. As part of Canada's Constitution, it deals with such significant issues as mobility rights, equality rights, and minority language educational rights.

Minority groups in Canada, in particular Native and French-speaking groups, are demanding recognition and equality in every area, including that of education. Quebec, the predominantly French-speaking Province, is taking the lead in addressing language and cultural issues, but several other cultural groups are also addressing issues of equality and respect. A special group is composed of people who are deaf. ASL has been declared one of the official languages of instruction for Deaf students in three Provinces. It is expected that others will follow.

It is against this background that all Canadian educators are beginning to examine more carefully the structure and content of their educational systems. Educators of the hearing handicapped are also being forced to examine educational principles and practices. The Canadian Deaf population views itself as having minority status and as such, has largely been ignored. In the past, "prejudice perpetuated deaf people's isolation from one another and from the general community" (Winzer, 1983, p. 155). Now however, deaf people are speaking out and becoming actively involved in the social structure of their communities and country. They have become teachers, hold government positions, have access to interpreters in the courts, have seen a Deaf member elected to a legislative assembly, and have most recently obtained a national news broadcast that is interpreted on the Canadian television network. Hard of hearing people, and those who use English, not ASL, as their main language of communication, are also defining the special needs of their group. Both Deaf and hard of hearing people are becoming increasingly involved in developing educational policy and improving educational systems. Problems still exist, but the situation is improving.

It is vital to realize that in Canada, responsibility for education is a Provincial rather than a federal responsibility. Indeed, technically, the federal government has no responsibility for educational policies or programs. This results in a diversity of Provincial services, and contributes to the growth of innovative and creative solutions to meet the very different needs of different areas in the country. On the other hand, this decentralized administrative control has contributed to a lack of continuity and cohesive development across the country as a whole. Each Province depends on its own government for the establishment of educational funding policy and legislation and as a result, facilities and systems differ greatly. Although the Provincial governments directly control a few schools, including Provincial schools for deaf students, most educational facilities are run by local school boards. The positive and negative conditions created by this diversity affect all of special education in a very direct way, and can be seen clearly upon closer examination of the education programs for those students with impaired hearing.

It has been estimated that there are over 200,000 profoundly deaf people in Canada, and an additional 1,500,000 with milder hearing impairments (Rodda & Hiron, 1989). The remainder of this chapter will describe the Canadian system that is presently in place for educating deaf and hard of hearing people, and will also address the issues, concerns, and accomplishments that are distinctly Canadian.

A Brief History

The most comprehensive article to address the historical developments of the education of hearing impaired people in Canada was written by B. R. Clarke and M. Winzer in 1983. Clarke, then Director of a University program for training teachers, and Winzer, a teacher and historian, describe in some detail the people, events, and conditions that gave rise to the present situation. Much of the following summary is taken from their work.

The earliest immigration into Canada and the earliest settlement growth took place on the eastern seaboard. The early history of education of the deaf focuses entirely on this part of Canada. It was not until the early twentieth century that the railroad opened the West to new populations, which in turn, allowed for the rise of new programs for deaf students.

The eastern region was the home of the first school for the deaf. It opened in 1831 in Champlain, Quebec, but closed five years later due to lack of funds. Operating costs, in fact, became a crucial issue for many of the schools and classes that opened throughout the nineteenth century, as schools in Prince Edward Island, New Brunswick, and Quebec lived rather short lives. In many cases these new endeavors were entirely dependent on the goodwill and financial assistance of private benefactors, although by the 1860s some Provincial governments were giving grants in aid.

This Quebec school was started by Ronald McDonald, who was sent to visit schools for the deaf in New York and Philadelphia. He was trained and supervised by Thomas Hopkins Gallaudet and Laurent Clerc. Thus began a practice that existed for close to 130 years: the formal training of teachers outside the boundaries of Canada. The United States, because of its close proximity, and Britain, because of its cultural, historical, and Commonwealth ties, were both instrumental in influencing early trends and policies through these teacher education contacts. Canada now has its own well-established training programs, but the early American and British influence can still be seen in the schools.

The early schools were usually founded by someone with a vested interest in educating deaf children, either parents of deaf children, or deaf people themselves. The earliest permanent Canadian school for the deaf was opened in Montreal, Quebec in 1848. In Nova Scotia, the private institution that opened in 1856 in Halifax, has been replaced by the Atlantic Provinces Resource Center for the Hearing Handicapped in Amherst, a facility that now serves the four Atlantic Provinces with on-campus and outreach programs. Deaf people were instrumental in establishing these early schools, and in most cases manual communication was used by the teachers. After visits to schools in Europe and the Milan Conference in 1880, however, changes occurred and oral instructional methods became predominant.

In the west, a very young Vancouver began a day school for deaf children as early as 1888, but it lasted for only one year. Almost 30 years later, another day class was established by the Vancouver School Board. This institution was known as the Jericho Hill School for the Deaf. The school received a great deal of support from the government and the Deaf community, and built one of the most up-to-date educational facilities available anywhere in the world. It incorporated the latest in technological advances, including the use of real-time captioning and video screens in all classrooms. Deaf students shared resources and facilities with hearing children.

Other western schools were established: in Saskatchewan in 1914, in Alberta in 1956, in Manitoba in 1958. In Ontario, back east, the Milton school started in 1963 and in 1972 there was enough demand in southern Ontario for a school in London. The Saskatchewan school closed in 1991.

The fourteen schools that were in existence in the early 1970s all provided some kind of residential facility, an arrangement that assisted in solving the rather serious transportation problems that existed in the earlier years. Students in the Maritime Provinces travelled many miles to the Halifax Institution, or even went so far as to go to the schools in Ontario and Quebec. For many years students from the West Coast travelled the 1,500 miles to the Saskatchewan and Manitoba schools, and students from Alberta travelled even further to Montreal. Today, students who have impaired hearing have the option of using educational services much closer to home and in their own Province. This option does not apply however, to those students from the Yukon and the Northwest Territories. If these students wish to receive their education in a residential school, they must leave their homes and travel to live at the schools or in foster homes in one of the Provinces to the south. The northern situation is unique, and deserves further attention later in this chapter.

In addition to residential schools, Canadian Provinces were also opening day classes for students. The first Province to make a deliberate and systematic attempt was Ontario: Toronto in 1924, Ottawa in 1928, and Hamilton in 1944. Eventually the Metropolitan Toronto Board in 1964 established the largest Canadian day school for deaf children. During the 1960s, increased parental pressure demanded that the locally accountable school boards take more responsibility for educating children with special needs and as a result, programs sprang up all across Canada. These included at least three distinctive types of programs (Clarke & Winzer, 1983, p. 44):

1. *Special classes for hard of hearing children.* These were often organized on the basis of partial or gradual integration of the hearing impaired child into the regular classroom, operating predominantly at the elementary level but sometimes extending to the secondary level. Teaching methods were mainly oral.
2. *Special classes for deaf children.* These tended to function more as separate classes, although permitting a degree of integration, and were essentially an alternative to special school placement. Instruction was carried out by either the oral or combined method.
3. *Special services.* Speechreading, auditory training, speech teaching, tutoring, remediation, counselling, and interpreting were made available to hearing impaired children in regular classes, generally on an individual basis.

Most day classes use auditory/oral or Signed English approaches to communication, whereas the schools for the deaf are now strong proponents of sign language. The Montreal Oral School, begun in 1950 by a small group of English-speaking parents, is perhaps the largest in Canada, with 203 day students and employing 29 classroom teachers, supervisors, and itinerant teachers. The Quebec Catholic school board also offers special French oral options to a large number of students. In British Columbia, the Vancouver Oral Center was established in 1960 and has now grown to meet the auditory/oral needs of over 60-70 families in various programs throughout the city. In 1981, this school received the Alexander Graham Bell Award for excellence in auditory/oral programming. Many other Canadian cities operate smaller oral programs.

It is interesting to note that many of the earliest teachers of the hearing impaired in Canada were immigrants from the United States or from Britain, and "in a country as undeveloped and isolated as Canada in the nineteenth century, a great deal of success of the programs was due to their unstinting and enthusiastic efforts. The outstanding contributions of these teachers during the beginnings of Canadian education of the deaf are not well chronicled and these highly distinguished achievements have generally not received the acclaim they warrant." (Clarke & Winzer, 1983, p. 40). In the early 1970s teachers decided to form a national organization that would provide at least some solution to the problem of how to foster and develop useful and worthy communication across 5000 miles of country. The Association for Canadian Educators of the Hearing Impaired was established in 1973.

By the early 1970s Canadian children with hearing difficulties could choose from a variety of educational options. Students could learn in manual or in oral settings; they could be integrated into regular classes or they could attend a residential school for the deaf. Provincial governments took more responsibility for the education of these students. At the same time teacher training opportunities were increasing. If years previous to 1970 could be described as years of building, then perhaps the next twenty could be described as years of change and development. These were years strongly influenced by a number of things, some distinctively Canadian, some international:

- The incredibly strong growth within the Deaf communities and their cohesive support for their outspoken leaders
- The recognition by leading linguists that American Sign Language is a language in its own right
- The appearance of legislation requiring students to be educate within the least restrictive environment
- The growth of specialized telecommunication devices and medical improvements

♦ Specifically in Canada, the impact of the Canadian Charter of Rights and Freedoms of 1982.

In the following sections, we will examine the Canadian situation as it now exists and as it has been influenced by these important forces. The sections include: educational systems; preschool and postsecondary education; communication methodology; the curriculum; northern education; and teacher training and research. The final section will highlight some of the issues that are distinctly Canadian and attempt to give some indication of future directions.

The Current Situation
Schools for the Deaf

As of 1990, there were eight residential schools for the deaf in Canada: Jericho Hill School for the Deaf in Vancouver, British Columbia; the Alberta School for the Deaf in Edmonton; the Manitoba School for the Deaf in Winnipeg; the Belleville, Milton, and London schools in Ontario; the Interprovincial School for the Deaf in Amherst, Nova Scotia; and the School for the Deaf in Newfoundland. These schools allow students an opportunity to live in dorms during the week, and to stay with foster families on weekends. Except for the Vancouver School, which has recently come under the jurisdiction of a local school board, all these schools are operated by their respective Provincial governments. Influenced by major funding problems and government cutbacks, some of these schools have become incredibly expensive to operate as the cost per student has increased significantly in recent years. Provincial governments are continuously investigating the feasibility of maintaining these expensive facilities, and the schools find themselves constantly providing rationale for their existence. In 1991, the Saskatchewan School for the Deaf lost its battle and was forced to close.

The Impact of Mainstreaming

The moves to close the schools for the Deaf were facilitated by the concurrent move in educational fields to place students with special needs in the least restrictive environment. In most instances, this concept was equated with integration within the public schools systems and a strong wish for "normalization" to absorb special needs students into the mainstream of society. Educators were encouraged to open regular classrooms so that special needs students could function within them, and although adequate support services were often recommended, the reality of mainstreaming proved otherwise. Many students were placed in educational situations without appropriately trained teachers or consultants, and without adequate communication services in place.

In British Columbia, for example, most of the population is concentrated in the southern regions. In middle and northern areas, communities are isolated by great distances. Serving the needs of students within these communities is very difficult. Many deaf students can often be served better by being placed in a residential environment, where access to support services and educational options is more readily available. On the other hand, living away from family and community can often be a great hardship.

There are, however, large numbers of students still being served in their home communities throughout the Province. The School for the Deaf in Vancouver has just appointed a program consultant for Outreach Services to attend to the needs and concerns of these students and their teachers.

The Influence of the Deaf Community

It is absolutely essential that the move towards integration be seen in juxtaposition with the move towards cultural unity within the Deaf community. The protests against the school closures have been loud and strong, and in some cases their outcry has prevented other schools from closing. The schools are seen as the "home" of the Deaf culture and language, and as essential units for the organization and delivery of services to the Deaf community. Deaf Canadians are determined to maintain their cultural heritage within these educational boundaries. It is not surprising to see that there are many parallels between what is happening in Canada and what is happening in our neighbor to the south, the United States. Many of the best educated Canadian Deaf students are graduates of Gallaudet College, and the bond between Deaf communities on both sides of the border is strong.

There are parallels too, between the Deaf and other linguistic and cultural minorities. The Deaf community in Canada needs to have American/Canadian Sign Language recognized. Canadian Deaf groups are extremely vocal, and recognition and use of ASL is often seen as a civil and fundamental rights issue. The Native and French communities demand rights and language unique to their own cultural heritage. All minority groups, including the Deaf, feel passionately about these critical problems. Promoting "the efficacy of bilingual education in the Canadian context should of course strike a resonant chord for many citizens who should be very sympathetic to this apparently reasonable objective" (MacDougall, 1989, p. 8).

On Friday, May 12, 1989, deaf people across Canada staged the first ever massive protest against the system of deaf education in Canada. They asked that their fundamental rights be recognized, made an emotional plea for recognition of ASL in the school system, and demanded a greater voice in decisions that directly affected their future (MacDougall, 1989).

In 1990, the Provincial legislature in Ontario called for a thorough review of Ontario educational programs for deaf and hard of hearing students, which resulted in a 205-page report that scrutinized the system and suggested recommendations. It is perhaps the "most significant document in education

of the deaf in Canada to be published since the early 1950s" (Rodda, 1990, p. 43). Even though it deals only with one Province, the document provides more information on Canadian systems of education than has ever been available before, and so deserves a brief elaboration.

In 1989, an advisory committee was established under the Canadian Hearing Society, and both internal and external review teams were responsible for data collection and analysis. Of the 38 recommendations made by the internal reviewers, and the 57 by the external reviewers, most differed "only in focus and emphasis" (Rodda, 1990, p. 44). There was extremely wide consensus on the issues involved. A direct result of this report was that ASL was recognized by the Ontario legislature as one of the official languages of instruction in Ontario. Alberta passed similar legislation in the spring of 1990 and several other Canadian Provinces followed suit. Beginning in the fall of 1991, the Province of Ontario also established a pilot program using ASL as the language of instruction in what is being called a "bilingual, bicultural" educational setting.

Most Canadian Provincial schools for the deaf are at this time reviewing their policies on communication systems employed in their classrooms. Because of the scarcity of information on the efficacy of using an "English-as-a-second language" approach, schools are attempting to meet the challenge of providing the right balance between the use of Signed English and ASL. Until recently, total communication has prevailed, with emphasis on the use of English in the classroom as the only language of instruction. Educators are adamant in their wishes for wanting to provide deaf students with the best education possible, and at the same time, they are cautiously hesitant in making profound changes before the research data is available.

There are at least three areas, however, where schools are implementing immediate change: the recruitment of deaf teachers, the upgrading of sign language skills for the professional staff, and the incorporation of Deaf Studies courses into the curriculum. All Provincial schools have deaf teachers on their staffs, but Alberta has the greatest number with fully 60 percent. Some Provinces also have in place a mandatory skill testing evaluation for all their teachers, and most provide in-services and workshops on an ongoing basis.

The Public School Systems

The public school systems are also undergoing change, although the situation seems to be somewhat more stable. In all of the major centers in Canada, students have options. In all Provinces, both oral and English sign language communication classes can be found. At the schoolage level, students can access special classes most frequently taught by a trained teacher of the deaf, and students can be integrated according to their capabilities. Some students are fully integrated into their home school situations, and are seen by an itinerant teacher of the deaf on a weekly or a monthly basis depending on their needs. Other students may be partially integrated for some subjects, and yet others remain in the special class for all their academic work.

Many of these students using either oral or signed communication, need to have access to qualified educational interpreters. Interpreters in general, are in great demand across Canada, and it is becoming increasingly evident that working in classrooms requires a number of very important skills. These people are often called upon to become tutors and support people. Some students are able to access oral or sign interpreters but in fact the majority of students are learning with the assistance of minimally competent teacher aides. The need to define responsibilities and to develop training programs has been a big challenge in the 1990s.

A variety of educational options, however, exists only in the larger populated centers of Canada. The situation for rural areas is some-

what different. If trained educational consultants are hired, they are usually based in communities where facilities and support systems are at a minimum, and their responsibilities vary widely. They may be required to consult with teachers, work with students on an individual basis, or provide and arrange access to testing and educational resources. In some instances, a trained teacher may be hired if there are more than two or three hearing impaired students in a school and if establishing a class is a feasible alternative.

A consultant outside the major centers of any Province however, may have as many as 100 students on his or her caseload, with no more than one or two in any one school. A survey taken in Alberta (ERC, 1989-90) has provided the most comprehensive information about students with impaired hearing in any of the Canadian Provinces. Researchers contacted school administrators, teachers, and parents and compiled a nearly complete account of the "number and location of students with impaired hearing and a broad sampling of the characteristics of the schools in which they are taught" (p. 2).

The total number of students with impaired hearing amounted to 1,413, which is a rate of 3.0 per 1,000 Alberta students. The researchers state that this rate is lower than expected and one reason for this may be the under-reporting of cases of middle ear infection (otitis media) which is very common in the Province. Although the distribution of students varies by geography and chronology, "most students attend classes with no other student similarly impaired" (p. 2). "Of the 505 (teachers) who completed questionnaires on a total of 878 students with impaired hearing, more than two-thirds (68.7 percent) had only one hearing impaired student in their classrooms. Forty-nine (9.7 percent) had two students, so nearly four out of five teachers had only one or two students who were hearing impaired in their classes. It must be remembered that hearing losses for these students range from mild to profound. The majority of the students receive their language and communication through the use of their residual hearing. This distribution of students clearly indicates the need to design appropriate teacher training programs, to develop a network of support systems for teachers and students, and to maintain options in educational programming.

It would be unfair to give the reader the impression that all students with hearing losses are being adequately served. This is not the case. Services provided to these students depend entirely on several factors: (1) whether or not an identification process is in place, and its success rate, (2) the abilities and willingness of the school personnel to recognize the needs of these students, (3) the funding available for service provision, and (4) the availability of trained and competent teachers, consultants, and support staff. Across Canada these factors vary a great deal. At the very least, however, each Province has a coordinator for these special services. In the Maritimes these responsibilities are maintained at the Atlantic Provinces Resource Center in Amherst.

Northern Education

Canada is an extremely large country, and much of the chapter up to this point has dealt with educational concerns as they exist for the southern ten Provinces. To the north however, stretches a vast region divided into two parts. The Northwest Territories (NWT) encompasses four time zones and covers 3,376,698 square kilometers. The population is 51,744, with 13,400 students registered in the K-12 educational system (Donahue, 1989). The second part, the Yukon, is the seventh largest Canadian land area, and its population of 26,000 is distributed among 25 communities. Twenty thousand are concentrated in the capital city of Whitehorse.

The northern region of Canada has a very high incidence of hearing loss; many of these deficits are the results of recurring and untreated middle ear infections. In a study by the Baffin Divisional Board of the NWT, 100

students out of 3,144 students were identified as having hearing losses. These students attended fourteen different community schools and were spread out over more than 500,000 square kilometers. At a school in Keewatin, 60 out of 100 students were found to have impaired hearing. Thirty of these had moderate to severe losses (Donahue, 1989, p. 35). Over three-quarters of the school population is Native American.

In the northern region, the educational system is especially cognizant of the very different cultural needs that influence both the content of the curriculum and the service delivery model. Especially for children with impaired hearing, English is already a second language, as their first language may be any one of a number of different Native languages. This means that educators must be especially sensitive to the complicated needs of these students.

In addition to the cultural concerns, the school population itself is often in transition as economic fluctuations take place. In certain communities the school population may double in one year but face declining enrollments the next, as families move, looking for employment. Students may have already lived in several communities by the time they are six or seven years old. In addition, teachers must be aware of the often devastating effects of alcohol. A recent study indicated that "the incidence of Fetal Alcohol Syndrome in the general population is 1.90 per 1,000 births, whereas in the Yukon the incidence is 46 per 1,000 births. The resultant degrees of mental handicaps form a significant number of students" (McFarlane, 1989, p. 16). Many of these students are also hearing impaired.

Previously, students with special needs were sent to residential schools in the southern Provinces. In recent years in the northern region, recognition has been given to the fact that students should be encouraged to stay at home and be educated within their own family and community schools. In many instances the financial cost is much less, when provision is made for students to be educated with their peers, and this remains a factor that has influenced the design of the educational system. Many students with hearing loss are often not identified, but those who are, are often found to be fully integrated into the regular classrooms, where they are taught by regular teachers of hearing children. Depending on their specific needs, however, they and their teachers will have access to various kinds of support: FM systems, in-services, and access to special needs consultants. It is often difficult to hire trained teachers to work with hearing impaired students in the north; as a result, the existence of qualified personnel varies greatly. People who are hired may act as itinerant teachers and provide consultation, programming, or access to other support services. Provincial Universities often send faculty to the northern region to provide additional short courses and services as needed and requested. Because of the geographical isolation and adverse climatic conditions, providing support to teachers is an essential component of this system.

Curriculum

Two concepts characterize the curricular aspects of the education of the hearing impaired in Canada: individualization and the provision of options.

In all Provinces, hearing impaired students are provided with individual educational plans (IEPs), where both long- and short-term goals are established with parental input. In most cases parents must, at the very least, meet with the teachers to sign the plans. For the most part, these plans are supposed to cover all areas of the child's development—physical, intellectual, and social-emotional. In reality, however, there is a tendency for the plans to emphasize the remediation of the specific student deficits, including the incorporation of speech and language goals and the statement of any behavioral changes that might be required. Placing students in settings that focus on remediating deficits seems to be a typical failing of the education of the deaf.

As yet, one seldom sees goals that build on the strengths and abilities of these students.

In most cases, our educational settings are providing curricular options for deaf and hearing impaired students, and in many ways these become tied to the educational settings. For those students who are capable of doing work that is on a level equal with that of their hearing peers, and who prefer to be integrated into the regular school system, the curricular needs and expectations are the same as for hearing students. Some students require additional help and a modified or slower-paced curriculum. This option can be provided when the trained teacher of the deaf acts as a consultant or as a part-time teacher. In schools for the deaf, programs often provide a variety of streams—advanced academic, regular academic, and vocational, which can be tailored to fit the needs of the students.

The special needs of one group of deaf and hard of hearing students, those who are gifted, are being overlooked in Canadian education at this time. No formal identification procedures are in place, nor are there any special programs or curricular guides available to meet their needs (Yewchuk & Bibby, 1990). Since the education of gifted students is, in itself, a relatively new field, looking at gifted students who are also hearing impaired is also just emerging. Individual teachers who are sensitive and aware of the special talents of their students, are very often extremely adept in providing opportunities and challenges that go beyond the published curriculum. Further research is necessary, however, to ensure that these students are not being neglected "because they are smart enough to learn anyway". This is an inaccurate but popular myth about gifted people.

Curricular materials are widely available and resources continue to be developed. Computer programming, on-screen video captioning, and other technological advances are being used in the classroom. For an overview of materials and programs that might be found in Canadian schools, the reader is referred to Bunch (1987). This book focuses primarily on programs specifically developed for hearing impaired students.

One of the newest areas of curricular development is taking place in the area of sex education. A recent study by Sobsey & Varnhagen (1988) has enabled us to recognize that the incidence of sexual abuse among handicapped students is many times higher than that of the general population. This situation includes people who are hearing impaired. At the same time that educators of hearing children are reassessing their sex education programs in schools for the deaf, questioning whether or not these courses should be mandatory, some Canadian educators are adapting and developing materials especially for use with hearing impaired students. In Nova Scotia, for example, the Cumberland County Family Planning Association produced a video on sexuality for deaf and hard of hearing teenagers and their families (Franchi, L. & Bangs, D., 1989).

One weakness is apparent in our educational system regarding curricular development: As teachers of hearing impaired students we are extremely lax in keeping up with current research in the field. In general, teachers of the deaf do not make time to read journals in other areas, and as a result can become somewhat isolated and unaware of exciting changes occurring in regular education. These advances often have direct implications for the education of deaf and hard of hearing students. Given the many demands faced by teachers, this tendency is not surprising; it is, however, a cause for some concern and once again, provides a challenge for teachers in the field.

Infant and Preschool Education

Children with hearing impairments are most often diagnosed in medical facilities. Routine infant screening programs exist in well-baby clinics and health units throughout each Province, but there are still significant numbers of children who are not diagnosed or provided with intervention programs prior to entry into the school system.

For infants who are identified as having a hearing impairment, a variety of services are provided to these children across Canada. Facilities and options differ, as does the quality of the programs. Within the major centers, parents have access to informed and trained personnel who can answer questions not only about their child's hearing loss, but also about services that they might access. All Provinces provide the following services in one form or another, but the method of delivery varies depending upon the geographical situations: (1) parent education classes and support services; (2) home training programs; (3) access to professionals working specifically with hearing impaired children such as audiologists, speech/language clinicians, trained teachers, and counsellors. At the age of three, most children are able to attend specialized half-day programs that focus on child development, stressing early childhood needs in addition to the development of remedial skills. In some cases, these children are able to access the regular day care programs where integration with hearing peers takes place. For families not living in densely populated areas, itinerant services are often available, but continuing and ongoing support systems are sometimes difficult to maintain.

Home training programs are also faced with the need to service people across large distances. Some Canadian families make use of programs like those available from the John Tracy Clinic correspondence courses. The Province of Newfoundland has developed an outreach program that provides a distance education package for parents of preschool hearing impaired children. The program makes use of video units and speech trainers. In addition, support is provided by a trained teacher of the deaf who does home visits and provides telephone support, and on-campus workshops. Developments in computer technology will very soon provide distance education with other exciting options.

All Provinces offer options to families in terms of communication methods. Programs are available using auditory/oral methods, as well as those which offer a Signed English base. A few Canadian Provinces are developing programs where ASL is supported as a first language.

During recent years, educators have also encouraged parents to meet and talk with deaf adults as an integral part of their growing understanding of deafness. In some instances, home training programs encourage deaf parents to work closely with hearing parents as they help their child develop communication skills. At least three Provinces, British Columbia, Alberta, and Manitoba, have also developed programs that specifically recognize the needs of hearing children of deaf adults. These children can access language and speech play programs that address their needs for verbal role models, and the deaf parents of these children can become involved in support groups.

Financial support for early childhood programs comes from the Provincial Department of Education for children between the ages of two years and five months, to five years and five months. The Provincial Department of Health funds early intervention programs, for children from birth to three years of age. Perhaps one of the most critical issues facing these programs today is the need for specially trained personnel. Since communication is one of the key issues, it is critical that the specialists involved have a good understanding of the impact of hearing loss on the child and family. Furthermore, they must have the skills needed to help develop audition, speech, and language, so that this critical time is not lost and the child has an opportunity to reach the fullest expression of his or her potential. Counsellors, speech/language clinicians, and early childhood teachers are readily available, but few have the background in deafness that can meet the specialized educational demand of these children and their families. Some University training programs are attempting to meet these needs by offering degrees that allow specialization in both early childhood

and special education, but as yet these are few.

Parent counselling is seen as a critical component of early childhood intervention systems, but services are still lacking in many Provinces. The Children's Hospital and Diagnostic Center in Vancouver, British Columbia, developed a "nondirective, supportive, parenting-skills programming oriented around the family of the hearing impaired child" (Rodda, 1986). Furthermore, at the University of Alberta, in Edmonton, the Department of Educational Psychology offered the first training course in parent counseling for families of hearing impaired children in the summer of 1982. In addition, summer camps are beginning to be held for families. The Deaf Children's Society in British Columbia was instrumental in developing the camping concept and the Society's Deaf director has written an informative book on the topic of families (Freeman et al., 1981). The camps provide parents and children with the opportunity to spend time with each other and with other families who share similar experiences. All ages may participate in short courses, discussion groups, and seminars that are offered daily throughout the week-long camp.

Postsecondary Education

In 1989, the first international conference on postsecondary education was held in Edmonton, Alberta. A description of that conference has been published (Wolf-Schein & Schein, 1991). The conference was a joint venture between the University of Alberta and Gallaudet University and grew out of a perceived and urgent need to allow formal opportunities to discuss concerns about issues related to upgrading and furthering educational opportunities for deaf and hard of hearing students.

Because of the lack of federal control over educational policy, Canada finds itself hard-pressed to meet the needs of young deaf adults as they attempt to gain further training, education, and experience in preparation for future jobs. In the last twenty years, however, there has been a tremendous growth in program development at the community college level. It is important to mention two exemplary programs that have developed recently, to assist in the development of literacy skills and job placement for people with hearing handicaps. These programs have been established to explore the needs of the adult deaf. Given government seed money in 1990 during the International Year of Literacy, one program was set up in Victoria, British Columbia. The purpose of the program was to provide tutorial support, appropriate learning assessments, liaison, advocacy, and in-service for any deaf and hard of hearing adult student enrolled in any of the community's postsecondary programs. In the early 1990s, the program was directed by Karen Taylor and Denise Chow, and served students between the ages of 20 and 75. Most were 25 to 30 years old. In line with other adult literacy programs for hearing adults, the program aimed to set up offices in a less intimidating storefront setting in a nearby mall, thus promoting its philosophy of increasing the deaf and hard of hearing person's literacy skills.

In Manitoba, the Deaf Human Services Worker Training Program project (Evans, G., & Mitchell, L., 1991) was a joint venture of the Manitoba Government and the Children's Home of Winnipeg. Established in 1986, this project trained twelve Deaf adults in human service occupations and did a complete evaluation of its successes and failures, its training model, the use of ASL, and its impact on other agencies. Future recommendations are also included.

The quality of postsecondary programs across Canada is inconsistent, however, mainly due to the fact that each Province is responsible for meeting its own educational needs, and thus sources of funding vary. In addition, the method of delivery and the availability of means for delivery differ greatly (Rodda & Hiron, 1989).

For many years, students who graduated from Canadian schools went to Gallaudet University for further education. In 1984, for example, over 100 Canadian students were enrolled at Gallaudet, whereas only about 30 were attending postsecondary programs in Canada. In the early 1980s, the combination of increasing parental advocacy, increased legislated opportunities to all students with handicaps, and the focus on human rights led the Canadian Federal Government Department of the Secretary of State to create three centres of specialization in Canada—in Alberta, Ontario and Nova Scotia. These centers were mandated to "address barriers facing deaf students in each region of the country, and to improve postsecondary education opportunities for disabled Canadians through research, development of support services and innovative programming" (Rodda & Hiron, 1989).

The University of Alberta in Edmonton has concentrated its efforts on seeking ways to improve access to Universities and has specifically focused on postsecondary educational opportunities. The University of Western Ontario in London has addressed the educational problems associated with communication difficulties, and St. Mary's University in Nova Scotia has dealt with the availability of support services for handicapped students, including those with impaired hearing.

Teacher Training

There are four teacher training programs in Canada, two in the western Provinces of British Columbia and Alberta and two in the east, in Ontario and Nova Scotia. These programs are a minimum of one year in length and provide basic course work and practica which enable teachers to apply for professional certification through the Association of Canadian Educators of the Hearing Impaired (ACEHI). ACEHI has set minimum certification standards for training teachers, incorporating course work in language, speech, audiology, curriculum, and sign language. A specified number of hours of supervised practice teaching is mandatory.

All training programs are University-based, meaning that students are able to obtain either a Diploma or a Master's degree after the completion of an undergraduate degree. The University of Moncton, which bases its program at the Amherst Provincial Resource Center, and the University of Alberta offer course-based Master's degrees. In addition, the University of Alberta provides options which allow students to complete a Diploma or a thesis-based Master's degree. The University of British Columbia has had a Master's route available in 1992, and York University in Ontario offers a Master's degree in Deafness Studies.

In order to teach in any of the Provinces, regular teacher certification is mandatory. Most teachers training to become teachers of the deaf and hard of hearing have therefore already completed undergraduate education degrees and are pursuing this as an area of specialization. Some of these students already have several years of experience teaching hearing children, while others are just beginning their careers. Each of these students has specialized in one of three areas: pre-school education, elementary education, or secondary education.

University faculty in charge of the training programs are professors in education faculties who have specialized training and experience in working with deaf and hard of hearing people. In some cases, faculty in other departments such as audiology, linguistics, reading, or speech rehabilitation are invited to instruct or assist with instruction of some courses. All University programs invite teachers of the deaf in the field to participate as guest lecturers and in some instances to offer specialized courses as guest instructors. The University of Alberta has hired the first adjunct professor who is deaf, and several deaf people in the educational system are actively involved as members of advisory committees.

All training programs are extremely dependent on trained teachers in the field because these are the people who act as cooperating and supervising teachers for students placed in their classrooms for practica. These practicing teachers provide feedback to the students on a regular basis, and share their knowledge and experience on an ongoing basis. The cooperating teachers take their responsibilities very seriously and provide excellent role models for the students.

Teacher education faces many challenges. Perhaps the most daunting is that of providing a comprehensive basic training in such a short period of time—one year. In order to ensure that basic competency requirements are met, the University of Alberta, for example, requires that students enter the program with the equivalent of an "introduction to deafness" course and basic course and skill development in sign language. Issues regarding exit criteria are being discussed in conjunction with ACEHI. All University programs are attempting to balance basic training with the need to provide students with some specialization in areas such as reading, behavior, multiply handicapped students, team teaching, consulting, and communication development. The role of the teacher is changing as students' needs increase and as models for integration attempt to provide for these students' specialized needs.

Research

The major Canadian research center on deafness studies is located at the University of Alberta in Edmonton. A Chair of Deafness Studies, the second in the world, was established in 1988. (The other Chair is at Gallaudet University in Washington, D.C.) The Chair was established through a $1.2 million endowment in honor of Dr. David Peikoff, a famous Canadian deaf leader. Its purpose is to encourage the undertaking of research and related projects that will be of benefit to deaf and hard of hearing Canadians.

By 1991, the Chair had undertaken research and published extensively in the areas of mediated communication (VLI - visual language interpreting and communication aides) and postsecondary education. In addition, extensive national and Provincial demographic information has been collected. Under contract from Statistics Canada, the Chair analyzed data on hearing impairment from the Health and Activities Limitation Survey (HALS), a post-censal study of Canada's disabled population conducted in 1986-87. The results await publication under the title Canadians with Impaired Hearing. The Chair has also established the Alberta Disability Database in response to a need for accurate and up-to-date information (Report from the David Peikoff Chair of Deafness Studies).

In 1991, a Government grant provided an opportunity for a research seminar to be held in conjunction with the ACEHI Convention in Calgary, Alberta. Twenty invited participants discussed the status and focus of research in hearing disabilities in Canada and suggested proposals and ideas for future directions. These included the following areas, listed in alphabetical order: assessment, communication technology, disability statistics, educational interpreting, language and cultural issues, literacy, language development and linguistic competence, mental health, postsecondary education and adult learning, teachers and researchers in schools, and teacher education and classroom settings.

In addition to these specific ideas for the direction of future research, ongoing projects at the various Universities involve investigation into issues related to mainstreaming, teaching and learning English as a second language, the impact of ASL as a first language of instruction, the prevalence of hearing impairment among the Northern native population, giftedness among hearing impaired students, and sexual abuse.

Conclusion

Canada is facing challenging times in the education of deaf and hard of hearing people, both students and adults. Within a wide variety of options, the opinions and perspectives of educators can differ greatly,

and perhaps that is Canada's special strength. Diversity of perspective encourages change and growth. The common goal, however, is to better the educational environment so that each deaf and hard of hearing student can develop to the best of his or her potential.

References

Bunch, G. (1987). *The curriculum and the hearing impaired student.* Toronto: College Hill.

Clarke, B., & Winzer. (1983). A concise history of the education of the deaf in Canada. *ACEHI Journal, 9*(1), 36-51.

Donahue, G. (1989). Special education in the Northwest Territories. In M. Csapo & L. Goguen (Eds.), *Special education across Canada: Issues and concerns for the '90s.* (pp. 29-37). Vancouver, B.C.: Center for Human Development and Research.

ERC. (1990).

Evans, G., & Mitchell, L. (1991). The deaf human service worker training program: An alternative postsecondary model. In E. Wolf-Schein & J. Schein (Eds.), *Postsecondary education for deaf students.* (pp. 186-201). Edmonton: University of Alberta.

Franchi, L. & Bangs, D. (1989). *Loving yourself.* Amherst, Nova Scotia: Cumberland County Family Planning.

Freeman, R.D., Carbin, C., & Boese, R.J. (1981). *Can't your child hear? A guide for those who care about deaf children.* Baltimore: University Park Press.

MacDougall, J.C. (1989). Deaf Canadians in revolt. In E. Wolf-Schein & J. Schein (Eds.) Edmonton: University of Alberta. *Postsecondary education for deaf students.* (pp. 79-88).

McFarlane, P. (1989). Special education in the Yukon. In M. Csapo & L. Goguen (Eds.), *Special education across Canada: Issues and concerns for the '90s.* (pp. 15-18). Vancouver, B.C.: Center for Human Development and Research.

Ojile, E., & Carver, R. (1987). Education of the deaf in Nigeria and Canada: A comparison. *ACEHI, 13*(3), 96-103.

Report from the David Peikoff Chair of Deafness Studies: January 1989 through August, 1991. (1991). Edmonton, Alberta: University of Alberta.

Rodda, M. (1986). Canada: Preschool programs for the hearing impaired. *Gallaudet encyclopedia of deafness.* New York: McGraw-Hill.

Rodda, M. (1990). Review of Ontario education programs for deaf and hard of hearing students. Program Implementation and Review Branch, Ministry of Education, Government of Ontario, Queen's Park, Toronto, ON. 1989. *ACEHI, 16*(1), 43-44.

Rodda, M., & Hiron, C. (1989). Postsecondary educational services for deaf and hard of hearing students in Canada: A survey of need. *ACEHI, 15*(2), 44-56.

Sobsey, R., & Varnhagen, C. (1988). *Sexual abuse, assault and exploitation of persons with disabilities.* Ottawa, Ontario: Health and Welfare, Canada.

Winzer, M. (1983). Educational reform in Upper Canada: John Barrett McGann and the "deaf mutes". *ACEHI, 9*(3), 155-169.

Wolf-Schein, E.G., & Schein, J.D. (Eds.). (1991). *Postsecondary education for deaf students.* Edmonton, Alberta: University of Alberta.

Yewchuk, C., & Bibby, M.A. (1988). A comparison of parent and teacher nomination of gifted hearing impaired students. *American Annals of the Deaf, 133*(5), 344-348.

Historical Development of the Education of People With Hearing Disabilities in the Czech Republic and Slovakia*

by Milada Smutná

* This chapter was completed before Czechoslovakia was divided into the Czech Republic and Slovakia. The services discussed continue to exist in the two countries.

The History of the Founding of Schools for People with Hearing Disabilities

The first two schools for the deaf in Bohemia and Moravia were founded in Prague in 1786 and in Brno in 1832. The first schools of this type in Slovakia were founded at Liptovsky Mikulas in 1835 and in Bratislava in 1836. Most of these institutions were private and were operated and supported by charitable associations. Later the schools in Slovakia were state-run.

In 1835 there were only ten institutions for the deaf in the whole Austrian monarchy. These schools were located in Vienna, Milan, Vacov, Linz, Graz, Brixen, Prague, Brno, Lwow, and Salzburg. Three hundred and ninety pupils were enrolled in these ten schools. The total number of deaf children in the whole Austrian monarchy was estimated to be about five thousand. Most of them received no education. Because of monetary limitations, it was impossible to build schools to educate all of the deaf children in the country.

Doctor Czech proposed that priests and teachers teach deaf children in their homes. In 1835 he sent the Austrian government in Vienna a memorandum in which he stated that the deaf have the right to an education and that the state is obliged to provide the education free of charge. The memorandum was distributed to the governments of all the states of Europe and America. The Austrian government approved Czech's proposal. After that, many deaf children in the country were provided a basic education through home-schooling by Czech village priests and teachers.

Prague Institution for the Deaf and Dumb

The first institution for the deaf located in Prague has a long and interesting history. The story begins when members of the Prague Masonic Lodge, "At Seven Stars," headed by Kaspar Herman, the Count of Kunigl, decided to found in Prague a home for orphans, dedicated to the memory of Emperor Joseph II of Austria's visit to Bohemia. (The Emperor was observing a military exercise in Bohemia.)

On the 16th of September 1786 a special deputation led by Count Kunigl went to the military camp at Hloubetin to inform the Emperor of their intention to establish the orphanage. Emperor Joseph II recommended that instead of an orphanage, which had already been established in Prague in 1773, a school for the deaf be founded. He was well disposed towards this branch of education, since he had observed children who were deaf being taught at the Paris School for the Deaf established by Abbé Charles-Michel de l'Épée. Earlier, Joseph II had ordered the creation of a school for the deaf in Vienna.

The members of the Masonic lodge gladly complied with the Emperor's wish. In a short span of time a plan to develop the institution was completed and was approved at the highest Cabinet level on November 28, 1786. The school was officially opened on December 7, 1786.

Count Kunigl was charged with the control of the institution and Karel Berger was appointed headmaster. Six pupils (three males and three females) were admitted to the school. The youngest pupil was eight-year-old Jan Krimlak, and the oldest, a thirty-six-year-old journeyman shoemaker, Karel Vocasek.

Two floors of a house called "At the Stone Table" were rented and used as a school building. In addition, a boarding house in the Cattle Market (now Charles Square) was also used for school purposes. Count Kunigl lived on the first floor of the house.

In the course of time, the number of pupils enrolled in the school began to increase and because of the increasing enrollment, it was necessary on several occasions to relocate the school to new facilities. The different sites of the school are detailed below:

1786–1794   "The House at the Stone Table," land registry 671 in the Cattle Market district. The rooms were rented.

1794–1795   A house in the Cattle Market district (later the Palace of Charity), land registry 314. The rooms were rented.

1795–1797   A house called Zetelbersky, land registry 143, Chomutov. The school was temporarily moved there when Karel Berger was appointed headmaster.

1797–1831   Houses No. 478 and 479 on Lipova Street in Prague - the first buildings bought for school purposes.

1831–1838   House No. 669 at the corner of Charles Square and Zitna Street. A new building was purchased because of the ever-increasing number of pupils. This building was later reconstructed to accommodate 137 pupils.

[No information was available for the years between 1838 and 1902—Ed.]

1902–1919   House No. 104 on Holeckova Street. The structure was built between 1900–1902 to house the school. Frantisek Storek was the architect.

1919–1929   Children's Home, land registry 4, at Old Dejvice (now called Prague). The building on Holeckova Street was taken over by the State Statistical Board.

The funds needed to run the school were obtained by collections, donations, inheritances, grants, foundations, and other sources. It was not until 1857 that the institution was partially supported by public monies. Since 1857 the school has been regularly subsidized by state agencies such as the Provincial Committee, the Ministry of Social Welfare, the Ministry of Health, and municipal authority of the city of Prague. Listed below are the school's administrators since its inception:

1786–1791   Kaspar Herman, Count Kunigl
1791–1796   Count Filip Svet-Spork
1796–1801   Jan Justin, Doctor of Law
1801–1807   Wolfgang, Free-born Lord of Damnice
1807–1810   Jan, Baron of Weinling
1810–1817   Jan Limbeck, Knight of Lilien
1817–1821   Frantisek Nemecek, Doctor of Philosophy, University Professor
1821–1823   Mikulas Titze, Doctor, University Professor
1823–1849   Josef Herget
1849–1855   Knight of Sacher-Masoch
1855–1866   Leopold, Baron of Hennet
1866–1899   Frantisek Schonborn, Cardinal
1899–1916   Leo Skebensky of Hrist, Cardinal
1916–1917   Emil Ott, Doctor, University Professor-unofficially in this post from 1877
1917–1918   Jaroslav Sobicka
1918–1928   Frantisek Ebrle
1928–1948   Antonin Schauer, Doctor of Law

In 1948 the school was transferred to state ownership and administration.

The first teacher and headmaster, Karel Berger (1743–1806), learned to teach the deaf at a school for the deaf in Vienna, where de L'Épée's methods were applied. Berger taught his deaf pupils in Prague letters, syllables, and words by the use of the manual alphabet. After the pupils had learned a certain number of vocabulary words, they then formulated simple sentences. Berger used both natural and artificial gestures to explain the meanings of words. He also tried to teach his pupils to speak. Classes lasted from 8 a.m. to noon. The following subjects were taught: the manual alphabet, letters, reading, German grammar, calligraphy, and the elements of religion.

The Leipzig School for the Deaf used the oral method of teaching the deaf originated by Heinicke. Heinicke's oral methods were introduced to the school by Ondrej Schwarz (1759–1799). His oral system concentrated on speech development.

Major contradictions and arguments naturally occurred between the proponents of the two pedagogues. The board of the institution was hesitant to decide on which pedagogy was favored. Finally as a compromise, older pupils were taught by the use of the manual method while the younger students were taught by the use of the oral method. Continuing arguments and contradictions concerning methodology caused Berger to resign as headmaster.

Under the leadership of the subsequent headmasters, especially Jan Mucke, the oral method won out. Jan Mucke (1770–1840) kept in touch with specialists abroad, studied special education literature, and made full use of the accumulated knowledge of the personnel at the school for the deaf in Prague. He wrote a number of treatises on issues in the education of the deaf. In one of his books he states:

If teaching deaf-and-dumb children is to bring any permanent benefit to society, develop their thinking processes and communicate with their environment and thus relieve their ill fortune, the oral methods concentrated on speech development must be used. The writing method alone is not sufficient. A written word without vocal speech remains a mere sign. It is the articulation of words and sentences that makes the written utterance meaningful and strengthens the memory. Do not let us regret time and effort spent on speech development even if the child's articulation is unpleasant and often difficult to understand. The more the child practices the articulation of speech, the more intelligible it will be. Without the fear of breaking the sequence of speech-sounds he or she can learn to write and think.

The greatest misery of the deaf-and-dumb is that they cannot make themselves understood. The teaching of speech and lipreading relieves their ill fortune.

While Jan Mucke was serving in the capacity of headmaster, the first deaf teacher of the deaf, Hubert Kauzner (1815–1856), was hired. He was a graduate of the Prague Academy of Painting. Among Mucke's most important decisions was the establishment of a Czech language department at the school in 1836. This was done on the basis of a 1835 government decree, which stated that Czech children could be taught in Czech. Until 1835 pupils were only taught in German.

Peter Veselsky (1811–1889) was the first pedagogue to accept the challenge of teaching the Czech language to deaf children. It is not an exaggeration to say that Veselsky was a true pioneer since he had no knowledge of previous methods used to teach Czech to the deaf. He prepared all of the teaching aids by himself. He wrote the first textbooks on teaching Czech to the deaf, which unfortunately were not preserved. He is alleged to have destroyed all of his textbooks when he left the school.

After the death of Jan Mucke, who had a strong influence on the methods used at the school, Vaclav Frost (1814–1865) became headmaster. At the beginning of his career he became acquainted with the methods used in the existing European institutions for the deaf. During his journeys and visits to different schools for the deaf he was most impressed by the pure oral method used by Bedrich Morich Hill (1805–1874) at the school in Weissfeld. Speech was used to teach all subjects. Frost used all aspects of the pure oral method and the gesture speech method to create the so-called combined method. The artificial gestures that had been used in the past were replaced by new signs that proved to be more convenient for teaching purposes. Frost's signs met with wide acceptance and were soon used in all similar institutions for the deaf in Bohemia, and also at some schools in the then Austrian-Hungarian monarchy. The combined method adapted by Frost is denoted as the Prague School Method in special education historical literature. This method continued to be used at the Prague School until 1932.

In the days of Vaclav Frost, Vaclav Kotatko (1810–1876), his successor as headmaster, taught in the Czech department.

Kotatko began to write textbooks about teaching the deaf. In 1859 he published *Preparatory Speech Exercises*; in 1860, *Special Speech Exercises*; and in 1864, a two-volume *Manual for the Deaf-and-Dumb* (the first volume was devoted to grammar, and the second contained articles and descriptions). The introductory section of his *Primer* (1871) covered language drills, gymnastics, and breathing exercises. The remainder of the book contained speech drills designed to develop consonant sounds arranged according to degree of difficulty. Vowels were gradually added to the consonant sounds. Words and short sentences were then formed. In 1871 he also supplemented his primer with a reader. In 1874 his volume of short stories for deaf-and-dumb children was published. It was designed as a reader for fifth graders. The archives of the school for the deaf holds other writings of Kotatko, including the *Homeland and Nature Study for Deaf-and-Dumb Pupils* and a *Reader for the Third Grade*. Kotatko ranks among the best teachers in surdopedagogy [education of the deaf], since other than Veselsky, he was the only author of Czech textbooks and teaching aids for students who were deaf.

His successor, Karel Kmoch (1839–1913), continued to support the use of the combined method. During his time as headmaster two important events occurred. First, in 1886 the hundredth anniversary of the founding of the school was celebrated. Kmoch called the jubilee "Contributions to the History of the Prague Private Institution for the Deaf-and-dumb." Second, between 1900 and 1902, a new building was constructed. This building is still in use.

Karel Maly (1846–1916) ranks among the best and most important Czech pedagogues to have taught at the Prague school. He initiated new and progressive methods of teaching the deaf. Maly made the deaf pupil the center of his teaching. His methods stemmed from the experiences and needs of the deaf pupil. Maly included his principles and methods in three voluminous books called *Speech Practicing*. Maly also revised the order in which speech-sounds are usually taught to children who are deaf.

School for the Deaf in Brno

The second school for the deaf was founded on October 4, 1832 in Brno. Many obstacles and difficulties had to be overcome in order to establish the school and to keep it running. It took 30 years to gather enough money to buy a suitable building and meet the school's operating costs. The state administration did not contribute a single crown; it only gave consent to establish the institution. The school was entirely dependent upon the charity of individuals. At that time people still thought that the deaf were not educable. The achievements of the students enrolled in schools in Prague, Paris, Vienna, Leipzig and elsewhere demonstrated that educated deaf people could be accomplished artisans and officials, and independent, contributing citizens.

Joseph Dittman of Traubenburg, a judge, was instrumental in the creation of the school. In his court he saw deaf people who had no education and who had committed crimes. They were unable to make themselves understood, and were lonely, homeless, and jobless. Dittman wanted to help them. He retired at the age of 61 and in 1822 became the protector of the deaf. He provided financial gifts aimed at the establishment of an institution for deaf children. In 1829, he collected sufficient moneys to purchase a house, No. 4 on Trnita Street. The first class of deaf children was educated there in 1832. Most of the deaf children were from poor families. Fourteen deaf children were provided an education free of charge. Because of a constant lack of financial resources at the time, the number of children enrolled could not be increased. Dittman worked for the institution until 1843.

Between 1850–1856 the school enrolled as many as 30 pupils. The children usually started school at the age of eight and were in school for four to six years. Tuition, board, and lodging expenses for each pupil amounted to 140 guilders.

The school curriculum included speech, lipreading, reading, writing, mathematics, and art. After classes were over for the day, an assistant teacher was responsible for pupil care. The headmaster and the assistant teacher were also responsible for instruction. The assistant teacher was provided free board and lodging and was paid 100 guilders a year for his work. Both Czech and German children were instructed only in German. At that time some people thought that the deaf were not able to learn Czech.

For many years (from 1833 to 1854) a German priest, Quido Lang, was the headmaster and teacher at the school.

In 1856 Jan Valisek was engaged as an assistant teacher (at that time the school had no headmaster). Valisek not only taught but also managed the institution. It was at that time that he began to teach deaf children from Czech families the Czech language. Czech and German children communicated with one another by means of the gesture speech (sign language).

In 1865 the school was moved to a larger building at No. 8 Trnita Street. Sixty pupils could be housed at the new location. Girls were admitted. The pupil capacity was still not sufficient to meet the demand, however. Money was collected from all over Moravia. The Moravian Diet also contributed funds. In 1875 it was possible to add a back wing to the main building. The institution then had the capacity to educate as many as 140 children. This was still not adequate. In response to the demand for educational services for deaf children, in 1890 the Moravian Province built two new schools for deaf Czech children at Ivancice and Lipnik-upon-Becva. These schools were opened in 1894. The Moravian Province provided funds for the two schools from public and state moneys. The school in Brno continued to teach German to children who were deaf. Later the Moravian Province founded two other schools for deaf children, one at Valasske Mezirici in 1911 and another at Sumperk in 1913. The private Moravian-

Silesian institution for the deaf was abolished and its pupils sent to the school at Sumperk. These four provincial schools in Moravia became a basis for the establishment of other schools for children with impaired hearing.

Historical Development of the Education of Children with Hearing Disabilities

The oldest school for the deaf in the Czech Republic, the Prague Institution for the Deaf-and-dumb, was founded in 1786. Children were first taught in the Czech language by Peter Veselsky in 1833. He wrote the first textbook which, unfortunately, has not been preserved. In 1871 he issued a primer which contained 17 exercises on the articulation of consonants and the vowels. In 1872 Jan Valisek, a teacher in the institution for the Deaf at Brno, published a book aimed at teaching articulation.

The first text to teach reading to deaf pupils was published at Hradec Kralove in 1886 by Josef Beran. The first part of the book contains a basic vocabulary of about 300 words and 155 pictures.

The first primer approved by the Central Education Authority was issued in 1920. It was developed by Ondrej Zajic.

A primer for the preparatory grades of the schools for the deaf was written by Ladislav Stejgerle in 1955.

Range and Kinds of Programs for People with Hearing Disabilities

Children with hearing disabilities do not attend regular schools. All of the basic schools for the deaf in Czech Republic and Slovakia are residential schools and provide for the overall care of children with hearing disabilities. The schools for children with hearing disabilities include kindergartens designed to educate children from the age of three. Organized within the schools are Czech language groups, book clubs, sign classes, and other groups.

Teaching speech is one of the essential parts of the educational program in the kindergarten. Various means and aids are used to teach the classes, including toys, pictures, gestures, speech, the manual alphabet, and videocassettes. Many of the children live at home and are at school only during school hours. The aim of these special kindergartens is to prepare the children to be independent, self-sustaining, and ready for basic school. The kindergarten program is the first stage in the education of the deaf.

The curriculum of the basic schools for children with hearing disabilities is similar to that used at regular schools for hearing children. Pupils are exempt from some subjects because of language difficulties.

Separate schools are provided for children with partial hearing and children who are deaf. The schools for the deaf are required to use the oral method only. Gestures are sometimes used by teachers. At present a new concept in the provision of special education services is being utilized. This focuses upon the pupils' academic ability instead of their hearing levels as the decisive factor in program placement. The new law seems to be very successful. Under the new law, sign language will be one of the several communication methodology options used to reach children with hearing disabilities.

There are no private schools for the deaf at the present. It is, however, possible that they will be founded in the future.

Opportunities for higher education for people with hearing disabilities, if they have finished compulsory education and find employment, is organized by the Union of the Disabled (the Council of People with Hearing Defects). This organization arranges various kinds of courses for the deaf, including lessons in the Czech language, speech development, and various hobby areas. The Union of the Disabled works cooperatively with other organizations and agencies to manage facilities and provide recreational opportunities for people with impaired hearing.

There are two secondary schools for pupils who are deaf in the country, a grammar school in Prague and a vocational school at Kremnica in Slovakia.

Grammar schools in the CSFR generally prepare students for study at a university. The curriculum of the Prague Grammar School for the Hearing Disabled is similar to that found in regular grammar schools. The grammar school is attended mainly by students with a partial hearing loss, who benefit from the use of hearing aids. It is hoped that these hard of hearing pupils will continue their education at regular secondary schools. It is hoped that capable students who are deaf will have the opportunity to study at the Prague Grammar School. After the completion of grammar school, students with hearing disabilities can continue their study at a university or they can take a job. Currently, regular secondary schools are not readily available to students with partial hearing in spite of the fact that many of these students could probably successfully complete a regular secondary school program.

The secondary vocational school at Kremnica provides students who are deaf with vocational training. Those who complete the vocational training program can be employed as foremen, office workers, social workers, accountants, and in positions in other fields that require a secondary education. Unfortunately, not all of those who complete vocational training can find an appropriate job.

After the completion of study at the grammar school and secondary vocational school the pupils complete the school-leaving examination.

Vocational trade schools exist to prepare students for a job. At the end of compulsory school attendance, which lasts nine years, most pupils attend vocational trade schools. The choice of trades for young people with hearing disabilities is rather limited and the "typical trades for people with hearing disabilities" prevail. Many of the "typical trades" are not very attractive to the majority of deaf students. The deaf person's career choice in Czechoslovakia is influenced by physicians, who may not recommend some trades because of unfounded safety reasons. The traditional trades of deaf people are tailor, dressmaker, housepainter, decorator, shoemaker, and metalworker.

Some large factories have now set up apprentice training centers for young people with hearing disabilities. The number of apprentices in individual trades depends on the needs of the factory. The trainees who finish the apprenticeship can easily find employment in these factories. If the deaf person proves his or her skill, the factory for whom they work will provide them with a flat or they can qualify for a cooperative flat when they start a family. The factories involved are in several fields, including electronics and locksmithing. The apprenticement program lasts for three years. During the first year of the apprenticeship, students spend alternate weeks in the classroom and on the job in the factory. The following year the students spend two weeks at the factory for each week in the classroom. The amount of time spent in the factory during the third year depends on the nature of the work. In every case, the time spent in the factory is lengthened and time in school shortened.

The apprenticeship classes are taught by the teachers from the factory. If necessary, an interpreter is utilized to explain difficult subject matter to the apprentice with impaired hearing. Companies employing deaf workers consider them to be good and reliable workers.

Vocational trade schools for the deaf are situated in each region. Most of the trainees are hired by the company that provided the apprenticeship.

The vocational trade school course and

apprenticeship requirements for the deaf person are the same as for any person with normal hearing.

Parent Education

Training and courses for parents of children with hearing disabilities are organized by the Association of Parents and Friends of Children with Hearing Disabilities, in cooperation with the Union of the Disabled. If a hearing defect is diagnosed in an infant, the doctor, phoniatrist, logopaedist [speech pathologist], and other specialists immediately begin to work directly with the child's parents. Under law in the Czech Republic and Slovakia, the child is in the care of health-service institutions until the age of three. After the age of three, the child is the responsibility of the school. All Czech and Slovak children who can profit from the use of a hearing aid are provided with one free of charge. The Union of People with Hearing Disabilities acquaints parents to the elements of sign language. Not all parents, however, are interested in their children learning sign language. Many are more interested in having their child develop intelligible speech.

Some schools have parent associations that provide lectures, seminars, and courses to acquaint parents with problems related to their child's hearing defect. Also included are discussions focusing on the link between education, the school, and the family. The parent association participates in the care and education of the deaf child until the end of compulsory school attendance.

The Union of the Disabled/Council of People with Hearing Disabilities in cooperation with the Ministry of Education, Ministry of Health, Ministry of Labor and Social Affairs, and other institutions and organizations holds seminars, courses, lectures, and organized vacations for parents and their hearing impaired children. The union works in cooperation with each respective school in the development of vacation programs. The Union of the Disabled/the Council of People with Hearing

Disabilities assists in the resolution of many issues not resolved by state organizations.

Methods of Communication

The oral method is the main method of communication applied in the Czech system of education for children who are deaf. In common conversation, however, sign language is used. In addition, the whole staff of the schools for the deaf have participated in sign language classes. At the present all teachers at schools for the deaf are supposed to have at least a basic knowledge of sign language.

Teaching has become more efficient with the introduction of video technology and the use of interpreters. A comprehensive experimental media center was founded on September 1, 1986. The center has prepared 40 video programs for use in schools for the deaf. Originally, the scheme was aimed at improving instruction in the three kindergarten grades and in first grade of basic school. The programs have worked well.

The deaf in the Czech Republic and Slovakia use several kinds of sign language. Among school children the so-called natural gestures can be seen. At present the aim is to unify Czech sign languages by means of video courses covering sign. Deaf adults use the common Czech sign language which has its own syntax and grammar. Interpreters use signed Czech which follows the sentence structure of the Czech language.

Secondary Education

Secondary education opportunities for the deaf are minimal when compared with the regular system of education. Secondary schools admit only partially hearing students. Deaf students are not permitted to study at regular secondary schools. Advanced technology in the form of hearing aids allows those with partial hearing to receive a better education than do the deaf.

Higher Education

Higher education opportunities are similar to those found in the secondary schools. Only late-deafened individuals or students with partial hearing who can profit from the use of a hearing aid are admitted.

Programs Available for the Preparation of Teachers

In 1983 pedagogical study in special education was divided into logopaedics and surdopaedics. Logopaedics remained as the basic subject and surdopaedics can be chosen by students as one of the several optional areas of specialization.

The following courses are taught: Teaching Speech to People with Hearing Disabilities and Visual Sign Languages of the Deaf. The two courses were included in a text entitled *Burdopaedics I*, published by Charles University in 1989.

Programs of study for teachers of the deaf have also been developed at other pedagogical colleges and faculties.

Certification

In the past a certificate to teach the deaf was not needed. Now graduates from the College of Special Pedagogics receive training appropriate to teach at schools for the deaf. In addition the teachers of the deaf are expected to know the elements of sign language. Not all current teachers of the deaf are qualified to instruct deaf children. Whether or not a teacher is qualified to teach the deaf is currently determined by the appropriate school committee.

Deaf Teachers of the Deaf

It is not possible at this time for a deaf person to work as a teacher of the deaf.

Since the deaf are not permitted to complete a secondary education and therefore cannot study at one of the institutions of higher learning, they are not allowed to work as teachers. But in practice deaf people sometimes teach various courses organized by the Union of People with Hearing Disabilities, with excellent results.

Vocational Education

Today in the Czech Republic and Slovakia, vocational education for deaf students provides only seven types of apprenticeship for boys and five for girls. Physicians and safety officers who often lack empathy and understanding of deafness and who must observe state standards of work safety play an important part in the selection of an apprenticeship for the student who is deaf. An organization's management approach often determines whether or not a deaf person will be admitted to a "forbidden" trade. Large companies seem more successful in organizing the training programs and providing jobs. With a movement towards the private enterprise system, it may become more difficult for the deaf to secure employment. In cooperation with the parents, education in vocational trade schools is now arranged through national committees and regional administrative authorities.

Current Problems and Future Trends in the Education of the Deaf

Organizations of deaf people and parents of children with hearing disabilities are constantly attempting to improve the education of deaf children in the Czech Republic and Slovakia. The current system of education is a serious obstacle to the improvement of the education of students who are deaf since it does not allow them to study at secondary schools and universities. The system of education has not succeeded in providing children who are deaf with an academic level and knowledge base that is typical of hearing children. This fact excludes deaf children from integrating into the mainstream.

Currently there are 20 schools for children with hearing disabilities in the Czech and Slovak Republics. Fourteen of them are in the Czech Republic and six in Slovakia. These schools enroll approximately 2,450 to 2,500 pupils a year.

Towns with schools for children with hearing disabilities are as follows:
In the CSR:
Prague (4 schools)
Hradec Kralove
Horicky u Nachoda
Plzen
Liberec
Ceske Budejovice
Vodnany
Brno
Ivancice u Brno
Kyjob
Valasske Mezirici
Olomouc - Kopecek
Ostrava - Portuba
Frydek - Mistek

In the SSR:
Bratislava (2 schools)
Lucenec
Kremnica
Presov
Levoca

Schools for the deaf have an organized sports program. Once a year sporting events for both deaf girls and boys are held in which the best students compete on behalf of their respective schools. Club sports are also active.

The aim of the different organizations, agencies, and parents is to provide deaf children with the same level of education that is provided to all hearing children. It is also hoped that deaf children will receive the same level of educational services currently provided for hard of hearing children.

Hopefully, in the future, the ability and knowledge of the individual child will be the decisive factor—not the degree of hearing disability; and thus the deaf person depending upon his or her capabilities would have rights equal to those of any other citizen in the country.

Education of the Deaf in Denmark

by Palle Vestberg

Introduction

When Thomas Hopkins Gallaudet traveled from America to England and France in 1815 in order to learn about the education of the deaf, he could have visited The Royal Institute for Deafmutes at Solvgade in Copenhagen, Denmark, which celebrated its tenth year of existence that year.

In 1815 the Royal Institute had four teachers and 35 students. Thirteen of the 35 students successfully passed their final examination that year and left the institute with certificates of approval. Andreas Moller, who became deaf at the age of two, was one of the thirteen graduates. A few years after graduation he became a teacher at the Institute, and in 1824 Moller went back to his native country of Norway and founded Norway's first school for the deaf in Trondheim.

Today the 1000-year-old kingdom of Denmark has 5,000,000 inhabitants who speak Danish, and 3,000 deaf persons who use sign language.

Historical Development

The 75-Year Reign of the Sign Language Method (1805–1880)

In the spring of 1803 a young Danish physician, Peter Atke Castberg, left Copenhagen to visit schools for the deaf in Germany, Austria, Hungary, and France. His goal was to study their various methods of instructing the deaf and to make a proposal for the organization of a Danish institute for the deaf.

At the same time the Danish government conducted a nationwide survey on "deafmutes" (figures provided by ministers of religion) which indicated that there were 515 deaf persons out of a total population of 820,623 or a ratio of 1:1593. This is very close to the ratio that is accepted today.

In 1805, after his return, Castberg submitted a proposal to the government to establish a national educational institute for the deaf patterned after the French method of teaching the deaf. The French method was based upon the use of the natural sign language of the deaf. Castberg did not wait for the proper authorities to consider his suggestions, but immediately started tutoring two deaf pupils. On January 18, 1806, the two deaf students sat for a public examination. The deaf students' successful results on the examination were reported in the newspapers of the time.

On January 28, 1806, the first public education program for the deaf in Denmark was started in a classroom of a school administered by the poor-law authorities. Eight pupils, five boys and three girls, between seven and thirteen years of age, attended the school. Castberg hired two teachers to conduct classes at the school, one of whom was deaf.

One year later the number of students in the school had increased to ten and the school was moved to its own building (next to the Royal Distillery). The school was formally founded April 17, 1807, as the Royal Institute for Deafmutes.

The beginning of the education of the deaf in Denmark is described in some detail to indicate the careful educational planning that was characteristic of Denmark at the beginning of the nineteenth century. It seems as though great effort was taken to ensure that the proper educational choices were made. The abilities of adult deaf persons as teachers of the deaf were appreciated. Sign language and written Danish were considered to be of fundamental value in communicating with the deaf. The first primer to be used with the deaf was published in 1806 and the manual alphabet was printed 1808. During that same year Castberg wrote his first treatise on the necessity of using sign language to educate the deaf.

For the next 70 years methods of teaching the deaf in Denmark were based on

Castberg's ideas. Finally, during the last decades of the century, general opinion throughout the world changed in favor of the oral method of instructing the deaf.

An interesting by-product of the education of the deaf in Denmark during this period was the invention of the typewriter by R. Malling Hansen, director of the Royal Institute for the Deaf. In 1870 his typewriter became the first commercially sold "writing machine" in the world. The principles of the world's first typewriter were founded on comparative studies of the speed of handwriting and the use of the manual alphabet.

Ninety Years of Oralism (1880–1970)

As a consequence of a widespread opinion among teachers of the deaf that sign language was a threat to oralism, the Danish government decided to build a new oral institute for deaf. The new school was built 100 miles away from the old institute and it was staffed with new teachers who did not know sign language.

The new institute, which was built in the rather small town of Fredericia, opened in 1880 with Georg Jorgensen as its director. He had studied the oral method of teaching the deaf in Germany and successfully practiced its use for several years with specially selected deaf pupils in Copenhagen.

Ten years later, in 1890, another new school for the deaf was founded in the small town of Nyborg, which was geographically (and also ideologically) halfway between the other two schools. The purpose of this school was to educate children with usable residual hearing, who had been postlingually deafened. It was called the school for "un-real deafmutes."

These pupils were supposed to be able to profit from an oral approach, but the director, Georg Forchhammer, who was a polytechnical engineer, found that instructing by means of pure oral Danish was a very incomplete

method of communication. Since the manual alphabet is not congruent with speech, in 1890 he developed a phonetically based system of thirteen hand positions that filled in the consonants that were visually ambiguous or invisible through speechreading. The hand positions were meant to be decoded at the same time as one was speechreading, hence the name of the system: the Mouth-Hand-System. Sixty-six years later this system inspired Dr. R. Orin Cornett while working at Gallaudet College in the United States to develop a system of hand positions called Cued Speech.

In 1909 Georg Forchhammer became director of the oral Royal Institute for Deafmutes in Fredericia. Since 1909 various mixtures of the methods of instructing deaf students have been used in the schools for the deaf in Denmark.

In the 1920s a special method of communicating with the deaf that was based on contemporary learning theory was developed at the Copenhagen Institute and accepted by other schools. The concept was to make the reception of spoken Danish more understandable than was possible with the Mouth-Hand-System. After a short delay, speech was followed by signs in the hope that the brain, through a conditioned response, would build up associations between words and signs.

The field of audiology had a strong influence on the education of the deaf in Denmark in the 1950s and 1960s. Also during this period the concept of mainstreaming influenced ideas about communication in schools and programs for the deaf. Danish Hearing Aid Manufacturers (Oticon, Widex, and Danavox) assumed a leading position in the amplification of hearing-impaired children worldwide.

Twenty Years of Total Communication (1970–1990)

In the 1970s, as the poor results of the oral/aural approach became known, a new sign language research and teaching institute, the Center of Total Communication for the Deaf, was established. Due to this center Danish Sign Language is now intensively studied, described, and taught to many professionals in the field of deafness.

At the same time, society's attitude towards the deaf started to change. The deaf have come to be viewed as a minority group with its own language and culture and not just a group of handicapped people. This change in the attitude of Danish society has led hearing people to a growing awareness and recognition of deafness and deaf people and the rights of minorities. This has also led to demands by the deaf community to have an influence on the decisions that concern the communication strategies and methods of teaching language to be used in schools for the deaf.

In 1989 the Danish Secretary of Education appointed a committee charged to consider the part sign language should play in the curricula of schools for the deaf. Should sign language become more than just a means of communication? The secretary also took measures to ensure that teachers of the deaf were better prepared in the use of sign language by requiring all teachers of the deaf to complete a qualifying sign language course.

Educational Services for the Deaf in the 1990s

Communication Methodology

The official policy today is to provide the family of each deaf child the opportunity to choose among different communication modalities and to use whatever combination of communication modalities best ensures optimal familial interaction and overall child development.

All deaf infants are provided with hearing aids and the parents are encouraged to stimulate the infant's hearing and speech. In addition, parents are informed of the strengths and weaknesses of all of the different communication methodologies that are available to their deaf child. Eventually the parent will have enough information about the different options available, including sign language and sign and speech combinations, to make a decision concerning which method of communication is best for their child.

Usually the parents will join a parent group for mutual support and for the opportunity to discuss all kinds of subjects, especially communication modalities. They may take courses in Danish Sign Language, or learn about simultaneous or total communication. Through these experiences the parents will discover what communication methodology is best for their child. Observations of the fluent communication between deaf mothers and their deaf babies also has had a strong influence on the thinking and choices of hearing parents of deaf children.

Recently a number of hearing parents have decided to use sign language with their deaf children from a very early age. Many parents of deaf children enroll their child part-time in a day-care center that uses sign language.

As a result of this early investment in the use of sign language many parents are able to communicate on age-appropriate topics with their deaf youngsters during those early and most important years for language development. Because of early parental decisions and efforts, many deaf children have fully functional language systems and demonstrate self-confident, outgoing, and assertive personalities by the time they reach school age. These children expect to be fluent expressively and receptively when communicating with others.

These changes in Danish policy demand that teachers in schools for the deaf be competent in the use of sign language. Parents now expect that their deaf children will be able to follow the regular public school curriculum. These expectations create new challenges for teachers and administrators of the schools for the deaf.

Response of Schools and the Government

The schools for the deaf that were mainly oral/aural until the 1960s began in the 1970s to accept the philosophy of total communication and different possible forms of combined communication (Hansen, 1980). During the 1980s interest in the sign language used by the adult deaf community has increased (Hansen, 1987). A few deaf persons have been educated as teachers and work at schools and in programs for deaf children.

The current official government policy is to encourage the use of sign language. The linguistics of Danish Sign Language is being studied intensively (Engberg-Pedersen, 1979, 1986, 1989; Kjaer Sorensen, 1975; Kjaer Sorensen & Hansen, 1976). Other developments planned include improvement in teacher sign competency, bilingual education of the deaf, and the recognition of sign language study as a subject in its own right (Hansen, 1987).

Parent Education and Guidance

Prelingual hearing losses are usually recognized during the first one and one-half years of the infant's life. The nearest hospital audiological department provides a hearing aid. Parents of deaf children are offered continual psychological and pedagogical guidance, individually or in groups, from specially trained psychologists and language, speech, and hearing therapists in one of the three regional units for parents of hearing impaired children. Semiannual evaluations of each child's development and progress are part of the program. Parents and their children are offered language and communication training at a center, or experts will visit them at home and provide individual training and counseling. Also, the parents are invited to attend courses in audiology and communication. Parent organizations also offer a variety of activities for the parents of deaf children.

In Denmark expenses incurred as a result of a person's disability are covered by social security. Expenses covered include hearing aids, materials and books for language training courses, transportation, a teletypewriter, a videorecorder, and so on. If both parents work full-time, the mother (or the father) is offered financial compensation if she or he chooses to continue maternity leave or wants to work part-time and take care of the baby. Also, the child's attendance at a special day-care center is paid for by the State.

From the age of three, children with a severe hearing loss are offered group day-care services manned by qualified personnel. All of the children in the group are deaf.

Options for Children 6–16 Years Old

Special Programs in Schools for Hearing Children

Many public schools have mainstreamed students with various degrees of hearing loss into regular classrooms. Depending upon individual needs, these children are provided with itinerant services by speech and hearing therapists. Some of the mainstream classrooms that include deaf children also have a teacher assistant. A few students have sign language interpreters. Individual arrangements are made depending on the student's needs and the availability of resources. The deaf students who are mainstreamed follow the normal curriculum used by hearing students. In some cases the deaf child is one or more years behind in the curriculum.

Those deaf students who cannot follow the normal public school curriculum are offered day programs that are located in ten special education centers found throughout Denmark. These centers contain classes for both hearing and deaf students. This permits the deaf student to be in a full-time special education classroom and at the same time experience a regular public school environment. The deaf students have the choice of socializing with deaf and/or hearing agemates according to their individual needs and preferences. Since the deaf students come from rather large geographical areas they are transported to school in small buses or taxis.

Residential Schools for the Deaf

The three residential schools for deaf children in Denmark are situated in the cities of Copenhagen, Fredericia, and Aalborg. Most of the students in the residential schools are day students and travel to the schools daily in small buses or taxis. Each school has about 100 students and a ratio of approximately one teacher per two or three deaf children. Most of the classes contain groups of four to six deaf children and two teachers. This arrangement allows for individual tutoring in special subjects.

Normally, six to eight residential students live together in small houses near the school. Each house has a small, specially trained staff, who are responsible for leisure-time activities. Almost all of the children in these houses return to their permanent homes each weekend, on holidays, and during the summertime.

Curriculum in Special Schools and Classes

There is no special, obligatory curriculum for deaf pupils in Denmark. The subject matter and number of lessons covered is the same for deaf pupils as for hearing students.

The teacher is free to plan lessons within the scope and sequence of the general curriculum. The goals and levels of difficulty in each subject area taught are adjusted to meet the individual needs of each student. Teachers normally use teacher-made materials to supplement the few books made especially for deaf students that are available in the schools for the deaf.

Usually the teacher will teach several subjects and lessons to the same group of children each day. The teacher of the deaf may teach the same group of children for several years or throughout their elementary school years.

Options for Young People 16–19 Years Old

The basic compulsory education program for hearing children in Denmark lasts for nine years. At the completion of the compulsory education program the students can go on to general advanced education (called HF [folk-high] and Gymnasium) for two or three years or leave school and start vocational training.

The basic compulsory education program for deaf students usually continues for ten years. Most then go to the residential school for deaf students in Nyborg for two or three or more years. A few attend mainstreamed programs in an ordinary HF or Gymnasium with the assistance of a sign language interpreter. Others leave school and start vocational training.

Academic Performance

Studies completed in the 1970s of the academic performance of deaf students aged 16–18 enrolled in traditional oral and/or manual programs for deaf indicated that only a small fraction performed at a level equal to or above that of the average ten- or eleven-year-old hearing students in most school subjects (Vestberg, 1973). The few who performed at age level were very gifted and/or were not born with a profound hearing loss.

The majority of the deaf children who had hearing parents seemed to progress very slowly in their ability to use sign language (Kjaer Sorensen & Hansen, 1976).

The rather disappointing school achievement, especially in the area of written and spoken Danish, of the majority of deaf students has forced parents and teachers to reconsider the means and ends of the educational process. Early recognition of the interactive and communicative needs of the young deaf child is now the primary focus.

Most of the parents of the new generation of deaf students now attending school expose their children to some form of sign language at a very early age. The results so far of this early exposure to signs are promising. Many deaf youngsters now in the middle grades have already achieved a higher reading and writing level than the majority of 16-year-old deaf students did 15 years ago.

What remains to be done is the completion of a comprehensive study that can tell us to what extent this immediate impression of improved performances by some of the children can be confirmed by tests used with the general school population.

Vocational Education

A generation ago vocational education for most deaf people in Denmark was restricted to a few occupations traditionally considered appropriate for deaf individuals. During their school years, deaf girls and boys were required to make an early decision concerning how they wanted to make a living for the rest of their lives.

Although there are no longer any special vocational schools for the deaf, many career opportunities are now open to deaf persons and there are very few career limits. The competition for admittance to some programs is great. This places a heavy demand on the abilities, aptitudes, and skills of the deaf person. Because of the intense competition many young deaf people are forced to leave school and seek employment.

Unfortunately, the large increase in unemployment in this part of the world has had a heavy impact among young people in general, and among the deaf in particular. Today it is increasingly more difficult to find and keep a job or follow a vocational career plan.

After nine or ten years of basic education and two or three years of secondary education, most deaf people start their vocational careers by serving an apprenticeship in some industry or craft area. Others choose to extend their education for an additional year and attend a preparatory industrial school. Still others begin work as unskilled workers in different industries or trade areas.

The folk-high school, Castberggard, is a Danish tradition. Attending Castberggard is another possibility for young deaf people. A folk-high school is an informal liberal college with courses that are three to ten months in duration; it has no admission requirements or accredited programs. The students may take courses that continue for a few weeks or many months.

Qualified persons provide deaf people with vocational counseling and guidance. The vocational counselor helps the deaf person plan a career, search for a job, and make necessary job development and placement arrangements. The vocational counselors also arrange for sign language interpreters as is necessary. These services are free of charge.

Higher Education

Colleges and universities are open on an equal opportunity basis to interested and gifted deaf students. Sign language interpretation is provided for lectures, discussions, and so on.

There are no institutions of higher education in Denmark designed especially for deaf students. Only a few individuals have been able to get the financial grants necessary to attend Gallaudet University in the United States.

Some deaf persons have had successful professional careers. Deaf professionals include a certified public accountant, graduate student in agriculture, social worker, teacher, engineer, psychologist, and architect.

Hopefully, the new view of a deaf adult as an important resource person and role model for deaf boys and girls will encourage more deaf students to invest their time and efforts in obtaining an advanced education.

Teachers of the Deaf

In order to become a teacher of the deaf one must first qualify as a regular classroom teacher by completing a four-year course of study at a teacher training college. At the completion of the four-year teacher preparation program, the individual can apply for a position as a teacher at one of the schools for the deaf.

If accepted, the person begins as an assistant teacher and concurrently enrolls in a special education preparation program one day a week for two years. Traditionally, one-third of the lessons in this program is spent on learning sign communication. A revised program has been instituted that requires the teacher in training to complete a program that is 26 weeks in length. Nineteen of the 26 weeks concentrate on training in the use of sign language.

To become a speech and hearing therapist, students must continue their education one day a week for three more years. This is in addition to the training previously completed to become a teacher of the deaf.

Up to the present time only a few deaf persons have completed the college program to prepare teachers and have found employment as teachers of deaf children.

Little is done to encourage deaf students to pursue a teaching career, and most of the deaf persons who are employed by schools for the deaf are not teachers but hold less prestigious and influential jobs. The growing recognition of the importance of sign language in the educational process, however, has led to the development of teacher aide positions for some deaf persons who have not completed a proper education.

The Center of Total Communication for the Deaf, which provides classes in sign language for parents, teachers, and interpreters, is rather exceptional in that 35 of the teachers and other staff members are deaf.

Also Castberggard, the folk-high school for the deaf, is an exception to the rule since several of the teachers and the assistant director are deaf.

Current Trends and the Future

Dissatisfaction with the rather poor results of oral/aural and simultaneous methods of communication has eased the way for the discussion of alternatives. One of the alternatives now being discussed and developed in Denmark, as it is in other countries, is a bilingual approach to the education of the deaf.

One of the important conditions necessary for radical changes to occur in the policies that govern the education of the deaf in Denmark is a change in society's attitude towards deafness and deaf people. As long as deaf people and their language were considered as second rank, educational endeavors were aimed at freeing children of the "burden" of deafness and providing them with access to the hearing world.

An important change in attitude on the part of many is the acknowledgement that deaf people can be equal to hearing people if allowed to compete on an equal basis. This has led society to the recognition of the importance of sign language and an appreciation of the deaf as a rich societal resource.

The deaf community is now looked at not as an obstacle to integration into the larger hearing society, but as a place where people deprived of hearing can find fulfillment, and a platform from which many of the advantages of the hearing world can be approached and achieved.

As society finally accepts deafness as a given life condition for some people, it will accept the special ways and means that are necessary for the deaf to have an equal opportunity for a satisfying life situation. This acceptance of the deaf will lead to a societal attitude that views deafness not as just a lack of hearing in an individual, but as a positive personality variable in its own right; one that can provide a unique contribution to an individual's character—something, in fact, that cannot be experienced by people who hear (Vestberg, 1989).

Rephrasing some of the difficult and controversial questions about the education of the deaf in the framework of bilingualism may lead to new ways of looking at the different issues that confront parents and educators. This may in turn cause a re-evaluation of current pedagogy and lead to successful alternative measures.

One of the consequences of the bilingual approach may be that schools will consider sign language not only as an alternative for students who are oral/aural failures, but as the primary language vehicle for deaf children and an integral part of the curriculum in its own right. This change, if it becomes widespread, will create a demand for teachers of the deaf whose primary language is sign.

Also, the acceptance of sign language as the deaf child's primary language will result in the use of sign language as a major medium for subject matter instruction.

Another consequence of the use of sign language as the instructional language of the deaf, and Danish as the deaf child's second language, may be increased literacy. Because the Danish language has limited accessibility through the use of lipreading (aided by the Mouth-Hand-System and the Manual Alphabet) and the use of residual hearing, very modest academic achievement gains were realized in the past with the use of the traditional oral method of teaching the deaf. Danish seems to be more fully accessed through written and read language when the linguistic forms can be explained and understood in detail through the use of sign communication.

References

Engberg-Pedersen, E. (1979). Topics or topicalized nominals in Danish Sign Language? In
B. Frokjaer-Jensen (Ed.), *The sciences of deaf signing* (pp. 43-53). Copenhagen, Denmark:
Audiologopedic Research Group, University of Copenhagen.

Engberg-Pedersen, E. (1986). The use of space with verbs in Danish Sign Language. In B. T. Tervoort
(Ed.), *Signs of life: Proceedings of the Second European Congress on Sign Language Research*
(pp. 32-41). Amsterdam: Institute of General Linguistics.

Engberg-Pedersen, E. (1989). Pragmatics of non-manual behaviour in Danish Sign Language.
In *Proceedings from the Fourth International Symposium on Sign Language Research* (pp. 121-128).
Finland.

Engberg-Pederson, E., & Pedersen, A. (1985). Proforms in Danish Sign Language: The use in
figurative signing. In W. C. Stokoe & V. Volterra (Eds.), *SLR '83: Proceedings of the III
International Symposium on Sign Language Research* (pp. 202-209). Silver Springs, MD:
Linstok Press.

Hansen, B. (1975). Varieties in Danish Sign Language and grammatical features of the original
sign language. In *Sign Language Studies 8.* 249-256.

Hansen, B. (1980a). *Aspects of deafness and total communication.* Copenhagen, Denmark: Doves
Center for Total Kommunikation.

Hansen, B. (1980b). Research on Danish Sign Language and its impact on the deaf community. In
C. Baker & R. Battison (Eds.), *Sign language and the deaf community* (pp. 245-263).
Silver Spring, MD: National Association for the Deaf.

Hansen, B. (1986). Sign language varieties and the TV-medium. In B. T. Tervoort (Ed.), *Signs of life:
Proceedings of the Second European Congress on Sign Language Research* (pp. 147-153).
Amsterdam: Institute of General Linguistics.

Hansen, B. (1987). Sign language and bilingualism: A focus on an experimental approach to the
teaching of deaf children in Denmark. In J. Kyle (Ed.), *Sign and school: Multilingual matters*
(pp. 81-88). Clevedon.

Hansen, B., & Engberg-Pedersen, E. (1984). Danish Sign Language. In F. Loncke, P. Boyes-Braem,
& E. Lebrun (Eds.), *Recent research on European sign language* (pp. 61-72). Lisse, the
Netherlands: Swets and Zeitlinger.

Holm, A., Gudman, S., Rasmussen, J.W., & Vestberg, P. (Eds.). (1983). *Doveundervisning i Danmark
1807–1982.* Copenhagen, Denmark: Doveforsorgens Historiske Selskab.

Kjaer Sorensen, R. (1975). Indications of regular syntax in deaf Danish school children's language.
Sign Language Studies, 8, 257-63.

Kjaer Sorensen, R., & Hansen, B. (1976). *The sign language of deaf children in Denmark.* Copenhagen,
Denmark: Doves Center for Total Kommunikation.

Vestberg, P. (1973). Evaluation of reading achievements of deaf children. In E. Kampp, *Evaluation
of hearing handicapped children.* Ebeltoft, Denmark: Fifth Danavox Symposium.

Vestberg, P. (1989). *Beyond stereotypes: Perspectives on the personality characteristics of deaf
people.* Gallaudet Research Institute Working Paper 89-2. Washington, DC: Gallaudet
University.

[Except for Holm et al., 1983, only English texts are included.]

The Education of the Hearing Impaired in Egypt

by Waguida El Bakary, Ed.D.

Introduction

The education of the hearing impaired in Egypt is the responsibility of the National Ministry of Education through the Special Education Department and its Division for the Education of the Hearing Impaired. Thirty-five public schools for the hearing impaired are found in 24 out of the 26 governorates of Egypt.

The Ministry builds and equips schools, provides specialized teachers, sets and modifies curricula, conducts pre-service and in-service teacher training, and supervises and monitors schools. The Ministry of Education aims to prepare the handicapped children for life after school by providing them with information, skills, morals, and directions (Nagdi, 1986, pp. 7-8).

The issuance of Law Number 68 in 1968, which included statutes for the creation of special schools for the handicapped, ushered in a new era in the education of the handicapped in Egypt. The law mandated that the education of the handicapped be compulsory through grade eight. Since the enactment of the law, enrollment in the special schools has increased significantly. In spite of the increases, it is estimated that the schools for the handicapped can accommodate only 1 to 1.5 percent of the population of handicapped schoolage children in Egypt (Mina, 1983, p. 106).

Schools

The following table provides national statistics on the number of schools and teachers of the hearing impaired teachers in Egypt in 1989-90.

Table 1. Number of Schools for the Hearing Impaired, Hearing Impaired Students, and Teachers of the Hearing Impaired in Egypt

During the 1989-1990 School Year

Item	Number
Number of schools	35
Number of students	5,144
Number of teachers	836

Compiled from the following sources: Ministry of Education, n.d. a, p. 1, and Ministry of Education, n.d. b, pp. 1-2.

For a complete list of schools please refer to Appendix A. It is interesting to note that 85 percent of schools for the hearing impaired are called "Al-Amal" or "Hope" schools.

There are no public schools for the hearing impaired at the nursery or kindergarten level in Egypt (Ibrahim, 1990). However, the Ministry of Social Work runs a few nurseries that include hearing impaired children (Abdel Gawwad, 1990).

There are a small number of schools for hearing impaired children who are beyond the fifth grade level. Preparatory level departments for hearing impaired children are available in some schools across the governorates (Abdel Gawwad, 1990). Experimental secondary level classes were opened in 1984-1985, when research showed that a percentage of the hearing impaired students could profit from continued study through the college level (Nagdi, 1986, p. 8). There are presently two secondary schools in Cairo and one in Alexandria that enroll hearing impaired students (Abdel Gawwad, 1990). Postsecondary educational opportunities at the national universities are not available at this point for hearing impaired students.

There are only a few private schools for the hearing impaired in Egypt. Two of the private schools are in Cairo (Abdel Gawwad, 1990).

Table 2 gives a breakdown of the number

of students in each stage of school: primary (elementary), preparatory (junior high), and secondary (high school).

Table 2. Distribution of Hearing Impaired Students in Egyptian Schools

Stage	No. of classes	No. of students
Primary	393	3,862
Preparatory	107	1,087
Secondary	11	195
Total	511	5,144

Source: Ministry of Education, n.d. a, p. 1.

The average number of students per class is twelve at the primary stage, fourteen to sixteen at the preparatory stage, and up to eighteen at the secondary stage (Fadel, 1990).

Curriculum

At the primary (elementary) stage the curriculum in schools for the hearing impaired is, with few exceptions, the same as that used in the regular schools. Table 3 presents details on the primary stage curriculum at schools for the hearing impaired in Egypt.

Although the curriculum for hearing impaired students is similar to that of normal students, the speed with which they are expected to cover the curriculum is different. For example, the hearing impaired student is expected to complete the grade one curriculum in two years rather than one. The first five years of the basic education stage for normal children takes the hearing impaired students eight years to complete. See Table 4 for a comparison.

Table 3. Primary (Elementary) Stage Curriculum of Schools for Hearing Impaired in Egypt

Subject	Hours Per Week Grade							
	1	2	3	4	5	6	7	8
Religion	2	2	2	2	2	2	2	2
Arabic and pronunciation	14	14	12	12	11	11	10	10
Mathematics	5	5	6	6	6	6	6	6
General knowledge for environmental activities	3	3	4	4	5	5	6	6
Physical education	3	3	3	3	3	3	3	3
Art & manual work	3	3	4	4	4	4	4	4
Agricultural education	1	1	2	2	2	2	2	2
Home economics	-	-	-	2	4	4	4	4
Music	1	1	1	1	1	1	1	1
Total hours/week	32	32	34	36	38	38	38	38

Source: Ministry of Education, 1990, p. 40.

Table 4. **A Comparison of Grade Levels Between Normal and Hearing Impaired Children**

Regular Grade Level	Equivalent Grade Level for Hearing Impaired Students
1st grade	1st grade
2nd grade	1st grade
3rd grade	1st grade
4th grade	2nd grade
5th grade	3rd grade
6th grade	3rd and 4th grades
7th grade	5th grade
8th grade	5th grade

Source: Abdel Gawwad, 1990.

The curriculum of the preparatory and secondary stages includes a heavy emphasis on vocational training and includes specialization in subjects such as carpentry, typing, knitting, sewing, engraving, mechanical repairs, and plumbing. For more details on the preparatory stage curriculum of schools for the hearing impaired in Egypt, please refer to Appendix B.

The communication systems used in the schools include the Arabic manual alphabet, sign language, and speechreading. The Total Communication philosophy is utilized (Abdel Gawwad, 1990).

Admission Procedures

Public schools for the hearing impaired accept deaf or severely hearing impaired students who are at least moderately intelligent and possess no other handicaps. A child is considered to be deaf if he or she has a 70 to 120 decibel hearing level in the better ear after treatment. A severe hearing problem is defined as a 50 to 70 decibel hearing level in the better ear after treatment (Ministry of Education, 1990, p. 13).

Day Schools

Certain procedures are followed in admitting hearing impaired students to public schools. These are:

1. A personal interview to ensure that the student does not suffer from multiple handicaps. Only children with hearing handicaps are eligible or enrollment in these schools.
2. The attainment of at least the age of six. However, due to a lack of awareness, some parents do not enroll their children until the age of eight.
3. A hearing examination. The hearing test is conducted at the Public Institute for Speech and Hearing in Embaba.
4. An intelligence test. The test is performed at a private clinic in Qubbah. The purpose of this test is to ensure that the child is not mentally retarded.
5. A three-week in-school observation period at the beginning of the academic year. If the student performs according to expectations during the three weeks of school, enrollment continues. If not, the file is reexamined, the parents are counseled, and referrals are made to other institutions (Fadel, 1990).

There are no official statistics available that compare the number of hearing impaired children enrolled in schools for the hearing impaired with the total number of hearing impaired children in the country. Mina (1983, p. 106) states that special education schools accommodate only 1 to 1.5 percent of the total number of handicapped children. Ministry of Education sources estimate that the number of children enrolled in schools for the hearing impaired is about one-third of the total population of hearing impaired children in Egypt (Abdel Gawwad, 1990). Dr. Salah Soliman, Professor and Chairman of the Department for Hearing at the Faculty of Medicine, Ain Shams University, estimates the number of hearing impaired children in Egypt to be two million (El Mahdi, 1990, p. 11).

Hearing impaired children in Egypt are not enrolled in school programs for the following reasons:

1. There is a lack of parental awareness of services for the hearing impaired. It is noteworthy that the majority of hearing impaired children in Egypt have parents who fall into the lower socioeconomic and cultural levels.

2. Egyptian schools for the handicapped do not accept students with multiple handicaps. There are three kinds of special education schools: schools for the hearing impaired, the visually impaired, and the mentally retarded. Those children with multiple handicaps are handled by private institutions.

3. There is a lack of space in the schools for the hearing impaired. These schools have waiting lists, and hearing impaired children may have to wait until the following year to be enrolled.

4. There is a shortage of residential programs in all schools for the hearing impaired (Abdel Gawwad, 1990).

Residential Programs

A select number of schools offer free residential programs for the hearing impaired. Because of the shortage of space in these residential schools, priority is given to students who live far away from the school and who would have to take two buses to get to the school (Fadel, 1990). Parents who cannot accept their children's hearing handicap are often those most eager to place their children in residential schools (Abdel Gawwad, 1990).

Condition of the Schools

The Ministry of Education faces numerous severe problems in administering the national system of public schools for normal and handicapped students in Egypt. These problems include financial, teacher, building, and material shortages. In light of the current dire situation, the fact that there are schools for the hearing impaired at all is an achievement.

It is not surprising then to find that conditions in schools for the hearing impaired are not optimum. Although the Ministry of Education issues directives on specifications for schools for the hearing impaired which include the ideal standards for buildings, equipment, educational services, and vocational activities (Aboul Laif, 1971; Ministry of Education, 1989), researchers have found that the conditions in schools for hearing impaired children leave much room for improvement. The findings of Dr. Samira Abou Zeid Abdou Nagdi support this fact (1986).

This researcher's visits to Ministry staff and principals of schools for the hearing impaired indicated that these schools need additional financing to upgrade their auditory training equipment, acquire more individual hearing aids, maintain equipment and machines for vocational training, develop curricula tailored to the needs of this special group, train specialized teachers and administrators, hire specialized staff, furnish residential programs, purchase educational materials and media, and provide financial aid to needy students and unemployed graduates (Abdel Gawwad, 1990; Fadel, 1990).

Employment Opportunities

The Egyptian People's Assembly (Parliament) has passed a law that obligates the Ministry of Manpower to reserve 5 percent of the positions in the government and the public sector for the handicapped. Although there is an occasional outcry in the People's Assembly about this percentage not being respected (Muawwad, Abdel Gawwad, Sherif, 1990, p. 8), this researcher was informed by the principal of the prestigious Al-Matariya School for the hearing impaired that its graduates have little difficulty obtaining jobs with the government or in the schools from which they graduated. Employment opportunities in factories are also available (Fadel, 1990).

Parent Education

There are no organized parent education programs designed to assist parents in dealing with their handicapped children. This lack of parental education is especially true in the case of parents of preschool-aged handicapped children. There are few voluntary support groups and the support groups that do exist are not yet highly organized. Hearing impaired students have organized some clubs that focus on sports and social activities (Abdel Gawwad, 1990). Some school administrators counsel parents of hearing impaired students who are having problems with socialization or academic progress (Fadel, 1990).

Until recently, the parents of handicapped children were not vocal. The problems of the handicapped were not in the forefront of the public's attention. However, there have been positive trends lately. Some parents of handicapped children, particularly those from the higher socioeconomic classes and those who have benefitted from living outside of Egypt, especially in western countries with developed services for the handicapped, are taking active steps to raise public consciousness. They are organizing support groups, building schools, attracting media coverage, lobbying the government for more and better services, and encouraging donations of equipment to the schools for the handicapped.

Occasionally parents of handicapped children describe in the national newspapers their plight and the absence of significant services for the handicapped. Recently one parent complained that he toured all the bookstores in Cairo to find a book on sign language and did not find a single volume (Idris, 1990, p. 11). The author visited the Ministry of Education's Library to find references on the hearing impaired. Only two books were found on the shelves.

Teacher Training

For a long time there were no special education departments offering teacher preparation at the national universities in Egypt. In September, 1991, Al-Azhar University was the first university in Egypt to start a program to prepare teachers of hearing impaired children. This center was headed by Dr. Farouk Sadek (Mehanna, 1990, p. 15). Before then, the Ministry of Education was the only provider of training to teach handicapped children.

The Ministry of Education offers a one-year national teacher training program for special education teachers. The program has different sections that target the preparation of teachers of children with mental, hearing, or visual handicaps. At the end of the year of study, the graduates receive a diploma in special education (Ministry of Education, 1990, p. 31). In 1990-1991, enrollment in the hearing impaired section of this program was 74 (Ibrahim, 1990). This is a small number compared with the actual numbers of teachers needed. It is not uncommon, therefore, to find teachers at schools for the hearing impaired who have had no formal training to teach hearing handicapped students. This is particularly true for teachers of academic content areas and vocational courses (Fadel, 1990).

Admission to the Ministry of Education special education teacher training program is competitive. To qualify, the applicant must be a teacher in the basic education stage, preferably at the primary level, with a minimum of three years of teaching experience. In addition, the teacher's performance evaluation during the past two years must not be less than "excellent." The permission of the teacher's employer and a successful personal interview are also required. Applicants must pledge that they will attend the session full-time and teach in a special education school for no less than three years after receiving the diploma. During the training program, the participants continue to receive their full teaching salary (Ministry of Education, 1990, p. 31).

A study of the Ministry of Education's special education teacher training program conducted in 1983 revealed that the predominant teaching method used in this program was lecture. The discussion method was used to a lesser extent. Research and practical application were not found to be primary methods of instruction. The student teachers surveyed recommended that the amount of time allocated for practicum and field visits be increased. They also recommended that the schools be equipped with educational media, curricular materials, and other resources required to teach the deaf. The student teachers would then be able use these instructional resources during their practica. The study concluded that the current program is far from ideal (Mina, 1983, pp. 117-118). Another study (Nagdi, 1990) revealed that special education schools suffer from a severe shortage of qualified teachers. The study also pointed out that the present level of special education teacher training is professionally inadequate (Nagdi, 1990).

These findings are all the more significant since the educational system for the handicapped in Egypt has a significant impact on similar programs in the other Arab World countries. Many of the educational programs for the hearing impaired children of other Arab countries were developed and are run by Egyptian specialists or native specialists who have been trained in Egypt (Mina, 1983, p. 107).

Future Directions

Positive developments are currently taking place in the area of educational and social services for the hearing impaired in Egypt. These developments are as follows:

1. The Division for the Education of the Hearing Impaired at the Ministry of Education is cognizant of the problems that exist in the schools for the hearing impaired. With USAID funds, the Division is making plans to send teachers and supervisors on missions abroad with the goal of obtaining information that will upgrade the facilities and equipment in schools for the hearing impaired in Egypt. A committee of educators and Ministry staff is at work improving current curricula and devising new special curricula for the hearing impaired (Abdel Gawwad, 1990).

2. More researchers are taking an interest in special education and are disseminating their findings and recommendations to Ministry of Education committees through journal articles and newspaper interviews.

3. President Hosni Mubarak declared the decade of 1989-1999 as the decade of the child. The year 1990 was targeted by Mrs. Mubarak as the Year of the Handicapped Child. Within this framework, in 1990 there were noticeable efforts by private citizens and public officials to remodel and reequip special education schools, and to expand services for and public awareness of the handicapped population.

4. A number of national conferences have addressed the issues of the handicapped. A conference entitled "Towards a Non-Handicapped Childhood" was held in November 1990 (El Mallakh, 1990, p. 11). Another conference entitled "Better Directions for Handicapped Children" was also held during the same month (Al-Ahram, 1990, p. 8).

5. Private efforts are being made to provide services for the handicapped. Parents of handicapped children and charitable organizations are taking

positive steps to establish private schools for the handicapped that will supplement and complement the government's efforts. Private efforts are providing funds to remodel schools and upgrade equipment. The Right to Live Society, the Integrated Care Society headed by Mrs. Mubarak, Mrs. Barrada and her project for a village for the handicapped, and the Rotary Club are examples of individuals and organizations that are volunteering their services.

6. Departments for special education in general and the hearing impaired in particular are being established for the first time as part of the National University system.

7. Public health awareness programs are being mounted in the mass media that focus on the prevention of handicaps through (a) better care during pregnancy, (b) good nutrition, (c) encouraging vaccinations to control early childhood diseases, (d) encouraging medical exams before marriage, and (e) discouraging the marriage of relatives. National news papers are taking a leading role in the conduct of the public awareness campaigns. Hardly a week passes without national coverage on two or three issues pertaining to the handicapped (El Mahdi, 1990, p. 11).

laws facilitate the employment of special education graduates. Traditionally, parent support groups have not been well organized or powerful. Recently these groups have become more of a political force. The only teacher training program that qualifies teachers to work with hearing impaired students is small and not very effective.

There is reason to believe that the recent interest shown by government, private organizations, and parents of the handicapped will result in more and better services for the hearing impaired students of Egypt in the future.

Summary

Schools for the hearing impaired in Egypt are administered by the Ministry of Education. The schools are insufficient in number to absorb all hearing impaired students and are not well equipped. The curriculum does not differ very much from that used in regular schools. Students with multiple handicaps or low IQ scores are not accepted in the schools for the hearing impaired. New

Appendices
Appendix A

Distribution of Schools for the Hearing Impaired in Egypt's Governorates

Governorate	School
Cairo	1. Al-Amal School, Matariya
	2. Al-Amal Qawmi School
	3. Al-Gamiía al-misriya lil summ
	4. Al-Amal School, Mounira
	5. Jannat al-atfal, Zinhum
	6. Al-Amal School, Abbasiya
	7. Al-Amal School, Shubra
	8. Al-Amal Primary School, Helwan
	9. Al-Amal Prep. School, Helwan
Alexandria	10. Al-Amal School, Hadara
	11. Al-Amal School, Janaklis
Al-Beheira	12. Al-Amal School, Damanhur
Al-Gharbeya	13. Al-Amal School, Tanta
	14. Al-Amal School, Al-Mahalla
Kafr El Sheikh	15. Al-Amal School, Kafr El Sheikh
Al-Menoufia	16. Al-Amal School, Shebin El Kom
Al-Qalyoubia	17. Al-Amal School, Banha
	18. Al-Amal School, Qanater El Khaireya
Al-Dakahlia	19. Al-Amal School, Al-Mansoura
Damietta	20. Al-Amal School, Damietta
Al-Sharkia	21. Al-Amal School, Zagazig
Port-Said	22. Al-Amal School, Port Said
Ismailia	23. Al-Amal School, Ismailia
Suez	24. Al-Amal School, Suez
Giza	25. Al-Amal School, Giza
Fayoum	26. Al-Amal School, Fayoum
Bani Sweif	27. Al-Amal School, Bani Sweif
Minia	28. Al-Amal School, Minia
Assiout	29. Al-Amal School, Assiut
Sohag	30. Al-Amal School, Sohag
Qena	31. Al-Amal School, Qena
Aswan	32. Al-Amal School, Aswan
Matrouh	33. Al-Amal School, Matrouh
Al-Wadi Al Gadid	34. Al-Amal School, Al-Wadi Al Gadid
North Sinai	35. Madrasat al-tarbia al khasa

Source: Ministry of Education, n.d. b.

Appendix B

Preparatory (Junior High) Stage Curriculum at Hearing Impaired Schools in Egypt 1989–1990

Subject	Hours Per Week		
	Grade 9	Grade 10	Grade 11
Religion	2	2	2
Arabic language	8	8	8
Mathematics	4	4	4
Science and hygiene	2	2	2
Social studies	2	2	2
Physical education	2	2	2
Vocational training	20	20	20
Total	40	40	40

Source: Ministry of Education, 1990, p. 41.

References

Abdel Gawwad, M. (1990, October 7 and 9). *Interview*. Cairo, Egypt.

Aboul Laif, H. K. (1971). *Al-taghizat al-lazima li-fasl amin* [Specifications for safe classrooms]. Cairo, Egypt: Ministry of Education.

El Mahdi, H. (1990, November 23). 60 milliun mu'awwaq fil 'alam bisabab hawadith al-tariq wal manzil [Sixty million handicapped in the world due to road and home accidents]. *Al-Ahram*.

El Mallakh, A. (1990, November 16). A'yad al-tufula ba'd liqa' al-qimma [Children's festivities after the summit meeting]. *Al-Ahram*.

Fadel, F. A. (1990, October 16). *Interview*. Cairo, Egypt.

Ibrahim, F. (1990, October 10). *Interview*. Cairo, Egypt.

Idris, F. A. (1990, June 18). Ba'd an dukht [After I searched hard]. *Al-Ahram*.

Mehanna, M. (1990, October 10). Akhbaruhum [Their news]. *Al-Ahram*.

Mina, F. M. (1983). Birnamij i'dad mu'allimi al'atfal al'mu'awwaquin fi misr [The teacher preparation program for teachers of handicapped children in Egypt]. In *Majmu'at buhuth wa magalat fil tarbiya* [A collection of research articles in education]. Cairo, Egypt: Dar al-thaqafa lil tiba'a wal nashr.

Ministry of Education. (1989). *Muzakkira fi sha'n al-mutattalibat al-tarbawiya li madaris al-tarbiya al-sama'ia* [A memorandum on the educational specifications for hearing impaired schools]. Cairo, Egypt: Ministry of Education.

Ministry of Education. (1990). *Qarar wizari raqam 37 bi tarikh 28/1/1990 fi sha'n al-la'iha al-tan fiziya li madaris wa fusul al-tarbiya al khasa* [Ministerial Decree No. 37 dated January 28, 1990 concerning regulations for Special Education schools and classes]. Cairo, Egypt: The Author.

Ministry of Education. (n.d. a). *Bayan ihsa' li madaris al-tarbiya al-sama'iya 1989/90* [A statistical table on hearing impaired schools in 1989/90]. Cairo, Egypt: The Author.

Ministry of Education. (n.d. b). *Bayan 'an madaris al-tarbiya al-sama'iya wa 'anawinuha 1990/91* [Statistics on hearing impaired schools and their addresses in 1990/91]. Cairo, Egypt: The Author.

Mu'alagat al-atfal al-mu'awwaqin - nadwa dawliya 'anha ghadan [Treating handicapped children - An international seminar on this topic]. (1990, November 24). *Al-Ahram*.

Muawwad, M., Ali, A. G., and El Abd, S. (1990, March 3). Al-mutalaba bi tashdid al-riqaba 'ala mukhtalaf al-aghiza li daman ta-iin nisbat al 5% lil mu'awwaqin [The call to increase super vision on various organizations to ensure the employment of the 5% quota for the handicapped]. *Al-Ahram*.

Nagdi, S. A. Z. A. (1986, February). *Mada mula'amat al-imkanat wal taghizat al-mutaha fi madaris al-mu'awwaqin sama'iyan fil ta'lim al-asasi li ihtiyagatihum* [The extent to which facilities and equipment available in hearing impaired schools in basic education are suitable to their needs]. Paper presented at a conference, Cairo, Egypt.

Nagdi, S. A. Z. A. (1990, March). *Al-tarakumat wal tahaddiyat fi i'dad al-mu'allim* [The accumulations and challenges of teacher preparation]. Paper presented at a conference, Alexandria, Egypt.

Education of the Deaf in El Salvador

by Dr. Jess Freeman King

    This chapter is dedicated to the teachers of the deaf in El Salvador, the beautiful people who so graciously touched my life and invited me into theirs.

Education of the Deaf in El Salvador

The current status of education of the deaf in El Salvador cannot be understood without a historical sketch of the Central American region. The interdependence of the Central American nations is evident and vital. To understand the current educational situation one must be cognizant of El Salvador's fiercely independent nature.

Historical Background

The roots of the educational, economic, and political status of Central America stretch back to the mother tree of colonial Spain. Central America, unlike Mexico and Peru, played only a minor role in the designs of the massive Spanish empire. Because of the various indigenous groups in the conquered and Spanish-occupied areas, the Spanish subdued the region in stages, necessitating that a new government be established with each subsequent conquest. The inherent result of this policy was a lack of centralization which fostered town councils as the most important governing body. Municipalities assumed the day-to-day governing authority (Blachman, Leongrane, & Sharpe, 1986, p. 4).

Following closely on the heels of conquest were the missionary efforts of the Catholic Church, aimed at dispelling beliefs in the old Indian gods and introducing Christianity. The Franciscans and Dominicans, in particular, were instrumental in these missionary efforts, and by the latter part of the seventeenth century, the Church had become a powerful source of authority.

The social structure of the region at this time was dominated by a white elite composed of Spanish-born as well as locally born whose parents were from Spain. The lower class was composed of the indigenous peoples who functioned as the labor force. A third distinct social class was composed of those individuals who were of mixed indigenous

and white blood. This class usually worked as artisans, merchants, peddlers, and skilled laborers in the towns (Blachman, Leongrane, & Sharpe, 1986, p. 5). This emerging middle sector would gain political clout and importance in subsequent years, into the present.

Central America achieved independence from Spain and from Mexico during the 1920s and organized as a single political entity, the United Provinces of Central American (Costa Rica, Nicaragua, El Salvador, Honduras, and Guatemala), until the federation disintegrated in 1938.

As for El Salvador, it was originally settled by the Pipil Indians, who migrated south from Mexico. During the early part of the sixteenth century, the Indians were subjugated by the conquistadors of Spain and were placed under the direct control of the captaincy general of Guatemala. It would be three centuries before El Salvador declared its independence from Spain, ultimately becoming an independent nation in 1839 (Bonner, 1984, p. 20).

Following independence, El Salvador gradually polarized into two competing factions, the conservatives and the liberals. Such remains the case today, with these two extremes fractionalized into a variety of political parties with varying platforms along the political continuum.

Perhaps the classic lines penned by the poet Carl Sandburg are appropriate in fostering an understanding of the present educational, economic, and political situation in El Salvador, and the resultant impact on the education of the deaf:

The people, yes, the people,
Until the people are taken care of one
    way or another,
Until the people are solved somehow for
    the day and hour,
Until then one hears "Yes but the people
    what about the people?"

Seventy percent of El Salvador's people are rural peasants, stymied by poverty and illiteracy, as they have been for generations. In spite of government projects padded largely with American dollars, for the most part, social and economic progress has not filtered down to the peasants. In fact, some studies have placed the functional illiteracy rate at 90 percent among the peasants (Bonner, 1984, p. 17). The cold reality is that there are two starkly different worlds in El Salvador—one inhabited by the poor and illiterate, and the other by the middle class and the rich.

The plight, politically, educationally, and economically, of El Salvador is "the people" . . . the masses of people who comprise the bulk of the population . . . the masses who are poor, uneducated, and who, of necessity, prioritize daily subsistence far above education and literacy. This being the state of 90 percent of the population, one can confidently venture to guess what the state of the typical deaf person is in El Salvador.

Extent and Kind of Educational Services for the Deaf

At present, the educational opportunities for the deaf can be broken down into three basic types of programs:

1. **Large day class program for the deaf.** The main center for deaf children in El Salvador is located in the capital city of San Salvador and is called El Centro Audicion y Lenjuage. The funding for this program comes mainly from the federal government. The administrative staff includes a superintendent and a principal, along with a teaching faculty of approximately 20 full-time teachers, and a support staff that includes a part-time audiologist and a part-time school psychologist. The student enrollment is in the vicinity of 200 students, ranging in age from five to eighteen.

2. **Church-sponsored day class program in San Salvador.** This is a church-sponsored program that is funded by and housed at Iglesia Nazaret. This was the first program for deaf children in El Salvador to employ Total Communication. At present, there are between 20 and 25 students enrolled in the program, all of them being of preschool or elementary age. The faculty includes five teachers and one director, who also has teaching responsibilities. The majority of the students come from upper-middle-class and/or affluent families, who, for the most part, are actively involved in supporting the program.

3. **Public school programs.** Outside of the capital city of San Salvador, the only other educational programming for deaf children is in self-contained classes found in public schools. These classes also include children with mild to profound handicaps other than deafness, which also ranges from mild to profound. More times than not, the teachers of these self-contained classes have little knowledge of deafness.

Parent Education

Both the large day class program, El Centro Audicion y Lenjuage, and the smaller, church-sponsored program, Iglesia Nazaret, provide parents with psychological support and guidance services. The very active parent group at Iglesia Nazaret has taken the lead. Due to the large number of students at El Centro Audicion y Lenjuage and the fact that most of the parents of children in this program are from the lower socioeconomic strata and must rely on buses for transportation, the parent education opportunities via workshops and other ongoing educational activities are not optimal by any means. In contrast, because of the higher socioeconomic level of the parents and the smaller size of the program itself, the parents at Iglesia Nazaret appear to be a close-knit group, have higher aspirations for their children relative to education, for the most part have learned at least basic sign language, and are eager and able to participate in workshops and conferences that will further their understanding of deafness.

However, at present there is no nationwide parent organization.

Communication Methodology Utilized

Until the late 1980s, the philosophy embraced by educators of the deaf in El Salvador was of the oral persuasion. However, the Total Communication philosophy is presently being utilized at both El Centro Audicion y Lenjuage and Iglesia Nazaret. Both programs employ a combination of American Sign Language and native signs arranged to follow the syntax of spoken Spanish. Basically, what is utilized is a simultaneous system with an extensive use of grammatical markers. The public school programs in the rest of the country still, for the most part, rely on the oral method of instruction.

Academic Achievement of Deaf Children

Because of extremely limited availability of standardized testing, valid and reliable data of academic achievements of deaf children in El Salvador does not exist. The bulk of the standardized testing that has been conducted was completed at El Centro Audicion y Lenjuage and Iglesia Nazaret. Formalized and standardized achievement testing is nonexistent in the outlying programs.

Opportunities for Vocational Education

Deaf students who have finished their formal schooling are able to pursue vocational training at a limited number of schools in San Salvador and San Miguel. However, no organized interpreting network is available for these students.

Postsecondary Education Opportunities

Currently the opportunity for deaf students to pursue a high school education, for all practical purposes, is nonexistent. As is true of vocational education, neither an organized interpreting network nor a program to train interpreters is available. The typical education in El Salvador does not go beyond grade nine for the majority of the population. The adult literacy rate for the entire country as of the early 1980s was only 63 percent. The literacy rate in rural areas is only 30 percent (Bonner, 1984, p. 12). Thus, the student who is deaf cannot be adequately prepared for higher education.

Teachers of the Deaf

Opportunities for Deaf Individuals to Serve as Teachers of the Deaf

At present, in the entire country of El Salvador, there is only one deaf person involved in the direct delivery of educational services to students who are deaf. That person is the principal at El Centro Audicion y Lenjuage in San Salvador. Iglesia Nazaret employs an instructional assistant who is profoundly deaf. She received her formal education at the Louisiana School for the Deaf, then returned to El Salvador.

Availability of Teacher Preparation Programs

Presently, there are no college or university programs in El Salvador that offer teacher preparation programs in education of the deaf. The current teachers of the deaf were either educated in a teacher training program outside of El Salvador or studied Special Education in one of the local universities and then began teaching deaf children. These teachers have an extremely limited background and understanding of deafness.

Certification of Teachers of the Deaf

There do not exist, at the present time, standards for the certification of teachers of the deaf in El Salvador. The local universities do offer degrees in Special Education; however, there is minimal, if any, attention devoted to the education of the deaf.

Therefore, the majority of the Salvadoreans who are teachers of the deaf entered the classroom without proper certification and with only a limited understanding of the educational implications of deafness.

Significant Current Issues and Future Direction of the Education of the Deaf in El Salvador

Education of the deaf in El Salvador is at a critical crossroads, and unless the crisis is met fearlessly and with candor and honesty, the deaf children of El Salvador will continue to be lost educationally, socially, and emotionally.

To solve this problem a number of things must be addressed, including the need for a comprehensive nationwide identification process; the development of a model facility for deaf children that can act as a clearinghouse for information concerning deafness and the education of the deaf child; the establishment of a teacher preparation program on the university or college level; guidelines for programs already established or that will be established; the creation of a national parentsí organization; and cooperation and networking among the currently established programs.

Teachers, administrators, and parents in El Salvador desire quality and excellence in the educational programs for children who are deaf in El Salvador; but until unified programming, ongoing inservice opportunities for teachers and parents, and an established teacher education program exists, these dreams will never be realized.

Deaf children must be afforded opportunities for meaningful communication with teachers, parents, and their peer group. This is not happening in most of the public school programs in El Salvador. The large day class program in San Salvador, El Centro Audicion y Lenjuage, has had minimal success. However, the current situation must not be attributed to the administrators and teachers. The problem lies in the lack of teacher preparation and ongoing inservice training opportunities for those in the field.

It is the goal of educators of the deaf in El Salvador that the child who is deaf will be afforded an education that will prepare him or her to compete equally with the hearing students in the country. These educators believe that given an *equal* education and *equal* opportunities, the child who is deaf can compete. For this belief to become a reality, the issues of equal education and equal opportunities must be addressed by not only educators and parents, but by the central government that is responsible for the funding and by the society that dictates attitudes.

References

Blachman, M. J., Leongrane, W. M., and Sharpe, K. (1986). *Confronting revolution: Security through diplomacy in Central America.* New York: Pantheon Books.

Bonner, R., (1984). *Weakness and deceit: U.S. policy and El Salvador.* New York: The New York Times Book Co., Inc.

Education of the Deaf in France

by Dr. Denise Busquet

Historical Background

Any history of the education of the deaf in France will include a survey of the philosophies and methods used by educators who had the goal of freeing the deaf from their bond of ignorance and isolation through education and communication.

Before the eighteenth century in France, as in other European countries, some deaf individuals received tutoring. Historical documents concerning the education of deaf persons attest to isolated but brilliant results. The failures were not reported.

By the end of the eighteenth century in France, the education of the deaf took on a new direction and became a country-wide education system that later served as a model for the development of the education of the deaf and hard of hearing in many other countries.

A priest, Charles-Michel de l'Épée (1712-1789), was sensitized by the condition of the deaf in the lower classes. He found that they were hidden, humiliated, left uneducated, and often condemned to stay as the cruel and dangerous idiots often depicted in literature.

In 1760, the Abbé de l'Épée founded, in his own house, in the Rue des Moulins in Paris, the first free class for the deaf. He devoted his life and his fortune to teaching the deaf to speak, and to use a new language of his own invention, the language of methodical signs, or the language of gestures.

This mimetic language that de l'Épée developed had little in common with the dactylological system developed by the Spanish educator Pablo Bonet. It was truly a new mode of communication in which each gesture represented an idea, a word, or a phrase. The Abbé de l'Épée did not publish any information that detailed this new language. In 1808, however, the Abbé Sicard, his successor, compiled a dictionary of signs borrowed from Abbé de l'Épée and extended through his own practice.

Laurent Clerc, a brilliant deaf pupil of Sicard's, became a teacher of the deaf, first in France, then in the United States, where Thomas Gallaudet brought him in 1817 to teach Abbé Sicard's sign language to the deaf population. Clerc proceeded to help Gallaudet establish the first permanent school for the deaf in the United States. Thus was created a sign language system that was common to both America and France.

This language enabled the deaf to gain access to education and communication which, although limited to the deaf and their teachers, permitted an exchange of communication that had been denied to them up until then.

The use of Abbé de l'Épée's sign language system and the development of residential schools for the deaf created a separation between these institutions and the hearing world. It was so complete that it caused the deaf to be very isolated from the general society at the beginning of the nineteenth century.

Although Abbé de l'Épée had taught his students both verbal language and sign language simultaneously, eventually only sign language remained in the classrooms of the residential schools that developed rapidly at the time. Teachers in these institutes for the deaf realized that some of the children entrusted to them would be able to learn to speak, but in this closed-in environment, sign language prevailed.

From 1827 until 1850, various attempts to reintroduce speech instruction to the schools for the deaf were attempted, but all failed. Two doctors from the Institute for the Deaf at Rue Saint-Jacques in Paris, Dr. Itard and Dr. Blanchet, were among those who tried to bring the deaf and mute back into the world of speech. They advocated that the hearing and speech impaired be educated by the use of methodical and systematic exercises. They fought against the segregation of the deaf.

In 1848, Dr. Blanchet attempted to integrate students who were deaf into a normal school environment in the Paris school system. In addition to the integration of the deaf students among the hearing, this experiment proved to be valuable in that it provided students with a less expensive education, as opposed to the costly education provided by the residential schools for the deaf. Few scholarships were available to allow the students who were deaf to attend the institutions for the deaf. This experiment aimed at integrating the deaf and hearing students was not repeated and was not attempted again until a century later.

As an outcome of the 1880 Congress on the Education of the Deaf in Milan, the use of sign language to teach the deaf was officially banned. Yet the situation was quite paradoxical: Although sign language was supposedly banned from institutions for the deaf, in isolated schools for the deaf, sign language remained as the best means of communication between the deaf students. Few teachers knew how to sign and those who did use sign language did not do it well. Sign language was no longer the main vehicle of learning or means of the transmission of knowledge. It was considered to be a second-rate language. Sign language became more basic and varied from institution to institution, which made communication among the deaf from different regions of the country increasingly difficult, and caused the break-up of the deaf community.

It was not until the second half of the twentieth century that the oral system of educating the deaf, in vogue since the 1880 Milan International Congress on the Education of the Deaf, began to change.

Detection and Diagnosis

The education of a child who is deaf begins when the diagnosis of deafness is divulged. It is also the time when preliminary information is given to the family concerning the child's chances of being educated and making progress.

Except in the case of parents who are deaf themselves, the first question parents ask is: "Will the child speak?" At that point the answer to that question is very difficult to determine. Besides the fact that it is impossible to predict a baby's language acquisition potential, the answer can influence the parents' educational choices and choice of a system of communication to use with the child.

The doctor responsible for the diagnosis can only, when projecting into the future, provide resources information and possible educational options. The doctor must be quite conscious of the fact that, in the face of the handicap, he or she does not have complete control over the educational method to be used with the child.

Detection

For the past 30 years or so, in France as well as in most developed countries, the diagnosis of deafness is made earlier and earlier in the child's life. This is due to better information, better techniques, and the support and encouragement of state authorities.

Early detection by the state was encouraged through a decree dated April 15, 1976. This decree led to the creation and operation of *Centres d'Action Médico-Sociaux Précoces* (Centers for Early Socio-Medical Action). Ministerial Memorandums Nos. 77-033 and 78, dated January 24, 1977, defined the conditions for the detection and education of children from birth to the age of six.

Public information concerning the importance of early detection and diagnosis through the use of mass media has not been institutionalized as it has in some other European countries. The program of early detection remains cyclical. The system used in France is relatively efficient; however, its effect is unevenly felt throughout the different socio-economic groups.

General practitioners and pediatricians are becoming better and better informed about the importance of early detection and serve as intermediaries with the specialized centers. Doctors active in PMI (*Centres de Protection Maternelle et Infantile* [Centers for Mother and Child Protection]) also play an important role in the detection process, especially with lower-income families. Personnel at all early childcare institutions, such as day-care centers and kindergarten schools, are also vigilant, and their help is essential in the detection of deafness at an early age.

The degree of competence of health professionals and educators in detecting hearing loss at an early age is geographically uneven. It is higher in urban areas. In some regions systematic group hearing tests aimed at detecting hearing loss in children are given. Despite some good results, the system has not become generalized to the whole country because it is too complex and costly to set up. Instead, systematic testing of babies who are at a high risk of having a hearing loss is preferred by the state.

A few years ago, infant audiometry gained in popularity because of the use of a new testing procedure: the recording of provoked acoustical oto-signals (equipment of Dr. Kemp, England). This test provided a reliable detection method since the signals recorded indicate the effectiveness of the operation of the cochlea. It is a simple, non-invasive, fast, objective, reliable test that can be completed during the first few days of life.

The presence or lack of oto-signals leads to a conclusion that the outer, middle, and inner ear are either sound or malfunctioning. The absence of such signals leads the examiner to suspect a peripheral hearing loss equal to or more than 30 decibels. Confirmation of the diagnosis requires a complete audiological check-up.

This author has verified the reliability of this test, by comparing it to the usual audiological check-up procedures used on children below the age of six as applied at the CAMSP of La Norville (outside Paris). Five hundred children were tested in one year. Comparison of the results shows that the presence of acoustical oto-signals was always correlated with normal hearing except in cases of central deafness.

It can be concluded from this comparison that there are no false positive responses. This detection test is reliable, since it ensures efficient differentiation between normal subjects and doubtful cases. The general use of this test in the forthcoming years could well lower the age of the diagnosis of deafness in infants.

Diagnosis

A child who is suspected of having a hearing loss is not always automatically oriented towards the proper agency. The family's journey is often too long and paved with obstacles before a specialist is finally consulted.

The key person in the consultation process is the ORL doctor (ear-nose-throat) who performs the audiological examination. In France every audiologist is a medical doctor. Ideally, the audiological examination is performed in an audiophonological center, if there is one nearby.

In the 1960s, the Peysard Report defined locations and conditions necessary for the proper treatment of French children who are deaf and hard of hearing. *Centres régionaux d'Audiophonologie* (Regional Audiophonological Centers) that are located in each region provide the necessary equipment and competent personnel to conduct the audiological examination. The function of these centers is to make the initial audiological evaluation and produce periodic progress reports.

The deaf children return to these centers for periodic follow-up examinations. Some children who reside near such centers also complete their education in these centers.

Progress reports are completed by a competent multidisciplinary team made up of a doctor, an audioprothesist, a speech pathologist, an educator, and a psychologist. It is a different team from the one that has been treating the child. Since this team is not directly involved in the child's education, it can be more objective in evaluating the child's ability, an essential factor in determining the deaf child's placement and educational program.

Unfortunately, such centers do not exist in each region. Often it is still the family practitioner who first sees and treats the child who is deaf or hard of hearing.

Audiometric Tests for Children

To complete a comprehensive audiological examination, several tests are performed. The tests used depend on the child's age and how difficult it is to reach a diagnosis. Listed below are the audiological tests commonly used in France. Objective methods of assessing the child's hearing level are always used first.

- **Pure Tone Audiometry.** The sound stimuli presented consists of continuous pure tones, pulsated or wobbled tones, a broad range of frequencies, complex sounds, familiar or unusual sounds, and musical instruments or toys with different sound frequencies or intensities. The child responds to these sound stimuli in the following ways: by reflex action; through conscious and voluntary action including a verbal or motor response; through conscious and conditioned responses connected with procedures such as peep-show and play audiometry.
- **Speech Audiometry.** Speech audiometry consists of a systematic search for responses to words, phrases, and other sounds of different intensities. Speech audiometry includes tests of speech comprehension and discrimination. Objective, involuntary occupational tests serve as a complement to the behavioral tests listed above.
- **Recording of provoked acoustical oto-signals.** This test allows an analysis of the peripheral hearing system.
- **Impedance audiometry.** This includes tympanometry and tests of the stapedial reflex.
- **Recording of the stimulated potential of the cerebral trunk (BERA).** This test is systematically done whenever deafness is suspected after the completion of subjective tests.
- **Electrocochleography and recording of the stimulated potential of the cerebral hearing system (ERA).** These tests are only done in specific situations, in order to refine the diagnosis; for instance, if central deafness is suspected.

The limits of these objective methods must be recognized so as to avoid erroneous conclusions. Such methods can in no way replace subjective audiometry. Instead, these tests complement it. The information provided, when included with that of subjective audiometry, presents a comprehensive diagnosis of the child's hearing level. The scope and complexity of the auditory diagnosis would depend upon the child's age and symptoms. It is technically possible to diagnose a hearing loss from the time of birth.

Obviously, some errors in the diagnosis of a hearing loss are possible. If the diagnosis is in doubt, a new evaluation can be requested from another diagnosis center and the cost will be reimbursed by the National Health Insurance System.

Some families, traumatized by the news of the diagnosis of deafness in their child, go through several evaluations in search of a contradictory diagnosis that would satisfy them. The ties established among doctors throughout the country who specialize in this field usually help stop this erroneous practice.

General Evaluation

Once deafness has been diagnosed as precisely as possible and before defining the treatment plan, other types of evaluations may need to be completed. A determination of the etiology of the hearing loss is often important to parents and may prevent further health problems. Often, however, the determination of the cause of the deafness turns out not to be very useful. The cause of the deafness remains unknown in about 30 percent of the cases.

Other possible tests include an ear-nose-throat examination, a clinical search for malformations, a genetic work-up to search for familial antecedents, and an opthamological examination. Additional exams may also be requested, including an analysis of kidney function, an electrocardiogram, a chromosomic chart, a metabolic study, and so on.

Although a medical evaluation is important in order to reduce the parents' guilt feelings and need to know "why" their child became deaf, as well as not to ignore related possible health problems, it is not urgent.

On the other hand, the use of other tests is unavoidable. The goal of these tests is to evaluate the child's academic potential and to gather information needed to establish a treatment and an educational plan.

Language Evaluation

A language evaluation is indispensable in order to determine the deaf or hard of hearing child's mode of communication, current language level, speechreading ability, ability to use his or her residual hearing, the quality of the child's speech, and ability to attend.

Many tests are available to analyze the child's system of language reception and production. The use of multiple tests is not advisable, since it would lead to an inventory of useless information. What is important is to make good use of the information obtained from a few tests. Often it is the speech pathologist's past experience and imagination in the use of the tests that contributes to the quality and diversity of the information obtained.

The language tests commonly used in France include the following:

- *Test of Intellectual Level of Children from 18 Months to Five and One-Half Years of Age,* by S. Borel-Maisonny. (1946), re-standardized in 1971
- *Speech Development Test* by Madame Borel-Maisonny
- *Speech Evaluation Test* by C. Chevrie-Muller, A. M. Simon, and P. Decante, for children from four to eight years old 1981

- *Test of the Child's Syntactical Ability (N.S.S.T.)* by F. Wrill-Halpen, C. Chevrie-Muller, C. Guidet, for children from five to eight years old. 1983
- *Test of Read and Written Language (CALE)* by Andrée Girolami-Boulinier. 1974
- *Picture Vocabulary Test.* Y. Légé, P. Dague
- *Speech Tests.* D. Sadek-Khalil

Psychological Evaluation

The psychological evaluation includes tests that measure the deaf child's level of intelligence, including nonverbal intelligence (spatial abilities), reasoning ability, memory potential, and visual memory and psychomotor ability.

A variety of evaluation tools are used to conduct the psychological evaluation. In addition to being standardized for use with French children, some tests have been standardized for children who are deaf and hard of hearing. This was done to eliminate, as much as possible, the effect of French language deprivation. With the deaf and hard of hearing children who have good speech and writing ability, the use of tests with verbal content and directions can provide interesting information. The most commonly used tests that make up the psychological evaluation include:

- *Scale of Psychomotor Development for Infants.* O. Brunet, I. Lézine
- *Scale of Sensori-Motor Intelligence.* I. Casati, I. Lézine
- *Wechsler's Intelligence Scale for Children (WISC) and for Preschool and Elementary School Children (WPPSI).* D. Wechsler. This test originated in the United States but has a solid French standardization.
- *Performance Scale.* Borelli-Oléron
- *Test of Visual Perceptual Development.* M. Frostig

If it is deemed appropriate, neurological and psychiatric exams can be added to the diagnostic battery.

Finally, an analysis of the family situation will assist in determining the child's treatment plan and establishing a guidance and education plan for the family. A complete evaluation will profile the whole child and his or her family and not focus just on the deafness.

At this point a treatment and educational plan is developed. If the complete evaluation reveals that medical or surgical treatment is not required, which is true in most cases, the child will receive hearing aids and an educational plan.

Hearing Aids for Children

Research and practice indicate that deaf children, no matter whether they have a moderate, severe, or profound hearing loss, should be equipped with hearing aids at the earliest possible age. Most children suffering from a mild hearing loss are not equipped with hearing aids.

The particular hearing aid that is prescribed depends upon the child's ability to comprehend verbal messages. This will vary widely from one child to the next even if the measured hearing level of two children may seem identical. Total deafness is rare. With all children who are deaf, the use of a hearing aid on a trial basis is recommended. A cochlear implant will be considered only after the child fails to progress with a conventional hearing aid.

In France, hearing aids can only be prescribed by a doctor. Using a prescription supplied by the doctor, the actual fitting of the hearing aid is completed by a hearing aid specialist. The parents must contact the hearing aid specialist on their own. Facilities that provide hearing aids are private and independent from the diagnostic units. Hearing aid fittings are not done at hospitals. The fittings are done, however, under the strict supervision of the prescribing doctor and the speech pathologist. The speech pathologist does a follow-up on the success of the child's use of the hearing aid. Some of the specialized clinics that do the diagnostic testing work in partnership with particular hearing aid specialists, or even contract their services directly. The hearing aid specialist is responsible for all hearing aids used within the diagnostic unit. This facilitates collaboration among professionals and helps minimize the consequences of some family negligence concerning the child's use of a hearing aid. In most cases, a hearing aid is secured and placed on the child immediately after the diagnosis of deafness is complete. Deaf children vary in the length of time they need to adapt to the use of the hearing aid. The age of the child and other factors cause the time of adjustment to vary from child to child.

The permanent acquisition of the hearing aid takes place only after a trial period which can last from a few days to a few months. This adjustment period is not rushed and may require an introduction and sensitization to sound for a few weeks before the fitting of the hearing aid. Periodically, the hearing aid specialist will check the child's hearing aid to verify how well the hearing aid is working. His or her observations are compared to those made by the parents, the speech pathologist, and the educators in charge of the child's education. The medical specialist can also monitor the child's hearing level through the use of pure tone and speech audiometry.

Types of Hearing Aids Available in France

All children who are deaf now receive behind-the-ear hearing aids. Body-worn hearing aids are no longer used. Some deaf or hard of hearing adolescents can be fitted with in-the-ear hearing aids. If this type of hearing aid equipment meets the child's needs, it has the great advantage of being invisible and eliminating the stigma felt by some who wear hearing aids. Programmable hearing aids are preferred. These hearing aids can be adjusted according to the child's needs without having to resort to the purchase of new hearing aids. If feasible, two hearing aids are preferable to one, since they provide a stereophonic perception of sound and allow the child to detect the direction of the sound source.

The use of two hearing aids with very young children is very difficult and is not recommended. If there is little asymmetry between the sound threshold level of each ear, one hearing aid is the preferred first step.

Special Equipment

In cases of congenital defects of the outer and middle ears, implantable hearing aids are available. They allow direct stimulation of the bone without the interference of the skin. Results from this type of equipment are far superior to results obtained from the vibrator type fixed by the use of a headband.

In cases where conventional hearing aids fail and where deafness is total, a cochlear implant can be considered. This technology has been used in France for many years, although it remains controversial. Violent opposition has been common from associations of deaf adults, some parents of deaf children, and some specialists in infant audiology. Only recently has cochlear implant technology begun to be applied to children in a sensible and organized manner. Until recently the cost of the cochlear implant was charged to the family and often required a media campaign to collect the necessary funds. Cochlear implant surgery is now financed directly by state hospitals.

The family plays an essential role in the deaf child's success in the use of a hearing aid. Parents make frequent visits to the hearing aid specialist. The different professionals involved in the child's case seek information from the parents in order to better understand the child's reactions to the hearing aid in daily life. In order for a child to accept his or her hearing aid and get the most use from it, it is essential that the parents also accept the hearing aid and fully understand its importance.

Habilitation Equipment

The overwhelming majority of deaf children in France have their own individual hearing aids. Habilitation centers are also equipped with group amplification systems and FM systems aimed at giving deaf children the maximum personalized hearing environment possible. This should facilitate their ability to use sound. The amplification systems most frequently used today in France include:

- **Simple group and individual amplification systems.** These systems allow the children to discover real-life sounds and speech under excellent acoustical conditions, thanks to a very wide frequency range and a remarkably low signal-to-noise ratio. Professor Lafon is quoted as saying: "The table amplifier helps the child discover sound. The hearing aid helps the child recognize sound."
- **Filter and sound amplifiers.** The sound response curve of these amplifiers is modified by the use of filters chosen according to the child's hearing level and habilitation goals. The SUVAG Type I and SUVAG Type II sound filters are used with the Verbo-tonal method and offer multiple filter possibilities that can meet every child's needs. The SCR Company has recently developed this type of equipment for commercial distribution.
- **Special Sound Amplifiers.** Professor J.C. Lafon's transponder type of hearing aid with coding translates normally high sounds into low frequencies, which allows the child to hear phonetic signals that would normally be an inaudible part of the speech spectrum. This type of equipment is appropriate for deaf children with no hearing above 1,000 Hz. This

specialized amplification equipment, called Galaxie, has been on the market for some time. An individual hearing aid with the same specifications and characteristics is being tested.

♦ **Tactile vibration.** Tactile vibrators are often used with children who are profoundly deaf, in conjunction with several of the amplification devices discussed above. In the case of infants, the use of vibrating floors, which preserves their freedom of movement, is preferable to that of a body-worn vibrator.

Acoustical Transmission in Education

For a long time the ability of deaf children to perceive the teacher's speech has been the main goal of acoustical transmissions in the educational setting. At first, all classrooms in France were equipped with fixed amplification systems. The lack of flexibility of these fixed systems and the impossibility of real verbal exchanges quickly made these systems obsolete.

Today, wireless FM transmission systems are commonly used, either through the use of high frequency or infrared light modulation. Thanks to such devices, a deaf person can continue to perceive fully a speech signal with no reduction in intensity, no matter how distant the signal or the person speaking may be. Most special classes for deaf children, and ordinary classes where deaf children are integrated, are now equipped with FM systems.

Recently, Dupret and Lefévre from Montbéliard came up with a new wireless transmission device, which interprets sound signals automatically for people with a profound hearing loss. An electronic computer module is hidden under the individual's clothing and is linked to a hearing aid. The electronic module corrects the main shortcomings of the hearing aid: weak intensity, timing perturbation, and alteration of frequency selection. Its catchy name,

"Emily," and a vast advertising campaign have helped it to quickly become known by the general public. It is difficult as of yet to measure the effectiveness of the device because of its limited distribution.

Oral Methods

The resolutions of the 1880 Milan International Congress on the Education of the Deaf were implemented in France with particular vigor. Deaf teachers, who had been active in the institutes for the deaf up until then, were released from their positions. The strict oral method became the only method of teaching the deaf for over a century.

Thanks to constantly improving amplification devices, the acquisition of oral language is relatively simple for many deaf persons who have a moderate-to-severe hearing loss. The level of success is very different for those who are profoundly deaf. For this group, access to oral communication is neither spontaneous nor easy. Results depend very much on the quality of the deaf child's educational program. Many pedagogical theories have been presented and tried over the years by the French and professionals from other countries in order to find solutions to the low educational achievement level of profoundly deaf children.

Some of these theories met with little success and died out quickly, whereas others have become widespread and remain today as useful pedagogical tools in development of the speech of the deaf. Listed below are the distinctive characteristics of the communication methodologies most commonly used in France.

Oral-Graphic Method Used in the Institutes for the Deaf

The name is not universally accepted but it seems to be the most accurate definition. Pictured and printed French and the corresponding oral form are presented together.

The child is presented a stable reference point, thanks to the precise information found in the pictures and print representations. Acquisition of the French language can progress quite well with this form. With this methodology, the spoken language does not usually develop to a point where it can be used as a tool for the exchange of dialogue between the deaf child and others.

Auditory Methods

The auditory method, or the full use of the deaf child's residual hearing, is based on the fact that auditory training can help develop speech and eventually language in some children who are deaf.

Speechreading is part of the oral methodology, but is not systematically taught or stressed. Speechreading is even excluded in certain auditory training exercises. What is stressed in the oral methodology is speech reception and the control of speech production through audition.

After 1950, the first efficient electronic hearing aids brought about the rapid development of hearing habilitation techniques, thanks to many doctors and educators. These strategies were associated with new equipment invented by the promoters of the techniques (Perdoncim, Jouve, Tomatic, and so on) and were publicized as ways to conquer deafness. These techniques and equipment were viewed by parents as "miraculous remedies," but after many disappointing results, the strategies were strongly criticized by traditional educators and quickly abandoned. These techniques did contribute, however, by providing evidence of how important systematic auditory training was for speech development, speech reception, and speechreading.

The Borel-Maisonny Method

Madame Borel-Maisonny was the pioneer in the area of speech therapy in France. Her multidisciplinary knowledge and her clinical and pedagogical skill helped to improve the progress of a large number of speech and language impaired children. Year after year, she developed multiple educational techniques that assisted speech and language impaired children with a variety of symptoms and problems. She and her assistants applied her techniques to deaf and hard of hearing children with various degrees of success. Depending upon the hearing level of the child, the type of pedagogy used, a favorable family, and school environment, results were often excellent.

The Borel-Maisonny Method can be described as an articulatory method based on the postulate that the act of hearing requires an explicit knowledge of how the hearing and speech mechanism works. The sounds to be produced are described precisely to the child, with the help of drawings of each speech sound. The pictorial representation of sounds is introduced to the deaf child as early as possible. Recognition and memorization of phonemes is facilitated by association with a gesture or sign that illustrates each phoneme and how it is to be articulated. This visual display, or graphic representation of the sound, demonstrates the position of the speech organs.

This phonetic aspect is combined with the use of a device, the *phonaudioscope*, which amplifies messages and presents a visual picture of certain speech parameters, including the rhythm of the sound, the visual representations of the prosodic elements of sound inflection, and other factors found in proper articulation.

Verbo-tonal Method

The Verbo-tonal Method appeared in the mid-1960s. It was created by a Yugoslav linguist, Professor Guberina, and was praised by a number of parents who pressed the schools to adopt it. The attractive theoretical principles promoted by Dr. Guberina generated much hope among parents. It was very different from the methods of speech development in use at that time. Guberina's method was not based on articulatory description and did not call for analytical devices. The phonological system was learned unconsciously, by way of successive approximations. Priority was given to prosodic elements, and transcription was not a primary intent. In its initial phase, this method was presented primarily as an auditory training method.

According to Guberina, every deaf child possesses residual hearing that, by efficient training, can be used to develop speech perception and the acquisition of language. As a complement to developing the hearing potential, the perception of low acoustical components of speech through vibro-tactile sensitivity was also developed.

As the Verbo-tonal Method developed, it was enriched with new techniques based on the role of the body in speech production. Phonetic rhythms, both physical and musical, helped model oral expression, especially in its phonetic and prosodic parameters. Dramatization was used to vocalize the concepts discovered and experienced by the body.

After 1970, the Verbo-tonal Method was utilized in many centers. These centers, which favored the integration of deaf and hearing students, were connected to the National Education System. Some centers aimed at the use of the Verbo-tonal Method were created by parent groups and professional associations. The Verbo-tonal Method seemed to be most successful in improving deaf children's vocal quality, articulation ability, and prosody. However, the Verbo-tonal Method did not seem to help deaf children's performance in the areas of reading and writing.

Presently, the Verbo-tonal Method is used in combination with other instructional techniques. It remains as an excellent tool in the development of the speech of a profoundly deaf child.

Cued Speech

Cued Speech, developed by Cornett (USA) in 1960, is a series of hand signs designed to help make speechreading a complete language reception modality. It clarifies the ambiguities found in speechreading by using signs formed near the mouth that represent different speech sounds that are not visible or look similar while speechreading. The system was introduced and spread throughout France by a parents' association (ALPC) that attempted to promote its use in the home.

Professionals in the field have shown a growing interest in the Cued Speech system and have introduced it in some educational centers for the deaf without the prodding of the parent groups. ALPC also encouraged the use of Cued Speech in ordinary schools where profoundly deaf children are mainstreamed. As the teacher speaks, an interpreter translates the message using the Cued Speech sign system. A support system (CODALI) was created in Paris in 1986 to promote the mainstreaming of deaf children from kindergarten to twelfth grade with the use of Cued Speech interpreters. The interpreter's role was officially recognized, and an official diploma for Cued Speech interpreters was created by decree in 1987.

In addition to the methods and techniques described above, several other systems are used locally, but none of these other methods has gained national importance.

Communication Options

Title 3, Article 33, Law No. 91-73, dated January 18, 1989, reads: "In educating deaf youth, there is a right to freedom of choice between the use of bilingual communication (LSF or French Sign Language and French) and oral communication." The procedures, conditions, and processes needed to support the law have not been fully developed. The ensuing actions to be taken by specialized schools for the deaf and other programs to put the law into practice are under study. The law is very recent and represents an important evolution in the education of the deaf during the past several decades.

Oral Method Comes Under Attack

The oral method as defined by the 1880 Milan International Congress on the Education of the Deaf was the only official method of teaching the deaf in use in every French school for the deaf until the late 1970s. Until recently the use of sign language was forbidden.

The oral method, however, was utilized with deaf children in many ways. In residential schools for the deaf where the age of the children ranged from 3 to 21, the communication system most commonly used outside of the classroom was French Sign Language (LSF). Most educators do not know how to use French Sign Language. School material is taught by use of the oral methods, which include spoken and written French.

Deaf students in some day schools and in special mainstream classes within ordinary schools have no knowledge of signs and communicate only by the use of speech and spontaneous gestures.

In the early 1980s, the use of the oral method in France reached the crisis stage. The use of only one language and one method of teaching the deaf came under attack. Oralism was considered to have failed. The proponents of the oral system pushed what they labeled the "numerous educational, professional, and human success stories of oralism." These isolated models and examples of success could not be generalized to the deaf population at large. The majority of these success stories were the result of private one-on-one education, created and promoted by parents and a few pioneering speech pathologists, who claimed success with the use of better hearing aids and new speech therapy methods. Attempts at generalizing these successes to the total school-aged population of deaf children failed. Besides the disappointing academic and language development results, a comparison of the educational results achieved in other countries (Scandinavia, USA) contributed to the general dissatisfaction and created questions concerning the effectiveness of the oral method.

Bilingual Approach Developed

In 1979, the first experiment in the use of a bilingual approach was carried out in France at the Bossuet School in Paris. During the 1980s, bilingual methods of teaching the deaf spread, and by government decree, were officially accepted. The controversy over the best method to use to teach the deaf, which has plagued the education of the deaf for centuries, is now slowly being resolved, although a consensus concerning the ideal way to educate the deaf child has not yet been reached.

The bilingual method of educating the deaf is now legal and the resources needed for its implementation are available. Qualified personnel are being trained and certified to implement the bilingual method. It is now fully legal to train and hire deaf adults, which was not true in the early days of the bilingual movement.

Many ambiguities persist, however. Some centers for the education of the deaf have continued to follow the oral philosophy. Some oral schools have even hired "token" deaf persons. Other centers that use the bilingual method have not adapted their curriculum to meet the individual differences found in deaf and hard of hearing children, nor do these schools cater to the wishes of the parents.

Currently, a variety of educational placement and communication methodologies exist. The geographic distribution of school programs for the deaf does not always allow parents options in the choice of a communication methodology. Only the large metropolitan areas possess a variety of educational options within reasonable access. Only in these areas is a real choice possible, after consultation and agreement between parents and professionals. Everywhere else, deaf children are educated in school programs, not according to what educational option would be best for the child, but as a result of what option is available in the geographic region.

It is the intention of Decree No. 91-73 that every center for the education of deaf children will be able to meet the individual needs of each deaf child. Because of limited resources, it will be difficult for the smaller centers to provide a variety of educational options.

Variety of Methods Now Used

The table below describes the general evolution of the main communication systems used with the deaf. All of the communication methodologies that have been part of the evolutionary continuum are still in use to some extent in France today.

Table 1.

Monolingual (French)	Oralism
	Oralism + LPC (Cued Speech)
	Oralism + FS (Signed French)
	Oralism + FS + LPC (Cued Speech)
Bilingual System	French + LSF (French Sign Language)
	French + LSF + FS
	French + LSF + FS + LPC

Auditory training and speechreading are not part of each of the communication methodologies. The list of all possible communication options does not take into con-

sideration the priority to be given to each language within a bilingual system. Some individuals advocate learning LSF first, followed by written French, and finally spoken French. Others prefer that all be learned simultaneously. The simultaneous development of both LSF and French is very difficult to achieve.

In every case, learning and using French, the national language, remains the primary goal of the education of deaf and hard of hearing children. French is the agent of social, professional, and cultural integration of the deaf person into French society. Because of inadequate progress in the ability to read and write French, there is a feeling by many that the learning process needs to be carried out exclusively by the use of LSF. This is not currently being done.

After a review of all the educational methods that are now being implemented with deaf children in various degrees and unevenly throughout the country, it is clear that the choice of the appropriate communication and language system for each child has not often been achieved. The deaf child's future education has often depended upon the initial meeting between parents and specialists.

Guidelines for Placement

To create a more coherent and efficient system of educating deaf children in France, parents, educators, and the government must come to a consensus concerning what is best for each child. This goal can be reached only through a thorough evaluation of the results of all existing methods of teaching the deaf in France. All parties involved agree that an evaluation of the current situation is necessary, but there is no agreement on the means to be used to complete this evaluation.

Today, the following fundamental principles serve as guidelines for placement decisions:

- The choice between the use of one or two means of communication

(French alone, or French + LSF) is to be made by the parents. It is the duty of the institute for the deaf and the educators to guide and advise the family, but not to make the decision.

- At each school for the deaf the variety of communication methodologies that can be applied to each child must be accompanied by a set of consistent objectives and strategies.
- The deaf child can truly be considered to be bilingual only if provided all means necessary to acquiring both languages.
- Hearing aid fitting and auditory training continue to be essential elements in the education of deaf children.

Infant Habilitation

Infant habilitation is defined as the treatment and education of children from birth to the age of three. After a conference that was held in Paris in 1967, early childhood education has developed rapidly in France.

Profoundly deaf children are often diagnosed during the first year of life. A recent survey indicated that habilitation begins before the age of two for the majority of children with a severe or profound hearing loss.

Infant habilitation can be described as a period of diagnosis, study, stimulation, active observation, and evaluation. The objectives of early childhood education for deaf children are:

- To avoid if possible, or at least to reduce, the consequences of the hearing loss on the child's growth and development
- To allow the child to access communication and a language system at an early stage
- To set up the conditions necessary or a good adjustment to school and society

- To support the family in its role of raising a deaf child
- After the diagnosis, to develop a personalized habilitation plan

Follow-up is completed by a multidisciplinary team. Each specialist on the multidisciplinary team has a specific role. The speech pathologist acts as the referring specialist. He or she is in regular contact with the child several times a week. Other members of the multidisciplinary team are involved when needed by the child or the family.

The Family

Parental participation is indispensable. The parents are considered as vital members of the habilitation team. The specialist responsible for the child's management attempts to make the parents the primary educators of the child. Frequently, the very early diagnosis of a child's deafness, although necessary, causes great familial anxiety. This may make a successful parent-child relationship more difficult.

The Child

The infant is usually seen at least once a week and usually more often by a speech pathologist. Since language is only acquired through pleasurable experiences, the early childhood habilitation sessions must be appropriate. Each activity is presented in a play format, using natural materials and settings. Although the sessions can be intense, it is important to respect and take into account the deaf infant's creativity, desires, and wishes.

After eighteen months of age, the child who is deaf can participate in group activities aimed at developing:

- Interaction with other children in order to avoid the child experiencing one-to-one relationships with adults only

- Motor responses and rhythm
- Cognitive and creative activities

In the past, early childhood education for deaf infants focused upon the acquisition of spoken language. In the past few decades the use of sign language and the presence of deaf adults has modified the habilitation of infants who are deaf. Although there is now a general consensus concerning the importance of providing the child who is deaf with a means of communication at an early age, many specialists and parents remain divided about the way to achieve that goal.

In France today there exist several early childhood education programs that use a variety of systems to communicate with deaf infants. The different early childhood habilitation programs for deaf infants can be divided into those programs that use the oral method or the bilingual method.

Presently, the majority of early childhood centers in France use the oral method. Out of 100 early childhood institutes surveyed by A. Gourouben in 1991, 53 use the oral method and 40 the bilingual method. The bilingual centers require the hearing parents to learn LSF, although the opportunity to learn LSF is not always available within the center itself.

Both oral and bilingual options are available in some early childhood centers. The hearing specialists, in coordination with ear-nose-throat physicians and speech pathologists, are the first specialists to work with deaf infants. Several centers have opened special infant education departments and established private multidisciplinary treatment teams (audiological, psychomotor, psychological, and educational). The fact that diagnosis and habilitation can occur in the same location makes it easier for the specialists to exchange information and improve parental support. Critics state that the programs located in hospitals focus on the medical aspect of deafness and do not provide an appropriate environment for education and language development.

A law passed in April 1976 created CAMSP, or *Centres d'action médico-sociale précoce* (Centers for Socio-medical Treatment for Infants). These centers are responsible for the testing, diagnosis, and follow-up of deaf children from birth to the age of six. Some of these centers specialize on the diagnosis and treatment of the deaf and hard of hearing, and others work with all disabilities. Some of the specialized centers, which have been approved to care for children from birth to age twenty, have followed the cases of some children who are deaf from the time they were first diagnosed until adulthood.

A 1988 governmental decree modified the conditions necessary for the approval of infant centers designed to serve deaf and hard of hearing children. The centers that are legally approved to work with the deaf and hard of hearing children are called the SAFEP or *Services d'Accompagnement Familial et d'Éducation Précoce* (Centers for Family Support and Infant Habilitation). The other types of centers still exist.

The transition between infant education and higher schooling is delicate. Several educational options are available, and it is often difficult to determine which option corresponds best to the needs of the child who is deaf.

The Educational System
Residential Schools and Day Schools

Until the second half of this century, the great majority of deaf children in France were educated in residential schools. The system of residential schools was developed mostly for geographic reasons. Since the number of institutes for the deaf was limited and many of the deaf children resided far from the institutes, these schools had to have a residential component.

Segregation from the larger community and society was inevitable in spite of efforts of the institutes for the deaf to open the residential schools to the general public. This isolation jeopardized the deaf child's full integration into French society. Although sign language was not officially taught in these institutes, sign language was the most practical means of communication for the deaf students, both among themselves and with their teachers. Defenders of the oral philosophy of educating the deaf considered residential schools as a hindrance to the full development of oral education.

In the 1960s many new day schools for the deaf were created. At first they were limited to urban areas. Most had small numbers of children who are deaf and were created by hearing specialists. These day schools competed with the residential schools as the site of education for deaf students. In response to this competition the residential schools for the deaf opened day classes. After a few years the day schools and classes for the deaf, instead of enrolling a small percent of the total number of students who were deaf, enrolled the majority. This evolution in the site of the education of the deaf followed the new trend which indicated that parents were increasingly reluctant to be separated from their deaf children and wanted them to be educated as close to their homes as was possible. Many parents were involved in creating new rural centers for the education of the deaf children.

Mainstreaming

In France until comparatively recent times the education of all students who were deaf was completed in specialized residential and day schools. These schools had classes with small enrollments and highly specialized staffs. During the past few years there has been a strong movement in France and other countries to educate handicapped and non-handicapped children in the same classrooms. This movement has resulted in the integration of deaf children into regular public school classrooms.

The idea of mainstreaming the disabled is far from being new in France. The idea was first formulated by Blanchet in 1848, but it failed. By the late 1960s, however, mainstreaming was widely developed and was based upon a number of different models.

- With the support of a speech pathologist, many parents integrated their deaf children into regular classrooms. The newly created day schools for the deaf often encouraged mainstreaming children who were deaf for part of the school day.
- The opening of an important school program for deaf students in the north of France (Ronchin) in 1970, followed by the publication of the report *Rééducation sans frontiéres* (Education Without Borders) and the film *300 sourds en voie d'intégration* (The Progress of 300 Mainstreamed Deaf Students) played the role of catalyst for the mainstream movement. At that time the French Ministry of Education made the in-school mainstreaming of children who were deaf an official state policy.
- In 1970 the first of many school units that promoted in-school mainstreaming modeled after the Brussels school plan was developed on the outskirts of Paris. This educational unit provided a specialized education for the deaf and hard of hearing, while facilitating contact between the deaf and hearing students in the school.

These first mainstream programs for deaf students were the result of the efforts of determined specialists and parents. These groups created a non-profit organization to meet their goals.

The Verbo-tonal Method is often credited with advancing the status of mainstreaming all children with a hearing loss in France. Some specialists were convinced that by using the Verbo-tonal Method they could provide children who were deaf with an effective means of communication that would allow them to be educated in schools for hearing children.

The first mainstream programs were organized without legal support. In 1975 a law was enacted that officially recognized the basic principle of mainstreaming. The policies and procedures required to implement the law were not developed, however.

January, 1982, and 1983 memoranda from the Ministry of Education contributed to the recognition and extension of actions undertaken earlier in behalf of the mainstream concept. The 1982 and 1983 memoranda were further complemented by two memoranda published in January 1992 that encouraged maximum possible integration of the handicapped children into the regular public schools of France.

Presently, most French children who are deaf attend officially integrated schools. The integrated schools can vary greatly and are very diverse. Full mainstreaming or integration is considered to be achieved when the deaf child receives all of his or her instruction in classes with hearing children. If the deaf child receives part of his or her instruction in a special class and part in a regular classroom, it is considered to be partial mainstreaming.

The following variations in the degree and configuration of mainstreaming are found in France:

- Insertion of the child who is deaf in a special class within an ordinary school
- Mainstreaming the child who is deaf in all activities outside the classroom (lunch, recess, physical education, sports, and so on)
- Mainstreaming the child who is deaf in art and physical education classes
- Mainstreaming the child who is deaf in classes representing subjects and activities except for French
- Total mainstreaming of the child who is deaf in all regular public school classes with individual counseling
- Total integration of the child who is deaf into the ordinary classroom without counseling
- Mainstreaming the child who is deaf in classes with specialists who work with children with handicaps other than deafness

Recently some children who are deaf have been mainstreamed with the use of a sign language interpreter. The use of a sign interpreter is still a rare occurrence.

Schools for the Deaf and Hard of Hearing in France

Institutes for the deaf were the first schools developed in what has become the national school system for handicapped children.

The education of children who are deaf began in the nineteenth century. These schools were created locally and maintained by religious or charitable institutions. State and local government authorities took over the control of some of the institutes for the deaf at the beginning of the twentieth century. Many of the institutes for the deaf became important regionally.

The first school for the deaf was created in Paris in 1775 and later became the National Institute of Rue Saint-Jacques. One hundred and fifty-three institutes or schools for the deaf were created during the nineteenth century, either by the government or by religious organizations. Some have disappeared, but many have survived.

Schools for the Deaf in the Twentieth Century

The following schools for the deaf were created before the 1950s:
Public Schools:
- Four National Institutes under the authority of the Ministry of Health
- Five institutes (two national and three regional) under the authority of the Ministry of Education

Private Schools:

- Thirty-one schools for the deaf have a Catholic Church affiliation
- Two schools for the deaf have a Protestant church affiliation
- Ten private schools for the deaf were created without any religious affiliation

Through the years institutes for the deaf with a religious affiliation have become progressively less tied to the religion. Whereas in the past these schools for the deaf were staffed by personnel who were affiliated with the religious organization and filled with deaf students who were members of that church, these schools are now staffed mostly by lay persons and admit deaf children of many religious persuasions.

Beginning in 1950, a second phase in the education of deaf students followed more of a medical model, with the development of the fields of speech and language therapy. The education of deaf children became a team effort. Teachers affiliated with the National Education network were responsible for the development of the curriculum of the schools for the deaf. And the speech pathologists became the persons most responsible for the education of students who were deaf and hard of hearing.

Other Educational Options

Special classes for deaf and hard of hearing children were created in each of the 95 administrative départements in France. At first these classes were only for children with moderate to severe hearing losses. These special classes were located within ordinary public schools and were limited to an average enrollment of six to eight students. The deaf children enrolled in the special classes received specialized education and were mainstreamed part of the time.

These deaf students were integrated into classrooms for students who could hear for certain subjects, lunch, recess, league sports,

and other aspects of the curriculum. Several of the non-profit centers for the education of children who were deaf were established by parents. Most were day schools, and included some degree of mainstreaming. Many were created to promote a specific educational methodology or approach. Generally these centers are experimental.

Other children who are deaf, or who have a moderate to severe hearing loss, are enrolled in ordinary public schools and follow the existing curriculum without modification. Although full mainstreaming of deaf children is not new, it continues to be an individual and exceptional solution to the placement of deaf children in France. Many of the children fully integrated into a regular public school classroom come from the higher socio-economic groups and have received help from a speech pathologist.

The full integration of deaf children into ordinary classrooms has continued to expand. The old centers for the education of deaf children have given way to more complex units. New Care Centers were created after 1983. The new centers include a multidisciplinary team that follows the child from an early age to adulthood and focuses upon the whole child.

Beginning in the 1980s the concentration and centralization of deaf children in residential schools declined, and in its place children who are deaf are being educated in public school classrooms dispersed throughout the country.

Current Trends and Directions in the Education of the Deaf

In an effort to reorganize and vitalize the education of the deaf, the Ministries of Education and Social Affairs have conducted a series of surveys that have led to amendments in the law governing the education of the deaf in France. The amended law is called *annexe 24 quater.* Schools for the deaf are now governed by Decree No. 88-423, dated April 22, 1988.

The school or institute for the deaf is now defined as a comprehensive resource center that provides medical, paramedical, psycho-social, and educational services. While each unit in the resource center has a specific function and a specialized staff, the units work with one another to form a multi-disciplinary treatment team.

These resource centers include:

- a SEES, or *section d'éducation et d'enseignement spécialisés* (Specialized Teaching and Learning Section). This section provides specific learning programs in areas of language and communication. These programs are adapted to the needs of each child and are approved by the National Education system.
- a SEHA or *section d'éducation des handicaps associé.* This section provides education programs for deaf and hard of hearing children who have disabilities other than deafness. These additional handicaps may include behavioral disturbances, and intellectual, visual, or motor deficiencies.

The resource center may also provide the following services:

- a SAFEP, or *service d'accompagnement familial et d'éducation précoce* (a family support and infant education service section for parents and children from birth to the age of three)
- a SSEFIS, or *service de soutien á l'éducation familiale et á l'intégration scolaire* (a family education and in-school mainstreaming support service section for children over the age of three who go to an ordinary public school)

The services listed above can be organized and located within one of the comprehensive resource centers or can be created as an autonomous center.

In both types of centers for children who are deaf, the older centers and those recently created and licensed, children can be admitted at a very young age and continue to receive services until the age of fifteen or twenty, depending upon the services and training offered.

Some of these comprehensive resource centers for the education of the deaf are run by the state and are under the authority of the Ministry of Education or the Ministry of Social Affairs. Most of the centers, however, are run by private, non-profit organizations, licensed and supervised by the Ministry of Social Affairs. These resource centers are financed, for the most part, by the National Health Care System, which pays a fixed fee for each child admitted.

The Different Levels of Education

According to the latest census from the DEP (Directorate of Evaluations and Prospectives) there were 14,088 deaf and hard of hearing children in school programs for the deaf during the 1989-1990 academic year. They were educated as follows:

- 9,133 were educated in specialized centers for the education of the deaf
- 4,955 were mainstreamed into ordinary classrooms

Kindergarten

Kindergarten programs are highly developed in France. Most hearing children attend a kindergarten beginning at the age of three. The curriculum and educational strategies stress an active, open, flexible, and personalized education.

The admission of handicapped children into the kindergarten is highly supported. Mainstreaming a child who is deaf at this level might seem to present few problems, and for that reason measures must be instituted to ensure that the child who is deaf is not simply placed in a situation that encourages passive mainstreaming, but in a situation where he or she is able to profit from the experience.

In many cases the young child who is deaf is integrated into the regular kindergarten for part of the day and also receives an intensive specialized education program for at least two hours each day. The specialized program takes place either within the ordinary public school or in a specialized center. Formal ties and cooperation are established among the teachers, the specialists, and the parents. These ties are made concrete by a signed mainstream agreement.

Elementary School

At the elementary level the mainstream program for the child who is deaf must be carefully planned, since the curriculum of the elementary school program is more precisely defined. The choice between attendance in a specialized unit or a mainstream program depends on the language ability and academic level of the child who is deaf. If a specialized educational program is required, every effort will be made to keep the deaf child in contact with hearing children outside of the specialized school.

If the child is integrated into an ordinary school classroom, the provision of specialized support is essential. Again, as in the kindergarten, the parents, teachers, and specialists must work cooperatively to develop an agreed-upon written program of services. These centers for the education of the deaf have evolved in the direction of becoming more flexible and personalized in the provision of services. At the kindergarten and elementary level, there are centers in almost every *département* of France. New centers are planned for those areas where centers have not yet been established.

Junior High (Ages Eleven through Fifteen)

At the junior high school level, there are about 50 specialized state-run and private centers that provide educational services for students who are deaf. In addition, about 60 resource centers offer educational counseling and speech therapy to junior high school aged students who are mainstreamed. Most of these centers provide specialized educational programs. Very few specialized classes for children who are deaf are found in French junior high schools.

Within the regular education system several mainstream possibilities exist:

- Using the specialized center for the deaf as a base, mainstreaming takes place in a neighboring ordinary public school. Students remain in close touch with their base school, sometimes even residing there.
- Using a SSEFIS (described previously as specialized base of support), main streaming takes place, if possible, in a school near the child's residence.
- Ordinary public schools that have an existing organized mainstream process regularly admit a certain number of deaf and hard of hearing children and provide a personalized education program, follow-up, and support services.

High School (Ages Fifteen to Eighteen or Nineteen)

Approximately fifteen specialized centers in France provide a high school education to students who are deaf. Forty-five ordinary school units offer mainstreaming possibilities for deaf and hard of hearing high school students. The number of deaf students who reach this level of education is still very limited. Statistical data concerning this level of deaf students is imprecise because it is difficult to identify and count deaf students who have been successfully integrated into ordinary public schools and those who have registered for video teaching programs. Mainstreaming becomes increasingly difficult for students who are deaf at this level. Many deaf students whose aim is chiefly to pass the *baccalauréat* (high school graduation exam) prefer the specialized school track, because it often helps the student who is deaf to prepare for the exam over a four-year period instead of a three-year period.

Preprofessional and Professional Training

The great majority of students who are deaf receive preprofessional and professional training in specialized units. No preprofessional and professional training particularly designed for the deaf has been developed. Diplomas received at the completion of training are the same as for the non-handicapped. The qualifications are identical. Training programs usually prepare a person for a CAP, or *Certificat d'Aptitude Professionnelle* (Certificate of Professional Aptitude), or BEP, or *Brevet d'Enseignement Professionnel* (Professional Training Diploma).

Postsecondary Education

Postsecondary education opportunities for deaf persons are available only in mainstream programs. The development of support services for deaf students at postsecondary education programs is currently under consideration. Recently, universities have begun to initiate support services. The University of Chambéry has been the pioneer in this area. Support services offered by the University of Chambéry include tutoring, counseling, LSF interpreting, notetaking, and photocopying by volunteers. Other services such as LPC interpreting are under study. Some specialized centers provide persons who are deaf with a program of studies designed to prepare for the BTS, or *Brevet de Technicien Professionnel* (Professional Technician's Diploma).

Special support services are provided for deaf students at all examinations. These support services include the presence of a LSF or LPC interpreter, practical information provided in writing, extra time granted for written exams, and other needed services.

Administrative Considerations

In recent years, all handicapped children including children who are deaf or hard of hearing have received special legislative attention in France. These new regulations conform to the best current practices and research findings in the field. Experience gained while trying new models of education as opposed to the use of century-old, static methodologies has provided new revelations that have encouraged a more personalized treatment of each deaf child. One drawback of the new regulations is that they tend to slow down individual action, therefore limiting personal decisions.

Protection of Deaf Children and Benefits

Among the laws and decrees governing every aspect of the education of children who are deaf, is a listing of the benefits available to families in order to provide the additional support needed to raise a disabled child.

Every child or adolescent recognized as deaf or hard of hearing by the CDES (Regional Commission on Special Education) is covered by the National Health Insurance System. The National Health Insurance System covers all care within a school or center, as well as all habilitation or educational programs conducted in the home or at an educational resource center.

The CDES also determines the degree of the handicap based upon an official scale. Presently, the degree of the hearing disability is determined by the average loss in db. of the following frequencies: 500 Hz, 1,000 Hz, and 2,000 Hz. A moderate hearing loss corresponds to a 40-to-70 db. hearing loss. A severe hearing loss corresponds to a 70-to-90 db. hearing loss, and a profound hearing loss is defined as a 90-to-100 db. hearing loss.

A child is entitled to the following benefits, depending upon the degree of the handicap:

- **Special Education Benefit.** If the child has over a 50 db. hearing loss, the family receives a monthly benefit amount when the treatment program actually begins. This amount is increased if the child has multiple handicaps or if the handicap justifies the need for additional expenses.

- **Handicapped Identity Card.** If the child has over an 80 db. hearing loss, the family receives a Handicapped Identity Card which carries with it a number of advantages, including a reduction in the family's income tax.

The scale used to determine the degree of the handicap is being revised. Not only will the hearing level be considered, but also the individual's speech and language ability. All requests for benefits are processed by the CDES upon the submission of an application and the completion of an interview with the child and his or her family.

The cost of hearing aids is reimbursed as follows:

- 100 percent reimbursement for all children under sixteen years of age diagnosed to have a long-term hearing impairment. Reimbursement for the purchase of two individual hearing aids is covered by CDES. The government reimbursement rate has a ceiling, but it remains close to actual cost.

- For persons who are deaf over the age of sixteen, the CDES will reimburse the individual for one hearing aid at a rate much lower than the actual cost.

Additional expenses incurred for special education and habilitation services are entirely covered by the National Health Insurance System. Free transportation is provided for most deaf children who live far from a specialized center.

The Deaf in Society

Professional and Social Integration

Some deaf people have succeeded in finding employment and becoming members of a profession. However, many have not succeeded. Several legal texts have declared that the deaf have the right to equal employment opportunities. These declarations were often not put into practice. A law passed in July, 1987, concerning the hiring of the handicapped, indicated that the deaf should have equal opportunities for employment and not be subject to discriminatory practices. Provisions of the law called for a fund to be established for the employment of the handicapped.

The law requires that 6 percent of the employees of companies with 20 or more employees be handicapped. Companies can fulfill this legal requirement by hiring disabled workers or by making a contribution to the national fund for the hiring of the handicapped. This fund is managed by an association (AGEFIPH) that distributes large subsidies to companies who hire deaf and hard of hearing persons.

New Communication Technology

Recent technological advances have greatly facilitated and simplified the communication and social interaction of deaf and hard of hearing individuals. Amplified telephones are in wide use by hard of hearing persons.

Beginning in 1986, teletype devices for the deaf (the French "Minitel") have been widely available in France. The teletype devices have proven to be invaluable for the deaf person. This device has made the deaf individual much more independent by providing him or her with access to data including information, schedules, and reservation procedures for train, airline, hotels, and other services routinely used by the general public. Also available are special programs with specific information about deafness, and legislation that provides the deaf professional with training.

The teletype devices for the deaf provide the person who is deaf with a written communication system. It allows the deaf to communicate and interact with anyone who has a telephone and a teletype device.

Deaf and deaf-and-blind people will benefit greatly from services provided by the NUMERIS network (French numerical integrated service network). This is a national telephone relay system that allows deaf and hearing persons throughout France to communicate. TV sets are available that can be equipped with an adapter for headphones or an infrared amplification system that provides a quality listening environment for hard of hearing individuals.

For the person who is profoundly deaf, close-captioned TV programs such as those of the Antiope system are of great value. The number of closed-captioned TV programs is still very limited, and the level of the written language used in the captions may not be accessible to all deaf persons. Many assistive devices, including doorbell and telephone flashing light systems, fire and security flashing light systems, are also now available for deaf and hard of hearing individuals.

References

Aimard, P., & Morgon, A. (1985). *The deaf child. Que sais-je?* Paris: PUF.

Borel-Maisonny, S. (1973). *Perception and education, pedagogical and psychological news.* Switzerland: Delachaux and Niestlé.

Bouvet, D. (1982). *Speech of the deaf child.* Collection "Le Fil rouge". Paris: PUF.

Busquet, D., & Mottier, C. (1978). *The deaf child: Psychological development and re-education.* Paris: Les Cahiers Baillére.

Chouard, H. (1978). *Hearing without ears.* Collection "Un homme et son métier." Paris: Robert Laffont.

Coll, J. (1979). Understanding and helping the hearing-impaired child. Toulouse, France: Privat.

CTNERHI (Publications by). (1979, November 2,3,4; 1980). *The deaf child before age 3.* Paris: Acts of the International Conference of ANREDA.

Cuxac, C. (1983). *The language of the deaf.* Paris: Payot.

De l'Épée, Abbé. (1984). *The real way to teach the deaf and the mute.* Corpus of French language philosophy, Fayard. [Reprinted]

Dumont, A. (1988). *The speech pathologist and the deaf child.* Collection d'orthophonie. Paris: Masson.

Franco-American Foundation. (1991). *The deaf in society: Education and access.* Paris: Franco-American Conference of 16-18 October, 1991.

Lafon, J.-Cl. (Texts collected and presented by). (1971). Deafness in infants: Diagnosis, education, hearing aids. International Audiophonology Conference. Besançon, France: Camponovo. Besançon, 9-12 November, 1969.

Lafon, J.-Cl. (1985). *Hearing-impaired children.* Collection "Handicaps and Re-adaptation." Villeurbanne, France: Simep.

Lafosse, Ph., & Challier, G. (1990). *How to live with a hearing-impaired.* Paris: Josette Lyon.

Morgan, A., Aimard, P., & Daudet, N. (1976). *Education of the deaf infant.* Collection d'orthophonie. 2nd ed. Paris: Masson.

Moody, B. (1983-1990). *The language of signs.* (Vols. 1-3). Paris: Marketing.

Pelisse, J.-M. (1982). *101 pieces of advice to 2 million hearing-impaired.* Collection "101". Paris: Hachette.

Périer, O. (1987).   The child with a hearing impairment: Medical, educational, sociological, and psychological aspects. In *Acta Oto-Rhino-Laryngologica Belgica: Vol. 41. No. 2.* (pp. 125-420). Brussels, Belgium: Publications "Acta medica belgica."

Sadek-Khalil, D. (1968). *A language test, pedagogical and psychological news.* Neuchâtel, Switzerland: Delachaux and Niestlé.

Many articles concerning the education of the deaf appear regularly in the following publications:

Bulletin of Audiophonology, published by the *Association Franc-Comtoise d'Audiophonologi* (Association of Audiophonology of French-Comté) and the *Faculté de Médecine et de Pharmacie de Besançon* (University of Medicine and Pharmacy at Besançon).

Communicate, published by ANPEDA, 10 Quai de la Charente, 75019 Paris.

The Courier of Suresnes, Centre national d'études et de formation pour l'enfance inadaptée (National Center for Study and Training of Handicapped Children), 58-60 Avenue des Landes, 92150 Suresnes.

Re-adaptation, ONISEP, *Département diffusion adaptation,* B.P. 102.05, 75225 Paris Cedex 05.

Review of Laryngology-otology-rhinology, 114 Avenue d'Arés, 33074 Bordeaux Cedex.

Additional practical information can be obtained in the following documents:

French Annual Bulletin of Audiophonology, OCEP, 10 Avenue Parmentier, 75011 Paris.

Deaf Children, Blind Children, a publication of the Ministry of Social Affairs and Employment.

Young Hearing-Impaired. Centers, education, schooling, professional training, ONISEP, Department of Publications - Distribution, Re-adaption, 75635 Paris Cedex 13.

Education of the Deaf in Germany

by Gunther List, Manfred Wloka, Gudula List

I. History of the "German Method" of Educating the Deaf

by Gunther List

The unique tradition of the "oral dogma" that has lasted for more than 200 years in Germany, i.e., the concentration on oral language and the successful exclusion of sign language from all official communication, is a heritage that still has its effect on today's education of the deaf in Germany. Any descriptions of the present state of the education of the deaf in Germany must be preceded by an open account of this history.

Two key historical experiences during the last six decades will serve as guidelines for the historical review of the education of the deaf in Germany. The first historical change was the new linguistic paradigm introduced in the 1960s, which has slowly begun to open up the perception of the sociological problems caused by "deafness." This new linguistic paradigm is being examined on an interdisciplinary basis in Germany. The second key, although proceeding with even more difficulty, that must be considered in any historical perspective of the education of the deaf in Germany, was the racial persecution of the "hereditary ill" deaf that occurred between 1933 and 1945, during the years of the Nazi regime (Biesold, 1988). Although study of this period proceeds slowly and with difficulty, it is important to turn our attention to those who were the victims of the Nazi society's approach to the problem of deafness then and compare it with society's current approaches.

The following remarks do not intend to anticipate the yet unwritten critical history of the subject. For the time being one cannot do more than outline some of the basic conditions, without claiming integrity, especially in as far as the radically abridged history of the

twentieth century is concerned. It was seemingly more important to discuss the nature of the very premises that have formed the foundation of German education of the deaf in the eighteenth and nineteenth centuries, and that have remained principally unchanged ever since.

The level of knowledge of the accumulated history of German educational theory can only provide a limited information base for a critical reconstruction of the history of the education of the deaf. Essentially, the documented history lines up the internal data on the education of the deaf in a way to legitimize the product it represents. By focusing upon the subject of "deafness" historically, the historians have successfully excluded this subject from reports on general history. By doing this, the history of the education of the deaf in Germany applies a model of progress that stretches the history of the "German method" of teaching the deaf from the year 1770 to 1880. Between these time marks of European history of the education of the deaf, oralism was trumpeted as the nineteenth century's best philosophy and most successful method of teaching the deaf.

Heinecke's Oral Method

The strong self-confident conviction of the superiority of the so-called "German" method of teaching the deaf going back to the time of the founding the first schools for the deaf in Germany is, indeed, astonishing.

The former cantor from Hamburg, Samuel Heinicke (1728–1790), programmatically introduced the oral method at the school he founded in Leipzig about 1770. This followed previous private oral instruction provided to deaf children of aristocrats that dates back to the time of the Renaissance. By strictly aiming his education at the "demutement" of deaf people by the use and adaptation of the oral language of the hearing majority (Heinicke, reprinted 1912), supposedly Heinecke achieved success by means of articulation lessons. He is given credit for the

* This chapter has three distinct sections. At the conclusion of each section is a list of references for that particular section.

establishment of the methodology that supported the oralists' position that the oral approach was the socially acceptable and optimum method of educating the deaf.

Heinicke's oral method was opposed by Abbé de l'Épée (1712–1789), his contemporary, who developed a model of education that utilized the sign language of the deaf. This methodology controversy concerning the superiority of the oral method of Heinicke or the manual method of Abbé de l'Épée has continued for more than two centuries. Although the Parisian institute of de l'Épée and the manual philosophy ruled over the expansion of the education of the deaf throughout most of the countries of the world until late into the nineteenth century, in the end oralism dominated. The year 1880 marked the end of the manual epoch. After the Milan International Congress on the Education of the Deaf of 1880, which denounced the use of signs, the oral philosophy ruled the world until quite recently. Even France, the country that originated the "French" method which favored the use of sign language, changed to the "German method" (Lane, 1984; List, 1991).

It is understandable that the German supporters of the oral theory of educating the deaf took the turn of events as a confirmation of the validity of their theory. How did this remarkable change from a system of education that originally focused on the use of sign language to the use of "German" or oral method occur? People were seemingly satisfied to simply accept the oral method originated in Germany by Heinicke as the superior method. The dramatic quarrel about the superior methodology to use to educate the deaf that was fought out in Europe between 1770 and 1880, which reduced the discussion to the narrow view of a mere methods battle, could have, at the utmost, provoked detailed discussions that related to the general history of the human mind (Vahle, 1927).

This narrow methods battle clearly played down what we are currently most visibly confronted with in the history of oralism, and what is impressively reflected in the writing of oralism's history: society's approach to deafness. Full control of the education of the deaf was handed over to educational experts who were able to gain approval and control because of their competence in the use of the oral methodology. Concerned individuals, including deaf individuals, were reduced to mere objects, even products of the method's success. This group became socially identifiable only during moments of social crises. The deaf and their friends became identifiable as a group only when they were felt to be somewhat threatening. An example of this fact would be the fights that occurred between the Wilhelminian Empire and social democrats and during World War I (Schumann, 1940).

Thus, with the start of the oral epoch marked by the first International Congress on the Education of the Deaf held in 1880, the figure of the hearing "teacher of deaf-mutes" is once and for all moved to the frontline to "represent" "the deaf-mute" to the exterior world. Deaf persons no longer had a say in their own education or future. This was the same deaf-mute who, during the period of the Enlightenment 100 years earlier, had freed himself from his supposedly animal-like state of mind, and had been discovered to be a human being capable of learning. With their radically "different" approach to language, the use of sign language, the deaf proved that they could develop language and perform intellectually, provided that the torch, sign language that lit up a then pitch-dark chapter in the origin of language and the evolution of mankind, was utilized (Gessinger, 1989).

As de l'Épée demonstrated with his successes in educating deaf children at his school, the deaf could be educated and have a chance to determine their own social history. But these gains that brought the deaf population emancipation also brought about isolation, a retreat from integration, and repression by the larger community.

Using the framework of the history of the education of the deaf detailed in this paper, it is clear why the oral method of educating the deaf had to finally turn out as the more successful model. By means of strenuously ignoring sign language, German society was distracted from attention to the group character of the deaf to a large extent, and concentrated on the "enlightening" role of the hearing teacher of the deaf. The teacher of the deaf's task of training the individual deaf pupil's oral abilities was nothing short of a handicraft and made him the dominant figure in the oral education of the deaf from the very start. The teacher of the deaf was enmeshed in the aura of his secret trade ("arcanum") (Heinicke, 1912). In contrast, the "French" model inaugurated by de l'Épée, which in the beginning was widely utilized in the Catholic regions of Southern Germany, was much more flexible and child-centered. Even though this alternative model to the prevailing oral philosophy of educating the deaf was theoretically sound, well founded, and served deaf students well, it continued to be a methodology used with only a minority of the deaf pupils in Germany.

Up until 1880 the "French" system, which used the natural sign language of the deaf, seemed to work well (Presneau, 1985; Schumann, 1940). Yet no matter how well the deaf were able to unfold their own social and counter-culture history under the banner of the "French" model, as long as sign language was not recognized by German society as being a language equal in its grammatical complexity to oral German (this only happened in 1960), there was little hope of success in making it the dominant language of the deaf.

Not even the enlightened philosophical discovery that the deaf were capable of being educated did much to sway the general European perspective. Even on that point opinions varied. In spite of the fact that research indicated that the use of sign language was a successful means of educating the deaf, this research was disregarded. Hearing administrators and teachers focused upon the oral language development of the deaf child

with the aim of making the deaf child "normal" by making him or her speak.

Thus the edge is taken off of the question of why Heinicke, the oralist, personally played this exceptional role in the development of the education of the deaf. It is more efficient to ask what factors enabled German pedagogics to play such a leading role in the emancipation, repression, and evolution of the education of the deaf. The attempt to derive the triumph of oralism from the superiority of the "method" as the Germans tried to do during the modern industrial era, reveals that the supporters of oralism relied on the promise of success and not success itself. The method of teaching the deaf that focused on spoken language failed in most individual cases. Many oralists do not deny this fact (Wolfgart, 1967). The social validity of oralism can only be explained by looking at the "side effects" it produces beyond mere success or failure.

Up to the early 1990s not even preparatory work had been completed on the history of the education of the deaf in Germany. (For the first time, this author will be able to do detailed research on the history of the education of the deaf as part of a project sponsored by the Thyssen Foundation.)

The supporters of the oral method of teaching the deaf now use the term "modernization" movement to explain its function. The modernization movement is made up of an alliance of three different interest groups. In the end this movement granted more importance to the social "side effects" of the oral method than to how well the individual deaf person was educated. The interests of the German state were guided by the answers to the following questions: Did the education the deaf received assist them to assimilate into society? Did the deaf develop competence in the use of the spoken language? The success of the modernizationists resided in the fact that their public posture and educational front was very effective. Also, at a time of numerous social problems in Germany, including the controversy over the age of compulsory school attendance, society did not want to deal with the provocation of a linguistically and culturally "different" group.

If the "accomplishment" of oralism is understood in the context explained above, the success of Heinicke and the spread of his model to other countries, especially after 1880, can be answered.

Next, the different phases of the history of the education of the deaf in Germany will be outlined. The course of the evolution of the education of the deaf in Germany may well be used as an example of its development in other countries.

The Oral Method's Three Periods of Development

It was finally in the 1880s that the professionals advocating oralism and public sentiment coincided and turned the tide towards oralism. The time periods up to the 1880s, which includes the second and third phase of the education of the deaf, as well as the evolution of education in Germany overall, can be summarized as follows: Period One—expansion, no uniform ideology, a lack of funds, a lack of educational programs and services between the revolutions of 1789 and 1846; Period Two—expansion of programs and services which followed the course of the demographic and industrial development of Germany; Period Three—accumulated social programs which led to the turning point for the oralist philosophy.

The first period, or the foundation period, begins in 1770 and ends with Heinicke's death in 1790 (and in France with de l'Épée's death in 1789). The Vienna Institute, which started in 1779 and was influenced by the "French Method," was the only school for deaf children in all of the other German speaking regions during this period. How little Heinicke's rigid and labor-intensive oral method influenced public school policy during his lifetime becomes obvious when the directorate of his school in Leipzig is passed on to his widow after his death and she immediately proceeded to sacrifice the oral goals of her husband by providing the students who were deaf with a general education that favored the cheaper *Arbeitsschule* (work-school). After this change in the school program, sign language was again tolerated (Schumann, 1940).

Thus Heinicke's attempt at an oral education for deaf children varied greatly from later developments. His methodical oral program had failed at that point in history. He was light years away from that publicly inaugurated oralism, which started in 1811 with the establishment of the Seminary for Teachers of the Deaf at the Berlin School for the Deaf. During the second half of the nineteenth century, Heinicke's oral methodology of teaching the deaf was rediscovered and revered as the "right" method of educating the deaf. But in fact it was the socio-psychological motivation of the later authors of oralism that caused it to be much more successful than was Heinicke's original model, and that assured the continuity of his methodology. Oralism proved to be the modern solution to the social problem of the "deaf-mute."

It was not considered a coincidence that the main goal of the education of the deaf at the time, the preparation of students for the Protestant confirmation, led to the general acceptance of the oral method as introduced by Heinicke. Nor is it a coincidence that oralism first became popular in the Protestant regions of Germany. Not only is confirmation an outward sign that marked an important stage in the child's socialization, but it is an individual act that is uttered orally. To enable the deaf to participate in confirmation had to be a dominant goal of Protestant culture, which set the stage for the use of oralism to solve the problems of the deaf from then on. Within the framework of this model the individual deaf person was expected to comply with the goals of developing speech competency and abandoning his or her natural sign language community (List, 1990).

By 1880 the "modernization" movement was evidently already fully developed and invoked the oralist philosophy of how to educate the deaf in a socially acceptable manner. It was successfully introduced only through a combination of a high degree of professionalism on the one hand and public intervention on the other hand.

The authors of the history of German pedagogics of the deaf have reserved the period after the turn of the century as the time of the final triumph of the oral philosophy. The time between Heinicke's death and the 1860s seemed to be a period of overall confusion. As a matter of fact, only during the decade between 1860 and 1870 did the pressure on public education (with the final realization of compulsory school attendance) became strong enough to make the oralist group indispensable to the organization of education of the deaf in Germany. During this historical period professionals who supported the oral philosophy had the opportunity to offer the oral system as a solution to the education of a rising number of pupils who were deaf. In the past the oral method of teaching the deaf had been limited primarily to deaf children of a few bourgeois families.

As compared with the rigidity and lack of change during the first historical period, the relative open-mindedness of the second historical period was welcomed. Part of the reason for the openmindedness of this phase stems from the fact that in the Catholic-dominated southern part of Germany, the French model of the education of the deaf dominated for a few more decades. In the Protestant-controlled northern part of Germany, the past stronghold of the oralist option, much of the rigidity of Heinicke's oral methodology disappeared and in its place the schools used a variety of communication methodologies which included signed and spoken language. Instead of calling the historical phase a time of confusion concerning the proper ideology and methodology to use, it was in a sense a bowing to the reality of the children's needs and the needs of the larger society. No one

philosophy dominated the period and it could be considered as a time of flexibility and enlightened discoveries concerning the "educatability" of the "deaf-mute." It was a time to try a variety of methodologies aimed at educating the deaf.

These were the first steps taken in the direction of making German pedagogics on the education of the deaf more professional. The teacher preparation program was not yet committed to the direction of oralism. At the beginning of the nineteenth century, in response to civic needs, general teacher preparation in Germany developed a new humanistic direction. Little by little in the course of the following decades, this humanistic trend in teacher education was diminished. After 1850, elementary teachers, influenced by Pestalozzi and Hill, took a chance at a career as a teacher. At the same time elementary teachers were provided permanent status within the society. Those who favored the oral approach to the education of the deaf were able to firmly entrench their philosophy.

In the past the schools in Germany had always been under the control of the central government. At this time the central government loosened its control over the schools, and local control, run by school administrators who were in touch with the local scene, prevailed. This change to local control cut down on administrative trivia, allowed change to occur, and focused more fully upon the welfare of children. Teachers had more influence over educational matters.

All of these factors, local control, less central bureaucracy, and a cooperative model of education, came together to form one functional unit during the second half of the nineteenth century. The "German" method of education became an attractive model to use to modernize the education of the deaf.

The Fourth Phase: The Oral Method's Final Triumph

The history of the education of the deaf since 1880 was based on this success. During this, its fourth phase, the history of the education of the deaf reached its peak and continued unabated until the beginning of World War I and the advent of "reform" pedagogics. This period was characterized by the formal introduction of compulsory school attendance for children who were deaf in Prussia in 1911 and the leading role played by educators of the deaf concerning the education of disabled children.

The contradictory achievement of the oral philosophy fully corresponded to the basic contradiction apparent in the politics of general education during the time of the Industrial Revolution. The general principle followed at the time was that education was for everyone, but, at the same time, school was used as a means of classification.

Under the banner of this official policy, schools for handicapped children, including schools for the deaf, were created. The profession of teaching the deaf was developed. Teachers of the deaf achieved a status equal to that of a regular elementary teacher. Teachers of the deaf were now thought of as experts and given the responsibility to educate deaf children as they saw fit.

At the same time the "deaf-mute," long since removed from the focus of social history, was rediscovered. The formation of the deaf child's oral abilities was considered the ideal way for the child who was deaf to become socially assimilated. If the child was not able to establish good oral skills, it was the child's fault and not the failure of the oral method. Many of the students in the schools for the deaf were oral failures and did not develop good oral skills.

Pedagogic Reforms Begin

The enlightening discovery that the "deaf-mute" was able to be educated was largely withdrawn. Thus, the German "teachers of deaf-mutes," while at the height of their social acceptance, found themselves in the middle of a crisis because of the fact that the oral pedagogy often failed to live up to its promise of successfully developing the speech of the children who were deaf.

Reform in pedagogics between the years 1914 and 1933 introduce a valid concern about the future of the education of deaf children in Germany. Sign language use was again permitted in the schools for the deaf. The permission to use sign language was not to acknowledge its equal value as a language, since it was restricted in use to before and after school and not during academic instruction. It was a tactical concession to the fact that the current state of affairs in the education of the deaf was not tenable. The purpose of using sign language was not to discover the true nature of the deaf child's linguistic, cultural, and social history, but to protect the established bastion of oral pedagogics more effectively from criticism as an ineffective system and to keep society from viewing the deaf as a group that was different.

The Nazi Regime

During the time of the Nazi regime, German society provided proof of the fact that it had no real concern for the education of the deaf or of deaf people in general when it followed the regretful role of actively destroying the social history of the deaf. The law, "prevention of offspring afflicted with a hereditary disease," which was passed on July 14, 1933, went much further than mere eugenics, which since 1880 had spread to other countries in addition to Germany. The law put into act the process of sterilizing all congenitally deaf individuals. This barbarous act entered the deaf in Germany into the general history of victims of Nazi atrocities. Deaf persons in Germany were not granted true acceptance into society, neither as a distinct cultural group nor as equal partners. One must go back in German history to the time before the advent of oralism to find a time when the deaf population was accepted.

References

Biesold, H. (1988). *Klagende Hände. Betroffenheit and Spätfolgen in bezug auf das Gesetz zur Verhütung erbkranken Nachwuches, dargestellt am Beispiel der "Taubstummen."* Solms-Oberbiel.

Deibbler, R. (1952). Die Entwicklung der deutschen Methode in ihrer Abhängigkeit von den zeitgenössischen geisteswissenschaftlichen Strömungen. *Neue Blätter für Taubstummenbildung 6,* 24-25, 69-70.

Fiebig, A. (1891). Die hundertjährige Marter der Taubstummen und ihrer Lehrer. *Ein Weck-und Mahnruf an die deutschen Regierungen.* Breslau.

Gessinger, J. (1989). Der Ursprung der Sprache aus der Stummheit. Psychologische und medizinische Aspekte der Sprachursprungsdebatte im 18. Jahrhundert. In Gessinger, J., & Rahden, W. (Eds.). *Theorien vom Ursprung der Sprache.* (Vols. 1-2).

Heidsiek, J. (1891). *Ein Notschrei der Taubstummen.* Breslau.

Heinicke, S. (1912). *Gesammelte Schriften.* Ed. Schumann, G. & Schumann, P. Leipzig.

Karth, J. (1902). Das Taubstummenbildungswesen im IX. Jahrhundert in den wichtigsten Staaten Europas. Ein Überblick über seine Entwickelung. *Im Verein mit ausländischen Vertretern des Taubstummenfaches.* Breslau.

Krohnert, O. (1966). Die sprachliche Bildung des Gehörlosen. *Geschichtliche Entwicklung und gegenwärtige Problematik.* Weinheim.

Lane, H. (1988). *When the mind hears: A history of the deaf.* New York. (Original work published 1984).

Leuchten, F. (1893). *Ein hundertjähriger Irrtum.* Hamburg.

List, G. (1990). Heinicke et líoralisme(un exemple de modernisation. In Couturier, L., & Karakostas, A. (Eds.). *Le pouvoir des signes.* Ouvrage édité à l'occasion de l'exposition "Le pouvoir des signes" commémorant le bicentenaire de l'institut de Jeunes Sourds de Paris. Paris.

List, G. (1991). Vom Triumph der "deutschen" Methode über die Gebärdensprache. Problemskizze zur Pädagogisierung der Gehörlosigkeit im 19. Jahrhundert. *Zeitschrift für Pädagogik, 37,* 245-266.

Lowe, A. (1983). Gehörlosenpädagogik. In Solarova, S. (Ed.). *Geschichte der Sonderpuadagogik.* Stuttgart.

Marcks, G. (Ed.). (1930). *Die Beschulung blinder, taubstummer und schwachsinniger Kinder mit den Bestimmungen über die Lehrkräfte an den Schulen für diese Kinder.* Amtliche Bestimmungen. Berlin.

Presneau, J-R. (1985). Oralisme ou langue des gestes: La formation des sourds au XIXe siècle. In

Borreil, J. (Ed.). *Les sauvages dans la cité: Auto-émancipation du peuple et instruction des prolétaires au XIX siècle.* Seyssel, France.

Schumann, P. (1940). *Geschichte des Taubstummenwesens vom deutschen Standpunkt aus dargestellt.* Frankfurt/M.

Stötzner, H. E. (1870). *Samuel Heinicke: Sein leben und wirken.* Leipzig.

Strümpell, L. (1910). Die Pädagogische Pathologie oder Die Lehre von den Fehlern der Kinder. *Eine Grundlegung . . . fortgeführt und erweitert von Dr. Alfred Spitzner.* (4th ed.). Leipzig.

Vahle, H. (1927). Die theoretische Gundlegung der Lautsprachmethode in ihrer historischen Entwicklung seit Heinicke. In Mittelstaedt, C., & Reich, F. (Eds.). *Samuel-Heinicke-Jubiläumstagung des Bundes Deutscher Taubstummenlehrer.* Kongress fur Taubstummen-Pädagogik und verwandte Gebiete unter Teilnahme von Fachgenossen aus dem Auslande Hamburg, 6-10 Juni, 1927. Leipzig.

Walther, E. (1882). Geschichte des Taubstummenbildungswesens. *Unter besonderer Berücksichtingung der Entwicklung des deutschen taubstummen-Unterrichts dargestellt . . . .* Bielefeld/Leipzig.

Wende, G. (1915). *Deutsche Taubstummenanstalten, -Schulen und - Heime in Wort und Bild.* Halle.

Wolfgart, H. (1967). Der taubstumme Mensch im Aspekt pädagogischer Anthropologie und Praxis. *Untersuchungen zur pädagogischen Anthropologie und zur Geschichte und Didaktik der "Früherziehung" des gehörlosen Kinds.* Dortmund.

II. Facts and Problems from Post-World War II to 1990 in Former West Germany

by Manfred Wloka

This is a report on the education of the deaf in the western part of now-unified Germany. This procedure seems sensible because of the almost entire lack of contact between East and West Germany from 1945 to 1990.

Demographic Data

The educational institutions for the deaf in West Germany have been divided into schools for the deaf, schools for the hard of hearing, and schools that combine the population of both groups. Particularly in the larger institutions, the deaf and hard of hearing have been educated under one roof, although in separate classes. A few of the larger schools have high school and vocational education programs, and units for the education of deaf children who have multiple disabilities. Some schools for the deaf and hard of hearing have combined with other special schools. Schools for the deaf have been combined with schools for language-impaired, physically handicapped, and the blind.

There are a total of 77 institutions for the deaf in the "old Bundeslander," distributed in cities and country throughout Germany according to the population. In the country-side where distances between homes and educational institutes are greater, boarding schools have been established. They are usually open from Monday through Friday. According to the latest statistical surveys, the total of deaf and hard of hearing students in special schools in Germany amounts to about 14,000. Roughly two-thirds of them are hard of hearing and have moderate to profound

hearing losses. There is a tendency in Germany to mainstream students with mild and moderate hearing losses into the regular public schools. This means that the actual number of hard of hearing persons of school age is considerably higher than these statistics suggest.

The German school system is subdivided into levels, which include preschool (or preparatory classes), primary school (four years), orientation period (two years), and different forms of secondary and vocational schools. Only the school for the deaf in Essen leads directly to matriculation. At present, only a few deaf and hard of hearing persons are engaged in university studies. Most are studying at the University of Hamburg and are majoring in the fields of psychology, education, law, and the technical sciences.

Programs for children who are deaf and hard of hearing usually start during the first year of life, or as soon as identified. Next, the deaf child enters a preschool or preparatory school. At the completion of preschool the child passes on to a primary school. Thereafter, the children go on to different forms of secondary education. In most cases children who are deaf enroll in the "Hauptschule" or orientation classes. A few attend high school. The enrollment in classes for children who are deaf ranges from five to nine students. Between six and ten is the normal enrollment of classes for hard of hearing children, and between four and eight pupils are enrolled in classes for children with multiple handicaps (Claubben, 1988).

After 1945, the education for the deaf received a new impetus. Twenty-four new institutions were founded after World War II, but only four of them were schools for the deaf. The trend in favor of schools for the hard of hearing, which has existed since the beginning of the century, continues. About half of the presently existing schools for the deaf were founded during the nineteenth century. Most of these schools now accept students with all degrees of hearing loss.

Roughly 2,500 persons are engaged in

teaching the deaf and hard of hearing in Germany. These teachers received their teacher preparation through the completion of university studies, followed by either basic or extension curricula. Students can enroll in studies aimed at preparing to be a teacher of the deaf in the cities of Hamburg, Dortmund, Cologne, Heidelberg, and Munich.

Early Socialization and Family Life

The family is just as important for the child who is deaf as it is for any hearing child in the community. The child receives the most important early input from his or her parents. Hearing parents, once they realize that they have a child who is deaf, are usually surprised or even shocked to the point of helplessness. They need assistance and advice in dealing with their deaf child. The general policy in Germany is to give parents advice about working with their deaf child at the earliest possible age in order to expedite language acquisition. Several agencies offer services to the parents to ensure early assessment, diagnosis, and education. These services involve parent counseling, language training in the home, treatment in clinics as outpatients, and enrollment in kindergarten and preschool classes.

Audiological services are supplied by independent audiological centers, otolaryngology clinics, and schools for the deaf and hard of hearing. It is in these centers that medical and psychological investigations are undertaken, and hearing aids are supplied and regularly serviced. Language training is provided to the parents at least once a month by a specially trained teacher who introduces them to play therapy and different activities aimed at stimulating the oral language development of the child. Clinics observe and educate the infants who are deaf every two to three months for periods of up to ten days. The curriculum of kindergarten and preschool classes includes language instruction, social and sensory stimulation, and free play. These

activities prepare the child for school and provide the information needed to ensure appropriate future placement decisions (Bund Deutscher Taubstummenlehrer, 1987).

Most of these agencies and institutions stress the concept that parents should give their child experiences that will provide him or her access to the world of hearing people. They advocate oral methods of language learning, supplemented by the use of modern hearing aids. Early goals of these educational programs include improvement in the young deaf child's ability to attend, speechread, speak, and use a hearing aid. All instruction is aimed at supporting "natural" oral language learning.

A new direction that focuses on the aural approach is just now becoming popular. Adherents of this approach to the education of the deaf believe that the hearing nerves can be activated by acoustic stimulation and the early use of hearing aids. The supporters of the aural methodology feel that even profoundly deaf children are able to acquire oral language naturally.

The concept of concentrating the early education of deaf children entirely on auditory perception is not applicable for many deaf children. Experience has shown that natural and fluent communication between the deaf child and his or her parents often cannot be achieved when a pure aural-oral education is practiced. Consequently, a different approach to the early education of children who are deaf that uses signs and oral language has been used in Hamburg since the early 1980s (Prillwitz, Wisch, & Wudtke, 1991; Prillwitz & Wudtke, 1988). This model includes traditional educational and language development strategies. The curriculum includes speechreading, speech development, and the training of residual hearing, supplemented by the use of conventional sign language and the manual alphabet.

The cooperation of parents in the early education of their child who is deaf is of course a crucial element for the success of any methodology used. The degree of parental engagement in the early education of their child is often considered as the major criteria for the child's academic success or failure. Although much of the early education of deaf children occurs in the home, the responsibility for language development cannot be attributed solely to the parents. Competent and well-prepared professionals in the field also play a critical role.

Life at Schools

School is compulsory for all children in Germany. This also applies to children who are deaf. Society is obliged to provide deaf children with adequate instruction in special schools.

Schools for the Deaf

Schools for the deaf are reserved for those children who possess a hearing loss that is so severe that it precludes their ability to perceive language through audition. The schools for the deaf have their own governing board, curricula, and methodology.

Schools for the Hard of Hearing

Children who, due to their hearing loss, are unable to follow instruction in a regular school but who are expected to acquire oral language competencies predominantly by the use of their residual hearing are referred to schools for the hard of hearing (Bund Deutscher Taubstummenlehrer, 1987).

The main educational goals for the children attending schools for the deaf and for the hard of hearing are to foster independence and successful integration into the community. This means that the student can utilize oral language skills, including sufficient language concepts, vocabulary, and syntax to be able to conduct life in a normal manner (Deutscher Bildungsrat, 1974).

Instruction in schools for the hard of hearing is predominantly aural and no system of signs (with the exception of graphic signs)

is used. To compensate for the disabilities caused by the hearing loss, speechreading, speech, and auditory skills are developed.

The curriculum used in the schools for the hard of hearing is similar to that used in regular public schools. Instruction aimed at improving language competencies (*Sprachausbau*) is the core of the curriculum. The goal of language instruction is the correction of any language development problems to the point that students meet normal standards in the areas of morphology, grammar, and syntax.

Language development or the term "forming" the language (*Sprachanbildung*) is at present, just as in the past, the predominant goal of the schools for the deaf and hard of hearing. Students are taught oral language without being able to hear themselves speak. At the same time students have to learn to "read" oral language from the lips of their interlocutors. Teachers of the deaf today normally do not use one method exclusively, but rather combine the particulars of many methods.

In principle, a teacher in the schools for the deaf is free to choose the instructional methods to be used and how the content will be organized. This even applies to the form of communication the teacher chooses to use. However, since German language competency is still the primary goal, the use of any manual language other than the phonetic manual system (cued speech) is still avoided by most teachers of the deaf in Germany. Signs and the manual alphabet have not yet made their entry into the schools for the deaf. Indeed, pressure by certain groups is mounting with respect to the application of other methods of educating the students enrolled in the schools for the deaf. The controversy concerning the use of either signed or spoken languages is still very strong. Yet substantial progress can be reported. In September 1982 teachers, parents, university professors, and representatives of the deaf community reached a consensus in favor of the use of oral methods and signs simultaneously (Munchner Gebardenpapier, 1982).

A main reason why signs are not commonly used as a medium for communication and instruction is that sign language has not yet become an obligatory part of the curriculum of institutions preparing teachers of the deaf.

The current teaching personnel's ideologically based disinterest in information about sign language has resulted in a remarkable absence of knowledge about the forms of signed communication and rejection of sign language as an independent symbol system and viable language. Signing has always been considered lacking in value or importance. Such opposition to signed communication is not based upon any rational or legitimate arguments.

Only recently has information about German sign language become available. About ten years ago a linguistic research program focusing upon German sign language was finally established at the "Zentrum fur Deutsche Gebardensprache und Kommunikation Gerhorloser" in Hamburg. As a consequence of sign language research, the pedagogy of oral education has been strained and teachers of the deaf disrupted. Official representatives of the oral faction discredit bilingual education and claim that it is harmful and will isolate the deaf. Eventually, German may be taught through the simultaneous use of signing and speech. This compromise is gaining ground. The development of a dictionary of German signs by deaf authors may be of great assistance (Maisch & Wisch, 1987, 1988).

The general aim of German education of the deaf, the integration of deaf people into the social and vocational context of the hearing majority, is still valid. After ten years of primary and secondary school (*Hauptschule*), students receive a certificate qualifying them for vocational education. In reality it is mainly for handcraft areas. A high school certificate earned after twelve years of schooling may lead to qualification as a professional. One example of a professional career would be engineering. Completion of the *Abitur* exam is a prerequisite for a deaf person who wants to continue on to higher education. At present it is only possible to complete the *Abitur* at the central vocational college for hearing impaired in Essen. Students who successfully complete the *Abitur* are entitled to enter university studies. They are then qualified to be a "technical assistant."

Hard of hearing students in Germany can reach the *Abitur* at schools for the hard of hearing in Munich, Hamburg, and Stegen near Fireburg. Hard of hearing students can obtain a high school certificate at eleven locations, deaf students at five locations.

The reluctance of some parents to be separated from their deaf children keeps some gifted children who are deaf from enrolling in a secondary education program. However, there is a growing tendency in Germany for deaf students to make use of higher education possibilities and opportunities.

Deaf Children with Multiple Disabilities

Due to better medical treatment, several of the past common causes of a hearing loss have been nearly eliminated or have decreased, but there has been a relative increase in the etiologies of deafness that are accompanied by multiple disabilities. Intellectual deficiencies, additional sensory deficiencies, central brain damage, and psychogenetic disorders are the secondary disabilities commonly found in children who are deaf. These multiple disabilities often compound the language learning difficulties associated with deafness. Schools for the deaf in Germany need to develop educational programs appropriate for this group of students, who often need practical life skills more than academic knowledge. All forms of communication, including the manual alphabet, signs, and speech may need to be used with children with multiple disabilities according to their individual needs.

Seven special institutions with residential facilities have been developed in Germany to meet the educational needs of this group of deaf children. Since the need for facilities for multi-handicapped children is greater than the capacity of the existing institutions, many schools for the deaf have arranged for special classes for children with multiple disabilities. A great problem, often unsolved, develops for deaf and hard of hearing persons with multiple disabilities after their formal schooling ends. This is the need for organized vocational training programs. Many of the deaf persons with multiple disabilities end up in group homes and sheltered workshops (*Berschutzende Werkstatten*).

Vocational Life and Instructional Training

The goal of educational institutions for the deaf in Germany is the successful integration of the deaf person into society. This implies the need for career or vocational education. After compulsory education ends at the age of eighteen, several German laws become activated: social legislation, laws regulating tuition aid (*Ausbildungsforderungsgesetz*), and laws concerning the seriously disabled (*Schwerbehindertengesetz*). These laws all describe the rights of disabled persons in general and of deaf and hard of hearing people in particular.

Notwithstanding the laws and rights guaranteed the handicapped, deaf and hard of hearing persons, and particularly individuals who are deaf, are in direct competition with non-handicapped persons for jobs. No special test accommodations have been established for persons who are deaf. Quality instruction and education is imperative if the deaf person is to compete equally. Therefore, one of the responsibilities of schools for the deaf is to prepare the deaf students for the particular requirements they will meet during later vocational training.

In comparison with hearing school-leavers, deaf school-leavers may have difficulty competing for available jobs because of problems encountered in attempting to communicate with instructors and employers, and less

experience and preparation in the handling of complicated situations. On the other hand, the person who is deaf may profit from increased visual and tactile abilities, more intensive concentration, and good general motivation.

Unfortunately, old prejudices towards the deaf and hard of hearing are still alive in German society. Therefore, schools, labor offices, parents, and of course deaf persons themselves must work to overcome these prejudices to ensure that deaf persons have a place in an organized apprenticeship program. Vocational education in Germany has a long tradition. The vocational programs are not aimed at the development of skill areas as in other countries but at preparation over a long period of time that leads to the development of a profession. Generally, the apprenticeship is organized according to a dual system. The practical on-the-job training part of the dual system is controlled by business enterprises, and the theoretical part of the training is offered by vocational schools. Although the relative importance of theory and practice may vary according to the particular occupational area in question, apprentices generally attend classes at a vocational school one or two days a week and receive practical experience at some business or factory for three or four days a week.

Vocational schooling is compulsory for deaf and hard of hearing apprentices, as it is for all others. In most cases, special schools for the deaf are responsible for the vocational instruction. The small number of deaf trainees and the broad spectrum of vocational content that needs to be covered create a difficult situation for the special vocational schools for the deaf. To overcome this difficulty, two forms of vocational instruction have evolved under the roof of the general schools for the deaf: In **mixed classes** (*Vielberufsklassen*), the deaf students receive general vocational instruction as a group and individual instruction in specialized career fields. In **specialized classes** (*Fachklassen*), deaf apprentices focus on different vocational areas, but not according to the years of vocational instruction completed as is the case in regular vocational schools. Generally, the vocational instruction is provided by teachers of the deaf.

In some densely populated regions with larger catchment areas, **central vocational schools** (*Zentralberufsschulen*) exist, which provide vocational instruction in more unusual vocational areas. In these schools education is often organized in instructional blocks consisting of courses three-to-five weeks in length taught by teachers of the deaf. The teachers of the deaf work cooperatively with teachers from the regular vocational schools, who do not have the qualifications needed to teach the deaf.

Another possibility for students who are deaf is to enroll in a **technical school** where both practical and theoretical professional training can be learned. Some deaf students use the technical school education as an introduction to the regular vocational preparation programs.

Profoundly deaf adolescents who have other problems that preclude them from finding an apprenticeship may enter a **special home** where vocational instruction along with recreational activities are offered (*Berufsbildungswerk*). Since the cost of the special home program is covered by the Office of Labor, admission to these homes depends on the recommendation of a vocational counselor. These institutes also offer preparatory courses for adolescents who are not yet ready to enter into organized vocational instruction or who need to explore their career potential. A certain climate of isolation and dependency is a disadvantage of these homes. The challenges that are to be expected on the job are not encountered at the special schools. This fact may lead the deaf person to fail in the workplace.

In the past, tailoring and shoemaking were prominent vocational areas for many deaf persons. Now persons who are deaf are involved in a broad spectrum of career areas. Deaf persons are currently employed in 55

vocational fields, including metal and woodworking, construction, textile manufacturing, leather work, printing, graphic design, food preparation, surveying, stonework, ceramics, horticulture, domestic science, lab and dental mechanics, and business administration (Bundesanstalt für Arbeit, 1985, 1996). However, in spite of the wide variety of job possibilities, due to increased dependence upon theoretical information in many fields, it has become more and more difficult to find adequate instruction in many vocational areas for students who are deaf. Electrical engineering would be a good example. If deaf or hard of hearing adolescents fail to gain sufficient knowledge in the fields of natural science and oral and written language during their years of formal schooling, their chances of passing the qualifying vocational examinations are low. To ensure that persons who are deaf take their rightful places as independent citizens in German society, new vocational training possibilities are needed.

Chances for Advanced Training and Academic Studies

The completion of a vocational program provides the person who is deaf, as is true for any person, a basis for his or her life work. Changes in technology and the economy lead to career changes and require workers to continue their education if they are to compete in the job market. The deaf worker may encounter the following problems while trying to adapt to change:

- Difficulty communicating and exchanging experiences with colleagues and superiors
- Difficulty participating in the supplementary instruction programs offered by firms
- Inability to take advantage of supplementary training courses offered by official institutions such as the chamber of industry, chamber of commerce, and trade unions

◆ Inability to profit from information supplied by public media about vocational areas

It is therefore vital to create special opportunities for deaf persons to obtain additional vocational knowledge and experience. Such opportunities are being provided by the special vocational homes located in Nurnberg, Winnenden, Husum, Munich, and Essen. The special vocational homes for the deaf offer supplementary vocational courses in the areas of computer technology, electrical technology, metal and wood craft, technical design, dental mechanics, surveying, cartography, domestic sciences, and other areas.

These courses normally take place on weekends and are financed by the Federal Office of Labor. Participants pay only part of the cost of travel and housing. Enrollment in and acceptance of these programs by deaf persons is high. These courses provide the person who is deaf with the knowledge and skill required to qualify for new career possibilities, and to make the workplace safer (Schulte & Straub, 1986).

The possibility for a person who is deaf to qualify for university study is still relatively limited. Only those students who have graduated from schools for the deaf and hard of hearing that include upper-level classes as part of the curriculum can qualify for university study. The central vocational school in Essen is the school for the deaf most likely to have the required upper-level classes as part of its curriculum.

Only a small number of deaf students decide upon an academic career. It is estimated that there are approximately 250 deaf and hard of hearing students currently engaged in studies at technical colleges and universities in Germany. Some of these students receive assistance from tutors and from interpreters and note takers during lectures. The lack of qualified interpreters is one of the reasons for the very low number of deaf persons enrolled in college. Besides the natural sciences an increasing number of deaf students are

enrolling in liberal and fine arts classes. Special education courses have the highest enrollment of students who are deaf.

Hamburg University has developed as a center for deaf students, presumably because the local *Zentrum fur Deutsche Gebardensprache und Kommunikation Gehorloser* makes it easier for the university to find interpreters. Presently, sixteen students are enrolled at Hamburg University in the fields of law, psychology, and special education. A German sign language curriculum and an instructional program for interpreters have been organized. In the long run, the number of hearing impaired persons with the academic preparation necessary to enter the university will increase, and as a consequence the general level of education of people who are deaf and hard of hearing will gradually improve.

Supplementary educational opportunities have been offered for many years by various institutions, including the school of the deaf. These educational opportunities include evening adult education classes (*Volkshochschulen*). The adult education programs offer a broad variety of lectures, courses, seminars, guided tours, and study groups that do not focus on vocational education but rather on more general areas of interest. The clubs and associations for the deaf play an important role in this context. They organize seminars and courses in order to develop the talents deaf persons need to serve the functions of the associations. These activities contribute much to the strengthening of the self-esteem and independence of individuals who are deaf.

Apart from intellectual and individual growth opportunities, these activities fulfill an important social function (Graf, 1967).

The Academic Training of Teachers of the Deaf in Germany

Teacher preparation in Germany follows prescribed laws. The basic state rules for the

University of Cologne or any other university preparing teachers are found in the "law of formation for teachers at state schools," the "regulations for first state exams for teachers at state schools," and in laws that dictate the curriculum of the programs designed to prepare teachers of the deaf and hard of hearing. People can study to be teachers of the deaf and hard of hearing at the following universities: Berlin, Hamburg, Cologne, Heidelberg, and Munich. The basic requirements for admittance to one of these programs includes the successful completion of the *Abitur* or an equivalent test of entry into a university, and several weeks of practical work in a special education school. There are two programs of study that lead to certification as a teacher of the deaf. One program requires eight to ten semesters or four to five years. A shorter program requires a reduced program of specialized studies in addition to the completion of a teacher preparation program designed for persons preparing to teach in regular public schools.

The complete course of studies in special education for a person planning to be a teacher of the deaf includes work in the field of general education, courses in one of the academic subject areas found in the regular public school curriculum, and work in two fields of special education. In addition to either the education of the deaf or the hard of hearing, the student must choose another area of special education (examples could be education of physically or mentally disabled individuals). Only rarely can a student choose to study both the education of the deaf and the hard of hearing. The preparation required to teach each group differs, the principal difference being in the language reception by the two groups.

The completion of academic exams at the end of the four to five years of study finishes the first part of the preparation program. In order to receive a state certificate as a special education teacher, a person must complete a supervised, two-year-long probationary period. At the completion of the two years of successful instruction, the individual must pass a final state exam for permanent certification.

Graduate studies in the education of the deaf or of the hard of hearing can also be completed by individuals who have already finished a teacher education program designed for teaching in the regular schools. This group must also complete another area of special education. For many years the only way to become a teacher of the deaf was to complete the two-year program of studies. During the late 1970s direct entry into special education became possible. This route requires more time to complete, but has the advantage of making available to the schools for the deaf persons who have general teaching experience. However, the first path to certification discussed is more prevalent.

Because of the many obstacles that must be overcome at this time, people who are deaf have little opportunity to become teachers of the deaf. Nevertheless, there is a small but growing number of deaf students enrolled in studies aimed at the preparation of teachers of the deaf. Although there is a historical tradition of having teachers who are deaf in schools for the deaf in Germany, presently the numbers of deaf teachers is very small. Presumably, this attitude will change when more deaf teachers make their way into the schools for the deaf and resume these old traditions.

The Community of the Deaf

It is well known that deafness may cause many problems in different social contexts. The speech communication deficiencies of some deaf persons causes serious communication barriers to exist between the deaf and hearing population. In spite of 200 years of efforts to teach oral language to the deaf, these barriers to fluent oral communication have not been eliminated. This is all the more true for those who were born deaf or became deaf before they were able to acquire language in the normal manner.

Years of experience indicate that partial integration of the deaf is very important for success in the workplace. As far as the deaf person's general participation in the social life of the country is concerned, enormous obstacles remain. Although the mass media have done a better job of informing the public about deafness, there is still a considerable lack of understanding about deafness on the part of the general public. The general public's lack of understanding and inability to communicate with individuals who are deaf have been the two main reasons that deaf persons, today and in the past, withdraw from the hearing society and remain within their own community.

In 1848 the first German association of deaf-mutes was founded in Berlin. Forty years later, also in Berlin, the first sports club for the deaf was established. Churches in Germany have a long tradition of caring for their deaf parishioners. The deaf parishioners formed clubs for the deaf. All of these organizations were and still are motivated by the goals of freeing their members from the isolation experienced when interacting with the hearing community, and of providing intellectual stimulation, entertainment, and support in vital contexts. Within their association and clubs, the deaf are not exposed to the strenuous requirements necessary to communicate with hearing people, but are free to communicate among one another in sign language while exchanging ideas and enjoying sporting activities. Because of the ease of communicating in their own language, deaf people do not feel handicapped at the club or association. Compared with the hearing population, a much larger percentage of the deaf population is involved in associations and clubs.

Before the unification of Germany in 1989, about 25,000 of the 60,000 deaf individuals who lived in the Federal Republic were members of clubs. Each geographical region has an association for the deaf, which usually follows the boundaries of the *Bundeslander*. These regional associations combine to make up a state-wide organization called the *Deutscher Gehorlosen Bund e.V.* This state-wide organization represents deaf people in Germany in all economic, social, vocational, and cultural activities (Deutsches Gehorlosen-Taschenbuch, 1989, 1990). The German sports association for the deaf with 130 local clubs and more than 10,000 members, and the Catholic Deaf Association with 3,000 members in 87 local clubs, are parts of this organization.

The *Deutsche Gehorlosen Bund* is related to UNO, UNESCO, the World Health Organization, and the International Labor Organization. The *Deutsche Gehorlosen Sportverband* represents the German deaf as a member of the Comite International Sports Silencieux (CISS).

To illustrate the variety of interests and activities promoted by clubs for the deaf, the *landesverband der Gehorlosen Berlin* may serve as an example: Two of the thirteen clubs for the deaf in Berlin are engaged in welfare activities, two in community life and travel, two in religious activities, and seven in sports. The sports involved include gymnastics, football, tennis, bowling, auto racing, and skating. The first club for the deaf to form was a swimming club founded in 1988. The high mobility of the deaf population, especially since the 1960s, has permitted the deaf to organize many meetings and events, not only on the national level, but also increasingly on the international level.

A movement to install cultural centers for the deaf at various places in Germany began around 1970. These centers offer opportunities to develop cultural pursuits. New theater groups, presenting themes from the world of the deaf, have been formed. A few years ago the *Deutsches Gehorlosen Theatre*, affiliated to *Deutscher Gehorlosen Bund*, celebrated its fortieth birthday.

A periodical called *Deutsche Gehorlosen Zeitung* is printed monthly with the purpose of informing people about the life of the deaf in Germany. The periodical lists club activities and sporting events. The well-known slogan "The home of the deaf is his club" expresses adequately what many deaf seek, a community of equals.

Public Life, Media, and Language Mediation

While in the past very little public attention was focused upon the deaf population, currently, attitudes are changing. Thanks to international contacts, the German deaf are recognizing the fact that they must present their concerns to the public. The general process of democratization in the Federal Republic of Germany after World War II has created new possibilities for the deaf to define their place in society. Laws were passed that gave the handicapped equal opportunities, and to some extent the paternalism of the past has been replaced by legitimate rights. It took some time before persons who were deaf affirmed and used those rights. Insight into the political process first had to be learned by the deaf community. As a result of the deaf population's newly gained courage and insistence, publicity and petitions, and negotiations with politicians forced the abandonment of the decision of the Federal Government to cancel free public transportation opportunities for the deaf and hard of hearing.

The Day of the Deaf, held in September of each year, promotes better understanding of the deaf and deafness through demonstrations, lectures, and public events. Television has become an important means of spreading information about deafness. The Bavarian Association of Parents of Hearing Impaired Children, in cooperation with associations of the deaf, managed to initiate a widely viewed TV program about the deaf and hard of hearing. This program, *Sehen statt Horen*, which presents political information and news from the deaf community, has been shown once a week since 1975. Whereas in the beginning of the TV program only announcements were presented in signed German with the remaining text subtitled, German Sign Language is now being used extensively. Since 1976 a Berlin TV channel

has been presenting programs using a sign language interpreter.

These public information sources have focused on the deaf community. This focus has attracted public attention to sign language. These successes have made it possible for teachers of the deaf to promote greater acceptance of signed German. The founding of the center for the study of German Sign Language in Hamburg and the publication of the first German Sign Language dictionary (Maisch & Wisch, 1987, 1988) were of great help in this respect.

Together with the growing attention to sign language, the need for interpreters has become more and more important. For many years the only persons who functioned as interpreters were hearing children of deaf parents. As the deaf population participates more in public life, the need for sign language interpreters paid by the state has grown substantially.

Nevertheless, the situation is still deplorable (Ebbinghaus & Hebbmann, 1980). Up to the present, interpreters are used only in emergency situations, including in court and at the police station. The current supply of interpreters does not permit deaf persons to participate fully in public life.

For most interpreters, interpreting is a sideline and not their main occupation. Therefore, these interpreters are not always available when needed. Currently the quantity and quality of interpreters remains inadequate. Sign language interpretation needs to be validated as a profession, and the State needs to establish an interpreter service system.

Certainly, research in German Sign Language is needed before sign language interpreters can reach the status and respect provided interpreters of different oral languages.

For a period of about fifteen years, research on the linguistics of German Sign Language has been in progress, mainly at the Hamburg center under its director, Siegmund Prillwitz. The results of completed studies of German Sign Language corroborate with the studies of sign languages of other countries.

With sufficient linguistic description of German Sign Language, it will be possible to develop a professional curriculum for the preparation of sign language interpreters and thus improve communication between deaf and hearing persons in Germany.

References

Bund Deutscher Taubstummenlehrer. (1987). *Statistische Nachrichten.* Heidelberg.

Bundesanstalt für Arbeit (Hrg.). (1985, 1996). *Orientierungsschrift zur Berufswahl für gehörlose und hochgradig schwerhörige Jugendliche.* Nürnberg.

Claubben, W.H. (1988) *Ergebnisse einer Umfrage zur Sprachentwicklung und zur Schulorganisation aus Schulen und vorschulischen Einrichtungen für Horgeschädigte im mitteleuropëischen Raum (ohne DDR). Hörgeschädigtenpädagogik 4.*

Deutscher Bildungsrat. (1974). *Gutachten und Studien der Bildungskommission. Sonderpädagogik 2.* Stuttgart: Gehörlose und Schwerhorige.

Deutsches Gehöriosen-Taschenbuch 1989/90. (1990). Essen.

Ebbinghaus, H., & Hebbmann, J. (1989). *Gehörlose, Gebärdensprache, Dolmetschen.* Chancen der integration einer sprachlichen Minderheit. Hamberg.

Graf, R. (1967). *Der Gehörlose und die Erwachsenenbildung.* München (Diss.).

Kommunikation mit Gehorlosen in Lautsprache und Gebärde. (Hrg.) (1982). *Bundesarbeitsgemeinschaft der Elternvertreter und Förderer Deutscher Gehörlosenschulen e.V.* ("Münchner Gebardenpapier"). München.

Maisch, G., & Wisch, F.H. (1987, 1988). *Gebärdenlexikon.* 2 Bände. Hamburg.

Prillwitz, S., Wisch, F.H., & Wudtke, H. (1991). *Zeig mit Deine Sprache.* Eiternbuch 1: Früherziehung gehörloser kinder in Lautsprache und Gebärden. Überarbeitete Auflage. Hamburg.

Prillwitz, S., & Wudtke, H. (1988). *Gebärden in der vorschulischen Erziehung gehörloser kinder.* Zehn Fallstudien zurkommunikativen Entwicklung gehörloser Kinder biszum Einschulungsalter. Hamburg.

Schulte, K., & Straubb, H.C. (1986). *Berufliche Fortbildung Hörgeschadigter, Ergebnisse eines Modellvorhabens.* (Hrg.) Der Bundesminister fur Arbeit und Sozialordnung. Heidelberg.

III. The Debate on German Sign Language and Perspectives for Interdisciplinary Research

by Gudula List

Even in Germany, where the oral method of teaching the deaf with its monolingual rationale has found particularly strong advocates in the past, bilingual concepts of educating the deaf will eventually prevail. Although many gains have been made in the education of the deaf, problems still remain. The deaf community's self-confidence as a language minority still needs to be consolidated. More precise knowledge about German Sign Language and the variants of signed German must be uncovered. Interdisciplinary research into the way German Sign Language is processed by the deaf is in its infancy. Sign language courses offered are geographically scattered and often not systematically developed. Sign language interpreting is far from being considered a professional area. German Sign Language interpreters require professional study and status. Finally, the curriculum used to prepare teachers of the deaf (now part of university programs but under the observation of the ministries of education) needs revision.

Revision of the curriculum of teacher preparation centers is threatening to some special education professors because the altered curriculum might bring to an end the continuation of oralism as the method of choice. Change in the academic curricula would also necessitate changes in the official regulations for state exams and certification requirements. Modification of the existing curricula is an extremely lengthy process, and the disputing parties are busy gathering their forces.

It is time for the deaf community to determine its own destiny and be involved in research and scientific discourse aimed at developing a more adequate education for deaf students in Germany.

The Current State of the Debate

The present scene of the education of the deaf can be described as a tripartite made up of a conservative wing that promotes oral education, a modernistic wing that promotes an accelerated form of pure oralism, and the wing that promotes the use of German Sign Language. Although these three groups disagree on many points, they all agree on the necessity of offering students who are deaf instruction in the use of the German language. Yet both the conservative and the modernistic group advocates of the oral method blame the group that promotes the use of sign language as being counterproductive by withholding the majority language, German, from children who are deaf and thus preventing their successful integration into the hearing and speaking society. Since the proponents of the oral movement have no proof of success in teaching German to the deaf, their accusations seem unwarranted.

Participants in the debate that support the oral philosophy include professionals in the academic discipline, university students, staff of the schools for the deaf, parents, audiologists, and hearing-aid technicians. Linguists, a growing number of social scientists, and of course the deaf themselves support the use of German Sign Language.

The majority of the professionals in special education, i.e., those who are responsible for teachers' training at the universities, belong to the conservative wing. Many of these individuals who have proven to be rather inflexible during the past decade or two have been replaced by individuals who support a more interactionally based concept of oral education. This new orientation coincides with a broader life span point of view that is not limited to the typical school years but includes early childhood education, parent counseling, and vocational education in later life (Jussen, 1985).

Research completed by this group of professionals does not focus upon methodology and the technology of teaching, but is predominantly empirical and looks at teacher competencies, forms of interaction, and achievement in school and later life. The results of these studies tend to be interpreted as the typical characteristics of the deaf. This tends to reinforce preconceptions of a profile that is seldom analyzed with respect to the conditions under which it evolved or by considering how different such a profile might look if oral language competencies were not regarded as the dominant factor involved in successful academic achievement or integration into society. This faction seems to think that persons who are deaf learn signs and integrate naturally into the deaf community without any problems. Furthermore, this group accepts the use of sign language outside of the school environment.

Many of the teachers at the schools for the deaf are on the side of the conservatives. However, after confronting often frustrating educational practices and student failure, a great many of the teachers are beginning to realize how much more productive the students' education could be if the natural language mode of the children, sign language, were taken into account. Although some teachers can use sign language, many lack proficiency. To complicate the situation further, the teachers are faced with insufficient opportunities to learn sign language. Yet in some schools for the deaf, some of the teachers are supportive of sign language and are ready to assist in the movement (Heidler, 1990).

The same holds true for the majority of students majoring in special education at the universities. Their curriculum is conservative. Sign courses are considered to be electives and not a required part of their studies. Most of the students feel the need to learn to sign, but have little opportunity to fulfill this need. The realization among students of the need to learn sign language may become the turning point in the development of education of the

deaf in Germany. It provides a signal that future teachers of the deaf will no longer face the situation of not being able to communicate with their students.

The modernistic wing of extreme oralism in Germany is made up of a coalition of a few professionals in special education, school teachers, and some specialists from audiology, clinical neurology, and hearing aid technology. Many parents of deaf children tend to be susceptible to the promise made by this coalition that their child will "hear" and "speak" if from an early age the child is submitted only to oral language. A whole team of medical and technical personnel, social workers, and pedagogical experts claims that they will be able to assist parents in eradicating the defect of deafness. This group states that the young deaf child can learn oral language if oralism "embraces the life of the child like an unmoveable clamp" (Diller, 1990, pp. 242, 256, trans.: G.L.). This group widely criticizes the use of sign language and states that nerve tissue in the temporal lobe will not develop if the child is subjected to signs and not stimulated orally within the very first years of life. Caretakers and teachers, even those who are known to favor oral education, are often accused of fostering deafness if the use of manual communication is not completely suppressed during the formative years.

Among the deaf community the modernistic wing finds little support. However, the deaf community is by no means unanimously on the side of the "sign language movement." Part of the deaf community (it is difficult to judge how many) belongs to the conservative wing. Obviously, the long years of paternalism of oral-oriented educators have left traces of doubt in their minds, and these doubts are reinforced by some of the leaders of the associations of the deaf. This is particularly true of those deaf persons who speak German quite well but are not fluent in the use of German Sign Language (*Deutsche Gebardensprache*: DDS).

Apparently, quite a few deaf persons do not agree with the concept that German Sign

Language is the natural language of the deaf. As long as the current system of educating the deaf withholds the means needed to build the concept of what "natural language" means, they will question the validity of German Sign Language as their natural language.

Statements about the different language systems used by the deaf often include the following:

- Spoken and written German is the true educational language
- Signed German (*Lautsprach-begleitendes Gebarden*: LBG) is "educated signing"
- Signed "language" is good for minor colloquial purposes among the deaf where "language" (*Gebarden sprache*) is put in quotation marks to make it clear that it is considered to be private, regional, unsystematic, and even "sage" (Muller, 1990).
- "German" Sign Language (where quotation marks are put around the nationality) is an artificial product constructed by linguists and scholars from outside the community.

Some call German Sign Language "HSG" to designate that it was developed in Hamburg and its *Zentrum fur Deutsche Gebardensprache und Kommunikation Gehorloser* and introduced to the deaf to create a situation that threatens to split the deaf community.

A large and growing part of the deaf community and their hearing friends support the sign language movement. Consciousness grows among the deaf community about the value of German Sign Language as the group's natural language, as a means of promoting self-confidence and a self-identity that does not focus upon the disability.

The sign language movement has received the support of academic researchers. In Germany, as in other countries, sign language study started with linguists interested in the structure and features of a manual language. Representatives of related academic disciplines have become engaged in research about sign languages. These researchers strive

to answer questions about the importance of sign language in the lives of deaf people, and the role of sign language in orally oriented societies.

It is important to note that, of the three factions discussed, currently the group that supports the sign language movement is receiving most of the support from the general public. The German public is indeed quite interested in this paradigmatic situation where the self-determination of a minority group is at stake. The Center in Hamburg must be given credit for the enormous amount of work they have done in promoting their cause. Particularly, the large congresses on German Sign Language that were organized in Hamburg received great publicity (Prillwitz, 1986; Prillwitz & Vollhaber, 1990, 1991).

Resolution of the debate among the three factions is far from being achieved. At present the most crucial controversy seems to be about the merits of German Sign Language (DGS) versus a coded German sign system (LBG). Instead of looking at qualities and merits, both sign systems are being sent to the battlefield as if they were competitors for the same goal and should battle until only one survives.

The modernistic wing places itself outside of this debate, since it is strictly against the use of any signing, except with deaf children who are not considered to be educable. This faction's position of disinterest in the debate exerts a strong influence. This group would support the use of coded German signs with multi-handicapped students. Again, the implication is that sign language is not for intelligent people.

The conservative wing, on the other hand, demonstrates its open-mindedness by endorsing the so-called *Munchner Gebardenpapier* (Braun et al., 1982), which claims the value of incorporating the use of coded German signs into the schools for the deaf. The main goal, or the development of spoken and written German language competency, is not questioned. This seemingly liberal attitude is proposed as a compromise and as a serious move towards meeting the needs of deaf people. However, it appears to be a half-hearted compromise since at least in the academic areas, it is felt by many that a signed oral language is not an alternative to the natural sign language, but is a totally different language system which may be useful in some instructional contexts, especially for those deaf students who have a good command of oral language. Clearly, the modernistic faction, while accepting a certain degree of manualism, is still focused upon the goal of developing oral and written German. This group feels that German Sign Language should be used only with those who cannot make productive use of its oral form.

The Importance of Interdisciplinary Research for Future Development

It would of course be naive to believe that theoretical linguistics, including research on language development and the use of German Sign Language, would be enough to settle these disagreements. The various arguments of each faction are too loaded with emotion and, in this complicated, historically conditioned situation, the situation calls for a thorough and interdisciplinary analysis of the whole sociocultural and sociohistorical context of the language development of the deaf.

The call for studying the whole spectrum of interdisciplinary approaches does not lessen the need for continued linguistic research on German Sign Language of the kind that has been ongoing in Germany during the past 20 years and emulated almost exclusively by Siegmund Prillwitz and the influential *Zentrum fur Deutsche Gebardensprache und Kommunikation Gehorloser* in Hamburg. Definitely, the registration and description of sign vocabulary and grammar continues to be an indispensable basis for projects, and of paramount importance to the deaf community to satisfy its linguistic conscience and concern for data on sign language.

Work at the center in Hamburg started by first becoming involved in the educational–political debate. Following the examples of North America and some of the more advanced European countries, efforts were undertaken to prove that the prejudices about sign language were wrong. The first educational programs to include signs were developed and implemented for families, early education programs, and local schools for the deaf (Prillwitz & Wudtke, 1989).

Since the mid-1980s the center has focused on the systematic registration of German Sign Language. Apart from the continued compilation of a sign dictionary and the initial stages of a descriptive sign grammar, major emphasis is currently aimed at the development of new technology for use in pursuing sign language research (Prillwitz et al., 1987; Schulmeister, 1990).

The center is also taking the lead in the development of practical sign language courses and the promotion of the use of interpreters. The development of an interpreter training program has led to fruitful cooperation between the Hamburg project group and the group at the Free University of Berlin (Ebbinghaus & Hebbmann, 1990). Deaf staff members at the center are engaged in plans for a video survey of signs used among persons who are deaf in the different regions of Germany. The result of the video survey of sign language will be transferred to a computer-based written form and submitted for structural analysis.

These activities should keep the center busy well into the next millennium. Meanwhile, an important part of the center's work concerns informing the broader public. The center's quarterly journal *Das Zeichen*, which acts as a forum for deaf and hearing readers, has met with active response. The publishing house of the center edits a series of books and videos, and also satisfies an urgent need for translations of important publications from other countries. Some of the works that have been translated include *Deaf Culture* by Padden and Humphries, *What the Hands*

Reveal about the Brain by Poizner, Klima, and Bellugi, and *Unlocking the Curriculum* by Johnson, Liddell, and Erting.

Scientific researchers from other disciplines of the social sciences have joined in the search for answers. In 1990, a working group of scholars—many from the University of Cologne, from the fields of anthropology, ethnology, philosophy, psychology of language, linguistics, sociology, and the history of education—was organized in North Rhine-Westfalia. The group has formed a documentation center. The mission of the working group is to stimulate and bring together the research potential of all German-speaking countries. Included are representatives from Hamburg, Berlin, Frankfurt, and Basel, where work is already under way. The German National Science Foundation is a source of support for these cooperative research projects. Most of these projects will involve deaf participants, both as native speakers and as co-workers who will have the chance to qualify themselves in academic contexts.

It will not be possible until the publication of the next edition of this book to be in a position to report on the possible outcomes of such endeavors. But a start has been made, and at least one project financed by the National Science Foundation is under way. The basic hypothesis of the project stems from the truism that primary language competency is a prerequisite for the establishment of the internal mechanisms needed for second language learning (List, 1989, 1990). The project aims at the study of the recoding processes underlying signing as primary language. The end goal is to develop the means necessary for facilitating cognitive and written language processes and production. Although ultimately aimed at instructional application, this is a first attempt at basic research on the psychological aspects of signing and hence should contribute to the ongoing debate on language universals and the status of sign language in Germany.

References

Braun, A., Donath, P., Gast, R., Keller, A., Rammel, G., & Tigges, J. (1982). *Kommunikation in Lautsprache und Gebärde (Münchner Gebärdenpapier) Hrg.* BAG Elternvertreter und Forderer Deutscher Gehörlosenschulen. München.

Diller, G. (1990). Des Frühforderkonzept an der Johannes—Vatter—Schule fur Gehörlose Friedberg/Hessen. Frühförderung gehörloser kinder nach den Grundsätzen muttersprachlich reflektierter Hörerziehung. Historische Entwicklung, theoretische Grundlagen und didaktisch-methodische Grundsätze. In Kröhnert, O., *Stiftung zur Förderung körperbehinderter Hochbegabter Vaduz (Hg.): Aufgaben und Probleme der Frühforderung gehörloser Kinder unter dem Aspekt der Begabungsentfaltung* (pp. 227-257). Bericht über das Internationale Symposion vom 10. bis 13. November in Hohenems, Österreich. Vaduz.

Ebbinghaus, H. (1988, 1989). Welche Schule für gehörlose Kinder? *Das Zeichen 6*, 98-108, 7, 58-64.

Ebbinghaus, H., & Hebbmann, J. (1990). *Gehörlose, Gebärdensprache, Dolmetschen.* Chancen der Integrationeiner sprachlichen Minderheit. Hamburg.

Heidler, H. (1990). *Gebärdensprache und Lautsprache.* Vortrag auf der 29. Bundestagung des Bundes Deutscher Taubstummenlehrer. Unpublished manuscript.

Jussen, H., et al. (1985). *Interaktionsmuster im Gehörlosenunterricht.* Opladen.

List, G. (1989). *Duality of patterning in signed and spoken language: A psychological perspective* (pp. 323-328). Sign Language Studies No. 65.

List, G. (1990). Schrift und Sprachbewubbtheit. Psychologische Reflexionen zum Leseniernen Gehörloser. In List, Gudula, & List, Gunther (Hg.), *Gebärde, Laut und graphisches Zeichen.* Schrifterwerb im Problemfeld von Mehrsprachigkeit (pp. 37-57). Wiesbaden.

Muller, W. (1990). Bedenken gegen einen Umgang nur mit Gebärdensprache (DGS). *Das Zeichen 13*, 283-285.

Prillwitz, S. (HG.). (1986). *Die Gebärde in Erziehung und Bildung Gehörloser.* Tagungsbericht zum Internationalen Kongrebb, November 1985. Hamburg.

Prillwitz, S., & Vollhaber, T. (Hg.) (1990). *Current trends in European sign language research. Proceedings of the 3rd European Congress on Sign Language Research, Hamburg July 26-29, 1989.* Hamburg.

Prillwitz, S., & Vollhaber, T. (Hg.) (1991). *Sign language research and application. Proceedings of the International Congress, Hamburg 1990.* Hamburg.

Prillwitz, S., & Wundtke, H. (1989). *Gebärden in der vorschulischen Erziehung gehörloser kinder.* 10 Fallstudienzurkommunikativ-sprachlichen Entwicklung gehorloser Kinder bis zum Einschulungsalter. Hamburg.

Prillwitz, S., et al. (1987). *Hamburg notation system for sign language: An introduction.* Hamburg.

Schulmeister, R. (1990). A computer dictionary with animated signs for the special field of computer technology. In Prillwitz, S., & Vollhaber, T., *Current trends in European sign language research. Proceedings of the 3rd European Congress on Sign Language Research, Hamburg. July 26-29, 1989* (pp. 381-189). Hamburg.

Historical Development of Education of the Deaf in Ghana

byAlexander D. Okyere and Mary J. Addo

Ghana National Association of the Deaf
Accra

Dedicated to

Dr. Andrew J. Foster, a great man, missionary, and educator of the deaf

All the pioneers who helped to improve deaf education in Ghana

Gallaudet University, Washington, D.C., the pioneer institution of higher education for the deaf in the world

All those who are helping to improve the education of the deaf worldwide.

About the Writers

Mary Joycelyn Addo (Miss) is a qualified teacher of the deaf. After completing her secondary education, Mary first came in contact with the deaf in 1971 when she began teaching at the Accra School for the Deaf. The Director of Special Education terminated Mary's appointment on the grounds that she was not a trained teacher or specialist.

Mary continued teaching in a hearing school. Between 1974 and 1976 she returned to school and obtained her post-secondary Teachers Certificate "A." She then returned to her former school to teach the deaf. Later, she obtained her diploma in home science education from the Winneba Specialist Training College, and then returned once more to the Accra School for the Deaf. In 1983 Miss Addo finally entered the College of Special Education, where she obtained a specialist certificate as a teacher of the deaf. She chaired the Home Science Department of the Secondary/Technical School for the Deaf at Mampong, Akwapim, until 1992 when she left for further coursework at the Winneba University College of Education, graduating with a Bachelor of Education in Home Economics and Mathematics.

Mary is one of the few pioneer interpreters for the deaf in Ghana. Having traveled widely with the deaf to most West African countries and Europe, Mary is featured regularly on Ghana National Television as the news interpreter for the deaf on the *Missing Link Programme.*

Alexander Daniel Okyere became deaf at the age of 26, when he was in his final year of training at the teacher training college at Bekwai-A Shanti. Alex appealed to the Ministry of Education for a job different from teaching, since he could not hear his hearing students when they talked. The Ministry posted Alex to the first school for the deaf at Mampong-Akwapim.

Alex taught the deaf in Ghana for fourteen years before entering Gallaudet University, where he obtained his B.A. in Economics. In 1983 he obtained his M.Ed. from Western Maryland College, Westminster, Maryland. Alex then returned to Ghana to offer his services to his deaf brothers and sisters. He now heads the Economics Department of the Secondary-Technical School for the Deaf, at Mampong. He also serves as the Vice President of the Ghana National Association of the Deaf and the First Vice President of the Ghana Federation of the Disabled.

Alex and Mary co-authored the paper entitled *Deaf Culture in Ghana.* They presented the paper during the Deaf Way Conference held at Gallaudet University in July, 1989.

A Tribute to Dr. Andrew Foster

In 1987, as a tribute to the life of Dr. Andrew Foster and to celebrate the thirtieth anniversary of the education of the deaf in Ghana, the authors of this chapter decided to write a book entitled *The Historical Development of Education of the Deaf in Ghana*. After conceiving the idea, the authors made a desperate effort to contact all the people who had helped Foster establish his school for the deaf in Ghana. These individuals included Reverend Konotey-Ahulu, Reverend H. D. Cobblah, Foster himself, and other educators of the deaf in Ghana. At that time Foster was in the United States.

One of the pioneers in the education of the deaf in Ghana, Reverend Konotey-Ahulu, had died. Other pioneers in the field who knew of the development of the education of the deaf in Ghana were contacted. Fortunately, Dr. Foster himself came to Ghana in September 1987, with the intention of conducting an interview on radio and television to mark the thirtieth anniversary of the establishment of the education of the deaf in Ghana. Foster's arrival was a "Great Coming." The authors were able to interview Foster about the founding of the first school for the deaf in the country.

It was a great shock when Dr. Foster died in December 1987 in an airplane crash, just a few months after that interview and his appearance on Ghanaian radio and television. He had been on his way to visit schools and Christian assemblies for the deaf that he had established in other African countries. His death left a deep sadness among the deaf of Ghana, and all that could be said was, "Foster, may your soul rest in peace. You are a great man."

Mary Joycelyn Addo and
Alexander Daniel Okyere

Introduction

History is a base upon which one evaluates performances of the past and actions of the present and the future. History that remains unwritten is more easily forgotten or adulterated.

Since no book that deals with the historical development of education of the deaf in Ghana has been developed, it seemed appropriate to create such a document to help both present and future generations, and especially those dealing with the deaf, understand the historical antecedents that established the education of the deaf in Ghana. The death of two key figures in the development of the education of the deaf, Reverend D. A. Konotey-Ahulu and Dr. Foster, have made the task timely and of greater importance.

The deaf, as a minority, are influenced from all angles by the majority hearing society. This fact makes it appropriate to write briefly about the geography and the educational system of Ghana.

Many people, too numerous to mention, helped make this work a reality. Yet, special gratitude and appreciation must be expressed to: Mr. S.A.K. Fiaxe, former headmaster of the School for the Deaf at Mampong-Akwapim and now an audiologist at the 37 Military Hospital in Accra; Rev. H.D. Cobblah; Godwin Amenumey, the president of the Ghana National Association of the Deaf; Samuel N. Adjei; Master Isaac Okyere; E.K. Antwi; Marion N. Obeng; Christiana Addo-Brown; Thomas K. Ansah; A.M. Oppong; Joseph Essel; the following headmasters of schools for the deaf: F.E. Ansah, E.A. Asamoah, S.A. Opoku; the Special Education Division of the Ghana Education Service; The College of Special Education; and Dr. H.W. Brelje, Director of Special Education: Hearing Impaired at Lewis & Clark College in Portland, Oregon, whose invitation to us to contribute a chapter to his book on deaf education gave us the final impetus. Our thanks also go to Mr. J. O. Appiah, who kindly accepted our invitation to write the Foreword, and to Dora Teteh, who helped with the typing.

Historical Development of the Education of the Deaf in Ghana

Geographical Background of Ghana

Ghana, which was the first African country south of the Sahara to gain independence, lies along the Gulf of Guinea on the West Coast of Africa. Ghana stretches between latitude 4.5° N at Cape Three Points on its southern border, and latitude 11° N at Bawku in the north. The Greenwich Meridian passes through Ghana's southeastern port city of Tema. The distance between the northernmost and southernmost points of the country is 672 kilometers, and between the eastern- and westernmost points is 536 kilometers. Ghana covers a total area of 239,460 square kilometers.

Ghana experiences a tropical climate with the highest temperature occurring between February and April. The southern part of the country has two wet seasons which occur between March and July and between September and October, while the north has only one wet season occurring between April or May and October. The country is well known for its minerals, with gold being the chief, and by which the country had its pre-independence name of the Gold Coast. It is also famous for its cocoa production.

Ghana Fact Sheets (1988) recorded that the 1984 population census showed that the country had a total population of 12,296,081 with a growth rate of 2.3 percent. There are over 40 languages and dialects spoken in Ghana, but English is the national language. The Ministry of Education encourages schools, especially those dealing with younger children, to make use of these local languages and dialects as much as possible.

Education in Ghana

In Ghana, almost every village is within walking distance of a school. Compulsory, fee-free first cycle (primary or elementary) education was introduced in Ghana in September 1961, while second cycle (secondary and technical) education became fee-free four years later in September 1965.

The central government provides the salaries and allowances of teachers and educational administrators, and the stationery and textbooks at the first cycle level. At the second cycle level, the government also is responsible for the provision and maintenance of school buildings and equipment. Tuition is free from the first cycle to the tertiary cycle, or the University. However, second cycle students are responsible for the purchase of their own stationery and textbooks.

Educational statistics released in the Ghana Fact Sheets (1988, p. 11) revealed that by 1985 there were 234 second cycle institutions with an enrollment of 130,454 students. The same source recorded that the 22 technical or vocational institutions had a student population of 24,500. The 39 teacher-training colleges in the country that provide initial teacher preparation were said to have an enrollment of 41,921 students. Additionally, there were six polytechnical institutes, two technical teachers' training colleges, twenty technical institutions, and six teacher-training, diploma-awarding institutions in the country.

There are three universities in the southern sector of Ghana. In 1985 these three universities had a total student population of 8,847 (Ghana Fact Sheets, 1988, pp. 11-12). Table 1 shows the breakdown of student enrollment in Ghana.

Table 1. Number and Enrollment in Educational Institutions in Ghana, 1986

Type of Institution	Number in the Country	Total Annual Enrollment
First Cycle Institutions		
Second Cycle Institutions	234	130,454
Technical/Vocational Inst.	22	24,500
Technical Institutions	20	
Polytechnics	6	
Teacher Training Colleges	39	41,921
Technical Teacher's Training	2	
Specialist Diploma-Awarding Institutions	6	3,000
University	3	8,847
Total	332	208,722

Table 2. Number of Special Educational Institutions in Ghana, 1990

Type of Institution	Number in the Country
Schools for the blind, first cycle	1
Integrated schools for the blind, second cycle	3
Schools for the deaf: First cycle	9
Unit schools	2
Second cycle	1
Schools for the mentally retarded	6
Rehabilitation centers	11
Total	33

Special Institutions

The special education institutions in the country include twelve schools for the deaf, three schools for the blind, and five schools for the mentally retarded. Table 2 provides a breakdown of the special institutions in Ghana. Two of the institutions for the mentally retarded are privately owned. Physically disabled persons who do not have additional disabilities are integrated with able-bodied persons at all educational levels. The school for the deaf at Mampong in the Eastern Region runs a special department for deaf-blind children. At the second cycle level the blind are integrated with the sighted in schools at Wenchi (BA), Wa (UWR), and at Okuapeman in the Eastern Region.

In addition, there are eleven rehabilitation centers. Eight of the rehabilitation centers are run by the government, and the remaining three are run by private organizations. These rehabilitation centers are responsible for the care and vocational training of all handicapped youth and adults.

The Present Trend in Public Education

Ghana began restructuring its educational system in 1987. This restructuring had started earlier on an experimental basis. The new structure intends to reduce from seventeen years to twelve years the number of post-nursery years students are required to attend school before they are ready to enter the university. The old system included six years of primary education, four years of middle school education, five years of secondary education at the GCE O'Level, and two years of sixth form education to prepare students for the university. In the new system, the child leaves the nursery school at the age of six, and spends six years in primary school. After the completion of primary school, the child completes three years in the junior secondary school (JSS). Those who pass out successfully from the JSS spend another three years in the senior secondary school (SSS). Those who successfully complete the senior secondary school enter the university. Based on past academic performances, teachers of the deaf have proposed that deaf children spend an extra year in both the JSS and SSS for the deaf.

The curriculum for the new structure is designed to include academic, pre-technical, and pre-vocational subjects. These subjects include mathematics, English, vernacular, home science, marine engineering, agriculture, and others.

Survey of Literature

No previous book on the historical development of the education of the deaf in Ghana has been written. Some information on the education of the deaf in Ghana has been developed by several individuals, either as a work project (Fiaxe, 1964) or for a seminar presentation (Foster, 1965; Aryee, 1972).

The object of these papers was not to present the history of the education of the deaf, but to focus on the achievement of the deaf, problems in educating the deaf (Aryee), and plans and proposals for the future of the education of the deaf (Markides, 1972). Although the authors did not thoroughly investigate the historical development of the education of the deaf, some of the facts mentioned in their writings or speeches are relevant. Following are some of the appropriate comments from these papers.

"Ghana is at present trying to do its best in the education and rehabilitation of the country's hearing impaired," declared D.T.K. Aryee in his address to the participants at a Commonwealth Conference in Accra in 1972. In the same speech, he mentioned that only "22% or 485 out of a total of 2,000 school-aged hearing impaired children were being educated in the eight schools for the deaf in 1972."

Earlier, Fiaxe (1964, p. 4) stated in a speech: "The purpose of the Christian Mission for Deaf Africans was to reach these deaf Africans with the Gospel." He explained further that "these people were doubly handicapped by deafness and illiteracy." He then called for the need to educate the deaf.

Foster also declared in 1965 (eight years after founding the first school for the deaf in Ghana), at a seminar at Ibadan University, that "there was no statistical basis to determine even approximately the number of deaf inhabitants in Ghana. Along with the lack of statistics relating to the prevalence of deafness in Africa, there is also an absence of information about the causes of deafness" (1965, p. 7).

Fiaxe also cites a report by two British officials, Dr. P. Henderson, Principal Medical Officer, and Mr. R. Howlett, Under-secretary of the British Ministry of Education, who arrived in Ghana on May 16, 1962, as part of the United Kingdom Ghana Mutual Technical Cooperation Scheme. Among their recommendations to the Ghana Minister of Education were suggestions that future schools for the handicapped be sited near already established secondary or technical institutions, and that all modern and commonly recognized methods of educating the handicapped in Britain and the United States of America be employed in the schools for the deaf in Ghana (1964, p. 7).

According to Fiaxe, these British officials stressed the need to train teachers for the schools for the deaf in Ghana at Manchester University in Great Britain, Gallaudet University in the United States, and locally. It was their recommendation that the site of the institution for training teachers of the handicapped be changed from the city of Minneba to Mampong Akwapim.

With regard to the incidence of deafness in Ghana, Dr. J. B. David, E.N.T. Consultant at the Korle Bu Teaching Hospital in Accra, stated that by 1964 all but four individuals that he had examined had sensory-neural deafness with positive Rinne's (1972). His survey indicated that there were a total of

2,469 deaf persons in Ghana. Another medical officer, Dr. Christopher Holborow, T.D.M.D.; FRCS, E.N.T. consultant at Westminster Hospital, London, stated at the 1972 Commonwealth Society for the Deaf Conference in Accra that, "on the whole the incidence numbers and main causes of deafness in Ghana are remarkably similar to those in countries in all parts of the world" (1972, p. 54). Like Foster, Dr. Holborow admitted to the difficulty involved in estimating the proportion of deaf people to the total population. By 1972, when Ghana's population was 8.5 million, Dr. Holborow estimated that there were 8,500 deaf people among the population.

Before Dr. David arrived in Ghana in 1954, there were no E.N.T. specialists in the country. Soon after his arrival, he was asked to survey the number of deaf people in the country. With the aid of social welfare personnel, he found less than 20 deaf children and adults. Because of the small number of deaf people uncovered by the survey, the Ministry of Health was advised that a school for the deaf was not an immediate need (1972, p. 62).

Another survey was conducted by an army commander, Lieutenant General Sir Alexander Drummond, in 1961. Lieutenant General Drummond used a mobile van to tour the whole country. His survey lasted two weeks. This survey reported that there were 1,200 deaf adults and children in Ghana. It was during that survey that 45 deaf individuals were found among the 400 inhabitants of a village called Adamorobe, which lies some 35 kilometers away from the capital of Ghana, Accra. The incidence of deafness in the village was very high and as a result Adamorobe was referred to as the "Deaf Village."

Despite several surveys conducted after 1954, Dr. Andrew Foster found that when he arrived in Ghana in 1957 there was no school for the deaf in Ghana nor any visible official interest in a school. According to Dr. Foster, a list of deaf children whose anxious parents had sought admission into a school for the blind was the only information available about the incidence of deafness (Foster, 1965).

The list contained the names of 23 deaf adults and children. Yet this did not dissuade Foster. For in 1965, he was relieved to find that a national scheme for the rehabilitation of the handicapped had registered 3,000 deaf people. Eight hundred of the 3000 were school-aged. Although past surveys of the deaf population in Ghana seemed to indicate a low incidence of deafness, by the time Foster left Ghana in 1965 the student enrollment at the school he had established had risen from 13 to 130, with 350 deaf pupils on a waiting list.

At the time this chapter was written, the problem of finding a reliable means by which to estimate the proportion of deaf persons in the population of Ghana still exists. It is some consolation that currently at least one school for the deaf can now be found in each of nine out of the ten regions of the country. Markides, a former principal of the Deaf Education Specialist Training College at Mampong-Akwapim, stated in his address to the Commonwealth Society for the Deaf Seminar in Accra (1972, p. 23), "One must not forget that there are thousands of persons in this country who are fully aware of the needs of deaf children and I am sure that this number is constantly increasing." He further stated that "it is mainly through the efforts of such enlightened people that this country can now boast of eight schools for the deaf." Since then, the number of schools for the deaf in the country has risen to twelve.

From all available information, both written and unwritten, there was no attempt to provide the deaf with any formal education or to develop reliable statistics on the incidence of deafness in Ghana, before Dr. Foster arrived in Ghana. Fiaxe (1964, p.1) stated that "before independence, the British Government did not leave any record of the number of handicapped persons in Ghana, although there were schools for handicapped people in Britain itself." However, before Dr. Foster came to Ghana, Ludwig Ahwere Bafo, a Ghanaian educator, had sent out a questionnaire with the purpose of identifying the number of deaf children in Ghana in need of an education. These questionnaires were misdirected to the School for the Blind so the needed census information was not available.

Dr. Foster's Mission and the First School for the Deaf in Ghana

On September 25, 1987, Reverend Dr. Andrew Foster returned to Ghana as part of his tour of the 22 African countries where he had established Christian Assemblies for the Deaf. The authors of this text were privileged to interview Dr. Foster the night before he was interviewed on Ghana National Radio and Television to mark the thirtieth anniversary of the founding of the first school for the deaf in the country.

Dr. Foster was asked why he chose Ghana for the establishment of the first school for the deaf in Africa. Dr. Foster replied that he had chosen Ghana because Ghana, along with Liberia and Nigeria, was a peaceful country where English was spoken, whereas most of Africa was in the birth throes of independence from colonialism (Addo & Okyere, personal communication, September, 1987). The achievement of independence in Ghana in 1957, therefore, was the major event that enabled Dr. Foster, missionary, to start his work in this country.

Fiaxe (1964, p. 1) stated, "The achievement of independence brought thrilling tales to this country — Ghana. Many schools for hearing children were established all over the country. Education became free, thus enabling even the poorest families to send their children to school." Perhaps this desire to educate every child including the handicapped was the reason why Dr. Foster said that some parents were anxiously seeking to admit their deaf children to a school for the blind.

Dr. Foster introduced himself as a young Afro-American missionary and educator of the deaf. He was a native of Birmingham, Alabama, in the United States of America. He became totally deaf from spinal meningitis at the age of eleven. He was the first black deaf person to graduate from Gallaudet University in Washington, D.C., and from Eastern Michigan University. During Foster's college days, he inquired about the status of deaf people in Africa and the opportunities to educate the deaf of Africa and to do missionary work among them. As a result of a lack of information about African deaf, in 1956 he founded and directed the United States Christian Mission for Deaf Africans (CMDA).

Through a speaking tour around America, Foster was able to raise enough money to be able to set off for West Africa in May 1957. Upon arrival in Ghana to start his project, Foster was encouraged by many Ghanaians. Among those who supported him, he recalled Henry Dashinor Cobblah, a Baptist pastor; Reverend D. A. Konotey-Ahulu, a Presbyterian minister; Mrs. Semanyo, director of Ghana Society for the Blind; Mr. Amoah, principal of the Akropong School for the Blind; Mr. J. Riby-Williams of the Department of Social Welfare; as well as some cabinet ministers including Mr. Kojo Botsio, Mr. K. A. Gbedemah, and Mr. C. T. Nylander (Addo & Okyere, personal communication, September, 1987).

Fiaxe (1964, p. 4) writes that with the help of Pastor Henry Dashinor Cobblah, who served as his interpreter, Andrew Foster toured the whole country, talked with the people of Ghana about his mission, and registered deaf children. Foster borrowed a classroom at the Osu Presbyterian Middle School for Boys, and after the school had ended its normal classes at 4:00 p.m., Foster educated deaf children. Dr. Foster's first school for the deaf was christened the Ghana Mission School for the Deaf. It was a day school and had an initial enrollment of thirteen deaf children and eleven deaf adults. Classes for the deaf children and deaf adults were held at different times.

Foster's school had a Board of Governors which included representatives of the Ministry of Education, the Presbyterian Church, the Methodist Church, a traditional ruler, a parent, and an older student. As headmaster of the school, Foster served as the secretary to the board. Foster recalled that Pastor H.D. Cobblah, Reverend Konotey-Ahulu, and Reverend Obeng of Aburi Akwapim were among the first board members. Reverend Obeng became the first chairman of the board and Seth Tetteh-Ocloo represented older students.

Foster stated that the enrollment of the school quickly increased by 50 percent, and the list of deaf children from distant towns and villages who attended the school soared to over fifty (Addo & Okyere, personal communication, September, 1987). This increase in school enrollment was made possible through radio announcements, newspaper advertisements, and articles. One of those deaf students from a distant town was the aforementioned Seth Tetteh-Ocloo. He, like Foster, became deaf at the age of seventeen years from spinal meningitis. Mr. Ocloo was later appointed as a teacher at the school (the first Ghanaian deaf teacher of the deaf). When applications for admission continued to pour in from different parts of the country, boarding facilities became a necessity. Searching around, Foster found an uncompleted house at Mampong on the cool Akwapim ridge. After renting and renovating the house, he moved the children's school there in January, 1959. The school for deaf adults and the church for the deaf remained at Osu.

The school for the adults, the church at Osu, and the school at Mampong were all under the management of Foster. Fiaxe, quoting from the Founder's Newsletter, explained that Foster was happy with the change in the location of the children's school because the move allowed for the accommodation of more deaf children from the countryside, the inclusion of vocational training, and the addition of a functional programme in speech and lipreading (1964, p. 5). When the enrollment at the Mampong school increased to about 100, and several hundred more were on a waiting list, Foster obtained a large site between Mampong and Tutu for a permanent school. In 1962, when the government decided to take over the growing project, Dr. Foster was made the school's first headmaster.

Meanwhile, the development of the Osu project (adults' classes) also continued. In 1965, a large house was rented as a Christian center for the deaf. The classes for deaf adults and the Church moved into this center. Some vocational courses were started for the older deaf youths and deaf adults. Later, deaf children in Accra were admitted to the center as day students. This school later developed into the present State School for the Deaf at Teshie.

The Church for the Deaf is still at Osu Presbyterian Middle School for Boys (where Foster started his first school) but the school for the adult deaf no longer exists.

Staffing the Ghana Mission School for the Deaf

Dr. Foster recalled some of the early teachers of the deaf, including Miss Florence Oteng, who was deaf; another victim of spinal meningitis, Miss Grace Tetteh (Mrs. Grace Amoah); and Mr. George Okae-Tetteh, who later established a school for the deaf at Bechem. Fiaxe added that persons with the Ghana Teachers' Certificate "A" were employed by the Ministry of Education to teach in the school for the deaf. Also, the Commonwealth Society for the Deaf offered scholarships annually to individuals who would train at the University of Manchester to be teachers of the deaf. After the successful completion of the University course, the teachers were awarded the University Certificate as a teacher of the deaf. Gallaudet University in Washington, D.C. also provided financial assistance that covered tuition, room, and board for a prospective teacher. In addition, the Danish Embassy in Ghana also gave notice of its intention to award a scholarship to train a Ghanaian teacher of the deaf in Denmark.

Investigation revealed that the late David Tettey Kwashie Aryee, former principal of the College of Special Education (Mampong-Akwapim), was the first of the pioneers who enjoyed the Commonwealth Society Scholarship Award to Manchester

University. Pastor H. D. Cobblah followed. Most of the teachers who went to Manchester were trained in audiology. The pioneer recipients of the Gallaudet University award included Dr. Seth Tetteh-Ocloo and Mr. Samuel Agorgli Kwaku Fiaxe. Mr. George Okae-Tetteh and Miss Vincential Diaba were among the first to enjoy the Danish Embassy award.

Curriculum of the Ghana Mission School for the Deaf

Education must be of use to the child and to society. The child must develop physically, mentally, spiritually, emotionally, and socially. In addition, the child must be equipped with skills that will enable him to earn a living after his education is complete. A curriculum that is planned with these goals in mind is likely to be successful.

The curriculum of the first school for the deaf in Ghana was geared mainly towards providing religious instruction (Aryee, 1972; Fiaxe, 1964). As a missionary, Dr. Foster's main focus when he came to Ghana was to "evangelize" the deaf (Aryee, 1972, p. 5).

However, Foster considered himself an educator as well as a missionary. Hence, he encouraged the students to learn other subjects in addition to religion. Fiaxe, who succeeded Foster as the second headmaster of the school, wrote that the syllabus designed for schools for the hearing children of the country was also used in the schools for the deaf. The subjects taught in the schools for the deaf included Bible knowledge, English language, reading, arithmetic, social studies, speech, writing, art, story-telling, and the vernacular languages (Ewe, Twi, Ga). The older boys and girls were provided with vocational training in the afternoon. The vocational subjects included carpentry, tailoring, dress-making, embroidery, and knitting. For recreational and athletic activities, the children played soccer, volleyball, basketball, table tennis, and practiced boxing (Fiaxe, 1972, pp. 6-7). Fiaxe

further stated that the children took part in track events. Through the completion of house duties, the children learned how to accomplish the chores of everyday life. These chores included cleaning their rooms, washing dishes, and mowing the lawns around the school.

During the 1966-1967 academic year, the first batch of students from the Ghana Mission School for the Deaf sat for the Middle School Leaving Certificate Examination. The examination was conducted by the West African Examinations Council. The deaf students completed the examination with the normally hearing pupils. Two out of the nine deaf candidates who completed the examination were successful.

Many factors may have contributed to the poor performance of the deaf students. Markides stated that one of the main factors was that many of the teachers in Foster's school were not qualified to teach the deaf. Some of the teachers who were qualified and who had trained locally and outside of Ghana had difficulty imparting knowledge to the deaf students (Markides, 1972). Another factor that might have accounted for the poor academic showing of the deaf students would be the number of years that the deaf children spent in school. In addition to the nursery school, the hearing child spends ten years in school. Foster's records indicated that there was no nursery program for the deaf students and that they spent nine years instead of ten in school. Six or seven of the deaf students who took the National examination the second year, the 1967–1968 academic year, passed.

Methods of Communication at the Ghana Mission School for the Deaf

During the 1965 Ibadan Conference, as Dr. Foster concluded his address to the participants on the topic "A General View of the Educational Status of the Deaf in Africa," he stated, "Finally, in all sincerity, I suggest that we allow no 'war of methods' from overseas to handicap our children further nor to divert our energy from facing Africa's own realities. We must fully utilize every known method of instruction and every means available" (Foster, 1965, p. 9).

Dr. Foster was well aware that the controversy over the proper way to educate deaf children was restricting deaf children's development overseas. He was also aware of the fact that the choice of the proper language to use as medium of instruction in the schools for the deaf was made even more difficult by the multiple languages used in Ghana. Foster was very careful not to insist on the use of any one particular method of communicating with the deaf at the Ghana Mission School for the Deaf. As Fiaxe had indicated previously, the syllabi of schools for hearing children was followed in the schools for the deaf, and the vernacular languages Ewe, Twi, and Ga were taught at the school. Interestingly, these languages could only be taught through the use of speech since Foster did not know the languages. One of the advantages Foster foresaw in moving the children's school for the deaf from Osu to Mampong was the ability to provide speech training to the deaf children at the new site. This proved that Foster, even though he was deaf, encouraged oralism.

In addition, when Foster was asked in 1987 whether he had any advice for the further improvement of the lot of the deaf in Ghana, he first recommended that all communication restrictions be removed: "A Total Communication philosophy that encourages the use of all methods and means should be utilized at all levels in all schools" (Addo & Okyere, personal communication, 1987). That was 30 years after he founded his first school in Ghana. Markides, a former principal of the Deaf Education Specialist Teacher Training College at Mampong, touching on the communication issue, wrote ". . . Ghana is facing a plethora of methods including the Rochester Method, the Combined Method, the Simultaneous Method, the Danish

Method, the Manual Method, and even recently Total Communication. We are truly international" (Markides, 1972, p. 24).

It is therefore obvious that the deaf children at the Ghana Mission School for the Deaf were not restricted to one method of communication.

Financing the Ghana Mission School for the Deaf

Addressing the participants at the Conference on the Education of the Deaf in Africa at Ibadan University in 1965, Foster said, "In many contemporary African countries, the goal is to provide a universal compulsory primary education. To what extent, if any, the deaf are included in that universality remains to be known" (1965, p. 8). As of the middle of the twentieth century the people in power in Africa have not included the deaf in their educational policies or planning. It was therefore necessary for Foster's school in Ghana to find other sources of financial support. Foster stated that at first his Mission had no funds with which to build a new school or to rent a big house.

Fiaxe (1964, p. 5) quoted the following from the Founder's Newsletter of December, 1959:

Christian Mission for Deaf Africans (CMDA) was born in the vision of a great need and continues under the Lord's enabling power. He has never failed us. While this work is not endowed or denominationally affiliated, the Lord has faithfully provided needed financial contributions from churches, classes, and individuals, as well as from grants from interested missions, charities and government agencies.

The same report (Fiaxe, 1964) added that the pupils of the Ghana Mission School for the Deaf paid a fee of $8.40 per month to cover their boarding expenses. Fiaxe and Foster stated that the National Trust Fund of

Ghana recognized the Christian Mission for Deaf Africans as a charitable organization and provided it with financial aid in the amount of $7,000.

In May 1960 the CMDA became affiliated with the Ghana Presbyterian Church. The affiliation became necessary because from 1952, new Missions ceased to be recognized as an Educational Unit by the Government (Fiaxe, 1964, p. 5). As a result of this action, the Ministry of Education of Ghana provided the CMDA with a grant of $9,206. After those grants were received the fee of $8.40 per month was abolished. Parents had to provide their deaf children with school uniforms. Salaries and wages were paid by the Ghana government after the State took over complete control of the school in 1961.

Present Trend in Education of the Deaf in Ghana

Number of Schools

At the moment, Ghana is divided into ten regions. All of these regions, except for the Upper East Region, have a school for the deaf that provides an educational program at the first cycle level. Figure 1 provides a map of Ghana divided into its regions.

Figure 1. Map of Ghana

As mentioned earlier, there are now twelve schools for the deaf in Ghana. The Eastern Region, where Foster's first school is located, now has four schools for the deaf. Two of these schools are residential and two are non-residential. The two non-residential schools are called Unit schools (in a "Unit" school, deaf children are integrated with hearing children). The only secondary-technical school for the deaf (the highest level educational institution for the deaf) in the whole country is also in the Eastern Region. The secondary-technical school is a residential school. The other residential school in this region is called the Demonstration School for the Deaf. This oral school for the deaf was built a few meters away from the school Foster established. Because of the fear that Foster's school would influence the new oral Demonstration School for the Deaf, the first school for the deaf in Ghana was phased out in 1979.

In addition to the normal elementary program, the Bechem School for the Deaf in the Brong-Ahafo region, has a special vocational program for the graduates of the post-middle school. The ages of deaf persons in this school range from two to twenty-six years. See Table 3 for a listing of each school, along with its location and enrollment.

Curriculum

The curriculum developed for schools for hearing children is still used in primary and middle schools for the deaf in Ghana. The content of the curriculum is similar to that of the Ghana Mission School for the Deaf described earlier.

Method of Communication

The Special Education Division of the Ministry of Education, which is responsible for the education of handicapped children, including the deaf, states that it has not yet decided on which mode of communication to use in the schools for the deaf in Ghana.

Table 3. **Location, Establishment, Date, Type, and Current Enrollment of Educational Institutions for the Deaf in Ghana**

Name of Institution	Location Town & Region	Date Establ.	R/NR*	Current Enrollment 84/85	85/86	87/88	88/89	Total	No. on Wait List in 1989
Demonstration School for the	Mampong AkwapimDeaf Eastern Region	1964	R	156	147	154	164	621	
State School For the Deaf	Teshie-Accra GT. Accra Region	1965	NR	120	127	123	136	506	19
WA School For the Deaf	WA, Upper West Region	1968	R	70	52	66	62	250	
Bechem School For the Deaf	Bechem Brong Ahafo	1969	R	168	201	232	231	832	35
Cape Coast School for the Deaf	Cape Coast Central Region	1970	R	120	97	90	96	403	
Sekonai School for the Deaf	Sekonai Wsetern Region	1971	R	120	181	114	129	644	5
Volta School for the Deaf	Hohoe Volta Region	1971	R	152	104	117	126	499	50
Kibi Unit School	Kibi Eastern Region	1975	R/NR	45	52	126	120	343	5
Koforidua Unit School	Koforidua Eastern Region	1975	R/NR	48	75	76	73	272	11
Secondary-Technical School for the Deaf	Mampong-Akwapim Eastern Region	1976	R	48	45	56	60	209	
Ashanti School for the Deaf	Jamasi Ashanti Region	1977	R	60	47	104	116	327	31
Savelugu School for the Deaf	Savelugu Northern Region	1978	R	78	92	92	134	296	
Total				1185	1320	1441	1447	5393	156

*R - Indicates Residential
*NR - Indicates Non-Residential

Although some schools for the deaf use the oral method and others use a Total Communication philosophy, the College of Special Education, which trains teachers of the deaf, emphasizes only the oral method of teaching the deaf.

Staffing

In 1965, the Deaf Education Specialist Teacher Training College was established at Mampong-Akwapim, in the Eastern Region of Ghana. During each two-year period from 1967 to 1985, about 20 teachers have graduated from the teacher training institution. In 1986 the duration of the training program was changed from two to three years. Also, the College has been upgraded and now awards diplomas.

The course content has been expanded to include information dealing with mental retardation and blindness as well as deafness. During the first two years of the program, all students are exposed to courses in the three areas of special education. During the final year of study, the students are required to major in one of the areas of disability and to take a position after graduation in that area.

Financing

As was mentioned earlier, education of the deaf and all other children in Ghana is fee-free at all levels. In addition to government support, the present schools for the deaf, including the Ghana Mission School for the Deaf, continue to benefit in kind and in cash from voluntary organizations. Some of the organizations that have provided contributions include the Catholic Relief Agency, Kristo Asafo Mission, World Vision International, and Rotary Club International. World Vision International, for example, has recently started providing school uniforms, assistance for agricultural projects, and the development and construction of water wells at select schools for the deaf. Private individuals have also donated.

Current Status and Future Needs

Thus far (1957–1990) no deaf person has entered any of the three universities in Ghana. Those who have attended a college or university have been trained outside of Ghana, usually in the United States. Because of a policy which seems to favour "oralism" and to discourage the deaf from teaching the deaf, those deaf who have completed their studies abroad and wish to teach have remained abroad.

Another area that requires special attention is the condition and control of the physical facilities of most of the schools for the deaf. The majority of these schools have been located for at least ten years in privately owned premises or rented buildings. An example would be the State School for the Deaf–Teshie-Accra, which has been housed in private facilities for over 25 years. Most of the schools for the deaf are in need of upgrading.

None of the schools for the deaf presently has access to psychologists, psychiatrists, vocational rehabilitation counselors, or other specialists. No technicians who can repair hearing aids are available.

Since Dr. David's original 1961 survey of the number of deaf people in Ghana, no other effort, at least in print, has been attempted. A new demographic study is urgently needed.

A meaningful program for the adult deaf and deaf children below the government social welfare rehabilitation age is also urgently needed.

Since there are still deaf adults who have never been to school and semi-literate deaf persons who are no longer in school, the school that Foster started for deaf adults should be revived.

References

Aryee, D.T.K. (1972, September). Address. In Kamm, Antony (Ed.), *Proceedings of the seminar on deafness*. Accra, Ghana: Commonwealth Society.

David, J.B. (1972, September). Address. In Kamm, Antony (Ed.), *Proceedings of the seminar on deafness*. Accra, Ghana: Commonwealth Society.

Fiaxe, S. A. K. (1964, May 22). *The education of the deaf in Ghana*. Gallaudet College, Washington,   D.C.

Foster, A. (Ed.) (1965). *Proceedings of the conference on the education of the deaf in Africa*. Ibadan, Nigeria: Toyobo Printing Press.

Ghana Fact Sheets. (1988, October).

Holborow, C. (1972, September). Address. In Kamm, Antony (Ed.), *Proceedings of the seminar on deafness*. Accra, Ghana: Commonwealth Society.

Markides, __. (1972, September). Address. In Kamm, Antony (Ed.), *Proceedings of the seminar on deafness*. Accra, Ghana: Commonwealth Society.

The Education of Deaf Children in Greece

by Venetta Lampropoulou, Ph.D.

Historical Development

Ancient Times

The existence of deaf people in ancient Greece and of that society's attitudes towards deafness has been documented mainly through the works of Greek philosophers and writers of the classical period. The general belief of the time was that the child who was born deaf could not be educated. Herodotus's works on the muses are considered to be some of the oldest sources written about deaf people. According to Herodotus, Krisos, the King of Lydus, had two sons, one of whom was hearing and the other deaf. Krisos tried to find a cure for his deaf son, but when he concluded that this was not possible and that his son would never speak, he considered his son hopeless, useless, and nonexistent (Herodotus, Muses, *Clio*, 85). The attitude of King Krisos is indicative of society's attitude towards deaf people at that time.

Herodotus, in his text, uses the words *deaf, speechless, mute,* and *hearing impaired,* and not the compound word *deaf-mute.* This fact might suggest that deafness and muteness were thought to be unrelated during his time.

The meaning given to the word *deaf* by various writers and scholars of classical times can lead to some assumptions regarding the beliefs about the position of deaf people in ancient Greek society. Homer, for example, in his *Iliad,* uses the word *deaf* to mean weak or powerless, as in the phrase ". . . because the arrow was deaf" (Homer, *Iliad,* l. 390). Sophocles, in his tragedy *Aias,* uses the word *deaf* to mean foolish.

Some of the Greek philosophers also dealt with deafness. Their theories may have had an influence on the general shaping of public opinion about deaf people.

Aristotle is one of the best known, and often misinterpreted, philosophers who has dealt with the subject. He considered the sense of hearing the most important of all of the senses because it contributed, as he stated, to the mental development of man. He thought that hearing was the main organ of instruction. Aristotle also believed that deafness was organically connected with speechlessness. According to this idea, he assumed that damage to the hearing organ would also cause damage to the speech organs (Aristotle, *Problems*). In another book, Aristotle stated that blind people were in a more advanced position mentally as compared to deaf people, because the blind could communicate with their environment (Aristotle, *De Sensibus*).

Such statements of Aristotle may have influenced some doctors and educators, who probably misinterpreted his ideas and thus did not attempt to educate the deaf. These people, assuming that the deaf were lacking the organ for instruction (hearing), together with Aristotle's assumption that the speech organs of the deaf were damaged, may have concluded that deaf children could not be educated. Some writers and educators have condemned Aristotle for his ideas and held him responsible for keeping the deaf in ignorance for more than 2000 years (Deland, 1931; Moores, 1978, 1996).

The fact is that Aristotle never referred to the education of deaf children in his works. He only placed high importance on the sense of hearing for instruction, which generally speaking, is true even today. He also stated that a child deaf from birth will not learn to speak, which is also true today to a great extent.

In Plato's *Dialogues,* we also find some useful information about the status of deaf people in Athenian society. In a dialogue between Theaetetus and Socrates, the latter expresses his idea that thought is expressed by people through speech, except if someone is deaf or speechless. Here, the philosopher is aware of the fact that deaf people do not speak. He also makes a distinction between deafness and speechlessness (Plato, *Theaetetus*).

In another of Plato's dialogues, Socrates, Hermogenus, and Cratylus talk about word-object correspondence and the arbitrary or natural symbols of this relationship. Here,

Socrates is talking about the use of sign language as a communication system among the deaf. According to Plato, sign language is a spontaneous tool since, as he stated, even the hearing people will use signs if they suddenly lose their speech (Plato, *Cratylus*). This statement of Plato is the first written statement about sign language. We can assume, from his dialogues, that deaf people and sign language were very much accepted by Athenian society.

In Sparta, according to Plutarch, all babies were inspected soon after birth and the handicapped ones were thrown into a gully of the mountain Tavgetus, known as Kaiadas or Apothetas (Plutarch, *Lycurgus*). Some writers have doubted Plutarch's statements, but given the militaristic ideology of Lycurgus's Sparta, the position of handicapped people could not have been as good as it was in other Greek cities of the same period. In Athens, for example, according to some reports, the non-slave handicapped people received an allowance (Lazanas, 1984).

During the Byzantine epoch, asylums and orphanages were established and children in need were protected and cared for. Some deaf children benefitted from these social and welfare programs, but education had not yet been provided for them (Lazanas, 1984).

Establishment of the First Schools

The education of deaf children in Greece began relatively late in comparison with other European countries, and this development has continued to be slow. This delay in the development of the education of the deaf can be attributed to a number of factors. Turkey's 400-year occupation of Greece from 1400 up to the mid-1800s may have been one of those factors. The political, social, and economic priorities of the newly independent Greek nation after the long Turkish occupation would be other factors.

In 1907, a rich landowner named Charalambos Spiliopoulos took the initiative to establish a school for deaf children in Athens. He went to a notary public to get all of the legal papers necessary for this purpose and on May 14, 1907, he obtained permission to establish a philanthropic asylum (Government Paper, 1907). But for some reason, most likely bureaucratic, his wishes did not materialize until after his death in 1937. Spiliopoulos left a substantial financial endowment and property for the establishment of the new school.

In the meantime, in 1922, after the defeat of the Greek army by Turkey and the destruction of the Greek civilization on the east coast of Turkey and in Constantinople (Istanbul), a ship carrying Greek refugee orphans from Turkey approached Pireas, the port of Athens. Among these orphans were ten deaf children. The American philanthropic organization, Near East Relief, which was helping Greek refugees from the east coast of Turkey who had arrived in Greece, established an orphanage for the refugee children in Athens, and later on the island of Syros. This organization took the responsibility of educating the ten deaf orphans. To accomplish this goal the Near East Relief Organization hired a teacher named Helen Palatidou. She was sent to the Clark School for the Deaf in the United States to receive training as a teacher of the deaf (Epetiris, 1950).

Helen Palatidou, herself a refugee from Turkey, was a young teacher with a good education and a great interest in working with the deaf. She studied at the Clark School for the Deaf from 1922 to 1923, and upon her return to Greece, began teaching the deaf orphans. The results of her teaching became well known in Greece, and the number of deaf students in her class soon increased. More teachers were also recruited to teach in the boarding school. Some of those who were recruited were also sent to the Clark School for the Deaf for training.

In 1932, the Near East Relief Organization met with the Ministry of Welfare to discuss the future of the school. At this meeting it was decided that the school would come under the auspices and support of the Ministry of Welfare. Later, in 1937, the property of Spiliopoulos was transferred over to this school. Today the school is known as The National Institute for the Protection of Deaf-Mutes (Government Paper, 1937). The school finally moved into a large new building and extended its services to include additional deaf children. Between the years 1956 and 1970, the National Institute for the Deaf (NID) established residential schools in five more cities.

Today, the NID provides a free education, residential facilities, and diagnostic and related services for deaf children from infancy to the age of fourteen to sixteen. It is supervised by the Ministry of Health and Welfare, through a board of directors that is appointed by the Ministry. Over the past years the NID has developed an in-service training program consisting of seminars on the education of the deaf and other professional activities for teachers.

Some teachers have played a leading role in the development of the National Institute for the Deaf. Besides Palatidou, one of the most important figures, according to the deaf people of Greece and NID records, was Helen Varitimidou. She went to the United States in 1945-1946 to receive her training as a teacher of the deaf. After her return to Greece, for a number of years she taught deaf students by the use of the oral method and trained new teachers of the deaf. She soon became the director of the NID. In 1948 she helped deaf graduates from her school establish the first association of deaf people in Greece. Helen Varitimidou was dedicated to her job and to her students.

Another influential figure at the National Institute for the Deaf was Vasilis Lazanas. He was not a teacher but a scholar with a great interest in deaf people. He was the administrative director of the NID from 1955 to 1979. He was also the first person in Greece to study the literature in the field extensively. Lazanas wrote many articles about the education of the deaf, vocational rehabilitation, and the position of deaf people in different societies. Most of his works have been included in a volume entitled *The Problems of the Deaf*. Vasilis Lazanas had been influenced by the oral method of teaching the deaf used at the NID and tried to convince his readers that deaf people could learn to talk (Lazanas, 1984).

Although the oral method of communication was used at the NID and the emphasis of the school was on the articulation of sounds and the development of speech, some of the teachers knew how to sign and, according to deaf graduates of the school, used signs unofficially in the classrooms. In the residence halls and schoolyard, the deaf students communicated among themselves by the use of sign language.

During World War II the National Institute's building was made into a hospital. The school was forced to move to a small building near the Acropolis. This period of time was as difficult for the NID as it was for the Greek people in general. It took years to recover from the setbacks caused by the war. It was not until about 1960 that the NID finally took back its original building and began to thrive again.

Meanwhile, another development took place in Greece that influenced the education of the deaf to a large extent. Andreas Kokkevis, a member of the Greek Parliament who had a deaf daughter, became very interested in the education of the deaf. From his position in Parliament and later as Minister of Health and Welfare (1964, 1974), he helped initiate legislative action and other measures favorable to the welfare of deaf children in Greece. In August 1956, Kokkevis proposed an addition to a law under discussion in the Parliament; the law passed and became the first law supporting the education of the deaf in Greece. According to this new law, public insurance organizations were required to pay the tuition of deaf children attending special schools (Parliament Records, 1956).

In September of the same year, 1956, Iro Kokkevis, the wife of Andreas, obtained a license and established a private school for deaf children in Glyfada, near Athens (Government Paper, 1956). This school was recognized by law as equal in accreditation to all public schools for hearing children (Government Paper, 1956).

Amalia Martinou, a teacher at the National Institute for the Deaf, was recruited to teach at this private school. She became the director for life and owned the school until 1986. At that time the administrative authority for the school was transferred to the State. Martinou was influenced by methods used in the British oral schools that she often visited. She and her teachers used the pure oral method and did not allow the students to use any sign language. According to graduates of Martinou's school, students had to "speak" all the time and learn how to read lips.

In 1966, with the help of Andreas Kokkevis and other parents, a junior high school program was added to the school. This school is now a public school, and its name is Public School for Deaf and Hard of Hearing of Argyroupolis. Argyroupolis is a southeastern suburb of Athens.

Another private, non-profit school was established in 1973, by an organization called the Institution for the Welfare and Education of Deaf and Hard of Hearing Children (Government Paper, 1973). The president of this organization, Sofia Starogianni, was the mother of two deaf sons. This oral residential school included preschool, elementary, and high school departments. The director of the school was Victoria Daousi, a Greek language teacher who was very skillful and dedicated to the education of deaf children. In 1982, the control of this school was given over to the State. This school, which consists of a separate preschool and elementary school, is known as The Public School for Deaf and Hard of Hearing of Philothei. Philothei is a northeastern suburb of Athens.

In reviewing the history and development of the first schools for the deaf, we can conclude that deaf education in Greece began relatively late. The early efforts were initiated by either philanthropic organizations or by individuals who had a direct interest in the field, such as parents of deaf children. The first teachers recruited to these newly established schools for the deaf were sent to oral schools for the deaf in the United States or England to obtain their training. This fact explains the strong oral tradition that is evident, even today, in most of the schools for the deaf in Greece.

Before 1975 the government played a minor role in the education of deaf children and in special eduation generally (Lampropoulou & Padeliadou, 1995). Until 1982 all existing schools for the deaf were private. As the number of students in these private schools increased, the problems these schools faced also increased. The problem of providing trained teachers of the deaf became more obvious as the number of deaf children and needed services and as programs for deaf children increased throughout the country.

Recent Developments and Major Forces

The government had little involvement in the early development of the education of the deaf in Greece (*Booklet of Information*, 1988, 1994). From 1975 until the present, however, parents of disabled children and people with disabilities themselves have lobbied and pressured the government to address the problems of disabled citizens and to take responsibility for the education of all children with disabilities, including the deaf.

Some very influential organizations have played a leading role in the lobbying and pressure activities. The first of these organizations, the Greek Union of Deaf-Mutes, which was founded in 1948, began to publish a newspaper in 1956. The problems of education of the deaf in Greece were raised constantly through this newspaper (The Problems of Education, 1956). As the deaf established more organizations in Athens and in other cities, the "voice" of the deaf in Greece grew louder.

In 1968 the Greek Federation of the Deaf was established as an umbrella organization that represented all deaf people of Greece. One of its main objectives was to improve the overall educational status of deaf children. The organization formed an educational committee dedicated to that goal. In 1986 a representative of the organization became the first deaf member of the board of trustees of the National Institute for the Deaf (*The World of Silence*, 1985).

The parents of deaf children also began to organize. In 1954 Iro Kokkevis and Sofia Starogianni, mothers of deaf children who were mentioned earlier, formed an organization dedicated to the welfare of the deaf. This organization undertook a number of actions and organized activities aimed at improving the educational system and the lives of deaf people in Greece. Their organization helped establish other organizations for the deaf that held meetings on different subjects. In 1965 the Association of the Parents of the National Institute for the Deaf was founded. These organizations of parents of deaf children and of deaf adults joined to compose a very powerful body that placed great pressure on the government to act in ways that would lead to improvement in the educational programs provided the deaf children of Greece.

As a result of this pressure, in 1975 a two-year course of study in special education was established at one of the Teachers' Academies (Government Paper, 1975). Unfortunately, this course of study provided only general information about children with special needs, and did not offer any kind of specialization. In 1976 an office for special education was established in the Ministry of Education (Government Paper, 1976). Soon after, a law providing for vocational rehabilitation for the handicapped was passed.

The first law for the education and vocational training of children with special needs was passed in 1981. This law was replaced in 1985 by Public Law 1655 (Government Papers, 1981, 1985).

During the 1980s, some rapid developments took place. In 1982 the parent organizations planned and presented a conference on the education of the deaf and invited specialists from several countries. Professors from the United States discussed the use of sign language as well as other current issues. These professors came from Gallaudet College, now Gallaudet University, in the United States. It was the first time that people in Greece who were involved in the education of deaf children had the opportunity to meet and listen to professors who were deaf. Another first was the use of interpreters for the deaf. Deaf people and parents indicated that the conference had a considerable impact.

In 1984, the first systematic study of the educational needs of deaf children in Greece was completed. In this study five different groups, including educators, parents, deaf adults, administrators, and governmental officials, were asked to assess the educational needs of deaf children in Greece. The major findings of the study were that there was a great need in Greece for development in the following areas: teacher training, curricula, diagnostic services, infant programs, and vocational training programs (Lampropoulou, 1985).

The results of this study were used by the National Institute for the Deaf to improve educational services for the deaf. The results of the study were also used by parent organizations of the deaf to make proposals to the Government for the development of new services and improvements in the existing educational system for deaf children in Greece.

Educational Provisions for Deaf Children
Demographic Data

Demographic data concerning the number of deaf children in Greece are not available. According to the figures given by the Ministry of Education's Office of Special Education, during the 1992–1993 academic year there were 1,760,000 students from the ages of three to eighteen attending school programs (preschool through high school) throughout Greece (Booklet of Information, 1994). Assuming that one school-aged child per thousand is deaf (Carhart, 1969), the estimated number of deaf children in Greece is about 1,760.

Another estimation can be drawn from the number of babies born each year in Greece. According to reports provided by gynecologists and pediatricians, between 130,000 and 140,000 children are born per year. Using Carhart's estimation again (one deaf child per thousand), the number of deaf babies born every year is around 140. Extrapolating this figure to include all deaf children, the overall number of deaf children from birth to age eighteen would indicate an estimated population of about 2,500. If we were to include children with moderate-to-severe hearing impairments and children with postlingual deafness, this number would be much higher.

The number of hearing impaired students who attended special programs for the deaf and hard of hearing during the academic year 1987–1988 was 707, while in 1988–1989 this number was 792 (Booklet of Information, 1988; Lampropoulou, 1990). Recent unpublished data from the Ministry of Education indicate a decline in the number of deaf students enrolled in school programs. According to these data, during the academic year 1995–1996, the overall number of deaf students attending the different educational programs, including infant programs, for deaf students was 712. Table 1 shows the breakdown of students and kinds of schools attended.

When one compares the estimated total number of school-aged deaf children to the number of deaf students currently attending the different special programs for the deaf in Greece, one can conclude that a relatively large number of deaf children are not presently receiving any special education services. These figures indicate that slightly under 30

Table 1. Professionals Working in Schools for the Deaf, Method of Communication, 1995–1996

Schools	No. of Student	No. of Teacher	Deaf Teacher	Sex Men	Women	Method of Comm.[1]	Other Specialists[2]
Infant Programs (NID)[3]	44	4	—	—	4	Total	4
Preschool Programs (ME)[4]	43	11	—	—	11	Oral*	—
Elem. Sch. Programs (NID)	177	46	5	4	42	Total	17
Elem. Sch. Programs (ME)	135	34	1	12	22	Oral*	6
Spec. Classes in R.S. (ME)5	49	8	—	3	5	Oral*	—
Junior High Schools (M.E.)	163	59	3	12	47	Oral*	3
High Schools (M.E.)	86	47	1	17	30	Oral*	—
Technical Schools (M.E.)	15	8	—	3	5	Oral*	—
Total 712	217	10	51	166		Oral	30

[1] Communication method
[2] Other specialists
[3] National Institute for the Deaf (Ministry of Health)
[4] Ministry of Education schools
[5] Regular schools for hearing students

* In some of these schools Total Communication in general is accepted and used to some extent by some teachers in their classes.

percent of the estimated 2,500 deaf children in Greece are enrolled in some kind of special program. According to findings, a large number of deaf children are attending regular schools without any special help, are misplaced in institutions designed for disabilities other than deafness, or simply remain at home (Lampropoulou, 1990).

Recent Legislation

The existing Public Law 1655/85 provides the philosophy, the structure, and the rules needed to develop and govern educational systems for students with special needs, including the deaf. Besides general goals, the goal of Public Law 1655/85 is to help students with special needs:

- to develop to the fullest extent possible and to maximize the use of their skills and abilities
- to integrate into the productive process
- to integrate into society at large (P.L. 1655/85, 1985)

According to the law, these goals can be realized through cooperation between special education programs and other social and scientific bodies.

The academic and vocational programs that make up special education are considered, according to the law, to be the responsibility of the State. The special schools are mainly a public school responsibility. The goal of these schools is to provide appropriate and quality educational services for children with special needs from the ages of three to eighteen.

P.L. 1655/85 states that the neighborhood school is the most desirable placement for a child with special needs. The law stipulates that each student should have an individualized education program designed and implemented by the regular classroom teacher. However, this mandate has not been enforced at the present time (Lampropoulou & Padeliadou, 1995). According to this law, if a student requires a more specialized program and additional support services, a special unit or class would be developed within a regular public school. The student would attend this class on a part-time basis, unless the student's special problems are so severe that he or she requires a full-time placement. Severe cases, according to this law, can best be handled in a special day or residential school setting. However, the most common placement for deaf students in Greece at the present time is the separate residental special school for the deaf or unit, or the special class within a regular school for hearing students (See Table 1).

This law also provides for the organizational structure of the special educational system. The Ministry of Education is responsible for the development, organization, and curriculum of the special schools. Within the Ministry of Education is the Office of Special Education. The Special Education Office has the duty of carrying out the mandate of the law in connection with the special schools. Attached to these bodies are special regional counselors whose role is to assist and advise the teachers and generally to support the special education programs of their region.

The directors and teachers of the special schools are responsible for the implementation of the curriculum and the daily functioning of the schools. As is the case with the special public schools, the private schools and institutes that are the responsibility of other Ministries, such as the Ministry of Health and Welfare, are also obliged to follow the Ministry of Education's National Curriculum and the mandates of Public Law 1655/85. However, the National Curriculum that the special schools have to follow is designed for students without disabilities, and no provisions are made for special adaptation.

Diagnostic and Intake Procedures

Students can be referred to a special school by a parent or by a regular public school teacher. According to the law, students must be diagnosed and evaluated by a Regional Medical–Pedagogical Center prior to their registration in a special program. One of these centers, the Medical–Pedagogical Center of the National Institute for the Deaf, provides a complete evaluation of deaf children of all ages. This center provides a team of specialists that includes an eye and ear specialist, an audiologist, a hearing aid specialist, a pediatrician, a psychologist, a social worker, a speech therapist, and a teacher of the deaf.

Children referred to the Medical–Pedagogical Center complete a comprehensive audiological, psychological, and academic assessment. Hearing aid selection, evaluation, and fitting are also provided by this center. A few audiological clinics that are usually attached to the Ear, Nose, and Throat (ENT) Clinics of children's hospitals in the major cities of Greece also provide young children with an audiological assessment and guidance in the selection of a proper hearing aid.

According to P.L. 1655/85, hearing aids should be provided free of charge to all hearing impaired school children. This part of the law has not been put into practice. At the present time, the parents of deaf children must purchase hearing aids for their children at a high cost directly from hearing aid dealers. In some instances, however, the cost of the hearing aid is covered by medical insurance.

Early Intervention and Parent Education

At the present time, newborn infants and young children are not routinely screened. Parents or pediatricians who suspect that an infant or a young child may have a hearing loss refer the child to an audiological clinic located in a children's hospital or to the Medical–(Pedagogical Center of the National Institute for the Deaf in Athens.

Nursery classes and preschool programs are often attached to elementary schools for the deaf. Children can be admitted to a nursery class, preschool program, or residential school at the age of three. Services for children younger than the age of three are limited in Greece. Parent-infant programs are provided by the National Institute for the Deaf and are found only in three large cities: Athens, Thessaloniki, and Patras. The infant programs of the NID, which were developed in 1986, provide guidance and educational services to about 40-50 families and their deaf infants (Lampropoulou, 1989).

Parents and their deaf infants visit these centers weekly. Usually the visits are on an individual basis, but periodically the parents of deaf infants meet as a group. The teacher of the deaf, with the assistance of the psychologist and social worker, provides guidance, diagnostic information, and additional information as needed. Advice on educational, communication, and technical matters, as well as on the general problems of coping with a deaf child in the home, are some of the areas covered by this guidance program.

One of the main goals of the entire program is to help parents develop, as early as possible, the skills required to communicate with their infants. The Total Communication philosophy is used in these programs. Sign language courses are offered to the parents by the center.

Although these positive developments in the area of early intervention are occurring in Greece at the present time, a large number of deaf infants and their parents are not benefiting from these services. Limitations in space, program availability, and the absence of a State policy concerning early infant screening, diagnosis, and intervention are the reasons for the lack of adequate numbers of parent-infant programs. The existing audiological clinics are not providing the needed guidance and services that parents require. They do not work cooperatively with the schools for the deaf and often, according to reports received from parents, instead refer the parents of deaf infants to speech therapists for private sessions at a high cost.

School Programs and Curricula

There are three types of schools for the deaf in Greece: residential schools, day schools or units, and special classes in schools for hearing students (see Table 2). All of these schools are part of one of two systems: a) the schools of the National Institute for the Deaf (NID), which is part of the Ministry of Health and Welfare, and b) the public schools (P.S.), which are governed by the Ministry of Education.

Schools of the National Institute for the Deaf

The schools of the NID are the oldest educational establishments for the deaf in Greece. They are considered to be semi-private, non-profit schools because they are governed by an independent board of directors appointed by the Ministry of Health and Welfare. They also are funded by this Ministry as well from other sources, such as bequests from wills and donations from wealthy contributors. Students in these schools do not pay any tuition. The same curriculum is used by the NID schools and by the public schools for the deaf.

Although the schools of the NID are all residential, they also accept day pupils. These schools, which are all at the elementary level, are located in different parts of Greece. Four of the six NID schools are located in the large cities of Athens, Thessaloniki, and Patras, and the remaining two are in the smaller cities of Serres in northern Greece and Kasteli, a town on the island of Crete. Children from the ages of six to eighteen attend the elementary schools. The corresponding age level for hearing students at the elementary school level is ages six to twelve. Attached to the schools of the NID are preschool and nursery programs as well as junior high and high schools that are administered by the Ministry of Education. These additional programs use the facilities and services of the NID.

As stated previously, the NID also provides infant programs for children under the age of three and their parents. There are three such programs in Athens, Thessaloniki, and Patras. Upon graduation from one of the elementary schools of the NID, the students

Table 2. Programs for Deaf Students in Greece, 1995-1996

Student Age Level*	Residential Schools (NID)[1]			Day Schools (ME)[2]			Special Classes in Reg. Schools (MA)		
	N.Pr[3]	N.S.[4]	N.T.[5]	N.Pr.	N.S.	N.T.	N.Pr.	N.S.	N.T.
Infant Programs (0-4)	3	44	4	—	—	—	—	—	—
Preschool Programs (4-6)	—	—	—	9	43	11	—	—	—
Elem. Programs (6-12)	6	177	46	7	135	34	6	49	8
Junior High Sch. (12-15)	—	—	—	3	134	45	2	29	14
High Schools (15-18)	—	—	—	3	81	43	1	5	4
Technical Schools (18-20)	—	—	—	2	15	8	—	—	—
Total	9	221	50	24	408	141	9	83	26

*Age range levels are for hearing students. Deaf students can usually stay longer in different programs depending on their need.

[1] NID = National Institute for the Deaf (Ministry of Health)
[2] ME = Ministry of Education schools
[3] N.Pr = number of programs
[4] N.S. = number of students
[5] N.T. = number of teachers

continue their education in public junior high schools for the deaf, controlled by the Ministry of Education. Compulsory education for all children in Greece, except for some groups of children with special needs, extends through the junior high school level.

Public Schools

The public schools for the deaf are all governed by the Ministry of Education. All of these schools were developed after 1982 (Booklet of Information, 1994). The public school system includes day schools or units and special classes. Residential facilities are not provided within the public school system. However, deaf students attending the public schools who need a place to reside can use the facilities of the NID or some other welfare residential home on a free-of-charge basis.

The public school system includes preschool, elementary, junior high, and high school programs for deaf children from the age of three to 25. Table 3 shows the location and kind of schools for the deaf in Greece. The large day school programs are located in Athens and Thessaloniki. Smaller units or classes are located in smaller cities and towns throughout the country. The day schools and the units are independent schools where deaf children do not mix with hearing children during school hours.

The special classes are usually based in a school for hearing children. The deaf students attend the special classes, either on a full-time or part-time basis according to their individual needs. The deaf students in the special classes usually spend part of the school day in classes designed for hearing students. Data collected for the academic year 1995-1996 indicates that there are two large elementary schools for deaf children in Athens and five smaller units in the cities of Volos, Ioannina, Hraklio, Thessaloniki, and Chalkis. Special preschool programs are located mainly in the large cities and are usually attached to the above elementary schools. Three special classes for deaf children are also located in the city of Thessaloniki, two of which are at the elementary and one at the junior high school level. There are also five special classes in hearing schools in other cities of Greece and three junior high and high school programs for deaf students in the large cities of Athens and Thessaloniki. Smaller junior and high school units are found in Patras and near Thessaloniki.

As is indicated in Table 1, during the academic year 1995–96, there were 712 students attending the different educational programs for the deaf in Greece. The number of deaf children attending school programs is very small when compared with the total number (1800-2500) of school-age deaf children in Greece. To provide special educational services to a larger percentage of deaf children will require the establishment of new programs for the deaf children now living in small towns or on the islands.

The age level of students, as shown in Table 3, is also a factor for consideration. The age span of children in programs for the deaf is as follows: preschool, ages three to five; elementary, five to eighteen; junior high and high school, thirteen to twenty-five. The age spread for hearing students is: preschool, three to five; elementary, five to twelve; junior and high school, twelve to eighteen. Deaf children remain in school programs much longer than do hearing students. This occurs for the following reasons: Normally, deaf children do not enter the special school at a very early age; the program of the special school is more flexible; and the pedagogy used follows a slower and more repetitive pace.

Condition of Service

According to the recent legislation (P.L. 1655/85) the average class size for a special class is eight or nine students. Table 1 shows that during the 1995-1996 academic year, the average teacher-to-pupil ratio was about one teacher per three pupils. The low teacher-to-pupil ratio gives the teachers of the deaf an excellent opportunity to provide each student

Table 3. **Characteristics of Deaf Students Attending Programs for the Deaf**

Schools	Number of Students	Age	Age Boys	Girls	Resident
Elem. NID[1] Athens I	65	5-16	29	36	34
Elem. NID Athens II	39	5-16	20	19	20
Elem. NID Thessaloniki	108	7-18	56	52	58
Elem. NID Patra	53	5-17	26	27	30
Elem. NID Kriti	11	7-16	5	6	9
Elem. NID Serres	20	5-16	10	10	13
Elem. NID Volos	7	7-15	4	3	7
Elem. PS Argiroupoli-Athens	67	5-16	39	28	
Elem. PS Philothei-Athens	26	6-16	20	6	13
Elem. SU[2] Chalkis	7	4-16	3	4	
Elem. SC[3]Thessaloniki I	13	9-15	4	9	
Elem. SC Ioannina	12	6-17	5	7	
Elem. SU Volos	4	7-14	2	2	
JH-HS Ag. Paraskevi-Athens	103	14-25	66	37	58
JH-HS Argiroupoli-Athens	78	13-25	36	42	
JH-HS Thessaloniki	50	13-22	30	20	19
JH-HS Patra	20	14-18	6	14	14
Pre-SC[4]Argiroupoli-Athens	12	3-5	9	3	
Pre-SC Ampelokipi-Athens	21	3-5	10	11	6
Pre-SC Philothei-Athens	9	3-5	6	3	
Pre-SC Thessaloniki	12	3-5	8	4	1
PRE-SC Patra	9	3-5	8	3	
Infant Programs NID	42	0-4	19	23	
Total	792	423	369	282	

[1]National Institute for the Deaf
[2]Special Unit, SC -
[3]Special Class
[4]Preschool

with an individualized program. However, reports from teachers and parents indicate that the special schools lack proper equipment, adequate hearing aids, necessary buildings, and appropriate curricula. Although some of the students use their personal hearing aids in the classroom, the lack of an adequate hearing aid repair service or hearing aid maintenance program is a serious problem.

The poor condition of the buildings that house the special schools and classrooms is also a problem. For example, the absence of soundproofing and environmental noise level controls are areas of real concern.

According to the law, the special schools and schools for the deaf must follow the same curriculum that is used in the regular schools. Some of the teachers have tried to modify the regular school curriculum in order to make it more accessible to their deaf students' needs. These curricular modifications are done on an individual basis and cannot be considered an organized effort at designing a curriculum appropriate for deaf children.

Several years ago the Ministry of Education formed a committee of teachers and specialists whose charge was to develop a language curriculum for deaf students. As a result, a curriculum for the development of Greek written language skills has been published and is used by teachers working with deaf pupils. This curriculum consists of six books for the teacher and six for the student (Lampropoulou et al., 1992). However, no curriculum has been developed for other subjects, so teachers have to follow the general school curricula for hearing students. Some of these teachers make their own adaptations in order to use the curricula with their deaf students.

Finally, appropriate tools to measure the academic achievement of deaf or hearing children have not been developed. Therefore, it is rather difficult to make any valid evaluation regarding the achievement level of deaf children in Greece. However, reports from parents, deaf adults, and teachers suggest that the over-all achievement level of deaf students graduating from high school is much lower than that of hearing students. As one would expect, the most problematic academic areas are reading and written language (Lampropoulou, 1993; Christodoulakos, 1985).

Communication Methodology

Until 1984 oralism was the only acceptable communication methodology used with deaf children in Greece (Christodoulakos, 1985). Things began to change in 1984. Seminars that looked at other communication methodologies and the poor achievement results of deaf pupils led the teachers and Board of Directors of the National Institute for the Deaf to decide to adopt the Total Communication philosophy. The teachers began taking courses in sign language and began using signs together with speech when communicating with the students in their classrooms.

These teachers are presently using signed Greek, which is a form of sign language that follows the syntax and grammar of the spoken Greek language. This sign system is not coded by the teachers and is generally employed in a loose sense. The manual alphabet is also used to supplement signed Greek.

Greek Sign Language, which is the native language of Greek deaf people, is used by the deaf personnel of the NID to communicate with deaf children when they are in the schoolyard and the dormitories. The NID often organizes sign courses for the personnel working at the Institute as well as for parents and other interested groups.

The public schools for the deaf mainly use the oral method of communication, as shown in Table 1. However, some of the teachers in these schools have reported to this writer that they have begun taking sign language courses and are using some signs in their classrooms.

Characteristics of Teacher Preparation Programs

During the 1995–1996 academic year there were a total of 217 teachers of the deaf working in schools and classes for deaf children. Of that total, 51 were men and 166 were women. The large number of female teachers indicates that the tradition that states that teaching the deaf is a woman's job holds. The majority of the teachers of the deaf at the NID, which is Greece's oldest school, are women. See Table 1 for further analysis of the professionals working in schools for the deaf.

Among the 217 teachers working in schools for the deaf are eleven teachers who are deaf. Seven are elementary school teachers and four are junior high or high school teachers (two art teachers and two chemistry teachers). The teaching profession, especially in the area of elementary education, is a rather new field for the deaf people in Greece.

According to reports from the Greek Federation of the Deaf, approximately ten deaf students are presently studying to become teachers at the different universities in Greece.

The lack of adequate teacher training is a serious problem in Greece. No university program designed to train teachers of deaf children has yet been developed. Only at the School of Humanities in the Department of Education at the University of Patras are courses offered in the area of the education of the deaf for students enrolled in an elementary education program. Graduate studies in Special Education and in deafness have been offered recently to a limited number of students by the same university. This new development has been received with much enthusiasm by the deaf community and by the parents of deaf children in Greece. However, most of the teachers presently working in the schools for the deaf have not received any formal training. Table 4 shows the amount of education received by teachers at different levels.

In order to overcome the shortage of teacher training opportunities, the NID did offer a one-year in-service course of study to prepare new teachers of the deaf. This program has been discontinued due to technical problems at NID. Another school, the Maraslios Academy, offers a two-year course in general special education for those individuals who wish to work with children enrolled in special programs. This course is general in nature and does not provide the specific training required to work successfully with deaf children. However, in keeping with present legislation, the degree received from Maraslios Academy is recognized as acceptable preparation for a position in a school for the deaf.

Table 4 indicates that very few of the teachers now working in schools for the deaf (8 of the 217) hold an M.A. or a Ph.D. degree in the education of the deaf. Some teachers (8 of the 217) have taken courses in the education of the deaf abroad and most of the rest have attended seminars or lectures related to their area of expertise. All of these teachers hold a degree in general education.

Table 4. Teacher Training

Schools	Doc.D.	M.A.	B.A.	C.A.	N.I.D.	G.S.E.	NT	Sem.	Each
Infant Programs					1	4			4
Preschool Programs						4	3	5	11
Elementary Schools (NID)[1]	1	1		1	46			46	46
Elementary Schools (ME)[2]	2				16	5	25	34	
Special Classes (ME)					1	5	3	4	8
Junior High Schools (ME)	1	3		4			30	25	59
High Schools (ME)				2			20	25	47
Technical Schools (ME)							8		8
Total	2	6	8		51	25	69	130	217

[1] National Institute for the Deaf (Ministry of Health)
[2] Ministry of Education schools

Doc.D. = Doctoral degree in deafness
M.A.   = Master's degree in Deaf Education
C.A.   = Bachelor's degree in Deaf Education
NID   = in-service courses of NID
G.S.E. = degree in General Special Education
NT   = no training
Sem   = Seminars
Teach = Total number of teachers

Vocational Education and Postsecondary Opportunities

According to the present legislation, the State is now responsible for the vocational education of students with special needs. Special vocational schools are to be established to meet the individual needs of such students (P.L. 1655/85, p.136). This part of the law has not yet been put into effect for deaf students. Instead, just a few minor programs have been introduced. Two small technical school programs have been developed by the Ministry of Education in the Athens area; these serve only fifteen students (Table 2). Lately, some local authorities have also developed vocational training programs for deaf students that are partially funded by the European Community programs. The local authority for Aryrouposis, a southeastern suburb of Athens, is very active in this area. This authority, together with the University of Patras, has developed programs for sign language interpreters and teachers. Another program developed by the local authority of Argyroupolis offers courses in computer operation and in graphic arts. These programs are considered by deaf people to be a good but limited start, and in no way provide the comprehensive vocational education programs that are needed.

The lack of vocational training is indicative of the vocational status of deaf people in Greece. The data presented in a recent study indicates that most of the deaf people in Greece are considered to be unskilled workers. The study also shows that deaf workers are underpaid (Lampropoulou, 1991, 1992).

Despite the shortcomings of Greece's special educational system, a number of deaf students manage to continue their education in the universities. According to reports from the Greek Federation of the Deaf, more than 20 students are presently attending university programs. More than 30 deaf people in Greece hold university degrees and work in a variety of professions. The universities, however, do not offer any support services for deaf students.

Current Issues and Future Trends

Educational services for deaf children in Greece are developing at a slow pace. Problems and shortcomings in existing services for deaf children are common. Some of the problems appear to be of a critical nature. One of the most pressing problems is the need to extend educational services to children who are not currently being served. In particular, programs for deaf children with multiple handicaps are virtually non-existent and must be established immediately (Lampropoulou, 1989).

There is an urgent need to develop comprehensive vocational training programs for deaf students. Such programs help deaf people advance their general occupational and financial status. The development of more teacher training programs at the university level that can produce teachers who can provide quality instruction to deaf students is another high priority need. A final critical need is the development of curricula that will provide an appropriate and accessible education for the deaf children of Greece.

The merits of the different communication methodologies used with deaf children are an issue that is often discussed in Greece at the present time. Parents, as expected, prefer the oral method, while the deaf community and the majority of the teachers of the deaf, including those from the oral schools, question the applicability of this method to the majority of deaf students. The National Institute for the Deaf with its change to the Total Communication philosophy began the movement away from the oral method. This change in communication philosophy now appears to be spreading to other schools as well.

Parents of deaf students and the deaf people of Greece themselves are becoming more militant and are demanding a better education for deaf children. These groups have recently organized meetings and conferences, and have drawn up policies covering all of the issues that have been mentioned above. These groups are emphatic about the need for quality services.

The integration of deaf people into the larger society and the mainstreaming of deaf children into the regular educational setting are becoming important issues in Greece. Deaf people, the majority of the teachers of the deaf, and many of the parents are skeptical about the value of integration and mainstreaming. They feel that the regular schools are not equipped to serve deaf students. They seem to prefer day schools or special classes in which deaf children are taught in separate groups (Lampropoulou & Padeliadou, 1997; Lampropoulou, 1995).

At this time, the government of Greece seems to have become more sensitive to the needs of special children. This recent sensitivity could be the result of renewed benevolence and moral responsibility for the citizenry of the country, or a result of pressure applied to the government by organizations consisting of parents of deaf children and deaf adults. This organized pressure, coupled with the activities of the European deaf community, has become a powerful force that should lead to a more optimistic future for the deaf of Greece.

References

Aristotle. *Problems.*

Aristotle. *De sensibus.*

Booklet of information. (1988, 1994). Athens, Greece: Special Education Office, Ministry of Education.

Carhart, R. (1969). *Human communication and its disorders.* Bethesda, MD: National Institute of Health, Public Health Service.

Christodoulakos, J. (1985, April). *Deafness: Myths and realities.* Proceedings of the First Panhellenic Congress for Deaf People. Athens, Greece.

Deland, F. (1931). *The story of lipreading.* Washington, DC: Volta Bureau.

Epitiris. (1950). Athens, Greece: *National Institute for the Deaf.*

   40 Years Union Booklet. (1988). Athens, Greece: Greek Union of Deaf-Mutes.

   Government Paper (ΦΕΚ) 68/15.3.1932, A.N. 1726/16-6-1937, 96/17-5-1907, 41/4-2-1907.

   Government Paper (ΦΕΚ) 185/6.9.1956, 243/12.12.1956.

   Government Paper (ΦΕΚ) 281/16.11.1956.

   Government Paper (ΦΕΚ) a.53/19.1.1973, 273/4.12.1975.

   Government Paper (ΦΕΚ) 202/1979 T.A., 80/31.3.1981, e/287/20.1.1982.

   Government Paper (ΦΕΚ) 167/30.9.85 A.T.

Herodotus. *Clio.*

Homer. *Iliad.*

Lampropoulou, V. (1985). *A needs assessment study for the education of the deaf children in Greece.* Unpublished doctoral dissertation, New York University, New York.

Lampropoulou, V. (1989a, July). *The history of deaf education in Greece.* Paper presented at the Deaf Way Conference. Washington, DC.

Lampropoulou, V. (1989b, July). *The vocational distribution of deaf people in Greece.* Poster presentation at the Deaf Way Conference. Washington, DC.

Lampropoulou, V. (1990, July, August). *Etiological distribution and characteristics of deaf children in Greece.* Paper presented at the 17th International Congress on Education of the Deaf, Rochester, NY.

Lampropoulou, V. (1992). *The socialeconomic status of deaf people in Greece.* The Journal of the British Association of Teachers of the Deaf, 16 (4), 90-96.

Lampropoulou, V. (1993). An evaluation of the written language of deaf students in Greece. (ΑΞΙΟΔΟΓΗΣΗ ΤΗΣ ΓΡΑΠΤΗΣ ΓΔΩΣΣΑΣ ΤΩΝ ΚΩΦΩΝ ΜΑΘΗΤΩΝ). *Glossa* (Γλωσσα), 30 (12), 40-50.

Lampropoulou, V. (1995, July). *The integration of deaf people in Greece: Results of a needs assessment study.* Paper presented at the 18th International Congress on Education of the Deaf. Tel Aviv, Israel.

Lampropoulou, V., & Padeliadou, S. (1995). Inclusive education: The Greek experience. In C. O'Hanlon (Ed.), *Inclusive education in Europe* (pp. 49-60). London: David Fulton.

Lampropoulou, V., & Padeliadou, S. (1997, March). Teachers of the deaf as compared with other groups of teachers on attitudes towards people with disabilities and inclusion. *American annals of the deaf.*

Lampropoulou, V., Alevizos, G., Balafouti, K., Samara, M., Filianou, A., Fitsiou, A., & Hatzopoulou, M. (1992). *Let's write.* Athens, Greece: Publication Company of School Books (O.E.D.B.).

Lazanas, V. (1984). *The problems of the deaf.* Athens, Greece.

Moores, D. (1978, 1996). *Educating the deaf: Psychology, principles and practices.* Boston: Houghton Mifflin Company.

Parliament Records. (1956, August). *The discussion of the act to support schools for the deaf.* Athens, Greece.

Plato. *Dialogues.* (Kratylus; Theaetetus, 206d.).

The problems of education. (1956, August). *Newspaper of the Deaf-Mutes.*

Public Law 1655/85. (1985). Organization of Publications of School Books. Athens, Greece: Ministry of Education.

Plutarhos. *Lycurgus.*

Sophocles. *Aias.*

The world of silence. (1985, February).

Education of the Deaf in Hungary

by Yvonne Csanyi

Historical Development

The First School for the Deaf

A rich nobleman who was impressed by the school for the deaf he had visited in Vienna convinced the Austro-Hungarian Hapsburg monarch to found in 1802 the first school for the deaf at Vac, forty kilometers south of Budapest.

All the other schools for the deaf that exist in Hungary were built after the turn of the twentieth century. At present there are six schools for the deaf, one for children with multiple handicaps, and one for mentally retarded children.

The First School for the Hard of Hearing

In 1925 a school for hard of hearing children was created. Also in existence is a school for hard of hearing children with multiple handicaps and mental retardation.

All of the schools for the hearing impaired in Hungary are residential schools. These residential schools contain kindergarten departments for children from the age of three to six or seven. The kindergarten program provides parents of hearing impaired children with guidance, counseling, and home training. Some of the kindergarten departments also provide the services of an itinerant teacher.

The curricula used in the schools for the deaf is established nationally and varies according to the needs of the hearing impaired child. Each of the following groups of hearing impaired children has a separate curriculum:

- deaf with normal intelligence
- educable mentally retarded deaf children
- trainable mentally retarded deaf children
- hard of hearing with normal intelligence
- hard of hearing with multiple handicaps

There is also a special curriculum for the special kindergartens for deaf children.

The total number of hearing impaired pupils in schools for the deaf and hard of hearing is 1,426. Of that total, 598 are girls, and 828 are boys. See Table 1 for a breakdown of numbers of children in various school placements.

Table 1. School Placement for Hearing Impaired Children in Hungary

	Kindergarten	School
Deaf	106	661
Deaf with Multiple Handicaps	11	120
Hard of Hearing	139	385
Hard of Hearing with Multiple Handicaps	9	84

The duration of the education program in the special schools, which differs from that found in ordinary schools, is as follows:

Public schools for hearing children:	8 years (6-14)
Schools for the deaf	10 years (6-16)
School for the hard of hearing:	8 or 9 years

The educational programs for hard of hearing children with better language skills continues for eight years, whereas the education programs for those hard of hearing children with language problems lasts nine years.

In Hungary there are no private schools for the deaf. Pupils who graduate from the special schools receive the same diploma as do graduates of the ordinary schools.

About 70 percent of the curricula of the schools for the deaf is similar to that of the ordinary schools. Some subjects found in the curriculum of the special schools are not part of the curriculum of the public schools. The special subjects include language (learning the mother tongue), auditory and rhythmical training, and individual speech therapy. Two qualified teachers of the deaf work each day with a group of five to seven children. One teacher works with the students during the morning hours and one in the afternoon.

Children with special problems in such areas as language achievement/dyspraxia, disturbed sensory-motor integration, and weak verbal memory may be taught in smaller groups or individually. Children with language acquisition problems are sent to a diagnostic center.

Mainstreaming started during the 1980s and is still in a state of development. Itinerant services for hearing impaired children have improved but are still ineffective. Most of the hard of hearing pupils attend public school since there is only one special school in the country for hard of hearing children. The integration of hard of hearing children is spontaneous and supported most often by a speech therapist. Currently there are no public school classes or resource rooms for the deaf in Hungary.

Parent Education

Home training and parental guidance services are provided at large audiological centers and at special schools for hearing impaired children. Unfortunately, parents are provided with very little psychological support. To meet the critical need for a parent association, in January 1990 such an organization, Parents for Hearing Impaired Children Association, was established. The goal of the association is to ensure that parents have a more important role in the education and development of their deaf children.

Communication Methodology

In Hungary the oral/aural communication methodology is used with deaf children who have normal intelligence and have no additional language acquisition problems. A natural approach to language acquisition that utilizes conversation, motivating situations, and reading is followed. Great emphasis is placed upon auditory training and a unisensorial approach. With deaf children with normal intelligence who have problems in the areas of speechreading, integration, verbal memory, and speech, a more analytical approach that stresses graphic methods and the use of the manual alphabet is utilized.

With the mentally handicapped deaf, the manual alphabet, graphic methods, and sign language are combined in an analytical way.

After the completion of ten years in a special school, about 50 percent of the deaf students have an overall academic achievement level similar to the level of normally hearing children. However, they may have certain difficulties in the areas of written language, reading, speech intelligibility, and good performance levels in math, geography, biology, and other subject areas. About 30 percent of the deaf children completing the special school curriculum have poor academic records but are still able to graduate. Around 20 percent of the deaf children have big gaps in their general knowledge and language abilities.

Vocational Education

In 1990, 67 percent of all hearing impaired children in Hungary attended vocational schools designed for hearing children, 26 percent attended mainstreamed classes, and 7 percent attended self-contained classes for the deaf. The staff of the vocational schools provides no job placement assistance for deaf students. The Hungarian Association of the Hearing Impaired provides a special placement service throughout the country. In the past there was no unemployment in Hungary. The employment situation has changed with the advent of changes in the structure of the government.

Higher Education

Completion of a high school program provides the hearing impaired with the possibility of seeking higher education. If hearing impaired students pass the high school final examinations, they may attend a college or university. The Training College that prepares special educators accepts deaf students. Currently, hearing handicapped persons are teaching the deaf in Hungary. All of the current deaf teachers of the deaf have excellent language competency.

Teacher Preparation Programs

At this time there is only one college that prepares teachers of the deaf. The training requires four years beyond the completion of high school. Certification requirements are:

- Four years study with a certain number of examinations
- A diploma
- A final state examination

All teachers of the deaf are also qualified to teach the mentally retarded. They receive training in both disabilities at the same time.

Significant Current Issues and Future Directions

In the future the national curricula may be less detailed, thus providing teachers with more freedom. This trend may lower graduation requirements. Smaller private schools or classes might appear. Mainstreamed education

for the deaf and itinerant services may play a more important role in the future.

The following Letter to the Editor was written by the author and printed in the Spring 1990 edition of *The Auricle* (pp. 5–6). Excerpted here in its entirety, it describes the present status of deaf education in Hungary.

Auditory training has a long tradition in Hungary. In the early thirties Gusztav Barczi (an otologist) introduced "the auditory awakening and auditory education method" and achieved excellent results by introducing groups of words of varying length and rhythm directly into the ears of deaf children. He became famous all over Europe and his methods were adopted by other countries, particularly Germany. As Professor Armin Lowe has written: ". . . Barczi was the last great representative of an auditory education that achieved results without the use of today's prosthetic aids, which were not available in his time." After World War II modern acoustic technology and techniques provided better performance and success. Nowadays each hearing-impaired Hungarian child is entitled to receive free of charge the best type of hearing aid available. These aids are imported from well-known Danish, Swiss and Austrian producers.

It must be emphasized, however, that technical assistance is only one step in the direction of approaching our object of improving the deaf child's auditory and language skills. The method used and its continuing usage is of equal importance.

Oral education also has a long tradition in Hungary. Several versions of the oral method are used. The classic or "constructive" oral method was used in schools for the deaf in Hungary up until 1978. The "constructive" oral method starts off with sounds only and then progresses to short words and finally to a great variety of similar sounding sentences. After six years of experimentation a new, more natural oral method of teaching the deaf that emphasized auditory stimulation was introduced. This so-called "conversation method" was developed from the work of van Uden (Netherlands). (A. van Uden, *A World of Language for Deaf Children*).

In Hungary, auditory training is considered a unisensory approach. Mothers of young hearing-impaired children are encouraged to speak as much as possible directly into the micro phone of the deaf child's behind-the-ear hearing aid. Melodious and essentially rhythmical speech, as well as singing and music, play an important part in the therapy process. In schools for the deaf every teacher has a special tool—a piece of thin fabric stretched over a metal frame—to keep the child from speech reading and thus not focusing upon the auditory stimuli.

In the "conversation method," auditory stimulation is integrated naturally into all of the lessons as often as is possible. The teacher observes each child's reactions to the auditory stimuli. It is repeated for those who fail to achieve the right response. A number of different types of auditory presentations are utilized:

(a) The auditory presentation can consist of the repetition of a word or sentence already known to the pupil. This is known as "reinforcement" and should come easily to the deaf child.

(b) "Differentiation" consists of a list of words or sentences that are known to the children. The deaf child merely decides which word has been used. The words can be in the form of actual objects, written sentences, pictures or maybe something memorized.

(c) Hearing without aid: An example would be when the teacher says: "Listen, do you know what happened to me yesterday?"

This last stage is usually reserved for children performing at the advanced level, but it is used occasionally with younger children since it seems to improve auditory processing skills.

Inspectors chart each deaf child's basic language skills each year in all of the schools for the deaf in Hungary. Data has been collected for ten years in the areas of speech reading skill, verbal memory, grammar usage and speech intelligibility.

The Auditory-Verbal method described is used only with children who exhibit no additional handicap. Children who have special problems with lip reading, articulation, sensory/ motor integration, or are below a certain level of intelligence are taught by other methods. Whether or not a more analytic approach stressing graphic presentation or the use of the manual alphabet and signs depends upon the abilities of each child.

Mainstreaming is a new trend in Hungary. The Training College has started a new program that includes experience working with two groups of deaf children. After an appropriate home-training period, one group of deaf children joins the kindergarten class designed for normally hearing children. The other group of deaf children starts their education at a special School for Deaf or Hard of Hearing and is main streamed after a certain number of years depending upon their performance. An individualized education plan is established for each deaf child after thoroughly testing his or her abilities, intelligence, personality and language skills. Depending on the child's needs, a shorter or longer period of supportive therapy is provided. Close contact is maintained with classroom teachers and parents, and follow-up evaluations are completed annually. Parents play an important part in the therapy program and are called upon to undertake extensive auditory and oral training with their deaf children.

Only one college provides preparation in this field. Thus all teachers of hearing-impaired children receive their training at the same college. Postgraduate courses are also available. All Hungarian teachers of the deaf speak a common language and use the same methods.

Yvonne Csanyi, Ph.D.

Training College of Teachers of the Handicapped

Budapest, Hungary

Education of the Deaf in India

Dhun D. Adenwalla

Biographical Information for Chapter Author

Name: Mrs. Dhun D. Adenwalla

Country: India
         Mailing Address: 18 Napier Road, Pune 411040 INDIA
         Email: aden_d@giaspn01.vsnl.net.in

Education: B.A. (Hons), Dip. Lib. (Bombay); PADA (London); CTD

Present Position: Hon. Principal, The Oral School for Deaf Children, 4/B Short Street, Calcutta, 700 016
         Education Consultant, Family Learning Program for Deaf Children, 18 Napier Road, Pune 411 040

Brief Description of Professional Experience:
     Founder and Principal, The Oral School for Deaf Children, Calcutta, since 1964.
     Education Consultant, Pune 411 040.
     Seminars, Conferences, and Meetings. International Center for Deafness, Gallaudet University, Washington, D.C.
     Commonwealth Society for the Deaf, London.
     Consultation Meeting, UNESCO, Paris.
     Lecturer at the Ali Yawar Jung National Institute for the Hearing Handicapped, Mumbai.
     Consultant, Schools where deaf children are mainstreamed.
     Rhode Island Hearing Assessment Project, implications of screening newborn using TEOE-Observer.

Historical Overview

India's first school for the deaf, The Bombay Institute for the Deaf and Mute, was set up by Catholic missionaries at Mazgaon, Bombay, in 1885, under the direction of Dr. Leon Meurin and Mr. T.H. Walsh. In 1893, the Calcutta Deaf and Dumb School was started by volunteers Messrs. E.D. Dutt, S. Shah, J.N. Bannerjee, and M.N. Majumdar, and is now entirely supported by the Government. The first principal of the school was Bannerjee, trained at Gallaudet College in Washington, D.C. In South India, the Florence Swainson School for the Deaf at Palayamkotai near Madras was started in 1897. In Delhi, the Lady Noyce School for the Deaf was founded in 1931. Between 1900 and 1947, when India became independent, 38 schools for the deaf were established. Presently, there are approximately 436 schools in the country, mostly in urban and semi-urban areas. Bombay and Madras have the greatest number of schools. A total of 30,000 deaf children are attending school in India. That includes children in integrated/mainstream programs.

Education for the Deaf

India's population is presently 844 million (Census of India, 1991). The population has increased 23.5 percent from the 1981 figure of 683 million. Although the category of handicapped and deaf people has not been enumerated, some sample surveys estimate that 12 percent of the population has at least one disability.

Table 1. Estimated Population of Children with Hearing and Speech Impairments

Year	Hearing Impaired AGE		Speech Impaired AGE	
	0-4	5-14	0-4	5-14
1991	160,000	565,000	218,000	800,000
1996	(Estimated)	595,000	(Estimated)	835,000

Source: N.K.Jangira, Education of children with hearing impairments in general schools, 1990.

Therefore the total number of potential school-going hearing impaired children in India is in the region of 1,365,000.

Education for the deaf is not compulsory, nor is it free. Most schools, residential and day, offer primary education and pre-vocational training. Presently, about ten schools for the deaf teach up to the class 10 level (complete secondary education). Of these, only one school for the deaf prepares students for the Indian Certificate of Secondary Education. The other schools for the deaf prepare students for the State Secondary School Certificate Examination. However, the Government of India's VIIIth Economic Plan envisages all schools for the deaf going up to the Class 10 level by the year 2000.

Children with mild cerebral palsy and learning disabilities are at times admitted to the schools for the deaf. There is a school in Bombay that teaches deaf and deaf-blind children.

A sample survey of 11,665 young people in three geographic regions of rural India revealed that 10.7 percent had a hearing impairment. The major cause of the hearing impairment was suppurative otitis media. The Government has started a scheme of training community health workers, Balwadi teachers (primary schools), Anganwadi workers (in charge of health, nutrition, and education), and social workers within the village communities in prevention, parent counseling, and integration.

The scattered population and limited facilities available for general education complicates the provision of educational programs for deaf children. The 1986 National Policy of Education places emphasis on the need for educational programs for hearing impaired children that stress integration/mainstreaming/inclusion. Reliable data is not available. The Government has set aside funds to assist organizations to implement integration of all handicapped children. This goal will not be achieved unless teachers in regular school programs are encouraged and helped to change their attitudes toward deaf children and are provided with frequent short-term training courses aimed at providing them the skills needed to effectively instruct hearing impaired children. The support services provided in these integrated/mainstream classrooms are inadequate. No resource room or itinerant services are available. The states of Maharashtra and Tamil Nadu have the largest number of students in mainstream settings. One teacher of the deaf is provided for every ten deaf students of varying ages. Because the deaf students find the fast-paced educational programs difficult, many drop out of school.

Another serious problem confronting the deaf student is the multilingual society. Thirty-three mother tongues are spoken in the different regions of India. In addition, there are about 700 dialects. Of all the regional languages, Hindi is the most widespread and commonly spoken. English continues to occupy a paradoxical position. In urban areas, English and the regional language are the media of instruction for the educated middle class. By the age of eight, an Indian city child is usually trilingual, speaking the mother tongue (the regional language), Hindi, and English. Thus the language the deaf child is required to learn varies from region to region and from school to school. In some schools, he is required to learn two languages.

System of General Education

The Central Government and the National Policy of Education provide broad guidelines regarding the pattern of education and curriculum. Each state under the Department of Education implements policy and detailed curricula. Education is compulsory and free up to the age of fourteen years. However, there are no local truant officers monitoring villages or urban neighbourhoods to ensure that children are in school. Quite a number of children are in the labor force. Government schools have been upgraded, but private schools are also in demand. They charge a fee or award scholarships. The state Government encourages private schools by providing ad hoc or annual grants and financial allowance for teachers of the deaf.

The present system of general education is described in Table 2.

An encouraging aspect of the report of the 1991 Census is that the rate of literacy among the general population has increased from 43.56 percent in 1981 to 52.11 percent in 1991. The state of Kerala leads with a literacy rate of 90.59 percent.

Academic Performance and Opportunities for Postsecondary Education

Very few deaf students reach the level of the school-leaving examination (secondary school). There is as yet no postsecondary or college program for deaf students. A minuscule number of deaf students are enrolled in undergraduate colleges, or the school/college of art. About 30 deaf students are studying or have studied in the United States at Gallaudet University or Seattle Central Community College.

In urban areas, deaf school-leavers have become qualified for the following job areas or professions through attendance at private institutions or by in-service training programs: computer technology, precision instrument assembly, pathology laboratory assistants, skilled and unskilled factory workers, welders, bookbinders, carpenters, artists, architects, designers, photographers, beauticians, hairdressers, tailors, and weavers. These school-leavers seem to be the privileged few who have had better educational opportunities.

The Indian Government has embarked upon an ambitious program for those students who live in villages and rural areas. The Government's Integrated Rural Development Program provides generous training schemes for self-employment. Depending upon the needs of the rural area, trades as diverse as carpentry, pottery, beekeeping, poultry farming, agriculture, and sericulture are taught to

Table 2. System of General Education in India

Stage	Age	Grade/Class
Preschool (Balwadi, Montessori, Kindergarten)	2-1/2 to 5	Nursery, KG, Balwadi, etc.
Primary/Elementary	5 to 11	1 to 5
Middle	12 to 14	6 to 8

Secondary
State Matriculation (SSC) or
    Central Board of Secondary Education (CBSE) or
    Indian Certificate of Secondary Education
	15 to 16	9 to 10

Higher Secondary or Junior College
    Higher Secondary Certificate awarded by State Board
    or the Central Board or the Indian Council
	16 to 18	11 to 12

Colleges and Professional Institutions, such as Arts, Science, Commerce, Technical Institutes, Medical, Agricultural, Law colleges, etc.	18 and upwards	Awarded by Bachelor of arts, Universities - science, commerce, engineering, law, medicine, etc.
Postgraduate Studies		Masters and Doctorate degrees

youth from rural areas, including those who have not attended school. However, the instructors involved in this program are not able to communicate adequately with deaf youth.

Vocational Training

There are seventeen Vocational Rehabilitation Centers and eleven Rural Rehabilitation Centers run by the Government. These centers provide basic training through practical demonstration. Due to communication problems, the instructors in these centers are not able to give verbal instructions to the deaf students and very few know sign language. Recently, however, a number of VRC instructors have attempted to learn sign language in order to communicate with their deaf students.

There is only one Government-run industrial training institute for the deaf and a few in the private sector. A number of general technical institutes could be adapted to train the hearing impaired. Three percent of the space in these general technical institutes is reserved for the handicapped. This quota is not utilized due to the fact that the deaf students lack the required entrance qualifications.

Employment exchanges reserve 3 percent of the available jobs for handicapped people. Again, these job positions are not utilized fully due to the deaf persons' lack of basic qualifications. A job development center is being set up by an Institute on Disability and Rehabilitation Research, Washington, D.C. This is a pilot project aimed at the vocational rehabilitation of the urban and rural disabled. The job development center will be linked with the existing Government District

Rehabilitation Centers and will stress assessment, the training of instructors, and vocational training in job areas suited to the rural environment. In order to train handicapped youth who live in the city, the JDC will conduct courses in high technology and other sophisticated fields of work.

Communication

Oralism came to India with the European missionaries, who set up the first school for the deaf in Bombay. India has an oral tradition of teaching the deaf, probably because the earliest teachers were trained at the University of Manchester and at Clark School in the United States. Oralism is still enforced in most schools because teachers find it more comfortable and parents are initially attracted to it. In actual fact, however, most deaf children and adults communicate among themselves in sign language, which is learned from peers, since, in schools, sign language is not taught and is actively suppressed.

Serious attempts to study Indian Sign Language began in 1977, and as a result a dictionary of Indian Sign Language was published in 1980. The study carried out by Vasishta establishes the fact that ISL is a highly structured language. This is indicated by its grammatical regularity. There is no doubt about the expressive capabilities of ISL. ISL developed indigenously in India and has little resemblance to ASL or European sign languages. Contrary to the opinion among hearing people, ISL has no relationship to hand gestures used in classical Indian dance forms. A phonetic hand alphabet of Indian languages somewhat similar to the American one-handed manual alphabet was developed by Ms. P. Bhide in 1975, and is being used by some schools in Bombay.

Recently a few schools in India have started using Total Communication. Ali Yavar Jung National Institute for the Hearing Handicapped (AYJNIHH) has begun research studies on a "sign system" to help develop the language of deaf people in India.

Self-Help Groups

The All India Federation of the Deaf under the leadership of Dr. Nandy was started in 1955 at Delhi. It is a multipurpose center that prepares the deaf for vocational training and self-employment. *The Deaf Way*, a periodical published by deaf people and started in 1997, highlights achievements and hurdles of the adult deaf.

The All India Sports Council for the Deaf and the Delhi Foundation for Deaf Women, with branches in the major cities, has provided opportunities to deaf youth in many areas.

The National Society for Equal Opportunity for the Handicapped (NASEOH) was started in 1970. It runs a vocational training center, presents annual awards, and publishes the NASEOH news.

Parents groups, such as Suniye, are scattered throughout the major cities, but they do not form a lobby strong enough to demand better educational opportunities for the deaf children. Often parents receive conflicting advice from teachers, doctors, and audiologists. Some parents are enrolled in the John Tracy Clinic Correspondence Course in English or Hindi. Available information regarding alternative methods of communication is negligible. Dissatisfaction with the present situation regarding educational programs for the deaf has led some groups to start their own schools. Examples would be the EAR Center in Bombay, The Oral School for Deaf Children in Calcutta, and Parents' Own Clinic. There are eighteen preschool programs and some children attend Montessori schools for two to four years.

Recreation and Cultural Activities

Clubs managed by deaf adults are active in all of the larger cities of India. Indoor games of chess, carrom, table-tennis, and so on are organized, and hobbies such as photography and sketching are popular.

Deaf artists and architects have made names for themselves. Talent has yet to be explored in the rural areas. In Calcutta, a group of young deaf people have formed a theatre of the deaf called The Action Players. They have had many successful shows, won awards, and performed in other cities. Four young deaf artists were invited to the National Theatre of the Deaf Summer School in the United States, and one artist performed with the Japanese Theatre of the Deaf in Tokyo. The Action Players have also appeared on television.

Ali Yavar Jung National Institute for the Hearing Handicapped (AYJNIHH) is now planning to have another Theatre of the Deaf in Bombay.

Technology

Body-worn and behind the ear (post-aural) hearing aids are being manufactured in India that have a frequency range of from 0.250 to 6.30 kHZ and an output of 136 dB SPL. Some of these hearing aids are digitally controlled. The Government distributes free hearing aids to children of low income groups. However, they are not always the model that is suited to the individual child's hearing loss. Accessories such as cords and batteries are not free, so the benefit derived from hearing aids for the profoundly deaf is minimal. Ear mold making is in its infancy, and ill-fitting ear molds is a major problem for those children in the oral-aural programs. Since 1996, however, new units for making molds have made great strides. Audiometers, group hearing aids, and speech (auditory) trainers are manufactured indigenously. Counseling services in the area of auditory management and educational audiology are in short supply, as are technicians skilled in making and fitting ear molds, and in making minor and major repairs to hearing aids.

Other Services
Media Services

Although television sets are more readily available now to the general public, even in community centers and rural areas, captioned television programming is not available. However, many films in the regional languages are subtitled in Hindi or English which allows for a wider viewing among the general public.

The commentary of a 20-minute Sunday program, *New Magazine for the Hearing Impaired*, is signed and fingerspelled (two-hand alphabet). The general reaction of deaf adults to this signed program is reserved, since it is not signed by a deaf person.

Assistive devices such as teletype devices for the deaf are not available but are in demand by the educated deaf. Presently, there are about five teletype devices for the deaf in India that have been imported from the United States.

Interpreter services are not available even in the major cities. In seminars, if the deaf are participating, a volunteer may interpret. There are no special provisions for the deaf such as induction loops in public places.

Legislation

Legislation dealing with the deaf relates to travel concessions, awards and scholarships, tax benefits, and job vacancies. Whereas the blind can travel free, deaf people have to pay a certain percentage for rail and bus tickets. A system of scholarships for education and in-service training for handicapped persons from low income groups was started in 1955. Tax benefits amount to a deduction of rupees 10,000, after the computation of total income. Economic assistance is also given in the form of small loans to handicapped people who are self-employed. Three percent of the vacancies in the employment field for class III and IV posts (typing, clerk, peon, etc.) are reserved for the handicapped, but often this percentage is not fully utilized. Apart from these benefits, the Government of India awards a national prize annually for the most efficient handicapped employee and the most outstanding employer.

Teacher Preparation

It is recommended that schools for the deaf employ trained teachers of the deaf, but this is not always possible due to the shortage of teachers. Many receive in-service training while working at schools for the deaf.

Diploma or certificate courses of one year's duration are conducted in twelve institutes. The requirement for entrance is a Higher Secondary Certificate or Graduate student status. Preference is given to those who have majored in psychology, education, or social work. A general teaching certificate is not a compulsory requirement.

The only institute offering B.Ed. program to prepare as a teacher of the deaf is the Ali Yavar Jung National Institute for the Hearing Handicapped. To qualify for admission, a candidate must hold a bachelor's degree in any subject and must have worked at a school for the deaf for two academic terms. Up to now, deaf people have not been trained as academic teachers of the deaf, but are employed in some schools as arts and craft teachers.

Sign language courses are not part of the Institute course of study. Lectures/tutorials are conducted in English and the regional language at the four regional centers of AYJNIHH located at Hyderabad, Calcutta, Delhi, and Bhubaneshwar. An M.Ed. in the area of deafness designed to meet the training needs of educators, researchers, and higher secondary teachers is planned for the future.

The Ali Yavar Jung National Institute for the Hearing Handicapped was established at Bombay in 1983 by the Ministry of Welfare, Government of India. The Institute is aimed at providing teachers, clinicians, and welfare workers the training needed to develop educational programs for the hearing impaired,

undertake basic and applied research, and develop public educational programs through the production of short films to be shown on television. Examples would include "Suniye" (Listen), "Ek Khel Sunmney Ka" (a listening game-group screening test using pure tone signals at different intensity levels), and "Yes, the Deaf Can." The Institute is equipped with clinical audiometers, impedance bridges, B&D audiometer, and additional equipment which is used for diagnostic and research purposes. The Institute provides extension services which reach out to rural and semi-rural areas, where health workers and "Anganwadi" workers are trained to identify deaf children and counsel families. The Institute's quarterly newsletter *NINAD* mentions that AYJNIHH is actively involved in the forthcoming NSS (National Sample Survey) of the hearing impaired population and claims, "There are more than 4 million hearing impaired people in India."

Significant Current Issues and Future Directions in the Education of the Deaf

The following research studies are needed to provide the basic information required to improve the quality of educational services for the deaf in India:

1. A survey of deaf children and adults to determine the numbers, causes of deafness, degree, extent, and age at onset.
2. The use of alternative approaches in the education of the deaf children in villages and cities.
3. A study of the causes of low academic achievement and the high student drop out rate.
4. A detailed study of communication and life style in a sample survey of deaf adults, adolescents, and their parents, in order to asses their needs, in both rural and urban areas.

5. A comprehensive and detailed study of the prevalent use of sign language and other modes of communication used among the deaf and their hearing peers.
6. A study of the most effective ways of communicating with deaf adults in employment and training situations.
7. A study of mobilizing "pressure" groups as a means by which the needs of the deaf would be better under stood by the general public and professionals.
8. The development of leadership programs for the deaf.
9. The restructuring of teacher training programs in order that ineffective systems are no longer perpetuated.
10. The development of better qualified teachers, books in regional languages, and refresher courses.
11. The provision of higher salaries for professionals.
12. The development of programs that provide active and realistic support to parents. Parents are now provided with unrealistic expectations of a "perfectly" talking deaf child, rather than a "thinking" well-adjusted deaf child. With the profusion of new technology, parents' hopes that their child will develop perfect speech have risen to unrealistic proportions.
13. The development of family and marriage counseling services for the deaf. (Most marriages in India are still arranged.)

In India's developing economy and aim for education for all, innovative thinking and new strategies for educating the deaf are needed to provide for an improved vision of the future. It is most encouraging to see that new rural programs, sponsored and encouraged by the Government, and the few urban special institutions/schools stand out like jewels, albeit educating a small number. But the signs are evident in the product of these schools -

young deaf people with outstanding ability and courage in their convictions.

References

Adenwalla, Dhun D. Chapter. In *Gallaudet encyclopedia of deaf people and deafness*. McGraw-Hill.

Adenwalla, Dhun D. Chapter. In *International view of deafness*.

Annual Report. (1990). Ministry of Human Resource Development, Department of Education, Government of India.

Jangira, N.K. (1990, December). *Education of children with hearing impairment in general schools: Manpower requirement*. Paper presented at Fourth Annual National Seminar on Manpower Development, Ali Yavar Jung National Institute for the Hearing Handicapped, Bombay, India.

Pamphlets. Ali Yavar Jung National Institute for the Hearing Handicapped. Bombay 400 050, India.

Programs and concessions for disabled persons. National Institute for the Orthopaedically Handicapped.

Report of the working group on the welfare of the handicapped for the VIIIth Five Year Plan. (1989). Ministry of Welfare, Government of India.

Report. (1991, March 26). *Times of India*.

Rose, Sreela. (1989, December). *Augmentative communication . . . at ISSAC*.

Roy, R., et al. (1986). *An attempt to rehabilitate the deaf in rural India*. Paper presented at the First Asian-Pacific Regional Conference on Deafness, Hong Kong.

Special schools in India. (1990). New Delhi, India: Rehabilitation Council.

Sr. Rita Mary. (1990, December). *Education of the deaf: Present status and future needs during the VIIIth plan*.

Stillman, Ian. (1990, December). *A need for training vocational instructors for the deaf*. Paper presented at Fourth Annual National Seminar on Manpower Development, Ali Yavar Jung National Institute for the Hearing Handicapped, Bombay, India.

Vasishta, Madan, et al. *An introduction to the Indian Sign language (with focus on Delhi)*. Sign Language Research, Inc.

Education of the Deaf in Israel: Past, Present, and Future

A. Zwiebel, Ph.D.

Head, Special Education Teacher's Training Program
School of Education
Bar Ilan University, Ramat Gan, Israel

*Supported by the Schnitzer Foundation
for Research on the Israeli Economy and Society
and Shema Organization for the Hearing Impaired

Introduction

The educational system for the deaf in Israel will soon be entering its seventh decade of existence. As with everything in this "old-new" land, the past is an inherent part of the present and cannot be severed from the heritage of thousands of years. This heritage includes educational institutions that have existed for hundreds of years in Jewish communities and deaf personalities who lived and worked in Jerusalem from the first century C.E.

One must evaluate the development of the current educational system in light of several basic facts. Since the system has a relatively short history and many of its founders and developers are still working in the field today, it is difficult to develop a historical perspective. The country is made up of a heterogeneous society of immigrants from developed and under-developed countries. The general educational system is still in the process of development and crystallization. The meager resources currently available present a serious challenge to the philosophy of a welfare society that proposes to supply all the educational and rehabilitation services needed by its citizens. Because the population is small and spread over a large geographical area and the professional services provided all groups and sectors are not equal, alternative solutions to service delivery problems are required.

About fifteen years before the actual establishment of the State of Israel, pioneer educators established the first educational institutions for the deaf in the State. Because of the German Jewish background and education of these early pioneers, the early schools for the deaf utilized the theories of the German oral schools for the deaf.

The educational framework has crystallized, expanded, and developed widely in the years following the establishment of the State. Educational policy has been influenced by several bodies: representatives of the deaf community, parents of deaf children, and educators and policy makers who have immi-

grated from various countries (mostly from America). Some of these individuals were hearing impaired themselves.

Academic researchers from the United States and other countries who are current on what is happening throughout the world in the field have visited Israel during the recent past and have strongly influenced the education of the deaf in Israel. Since the educational system is entirely public, centralized and controlled by the State Ministry of Education, it can change rapidly. Academic training institutions and public organizations for the education and rehabilitation of the deaf tend to be flexible, open to change, and not controlled by the central government.

The public Arab sector has an autonomous department located in the Ministry of Education. The Ministry of Education supervises and administers educational institutions for the Arab deaf. Also in the Arab sector is a private institution managed by the church. In Jerusalem, classes for hearing impaired Arabs are located in a combined Jewish-Arab school, and in Tel Aviv there are a few Arab pupils in a segregated school for the deaf. The policies of the public Arab educational system have been influenced by the same sources as were mentioned above.

History

A survey of the earliest history of the education of hearing impaired in Israel reveals that the deaf were viewed by ancient Jewish society as human beings who possessed all of the rights of any citizen in the community (Zwiebel & Wiesel, 1989). Limitations were imposed only upon those few deaf people who had no means of communication. Historical sources indicate that deafness was not considered as a cause of low cognitive performance. The inability to communicate was considered a prime factor. Those deaf people who could talk or communicate in some manner, and the hard of hearing, were considered to have the same rights as people who could hear. Emotional maturity was not considered an area of concern or discrepancy, even with the deaf who lacked the ability to communicate. The research cites many examples of deaf people who were learned and who had gained high status in the Jewish society.

During recent times, with the establishment of the State educational system, Israel has undergone a process of organization and institutionalization. Educational reform reached a peak with the passage of laws that call for universal free compulsory education. Concurrently, institutions that provided special education services were also developed.

In the years preceding the establishment of the State, a time of Jewish immigration, there was a period of cultural crystallization during which Hebrew was adopted and accepted as the common language.

The current system of special education had its origins at the beginning of the century with the founding of the School for the Blind in Jerusalem. Just 30 years later the first school for retarded children was founded. In 1932 the first Hebrew school for the deaf in Israel was established in Jerusalem. It was among the first schools devoted to special education. The school was established as part of the French "Alliance" network which was concerned with the education of Jews in Europe and the Middle Eastern countries. The director and founder of the Jerusalem Hebrew School for the Deaf was Mr. R. B. Hexter, a German Jew. He had previously directed a school for the Jewish deaf in Berlin, one of the first Jewish schools for the deaf in Europe.

The oral method, according to the German school philosophy, was the method of instruction. Deaf children from all over the country studied in Jerusalem and were housed with foster families. The use of the German or oral philosophy of teaching the deaf was to be expected, since the German immigrants who had reached Israel at the time of the growing Nazi persecution constituted the intellectual elite of Israel and knew no other system of teaching the deaf. It was also common knowledge that in the past deaf children from Israel were sent to Germany to be educated in Jewish residential schools for the deaf.

It was just a matter of time until education for the deaf expanded to other areas of the country, including Tel Aviv, Israel's largest city, which had a small community of deaf people. Children who were refugees and who had attended Jewish residential schools for the deaf in Europe arrived following the end of the Second World War. There were also deaf children who were not absorbed by schools for the deaf in Jerusalem and whose parents wanted them to study near their homes.

Mrs. B. Miller, a teacher from the Berlin School for the Deaf in Germany, was the pioneer teacher of the deaf in Tel Aviv. Her school, which was established in 1941, developed gradually from one class to a school with eight classes of deaf children ranging from the ages of six to fourteen years. The German oral method was used in this school and the school's curriculum placed great emphasis on speech development and the acquisition of basic concepts. After the founding of the State of Israel, the school became part of the national educational network which was established in 1948. In 1952 Mrs. Miller also started Israel's first kindergarten for deaf children from the ages of four to six.

In the early 1950s, a school for the deaf was established in Haifa to serve the population of the northern part of Israel. The school was founded by Dr. Tzelyuk, an ear, nose, and throat specialist, who was born in Germany. Dr. Tzelyuk's school also emphasized speech and language development.

Services for deaf infants also started in the 1950s with the development of the Micha Organization for the Treatment of Deaf Infants. This organization was established by Dr. A. Korin, an ear, nose, and throat specialist. The Micha Organization has consulting centers throughout the country. Its goals and services were summarized by Horovitz and Shefatya (1987). They indicated that these centers treat children from the age of six weeks to six years and follow the children's progress during their first year in elementary school. The Center's functions include diagnosis and follow-up, parental guidance, and hearing aid fitting and follow-up. The deaf children visit the center several times a week for services that include language, cognitive, and social-emotional development activities. Part of the center's responsibilities is to provide parents with information and assistance concerning the placement of their deaf children in one of the several different educational settings available. At the outset, the Micha centers and especially those in Tel Aviv promoted the oral method of teaching the deaf.

In Tel Aviv the oral approach is still dominant. Other centers follow a Total Communication approach or a modified oral approach that permits instruction in sign language.

In the 1960s, the education for the deaf expanded and diversified. The first element of this diversification was the integration of deaf children into classes for hearing children. The concept of integration was influenced by special educators who had emigrated from the United States and was supported by people in general education and by members of the scientific community.

Integrated kindergartens were opened for pre-schoolers. Deaf children comprised 25 percent of the pupils participating in the kindergarten classes. Although the deaf children had their own teacher for instruction in academic areas, most of their time was spent participating with hearing children in games and group activities. Most of the deaf children who attend these kindergartens have been involved with the Micha Organization from an early age.

The first classes for the deaf in regular public schools were established in the 1960s in Tel Aviv. These classes were composed of an average of nine deaf children. Each class had a special teacher and a teacher's aid. The deaf children were integrated into classes for hearing children in subjects such as art, handicrafts, and sports. Capable deaf children were integrated into regular classrooms for other

subjects as well. In general, these children had no additional handicaps, had usable residual hearing, relatively good speech, and supportive families. Generally the parents of the deaf children were at a high socio-economic level.

Side-by-side with the public school classes for deaf children, separate schools for the deaf were also expanding. A central school for deaf children from the southern region of Israel was established. These special schools provided the pupils with activities and facilities that were on a higher academic level than was possible to achieve in a regular public school with one or two classes for deaf children. On the other hand, the separate schools for the deaf enrolled many deaf children who had problems in addition to deafness. This increase in number of deaf children with multiple handicaps caused some parents to find these schools to be less desirable than they had in the past.

Because of the large number of diverse population groups and the difficulty collecting enough deaf children to constitute a cohort group, deaf children in Jerusalem had to be placed in regular public school classes. A number of classes composed of Arab deaf children were opened at the school for the deaf in Jerusalem. These classes were taught by Arab teachers who teach the Arabic language and culture.

In the late 1960s, the Shema Organization for the Education and Rehabilitation of Hearing Impaired Children and Youth was established by Dr. Mazur. The purposes of Shema were: to make the public aware of the needs and problems of hearing impaired children and youth; to introduce new ideas concerning the education and rehabilitation of hearing impaired children; to supply direct services to deaf children and their families; to provide guidance and counseling services to parents, children, and professional personnel in the field; to provide advice and counsel to government officials who are responsible for the development and purchase of educational materials; to enrich and improve existing services; to provide social and cultural activities for hearing impaired children and youth during after-school hours; and to identify, diagnose, and place the impaired children in suitable educational settings.

The work of Shema is handled by a professional staff skilled in the education of the deaf. The staff includes educators, psychologists, community social workers, guidance counselors, and speech therapists.

Each Shema Center has a diagnosis and therapy department, a district supervisory center, and a program for hearing impaired adolescents (HOD).

The services of each Shema center include: programs for hearing impaired children and youth; social and cultural activities, which help to relieve social isolation, foster personality development, positive self-image, and self confidence; diagnosis and therapy services which include identification, auditory training, speech therapy, hearing therapy, language development, community involvement in the purchase and maintenance of hearing aids; a District Supervisory Center that provides teachers of hearing impaired children in regular schools with services which include the testing, follow-up, and coordination of all professional staff, proper educational placement, planning of tutoring services, and in-service training for the special education staff.

Shema was established by parents of hearing impaired children and has received strong governmental support during its organizational and operational phases. Especially important was Shema's part in the establishment of classrooms for deaf children in public schools, the integration of deaf children into regular classes, and the creation of support services to meet the special needs of hard of hearing children. Shema has also helped develop various auxiliary services for deaf children. The organization has established social activities for hearing impaired children who are fully integrated in regular public school classrooms and have no hearing impaired peers.

In the 1970s and early 1980s, new trends in the education of the deaf in Israel appeared. The first of these trends was the increasing number of placement options available for the elementary-aged deaf children (ages 6–14). One of the new options was to place classes of deaf children in regular public schools. This option provided the deaf child with some degree of integration. The amount of integration depended upon the individual needs of each child. Another option for some deaf children was total integration into a regular public school classroom.

Most of the children who were referred by the treatment centers to a regular public school classroom were hard of hearing. The treatment centers continued to follow these children's progress and provide their families with counseling services. In addition, the deaf children who were fully integrated into a regular public school classroom were provided tutoring by a special teacher for three to four hours a week at the expense of the Ministry of Education. The Shema Organization has also established an administrative structure that provides supervisors who guide these special teachers.

In the 1970s, specialized psychological services and assessment tools for the deaf were developed. Norms for the deaf children in Israel were established on Snijders-Oomen Test of Intelligence (S.O.N.) (Zwiebel & Rand, 1978). Diagnostic tools and achievement tests were adapted for use with deaf children. The first demographic research that focused on the deaf children who were partially or fully integrated into the public schools of Israel was conducted (Zwiebel & Rand, 1978).

In light of worldwide trends, the experience of educators, and the results of research studies, there is a growing tendency towards moderation in the use of the oral approach to educate deaf children, the approach that was so dominant during Israel's first 35 years as a nation. Committees of specialists who have studied the topic have suggested the removal of restrictions against the use of sign language in schools for the deaf. Israeli sign language (ISL) is now in use and has been combined with oral communication.

The 1970s saw a significant breakthrough in the provision of high school education for the deaf. Attempts were made to establish high school programs that included diverse vocational tracks. The initiation of high school education for deaf pupils integrated into regular public high school has created the need to establish support services.

Various education and communication options have been used with the deaf high school students enrolled in comprehensive and vocational high schools. Much thought has gone into planning these educational delivery models, and attempts at new configurations have been tried. In the southern region of Israel where groups of deaf pupils have been integrated into regular high school classrooms, some teachers of the deaf have functioned as interpreters for regular classroom teachers.

Similar arrangements have been developed in the separate schools established for deaf male and female pupils who are part of the ultra-orthodox Jewish religious educational system. Because these children are not able to integrate into government-operated educational settings, they have often received lower quality educational services in the past.

The trend to integrate deaf children into regular public school programs that appeared during the 1980s did not include deaf children with multiple handicaps. These children are still found in segregated schools for the deaf. The number of deaf children who are partially integrated into public school classrooms has increased markedly during the past decade and more and includes more children with a severe hearing loss.

A summary of the historical development of the education of the deaf in Israel reveals several trends:

1. Various educational settings were developed according to chronological age: kindergarten, elementary, high school, and higher education. This development reflects fulfillment of the basic educational needs of the deaf.

2. Programs were developed according to the severity of the hearing impairment. Programs were first developed for the deaf, then the hard of hearing, and finally for those with mild to moderate hearing impairments.

3. Treatment programs and auxiliary lessons were established after the basic educational system for the deaf was organized.

4. The thrust behind the development of the educational and treatment programs for deaf children originated from the deaf community, experts in the field (some of whom are hearing impaired), sources from outside of the country, and subsequently from research developments within Israel.

5. There has been movement from extremism to moderation in the use of the oral method.

6. Manual channels of communication have emerged.

7. There has been a movement from segregated schools for the deaf to integrated regular public school classes.

Educational Programs

Dynamic historical developments have determined the site of the educational and treatment programs for the deaf in Israel and have shaped the direction of future trends. Educational services for the deaf are concentrated in the main cities of each region of the country.

Because of smaller numbers of children, educational programs for deaf children in the remote areas of Israel are individualized and under government supervision. As the deaf children from the remote areas get older, especially at the high school level, there is greater flexibility in designing each pupil's program. The student's diverse interests and abilities (vocational and comprehensive tracks) and small numbers make flexibility in scheduling each student's program a necessity.

At the pre-school level there is a tendency to integrate the deaf children into kindergartens near their parents' home. The children and their families receive training, guidance, and treatment at one of the Micha centers. Pre-schools that integrate hearing and deaf children exist in several places. Other deaf children and children with multiple handicaps are referred to special kindergarten classes in schools for the deaf.

At the elementary level, options for deaf include the following: placement in segregated schools for the deaf, placement in a classroom for deaf children in a regular public school that is partially integrated, and full integration into a regular public school classroom. There are still regions of the country where this variety of placement options does not exist.

High school programs for the deaf include several tracks. The vocational track allows for full integration and training of deaf students with both high and low ability levels. Some of the vocational options enable the deaf pupil to obtain a matriculation certificate. This allows the student the option of continuing his or her education or of finding employment. Possible vocational areas include automobile mechanics, mechanics, drafting, sign-making, graphics, fashion design, and bookkeeping. In Jerusalem a national dormitory and vocational training programs have been established to meet the individual needs of deaf children with multiple handicaps.

Most hearing impaired children with a slight hearing handicap are fully integrated into the general educational system. The three hours a week of intensive tutoring provided by the government does not satisfy their educational needs. The government has made certain concessions to hearing impaired pupils who choose to take the government matriculation examinations. These concessions focus mainly on the foreign language part of the examination. Hearing impaired students are exempt from the section of the test that includes conversation and listening and are allowed to answer in Hebrew in order

to prove comprehension of the text. The pupil taking the exam is also entitled to a sign language interpreter if he or she so desires.

Some technical and academic institutions providing higher education admit hearing impaired students. Interpreters and note takers are not provided. The hearing impaired students enrolled in higher education programs are entitled to auxiliary services and are provided with funds for photocopying and tutoring in special cases.

Although many of the educational programs for the deaf still use the oral method of instruction, a transition from the oral method to the use of sign language is beginning in many schools. The Total Communication philosophy has been implemented in some classes for the deaf that are located in regular public schools. In-service training in the use of sign language is now required of all current teachers of the deaf.

The National Insurance Law entitles the hearing impaired to receive State-funded vocational rehabilitation services. Financial allocations are determined on the basis of the severity of the hearing impairment. Rehabilitation services are provided to all sectors of the population including those just beginning their employment, those involved in a vocational program, and those enrolled in a university. Several vocational rehabilitation centers throughout Israel provide diagnostic services for the hearing impaired. These centers also provide placement and follow-up services.

The first follow-up research (Horowitz & Shefatya, 1987) of deaf graduates aged 17 to 25 found that this group had a tendency toward early entry into the labor force. More than one-third of those who entered the job market between the ages of 17 and 19 found employment as unskilled laborers. Most of the deaf individuals included in this population graduated from schools for the deaf. The study found that only 16.7 percent of the 17–19 year olds had matriculation certificates and that only 30 percent of the population was still in school. The percentage of deaf individuals who hold matriculation certificates or who are still in school is lower than the percentages found in surveys of the general population. The development of high school level vocational programs for the deaf during the last decade should increase the number of deaf persons who achieve matriculation certificates or continue their education in future years.

Teacher Preparation

Programs to prepare teachers of the deaf in Israel have improved over the years. As mentioned previously, the first educators of the deaf came from Germany. These educators headed the schools for the deaf and trained the teaching staff through on-the-job training or short in-service courses. In 1964 the Ministry of Education first attempted to set up a course of study designed to certify teachers of the deaf. The course consisted of 500 hours of instruction, which included field work and lectures on audiology, language, and speech acquisition, and pedagogy. At the same time Bar Ilan University in Ramat Gan offered students a special track aimed at preparing teachers of the deaf. Graduates of this program received a B.A. degree and a license to teach. The training provided general education philosophy and methodology, and the specific in-service and practical training required to teach specific handicapped groups. The program philosophy was based on the belief that the basic foundations of reading acquisition and general methods of teaching are invaluable tools for anyone working in any field of education, including the education of the deaf.

Towards the end of the 1970s a program for the preparation of teachers of the hearing impaired was established at Tel Aviv University. The program focused exclusively on the training of teachers of the hearing impaired and included courses in psychology, audiology, reading acquisition, teaching methods, and a program of practicum experiences. The major in teaching the deaf was

part of the Special Education department. Graduates of this program were required to complete an additional year of general teacher preparation in order to receive teacher certification. Raising the academic standards of the teacher training programs has both enriched the preparation and raised the quality of teachers of the deaf. Two teacher education colleges have established programs for those graduates of regular teacher training programs who are interested in specializing in the education of the hearing impaired.

The number of deaf teachers who are involved in teaching the deaf in Israel is negligible. Most of the deaf teachers teach subjects like arts and crafts, home economics, or sign language. As the trend towards the increased use of sign language strengthens, especially in the schools for the deaf, the number of deaf teachers will probably increase. The strong oral trend of the past, the high academic level of teacher preparation programs, and the lack of adequate auxiliary or support services for deaf college students probably accounts for the small number of deaf teachers of the deaf in Israel.

Programs to train therapists in psychology, social work, and speech, as well as those designed to prepare teachers of the deaf, have become more intense and academically rigorous. Part of the curriculum of the program to prepare psychologists and social workers who can work with the deaf consists of on-the-job training at Micha and Shema centers. The therapists at these centers provide parents with counseling, guidance, and support services. According to parental need, the treatment includes the dissemination of information, diagnosis, placement, and individual and group therapy.

The opening of the School for Communication Disorders at Tel Aviv University during the 1970s has resulted in the preparation of speech therapists who have the special training needed to work with hearing impaired children. These university graduates who can also provide guidance services are employed in educational programs sponsored by the Ministry of Education.

Statistical Data

The statistical data available on the education of the deaf in Israel is based upon three demographic studies: the first, completed during the 1970s (Zwiebel & Milgram, 1982); and two completed in the 1980s (Horowitz & Shefatya, 1987; Wiesel & Reichstein, 1990). Also useful are data from the Ministry of Education (Arbatz & Zwiebel, 1989).

The percentage of deaf children among the population has remained constant, with the data indicating that the number of deaf children has grown at the same rate as the population in general. Most of the growth has occurred in programs where the hearing impaired children have been integrated into the regular public school classroom. Schools for the deaf and self-contained segregated classes for the deaf in public schools have shown no growth.

A study completed during the 1970s (Zwiebel & Milgram, 1982), reported that the number of pupils enrolled in schools for the deaf was reported to be double the number of pupils found in the mainstream programs. With the establishment of the mainstream philosophy, the location of elementary-aged deaf children has shifted, and now an almost equal number are found in integrated public school classrooms as are found in schools for the deaf.

The 4,200 pupils found in educational programs for the deaf in Israel are divided in the following manner: One hundred and sixty-nine pupils from the age of 4 to 6 are located in 17 kindergartens; 750 pupils from the age of 6 to 14 are found in segregated schools for the deaf or segregated public school elementary programs in the four main geographical areas; about 200 hearing impaired pupils, ages 14 to 18, are enrolled in seven special high school programs, and about 3,100 pupils are enrolled in integrated public school kindergarten, elementary, or high school programs located near their place of residence.

A demographic study of pre-schoolers (4 to 6 years of age) conducted during 1984 found that 61 percent were male. Fifty-nine percent had a hearing level of 91db or more. Only 7 percent had a hearing level of less than 55db (Horowitz & Shefatya, 1987). Most were found to be hearing impaired from birth. Only 11 percent became hearing impaired after the age of one year.

Hereditary causes were found to be the reason for deafness in about 40 percent of the children. Twelve percent became deaf from the German measles or some other complications of the mother's pregnancy. And for 19 percent the cause of deafness was unknown. About two-thirds of the deaf children received treatment before the age of two. Eight percent of the hearing impaired children have at least one hearing impaired parent, and 27 percent have at least one deaf sibling.

When the intellectual level of the hearing impaired children was checked by a performance IQ test, IQ scores ranging from 46 to 135 were found. The average IQ score was 102.2 with a standard deviation of 17.5.

Multiple handicaps were uncovered in about 50 percent of the children diagnosed. The most frequently found handicaps in addition to deafness were visual and emotional problems and learning disabilities. Socio-economic indexes indicated that the hearing impaired children came from a wide range of economic strata with a tendency to asymmetry at the lower level.

Research done in the 1970s with elementary school-aged children presented similar results as those found in a later study of deaf pre-school children (Zwiebel & Milgram, 1982). The study was completed mainly on a population of severely hearing impaired children. As was true of the results of the earlier study, the overall potential cognitive level was average and the socio-economic level of the hearing impaired children was slightly lower than that of the general population. Fifty-two percent of the pupils were boys. Sixty percent of the hearing impaired students integrated into public school programs were girls.

A demographic study completed in 1990 studied children with a hearing level of 56db and above. The investigation looked at the hearing level of children in three kinds of educational settings: schools for the deaf, classes of deaf children located in public schools, and mainstream classrooms (Wiesel & Reichstein, 1990). Seventy-nine percent of the pupils in the residential schools for the deaf had a severe to profound hearing impairment, whereas 66.5 percent of the pupils in self-contained classes located in public schools and 34.1 percent of the students integrated into regular classes for hearing children had a severe to profound hearing impairment. It can be assumed that most hearing impaired pupils with less than a 55db hearing level are integrated into public school classrooms.

Those pupils integrated into regular public school classrooms tended to have better communication skills and generally came from families with a higher socio-economic status (Zwiebel & Allen, 1988). It was found that most of the deaf children who were mainstreamed were oral. The children from the schools for the deaf used sign language to communicate in school but only minimally to communicate within the family circle. It was found that deaf children who have hearing parents generally have more handicaps in addition to deafness than do deaf children who have deaf parents.

No surveys of hearing impaired pupils in high school, in the Arab sector or integrated into a regular classroom, have been completed. One may assume that the demographic picture of hearing impaired high school students is similar to that discovered to be true of elementary level pupils. It has been reported that the pupils from the Arab sector are mostly from low socio-economic backgrounds. The percentage of deafness among the Arab population is greater than the percentage of deafness among the Jewish population. Frequent intermarriage among relatives in the Arab sector may account for a higher rate of hereditary deafness.

Research Findings

Academic Achievement

The first study completed in the 1970s (Zwiebel & Milgram, 1982) found that elementary-aged hearing impaired children, when compared with hearing children, showed a four-year achievement delay in basic arithmetic skills. Another finding was that a significant percentage of those who had finished eight years of study were not able to read. This phenomenon was most evident among the children attending schools for the deaf.

A survey of achievement in reading comprehension revealed that hearing impaired pupils integrated into regular public school settings, and in segregated public school lower elementary classes had good scores, and hearing impaired students in upper grade segregated classes had satisfactory reading achievement scores. The reading achievement scores of students enrolled in schools for the deaf showed marked academic retardation (Horowitz & Shefatya, 1987). A strong connection was found between the socio-economic background of the parents, the existence of multiple handicaps, the sex of the pupil (girls score higher), and reading comprehension achievement scores. Academic achievement in arithmetic was evaluated only on the basis of exercises and not word problems. The results were similar to the achievement scores in reading comprehension. Again, there was a significant difference in the scores of children enrolled in the various educational settings.

Another study that compared the achievement scores of deaf and hearing elementary school pupils in the areas of arithmetic word problems and mathematical comprehension found that the achievement level of the deaf pupils was lower than that of the hearing pupils (Zwiebel, 1989a, 1989c; Zwiebel & Allen, 1988). The achievement level of hearing impaired pupils from schools for the deaf was two to five years behind that of the control group of hearing pupils. The achievement gap between the groups was smaller for classes of hearing impaired children found in regular public school settings and for pupils integrated into regular public school classrooms.   Only high achieving hearing impaired students in the mainstream seemed to reach an academic level equal to that of their hearing peers. According to national surveys, hearing impaired children's arithmetic achievement scores are similar to those of culturally disadvantaged pupils (Zwiebel, 1989a). When the demographic variables that favor a mainstream setting were controlled, there was still a statistically significant increase in achievement in a mainstream setting as compared with a segregated school for the deaf or a segregated self-contained class in a regular public school (Zwiebel & Allen, 1988).

Cognitive Ability

Studies indicate that kindergarten and elementary level hearing impaired children have average cognitive levels (Horowitz & Shefatya, 1987).   In studies carried out by Zwiebel and Rand (1978), Zwiebel and Milgram (1982) and Zwiebel and Martens (1985), the intelligence of deaf children was evaluated by the S.O.N. test, which was specifically designed to test the intelligence of hearing impaired children and evaluates a variety of intelligence skills.   The test has Israeli norms.   Although the test results indicated that the cognitive level of a 16- to 18-year-old group of hearing impaired students was in the average range, this age group had a larger number of students in the lower IQ levels than would be true of the population in general.

Zwiebel and Allen's study (1988) also indicated that there is a significant difference in the intelligence level of high school students from different educational settings.   More of the pupils who attended segregated schools for the deaf had lower intelligence levels.

Communicative Ability

In Zwiebel and Milgram's study (1982) the communication abilities of hearing impaired pupils educated by the use of the oral method were evaluated.   All of the students evaluated had severe to profound hearing impairments. Teachers were asked to evaluate their pupils' ability to understand or to be understood by family members and other people in their environment. The children's use of different communication channels was evaluated. The findings revealed that the speechreading performance of the orally educated children was a bit higher than those who used signs. It was also found that the oral students used manual communication only if they had deaf parents. Some use of manual communication was found in families where there were at least two deaf children. Scores on an index of general communication ability showed that the orally educated elementary students who were integrated into regular public school programs scored significantly higher than those hearing impaired pupils educated in a more segregated setting.

A study by Wiesel and Reichstein (1990) completed about ten years after the implementation of manual communication in various educational settings found that most of the hearing impaired children who were in schools exclusively for the deaf used sign language as their primary means of communication at home and at school.

Pupils who were integrated into regular public school classes did not use sign language at all. About one-third of the hearing impaired pupils who attended a segregated class in a regular school program communicated with their parents in sign language at least part of the time. In school, the majority of these students always used speech. The research also measured the hearing impaired students' ability to communicate and comprehend the conversation of strangers. A connection was found between the students' hearing level, educational setting, and their ability to communicate with and comprehend strangers. Except for those with a profound hearing loss, the communication ability of the pupils tested ranged from fair to good.

Horowitz and Shefatya (1987) found a highly significant relationship between preschool hearing impaired children's language test scores and their background variables. The significant variables were the parents' level of education, the presence of handicaps other than deafness, and the child's performance IQ score. A moderate relationship was found between the children's language scores and gender (girls scored higher), the hearing status of the parent (hearing impaired children of hearing impaired parents scored higher), and the age of the onset of the hearing impairment.

Emotional Adjustment

The Meadow-Kendall Social-Emotional Assessment Inventory for Deaf and Hearing-Impaired Students (SEAI) has been adapted for use with both school-aged hearing impaired children (Zwiebel & Wiesel, 1989) and preschool hearing impaired children (Zwiebel, 1989b). Several studies have been completed that compare the emotional adjustment of hearing impaired children in Israel with the emotional adjustment of their hearing peers and of hearing impaired children from other countries. Also, the emotional adjustment of hearing impaired children placed in different educational settings has been studied.

Using children aged 4 to 6, two studies found that hearing impaired children function below the test norm (Horowitz & Shefatya, 1987; Dyssegaard et al., 1987). Horowitz and Shefatya found that about one-third of the children scored much higher than the norm on the hyperactivity scale and had a tendency towards aggressive behavior. Dyssegaard et al. found that the pre-school hearing impaired children evaluated by the Meadow-Kendall Social-Emotional Assessment Inventory displayed poor functioning in all items related to sociability, communication, impulsivity, and compulsivity.

Zwiebel, Meadow-Orlans, and Dyssegaard (1986) found that school-aged hearing impaired children generally functioned better in all sub-tests of the adjustment test than did pre-school hearing impaired children. The scores on the Meadow-Kendall SEAI of hearing impaired children from the United States, Denmark, and Israel were very similar. Most of the hearing impaired children exhibited immature behaviors, depended upon teachers and peers, and had difficulty acting appropriately in social activities that required cooperation. Although Israeli children were found to be less impulsive than hearing impaired students from the United States and Denmark, their scores were low on this part of the test. Israeli children were found to be more anxious and less happy, and demonstrated more fears and less humor. Israeli hearing impaired children as well as Danish hearing impaired children were found to be "socialized," "internationalized," and "introverted."

Another study that compared the performance of hearing and deaf school-aged children in Israel and the United States on the Draw-A-Person test found that the performance of hearing children from the United States showed a higher ability to adapt, a better self-image, and increased impulse control (Zwiebel & Wolff, 1988). Deaf children from Israel were found to be less mature, more independent, and more compulsive than their American peers. On the other hand, the deaf children from the United States displayed more aggression.

Horowitz and Zwiebel in separate studies of kindergarten and school-age children found no difference in the adjustment level of hearing impaired pupils from integrated and segregated educational programs. Horowitz discovered that children with a severe hearing impairment scored higher on tests of adjustment than did those with a less severe hearing impairment. Girls were found to be better adjusted than boys.

Future Trends

Future trends in the education of the hearing impaired indicate increased polarization. More and more hearing impaired children are being integrated into regular public school classrooms. The hearing impaired children with a severe-to-profound hearing loss, with multiple handicaps, and from low socio-economic backgrounds are being concentrated in the segregated educational settings. High school settings are becoming more diverse. Hearing impaired high school graduates will continue to apply pressure for broadened opportunities for higher education or an improved level of vocational training. As a result, postsecondary education for the hearing impaired in Israel will expand.

The establishment of university programs for the hearing impaired that include all necessary auxiliary services is being discussed. Current trends point to the provision of more sign language interpreters in all educational settings and an expanded number of options for language acquisition. The influence of researchers and academia on educational policies and the treatment of the hearing impaired is growing.

The various educational settings for hearing impaired children found in this "old-new" country have reached the stage of consolidation after a long process of establishment, pioneering, and crystallization. The openness of the system and the establishment of methods of self-evaluation offer much promise for continued expansion and improvement in the education of the deaf in Israel in future years.

References

Arbatz, R., & Zwiebel, A. (1989). *Education for the hearing-impaired in Israel - Historical review,* Unpublished dissertation, Bar Ilan University, Ramat Gan, Israel. (Hebrew)

Dyssegaard, B., Meadow-Orlans, K.P., & Zwiebel, A. (1987). Mental health needs of deaf children in three countries. In Proceedings of the Xth World Federation of the Deaf Congress. Helsinki, Finland: Congress of the World Federation of the Deaf.

Horowitz, T., & Shefatya, L. (1987). *The MICHA study - integration, identity and affiliation: Achievement and adjustment of hearing-impaired children and youth.* Jerusalem, Israel: Henrietta Szold Institute. (Hebrew)

Wiesel, A., & Reichstein, R. (1990). *National demographic and assessment survey of hearing-impaired elementary school students: Israel 1983/84.* Washington, DC: Gallaudet Research Institute.

Zwiebel, A. (1989a). *Judaism and deafness: Humanistic heritage.* Paper presented at The Deaf Way Conference, Gallaudet University, Washington, DC.

Zwiebel, A. (1989b). Leitlinien fur die integration einzelner horbehinderter auf grundlage ihrer schulischen lernerfolge - Eine interkulturelle betrachtund. [The integration policy of hearing-impaired individuals in the light of their academic achievements: A crosscultural view]. In *Proceedings of the International Conference of Hearing-Impaired Pupils in Regular Schools.* Berlin, West Germany: Bundesgemeinschaft schwerhoriger kinder.

Zwiebel, A. (1989c). *Meadow-Kendall Social-Emotional Assessment Inventory of Preschool Age: Hebrew adaption and norms.* Tel Aviv, Israel: Shema. (Hebrew)

Zwiebel, A. (1989d). Poor academic achievements of deaf children: Is it inevitable? In *Studies in education [Iudim bechinuch].* (Hebrew)

Zwiebel, A., & Allen, T.E. (1988). Mathematics achievement of hearing-impaired students in different educational settings: Cross-cultural perspective. *The Volta Review, 90,* 287-293.

Zwiebel, A., & Martens, D.M. (1985). A comparison of intellectual structure in deaf and hearing children. *American Annals of the Deaf, 130,* 27-31.

Zwiebel, A., Meadow-Orlans, K.P., & Dyssegaard, B. (1986). A comparison of intellectual structure in deaf and hearing-impaired students in Israel, Denmark and the United States. *International Journal of Rehabilitation Research, 9,* 109-118.

Zwiebel, A., & Milgram, N. (1982). Cognitive and communicative development in deaf children. *Megamot Israel Journal of Behavioral Sciences, 27,* 382-396. (Hebrew)

Zwiebel, A., & Rand, Y. (1978). *S.O.N. test for Israeli deaf children: New norms and applications.* Ramat Gan, Israel: Publications of Bar Ilan University. (Hebrew)

Zwiebel, A., & Wiesel, A. (1989). *Meadow-Kendall Social-Emotional Assessment Inventory for School-Age Children: Hebrew adaptation and norms.* Tel Aviv, Israel: Shema. (Hebrew)

Zwiebel, A., & Wolff, T.B. (1988). Draw-A-Person as a reliable test for deaf children: Cross-cultural and deaf-hearing comparisons. *The ACEHI Journal, 14,* 91-104.

Education of the Deaf in Japan: Its Development and Current Issues

Michiko Tsuchiya
 Chief Researcher
 Information and Culture Center for the Deaf
 Tsukuba-shi

Historical Development

During ancient times in Japan, because of the belief in reincarnation, it was considered a misfortune to have a deaf child. Deaf children were commonly treated harshly or abandoned in the mountains.

Later, in the 1850s, the deaf child born to an affluent family was tutored at home or sent to a temple school. At the temple school, children were taught brush-writing and how to count on an abacus. Since it was generally believed that the deaf were uneducable, they were ignored and usually only learned how to read and inscribe their own name.

In 1858, while Japan was still in isolation because of the Shogunate rule, United States Commodore Matthew C. Perry first arrived in Japan with his armed warships. His arrival resulted in the overthrow of the ruling system and hence the opening up of Japan to the outside world.

In order to modernize Japan, the new government dispatched a mission to Europe and to the United States to gain an understanding of the international situation and to investigate the cultures and institutions of various countries. Employing education as a political instrument to speed up the modernization of the country, the new government issued the School Law of 1872, which made it compulsory that every child be enrolled in primary school.

Although this sudden change from a private to a public school system was dramatic, it was not until the 1940s that the law included anything about the education of the deaf.

The need to educate the deaf had been recommended by prominent men who returned from overseas missions. For example, in 1811, Yozo Yamao, a government official, developed the first proposal to establish schools for the deaf and for the blind. He had traveled to England and observed that deaf persons could be productive if educated appropriately.

The true history of education for the deaf in Japan finally began in 1875 when a primary school teacher in Kyoto taught two deaf children as part of his regular class.

In 1878, because of the increasing number of deaf children and blind children enrolled in regular schools in Kyoto, the first school for the deaf and blind was finally founded.

Taishiro Furukawa was the first teacher of the deaf in Japan. The courses he taught included reading, brush-writing, composition, grammar, geography, and arithmetic. Speech training was included in the course of study, since he believed that muteness was caused by a hearing impairment and could be remedied through speech training. His teaching was conducted mainly through the use of a manual communication system that he developed.

Around 1900, the Ministry of Education created an act that encouraged the establishment of more private schools for the deaf and blind. However, due to the lack of a successful methodology, very few schools were developed.

Schools for the deaf and schools for the blind were separated by law in 1923. Educators became aware that the deaf and the blind had different educational needs and should be educated in different settings. At about the same time each prefectural government was ordered to build and fund public schools for the deaf. As a result, 24 schools for the deaf were founded.

Reports from abroad of the success of oral education for the deaf affected the course of the education of the deaf in Japan. These reports led to many heated arguments during the period between 1910 and 1920 and finally led to a transition from the manual to the oral method of teaching the deaf.

Alexander Graham Bell, during a visit to Japan in 1898, lectured on the necessity of an appropriate education program for the deaf and the need for a teacher training program. Shuji Izawa, who had studied under Bell's father and later acted as his interpreter, introduced Bell's "visual speech" system to Japan.

A.K. Reischauer, a missionary to Japan,

asked the Clarke School for the Deaf in the United States to send a teacher to Tokyo to educate his deaf daughter. This event led to the creation in 1929 of a private oral school for the deaf.

Although the manual method of teaching the deaf was still in use, many teachers of the deaf at the time felt that it was difficult to teach deaf children the Japanese language by the use of the manual method. Bell's advocacy of the oral method and other encouraging stories such as the one about a father who succeeded in teaching his deaf daughter speech, resulted in the founding of an oral school for the deaf in the central part of Japan. Moreover, the resolution passed in 1880 at the International Congress on Education of the Deaf held in Milan, Italy, to ban the use of sign language encouraged the tendency toward oral communication.

Gradually more schools began to adopt the oral method in the belief that speech training would promise deaf children increased happiness in the future. Hence, without full debate on the advantages and disadvantages of different communication systems used to teach the deaf, oralism became the main method of educating the deaf in Japan.

Oralism reached its height of popularity in the 1930s. In 1932, it was reported that there were more than 50 oral classes. After World War II, the introduction of the aural method of teaching the deaf and the development of hearing aids complemented the oral method and led to the formation of oral classes in schools for the deaf nationwide.

At that time, the Japanese Association of Teachers of the Deaf persuaded the Ministry of Education and the United States Occupation Headquarters to implement compulsory education for the deaf at the elementary and lower secondary grade levels. The School Education Laws of 1947 made this request come true. This law completely changed the educational system of Japan. The law required each prefectural government to establish public schools for the deaf and required parents to enroll their deaf children between the age of six and fifteen in these schools.

However, since the schools for the deaf were not fully established at that time, implementation of the compulsory education law as it pertained to schools for deaf children lagged far behind the implementation of the law in regular public school programs. Implementation of the compulsory education law started in 1948 with the first grade of the elementary department and was gradually extended until full implementation in all grades was achieved in 1956.

During subsequent years several significant changes occurred in the education of the deaf in Japan. The 1970s introduced the concepts of mainstreaming, early intervention, and an awareness of the increasing number of deaf children with multiple disabilities.

The capstone event of the 1980s was the establishment of Tsukuba College of Technology in Tsukuba-shi, 60 kilometers north of Tokyo, the first institution of higher education for the deaf and blind in Japan.

Educational Services for the Deaf

There are a variety of educational services for the deaf in Japan.

It is the responsibility of the prefectural board of education to see that deaf children are placed in the appropriate educational setting. Placement decisions are based on the results of medical examinations and other data. An advisory committee on educational placement consisting of doctors, teachers, and other specialists assists in placement decisions.

The School Education Law indicates that the child must have an average hearing level of more than 100db in both ears to be eligible for entrance into a school for the deaf. Some children with an average hearing level of between 60 and 100db who have difficulty understanding normal speech with a hearing aid are also eligible to enter a school for the deaf. Other children, who are able to comprehend normal speech with the use of a hearing aid, attend a special class or a resource room in a regular school, or attend a class for hearing children. The children who attend a class for hearing children go through the grades with few support services.

There are 107 schools for the deaf in Japan. These schools generally have kindergarten, elementary, and lower and upper secondary departments. Some schools are limited to either an upper secondary or kindergarten department. Tables 1 and 2 show the breakdown of deaf and hard of hearing students at different levels.

Table 1. Deaf Children Enrolled in Schools for the Deaf, 1987

Kindergarten	1,766
Elementary	2,748
Lower Secondary	1,580
Upper Secondary	2,757
TOTAL	8,851

Table 2. Hard of Hearing Children Enrolled in Schools, 1987

School	Number of children	Number of classes
Elementary	1,268	384
Lower secondary	439	116
TOTAL	1,707	500

The schools for the deaf aim to provide an education that is equivalent to that provided in regular public schools and also offer various programs that enable deaf children to overcome the difficulties that arise from a hearing impairment.

Almost all of the kindergarten departments offer early education programs for deaf children aged three to five. In addition to the curriculum normally offered by regular kindergarten programs, the kindergarten programs at schools for the deaf include speech and language development, auditory training, and communication skills development.

Many of the kindergarten departments provide guidance and counsel to the parents of infants who are deaf.

In the elementary department, the emphasis is placed on the acquisition of subject matter. Work on language skills continues and appropriate attitudes are developed.

The lower secondary department curriculum builds upon the education completed in elementary school and also offers career guidance.

The upper secondary department offers a three-year regular academic program and a two-year advanced vocational training program. The latter provides a large variety of vocational training options including dressmaking, industrial crafts, hair-dressing, and dental laboratory.

Curriculum and Academic Achievement of Deaf Children

The schools for the deaf, in cooperation with neighborhood schools, plan school events including field days and club activities, which provide opportunities for deaf and hearing children to participate together in educational activities, and experiences that help bridge both worlds and develop mutual understanding.

A large percentage of the deaf children in Japan have difficulty with language acquisition. This accounts for the generally low academic achievement level of deaf children in Japan. At the completion of high school, the average academic achievement level of the deaf child in Japan is said to be equal to the average achievement level of an eleven-year-old hearing student.

In Japan, there is a term, "the nine-year-old's hurdle," that has been used among the educators of the deaf since the 1950s. It means that deaf children between the ages of eight and ten have difficulty thinking in abstract terms. Those who fail to break through the so-called "nine-year-old's hurdle" will have a difficult time academically. In general, however, the academic achievement level of deaf children after World War II shows progress when compared with that of the pre-war period.

Early Intervention and Parental Guidance

A preschool program for four- and five-year-old deaf children was started at a private oral school in Tokyo in 1922. Preschools were then opened in 1924 at schools for the deaf in Osaka and Chiba.

A television production entitled *The Television School for Young Deaf Children*, which is part of the educational television network of Japan, was started in 1961. During the following year this television program contributed to the founding of preschool programs nationwide. Educators of the deaf in Japan have insisted that early intervention is critical from the standpoint of language acquisition and general academic achievement.

Nearly one-half of all of the schools for the deaf, including the nursery schools, provide preschool programs for young deaf children aged birth to three. These programs are staffed by trained professionals.

The preschool programs, which are part of the kindergarten departments of schools for the deaf, emphasize individualized instruction. Deaf infants receive instruction from one to three times a week. The preschool program is based upon a philosophy that stresses the need for a good family environment, personality development, a language development program based on spoken Japanese, and the full development of any residual hearing.

The importance of parent education is stressed at the preschool level. To understand the needs of their deaf child, the parents are required to attend preschool with their deaf children.

Some hospitals and day care centers include special services for parents of deaf children. These special services include counseling and lectures on a variety of topics including the role of the parent, the implications of a hearing impairment, the effective use of hearing aids, language development, speech, and auditory training.

Children with Multiple Disabilities and Their Communication

The first class for deaf children with multiple disabilities was formed in 1959 in a school for the deaf. Since 1950 the number of children with multiple disabilities enrolled in schools for the deaf has gradually increased. One hundred and thirty-nine deaf children with multiple disabilities were enrolled in classes in 1972, and 212 in 1974.

In 1979 the Education Act for Children with Additional Disabilities was enacted for the construction of new schools. The act made the education of children with additional disabilities compulsory and allowed deaf children with additional disabilities to be educated in the schools for the deaf. Since the number of deaf children enrolled in schools for the deaf has declined over the past few years, ample room is available for the children with other disabilities. Table 3 illustrates the declining number of students in these schools.

Table 3. Trends in School Enrollment for Deaf Children, 1955–1987

Number	1955	1965	1975	1978	1979	1987
Schools	99	107	107	110	110	107
Children	18,694	19,684	13,897	12,303	11,911	8,851

Classes for deaf children with multiple disabilities are limited to five students. Educators of the deaf have found that it is imperative that communication methodologies other than the oral method be used in these classes.

The Tochigi Method, which was developed at a prefectural school for the deaf in Tokyo, begins at the kindergarten level with the use of speech only and later, as the student advances through the grades, incorporates signs with speech.

Another method used with deaf children with multiple disabilities is cued speech. Japanese cued speech was developed at the Kyoto School for the Deaf in 1961. Cued speech and the simultaneous use of signs and speech have been adopted as the method of choice by several schools for the deaf and by some kindergarten programs.

These newly introduced methods of communicating with deaf children have challenged the traditional oral method. A recent report indicates that approximately 70 percent of the schools for the deaf in Japan now allow some use of signs in the classroom.

Mainstreaming

Special classes for hard of hearing children, which utilize the regular public school curriculum, have been established in regular elementary and lower secondary schools. Occasionally it is necessary to develop special curricula to meet the individual needs of some of the hard of hearing students. These special classes are small in size and utilize an individualized approach. In addition to instruction in a special classroom, the hard of hearing students are often mainstreamed into a regular classroom for some portion of the school day, depending upon their individual needs. Speech and language development and auditory training are stressed in these special classes. The child's residual hearing is developed to the fullest extent possible.

The concept of mainstreaming was first introduced in the 1950s by deaf high school students who after graduation continued their education at a university or junior college. The few special classes located in public schools that existed before the 1950s had been forced into dissolution because of World War II.

In 1961, with financial assistance, an otolaryngologist made an effort to form a special class in a regular school in Okayama in western Japan. He strongly believed that hard of hearing children could integrate successfully into society and therefore should be provided an education that would more likely make integration possible.

The creation of the special class in Okayama became the topic of a special TV program. This publicity promoted the concept of special classes in regular public schools and resulted in a dramatic increase in the number of special classes throughout Japan. Table 4 illustrates this increase.

Table 4. Increase in Number of Special Classes in Japan

Year	1967		1973
Elementary	30	Preschool	3
Junior High School	3	Elementary	93
		Junior High School	21
		High School	1
TOTAL	33		118

During the 1970s the development of oral-aural training, the use of sophisticated hearing aids, and early intervention enabled some young deaf children to be mainstreamed into a regular school classroom after the completion of a kindergarten program or the first grade of an elementary department of a school for the deaf. A private oral school in Tokyo started mainstreaming deaf children at all grade levels from preschool through high school. The mainstreaming process eventually led to the gradual dissolution of the upper secondary department of the private oral school.

At the request of the Ministry of Education, the success of mainstreaming in schools for the deaf in Tokyo was surveyed. The survey concluded that mainstreaming did not necessarily promise every deaf child academic success. The results of the study indicated that the success of mainstreaming the deaf child required that the child possess a positive personality, excellent academic achievement, and good communication skills.

Successful integration of deaf children into regular school classrooms requires that teachers of the deaf assist and advise the regular classroom teacher. It also requires that parents form organizations for mutual support and the acquisition of information. Recently, however, most organizations for the parents of deaf children have been rather inactive.

Although a significant number of deaf and hard of hearing students have succeeded in mainstream classrooms, in recent years many have returned to schools for the deaf after completing lower secondary programs in regular schools.

A school for the deaf in Osaka completed a study on the problem. The results are listed in Table 5 below.

Tokyo metropolitan schools for the deaf report the same phenomenon. Roughly 20 percent of the total enrollment of schools for the deaf consists of deaf students who have returned from regular public school programs.

The main reasons cited by more than 60 percent of the students who returned to schools for the deaf are as follows:

1. Poor academic achievement at the regular schools
2. Failure on the regular high school entrance examination
3. Advice of career guidance counselors at the regular public schools
4. Social and emotional needs of the students and their parents

Thirty percent of the returning students stated that communication barriers and personal problems were the reasons for their return.

These returning students create special problems for teachers of the deaf. The near total lack of speech training in the regular school requires teachers of the deaf to spend additional time in the area of speech development. A socio-cultural program that allows the students to become accustomed to the deaf culture is also a necessity.

Vocational Training Programs

Since the inception of the first school for the deaf, education for the deaf in Japan has had the dual purposes of providing language development and vocational training. The upper secondary department of schools for the deaf offer a variety of vocational programs including printing, word-processing, dress-making, hair-dressing, dental technology, and

Table 5. Deaf Students Returning to Schools for the Deaf, 1982-1986

Department	1982	1983	1984	1985	1986	Total	Average Number per Year
Elementary	3	6	5	2	4	20	4.0
Junior H.S.	6	8	10	11	2	37	7.4
High School	13	34	35	25	24	131	26.8
TOTAL	22	48	50	41	30	191	38.2

others. Table 6 shows the number of deaf students enrolled in upper secondary departments of schools for the deaf.

Table 6. Deaf Students Enrolled in Upper Secondary Departments of the Schools for the Deaf, 1985

Kind of School	Year in School	Number Enrolled
Regular Program	Freshmen	712
	Junior	793
	Senior	851
Special Class		115
Advanced Program	First Year	293
	Second Year	257
	Third Year	27

Hair-dressing, dental technology, and other select occupational areas require completion of a special curriculum in order to qualify for a license or certificate. See Table 7 for a breakdown of the various vocational training courses offered.

Table 7. Vocational Training Courses Offered to Deaf Students, 1985

Courses	Number of Students Majoring	Percentage of All Deaf Students
Regular program	821	27.7
Dressmaking	602	20.3
Industrial crafts	570	19.3
Hair-dressing	301	10.1
Printing	161	5.4
Mechanics	141	4.8
Dental laboratory course	90	3.0
Metallic work	57	1.9
Design	63	1.8
Home economics	49	1.7
Pottery	16	0.5
Dyeing fabrics	15	0.5

Table 7. cont.

Courses	Number of Students Majoring	Percentage of All Deaf Students
Laundry	13	0.4
Oil painting	10	0.3
Bamboo craft	6	0.2
Others	19	3.2

To meet the demands of society in an information age, the vocational training programs offered to deaf students have been upgraded and reflect new knowledge and technology. A high percentage of the deaf children who complete the lower secondary education program continue their education at the upper secondary level. Most of those who finish the upper secondary level program find employment. The majority of students are employed in manufacturing plants or do clerical work. Tables 8, 9, and 10 show the number of graduates of lower and upper secondary departments, and the number of workers and kinds of work done.

Table 8. Disposition of Graduates of Lower Secondary Departments (Regular Program), 1987

Upper secondary school*	574
Education training institutions**	1
Employment	3
Others	4
TOTAL NUMBER OF GRADUATES	582

Notes: *Those who proceed to upper secondary institutions and educational training institutions including those students who work.

**Educational training institutions including vocational education facilities, special training schools, miscellaneous schools, and others.

Table 9. Disposition of Graduates of Upper Secondary Departments (Regular Program), 1987

Higher education institutions	277
Educational training institutions	61
Employment	361
Others	56
TOTAL NUMBER OF GRADUATES	**755**

Table 10. Type of Employment for Deaf Workers

	Male	Female	Total
Professional, technical work	3	2	5
Office work	2	29	31
Sales industry	0	2	2
Service industry	11	7	18
Skilled worker:			
Ceramic chemicals metal goods	9	10	19
Machine maker	103	43	146
Other manufacturing industry	56	72	128
Construction	3	0	3
Labor	4	0	4
Sub-total, Skilled	175	125	300
Others	2	3	5
TOTAL	**193**	**168**	**361**

From 1910 to 1969, deaf persons were able to become vocational teachers of the deaf by completing a vocational specialist training program. This program, which included training in either industrial crafts, dressmaking, or much later in oil painting, was the closest thing to a college program possible for a deaf adult.

The 1960 Employment Promotion Law for the Disabled was issued to promote the employment of the disabled in the public sector as well as in some large private sector firms, and to provide the funds necessary to promote the development of vocational training programs outside of the schools for the deaf. Compared to what was available in the past, this law has significantly broadened the variety of occupational opportunities available to deaf individuals.

Higher Education for the Deaf

Since the late 1950s, deaf students have been pursuing higher education opportunities at universities or junior colleges. The School Education Law, which requires a full compulsory education for all deaf students, has resulted in an annual increase in the number of deaf students enrolled in institutions of higher education.

No support services have been available to deaf undergraduates enrolled in the universities.

In the late 1960s, because of the increasing number of deaf students attending institutions of higher education, the traditional vocational training emphasis of the curricula of schools for the deaf shifted to a curricula that emphasized college preparation. This change in emphasis has occurred in the curriculum of all school departments. The upper secondary departments now provide both college preparation and vocational training programs.

The movement to establish an institution of higher education for the deaf in Japan started in 1975, the same year that the International Congress on the Education of the Deaf was held in Tokyo. It provided a good opportunity for Japanese people connected with the education of the deaf to become aware of developments in the education of the deaf worldwide. The level of education provided for the deaf in Japan stood equal with that provided by other advanced countries, except in the area of higher education. Higher education opportunities for the deaf in the United States were much more advanced.

As the result of the efforts of many people and the support of the Ministry of Education, Diet members, and other concerned organizations, the first college program for the deaf was founded in 1988 at Tsukuba, which is northwest of Tokyo. The department for students who are deaf at Tsukuba College of Technology, which was in many aspects modeled after the National Technical Institute of the Deaf in Rochester, New York, offers a three-year technical program. The program includes courses in commercial design, mechanics, architecture, electronics, and data processing. A maximum of ten students who are deaf are allowed in each class. The students are provided with all needed support services, including sign language interpreters, notetakers, captioned displays, and other assistive devices. Communication flexibility and the use of new technology guarantee that the deaf students will have access to the required information. The trends that are being established at Tsukuba College may cause a shift from the long-adopted oral method of teaching the deaf in Japan to a more open, flexible, and child-centered communication philosophy.

The establishment of the first institution of higher education for the deaf has apparently inspired students who are deaf to higher goals and aspirations. According to faculty members at the college, the academic achievement level of the students has gradually increased. However, those deaf students at the college who have come from the mainstream programs have the similar issues to confront as did the deaf children who returned to the schools for the deaf after being enrolled in a mainstream program.

Teacher Training Program

Until the 1940s only the national institutions of higher education such as Tokyo University offered a teacher training program that led to certification as a regular classroom teacher. Beginning in the late 1940s, the national universities accredited by the Ministry of Education offered preparation programs leading to certification of both regular and special education teachers.

However, in 1954, due to an insufficient number of prospective teachers of the deaf, the requirement that one must hold a special certificate to teach the deaf was dropped, and those who held only a regular teaching certificate were allowed to teach deaf children. This practice has continued until the present time.

At present there are three ways to obtain certification as a teacher of the deaf: 1) attend a university accredited by the Ministry of Education that offers a teacher training program at the undergraduate level; 2) complete the education requirements through a correspondence program that meets the requisites of the Certification Requirement Act; or 3) attend workshops or summer school programs designed for those who wish to achieve the credits necessary for certification, and pass a teacher qualification examination. Table 11 shows the number of staff working in schools for the deaf in 1987.

Table 11. Staff Working in the Schools for the Deaf, 1987

Full-time teachers	4,545
Full-time staff (excluding matrons)	1,507
Full-time matrons	900
TOTAL	6,952

Upon completion of an undergraduate program, six national universities currently confer a certificate in the education for the deaf. Two national universities offer a teacher training program at the graduate level.

The curriculum of the teacher preparation programs includes courses in the theory and practice of speech development, the psychology of deafness, the mechanisms of hearing, and practice teaching at a school for the deaf. Before World War II more hours were spent in practice teaching and less on theory. Today the content of the curricula at teacher training centers varies from university to university.

The Japanese system of certifying teachers of the deaf has seriously affected the integrity of the education of the deaf. About three percent of the total number of teachers of the deaf hired annually hold a certificate as a teacher of the deaf. Most of those hired have earned a regular certificate.

The six national universities that provide specialized preparation leading to certification as a teacher of the deaf have few practicum centers or laboratory schools where educational theory can be put into practice. None of the university programs designed to prepare teachers of the deaf include sign language courses. A recent report states that students in these programs often have little interest in teaching the deaf and have had few actual classroom experiences with deaf children that would help them become aware of the realities of teaching the deaf. Additional practicum activities with deaf children are needed to help these students understand what is expected of a teacher of deaf children.

The teacher training programs place little emphasis on the personal qualities needed for success as a teacher of the deaf. When one considers the diverse needs of deaf children today, it is clear that the quality of the existing training centers needs to be updated and upgraded.

As was previously stated, the present Certificate Requirement Act allows teachers who are certified to teach hearing children in a regular school classroom to be hired to teach deaf children in a regular classrooms, special classrooms, or schools for the deaf. It has long been pointed out that a teacher with a regular education certificate has little or no awareness of the needs of deaf children and very little knowledge of the educational implications of a hearing impairment.

In spite of the dramatic changes that have occurred in the field of education, this situation has continued for nearly three decades. With the dramatic and increased diversity of needs exhibited by deaf children today, it is imperative that all new teachers of the deaf be flexible, knowledgeable, well prepared, and able to provide quality education to the deaf children of Japan.

Summary

As has been discussed, the diverse needs of deaf children in Japan are a compelling reason for schools for the deaf to modify existing educational practices.

One of the characteristics of educational programs for the deaf after World War II is the emphasis placed upon individualized teaching methods. Enrollment in schools for the deaf decreased during the 1960s as more and more young deaf children received their education in regular public school classrooms. The lower birth rate in Japan in recent years has also contributed to a reduction in the number of children who are deaf. Because of these trends, schools for the deaf in Japan have become smaller, and therefore provide less employment possibilities for teachers of the deaf.

Conversely, the gradual increase in the number of deaf children with additional disabilities has increased the need for appropriate educational programming and for teachers qualified to work with this population.

The large number of deaf students who are returning to schools for the deaf from regular public school programs implies that there is a basic problem with the mainstream programs. Mainstream placement criteria need to be developed to help ensure proper placement decisions. Equal attention and resources need to be directed to students who complete their educational program in schools for the deaf.

The education of the deaf in Japan during the prewar period was rigid and predetermined as to the communication method utilized. The current trend in the education of the deaf reflects the complex needs of each deaf child and the necessity of flexibility when choosing the proper communication methodology.

The deaf community has long criticized the prevailing educational policy, which was based on oralism. Since 1988 a strong movement developed by organizations of the deaf and associations of parents and concerned individuals has pushed the Ministry of Education to investigate the communication systems used in the schools for the deaf.

This investigation was conducted by an appointed committee of educators and professionals. In 1993 the committee submitted a report to the Ministry of Education that recommended that manual communication be introduced to the schools for the deaf at the high school level. The policy on communication at the preschool, elementary, and lower secondary school level basically was not changed.

One year later, the Ministry of Education started a program aimed at teaching sign language to teachers of the deaf.

Most schools for the deaf have as an end goal the successful integration of the deaf student into Japanese society. With its open and student-centered communication policy, the Tsukuba College of Technology program for deaf adults should have a strong influence on the future course of the education of the deaf in Japan.

In a time of changing educational placement options and communication methodologies, the schools and classes for the deaf in Japan will need to seek new ways of providing educational services that will develop the full potential of each deaf child.

References

Association of Teachers of the Deaf. *List of the schools for the deaf and teachers.*

Ishii, T., et al. (1987). The teacher training programs. *Auditory Disorders, 42*(12).

Miyano, T., et al. (1988). Mainstreaming. *Auditory Disorders, 43*(2).

Obata, S. (1987). A comprehensive study of the education for the deaf. Tsukuba College of Technology.

Okayama Kindergarten, et al. (1987). Parental education. *Auditory Disorders, 42*(2).

Sato, H., et al. (1986). Educational programs for multiple-handicapped children. *Auditory Disorders, 42*(1).

Special education in Japan. (1988). Special Education Division, Elementary and Secondary Education Bureau, Ministry of Education, Science and Culture.

Tsuchiya, M. (1989). *The deaf Japanese and their self-identity.* Paper presented at The Deaf Way Conference, Gallaudet University, Washington, DC.

Watanabe, K., et al. (1987). Aspects of a communication mean. *Auditory Disorders, 42*(9).

Yokoyama, T., et al. (1988). Employment of deaf persons. *Auditory Disorders, 43*(3).

Note: *Auditory Disorders* is the only educational journal for teachers of the deaf in Japan. It has been published monthly since 1958 by the Association of Educational Research for the Deaf.

Special Education for the Deaf in Lebanon

Antoine Roumanos

220

The Social Question

Historical, Social, and Political Background

It is almost impossible to study a country's social institutions without studying its own specific historical, political, and economic framework.

In Lebanon, researchers agree that the feudal system was and still is the base that should be used as a starting point in the analysis of its social and political life.

Lebanon is a very small country with a land mass of approximately 10,400 kilometers and a population of 3,500,000. It has a multi-religious, multi-ethnic structure and is situated between the continents of Europe and Asia. It was occupied and governed by the dying Ottoman Empire at the end of the nineteenth century. When the Industrial Revolution began to produce its effects on the economic and political systems of Europe, Lebanon was not aware of the industrial movement or of any kind of new political system except the old feudal system, which was managed and even manipulated by the Ottoman Empire in order to maintain its domination.

By the end of the nineteenth century, and just before World War I began, European influence in the Middle East, started by missionary groups and educational institutions, convinced wealthy Lebanese people to donate money for the purpose of creating, developing, and supporting new social and welfare institutions. Some local religious groups, also supported by rich individuals, also created social, welfare, or charitable institutions.

The Turkish occupier at the time was only concerned with stealing all of the country's goods and in enrolling its manpower in the support of military efforts that left the country in total ruin.

After the war ended, wealthy groups organized associations and created the first Lebanese social and welfare organizations, which included orphanages, hospitals, and educational and vocational centers.

Turkey, which occupied Lebanon at the time, had made the mistake of siding with Germany. The victorious Allies, especially France and England, divided among themselves the territories occupied by the Turks. The French put Lebanon under their own mandate.

In some regards, the French mandate was profitable to the Lebanese people. It influenced education positively and helped to create welfare organizations which included hospitals. But the French maintained the feudal system, hidden under new political, economic, and social terms and concepts. The French governed by using Lebanese ethnic, religious, and confessional factions and manipulated them in order to manage the social and economic conflicts that naturally arise in a multi-confessional society. The French did little to improve the economic and social infrastructure of the country. On the contrary, they helped maintain the status quo by creating economic markets only for their goods and industries. The French treated the country as if it were an underdeveloped vassal to be pitied. All educational, welfare, or health-related institutions followed the prevailing patterns.

Lebanon acquired its independence from France in 1943, during a period of social, economic, and political chaos. The new social and economic life took a different orientation. The capital, Beirut, developed greatly at the expense of peripheral regions. It was considered as normal for the new independent state to give priority to the capital, the center of political power, at the expense of other regions in the country that were still under the influence of feudal leaders. The human migration from the villages to the city, especially the capital, was so quick and unorganized that it did not permit a well-planned development of the capital and its suburbs. The suburbs very quickly became the permanent residence for poor people who were employed and exploited by the people in power in the capital city and used as cheap manpower for emerging industries and services, especially in the trade and banking sectors. The Lebanese economy moved from an agricultural and small manufacturing economy to one of large industries and services. Arab neighbors, the Europeans, and other western countries invested in the country and used the country and its free economic system as a base from which to make profits and to conduct trade with other Middle Eastern and Asian countries.

The first twenty years of independence, or until the early 1960s, were troubled socially and politically. But in 1959 the government created a new office to handle all social services. The Office of Social Development was first designed as an independent entity but was soon integrated into the Ministry of Labor and Social Affairs, which had been created in 1952. By the mid-1960s new plans were developed and new social projects created.

Infrastructure of Social Services in Lebanon

From the beginning of the 1960s, Lebanon increased its efforts to develop its infrastructure. This effort led to the construction of some of the basic institutions that are considered to be the real starting point of social work in the country. Clubs, associations, welfare institutions, special education institutions, and cultural centers were created and spread across the country.

Yet the rapid development, opulence, and improved conditions in Lebanon before the civil war exploded in 1975 could not hide the lack of well-organized and well-managed social institutions. The number of social institutions that were established were less than was needed. The institutions were in a weak and precarious condition. At the time the infrastructure of the country was very weak and insignificant.

From 1960 to 1978, the number of social institutions tripled. There was an increase from 307 institutions in 1960 to 1,302 institu-

tions in 1978. Social institutions spread throughout the country, including those concerned with family care, public health, environment, care of women and children, and special education. The greatest number of institutions were devoted to family care, public health, and environmental services. Of the 1,302 institutions in 1978, only 30 focused on special education. Because of the narrow understanding of the concept of social services dictated by the classical religious concept of charity, the contribution and influence of services and institutions was limited and localized.

In 1978, the majority of the employees working in social institutions (about 61.2 percent) had no area of specialization or education. Those who had an area of specialization in the fields of the social sciences represented only 3.3 percent of the total population of employees. Although this information was compiled in 1978, it is probably still valid.

A significant fact is that the percentage of the employees whose education is below the primary level is decreasing each year. The great majority of employees have completed either a secondary or technical education. Those who have achieved a University education represent a relatively low percentage.

Some important facts include:
- The increase in the number of social institutions is directly connected to a new understanding of the concept of social service or social needs and finally has moved away from the ancient concept of pity.
- The new understanding of social service has not given rise to the construction of modern social institutions or the efficient operation of existing social institutions.
- Activities in the social field are still private, spontaneous, and inefficient.
- The majority of the activities of the social institutions are crisis-oriented and are not built upon detailed programs or knowledge of basic needs.

- The concepts of development, participation, partnership, and motivation are replacing pity, charity, service, and paternity.
- Fund raising activities of the social institutions are based upon an emotional appeal and not upon results and follow-up data.

The majority of the social services agencies are unable to develop and prosper because of a lack of planning, well-documented projects, specialized personnel, and adequate funding.

Special Education in Lebanon

The specialized institutions (for handicapped persons, mentally retarded persons, and the like) represent only 2.3 percent of the total number of social and welfare institutions.

Historical Background of Special Education in Lebanon

Historically, special education in Lebanon has been a private matter. The education of the deaf was not mentioned in the literature before the 1950s. Deaf people were uneducated and under the care of their families.

Governmental Contribution to Special Education

By the end of the 1950s, Lebanese independence from the control of other states was largely achieved. New plans for economic and social development were produced. The government created, in 1959, the Office for Social Development (OSD) and charged it with the task of handling all social services in the country.

The office was to be part of the Ministry of Labor and Social Affairs, but run as an inde-

pendent office with its own mission and funding. This independence would allow the office to be very flexible; deal directly and freely with individuals, groups, and institutions; close deals; make contracts; and even spend money without going through a long and complicated bureaucratic process.

The goals and tasks of the newly created office were specified in the governmental decree that created it. The goals were as follows:

1. Develop a long-range plan for social development in the country and supervise its realization.
2. Study the social problems in the country and develop the budget needed to solve the problems.
3. Support on-going private social projects. Coordinate the existing social projects and create new ones with the help of the private institutions.
4. Support technical schools, and orient youth towards technical and vocational training.

In the beginning the government allocated a respectable amount of funds to run the newly created office. But as time passed, the budget decreased to the point that the Office for Social Development could no longer fulfill its mission. The office tried its best to conduct projects that could be divided into two categories: those developed by private institutions, and projects created by the office.

The whole system operated as best as it could until the beginning of the internal war of 1975. As was true of all governmental services and ministries, the office's services were seriously curtailed by the war. Political parties or military factions replaced formal representational government but not its basic functions. The whole situation deteriorated to a very primitive level. Destruction and desolation of the country aggravated the situation in critical ways.

On September 1, 1977, the government issued Legislative Decree Number 431, that created as part of the Office for Social Development, another office called The Office of Handicapped Affairs. The newly created office was developed to handle all affairs related to handicapped people and their special education. The office was to deal with education and vocational training, and with all the institutions working in this specific field.

But the creation of the office came too late. The war had begun two years before. The efficiency of the Office for Handicapped Affairs was very limited since the role of the Office for Social Development was decreasing. No significant changes could be made. The office was able to function but with a reduced number of personnel.

The Actual Situation of the Handicapped Population

Statistical data on the plight of the handicapped population in Lebanon is either not available or very hard to locate. Because of the Lebanese multi-confessional society, and because of the limited vision of government leaders, no one dares to conduct such research. Everyone is afraid of how any statistics might be used to foster political or military ends. The last census of the general population was completed in 1933.

The only governmental institution (Ministry of Plan) that provided official statistical data was completely dismantled during the war and no longer exists. Data on special education has never been a priority area in the minds of government officials and planners.

During the past sixteen years, several non-governmental, foreign, and local institutions have tried to conduct some statistical research that applied to the disabled population of Lebanon. The published results were judged to be inaccurate and demonstrated the difficulties encountered in trying to accomplish such research. These difficulties included the procedures utilized and the rapid demographic, cultural, and even physical transformations found in the population of the country.

The latest statistical data, completed in 1981 and published in French by Caritas-Liban under the title of *Les Handicapés au Liban* (*Handicapped People in Lebanon*), provide the best figures available concerning the total handicapped population and especially the deaf population in the country. These figures are only an estimation of the real figures. Even if these statistics are not accurate, they can provide an idea of the size of the handicapped population in Lebanon.

The Handicapped Population as a Whole

The estimated total handicapped population is about 106,355 persons or approximately 3.04 percent of the total population of the country. These figures probably underestimate the true handicapped population when one compares the population to that of other countries similar to Lebanon. Five percent is the usual figure used to estimate the handicapped population. Deafness represents about 8.76 percent of the total handicapped population and only 0.27 percent of the total population of the country.

Only 5,236 handicapped persons, or 4.69 percent of the handicapped population, are receiving services from an educational, therapeutic, or vocational institution.

The Deaf Population in Particular

Of the total number of 9,313 deaf people, slightly more lived in urban settings than rural settings. Over 60 percent of the population was twenty years old or more. There were almost twice as many males than females.

Only four percent of the deaf population is receiving the services of an educational or vocational institution. Only 27 out of about 5,526 deaf adults are served by institutions.

No research is available concerning the 99.61 percent of the total adult deaf population (from 14 years and up) which is not served by the system of institutions. Anecdotal information indicates that they are living miserable lives inside of their own micro-societies, are misunderstood, probably mistreated, not respected, and under-valued.

They have little communication and relationships with others and if able to find work are probably exploited.

A study published in 1981 (Caritas-Liban, 1981) surveyed 3,537 deaf persons of school age. Only 409 of those children were involved in educational programs. Since all existing Lebanese institutions are at capacity, the drastic lack of special education facilities for deaf children is clear.

The Multi-Handicapped Population

There are about 8,499 multi-handicapped persons in Lebanon. One thousand, three hundred and twenty three of them are primarily deaf. These deaf people probably have been part of the count of other categories since their deafness was considered as a secondary handicap. No institution in Lebanon takes care of multi-handicapped persons, and no research is available about this population. Most probably, the multi-handicapped are disseminated throughout the society, live with their families, and encounter severe social, psychological, and physical conditions.

The Special Education System and Lebanese Institutions for the Deaf

Special education institutions for the deaf did not exist in Lebanon before the late 1950s and early 1960s. After the first institution was created in the late 1950s, the development of others quickly followed.

Practically all of the large institutions for the deaf were created between the years 1956 and 1965. Education was the focus of all of the institutions for the deaf. The curricula was largely copied from that of existing normal public school programs. For a while, it seemed as though the newly created institutions would be capable of handling all of the educational needs. The true aim of these educational institutions was to get deaf people off of the streets and provide an education instead of leaving them to wander the streets or be hidden away by their families without care or education. At the time, at the institutions that were created, no trained personnel were available who could provide special education, no assistive devices were available, and no curricula existed. The only thing that did exist was the enthusiasm of many people to do something for a group who had nothing at all. See Appendix A for a listing of institutions for the education of the deaf.

The educational need, which seemed partially satisfied in the 1960s, reappeared stronger than ever in the 1970s and in the early 1980s when newly conducted research provided statistics that confirmed what the specialists had always suspected—that there were large numbers of deaf people not being served by the institutions. Many were young deaf children who were capable of profiting from schooling. Others were of such ages and stages of development that their education was badly compromised but still possible. Huge numbers, who were in age categories that made it impossible for them to be eligible for special education, were left without any educational services at all.

The reasons why many deaf individuals were not receiving educational services included the following: the family's preference to hide the disability discovered in one of its members; the distance between the home and the institution was too great since practically all of the institutions were established in or near the capital; the other region of the country was not served at all, especially the remote areas of the country; ignorance coupled with the Eastern belief in fate; the high cost of room and board and the education. Some of the reasons stated above continue. Other reasons have been largely attenuated by a new awareness of the needs of the deaf. The internal war, which at some periods has assumed the form of a civil and religious war, has aggravated the situation and created additional reasons why the deaf have not been provided an education.

The Cost of Special Education

With the creation of the Office of Social Development in 1959, the Lebanese government ceased its involvement in special education. The budget of the Office of Social Development was so small that it was impossible for the office to handle the need.

Because of the huge workload and need, the office, instead of creating its own special education institutions and its own social services, preferred to utilize existing institutions to provide social services or special education. The majority of the existing institutions were affiliated with the Christian or Moslem religions or a private organization. Some were initiated by a foreign country but the majority were created by groups within the country.

It was the responsibility of the Office of Social Development to examine, diagnose, and send qualified persons to the institutions. The office would pay a daily fee for the person enrolled which would cover board and room, education, assistive devices, and other necessary expenses. This system is still in effect.

With the advent of the education of the deaf in Lebanon, the Office of Social Development proposed to provide nearly 80 percent of the real costs of those who were enrolled in the special education institutions. The institution would have to bear the other 20 percent of the costs. The daily governmental rate was calculated by a team of specialists and institutional representatives who took into consideration several factors that influenced costs.

For a number of years the office was able to honor its commitments to the special education institutions. But as the years proceeded, developments in the field, new technologies, the need for more and more specialized personnel, and the great increase in the inflation rate caused by the internal war caused the costs to escalate. The Lebanese pound has lost approximately 98 percent of its buying power since 1984. Although the government's contribution to the cost of special education has been revised upward periodically, the government's percentage of the total costs has continued to decrease. The recent governmental share does not cover more than 5 to 10 percent of the actual costs.

Therefore, each institution, big or small, equipped or not, with trained or untrained personnel, is forced to raise the funds needed to support the social, instructional, educational, medical, technological, nutritional, and personnel costs of the institution. Clearly, this is a nearly impossible situation.

Institutions for the Handicapped: Problems and Difficulties

Great differences exist in the quality of personnel, equipment, and education provided by the institutions for the deaf.

There seem to be four levels of difficulties that the institutions are facing.

- The first level of difficulties deals with the provision of the normal basic needs of life, including proper nutrition, clothing, personal safety, personal health, and health care.
- The second level of difficulties deals with instructional practices and includes the qualifications of the teachers and the availability of needed materials, equipment, books, and other instructional tools.
- The third level of difficulties focuses upon the provision of an adequate number of qualified personnel including special teachers, special medical and paramedical personnel, language specialists, social workers, and others, and providing the preservice and inservice training they require.
- The fourth level of difficulties deals with the goal of the full integration of deaf people into society, the right to vocational training, the right to personal and social security,

independence, autonomy, and especially the protection from exploitation.

In Lebanon, there is probably no institution for the deaf that has resolved all of the difficulties mentioned in the four levels. The majority of schools for the deaf are still struggling with the difficulties attached to the first or the second level and have not even begun to face the difficulties associated with the other levels. Since little help is available, deaf people are struggling to survive in Lebanese society today and have very little control over the direction of their lives.

The governmental contribution that is supposed to cover at least 80 percent of the cost of special education of a deaf child, covers only about 5 percent of the institutional cost. The amount paid per day barely covers breakfast expenses. The educational program receives no assistance in the areas of national research on programs and procedures, trained professionals, acquiring special equipment, and funds to maintain existing equipment. The government does not assist deaf people. Deaf people have difficulty passing exams because of certain verbal requirements. They are restricted in their choice of work. There is an absence of laws needed to guarantee a deaf person's rights as an individual and as a citizen. The danger of the exploitation of deaf people, the intolerance and the incomprehension of the whole society, the inaccessibility of information on the environment, culture, and so on, are not of any help when it comes to deaf individuals or to professionals working in the field.

Special Education for the Deaf in Lebanon:
The Type and Extent of Educational Services for the Deaf

Day School versus Residential School

Until recently education of the deaf was available only to those between the ages of six and eighteen. Recent improvements in the educational system have lowered the beginning age to three. There is little concern about vocational training in the schools for the deaf.

All of the schools for the deaf in Lebanon act as relatively independent centers for those who live in the neighborhood of the school. For those who travel by school bus, the centers act as day schools. Those who live too far from the institution to use the inadequate school bus services reside at the school. Usually the group in residence is sent home every other weekend. Children whose family situation is not favorable may stay at the school and return home only for long vacations. Some may not go home at all but stay at the institution permanently. If school personnel suspect abusive treatment or a poor home environment, the student may stay at the school.

Timetables

As in most schools, the yearly school calendar is usually divided into three working terms, short holidays, and one long summer vacation.

1. First Term: October–December, followed by a two-week holiday for Christmas and the new year.
2. Second Term: January–April, followed by a two-week vacation for Easter.
3. Third Term: May–July, followed by a two-month summer vacation.

Usually, the schools for the deaf are in session for five days per week. The weekend begins at Friday noon and ends on Monday morning.

Classes run from 8:30 a.m. to 4:00 p.m. Class work is completed during three periods of instruction:

Period 1: 8:30 to 10:30, followed by a short break (10:30-11:00)

Period 2: 11:00 to 12:30, followed by lunch and a relatively long rest period (12:30-2:00)

Period 3: 2:00–4:00

Extent of the Programs

Kindergarten and Primary School

For many reasons, the educational programs of many of the schools for the deaf have not extended beyond the kindergarten and primary school levels. Some of the schools have developed a vocational program which starts at the end of the primary level or a bit higher. All institutions for the deaf are required to accept deaf people who have not reached the end of the primary level or who have never been in school.

Reasons why the education of the deaf in Lebanon has not reached beyond the primary level:

1. Historical Reasons
    - The relatively short history of special education for the deaf. Educational programs for the deaf did not begin until the 1960s. Teaching methods appropriate to teach the deaf have not yet been established.
    - The tendency to copy European practices, systems, and methods.
    - All Lebanese institutions for the deaf are small and forced to do everything on their own.
    - The lack of homogeneous age grouping of students has made

student progress difficult. Until recently, schools were still enrolling older students with no past educational experience.
    - The fifteen-year war forced schools for the deaf to close for variable periods of time almost every year. The schools were not able to be open for more than three months at a time during a two-year period and have not been able to operate on a continuous basis.

2. Cultural Reasons
    - Deaf children often do not enroll in the schools for the deaf until they are older and have missed many important years of education.
    - The diagnosis of deafness is not always made at an early age partly because of parent ignorance but mostly because of the absence of an early identification program in hospitals, pediatric clinics, and normal public schools.
    - The tendency of parents not to believe in their deaf child's potential.
    - The absence of a sufficient number of deaf adult role models who can provide parents of deaf children with hope.

3. Economic Reasons
    - The deaf children who reach the institutions for the deaf usually come from families with a low social and economic status.
    - The majority of the schools for the deaf do not have the financial resources needed to provide an adequate educational program. Many of the schools have poorly equipped classrooms and poorly trained and underpaid teachers and other personnel.

4. Educational Reasons

- The educational program is based upon the oral-aural approach. Until very recently, no signs were used or even permitted, especially in class rooms.
- The main problem with the educational program is the continuing debate about what can be defined as "the language education" versus "the language of education." The school system has assumed that a deaf child can learn both spoken and written forms of oral language of the country and academic content through the use of the written form of the same language.
- The absence of a sufficient number of specialized personnel, including audiologists and speech therapists, to man the whole Lebanese institutional system. There is only one University Institute to provide education and training for specialized educators. Students are trained to work with all kinds of handicapped people and do not specialize in the education of the deaf. Furthermore, the Institute did not open its doors until 1986. Even if adequate funds were available to pay the special teachers, sufficient numbers of personnel are not available.
- The use of the Arabic language complicates the whole system.

Arabic Languages an Added Complication

Each Arabic country has two Arabic languages. One is a dialect used in informal situations and daily communication, and is practically never written. In fact, it has no established orthographic rules. Writers who have tried some essays using the Lebanese dialect have each written in a different manner. The other Arabic language is the "pure" literature language and is used only in formal situations such as for speeches, TV, and radio, and for written Arabic found in letters, books, and newspapers. It has been proven that the two systems of Arabic, even though the lexicons have some resemblance, are not at all alike when it comes to grammatical and syntactic matters.

The existence of the two forms of the language makes it very difficult for the deaf to learn Arabic. The deaf students must learn to communicate verbally with one form and to read and write with the other. The situation becomes more complicated when the deaf child has developed the use of signs before coming to school. Signs are not used in most schools because of the prevailing philosophy that requires the deaf child to learn the verbal Arabic dialect first, and then two years later, learn the formal Arabic dialect required for reading and writing.

It has been noted that the grammatical and syntactical mistakes committed in speaking or writing Arabic are directly influenced by the sign system used by the deaf person.

Post-Primary Schools

Very few deaf students have been able to go beyond kindergarten and the primary levels of instruction. Rarer yet is the small number of deaf people who have been able to continue through the many years of general instruction that lead to high school completion and then go on to the University. By the time deaf students reach that grade they are usually at an age when they are no longer interested in a general education, and are more interested in some form of vocational training that will lead directly to a job.

Achievements of Deaf People

Some deaf individuals have been able to continue their education and complete higher grade levels. One of them, a female from a wealthy family, was educated in French. French is the second most common language spoken at home by a great number of families. French is the language of education for some topics, especially mathematics and sciences in high school. French is even used to teach history and geography in some schools. French language learning is provided in practically all primary schools and given the same importance as Arabic. (The English language is the third language to be learned and is introduced after the primary level in some cases or as part of the primary level in other cases.)

This deaf student left the special education system just after the end of the primary school and registered, with the help of the family and the special education institution, in a public school in Lebanon. There, she completed her high school education and learned English through the use of a private tutor. She then traveled to the United States and registered in Gallaudet University. She received her degree in chemistry from the University.

Although this case is not unique in the Lebanese annals, very few deaf persons have been able to accomplish this task. Other deaf persons who were educated in the use of the French language have continued their education in France. None of them has gone beyond the secondary education level. Some of them failed to continue beyond the first or second year of secondary school.

The Lebanese students' vocational training pursuits in France have not been successful either. The French special education system does not offer many vocational education opportunities.

Of all of the deaf students who have been educated in the Arabic language and who continued their education in Lebanon, only one female student was able to reach the secondary school level. This student from a poor family finished primary school in a special education center and then was mainstreamed into a normal public school program. Her educational progress was followed by the special school located in the area where she lived. She demonstrated exceptional learning and adaptation capacities. Along with the Arabic language, she learned French

and English. Course work in both French and English are normally required by all high schools in Lebanon. Her achievements were more than satisfactory and she is continuing her education in the public school system with the hope of entering the University.

Program Content and Teaching Methods

Program Content

In kindergarten and the primary school, deaf students learn the same subjects that are usually part of the curriculum of the public school. The kindergarten level is two years in length and begins when the child reaches the age of three. One of the goals of this level is for the deaf child to learn how to get along with his or her peers and function in groups. The acquisition of the basic skills needed to allow their children to continue their education to the next level is another goal.

For the general curriculum, the primary school level starts after the child has completed the two years of kindergarten and has reached the age of five or six. Primary school is divided into three cycles, each two years in length. The first cycle is aimed at achieving skill in reading, writing, counting, and some basic computing. During the second cycle, work in the area of reading, writing, and mathematics is continued. Some basic information in the areas of science, history, and geography is introduced. During the third cycle the child should perfect the ability to express his or herself, communicate, calculate, and acquire basic knowledge of the human and material environments.

The Lebanese deaf student is also expected to achieve all of the knowledge discussed above.

Teaching Methods

The First Historical Period

When special education started in

Lebanon in the mid-1950s and early 1960s, no educational infrastructure existed. The only model to emulate was the normal public school program and its traditional teaching methods. At first, teachers of the deaf tried to follow the model used in the public school system. This approach failed for the following reasons:

- Because of the differing ages, the curriculum designed for normal public school children was not appropriate for deaf children. It is very difficult to teach deaf children who are eight, nine, or even older with books designed for three- or four-year-old children. Often, fourteen-year-old deaf students were being taught with materials used to teach six- or seven-year-old hearing children.
- Traditional teaching methods based on a homogeneous group approach could not be applied successfully to a very disparate group of deaf children.
- The language-teaching process designed for hearing children is based on the fact that they have already acquired language, the mother tongue, at home. This is not true of deaf children who usually arrive at school without any language at all, except for a sign system of their own design which is not used in the classroom.

The Second Historical Period

As was indicated, the first period in the history of the education of the deaf was a dismal failure. Beginning with the 1970s educators of the deaf had to radically change their approach. Instead of revising their approach to include the sign language used by the deaf, European practices influenced the most talented educators to develop the education system in the following ways:

1. The educators tried to increase and improve the deaf children's language learning by equipping the schools with group and individual hearing aids. The focus was on auditory training or the development of the deaf student's residual hearing, speechreading skill, and speech potential.
2. The educators invented new programs largely adapted to be used with deaf children.
3. New instructional approaches that were radically different from what was used in the normal public school were developed. The educators created new teaching material for each group and often for each child, because the materials originally created for hearing children in the public schools did not work well with deaf children.

The second historical period of the education of the deaf in Lebanon also ended with failure. Schools that invested heavily in equipment found that it was expensive and difficult to maintain. There were not enough educational specialists who knew how to use the equipment and not enough technicians who knew how to maintain it. The schools for the deaf could not provide the instructional program or purchase materials needed to support the equipment or to complete the system.

The new materials were so "adapted" and the teaching so individualized that the risk was large that inexperienced and poorly trained teachers would depend upon the hand-outs and little real learning would occur. The difficulties experienced in the language learning process aggravated the problem. Deaf students did not have sufficient language background to support the acquisition of new information. The teaching process was very difficult to maintain year after year, especially when new teaching materials that were needed were not available.

The Third Historical Period

The third historical period in the education of the deaf began in the 1980s. Since the advent of the third historical period, the schools for the deaf have been able to obtain more equipment and materials and hire additional specialized professionals. New mainstream and early education programs have been developed.

Lebanese Experience with Mainstream Programs

By the end of the 1970s, some of the professionals working in the field of deafness who had trained in France pushed for the creation of mainstream programs. Because of the dismal state of the education of the deaf at the time, these professionals easily succeeded in convincing the administrators of programs for the deaf that mainstreaming was the answer to their problems.

Which deaf students would be enrolled in the mainstream programs was based on several factors: the academic achievement level of the deaf student, the deaf child's level of language development, and his or her ability to adapt to the academic system as a whole. The public school programs were contacted and their administrators and pedagogic teams were convinced of the necessity to experiment with the idea of mainstreaming. The teachers were prepared to accept the presence of deaf children in their classrooms. Yet it was not enough to assure that the experience would be a success, since the public school systems were not prepared to support mainstreaming.

At first deaf children were accepted into schools for the deaf at the age of six. The age of entrance was later lowered to three. In spite of the advent of early education programs, language learning problems were still encountered. The need for specialized materials, equipment, and personnel was still apparent.

The presence of deaf children was tolerated, but the faculty and administrators of the public schools could not grasp the totality of the deaf children's learning problems. Moreover, neither the special education school nor the parents could provide the

public schools with the follow-up and support services the deaf children needed. Left to their own devices, most of the deaf children were unable to cope with the mainstream environment and returned to the special education centers and schools for the deaf.

At the beginning of the 1980s, about 30 deaf children were involved in mainstream programs. In later years this number dropped to no more than seven or eight.

Lebanese Experience with Early Education Programs

Deaf children's experience with early education programs was much more favorable than was the mainstream experience.

Early education programs for the deaf began at practically the same time as did the mainstream programs. As with mainstreaming, the early childhood movement was influenced by European practices. Some of these experimental centers for the deaf were staffed by early childhood professionals. Often the staff might include a speech therapist and a clinical psychologist who could provide services for parents and their young deaf child.

At first the programs seemed to be a great success. Parents were enthusiastic and the deaf children seemed to be progressing, especially when the parents were completely involved in the educational process. It seemed at that time that the whole educational program for deaf children in Lebanon would be transformed by the success of the early education programs. But the high expectations were not at all confirmed.

For many reasons, the deaf children who were involved in the early education process were not able to integrate better into the educational system. They experienced the same kind of problems in language learning as did deaf children who were not involved in an early education program.

Some reasons for these results relate to the difficulties found in applying such programs to a country undergoing an internal military conflict. Other reasons were related to the lack of inventiveness, creativity, and success of the early childhood educators in sustaining the learning environment and continuing to provide appropriate materials.

Communication Methodology

The Influence of European Practices

Even in the relatively most advanced schools for the deaf, the oral approach is still applied in its most classical form. All other methodologies or techniques used to teach the deaf except for cued speech, which developed cues to be used with Arabic in 1988, are not used at all in Lebanon. The "cues" were borrowed from the French "Support Signs" created and used by Mrs. Borel-Maisonny, the famous French speech therapist. Mrs. Borel-Maisonny created a system of visual representation for all phonetic characteristics of the French language. She used it at first with mentally retarded persons, then with children who suffered language pathologies (dyslexia and so on), and afterwards with deaf people.

A manual alphabet to use with Arabic was not initiated until the Congress of Amman in 1986. The Verbo-Tonal Method of Guberina could not be applied because of a lack of trained personnel and the needed equipment.

Into the 1990s the status quo continues with little change. At the beginning of the 1980s the time seemed ripe for change.

Because Lebanese educators of the deaf are not acquainted with successful or innovative practices in other parts of the world, they have to wait until the European practitioners, influenced at first by American practices and especially by professionals from Gallaudet University, began to address the severe shortcomings of the oral approach.

French research has indicated that 100 years of condemnation of the use of sign language has not prevented the deaf people of France from continuing to sign with each other and to feel satisfied and fulfilled by the use of this type of communication. Moreover, neither the condemnation of sign language

nor technological and pedagogical improvements in the education of the deaf could ameliorate the achievements of deaf people. The willingness of others to ignore, misinterpret, and misjudge the sign language used by deaf people proceeded from a basis of total ignorance of the fact that the acquisition of a second language necessarily depends upon the use of one's first language (the mother tongue). Some researchers and professionals have stated that a bilingual approach to the education of the deaf is the only solution to the deaf person's language learning problems.

Rehabilitation of the Sign Language Used by Deaf People

At almost the same time, Lebanese professionals were arriving at the same conclusions as did the French concerning the use of a bilingual approach. Whereas French researchers could lean on a relatively well-documented tradition of the use of signs by the deaf people of France as well as the presence of active deaf individuals and deaf communities, Lebanese professionals had no precedent to start with. In Lebanon there are no culturally active deaf communities that support centers for the education of the deaf and residential schools for the deaf. There is no tradition that acknowledges and recognizes the value of sign language. Instead, there exists a relatively long tradition of ignoring the sign language used by the deaf, or merely tolerating its existence. Furthermore, most hearing educators of the deaf continue to use the oral-aural methodology to the present day.

The most advanced centers for the deaf are experimenting with new methods and philosophies. These programs discovered that the oral-aural methodology does not provide good results at all levels and especially during the early childhood years. For many children to be successful academically, these centers found that signs, mime, gestures, and body expression must be used. The Total Communication philosophy, or the importance of being very attentive to the whole child and to the use of the totality of available communication strategies to educate the deaf child, is gaining prominence. Programs that use the Total Communication approach have encouraged parents to use all of the possible ways to communicate with their child.

Introduction of Deaf Educators to the Educational Process

Schools for the deaf count among their staff some poorly educated deaf adults who work as servants, domestics, and service personnel in the kitchen or in other departments. Some of the deaf adults live at the schools for the deaf and assume minor tasks in the dorms or with after-school activities. Deaf adults have been used as teacher assistants because they presented a positive role model, especially for small deaf children. The deaf adults were able to communicate more successfully with the deaf children than were many of the hearing educators. The deaf adults understood the children and were able to better respond to their needs. The deaf adults were able to positively influence the deaf children's behavior as well as their academic achievement. Very quickly, the presence of deaf adults in the schools for the deaf became an educational necessity, and they were given the opportunity to join pedagogic teams even if they did not have the appropriate academic training or diploma.

At first, job openings for deaf adults at the schools for the deaf were limited to insignificant tasks accomplished during the school day. But very quickly deaf adults were designated to take charge of after-school activities, especially for those deaf students who had previously ended their primary education. The deaf adults succeeded very well in all of the tasks assigned.

By the mid-1980s, deaf adults had become full members of pedagogic teams and were given responsibilities for the instructional process.

The following roles were performed by deaf adults:

1. In each class, a hearing educator was teamed with a deaf adult. The deaf person was given the responsibility of teaching some academic topics, especially the vocational subjects. The educator who was deaf had the responsibility of working with the whole class, especially when the hearing educator was working with individual students. Language development activities were still the privilege of the hearing teacher.
2. With the new awareness of the important role of sign language, deaf educators have been designated as sign language teachers. New procedures have been created that permit the hearing and deaf educators to work on the same topics. The author of this chapter, and the pedagogic team he leads, have created a method to teach reading skills to deaf children that relies especially on the use of a hearing and deaf educator as a team. They both work on the same topic, telling the children a story, but each teacher uses different tools. The educator who is deaf uses signs, mime, and images, whereas the hearing educator uses verbal and written languages.

Current Trends and Future Issues in the Education of the Deaf

The introduction of deaf persons into the educational process could not have succeeded without some radical changes in people's concept of deaf individuals and the value of the education of the deaf. In addition, the rebirth and acceptance of the sign language used by the deaf people of Lebanon has been a critical factor.

The Training of Deaf Professionals

All observations provide evidence of the success of deaf adults in the role of educators in schools for the deaf. The lack of the opportunity and availability of the technical training required to become a teacher of the deaf is a current factor that limits deaf adults from careers as teachers of the deaf. Due to the poor educational system that now exists, deaf persons are not able to achieve the background and knowledge needed to complete the level of education required to become a teacher of the deaf.

Since there were no programs to prepare deaf adults to become teachers, one of the schools for the deaf, the Institut de Ré-Education Audio-Phoneé-Tique, prepared a 200-hour training session for the deaf adults who were currently working in centers for the education for the deaf. The training program was designed to address the deaf persons' lack of opportunity to gain the technical and pedagogical knowledge in education in general and especially in the education of the deaf required to become a teacher of the deaf. The training program was launched in 1991.

See Appendix B for a description of the curriculum used to train hearing educators of the deaf.

Research on the Sign language Used by Deaf People in Lebanon

Because of the relatively long-term use of the oral method to teach the deaf in Lebanon, the sign language used by deaf people in Lebanon has been totally ignored. Recently, professionals, school principals, and school directors have become more convinced of the necessity to know more about the sign language used by deaf people in Lebanon. Their assumption is that the sign language could be profitably integrated into the whole learning process. The use of sign language could possibly improve the deaf person's oral and written language acquisition as well as his self-image and general academic achievement.

Lebanese professionals are also convinced that the use of sign language in the educational process is perhaps the only way to escape from the dilemma of "language acquisition" vs. "acquisition of language." Research findings on bilingual and bicultural education of the deaf are being studied. The fact that educators who are deaf are enjoying the same status as the educators who hear has definitely promoted the introduction of sign language into the educational process.

Following are arguments to support the use of sign language in education of the deaf.

- Pedagogical arguments: Society's recognition of sign language as a bona fide language is helping to develop the image that the deaf person is different but not deficient and that it is worth while to stress his or her abilities rather than disabilities. It is easy to imagine the positive consequences of this change in attitude on the acceptance of the deaf person by his family and on the growth of his or her self-concept. Sign language might be the only and certainly the simplest way for family members to communicate fluently with the deaf child in an atmosphere of joy and contentment for all family members. The parents can then truly play the role of loving parents and not the role of teacher substitutes who focus on the child's acquisition of oral language. Schools also can profit from the use of sign language during indoor and outdoor activities.
- Linguistic arguments: Sign language is also the only language system the deaf child can use to manipulate language symbols as any hearing person would normally manipulate the spoken language. Sign language would allow the child to obtain necessary feedback in order to correct and/or proceed, to express freely

without internal or external obstacles, and to identify and take positions on issues. Sign language is the natural way for the deaf person to discover the social and linguistic rules of communication. Sign language permits a deaf person to gain natural and normal access to language in general, and to frame communications between parent and child in a manner similar to that which a hearing person does with the oral language. Many researchers are emphasizing the "critical period" for language acquisition and how sign language meets the deaf child's need for a native language. That first language (sign language) learned at an early age can be used to learn other languages.

- Bilingualism as a general concept of language learning, as well as a specific educational method in the education of the deaf, relies on a very simple idea: the use of signs, the language of the child's peers and of the deaf adults in his community, at a very early age. Sign language will introduce the child to a usable language system instead of being denied access to one. When the specific language rules are established by means of sign language, the second language acquisition process will profit enormously.

- Social arguments: When using their mother tongue (sign language), deaf people can identify with others, and constitute a linguistic community. The cultural identity achieved assists the deaf persons in improving their achievement and fostering their integration into the larger society.

Even though a large majority of teachers, school principals, and directors seem to be convinced of the need for research on deaf people's use of sign language to communicate, sign language research in Lebanon is still non-

existent. A questionnaire entitled "Role of Sign in the Education of the Deaf" was passed out to participants after a two-day work session, organized on February 11–12, 1988, for all the centers of education for the deaf in Lebanon. The results clearly indicate a new awareness of the value of sign language among all professionals and a radical change in their view of sign language. It showed, too, the willingness and perhaps enthusiasm of these groups to conduct scientific research on the signs used by Lebanese deaf people as a first step toward integrating signs into the educational process. Years of war have prevented practical moves in that direction.

Currently there is little or no published information on the sign languages used in neighboring Arab countries. With the help of an American researcher, Dr. James Woodward, from Gallaudet University Research Center, and Gallaudet University International Center for Deafness (ICD), the author of this chapter has drafted a research project on Lebanese sign language. The project has five major objectives:

1. Accomplish an in-depth collection and analysis of formational, lexical, and grammatical data on the sign language varieties used by deaf people in Lebanon.
2. Train Lebanese deaf professionals and members of the deaf community in the scientific study of the structure of the sign languages and the deaf culture.
3. The preparation of material for the teaching of Lebanese Sign Language.
4. Selection and training of prospective teachers of Lebanese Sign Language.
5. The selection and training of prospective spoken Arabic/Lebanese Sign Interpreters.

The project is designated to be implemented in three stages of approximately one year each. The first stage will focus on basic research on sign language varieties used in Lebanon and will result in the completion of objectives one and two. The second stage will focus on language teaching and will result in the completion of objectives three and four. The third stage will focus on the initial training of interpreters and will result in the completion of objective five.

Problems that have plagued the education of the deaf are being addressed. Educational assistants who are deaf and who work in the Institut de Ré-Éducation Audio-Phoné-Tique are being trained to instruct deaf children. Teacher preparation will be available to deaf and hearing persons in other locations in Lebanon in the near future.

Additional funds to support foreign researchers and specialists who are willing to travel to Lebanon and work with local professionals are needed. The study of local Lebanese sign languages requires the cooperation of a number of individuals, including local deaf people who already know sign language but who have no training in linguistics; local hearing people who control the educational and social welfare institutions for the deaf, but who have little or no knowledge of the local sign language; local linguists who know linguistic theory but who have had no training in sign language; and foreign sign language linguists who know about the general grammar and use of sign language but who know little or nothing about the situation in Lebanon.

When we examine what is known about Lebanese sign language, we see that the type of cooperation described above is necessary if Lebanon is to move from its strong tradition of oralism to the acceptance and use of sign language to educate deaf people and to foster the social integration of deaf people into mainstream Lebanese society.

The application of bilingual methodology in the education of deaf children in Lebanon is at the present non-existent. As the bilingual bicultural approach to the education of the deaf becomes known and accepted by professionals and parents, it could very well become the most commonly accepted methodology used to teach deaf children in the twenty-first century.

Appendices
Appendix A

Existing Institutions for the Education of the Deaf

1. Lebanese School for the Blind and the Deaf. Baabda. South-Metn. Mount-Lebanon. Started its activities in 1956-1957.

2. Institute for Audio-Phonetic Reeducation. Aï n-Aar. North-Metn. Mount-Lebanon. Started its activities in 1960.

3. Father Andeweï g Institute for the Deaf and Mute. Loueizeh. South-Metn. Mount-Lebanon. Started its activities in 1959.

4. House of the Deaf Children. Father Robert's Institute. Shayleh. Kesrouane. Mount-Lebanon. Started its activities in 1959.

5. El Kafa'at Institution for Rehabilitation. Hadath. South-Metn. Mount-Lebanon. Started its activities in 1976.

6. Assembly for the Development of Human Potentialities. El Bayan Institute for the Deaf. El-Ouza'y. Beirut. Started its activities in 1977.

7. House of the Orphan Welfare. Any-El-Helweh, Sayda. South-Lebanon. Started its activities in 1977.

8. Friends of the Handicapped Association. El-Kobbeh, Tripoli. North-Lebanon. Started its activities in 1988.

9. Psychological, Pedagogical and Social Orientation Center. Tripoli. North-Lebanon. Started its activities in 1989.

10. Mabarrat of the Woman Islamic League. El-Mounla, Tripoli. North-Lebanon. Started its activities in 1987.

11. Preventive and Pedagogic Center for Parents. Zahleh, Bekaa. Started its activity in 1985.

12. Armenian Association for the Blind. Bourj-Hammoud. North-Metn. Mount-Lebanon.

Appendix B

The Curriculum of the Training Program for Educators of the Deaf

1. Theory and practice of social services (10 hours). History of social institutions in Lebanon. Special education in Lebanon. Special education for the deaf. Functions of an educational center for the deaf.

2. Audiology (6 hours). Anatomy and physiology of the ear. The hearing function. Pathologies of the ear. Causes of deafness. Corrective interventions. Measurement of hearing. Collective and individual assistive devices.

3. Speech therapy (12 hours). Language and communication. Systems of codification. Sign Language, verbal language, written language. Pathologies of language. Reeducation of languages.

4. School and educational psychology (26 hours). Developmental psychology. Child development process. Psychopedagogy of a specialized center. Differential psychology (hearing-deaf). Female psychology.

5. Jobs frequently encountered in deaf centers (20 hours). Nurse. Psychologist and psychiatrist. Specialized educator. Social worker. Audiologist. Generalist. Speech therapist.

6. Analysis of practice (40 hours). Case studies. Exposition techniques. Writing reports. Case studies in centers for the deaf. Discussions on psychopedagogic relationships.

7. Classical topics recapitulation (40 hours). Arabic and Arabic grammar. French. Mathematics.

8. Manual educational activities (14 hours). Cartoonage. Ceramics.

9. Body expression (12 hours). Rhythmics, yoga, corporal expression.

10. Ethics and morality of professional practice (6 hours).

11. First aid (14 hours).

12. Visits to working institutions in Lebanon.

References

Caritas-Liban. (1981). *Les handicapés au Liban.* [The handicapped of Lebanon]. Statistical study directed by Akiki, Issam. Caritas.

Chamoun, M. (1970). Enfance inadaptée et ré-éducation au Liban. [Handicapped children and special education in Lebanon]. *Travaux Et Jours, 36.*

Chamoun, M. (1972, Janviers-Mars). Pour ré-éduquer. [To reeducate]. *Travaux Et Jours, 42.*

Chamoun, M. (1985). La ré-éducation de l'enfant sourd dans les pays arabes. [The reeducation of he deaf child in Arabic countries]. *Annales de Psychologie et des Sciences de l'Education.* (Vol. 1). Université Saint-Joseph. Faculté des Lettres et des Sciences Humains.

Collectif. (1979). *Seminars and work sessions in the field of the social service training. Examples and case studies.* Prepared for publication by Dr. El-Housaï ny, Hachem. Hadath, Lebanon: Social Training Center Publications. (Original text in Arabic).

Collectif. (1979). *Technical supervision in the field of the social service training. Concepts and examples.* Prepared for publication by Hadda, Frida. Hadath, Lebanon: Social Training Center Publications. (Original text in Arabic).

Collectif. (1980). *A study of the social services' functions and the conditions of its employees in Lebanon, 1978–1979. Ground research.* Part One: Exposition and analysis of results. Part Two: Statistical tables and diagrams. Prepared by the technical staff of the Social Training Center. 1980. Hadath, Lebanon: Social Training Center Publications. (Original text in Arabic).

Collectif. (1980). *Listing of the social institutions in Lebanon 1978–1979.* Prepared by the technical staff of the Social Training Center. Hadath, Lebanon: Social Training Center Publications. (Original text in Arabic).

Collectif. (1981). *Seminars and work sessions for development.* Prepared for publication by Dr. El-Housaï ny, Hachem. Hadath, Lebanon: Social Training Center Publications. (Original text in Arabic).

Collectif. (1987). *Lebanon, the reality and the need for rehabilitation and development. Final condensed report on the global scanning of the basic needs of Lebanese villages, counties and cities.* Hariri Institution. (Original text in Arabic).

Collectif. (1988). *Proceedings of The First Congess for Communication Disabilities in Lebanon.* Under the Patronage of Public Health Faculty, Lebanese University, and Model Handicapped Center. Sayda, May 20–22, 1988. Sayda, Lebanon: Orphan Welfare Association. (Original text in Arabic).

Ken'ana Abi-Abdallah, N. (1981). *Social service in Lebanon.* Hadath, Lebanon: Social Training Center Publications. (Original text in Arabic).

National Council for the Social Services in Lebanon. Association of the Social and Technical Institutions. (1983, April). Actual status of the Social Services Institutions in Lebanon and their future aspirations; Drawing a global representation of a social and developmental politic to be carried out by the governmental and private sectors. In *Proceedings of the Third National Congress of Social Work in Lebanon.* Beirut, April 11–15, 1983. (Original texts in Arabic).

Roumanos, A. (1982, August 28–September 3). Education of deaf children. *AL-NAHAR.* (Original text in Arabic).

Roumanos, A. (1983, April 11–15). *Situation of the deaf in Lebanon.* Lecture to the Third National Congress of Social Action. (Original text in Arabic).

Roumanos, A. (1986, November 13–14). *Handicap and society.* Lecture to the First Congress of Social Prevention. Batroun, North Lebanon. (Original text in Arabic).

Roumanos, A. (1988, February 11–12). *The role of sign in the education of the deaf. Sign at the service of language.* Work session organized with the collaboration of the World Rehabilitation Fund (WRF) for all Lebanese Institutions working in the field of deafness. Unpublished. (Original text in Arabic).

Roumanos, A. (1988, May 20–22). *Early education of deaf children.* Lecture to the First Conference for Communication Disabilities in Lebanon. Saï da, South Lebanon. (Original text in Arabic).

Roumanos, A., & Woodward, J. *A study of Lebanese sign language.* Research project, unpublished.

The Lives of the Deaf in Nepal

Lion Sita Ram Maskey, Founder
Jaljala Shishu Sadan

(From a paper submitted to the Twelfth International Congress on Education for the Deaf, Rochester, N.Y., July and August, 1990)

Introduction

Nepal, the home of Mt. Everest, is a land-locked country, sandwiched between China to the north, and India to the east, west, and south. Although Nepal, surrounded by the beautiful Himalayas as well as by green mountains, is rich in natural beauty, it is the third poorest country in the world. The total population of Nepal is 18.5 million, with an annual rate of growth of 2.6 percent. Only 35 percent of the people of Nepal are literate. The per capita income of a person in Nepal is $145 US. Eighty-three percent of the people live in rural areas, and 94 percent of the people depend on agriculture for subsistence. The people of Nepal have to struggle daily for food, shelter, and clothing. Illiteracy and poverty have retarded the economic growth of the country. More than 40 percent of the people fall below the poverty line. The majority of the rural people lives a hand-to-mouth existence and finds it difficult to educate their children. Since conditions are so difficult for normal children, the education of the handicapped is out of the question.

History of the Education of the Deaf

The history of the development of education in Nepal is a short one. Education was formally introduced in 1943 under the cruel regime of the dictator Rana, and was reserved for the members of the royal family. However, the political change that took place in 1950 provided an opportunity for the public to get an education. About three million children are studying in 19,893 schools. The number of teachers who instruct them totals 85,843. See Table 1 for further details on education in Nepal.

Table 1. Education in Nepal

Condition	School	Teachers	Students
Normal	19,893	85,843	2,907,687
Blind	15	31	175
Deaf	4 + 2*	49	383

* One private deaf school at Dharan and one deaf school run by social club, Pokhara.
Source: Ministry of Education, HMG/Nepal.

Those who are handicapped, blind, and deaf have received the opportunity to be educated only during the last few decades. The first school for the deaf was established in 1966 in Kathmandu. There are only a handful of social organizations that serve the blind, deaf, and other handicapped children. The six schools for the deaf enroll 383 deaf students. There are 15 schools for the blind with an enrollment of 175. In Table 2, the current statistical data shows that the total number of handicapped children is 77,623. Twenty-one percent are blind, 28.92 percent have other disabilities, and 49.9 percent of the total handicapped population are deaf. The current number of schools for the deaf is inadequate to meet the need.

Table 2. Disabled Individuals in Nepal

	Male	Female	Total	Percent
Deaf/Mute	22,594	16,201	38,795	49.97
Blind	8,113	8,285	16,398	21.11
Other Disabled	14,505	7,925	22,430	28.92
Total	45,212	32,411	77,623	

Source: Central Bureau of Statistics, Nepal.

Table 3. Comparative Study of Services for Blind and Deaf People in Nepal

	Male	Female	Total	Percent	School	Teachers
Blind	8,113	8,285	16,398	21.11	15	31
Deaf	22,594	16,201	38,795	49.97	2	49
	Male	Female	Total	Hospital	Bed	Doctor
Blind	122	53	175	16	750	50
Deaf	274	109	383	6	50	18

Source: Central Bureau of Statistics, Ministry of Education and Health, HMG/Nepal.

Tables 1, 2, and 3 illustrate vision and hearing projects in Nepal and show that there is a vast difference between these two. The total number of deaf students exceeds the number of blind students, although there are fewer schools for the deaf than for the blind. Also, the number of deaf students studying in schools for the deaf is greater than the number of blind students. Similarly, the number of ENT (ear, nose, and throat) services in hospitals, the number of beds, and the number of ENT doctors are far fewer than medical services for the blind. There are more vision projects run by the government as well as by the NGOs (non-government organizations) than projects concerning hearing impairments in Nepal.

Although the first school for the deaf was established in 1966, there were very few students at the outset and only the oral method was used to teach the deaf, due to the lack of knowledge of modern techniques used in highly developed countries. Gradually, the number of deaf students enrolled increased over each academic session. Four schools for the deaf were developed, one in each region: Surkhet, Bhairahawa, Rajbiraj, and Kathmandu. There are also two private schools, one in Pokhara, which is run by the Shrijan Yuwa Club, and one in Dharan, named the Jaljala Shishu Sadan and run by Mrs. Radha Maskey and Mr. Sita Ram Maskey. Table 4 shows enrollments and other data about these schools.

Table 4. Schools for the Deaf in Nepal

	Girls	Boys	Total	Teachers	Hostel
Surkhet (Estd. 1980)	8	40	48	7	x
Bhairahawa (Estd. 1976)	18	50	68	7	25
Pokhara (Estd. 1987)	9	18	27	3	-
Kathmandu (Estd. 1966)	57	118	175	19	24
Rajbiraj (Estd. 1984)	10	30	40	7	20
Dharan (Estd. 1985)	9	13	22	5	3

Source: Collected by author.

The interest of the children towards education could not be developed due to lack of an appropriate school program. Thus, vocational education areas including knitting, sewing, carpentry, painting, metal work, and printing, as well as sign language classes were introduced into the schools. Sign language classes made it possible for the deaf children to communicate with each other. The use of the Total Communication philosophy was emphasized only after 1985. For the first time, a Nepalese sign language dictionary was published in 1987 by the school for the deaf in Kathmandu, with the assistance of Peace

Corps Volunteer Patricia Ross. Similarly, a manual alphabet of Nepali letters was introduced by the Kathmandu Association of the Deaf. Sign language and the manual alphabet are now used in most of the schools for the deaf in the country.

Advocacy and Social Services

In 1980, the deaf of Nepal formed an ad-hoc committee with a view toward establishing a nationwide association of the deaf. The central government discouraged the development of a Nepal Association of the Deaf in the absence of a concrete governmental policy towards the education of the deaf. The lack of improvement in deaf people's employment opportunities, social values, and financial conditions hindered their development. Consultation from other countries has led to inspiration and enthusiasm among the deaf population. Efforts have been renewed by contacts with the deaf people at home and abroad and have led to the formation of a developed national association. Deaf persons have now developed clubs and associations in Kathmandu, Bhairahawa, Dharan, and Pokhara.

Although the Kathmandu Association for the Deaf was formed in 1980, it has been actively serving the deaf population only since 1984. The association, containing 74 members, has been engaged in arranging cultural programs, sports competition, health service programs, mountaineering training, books and video collections, and publication of a yearly calendar. Every year the Nepalese deaf receive training in mountaineering at various places in India. In 1987, for the first time, a deaf person from Nepal participated in the Tenth World Federation of the Deaf, held in Finland. Four deaf people participated in the Deaf Way Conference held in Washington, D.C., in 1989. This was the third time that two deaf persons from Nepal had participated in international congresses.

Deaf Hindered by Attitudes of the Public

In Nepal, disabled children are considered to be burdens to their already poor parents. Due to the social stigma attached to a disability, the parents of a disabled child do not want to let others know about the existence of such children. As a result, disabled people suffer from increased depression, inferiority complexes, and an inability to join society. There are still many people who believe that a disability is the prank of destiny and the dispensation of providence; to be deaf or to have any kind of disability is a result of the curse of God. Most of the people are not aware of current scientific progress. The parents cannot comprehend the fact that their deaf children could study, support themselves, and depend on their intelligence and abilities. It is considered a pointless investment to educate a person who is deaf. Parents forbid their hearing children to play with a deaf child in the neighborhood. If there are normal and deaf children in the same family, the deaf children are discriminated against by their own brothers and sisters. The deaf have to stay in seclusion, deprived of common human rights and opportunities, including a normal family life. Deaf men are restricted to labor in work such as portering, ploughing, and plumbing. It is quite clear that the parents of the deaf children of Nepal see no monetary benefit to be gained by educating their deaf children.

The condition of deaf women is even worse and is pathetic and deplorable. Their life is similar to that of a slave. Marriage is not even contemplated by the conservative society of Nepal. If it occurs at all, wealth plays a vital role in a marriage between a hearing and deaf person. Only a rich deaf person may be successful in finding a life partner.

The deaf children of Nepal never get the opportunity to become full contributing members of society. Even if they are intelligent, they do not receive the opportunity to realize their potential. Getting a job is equally impossible for the deaf in Nepal. No deaf person is employed in the civil service at present. Only nine deaf persons in the entire kingdom are employed by a semi-governmental organization. Apart from those engaged in agriculture, few deaf persons work for private businesses.

Due to the irregularities and corruption of past government institutions, disabled people have received little help. The plight of the disabled is worsening daily. Embezzlers often become millionaires at their expense. If it were possible for government and social welfare organizations to receive help from developed countries, the disabled could benefit greatly.

Conclusion

In view of all of this, disabled people living in Third World countries face similar problems. As the people of developed countries are progressing rapidly, the people of underdeveloped countries like Nepal are struggling for the basic and minimum needs of life. It is an absolute necessity for the developed countries of the world to give serious attention to the collective development of the deaf people of underdeveloped countries, who are suffering from the pangs of hunger and ignorance.

Therefore, I want to make an impassioned appeal to the deaf people of the world as well as those working in this field to contribute their part in the creation of a universal domicile of peace. The people of the whole world have a passionate desire for peace. So, every community is obliged to provide a substantial contribution for world peace.

The Education of Deaf Children in the Netherlands

Harry Knoors
Rudolf Mees Institute for the Deaf
Rotterdam, The Netherlands

Introduction

The education of deaf children in the Netherlands has had a long and often complicated history. The current situation is even more complicated, because of differences in the educational philosophy and practices of the five schools for the deaf in the country and the tremendous number of new developments that have occurred in the education of the deaf during the last decade.

History

In 1790 the Reverend Henri Daniel Guyot established, with the help of some friends, the first institute for the education of deaf children in the Netherlands. That first school is presently called the Royal Institute for the Deaf "H. D. Guyot" and is located at Haren near Groningen, a town in the northern-most part of the country.

In 1784 Guyot had visited Paris and there came into contact with the Abbé de L'Épée. Guyot attended lessons at Abbé de L'Épée's National Institution for the Deaf for nine months. When he returned to Groningen in 1785, he taught private lessons to a growing number of deaf pupils. At his school in Groningen, Guyot followed de L'Épée's philosophy of teaching the deaf. Manual signs were used as a representation of the spoken Dutch language. Thirteen pupils were enrolled in the school when it was established in 1790.

Forty years later, in 1830, the priest Marinus van Beek established the second school for the deaf in the southern part of the Netherlands, the present Institute for the Deaf at Sint Michielsgestel. Van Beek also developed a sign system, Dutch-in-signs, that was used to teach the deaf children at his school. The deaf children acquired the Dutch language through reading.

In Germany the so-called pure oral method of teaching the deaf gained ground very quickly. It was soon introduced in the

Netherlands as well. Adherents of this method claimed that deaf children could be taught to speak and speechread. The use of signs was seen as a threat to the development of these skills. Dr. Polano, a physician from Rotterdam who had two deaf children, hired David Hirsch, an oral teacher of the deaf from a school for the deaf in Aachen, Germany, to teach his children. In 1853 Hirsch arrived in Rotterdam and established the first oral school for deaf children in the Netherlands, the Institute for Education of the Deaf and Dumb. Today the school is called the Rudolf Mees Institute.

In 1888 a Protestant school called Effatha was established as the fourth school for the deaf in the Netherlands. It was situated at Voorburg near The Hague. In 1911 in Amsterdam the J. C. Ammanschool for the Deaf was established. This school was administered by the local authorities. From the beginning the Effatha, the J. C. Ammanschool schools, and the Rudolph Mees Institute in Rotterdam were established as oral schools for the deaf. In 1880 after the Milan International Congress on the Education of the Deaf, the Groningen Institute changed to an oral school for the deaf, and finally in 1906 the school at Sint Michielsgestel followed the Groningen Institute's lead and renounced the manual method of teaching the deaf. Educators of the deaf had become convinced that it was possible to develop the reading ability of deaf children after they had learned to speak.

The era of oralism would last until the start of the 1980s. Until then, educators sought ways to increase the effectiveness of the oral method.

The oralists first looked at technology as a way of increasing the effectiveness of oralism. Several types of individual hearing aids as well as group amplification systems were implemented on a large scale.

Next, the advocates of the oral system of communication tried to improve the didactics of the oral method. The "maternal reflective method" created by Van Uden (1977) and his colleagues was a natural method of language learning that departed from the essentially behavioristic view of language acquisition of the past, which stressed imitation and correction. In the maternal reflective method, the principles of mother-child interaction and communication (modeling, expanding language of the child) were applied to the classroom setting. It was claimed that the maternal reflective method was most effective if implemented at a very young age and without the use of any form of manual communication.

During the 1960s the concept of differentiation was introduced. It was acknowledged that not all deaf children could be successfully educated by the oral method. The term "oral failures" came into existence. Although their number rose steadily, the *ability* of the children considered to be oral failures was questioned, not the *method*. Additional learning disabilities (dysphasia, dyspraxia, sensoneural integration problems) were held responsible for their failure (Van Uden, 1981). To communicate with the oral failures, written Dutch and fingerspelling were used heavily. In order to avoid the spread of fingerspelling among all of the deaf children, the pupils at the Sint Michielsgestel Institute were placed in separate schools and signs could be used only to communicate with mentally retarded deaf children.

Somewhere around 1979 and 1980, things began to change drastically. The results of research on the mechanisms of first language acquisition made it clear to many that the oral method of teaching the deaf could no longer be prolonged. The philosophy of Total Communication, which had originated in the United States, spread to the Netherlands. Deaf adults attempted to obtain equal rights in Dutch society. Interest arose in the Sign Language of the Netherlands. All of these factors led to the reintroduction of signs in all of the schools for the deaf except for the one at Sint Michielsgestel. The Dutch Foundation for the Deaf and Hard-of-hearing Child in Amsterdam (an audiological center with a parent-guidance program and a research department) and the Royal Institute "Guyot" in Haren were pioneers in this movement.

Current Situation

In the Netherlands deaf and hard of hearing children are taught separately. Deaf children, defined functionally as those who have to perceive the spoken language visually, even with the best amplification equipment, attend the five schools for the deaf already mentioned. Hard of hearing children attend one of more than 30 schools for children with hearing and language problems. More and more of the hard of hearing children are being mainstreamed after a few years of special education.

Deafness is detected fairly early in the Netherlands. By the age of nine months the Ewing test, a test of auditory acuity, is administered to 72 percent of all infants (van der Lem, 1983). If a profound hearing loss is detected and confirmed, the parents of the deaf child are encouraged to take part in a parent guidance program. The schools for the deaf in Groningen, Rotterdam, Sint Michielsgestel, and Voorburg have parent guidance programs. In Amsterdam the parent guidance program is managed by the Dutch Foundation for the Deaf and Hard-of-hearing Child.

At the age of three, deaf children are enrolled in the kindergarten programs of the schools for the deaf. Legally, it is possible for deaf children to continue to attend a school for the deaf until the age of twenty. Many of the deaf students leave the school for the deaf before that age in order to attend a postsecondary program or other educational program that is part of a regular public school. In 1985 nearly 1200 deaf children were being educated at the five schools for the deaf (Onderwijs aan doven, 1986). The institute in Sint Michielsgestel is the largest and enrolls about 450 pupils.

All of the schools have departments for deaf children with multiple handicaps. The

Sint Michielsgestel school houses the only department in our country for deaf-blind children. The schools for the deaf in Groningen, Voorburg, and Sint Michielsgestel are partly residential. The schools in Amsterdam and Rotterdam are day schools.

Language Policy

As is the case in many countries, the policy that dictates what language methodology will be used to educate the deaf children of the Netherlands is a heavily debated issue. The subject of this debate is no longer the question of whether or not deaf children should be educated exclusively by the oral method. Although in practice that issue has been settled, the institute in Sint Michielsgestel continues to use the oral method. The maternal reflective method developed at the school is still in use. The differentiation concept mentioned earlier also continues to be practiced. The four other schools for the deaf have switched to the Total Communication philosophy.

The center of debate today is focused on what form of sign language should be implemented to carry out the Total Communication philosophy. Currently, the teachers in the four schools for the deaf that use the Total Communication philosophy use spoken Dutch and some form of Signed Dutch (SD), which might be better described as Pidgin Sign Dutch, to communicate with their deaf pupils. Signs are used especially for content words and for some functors (e.g., prepositions). Bound morphemes are not being signed. The signs that the teachers use stem from the lexicon of the Sign Language of the Netherlands (SLN). A minimum number of invented signs are permitted. Deaf adults are currently teaching SLN classes for teachers and parents. These courses are still in the process of development.

Some pedagogues claim that Signed Dutch (SD) is the best way to educate deaf children. It is their view that the manual component of SD will decrease as the children

get older and at the same time the child's use of oral expression will potentially increase.

Others point to the fact that at the time of the introduction of SD, research completed in the United States indicated that simultaneous communication might be a compromise at best. These critics point out that the production and perception of simultaneous communication is hampered by several fundamental problems, such as the synchronization of the speed of speech and sign and the combination of sequential and simultaneous ordering principles. Because of these problems, teachers and parents have been warned not to hold high expectations concerning the success of the use of SD as a means of improving the language competency of deaf children (Harder & Knoors, 1987).

The nearly complete lack of research on the use of SLN and a bilingual approach to teaching deaf children made it necessary to choose SD as the sign methodology of choice. After studies by Tervoort (1953, 1967) of the manual communication of orally educated deaf children, all research on manual communication and SLN came to a halt.

During the period between 1980 and 1990, research studies on the topic of SLN completed by linguists and psychologists filled in much of the gap in our knowledge of SLN. Many of the major properties of the manual communication of deaf adults have now been outlined (Schermer, 1985). Work focusing on the description of the lexicon of SLN is still in progress (Timmerman & Mans, 1990). Research attention is also aimed at the different aspects of the phonological system of SLN, the system of verb agreement, non-manual components, time indication, and the formations of compounds. (For summaries of this research see Schermer, Harder, & Bos, 1987; Schermer, 1989.) Finally, research into the acquisition of SLN by native signers and non-native signers has begun (Mills & Coerts, 1990; Knoors, 1989a, 1990; Loncke, Hoiting, Knoors, & Moerman, 1988).

Our increased knowledge of SLN, in combination with the acknowledgement that simultaneous communication is but one of several possible options that can be used to carry out the Total Communication philosophy, has recently led to substantial support for a bilingual model of education for the deaf in the Netherlands (Knoors, 1989b). In the bilingual model SLN is viewed as the first language of deaf children. Research indicates that SLN is a language in itself and an excellent means by which information about subjects like mathematics, history, biology, and geography can be transmitted effectively. Dutch would then be taught as a second language. Mastery of the written form of Dutch would have the highest priority for deaf children in the Netherlands.

During the last few years the four schools for the deaf that follow the philosophy of Total Communication have hired deaf adults to work in the classroom. For example, the Rotterdam Institute currently employs six deaf adults. All but one are employed on a part-time basis (the institute staff numbers almost 90 full- and part-time employees). One of the deaf adults has been hired as a teacher (the only deaf teacher in the Netherlands), three as teacher assistants, and two as sign language teachers. The employment of deaf adults in the schools for the deaf has, in a way, unconsciously introduced the bilingual education model to the schools since most of the deaf adults use SLN to communicate with deaf pupils. Although no well-designed and researched bilingual education program has been implemented at this time, the country is on the eve of implementing such a model. No doubt, such a project will once again intensify the debate over the proper language policy to be used in the education of the deaf in the Netherlands.

Educational Developments

The education of the deaf in the Netherlands has undergone significant changes during the last ten years, not only because of the reintroduction of signs, but also because of an increased rate of educational experimentation. Some of these educational innovations are summarized below.

Language Teaching

For many years language instruction was partially isolated from the teaching of other school subjects such as geography, biology, and so forth. The two approaches usually used in language instruction in the Netherlands are also commonly used abroad (see McAnally, Rose, & Quigley, 1987). Some schools adopted a structured language approach. The most extreme example of the structured language approach is the use of the Fitzgerald Key, which was also very popular in the United States for many years. In the Netherlands, the institute Effatha at Voorburg has been known for its structured method of teaching language to deaf children.

Other schools use what is referred to as the natural language approach. Adherents of the natural language approach try to incorporate in the teaching process as many principles of normal parent-child communication and normal first language acquisition as is possible. The institute of Sint Michielsgestel is noted for a natural language teaching approach, the maternal reflective method. The other schools for the deaf have been much less dogmatic on this issue.

All methods of teaching language to deaf children in the Netherlands have been characterized by the heavy emphasis placed upon the use of daily experiences for language content, metalinguistics, and other language activities. The personal experiences of the deaf children were used as the starting point for teaching language and academic subjects. As a consequence, curriculum content was highly coincidental and indicated a lack of planning and focus.

In 1982 pedagogues, linguists, and psychologists from the schools for the deaf in the Netherlands met with Peter Blackwell and the staff of the Rhode Island School for the

Deaf in the United States to learn about the language and learning curriculum of the Rhode Island School for the Deaf (Blackwell et al., 1978). This curriculum included the latest insights in language and literacy development and curriculum design. Since the Blackwell workshop, language learning and general learning are now integrated and a planning and goal-setting process has been initiated. Language, reading, writing, and subject-area content goals and an accompanying evaluation process have been developed.

Some of the departments of three Dutch schools for the deaf that use the Total Communication philosophy have adopted the Rhode Island curriculum. The schools in Voorburg and Amsterdam were the first to adopt the new curriculum and the school in Rotterdam followed some years later. Since its inception all three schools have continuously modified the original curriculum. The revised language and learning curricula of the School for the Deaf in Amsterdam has been published (Harder, 1989). The language development part of the curriculum has been evaluated and found to be most satisfactory (Harder, 1990).

Reading

The level of proficiency in reading comprehension of deaf children in the Netherlands is quite similar to the published reading comprehension level of deaf children in other countries (for the Netherlands, see IJsseldijk, 1987; Knoors, 1983; de Groot, 1981. For results abroad see Conrad, 1979, as an example). IJsseldijk claims that the level of reading comprehension of the pupils of the Institute at Sint Michielsgestel is higher than that of deaf children in other countries. However, close inspection of his research results does not warrant this conclusion.

To improve the reading proficiency of deaf children in the Netherlands, three research projects have been undertaken.

The first of these projects tried to answer the question of whether or not deaf children should be obliged to translate written text into a speech code in order to understand the text. The results of the study indicated that it was not necessary. The research showed that many deaf children could read well by translating the written words mentally into signs (Pijfers, 1989).

A second research project attempted to train deaf children to use speech as a mediating code when reading words, sentences, and stories. The results concluded that such training was possible, but that the training did not improve the children's understanding of word meaning. On the other hand, the children's memory for written word sequences did improve. It is possible that this improvement in memory for word sequences will help in the comprehension of written sentences and texts. Finally, writing the words down several times seemed to be the best guarantee that the orthographic structure of written words would be learned. Whether or not knowledge of the orthographic structure of words really helps in understanding the meaning of words could not be established (Schaper, 1989).

The last of the three research projects attempted to restructure the methods of teaching reading to deaf children in such a way that word and simple sentence comprehension would be improved. The project was completed at the Rudolf Mees Institute by researchers from the University of Utrecht. These researchers rejected the global method of teaching reading. Instead, they believed in a step-by-step process by which the young deaf child was first taught letters, then written words, phrases, and finally sentences. For each of these structures, the child was to analyze each part and then synthesize the parts into the whole. When analyzing the parts of the whole, the child was to compare one part with each other part.

During the preschool years while the child was in the letter state, no meaning was attached to the letter sequences. Analysis of form was heavily stressed. Only after the children were able to build letters from their component parts, compare one letter to another, and compare the sequence of the different letters, were these sequences given meaning by attaching signs to them. Speech and writing were both heavily taught as mediating codes. In doing this, the researchers tried to strengthen the deaf children's skill at visually analyzing and synthesizing language. Hopefully, this will avoid dependence upon guessing strategies and increase step-by-step multi-modal integration of the written word, the sign, and the spoken word (Quadvlieg, 1989).

Oral Skills

The institute at Sint Michielsgestel, in cooperation with the University of Nijmegen, continues to conduct research aimed at improving the quality of oral skills such as speech intelligibility and speechreading efficiency.

Some years ago, Maassen (1985) found that artificial correction of the suprasegmental aspects of the speech of deaf children did improve speech intelligibility, but correction of the segmental aspects of speech, especially vowels, had a much greater effect on intelligibility. As a result of this research, Sint Michielsgestel has developed what is called Visual Speech Apparatus (VSA), which consists of a digital signal processor, an IBM-compatible AT computer and an Amiga-2000 computer for graphic representations. The goal of the VSA is to provide deaf children with visual information and feedback about their speech. The emphasis is on the production of vowels. Means by which optimal use of residual hearing and/or tactile feedback can be accomplished have been established. Research is being conducted to discover the effectiveness of the VSA as a speech therapy tool (Povel & Wansink, 1986; Povel & Arends, 1989).

To improve speechreading skills, IJsseldijk (1989) has developed a training program that uses a computer linked with interactive videodisc equipment. With this equipment the individual deaf child can practice speechreading phonemes, words, phrases, and sentences under different conditions, such as viewing the face on the screen at different angles, manipulating the rate of speech, showing the lips only, and other variables. The computer provides the child with feedback and registers his or her answers. The equipment can also be used for diagnostic purposes (IJsseldijk, 1989).

Social-Emotional Development

As is true of deaf children in other countries, some of the deaf children in the Netherlands experience problems in social and emotional development. In some cases these problems may lead to severe psychotic symptoms. Two developments have taken place in recent years that may assist in preventing or solving many social and emotional problems.

In the area of prevention, the Paths curriculum developed by Mark Greenberg of the United States has received a lot of attention (Greenberg et al., 1987). The aim of this program is to prevent psychosocial difficulties by the orderly development of the psychosocial coping skills of deaf children. Greenberg has lectured in the Netherlands on several occasions and was invited to train some of our teachers in the use of the Paths curriculum. An organization of parents of deaf children in our country, FODOK, made it possible to translate the Paths program from English into Dutch. FODOK also appointed a pedagogue whose task was to coordinate the several Paths projects currently underway in schools for the deaf and hard of hearing in the Netherlands and in the Dutch-speaking part of Belgium.

FODOK has also played a crucial role in the treatment of mental health problems. FODOK has fostered a research project that is being conducted by the Dutch Foundation for the Deaf and Hard-of-hearing Child. This project is aimed at discovering which psychiatric problems are experienced by deaf children and how these problems can be detected and treated successfully (Beck & De Jong, 1989). Therapists are also experimenting with several therapeutic approaches.

Secondary and Postsecondary Education

Secondary education possibilities for deaf students vary according to the school for the deaf that they have attended. With the exception of the school for the deaf in Amsterdam, all Dutch schools for the deaf offer their pupils a vocational training program and the possibility of achieving a regular diploma. In order to achieve a regular diploma, the schools in Rotterdam and Groningen work cooperatively with regular secondary schools (Onderwijs ann doven, 1986).

In Rotterdam the high school students are mainstreamed into regular secondary school classes. Pupils are also provided individualized assistance by peripatetic teachers. Interpreters are not available at the Rotterdam secondary school. Research designed to evaluate this approach has demonstrated that mainstreaming led to acceptable academic results, but major problems in communication and social-emotional well-being (van den Broek, van den Broek, Gresnigt, & Rond, 1986). These problems have caused the Rotterdam school to change its policy. Today cooperation between the school for the deaf and regular public secondary school is symbiotic. The deaf pupils receive their vocational training at the regular secondary schools (teachers of the deaf accompany them), and they complete academic subjects at the schools for the deaf.

If pupils choose to follow a more theoretically oriented curriculum, that option is available at all schools for the deaf except for the one in Amsterdam. The school in Amsterdam has a secondary education program for students with hearing or language problems.

Those students who want to follow a more theoretically oriented curriculum that will prepare them for a teacher education or university program attend regular public school for their secondary and postsecondary education. Peripatetic teachers will provide these students with assistance. Interpreters are available several hours per week. The training of interpreters began in 1986. Currently the Netherlands has a tremendous shortage of interpreters.

More efficient use of scarce interpreter resources is one of the advantages of a centrally organized postsecondary education program for the deaf (CEGOBO) that has been proposed by the Youth Committee of the National Council of the Deaf. This organization holds the view that the relatively small numbers of deaf adolescents who want to follow a postsecondary education should be concentrated in the central part of our country near the several existing universities and other schools that provide postsecondary education (Pattipeiluhu, 1989).

Teacher Training

There is no such thing in the Netherlands as a separate teacher training program designed to prepare teachers of the deaf. The teacher training institutions in the Netherlands, called PABO (not part of a university), prepare teachers for both regular and special education programs. The parts of the PABO program curriculum that are aimed at special education provide general information only. Students learn the pedagogical principles of teaching children with a handicap. After completing their training, these new teachers receive appointments to either regular schools or special schools.

If the new teacher finds employment at one of the five schools for the deaf, he or she is required to follow a one-year-long in-service training program. The in-service training consists of a few hours of class time per week. Classes are conducted after the normal work day is completed.

During the two years after the completion of the in-service training, teachers of the deaf and teachers of children with hearing and language problems enroll in a series of evening courses. These courses are organized by two schools. One of these schools, the *Seminarium voor Orthopedagogiek* in Zeist, provides courses for all of the teachers from schools in the middle and northern parts of the country; the other school, *Katholieke Leergangen*, does the same for the schools in the southern part of the Netherlands. The course of study includes courses in linguistics, language development and language teaching, speech therapy, psychology, and methods of teaching the deaf.

This teacher training model will probably change in the near future. What the future teacher training program will look like is still not known in detail, but it is expected that before the last year of training the students will be required to choose between a career as a regular teacher or special teacher. The student's decision will shape the curriculum of the last year of study.

At this time only one deaf person in the Netherlands is employed as a teacher of the deaf. Two deaf people are currently studying to become teachers of the deaf. It is expected that the number of deaf teachers of the deaf will rise in the future.

Conclusion

In conclusion two basic points should be stressed again. First, the education of the deaf in the Netherlands no longer follows the oral method of teaching the deaf exclusively, as has been the belief of many educators abroad. Instead, a great variety of methods of communication are now utilized.

Second, since 1980 the education of the deaf in our country is no longer static, but very dynamic. This dynamism needs to be preserved and fostered. Continuation of the current step-by-step progress should benefit deaf pupils in the Netherlands by producing improved education services.

References

Beck, G. & De Jong, E. (1989). Psychische hulpverlening aan dove kinderen en adolescenten. [Mental health therapy for deaf children and adolescents]. In A.P.M. Van Hagen & H. Knoors (Eds.), *Onderwijs aan doven*. (pp. 159-172). Lisse-Amsterdam: Swets and Zeitlinger.

Blackwell, P.P., et al. (1978). *Sentences and other systems: A language learning curriculum foR hearing-impaired children*. Washington, DC: A. G. Bell Association for the Deaf.

Broek, P. van den, et al. (1986). Plaatsign van dove leerlingen in het regulier voortgezet onderwijs. [Mainstreaming of deaf pupils in schools for secondary education]. *Leiden Psychological Reports*. Leiden University, Department of Psychology.

Conrad, R. (1979). *The deaf schoolchild*. London: Harper and Row.

Greenberg, M.T., Kusche, C. A., Calderon, R., & Gustafson, R. (1987). *Path-curriculum*. Seattle, WA: University of Washington Press.

Groot, J.B.L. de. (1981). *Onderzoek naar de woordenschat en het begrijpend leesniveau bij leerlingen van het Rudolf Mees Instituut*. [Research into the lexicon and reading achievement of pupils of the Rudolf Mees Institute]. Rotterdam, The Netherlands: RMI Publications.

Harder, R. (1989). Werken aan een taal-leercurriculum. [Working on a language-learning curriculum]. Amsterdam. *Ammanschool*: NSDSK.

Harder, R. (1990). *Taal-leercurriculum, deel 1,2*. [Language-learning curriculum, part 1,2]. Amsterdam: NSDSK.

Harder, R., & Knoors, H. (1987). Consolidation of method or future changes? Use of signs in the education of the deaf in the Netherlands. In J. Kyle (Ed.), *Sign and School: Using signs in deaf children's development*. Clevedon/Philadelphia: Multilingual Matters Ltd.

IJsseldikj, F. (1987). De ontwikkeling van het begrijpend lezen bij dove leerlingen. [The development of reading ability in deaf pupils]. *Van Horen Zeggen*, 29 (3), 102-109.

IJsseldijk, F. (1989). Liplezen via beeldplaat en computer. [Lipreading by videodisc and computer]. In A.P.M. Van Hagen & H. Knoors. (Eds.), *Onderwijs aan doven* (pp. 127-143). Lisse-Amsterdam: Swets and Zeitlinger.

Knoors, H. (1983). *Onderzoek naar de leesprestaties en leesvorderingen van dove leerlingen van het Rudolf Mees Instituut*. [Research into the development of reading ability in deaf pupils of the Rudolf Mees Institute.] Rotterdam, The Netherlands: RMI Publications.

Knoors, H. (1989a). Verwerving van congruentie in Nederlandse Gebarentaal door dove kinderen zonder primair gebarentaalaanbod. [Acquisition of verb agreement in Sign Language of the Netherlands by deaf, non-native signing children]. In A.P.M. Van Hagen & H. Knoors (Eds.), *Onderwijs aan doven* (pp. 29-42). Lisse-Amsterdam: Swets and Zeitlinger.

Knoors, H. (1989b). Dove kinderen: naar opvoeding en onderwijs in twee talen en twee culturen. [Deaf children: Towards raising and educating them in two languages and two cultures]. *Tijdschrift voor Orthopedagogiek, XXVIII*, 239-246.

Knoors, H. (1990). De gebaarruimte benoemen. Benoeming van abstracte plaatspunten door late gebarentaalverwervers. [Nominal establishment by late sign language learners]. *Van Horen Zeggen*, 30 (4), 156-163.

Lem, G. J. van der. (1983). Gezinsbegeleiding en communicatieve vaardigheden. [Parent-Guidance and communication skills]. In B. T. Tervoort (Ed.), *Hand over hand* (pp. 83-89). Muiderberg, The Netherlands: Coutinho.

Loncke, F., et al. (1988). Native and non-native language acquisition: The case of signing deaf children. In F.Van Besien (Ed.), *First language acquisition*. Gent-Antwerpen, Belgium: ABLA- papers 13.

Maassen, B. (1985). *Artificial corrections to deaf speech, studies in intelligibility*. Dissertation, Katholiek Universiteit van Nijmegen.

McAnally, P.L., Rose, S., & Quigley, S.P. (1987). *Language learning practices with deaf children*. Boston: College Hill Press.

Mills, A.E., & Coerts, J. (1990). Functions and forms of bilingual input: Children learning a sign language as one of their first languages. In S. Prillwitz & T. Vollhaber (Eds.), *Current trends in European sign language research*. Proceedings of the 3rd European Congress on Sign Language Research. (pp. 151-162). Hamburg, Germany: Signum Press.

Onderwijs aan doven. [Education of the Deaf]. (1986). Publikatie van het Ministerie van Onderwijs en Wetenschappen.

Pattipeiluhu, S. (1989). Dove jongeren en hun beroepsopleidingen. [Young deaf people and their vocational training]. In A.P.M. Van Hagen & H. Knoors (Eds.), *Onderwijs aan doven*. (pp. 193-202). Lisse-Amsterdam: Swets and Zeitlinger.

Pijfers, L. (1989). Informatieverwerking en lezen. [Information processing and reading]. In A.P.M. Van Hagen & H. Knoors (Eds.), *Onderwijs aan doven*. (pp. 59-73). Lisse-Amsterdam: Swets and Zeitlinger.

Povel, D. J., & Arends, N. (1989). De Visuele Spraakafbeelder, een hulpmiddel voor het spraakonderwijs en dove kinderen. [The Visual Speech Apparatus, an aid in teaching speech to hearing-impaired children]. In A.P.M. Van Hagen & H. Knoors (Eds.), *Onderwijs aan doven*. (pp. 145-158). Lisse-Amsterdam: Swets and Zeitlinger.

Povel, D. J., & Wansink, M. (1986). A computer controlled vowel corrector for the hearing-impaired. *Journal of Speech and Hearing Research*, 29, 99-105.

Quadvlieg, G.J.M. (1989). Ontwikkeling van een synthetiserend-concluderende leesstrategie binnen een balansmodel. [Development of a synthetic-concluding reading strategy]. In A.P.M. Van Hagen & H. Knoors (Eds.), *Onderwijs aan doven*. (pp. 87-110). Lisse-Amsterdam: Swets and Zeitlinger.

Schaper, M. (1989). Ontwikkeling van een leeswordenschat. [Development of orthographic vocabulary]. In A.P.M. Van Hagen & H. Knoors (Eds.), *Onderwijs aan doven*. (pp. 73-86). Lisse-Amsterdam: Swets and Zeitlinger.

Schermer, G. (1985). Analysis of natural discourse of deaf adults in The Netherlands: Observations on Dutch Sign Language. In W. Stokoe & V. Volterra (Eds.), *SLR'83: Proceedings of the III International Symposium on Sign Language Research*. Silver Spring, MD: Linstok Press.

Schermer, G. (1989). Onderaoek naar kenmerken van de grammatica van Nederlandse Gebarentaal. [Research into features of the grammar of Sign Language of The Netherlands]. In A.P.M. Van Hagen & H. Knoors (Eds.), *Onderwijs aan doven*. (pp. 11-28). Lisse-Amsterdam: Swets and Zeitlinger.

Schermer, G., Harder, R., & Bos, H. (1987). Nederlandse Gebarentaal nader bekeken. [Looking into the Sign Language of The Netherlands]. In R. Appel (Ed.), *You me linguistics fun*. (pp. 69-82). Amsterdam: VU-Boekerij. Toegepaste Taalwetenschap in artikelen, Special 2.

Tervoort, B.T. (1953). *Structurele analyse van visueel taalgebruik binnen een groep dove kinderen*. [Structural analysis of visual language within a group of deaf children]. Dissertation. Amsterdam: Universiteit van Amsterdam.

Tervoort, B.T. (1967, 1975). *Developmental features of visual communication: A psycholinguistic analysis of deaf children's growth in communicative capacity*. Amsterdam: North Holland Publishing Company.

Timmerman, D., & Mans, H. (1990). On view: A national lexicon of Sign Language of the Netherlands. In S. Prillwitz & T. Vollhaber (Eds.), *Current trends in European sign language research. Proceedings of the 3rd European Congress on Sign Language Research* (pp. 391-401). Hamburg, Germany: Signum Press.

Van Uden, A. (1977). *A world of language for deaf children. Part 1. Basic principles: A maternal reflective method.* Rotterdam, The Netherlands: Rotterdam University Press.

Van Uden, A. (1981). *Diagnostic testing of deaf children: The syndrome of dyspraxia.* Lisse, The Netherlands: Swets and Zeitlinger.

Education of the Deaf in Nigeria: Past, Present, and Future

by Dr. Emmanuel Ojile
Senior Lecturer

University of Jos, Nigeria
Special Education Department
P.M.B. 2084
Jos, Plateau State, Nigeria

Background

The country of Nigeria in West Africa occupies an area of 923,768 square kilometers, or 356,700 square miles. Nigeria is about the size of California, Nevada, and Arizona combined. It is estimated that the population of Nigeria ranges from 100 to 150 million people. In Nigeria there exist about 450 tribal groups that speak 250 languages. The three dominant tribes in Nigeria are the Yorubas in the west, the Ibos in the east, and the Hausas-Fulanis in the north. Nigeria can be described as one of the largest African countries with vast natural resources, including ample fertile soil; minerals, including oil; and a substantial potential workforce. A definite Nigerian political structure has yet to emerge. This lack of a political structure has had a profound influence on the course of special education and the education of the deaf in Nigeria.

Origin of Schools for the Deaf in Nigeria (1950–1975)

The oldest school for the deaf in Nigeria is the Wesley Methodist School for the Deaf in Lagos. It was established in 1958 by the Lagos Society for the Care of the Deaf. The school is run by a board of management sponsored by the Wesley Methodist Mission Society. The school is supported by the federal government and the Lagos state government.

In 1968 a nursery school for the deaf was started in Lagos by the Wesley Society. The nursery serves as a feeder school for the Wesley Methodist School for the Deaf.

The late Rev. (Dr.) Andrew Foster, a missionary and graduate of Gallaudet University in Washington, D.C., came to West Africa in the late 1950s. Foster travelled extensively in Nigeria with the purpose of identifying key deaf people in the country. Among those he identified were Mr. Ezekiel Sambo, Mr. Gabriel Adepoju, Mr. Theophilus Nwakpa, Mr. James Agazie, and Dr. Peter Mba. Initially, Dr. Foster sent these individuals to his already functioning school for the deaf in Ghana to complete a course of study leading to certification. When these men returned to Nigeria after receiving their certificates, they were sent to schools for the deaf that had been recently opened by Foster. The record indicates that in the early 1960s, Dr. Foster opened missionary schools for the deaf in Kaduna, a city in the northern portion of Nigeria; in Enugu, a city in eastern Nigeria, and in Ibadan, a city in the western part of Nigeria. The individuals sent to these schools functioned as administrators, headmasters, and clerks.

Today there is no trace of Foster's missionary school for the deaf in Kaduna. The Enugu Missionary School for the Deaf, established in 1962 by Foster, was merged with classes for the deaf established by the Enugu Municipal Council in 1964. The school was closed in 1967 because of the Nigerian civil war. In 1976, at the end of the civil war, the school was taken over by the state and by various organizations, including Dr. Foster's Mission. These organizations assisted in restoring the school and overcoming the losses that the school had suffered during the war. In 1977 the school became a residential institution with an enrollment of 30 children. The school had 45 other children on a waiting list. In 1972 The New Society for the Care of the Deaf was formed in Enugu. Its goal was to help the school in Enugu progress by working with the authorities. Since 1977, the school seems to have ceased operations. Perhaps the students enrolled in the school were merged with those of two other state-owned schools located in the then Anambra State, then called the East Central State of Nigeria.

The Ibadan Mission School for the Deaf, which was opened in 1960 by Rev. (Dr.) Foster, preceded the founding of the Enugu Mission School. Dr. Foster served as the school's Director General. The school also had a constituted Board of Management. Originally housed in a rental building, the school was later moved to permanent quarters. In 1972 the school had an enrollment of about 80 deaf pupils. In later years, the enrollment of the school numbered about 300 deaf pupils. Most of its graduates have gone on to learn trades at nearby vocational training centers. The school was later merged with the current Ibadan School for the Deaf.

Even though Dr. Foster did not succeed in establishing a permanent school for the deaf in Nigeria, he must be remembered for his pioneering efforts. Moreover, he was instrumental in educating the deaf individuals who later became the pioneers of the education of the deaf in Nigeria. These pioneers started State schools for the deaf or were instrumental in the establishment of other schools for the deaf in Nigeria.

In 1958, the Oji River School for the Handicapped in the Anambra state of Nigeria was opened by the Anglican Mission and housed at its rehabilitation center. The school had an initial enrollment of eleven children and was used as a practicum site by teachers who were being trained at the mission. It was closed in 1967 in the wake of the Nigerian civil war. The war caused substantial damage to the facilities. The school reopened after the civil war. It admitted children between the ages of seven and ten and was under the administration of Nigeria's then East Central State Government. Several of the students who graduated from the school passed the government examination required to obtain the primary school leaving certificate. Those who passed the examination were admitted to vocational training programs. As of 1985, the enrollment of deaf pupils at the school stood at 125, with several on a waiting list.

The Ibadan School for the Deaf was founded in 1964 through the efforts of Mrs. Oyesola. Mrs. Oyesola, who was a leader in the Girls Brigade, met a deaf girl, Seliatu, during an activity organized by the Girls Brigade of Ibadan. Seliatu, a homeless girl and probably a beggar, was scorned and ignored by the other girls of Oyesola's group. Mrs. Oyesola was compassionate and adopted Seliatu. An American women's group in Ibadan recog-

nized Oyesola's concern for Seliatu and noted the communication barrier between the children in Oyesola's group and Seliatu. The American women's group made it possible for Oyesola to receive a scholarship to train to be a teacher of the deaf at Gallaudet University, Washington, D.C. After her return from Gallaudet, she started a class of three deaf boys and Seliatu in her home. She called it the Home for the Young Deaf. In September of 1963, she applied for and was granted permission by the Western State Government of Nigeria to establish a private school for the deaf. This act paved the way for the later opening of the Ibadan School for the Deaf. As of 1985, the total enrollment of the Ibadan School for the Deaf stood at 240 deaf pupils.

The Kwara State School for the Deaf and Blind–Ilorin, formerly under the administration of Mr. Gabriel Adepoju, was established in 1974. Mr. Adepoju, one of the deaf pupils trained by Dr. Foster, attended Gallaudet University in Washington, D.C. He received a B.A. and an M.Ed. in the education of the deaf and a Ph.D. in Special Education Administration. Upon his return to Nigeria, he worked to establish a school for the deaf in his home State. Through his influence and personal devotion, the number of staff members and student enrollment has expanded greatly.

In 1975, the Catholic Mission under the leadership of Rev. Sister Gwen Legault established the current St. Francis School for the Deaf and Blind at Vandekiya in the Benue State. The school started with few deaf students, but by 1987, 76 pupils had enrolled. For a number of years, the school came under the administrative control of the Benue State Ministry of Education, but in 1984 administrative control of the school once again reverted to the Catholic Mission.

To summarize, the years 1958 to 1975 marked the beginning of a series of attempts by various missionaries and the government to establish schools for the deaf in Nigeria. It was after 1975 that the strong impact of the government's entry into the field of Special

Education in general and education of the deaf in particular began to be felt.

The Years 1975–1985

The year 1975 witnessed a turning point in education of the handicapped, including the deaf, in Nigeria. Certain significant developments coerced the government into a change of attitude. The 1978 Ogbu Report on Special Education in Nigeria and the United Nation's report of 1976 pointed to the following special education needs: 1) a program designed to identify the handicapped; 2) the provision of educational facilities for the handicapped; and 3) the training of specialist teachers capable of handling the various educational needs of the handicapped (Onuegbu, 1988).

Ojile (1989a, 1989b) also observed that the Nigerian civil war, which ended in 1970, had a substantial role in the government's change in attitude. Following the cease-fire, there were great hardships in the country. Many were deafened and crippled by gun fire and exploding bombs. Illness, malnutrition, and infectious diseases ravaged refugee camps and caused deafness, blindness, mental retardation, and other handicapping conditions. In its Third National Development Plan (1975–1980), the Federal Government made the following statement about the handicapped:

> The problem of providing services for children who are handicapped as a result of disabilities such as blindness, deafness, and dumbness has become more complex with the growing awareness and needs of these individuals. The current levels of effort have proved inadequate in meeting current needs and argues for a change which will improve the situation both qualitatively and quantitatively. (Federal Ministry of Information's Republic of Nigeria, National Policy on Education, 1977, revised 1981)

In a landmark policy declaration, the government stated that it was the National Policy of Nigeria (Section 8:55-5) to make provision for Special Education. This policy recognized the importance of integrating the handicapped into society, providing both a free education for all handicapped and teachers trained to work with the handicapped. The government for the first time assumed the full responsibility for the education of the handicapped. Federal and State Coordinators of Special Education were appointed to monitor the progress of the schools for the handicapped. Between 1976 and 1977 alone, twelve schools that admit deaf persons were established by State governments (see Appendix A). One of these schools was the Plateau School for the Deaf, Jos, spearheaded by Mr. Ezekiel Sambo, another student of the late Dr. Foster.

Between the years 1978 and 1985, further efforts were made by the government to establish additional schools for the deaf or other handicapped groups. Out of the 24 schools for the deaf established within this time period, only four were established by missionaries (see Appendix A). For the first time the Church Missions in Many Lands (CMML) established a school for the handicapped in Iyale, Benue State. Three other mission schools for the handicapped were opened in Cross River State by Catholic missionaries.

By 1985, through the efforts of State governments or missions, seventeen states in Nigeria had established special schools that enrolled deaf persons. Oyo State continues to lead the other States with the establishment of a total of eighteen schools or units for the deaf.

Categories of Schools for the Deaf

It must be noted that the emphasis was not placed upon opening schools or units for the deaf alone, but on opening special schools where all handicapped persons, including the physically handicapped, deaf, blind, mentally retarded, and learning disabled could be educated together.

The four broad categories of educational facilities for the deaf in Nigeria are based on different admission procedures and curricular objectives. The four categories are as follows:

1) **Schools for the Deaf.** All students admitted to such a program are deaf, and the curricular emphasis is on academic training.

2) **Deaf Unit.** Located adjacent to a normal public school, these schools may have deaf students mainstreamed into a regular classroom or self-contained classrooms for deaf students. These schools also emphasize academic training.

3) **School for the Handicapped.** All handicapped persons, including physically handicapped, deaf, blind, mentally retarded, and learning disabled, are educated in the same school. These schools emphasize academic training.

4) **Special Education Center.** These schools admit all handicapped persons. The students learn vocational skills in addition to regular academic work.

Methods of Communication

The formal system used to educate the deaf in Nigeria has been imported from other countries. The communication method of the exporting country was often adopted. The Wesley Methodist School for the Deaf–Surlere, Lagos, which is considered the first school for the deaf in Nigeria and was opened by the Lagos Society for the Care of the Deaf, and assisted by British Methodist church missionaries, introduced to Nigeria the oral method of teaching the deaf, which was popular in Britain.

The arrival in Nigeria of American church missionary Rev. (Dr.) Foster, who started schools for the deaf in Ibadan, Enugu, and Kaduna, introduced the American manual method of communicating with the deaf to Nigeria. Initially, it appeared as though the oral method of teaching the deaf would prevail, but the work of Mrs. Oyesola, Dr. Peter Mba, Mr. Gabriel Adepoju, and Mr. Ezekiel Sambo, all of whom had acquired their training in the United States, strengthened the use of the American manual method of teaching the deaf. These pioneers advocated educating deaf children through the use of the Total Communication philosophy, which includes the use of sign language.

Between 1984–1985, Ojile completed a survey of the method of communication used in the existing educational facilities for the deaf in Nigeria. He observed that the 43 schools that enroll deaf students acknowledged adherence to the Total Communication philosophy, which includes the use of sign language, reading, and amplification (see Table 1). Even the Wesley School for the Deaf in Lagos, which formerly used the oral method of communication with the deaf, now follows the Total Communication philosophy. Because of the unavailability of interpreters, it is most likely that some units that have deaf students mainstreamed into regular public school classes will be forced to rely on speech, speechreading, and writing. Outside of the mainstreamed environment, the vast majority of deaf students in Nigeria communicate through the use of sign language.

Table 1. Method of Communication Used in Schools for the Deaf in Nigeria (1984–1985)

Number of Schools	Method of Communication	Number of Programs
1	Oral/Aural method only	0 (0%)
2	Local Signs	0 (0%)
3	Total Communication (American Sign Language, Reading and Amplifications)	43 (100%)
Total Numbers of Responding Schools =		43
Total Percentage		100%

Postsecondary Educational Opportunities

Because of the need to train specialists to teach in the schools for the handicapped, in 1974 the Federal Government made funding available to enable the Faculty of Education at the University of Ibadan, Nigeria, to begin a certification program. This program has been upgraded and now offers degrees in Special Education. The department has the authority to confer the B.A., M.A., and Ph.D. degrees in Special Education.

There are three other postsecondary institutions in Nigeria that offer programs in Special Education (see Appendix B). These include: 1) the University of Jos, Special Education Department. It was opened in 1977 under the leadership of Professor Cooper, a British subject. Like the University of Ibadan, it has the authority to confer the B.A., M.A., and Ph.D. degrees in all areas of Special Education; 2) the Federal Advanced Teachers College, Ibadan, converted in 1977 to the Federal College of Special Education, Oyo. The college offers a three-year Nigerian Advanced Teachers Certificate (NCE) in all categories of Special Education; and 3) the Kaduna Polytechnic Institute, a technical postsecondary institution owned jointly by the ten northern states of Nigeria. It also has a three-year program that offers an introductory course in Special Education. The first director was Dr. Kim Sykes, an American. This program at the moment offers a degree program and post-degree program in rehabilitation, general Special Education Management, and administration in areas of the blind and the deaf under Nigerian Special Educators Leadership.

The existing postsecondary institutions in Nigeria do not discriminate against handicapped college students. The three schools admit all qualified deaf or handicapped persons into their programs; however, the institutions are very competitive and provide limited enrollment possibilities. The percentages of deaf Nigerians receiving postsecondary educational training has increased greatly from the past when no such programs existed. For years Gallaudet University in Washington, D.C., and to a lesser extent other postsecondary programs in the United States, were the only options for higher education available to deaf persons from Nigeria.

Services for handicapped students in the higher education institutions in Nigeria have many persistent problems. One such problem is the inadequate provision of support services, including the availability of interpreters for the deaf. Ojile (1988) also observed that deaf students have no choice concerning the selection of a field of study. This implies that any deaf student enrolled in an institution of higher education must select Special Education as his/her major even though the student may have the necessary skills required to study computer science, business management, science, law, or some other field. This narrow range of options suppresses the interest and motivation of the deaf individual.

Obstacles to Progress

The obstacles that influence progress in Special Education in Nigeria are as follows (see Ojile, 1988, 1989a, 1989b):

Law, Legislation, and Politics

Although the 1974 government decree and the 1977 National Policy on Special Education, revised in 1981, set out the necessary blueprint for the effective implementation of Special Education, including the education of the deaf, this laudable scheme has proven to be a flop (Nwaogu, 1988). In addition, Ojile (1989) noted that frequent changes in the government and political instability in the country make any Special Education law or policy vulnerable and implementation difficult. Each successive Nigerian government has set up its own priorities. If the government in power is not favorably disposed towards Special Education, very often progress made during earlier administrations is eroded, and at worst, halted. At times the government has taken money earmarked annually for the development of programs in Special Education and used the money to fund different projects. This has led to an economic crunch for many of the special schools and institutions. It is hoped that political stability, permanent policies, and effective laws and legislation guiding the operation of Special Education, including education of the deaf, will come into being.

Lack of Census

Ojile (1989b) noted earlier the urgent need to conduct a census of the number of handicapped individuals living in Nigeria. Thus far the number of deaf, blind, crippled, mentally retarded, and learning disabled individuals in the country is unknown. In addition, the distribution of the handicapped, the number participating in an educational program, and the number on waiting lists is unknown. A census count would provide useful data for meaningful planning and implementation of educational services for the deaf.

Teacher Qualifications

In a comparison of the education of the deaf in Nigeria and Canada, Ojile (1986, cited in Ojile & Carver, 1987) reported the percentage of teachers of the deaf in Nigeria who have achieved the following educational level: master's degree, 6 percent; bachelor's degree, 11 percent; the Nigerian Certificate of Education (NCE), 19 percent; Certificate or Diploma, 31 percent; Grade II or I certification (traditionally the minimum teaching qualification at the elementary level in Nigeria), 24 percent. Ojile (1986) found that 37 percent of the teachers who work with the deaf in Nigeria lack the specialized training and knowledge required to teach the deaf. Nigeria has an urgent need for more trained teachers

of the deaf at the elementary, secondary, and postsecondary level.

Provision of Support Services

Nigerian schools for the deaf lack the following support services: periodic audiological evaluations, hearing aid evaluation, speech training, auditory training, psychological evaluations, and counseling services. This lack of support services can be blamed on insufficient funds available to purchase equipment such as audiometers, speech spectrographic displays, otoscopes, monofonotors, auditory trainers, visipitch trainers, oscilloscopes, and hearing aids, and to train and hire qualified personnel, such as audiologists, speech clinicians, counselors, and psychologists.

The consequences of not providing these needed services include the following:

1. Many of the deaf children in the schools for the deaf have never been evaluated to determine the cause and extent of their hearing loss. Consequently the schools for the deaf cannot discern whether or not the hearing loss can be remediated.
2. Those children with moderate hearing loss who could benefit from auditory and speech training through the use of fitted hearing aids and the cultivation of their residual hearing do not receive these services.
3. Deaf students with serious academic difficulties are not diagnosed to determine the cause of their learning problems. Others have been wrongly diagnosed and placed in classes in which they do not belong.
4. With the current state of the art, it is difficult to determine the student's academic achievement level. Regrettably, Nigeria has no knowledge of the educational attainment level of its deaf population. Presently it is not possible to ascertain whether or not the current educational curricula used in the schools for the deaf is adequate.

5. The absence of counseling and psychological services implies also that the hearing parents of deaf children are not provided the appropriate guidance and counseling required to relate effectively with their deaf children. Most of the parents of the deaf children are illiterate or semi-literate and may not be able to use the sign language that their deaf children have acquired as their first language. Serious communication problems exist in the deaf child's home environment. Parent education that includes basic information about deafness and sign language courses that would assist the parents and help alleviate this communication gap is needed. Intensive psychological and counseling services need to be implemented in the existing programs and institutions for the deaf.

The Future

Alake (1985) described the condition of the young Nigerian deaf school leaver as pitiful. He observed that little has been done by the government to alleviate the poor situation of deaf school leavers. Only those deaf school leavers who are fortunate enough to know influential people find employment. While employment possibilities might not appear too rosy for many deaf people in Nigeria, available statistics indicate that qualified deaf people do have a good opportunity to obtain satisfactory employment. Two deaf Nigerians, Mr. Gabriel Adepoju and Mr. Ezekiel Sambo, have served as principals of their respective State schools for the deaf. Another deaf person, Dr. Peter Okoro Mba, was at one time the head of the Department of Special Education at the University of Ibadan in Nigeria. Other deaf people, such as Dr. Eunice Alade and Mr. Pius Swem, have joined the Faculty of the University of Ibadan and the University of Jos in Nigeria.

Another deaf gentleman, Mr. Idris Dodo, has coordinated programs and taught at Kaduna Polytechnic, a postsecondary career program in Nigeria. Other deaf people can be found teaching in schools for the deaf, working for private firms, or running their own businesses. The numbers of deaf people in the labor force of Nigeria with responsible positions is meagre when compared to the number of deaf people who hold top level jobs in countries such as the United States and Canada. Nonetheless, when comparing the job possibilities in Nigeria with those in other developing countries or surrounding African states, Nigeria fares far better. In many African and developing countries there is still an open disregard for the dignity of deaf people.

In conclusion, today there are many qualified and highly trained deaf Nigerians scattered across North America. Even though many of these individuals may not want to return to Nigeria, it is expected that others will one day return to contribute their share towards the development of the education of the deaf in Nigeria. It would appear that in the face of all of the turbulence, political instability, absence of laws and legislation, and existing poverty, the education of the deaf in Nigeria has come to stay. In the words of Onwuegbu (1988), "It will be very difficult now for anybody to kill it."

Appendices
Appendix A

Schools for the Handicapped in Nigeria, 1985

Name of School	State	Date Opened	Established By
Wesley School for Deaf, Surulere	Lagos	1958	Humanitarians/ Missions/Govt.
Special Education Center, Oji River, Enugu	Anambra	1958	Missionary/ Government
Ibadan School for the Deaf, Ibadan	OYO	1963	Individual
Special Educ. Center, Ogbunike	Anambra	1964	Missionary/ Government
Kwara State School for the Deaf, Ilorin	Kwara	1974	Government
St. Francis School for the Handicapped, Vandekiya	Benue	1975	Individuals/ Missionary
UMC Dean Unit, Oke-Ado, Ibadan	OYO	1976	Government
Oniyanrin Special Unit, Ibadan	OYO	1976	Government
Eruwa School for the Deaf, Eruwa	OYO	1976	Government
School for the Handicapped, Tudun, Maliki	Kano	1977	Government
Plateau School for the Deaf, Jos	Plateau	1977	Government
Ondo School for the Deaf, Akure	Ondo	1977	Government
The Community School for the Handicapped, Ogbomoso	OYO	1977	Government
Special Education Unit, Ayegbaju-Ile-Ife	OYO	1977	Government
Handicapped School, Iwo	OYO	1977	Government
Spec. Educ. Unit, Thru St. Philips Anglican School, Ilaro, Ife	OYO	1977	Missionary/ Government
School for the Handicapped Children, Ibereokodo, Abeokuta	Ogun	1977	Government

Name of School	State	Date Opened	Established By
Special Education Center, Orlu	Imo	1977	Government
Special School, Ikoyi	OYO	1978	Government
H L A Spec. Educ. Unit, Agodi	OYO	1978	Government
Kaduna State School for the Deaf	Kaduna	1979	Government
Special School for the Handicapped, Ilesa	OYO	1979	Individual/ Government
Deaf Unit, Methodist Grammar School, Bodiga Ibadan	OYO	1979	Missionary/ Government
Lagelu Spe. Educ. Unit, Lalupon	OYO	1980	Government
Ijokodo High School Deaf Unit, Ibadan	OYO	1980	Government
Omoyemi Special Unit, Apevin, Ibadan	OYO	1980	Government
Spe. Educ. Center, Jada	Gongola	1981	Government
School for the Handicapped Child, Benin City	Bendel	1981	Government
School for the Handicapped, Roni, Kano	Kano	1982	Government
C M M L Special School, Iyale	Benue	1982	Missionary
Niger State School for the Deaf, Minna	Niger	1983	Government
St. Louis Center, Ifuho, Ikot Ekpene	Cross River	1983	Government
The Child Special School, Ikot Ekpene	Cross River	1983	Catholic Missionary
Sokoto State School for the Handicapped	Sokoto	1984	Government
Ogbomoso Grammar School, Deaf Unit	OYO	1984	Government
Seventh Day Adventist Grammar School, Deaf Unit, Iwo	OYO	1984	Missionary/ Government

Name of School	State	Date Opened	Established By
Imo State Secondary School for the Deaf, Ofa-Kala Orodo	Imo	1984	Government
School for the Handicapped, Bauchi	Bauchi	1984	Government
Good Shepherd Spec. Educ. Center, Ogoja	Cross River	1985	Catholic/ Missionary
All Saints Special School, Osogbu	OYO	1985	Missionary/ Government
School for the Deaf, Ijebu-Ode	Ogun		Government
School for Handicapped Children, Ilaro, Ogun	Ogun		Government
School for Handicapped Children, Sagamu-Remo	Ogun		Government

Total number of schools - 43

Appendix B

Postsecondary Facilities Admitting Deaf Individuals

Institution	Date Established	Level of Training
University of Ibadan, Nigeria B.A./M.A./Ph.D.	1974	Cert/Diploma
University of Jos, Nigeria B.A./.M.A./Ph.D.	1977	Cert/Diploma
Federal Advance Special Teachers College, OYO, Nigeria	1977	NCE*
Kaduna Polytechnic, Nigeria		Diploma/Advance

* Nigerian Advance Certificate of Education

References

Alake, S.F. (1985). Primary education for deaf children in Nigeria. In I.G. Taylor (Ed.), *The education of the deaf: Current perspectives, Vol. IV.* New York: Croom Helm & Associates.

Federal Republic of Nigeria National Policy on Education. 1977, 1981. (1977, 1981). Lagos, Nigeria: Federal Ministry of Information.

Nwaogu, P.O. (1988). The provision of national policy on education-special education. In O.C. Obosi (Ed.), *Development of special education in Nigeria.* Ibadan, Nigeria: Fountain Books Limited.

Ojile, O.E. (1985). *An updated list of educational programs for the hearing impaired in Nigeria.* Unpublished research, University of Jos, Special Education Department.

Ojile, O.E. (1986). *Teacher's qualification, method of instruction and provision of related services in Nigerian deaf schools.* List of faculty research, Jos, Nigeria: University of Jos.

Ojile, O.E. (1988). Educating the handicapped at the post-secondary level in Africa: The current states and problems. In D. Knapke & C. Lendman (Eds.), *Proceedings of the 1988 AHSSPPE conference association on handicapped student service programs in post-secondary education* (pp. 264-271). Columbus, OH.

Ojile, O.E. (1989a). *Education of the deaf in Nigeria: Historical perspective.* Paper presented at the Deaf Way: An International Festival and Conference on Language, Culture and History of Deaf People, Gallaudet University, Washington, DC.

Ojile, O.E. (1989b). Special education, deaf education in Nigeria: Development, administration and problems. In E.G. Wolf-Schein and J. D. Schein (Eds.), *Post secondary education of deaf students* (pp. 264-271). Edmonton, Canada: University of Alberta Press.

Ojile, O.E., & Carver, E. (1987). Education of the deaf in Nigeria and Canada: A comparison. *The ACEHI/LA Revue ACEDA, 13,* 96-103.

Onwuegbu, I.D. (1988). Development of special education in Nigeria. In O.C. Abosi (Ed.), *Development of special education in Nigeria* (pp. 5-12). Ibadan, Nigeria: Fountains Books Limited.

Education of the Deaf in Norway

by Knut Arnesen

Historical Development of the Education of the Deaf in Norway

The First Schools for the Deaf

Deaf children were the first group to receive special education in Norway. The first school for the deaf was established in Trondheim in the middle of Norway in 1825 as a result of efforts made by a young deaf man, Andreas Christian Moller. He had been educated for some years at the Royal Institute for the Deaf in Copenhagen. The king of Sweden and Norway, Carl Johan I, formerly General Jean Baptiste Bonaparte of the army of Napoleon I, had decided that 30 "deaf and dumb" boys from the age of eight, and girls from the age of seven were to receive an education that would turn them into "useful citizens" at the school in Trondheim. Knowledge of sign language was the main qualification required of the teachers. Expenses were shared by the government, the home county of the pupils, and from money collected in churches all over the country.

In 1848, Fredrik Glad Balchen founded the first private school for the deaf in Oslo. Two more private schools were established soon after. Private schools meant the introduction of the oral method in the country, as this method was used in private schools in most other countries. With a grant from Parliament, Balchen went to Germany to study and was strongly influenced by Moritz Hill in Weisenfels. He was acquainted with other new pedagogical ideas as well.

Oralism gradually became the method used by all schools for the deaf in the nineteenth century. An article written by Sigvald Skavian, principal of the school in Trondheim in 1875, opposed the oral method of education for the deaf by advocating that sign language has a grammatical structure fully capable of expressing complex and intimate thoughts and ideas. In his view the question of the choice of method was a question of individual needs and preferences.

By the end of the century, there were schools for the deaf all over the country except in the northern regions, where lack of sun and light in winter made lipreading and thus the oral method inapplicable and useless.

Legislation and Special Education

Up until 1881 there was no law securing the right to special education for deaf children. A law passed by Parliament in 1881 stated that all "abnormal" children, such as the blind, the deaf, and the mentally retarded were entitled to eight years of education, in state, municipal, or private schools. Vocational training played an important part in these schools. This law meant a great step forward in the education of the deaf and in the lives of deaf people.

According to this law, the schools for the deaf were to use "one known method only, either the oral method or the manual method." A method that was a mixture of both oral and manual would not be tolerated. Each school was given the option and decided for itself which method to follow.

In the middle of the twentieth century, there was still a strong emphasis on segregated special schools for all handicapped children, as well as for children with mild learning disabilities and speech disorders. In the mid-1970s, mainstreaming became the aim of all education and this law concerning special schools was abolished. Since 1976, the general law of education concerning children in Norway takes care of the rights of handicapped children as well as children with no specific educational needs.

Theoretically there are no age limits regarding the right to education for deaf people. Infants are entitled to proper assistance, and their parents, to education and guidance. Deaf students up to the age of twenty are guaranteed an education. Adults have a right to receive an education that will enable them to function better at work and in society as a whole. The law states that all deaf children should be provided with a free, appropriate public education.

The extent and the quality of this education, however, are not regulated by law. Parents have the right to refuse special education services for their child if they find them to be inappropriate. In the opposite case, when the child does not receive the kind or extent of special education that parents find suitable, their only option as private citizens is to sue the state.

Deaf Preschool Children: Education and Parent Guidance

The importance of early diagnosis and habilitation of deaf children has been recognized among teachers of the deaf for a long time. The average age of discovery of hearing loss still ranges from between six months and three years. Parents, especially mothers, are the first to report their suspicion that their child has a hearing loss. With improved cooperation between parents and the medical profession, the age of diagnosis has been reduced significantly. Parents are also found to be very good at identifying the extent and kind of hearing loss of their child.

Parent guidance programs are available mostly to parents in the central parts of the country. With special education being the responsibility of the municipal authorities of small communities, information on the availability of parent guidance services to parents in small communities is lacking.

The impact of parent participation in setting up a program for young deaf children is vital. By using the parents and especially the mother as the main source of information and expertise on her deaf baby, professionals receive the most reliable and extensive information concerning the child. Parents are included in the team of professionals that collaborate and take a shared responsibility for

the development of an educational program and for the decisions made concerning the deaf child's future life.

Special education programs for deaf infants were established in Oslo during the early 1950s. These programs were inspired by the John Tracy Clinic, located in the state of California in the United States. Today there are thirteen kindergartens for hearing impaired children in Norway. In a sparsely populated country like Norway, however, this means that most deaf and hard of hearing preschool children attend nursery schools and kindergartens with hearing children. Most of the children who are mainstreamed in this way regularly visit a program for hearing impaired children in order to learn sign communication as well as oral communication. The deaf and hard of hearing children attend kindergartens for hearing impaired children, from the time their hearing loss is first discovered. The curriculum of these kindergarten programs is quite similar to that found in an ordinary kindergarten for hearing children, except for the special emphasis on language acquisition. One of the aims of these programs is to employ deaf adults as well as special teachers to provide language models for the children to identify with.

Methods of Communication

The focus of the education programs for deaf and hard of hearing children is language acquisition and individual and social development. These goals cannot be considered separately, and are the primary goals.

In Norway opinions have varied among teachers of the deaf and others interested in the education of the deaf concerning the proper approach and method of teaching language. Deaf children often have been presented with a variety of linguistic modalities simultaneously to develop their oral and written language. When the first school for the deaf at Trondheim was established in 1825, the manual approach of teaching the deaf was used. This method used sign language and writing. Oralism was introduced to Norway as well as to other Scandinavian countries in 1848 with the founding of the school for the deaf in Oslo.

The controversy between manualism and oralism started at that time and has continued up until recent times. The impact of the resolution to support oralism that came from the 1880 International Conference on the Education of the Deaf in Milan also affected the education of the deaf in Norway.

However, it must be stated that the education of the deaf has not followed a path of completely independent development. The changes that have occurred in the education of the deaf have paralleled changes in education generally and also have been due to research findings, political trends, and changes in society.

During the first decades of this century, the oral approach became the basis of the education of the deaf. From this basic ideology the constructive method developed, which used the single phoneme as the foundation for the development of language. This method followed the teaching practices of Vatter in Germany. When the child could master some phonemes in relationship to speech, lipreading, reading, and writing, the next step would be the process of putting the phonemes together to make syllables and finally words and sentences.

This constructive method did not suddenly disappear, but gradually evolved from being a method applied to children in a very rigid manner, to one that was less rigidly applied concerning the performance required of the child and the teaching procedures utilized.

During the 1930s and 1940s, psychological and educational research revealed a new view of child development. By the late 1930s, Norway had developed a national curriculum based on the new philosophy.

As the needs of each child were considered, teachers became more flexible and child-centered when considering the children's need for self-expression, whether it was done orally or manually. In many classrooms, the teachers provided a special time for conversation. The children were allowed to express themselves naturally. Teachers also became more aware that children's concepts were not only based on single experiences but were due to a number of experiences and to practice. A result of this new awareness on the part of teachers was an increasing development and use of learning materials designed for multisensory stimulation.

Although the constructive method did not totally disappear, the changes in teaching procedures created a new method. This new method is often referred to as the traditional method. The learning theory behind the traditional method, as it was with the constructive method, is that learning proceeds from parts to wholes and that children learn by repetition and practice. In regard to language development this was considered to be a synthetic method, which meant to go from words to sentences. However, in regard to speech, teachers often had to break the words into syllables and phonemes, so the method can also be said to be analytic. Even if psychology has for a long time advocated field theories of learning, which postulate that learning encompasses total situations and proceeds from more global concepts to the understanding of its parts, in classrooms for the deaf the idea of developing parts of language and speech more or less in isolation and stringing them together according to certain rules still has a strong following. Arguments based upon deaf children's slow progress, limited vocabulary, and poor conceptual understanding have been raised in opposition to this method. In defense of the method, many deaf children have benefited from its use.

After World War II, sound amplification systems had a great impact upon schools for the deaf. Many classrooms were equipped with group hearing aids, and it became common for the pupils to wear individual hearing aids. Amplification and pre-school training seemed to "produce" a new type of deaf child. The characteristic feature of these deaf and hard of hearing children was the ability to pick up language quite quickly, and they acquired nearly natural written and spoken language patterns. In the past many teachers had been aware of differences in the amount of residual hearing found among their students, mainly because of observed differences in speech intelligibility, but with the advent of group and individual sound amplification, this difference became more obvious. Auditory training became a special subject, often taught separately, as was true of articulation. This led to a very strong belief in the use of an aural-oral approach to the education of deaf children.

In order to offer these children a "better" language environment, special classes in which deaf and hard of hearing children were integrated with hearing children in regular public schools were established throughout the country. This radical change from an emphasis on visual and tactile stimuli to a strong emphasis on auditory stimuli took place.

The differentiation between the profoundly deaf on one hand and the partially hearing on the other led to a noticeable decrease in the total number of students attending schools for the deaf. Not only did the schools for the deaf experience a change in the quantity of students, but also in quality. The schools for the deaf enrolled more children with profound hearing loss and additional handicaps. This change in the composition of students also led to a temporary decline in the use of auditory training in the late 1970s and the 1980s. In the 1990s the concentration on auditory training, in spite of better equipment constantly coming on the market, continues to decline.

As was discussed previously, historically, the approach to the education of the deaf that used conventional sign language primarily was the main mode of communication for many years or until the oral philosophy started to take over in the middle of the nineteenth century. In 1881 Norway passed its first special education legislation, which provided all deaf, blind, and mentally retarded children

with a minimum of eight years of education. The law included a statute that stated that deaf children were to be educated by the use of an oral approach. However, the change in the student population in our schools for the deaf in the 1960s created a favorable climate for the use of sign language again. Sign language courses for teachers and parents were started all over the country.

The Norwegian psychiatrist Basilier had a great influence on the movement towards the use of sign language. He very strongly advocated the deaf child's need for communication. From the start, sign language became more and more accepted among those working in the education of the deaf. An important educational goal is still to teach the deaf students the Norwegian language. In order to help the students develop skill in the use of Norwegian, a sign language based on the structure of the Norwegian language was created. Deaf students then had to learn Signed Norwegian instead of Norwegian Sign Language. During the 1970s, most teachers of the deaf turned to the use of both sign and speech. The Total Communication philosophy, which tried to combine oralism and manualism, was in favor.

There are two categories of manual communication used in Norway. The first category consists of manual communication that is independent of oral languages. This category can be referred to as sign languages. The second category consists of manual communication that is derived from oral languages and can be referred to as sign systems. Signed Norwegian belongs to this second category.

Furth (1973) stated that with the exception of the few deaf children born to deaf parents, the vast majority of deaf children are not exposed to sign language at home. As a consequence, during the years in which hearing children assimilate the language of their society, deaf children are not exposed to any consistent linguistic system. Because of the fact that over 90 percent of deaf children are born to hearing parents, the child and the parents must manage as well as they can by the use of spontaneous gestures that do not go beyond the level of concrete expression or pointing, and cannot be called a conventional language system. These gestures are, of course, communication, but they are not a language in the sense of a formal linguistic system.

What Furth said (1973) is one of the reasons why many people advocated using Signed Norwegian. The idea was that if parents and teachers used this system consistently in connection with amplification and lipreading, their deaf children would attain a nearly normal level of language development.

In those cases where the system was practiced consistently from the early childhood years on, some very promising results have been documented. However, in many cases the system became so rigid that it hampered communication. Often the use of Signed Norwegian concentrated more on how to sign correctly than on creating the conditions necessary for natural communication and conversation to occur.

A main argument against the use of Signed Norwegian has been that it is difficult for a child to deal with several sensory modalities at the same time.

Nowadays linguists and psychologists are interested in the sign language used by the deaf community. Many say that the most natural and effective language for all deaf children is the language used by the adult deaf community. Experience and research indicate that deaf children of deaf parents develop sign language at the same rate as hearing children develop speech. Bellugi (1980) said that the study of the language acquisition of deaf children of deaf parents is the same as a study of normal language acquisition in hearing children.

However, because over 90 percent of deaf children are born to hearing parents, a possible strategy for hearing parents of a deaf child would be to learn sign language and use it with their child from an early age and thus develop a base from which the deaf child can learn the dominant language of society. "Even with the best possible early identifica-

tion programs, this input will not be present from birth. This fact alone indicates that this is not a normal language acquisition process. Nor does this approach deal with the many other issues of linguistics features involved in language acquisition, including the naturalness of the interactive process, and the impact on the parents, who while in the process of dealing with the discovery of deafness in their child are asked to learn and use a new language" (Blackwell, Engen, Fischgrund, & Zarcadoolas, 1978). Other problems that have an impact on language acquisition include extended family grief and guilt.

Ahlgren (1982) advocates that the deaf child must go from monolingualism to bilingualism, which assumes that all deaf children have to grow up in an environment where the sign language of the deaf community is the dominant language. The dominant language of the society, like Norwegian or Swedish, has to be learned as a second language.

This view of language acquisition should produce big changes in our teaching methods. Ahlgren (1982) says that it is important that teachers of the deaf have a good knowledge of their "mother tongue" and that they are fluent in the use of sign language. She realizes, however, that many teachers are not fluent in sign language. She proposes that a good place to start would be with an exchange of languages between teacher and children in the classroom in order that both the teacher of the deaf and the deaf children become bilingual.

Blackwell, Engen, Fischgrund, and Zarcadoolas (1978) say that it should be noted that all second language methods today are designed on the assumption that the learner has already acquired another oral language. Ahlgren (1982) has never really considered the level of sign language competency that the child might need to begin learning Swedish or Norwegian as a second language. In addition, it is important to consider which language can provide the soundest basis for reading instruction and the acquisition of knowledge through reading.

Schools for the Deaf and the Deaf Community

In Norway strong emphasis has been put on the importance of letting every handicapped child stay in his or her local school. Organizations for the deaf, however, are strongly opposed to the idea of mainstreaming deaf children. These organizations defend the right of deaf children to be placed in an educational setting where sign language is used by both the deaf children and adults. The deaf community feels that schools for the deaf are crucial and cannot be replaced by the local school where the deaf child is often the only person to whom sign language is a natural language. The Norwegian Association for the Deaf also points out that in a sparsely populated country like Norway, deaf children are scattered throughout the country, making it impossible to find a trained teacher of the deaf for each child.

Since the fall of 1987, the main arguments deaf persons and professionals in the field propose in favor of the schools for the deaf are as follows:

- Deaf children need the kind of educational setting that a school for the deaf provides in order to have optimal learning conditions.
- Only the schools for the deaf can provide the necessary surroundings for a deaf child to learn sign language, which is the basis for his or her sound intellectual, social, and emotional development.
- Freedom of choice in the selection of the educational setting that most appropriately meets the needs of deaf children is essential. Schools for the deaf need to be one of the options available. The child and his or her family must have the right to choose between a mainstream placement option and a school for the deaf.

The deaf community, parents, and professionals all stand as a united front on this

issue. In June 1991, a task force representing both parents and professionals was established by the Department of Education. The goals of this task force were to:

- describe educational needs that are peculiar to deaf children
- provide suggestions concerning the establishment of an educational system that effectively serves all areas of Norway
- describe what a "center of competence," formerly the school for the deaf, should look like.

Schools for the Deaf Are No Longer Needed

In 1987 the Norwegian Parliament declared that the state would no longer support schools for the handicapped. No exceptions were made for any disabled group including the deaf. It was stated that the step-by-step process of the integration of handicapped people into society would be fulfilled by the abolition of state schools for the handicapped. To replace the schools, local agencies were given the responsibility of taking over and providing both free special education and care for disabled children. This program was especially aimed at children with learning disabilities who live in homes with poor social environments. The state felt that for many of these children, their life condition would improve if they were allowed to stay in a foster home or at a home with special support services instead of being sent away to an institution.

The target group for this school reform was not primarily deaf children or children with communication problems. This change in Norway's special education delivery system, together with the eradication of homes for the mentally retarded, has been named the "twin reform." Politically, it is motivated by economic reasons. Norway's welfare state is gradually being reduced. State responsibility for special services is to be reduced to a minimum. Education is to become a local responsibility both financially and pedagogically.

The state schools for special education are supposed to emerge with a new role and be considered as "centers of competence" with broad theoretical and practical knowledge, and considered as interim facilities. These centers are not supposed to receive clients for a short period of time and should be regarded as a last resort for services, and utilized only after it has been determined that the child's educational problems can no longer be handled at the local school. The special residential schools are to turn into guidance and counseling centers that people can turn to for the highest expertise in the country in each area of disability. Five "centers of competence" will be established, two for the hearing impaired, two for the visually impaired, and one for communicative disturbances.

The Situation Today

Since about 1970, there has been a strong political movement in Norway towards the mainstreaming and integration of all groups of handicapped people into society. This idea has strongly influenced the educational system in general and the field of special education in particular. Between 90 and 100 percent of all mentally retarded children and young adults in Norway live at home and receive their education at their local school. Elderly mentally retarded people are scheduled to leave the huge institutions for the mentally retarded and return to their home communities during the next few years.

Since 1976, when the Special Education Act was abolished, one law concerning the educational rights of children in Norway applies to all children, regardless of their mental or physical handicap. This education act has greatly encouraged the integration or mainstreaming of handicapped children into normal schools.

Reports made by independent educational experts within the OECD state that the Norwegian educational system has been decentralized to such a degree that the experts fear that National standards can no longer be maintained. This criticism has not been fully recognized by the state authorities in Norway but is heavily supported by teachers.

School legislation now gives the parents of all children the right to decide what kind of education is appropriate for their child. The advice of professionals may be taken into consideration by the parents, but is not decisive in the decision-making process except when the child's health or welfare is seriously threatened or endangered. Local authorities are required to provide the kind of educational program the parents want at their local school. Lack of money is the only obstacle that can cause municipal authorities to disregard parents' wishes.

Unless schools for the deaf can prove that they are superior to the program provided by the ordinary public school, the Norwegian Parliament decree that schools for the deaf will no longer exist will stand.

The statement of the Norwegian Parliament has caused great concern and alarm among the deaf, teachers of the deaf, and parents. The Department of Education plan to close the schools for the deaf has the support of the Secretary of Finance and will save a considerable amount of money. The state schools for special education cost a total of about 40 million pounds a year, to educate approximately 1,100 pupils. That means that it costs about 36,000 pounds to educate each pupil.

Since schools are primarily available to children living in certain areas, deaf children can obtain the optimum education in central areas of the country. Norway is challenged to come up with a new system that will distribute the means of education in a more equitable way.

According to the official National plans for the reorganization of the schools for the handicapped, some of the schools for the deaf are supposed to be transferred to municipal ownership and not closed completely. The main objection to this plan is that each municipality is too small a unit to run a school for the deaf when only one or two deaf pupils may reside in the local area.

What's Going On at the Schools for the Deaf?

Currently the schools for the deaf have about 350 pupils. That figure also includes preschools. About one half of the 350 pupils reside at the schools. The other half of the deaf students, although they do not reside at the school, stay at the school during most of their free time in order to share the company of other children and adults who sign. More and more deaf people have been employed by the schools for the deaf. Fifteen deaf persons work at the school in Oslo, both as teachers and in other roles.

In the 1990s there also was an increasing awareness of the needs of hearing impaired children with multiple handicaps. Three of the schools for the deaf now enroll deaf-blind children in addition to the deaf and hard of hearing. There is no suitable program in Norway for deaf children who have psychiatric problems. People are currently working on the problem and intend to make state authorities aware of this need.

Most of the schools for the deaf serve as resource centers and offer services to the local schools. For example, as soon as a child is identified as deaf, the Skadalen School for the Deaf in Oslo offers parents a guidance program. This program started in 1960.

Some of the schools also function as resource centers and provide services to local schools, kindergartens, and families living in areas distant from the school for the deaf. These services are rendered by multidisciplinary teams of teachers, social workers, psychologists, and medical personnel.

The schools for the deaf in Norway are very well equipped with all needed equipment and materials. Adequate financial resources are available. The teachers are well educated and there are often two teachers in a classroom of four or five deaf students. The staff-to-student ratio is also low among support staff.

The low faculty-to-student ratio enables the teachers to individualize the education provided the deaf children. The individualized approach does limit the process of group dynamics and interactions between the deaf children.

Teacher Training
Introduction

Since 1961 in Norway there has existed a solid system of preparing special education teachers. In that year, the Postgraduate Teacher Training Center for Special Education was established. This center coordinates training activities and provides teachers with the opportunity to expand their skills in special education, become aware of research findings, and gain practical experience. Before 1961 postgraduate education in most areas of special education was limited to one year or less. The programs were not sufficient in terms of quality or quantity. In order to accomplish the goal of providing a quality education for all disabled persons in Norway, the skill of teachers involved with this population had to be raised.

The Basic Structure of the Norwegian Special Education System

The creation of the Postgraduate Teacher Training Center for Special Education (now the Advanced College of Special Education) in 1961 gave teachers the possibility of a two-year postgraduate course of study. The first year of study (Part One) was the same for all enrolled, and the second year (Part Two) was divided into five specialized courses. In 1976 a new program (Part Three) leading to a level of study approaching that of a Ph.D. program was initiated. This course of study was started at the Postgraduate Teacher Training Center for Special Education and consisted of a two-year-long, full-time course of study that built upon the course work completed in Part Two.

Admission Qualifications

A requirement for entry into Part One of the special education preparation program is the completion of a recognized regular teacher training program and, preferably, previous experience as a teacher. The majority of the people who begin the first part of the special education preparation program have completed training designed for a general teacher or a preschool teacher. However, a rising number of individuals have either completed the education required to become a qualified subject matter teacher or hold a degree from a university. In a few special cases, applicants with a background in physio-therapy, work therapy, or a similar area have been accepted.

Some Basic Principles and Problems

Hopefully, it is evident from the description above that graduate and postgraduate courses in special education in Norway are available only to those individuals who are already qualified as teachers. This means that the Advanced College of Special Education does not accept students after they have taken what in Norway is called *examen artium* (this corresponds to A-levels). They must have first completed a three-year teacher training program or a similar course of study and have experience as a teacher. (There are certain exceptions to this basic rule.)

An important principle in Norwegian school policy and National policy during the past 230 years falls under the heading of decentralization. This concept has influenced the area of special education, not the least the decentralization that has taken place in graduate and postgraduate education.

Today we find ten different teachers' training colleges involved in different ways of preparing special education teachers. There has also been a general decentralization with regards to the division of responsibility for the completion of scientific research. The Advanced College of Special Education has established external stipend positions whereby highly skilled practicing special educators can use half of their work time as stipend-students at the Advanced College. These teachers work on research projects in the district where they are employed. The guidelines for Part Three studies (Ph.D.) stress that it is preferred that the students enrolled conduct scientific research in the district or at the institution where they have been working. The concept of integration that is found throughout Norwegian school policy is an important part of the decentralization principle.

This principle provides as many children, young adults, and elderly people as possible with the option of being educated near their home. The desegregation and decentralization philosophy can only be realized with maximum mobilization of resources at the local level. This means that preparation in special education will need to be an integral part of every teacher's basic training in the near future. At the moment, in Norway, there is an intense debate about how these aims can be achieved.

References

Arnesen, K. (1983). *Language acquisition and deaf children.* Paper presented at the European Conference on Deaf Education, Sigtura, Sweden.

Arnesen, K., & Simonsen, E. (1989). From Andreas Miller to project S. *Special Pedagogible.*

Befornig, E. (1978). *Teacher training.* Paper presented at International Conference, Scotland.

Bellugi, U., & Studdert-Kennedy, M. (Eds.). (1980). *Signed and spoken language: Biological constraints on linguistic form.* Weinheim, German Democratic Republic: Verlag Chemie.

Blackwell, P., Engen, E., Fischgrund, J., & Zarcadoolas, C. (1978). *Sentences and other systems.* Washington, DC: Alexander Graham Bell Association of the Deaf.

Furth, H.G. (1973). *Deafness and learning.* Belmont, CA: Wadsworth.

Simonsen, E. (1989). *Education of deaf children in Norway.* Paper presented at International Conference, Rotterdam, The Netherlands.

Instruction of Persons with Hearing Defects in Poland

Urszula Eckert

The M. Grzegorzewska Higher School of Special Pedagogies in Warsaw

Introduction

In compliance with the suggestion of the initiator and editor of the book, Dr. H. William Brelje, we present in this paper some aspects relating to Poland's educational system for persons with hearing defects. Most of the material contained has been prepared by Urszula Eckert, assistant professor at the Warsaw and Head of the Institution of Surdo-pedagogics at this College. The section on care of children with auditory defects was developed in part by Ewa Kulczycka, M.A. assistant at the Institution of Surdo-pedagogics.

The first part of the paper will include a discussion of terms as the terms are interpreted and used in our country.

This chapter will discuss both deaf and hard of hearing persons. In Poland, according to special pedagogics, the term deaf is defined as "children, young people, and adults who have such a severe hearing defect that it is impossible for them to receive auditorially the world of sounds, and develop normal speech by means of the sense of hearing." Using this definition, a deaf person is one who receives information chiefly by visual means. The most significant social implication of this lack of hearing is the great difficulty the individual has in mastering the common means of inter-human communication — oral speech — through the imitation of heard speech. This, in turn, leads to difficulties in logical thinking and relations with the society.

Efficiency training is the restitution of impaired functions (auditory training, motor exercises of the speech organs, manual exercises, and so on).

In this paper the terms *revalidation* and *rehabilitation* will be used interchangeably. Children with hearing defects are included in the educational system, just as are their hearing peers. *Special education* is defined as the instructional methods and appliances adapted to meet the developmental needs and limitations of children with special needs.

Mostly, special instruction takes place in special establishments. These include: independent day kindergartens, special schools for commuting children, or residential schools and centers that include kindergartens, and dormitories where a majority of the pupils live.

The special education system demands the participation of teachers who hold suitable qualifications in special pedagogics. Special instruction is also provided to children who have less severe disabilities in normal kindergarten and schools. These children are integrated into the regular education system.

Instruction of children with hearing defects follows several organizational patterns which include special kindergartens, special schools, and public schools for hearing children.

Among the existing educational services are special kindergartens, schools for the deaf, schools for the mentally handicapped deaf, schools for the hard of hearing, and schools for those who are hard of hearing and mentally handicapped. The instruction of the deaf-blind takes place within educational facilities for the blind. The special education system for children and youth with hearing defects is composed of three-year kindergartens, eight-year primary schools, and three-to-five-year secondary schools.

Integration as it is understood by special pedagogics is defined as a system designed to integrate persons with disabilities into the larger society. The philosophical statement would be that a person with disabilities should be provided the same considerations true of a normal individual (except for cases of deep mental handicaps) (Lipkowski, 1976).

Educational integration means that disabled individuals will be educated with fully efficient persons within the normal educational system. Integration aims to prevent and minimize the problem of isolation. It is possible for children and young people with hearing defects to take part in the integrated education system.

Surdo-pedagogics is a branch of special pedagogics that deals with the theory and practice of educating deaf and hard of hearing persons. The term *surdo-pedagogics* is of Latin origin, and derives from *surdus* or "deaf." The term *surdo-pedagogics* is used interchangeably with the term "education of the deaf and hard of hearing." In Poland *surdo-psychology* is also used to denote the psychology of persons with hearing defects, and the term *surdo-logopaedics* is used to denote the science of teaching speech and resolving speech defects in people with hearing defects.

History of Instruction of Persons with Hearing Defects in Poland

In Poland it is difficult to trace the beginnings of the care and education of persons with hearing defects. Mention is made of the care of handicapped people in monastery and church records that date back to as early as the tenth century. In the beginning, these services were limited to refuges (shelters). Organized care at that time bore more of a charitable character than an educational one. In the course of time persons were separated according to the type of impairment; e.g., the mentally handicapped, the blind, and the deaf. It is conjectured that deaf persons, because of their communication difficulties, were treated as mentally handicapped.[1]

Poland had access to information on the origins and methods of instructing the deaf throughout Europe. During the first half of the eighteenth century a growing interest in the education of the deaf in Poland was noted. In 1754, the Polish King Stanislaw Leszczynski participated in a demonstration by Pereira (Schuman, 1940) of the instruction of a deaf person. Another Pole, Michal Bohusz, visited the Charles Michel de l'Épée Institute in Paris. Charles Michel de l'Épée was the creator of the sign method (Wolfgang, 1825). Next, in 1784 Prince Stanislaw Poniatowski visited a school in Leipzig directed by Samuel Heinicke, who was the creator of the oral method of teaching the deaf (Nurowski, 1983).

At the beginning of the nineteenth century, the idea to found an institute for the deaf-mute in Poland emerged. This idea was fostered by the Catholic Bishop Jan Nepomucen Kossakowski from Vilnius. He dispatched Zygmunt Anzelm to Vienna to gain knowledge about the formation of a school for the deaf.

Upon his return, Anzelm was called to Petersburg by the Russian Empress. In 1806 a school for the deaf was organized at Pavlovsk near Petersburg. At that time Poland, as a consequence of enemy invasions, had lost its independence and was partitioned among Russia, Prussia, and Austria. The partition of Poland lasted from 1772 until 1918, or for nearly 150 years. Other attempts at forming a school for the deaf undertaken during the partition period were not successful. However, these attempts did cause a growing awareness of the necessity to organize services for the protection and education of deaf children.

The first successful attempt at founding such a school occurred in the territory of the Congress Kingdom of Poland[2] by a priest, Jakub Falkowski, first in 1816 at Szczuczn, and later in 1817 in Warsaw.

The year 1817, the year during which J. Falkowski founded the Institute for the Deaf-Mute in Warsaw, constitutes the beginning of an organized care and education system for people with hearing defects in Poland. Activities of the Institute were varied. Its basic activity was instruction. And for this reason the school's teachers developed text books. In 1817 the first manual entitled *Elementary reading book for children starting to learn, especially for those being deaf-mute* was published. Its author was J. Falkowski, Rector of the Institute. Other text books were prepared by the pedagogical board of the Institute.

During the school for the deaf's first few years of existence, training in the area of lithography was introduced in order to prepare pupils for professional work. The instructor of the training program was Jan Siestrzynski, who was a physician, lithographer, and also a phonetician.

Jan Siestrzynski developed theoretical and practical guidelines for teaching speech. They were contained in his voluminous work bearing the title *Theory and Mechanism of the Speech* (Siestrzynski, 1820).

During the nineteenth century other schools for the deaf on Polish territory were established under the rule of foreign countries. In 1830 in the territory annexed by Austria, a school was founded in Lvov. In 1832 in the territory annexed by Prussia, a class for deaf children was started in Poznan. In 1833 in the territory occupied by Russia, a school for the deaf was established in Vilnius. The Vilnius school was established and re-established on several occasions. In 1870 the first school for Jewish children who were deaf was founded in Lodz (Nurowski, 1983).

During the years 1817–1917 eight schools for the deaf were established in Polish territories under foreign rule. Most of the schools were boarding schools, designed for children traveling from distant localities.

After the First World War, when Poland regained its independence, the education system in the devastated country was organized and initiated, including schools for the deaf. The prime mover of the organization of special schools was Maria Grzegorzewska (1888–1967), who was the founder of special pedagogics[3] in Poland. New centers were established, and schools that had closed were re-established (e.g., in Vilnius). The schools for the deaf were co-educational, state or privately owned, and some founded by a religious group (e.g., for Jewish children). In some schools vocational training designed to prepare shoemakers, tailors, joiners, and printers was established.

During the period between World War I and World War II (1918–1939), despite many urgent needs in all areas of the country's life, fourteen schools for the deaf, attended by nearly 1500 pupils, were established. Also, in 1919 a kindergarten for deaf pupils was started, and in 1934 a vocational school for the deaf was begun.

Although a few deaf pupils have graduated from normal primary schools, most of the instruction takes place in special schools. The alumni of these schools are prepared for professions and work in workshops of hearing artisans.

During the Second World War Germany and the Soviet Union occupied and partitioned Poland and proceeded to destroy the Polish people and its culture. Many millions of Polish citizens lost their lives due to famine, disease, war, or imprisonment in concentration camps. In the framework of denationalization Polish schools were closed.

Solely in a small territory called General Gubernia (German-occupied Poland) did schools using the Polish language and a few special schools exist. One of the special schools was the institute for the Deaf-mute and the Blind in Warsaw. It was a small school serving mainly deaf children from Warsaw.

Polish teachers who carried out instruction in this clandestine school were in real jeopardy. If they were detected the teachers and pupils could face stiff penalties including a death sentence. After the Second World War, when Poland again regained its independence, the education system was re-initiated. It was a difficult task because of great shortages and devastation. Many school buildings lay in ruins or were used as warehouses. Only those school buildings that the Germans had used to educate their children were in good shape.

There was a shortage of teachers since many of the teachers had died, been murdered, or remained in exile. No new teachers were trained during the five war years.

With the great enthusiasm which accompanied independence, the Poles were mobilized and started the reconstruction of their ravaged country. The rebuilding of the educational system was also started, including the reestablishment of schools for the deaf. Unfortunately some institutions with a long history, including the institutes for deaf-mutes in Lvov and Vilnius, remained as territories of Soviet Russia as determined by accords of the Yalta and Potsdam conferences of 1945.

As a result of many long-term organizational steps, the education system for persons with hearing defects began to function and to expand. The system grew not only numerically, but qualitatively as well. The scope of care and instruction broadened. Until 1945, the needs of only the school-aged deaf child were attended to. It became clear that the habituation process should be begun as early as possible. The education of preschool deaf children was started soon after the date the diagnosis was made. Many forms of vocational training were introduced. A whole network of special vocational schools were set up, including primary vocational schools, secondary schools, and technical schools.[4] Youths with hearing defects also made use of public schools and workshops, or took lessons in vocational schools for hearing pupils.

Due to a more comprehensive diagnosis of the children's needs, the profile of the special education centers changed. The diagnosis took into account the level and type of the disability and the age of the child.

The present system includes kindergartens and schools for deaf children, and separate schools for deaf children who are mentally handicapped. Deaf and blind children are educated in schools for the blind.

In 1957 schools for the deaf were separated from schools for hard of hearing pupils. And since 1977 a school and instructional center for hard of hearing children who are mentally handicapped has been in existence.

In 1938 at the Lvov Institute for Deaf and Mutes two classes for hard of hearing pupils were established and furnished with hearing devices (Kempa, 1939). These classes were stopped during the war. After the war deaf and hard of hearing children were educated separately.[5] Now the majority of hard of hearing children complete their lessons in public schools. A few, often those with additional disabilities, are educated in schools for the deaf.

Today in Poland there is a growing trend towards integrating children with various disabilities into the public school system.

Currently it is estimated that 80 percent of deaf children and 20 percent of hard of hearing children attend special schools, with the others attending public schools (Nurowski, 1983).

The lack of audio-visual equipment and hearing devices is creating a huge problem. This equipment is very expensive and the state needs the available foreign currencies for higher priorities. Thus, the waiting period for hearing aids and other devices may extend for a year or more and causes a delay in the habilitation process.

The organization that is statutorily responsible for dealing with problems of persons with hearing defects in Poland is the Polish Association of the Deaf. Within its framework there are 25 regional sections and 153 territorial circles. Its services include rehabilitation and consulting centers, training and manufacturing establishments, clubs and community centers. The Association has also established care centers in enterprises where persons with hearing defects are employed.

Elements of the Care System for Persons with Hearing Defects

Up to the time of the Second World War, services were limited to special primary schools and a few vocational schools. After the war, services for persons with hearing defects have increased in number and variety. This paper includes information on the leading forms of services existing in Poland.

During the second half of this century greater attention has been directed towards the earliest phase of a child's development. Because of the significance of the early stages of development in the life of an individual, various actions have been undertaken to ensure that children with disabilities are diagnosed at an early age.

Early intervention services have been developed. This early validation/habilitation is carried out within the child's environment.

Hence, the role and attitude of parents in this habilitation process is very important.

Guidance for Parents

From the time of the formation of a special education system in Poland, the important role played by parents in the early habilitation of deaf children has been recognized.

One of the first teachers of deaf children, Jan Siestrzynski (1788–1824), emphasized the role of parents in the habilitation process. In his "Guidelines for Parents" he stated:

> ... no one can contribute to a deaf child more than its parents ....
>
> ... It is for you, parents, that I am putting down these several guidelines.
>
> Whenever you perceive that your child has a hearing defect, and feel that the deafness cannot be cured, do consider the child as deaf only, not mute .... You can carry on almost as well by means of the sense of feel and vision as by hearing. After all, you do not know the degree of your child's hearing loss. The child may have residual hearing even though it may not be enough to differentiate ordinary speech. Speak to the child. Provide experiences with different sounds including songs and bells.[6]

Siestrzynski's early advice does not mean, however, that the problem of hearing impairment was duly appreciated. Up to the time of the Second World War, preschool education for the deaf child did not exist, and a majority of deaf pupils were enrolled in residential schools. It was not until after the Second World War that the importance of the role of parents in the habilitation process was perceived. The role of the John Tracy Clinic in stimulating the significance cannot be overlooked. The "Correspondence Course for Parents of Little Deaf Children," first published in Los Angeles in 1954, was translated into Polish by the pediatric otolaryngologist Maria Goralowna, and published in Warsaw in 1964 by the Polish Association of the Deaf.

In 1962 M. Goralowna's pamphlet entitled "What to do? My child does not hear," was published. This was the first paper published in Poland that presented the Polish medical establishment's point of view about the substance and etiology of hearing defects in children. The paper contained practical guidelines and examples of how to work with a deaf child, how to use a hearing device, and other topics.

Also during the 1960s information centers for the habilitation of children with hearing defects were organized. The first centers were set up in 1960 in Katowice (founder, K. Glogowski) and Wroclaw (founder, M. Kempa) (Kirejczyk, 1977). In 1963 in Warsaw a Central Information Bureau for Audiology and Rehabilitation was established.

The main task of these information centers was the early treatment of children with hearing defects and their parents. These centers employ audiologists, laryngologists, psychologists, educators, logopaedists, technicians, and others. A network of 21 of these rehabilitation centers has been developed. These centers care for about 10,000 hearing impaired children.

The centers were also interested in possible genetic transmissions of deafness and prenatal problems.

Depending upon staff expertise, these information centers conduct diagnostic services, habilitation services, training activities, and publicity campaigns. The main thrust of the centers is focused on early diagnosis, and early habilitation.[7] The centers' actions take various forms. The centers have contacts with maternity clinics, train nurse-midwives, and inform the public about the consequences of hearing defects and possible means of extenuating the effects of the hearing defect. Nurses are trained to perform simple examinations of young children's hearing level. The information centers provide maternity clinics with booklets that provide appropriate information. These materials contain information about a young child's reaction to sound. Also provided are lists of the names and addresses of the nearest laryngology and rehabilitation centers to contact if a child does not react to sounds. Most often, such booklets are handed to mothers as they leave the maternity ward with their new-born baby.

Midwives visiting babies and their mothers are, in many regions of the country, required to carry out hearing screenings and to watch the child's behavior to sound. Despite all of the above the percentage of deaf children diagnosed at an early age is not great.

According to data issued by the Institute of Mother and Child in Warsaw, only 7 percent of children with a hearing defect are detected during the first year of life. About 50 percent of hearing defects in children are detected during the first three years of life. About 60 percent of hearing defects are detected by the parents themselves. The parents become alarmed if the child does not start to babble between its eighth and twelfth month of life or attempt to speak by the age of two (Sobieszczanska, 1989).

Research showed that in only 12 percent of the cases did parents indicate that the lack of speech was the predictor of the child's hearing defect (Eckert, 1986). Eighty percent of the parents were more alarmed by the child's lack of reaction to sounds. Often the young child's reaction to the vibrations caused by a loud sound source are incorrectly received by parents as true reactions to sounds.

Early medical examinations of young children that include hearing evaluations increase the percentage of children detected as possessing a hearing defect. The staff of the rehabilitation center then attempts to contact the homes of the children identified as having a hearing defect as soon and often as possible. Some rehabilitation centers conduct weekly visits and in others, the visits are less frequent. These visits provide the evaluation center employee a better opportunity to know the home environment, as well as to work directly with the child and the parents.

Working cooperatively with the parents has become an important element of the habilitation process (Eckert, 1977). Part of the rehabilitation worker's responsibility is to assist the parent in the process of accepting their child's disability without rejecting the child or becoming overprotective.

The parents who have not been able to accept their child's hearing impairment require special help. These parents need to recover confidence in themselves and their children. They need to be helped to understand their role in their child's habilitation process. Only after the parents' attitude has changed are they allowed to take an active part in the habilitation process. Parents receive assistance from specialists, including special educators, psychologists, logopaedists, and laryngologists who work in the habilitation centers for children with hearing defects, or in the special kindergartens.

The specialists help parents as follows:

- help overcome the stress caused by the fact that their child has a hearing defect
- inform the parents about the limitations and possibilities in the child's development
- help the parents form an attitude of acceptance of the child's hearing dis ability
- instruct parents about the forms and methods of habilitation
- discuss the educational difficulties faced by the child with a hearing defect and the means of overcoming these difficulties
- familiarize the parents with professional literature that deals with the problems of habilitating and educating the hearing impaired child
- include the parents and families of the hearing impaired child in a cooperative effort aimed at the habilitation of and the development of self-dependency within the society.

In addition to assistance on an individual basis parents are provided two- or three-week courses and summer family vacation experiences. Support groups made up of parents of children with hearing defects and counseling by mail are available.

Currently in Poland there is an urgent need to increase the number of specialists involved in the diagnostic processes, in order to obtain a more complete and comprehensive diagnosis.

At present the main elements of a diagnosis are the results of the children's audiological examination and level of intellectual development. These data constitute the base used to begin the habilitation process. Often the diagnostic results do not match the efforts put into the habilitation processes. Often not detected are existing additional defects which have an inhibitory influence on a child's development. This is especially true for those children whose etiology indicates that meningitis or encephalitis was the cause of their disability.

As is indicated by a report on research completed through Polish-American scientific cooperation (Borkowska-Gaertig, 1976), greater attention was paid to this problem in the 1970s. The research indicated that apart from the hearing defects, the children suffered from microinjuries of the brain which caused many micro-disorders in the developmental process.

Deaf children with additional impairments require comprehensive medical, pedagogical, and psycho-social diagnosis, and solutions, and parental cooperation. The early habilitation of the child with a hearing defect is recognized as crucial to the child's development and is conducted as follows:

- individually with parents and their child at home, or as an out-patient in a rehabilitation center
- with children attending a special kindergarten for children with hearing defects
- by habilitation centers in cooperation with residential nurseries or kindergartens for hearing children

On a weekly basis or as often as is possible, a logopaedist or special educator from a local service center will provide services to the kindergarten where the child with a hearing defect is enrolled. The counseling centers mainly service hearing impaired children of a preschool age and hearing impaired children educated in an integrated system.

Care of Small Children with Auditory Defects

This section is devoted to a discussion of the means of improving surdo-pedagogical care of small children in Poland. These propositions may seem naive in this period of limited organizational and financial capabilities, but it is necessary to write about the requirements of an adequate surdo-pedagogics program in order to outline its future development.

To answer the question of what should be changed in the current system of care of children with hearing defects requires a complex investigation of the current situation.

First, the problem of facilitating the proper otolaryngological diagnosis of small children which in turn stimulates the efficiency of surdo-pedagogical education needs discussion. Next, the development of centers for surdo-pedagogical diagnosis based on foreign experience should be reviewed. Thirdly, the problem of developing a system for the surdo-pedagogical education of tutors of children with impaired hearing needs examination. Finally, the issue of the financial conditions of Polish surdo-pedagogics needs to be addressed.

The main problem in Poland is to develop a system of regular care for the small deaf child. This system needs to be based upon the following prime factors:

- early detection of the hearing defect and prompt habilitation
- early and full application of proper hearing aids
- planned, systematic assistance of parents by appropriate specialists

Early detection of a hearing defect requires a higher level of pediatric care beginning with the neonate, infants and children between the ages of two and four (Eckert, 1986). A more detailed early assessment would aid in the early detection of any defect, and avoid or minimize any retardation of early development. The physician who observes any deviation from the normal auditory behavior of the small child would then refer the child to an otolaryngologist for a more specialized investigation of the auditory system. During the stages of child development, it is usually the parents who first become concerned about their child's normal development. Thus, pediatricians, midwives, and environmental nurses must be taught not to neglect concerns of parents. Medical personnel should provide increased attention to families that are at a higher risk of having children with an auditory defect.

General auditory investigations require neither specialized equipment nor specialized training. When fully trained and aware of the importance of an early auditory diagnosis, the proper specialists should have no difficulty in conducting preliminary tests. Any indications of a possible hearing defect should be promptly followed up, since any time lost in early detection is to the detriment of the infant's development. Hence, emphasis need to be given to audiological issues in the preparation of pediatricians and midwives.

Pediatric care does exist in Poland, but is still unsatisfactory in the area of the assessment of auditory defects.

Poland currently lacks adequate diagnostic centers. It is hoped that the assistance of renowned diagnostic centers in other countries will make it possible to use and develop new diagnostic tools, and also novel habilitation methods.

The introduction of new diagnostic tools will begin with a detailed assessment of children with hearing defects. This will lead to more efficient diagnosis of dyspraxia and other disorders. The diagnosis of dyspraxia still provides problems. A full diagnosis employing modern methods will permit the development of early education programs for children with auditory defects.

Cooperation is planned with leading European centers (e.g., Sint Michelsgestel, The Netherlands; Heidelberg, Germany; Budapest, Hungary; and Meggen, Switzerland) to develop a full early identification and training model. This project has been planned for several years and will cover the preparation of staff, different forms of care for families, and methods and programs of habilitation.

It is expected that these changes will bring about revisions in the structure of the educational system in Poland. The current relative autonomy of schools, in the selection of institutional methods, staff, curriculum, work organization, and so on, is not providing satisfactory results. Schools are not differentiated according to the disabilities and capabilities of the children. Currently, separate schools exist only for mentally handicapped children with auditory defects. No program differentiation has been made as of yet concerning the use of different communication methods. Presently all children, no matter what their disability, are taught by the use of the same communication system. An example might be a child with dyspraxia taught by the same communication system as children who are able to speak in full phrases without any difficulty.

The current system does not involve parents in the habilitation process. We still tend to believe in the parents' good intentions, and are moved by mothers' tears and their assurance that they will devote their time and energy to the well-being of their hearing impaired child. Alas, the difficulties of everyday life do not always permit efficient care, and parents with good intentions sometimes make errors that make it more difficult to work with the child. During this time of economic hardships in Poland, parents often struggle to meet the material demands of the family. Often, they are forced to undertake additional employment. On the other hand, the tutors of their deaf children frequently pose higher demands than they can achieve. Parents are accustomed to the additional benefits available if one has a handicapped child, including free-of-charge hearing aids and other types of social benefits (e.g., reimbursement of the cost of traveling with the child). Parental ties with the child are often loosened by the placement of the hearing impaired child in a residential school. It is hoped that by overcoming the barriers to integration many more children will remain with their families and attend local schools. To foster integration, the importance of educating parents becomes more pronounced. Diagnostic centers similar to the John Tracy Clinic and others, with specialists engaged in presenting a variety of surdo-pedagogic courses that acquaint the parent with child's environment, teach the parent proper practice and theory of dealing with their deaf child, and provide the parent with opportunities to observe the way the child communicates are needed. The activities should foster communication skills, proper methods, procedures, and promote better schools.

Financial issues are also important. Maintaining comprehensive diagnostic centers using public funds, similar to the John Tracy Clinic, is currently impossible. The parents of our hearing impaired children are not wealthy, and the tradition of charity disappeared 50 years ago.

Hearing aids are in great demand. Saturation of this market is mainly a financial issue. Polish surdo-pedagogics, aware of the role of these devices, have had but minimal influence upon the purchase of hearing aids for auditorily impaired children. The waiting period for the receipt of a hearing aid is still far too long. Meeting the demand under current conditions will be difficult.

The same is true for the preparation of caring surdo-pedagogical staff. There is a dearth of qualified teachers, tutors, supervisors and administrators, social workers, sign language interpreters, and so on. The lack of adequate financing plays a crucial role, but success often also rests with the good will of individuals. It is hoped that these good intentions will lead to hope for a better future. Although surdo-pedagogics seems to have

financial difficulties all over the world, the education of the deaf is continuing to improve. It should be the same in Poland.

The Educational System

Preschools and Kindergartens

The majority of preschool-aged deaf children in Poland attend special kindergartens. There are kindergartens for deaf children and hard of hearing children (Eckert, 1985). These preschool establishments are part of the general education system. The preschools include children with hearing defects from three to seven years of age. Kindergarten attendance is not obligatory. It is a decision of the parents and a qualifying board, composed of an educator, psychologist, and audiologist. A kindergarten group of deaf children usually consists of six to eight children.

The special kindergarten may be an independent unit, organizationally placed at a kindergarten for hearing children as a sequence of parallel groups, or it may be part of a special education center for deaf or hard of hearing children.

A kindergarten for the deaf conducts a special program. A kindergarten for hard of hearing children has a general program. Each is adapted to the developmental possibilities of its wards. Individual habilitation of the hearing impaired child is included as part of the class schedule. To alleviate the effects of the hearing defect, appropriate organizational forms are used, as well as special education methods and technical equipment adapted to individual needs.

The special kindergarten continues the educational course of the preschool, and if the child attended, the work of the habilitation center. The aim of the special kindergarten is to foster the comprehensive development of the child, to ensure early and complex habilitation, and to provide readiness for further schooling.

Deaf children, and especially hard of hearing children, are also enrolled in public kindergartens, either individually or in parallel special groups. Children from a special kindergarten, under certain conditions, may transfer to a kindergarten for hearing children, and also hearing impaired children enrolled in public kindergartens can transfer back to a special kindergarten.

Persons teaching in a special kindergarten should have pedagogical training in preschool education, and in the field of surdo-pedagogics. Other specialists employed at the special kindergarten are logopaedists, psychologists, and laryngologists.

Currently the kindergartens and special schools are state-owned and are subordinate to the authority of the appropriate educational administrative unit.

Special Primary Schools

The next organizational form is the special primary school. In Poland primary school consists of eight grades, and enrolls children seven to fifteen years old.

There are special primary schools for children with the following hearing defects:
- deaf children
- deaf and mentally handicapped children
- hard of hearing children
- hard of hearing and mentally handicapped children, special classes in public schools

Attendance at primary school is obligatory.

A qualifying board makes placement decisions. There are six to eight pupils (deaf or hard of hearing) in a class. There are special primary schools for deaf pupils who have a profound hearing loss (approx. 90 db, or more), and who for want of, or in spite of, an early habilitation program did not develop a proper personality or master oral speech to an extent which would allow them to attend a public school (for hearing pupils) and communicate orally with their peer group. Pupils with multiple handicaps attend the primary school for deaf and mentally handicapped students.

In both types of special schools a special program is utilized that is adapted to the pupils' developmental disorders. The curriculum, in contrast to that found in public schools, does not include classes in a foreign language and in music. The special schools' curriculum includes calisthenics and special training in speech development and auditory training.

The goals of the special schools are to develop the pupil's full potential to be an independent citizen, foster vocational training, and promote social development and communication skills.

In addition to oral and written language and to facilitate communication, dactylography and sign language are also introduced in the special schools. In schools for the mentally handicapped deaf, a mixed method adapted to each pupil's individual needs is utilized. Instruction and education in the special schools is based upon an experiential model that utilizes the pupil's environment.

The schools for the hard of hearing are attended by children with hearing defects that restrict the reception of aural information. The curriculum is similar to the one used in schools for mentally handicapped hearing pupils. Alumni of these schools are directed, according to existing possibilities, to a vocational school for the mentally handicapped, or to a cooperative for disabled persons.

Deaf and blind children are educated in preschools and schools for blind children.

The faculty of the special primary schools, or public school classes, are trained in the field of pedagogics for the deaf and hard of hearing. These special schools also employ logopaedists, psychologists, technicians who maintain electro-acoustical equipment, and health service staff (otolaryngologists, pediatricians, nurses).

Deaf children, and especially those who are hard of hearing and who attend public schools, have rights equal to those of their hearing peers. The hearing impaired children in public schools benefit from the help of rehabilitation centers, especially in the areas of improving their auditory training and speech development, and tutoring in subject matter areas.

All of the special schools have residential facilities for pupils traveling from distant locations. The residential schools have 24-hour care and full instructional programs designed to ensure maximum results from the habilitation process. The special schools employ educators who possess the pedagogy required to habilitate children and youth with hearing defects.

Secondary Schools

Those hearing impaired pupils who finished primary school may enter secondary schools. These secondary schools are chiefly special vocational schools with a program of study three-to-five years in length. Completion of these programs of study qualifies the students for several possible degrees.

Deaf people who have mastered oral speech, and especially those who are hard of hearing, may also enroll for professional training in vocational schools designed for hearing persons. Those hearing impaired persons who complete vocational training in a regular vocational school are generally alumni of primary schools for hearing pupils, or the alumni from schools for hard of hearing pupils. The hearing impaired graduates of these schools may also enter secondary schools. Certificates from secondary schools entitle these students to apply for high school or university studies.

In Poland a few deaf youth, and a majority of the hard of hearing youth study with hearing youth, study with hearing youth in various kinds of secondary schools. A few hearing impaired students graduate from the universities. The number of people with hearing defects in Poland is set at approximately 80,000 persons. The numbers of school-aged hearing impaired children in different age groups is listed below:

Children up to
the age of three   approx. 1,000

Children from three
to five years of age   approx. 1,600

Children from six to
eighteen years of age   approx. 11,000

(Polish Association of the Deaf, 1989)

Within the framework of the Polish special education system exists the following educational establishments for persons with hearing defects:

- 10 kindergartens, mainly connected with special schools
- 27 primary schools, 22 schools for the deaf, and 5 for the hard of hearing
- 15 basic vocational schools for the deaf
- 1 technical school
- 1 secondary school

(Hulek, 1989)

These establishments educate and train approximately 4,500 persons.

It is estimated that 80 percent of all deaf children and 20 percent of all hard of hearing children in Poland attend special schools. The remainder are integrated into the public school system.

Integration of Hearing Impaired Students into Public Schools

The integration of hearing impaired students into the public schools has occurred for some time but not in large numbers. There is a broad need for the increased integration of hearing impaired children into the public school system. The increased need is associated with two phenomena:

- earlier and more comprehensive diagnosis and detection of an auditory disorder, and a resulting need to ensure appropriate habilitation
- acknowledgment of the negative emotional and social implications of segregation (special schools) on hearing impaired individuals

The first enactment relating to school integration was issued by the Ministry of Education in 1962. A comprehensive set of regulations concerning integration was issued by the educational authorities in 1973, and further regulations have been added in subsequent years.

Integration of hearing impaired children into the public school system is realized as follows:

- special groups of children with hearing defects are enrolled in kindergartens for hearing children, and in special classes for children with hearing defects in public school buildings. The classrooms for children with a hearing defect are equipped with appropriate assistive listening devices, and lessons are conducted by a teacher trained in pedagogics designed to teach deaf and hard of hearing pupils. Hearing and hearing impaired pupils come together during recess, in some classes (e.g., physical education, fine arts classes), or during jointly organized excursions or other events.

- children with hearing defects are educated in kindergartens or in a school for hearing pupils, and are treated equally. Most often these are children who were coached by parents under the guidance of a rehabilitation center, who have attained a habilitation level that enables them to successfully learn jointly with hearing pupils.

In 1989 almost 1,000 deaf pupils and 3,500 hard of hearing pupils were educated in kindergartens and schools for hearing pupils (Hulek, 1989). These pupils often remain under the care of a counseling center.

Difficulties Fulfilling the Curriculum at a Special School for Children with Auditory Defects

Since the end of World War II, Polish surdo-pedagogics have utilized several approaches to curriculum development. Initially, each school prepared its own curriculum. The main advantage of this system was that the curriculum could be adapted to meet the conditions that existed in each school. The skills of the pupils, teaching staff, educational aids, and other factors could be taken into consideration in determining and implementing the curriculum. The negative factor in this approach was that the variety of approaches made it difficult for all pupils to be at the same academic level when moving on to post-primary schools. This situation lasted till 1966. Over the next twelve years, draft curricula were developed, subject to approval of the Ministry of Education, that were situated somewhere in between an independently devised school curricula and a national curriculum. In 1978 the Ministry of Education introduced a unified special curriculum for all special schools for deaf children. The special curricula was also used in special schools for mentally handicapped children who were deaf or hard of hearing.

Recently, more flexibility in the implementation of the uniform curriculum has been permitted. One of the reasons for the increased curricular flexibility was that the development of more comprehensive diagnoses of children with hearing defects uncovered additional handicapping conditions.

Thus, it became necessary to revise the curriculum of the special schools to meet the needs of the students with additional disabilities. The pedagogic council presently has the right to modify the curriculum in force and some schools have utilized this opportunity.

Difficulties encountered in implementing the national curriculum for deaf children has inspired changes. Investigations[8] have shown that the academic accomplishments of hearing impaired children are inferior when compared with those of children in regular education. The good results achieved by normal children are counterbalanced by mediocre results for children with impaired hearing. The speech skills of the deaf individuals have an effect on the future ability of the person to successfully integrate into society.[9]

The academic achievement level of the auditorially impaired children who are integrated into public schools is much higher than that of their peers who are educated in special schools. Wider use of the integration of deaf children into regular public school classes will improve academic results (Kirejczyk, 1970). Not all hearing impaired children are suited for education in the open system. The successful integration of the hearing impaired child depends upon the attitude of the child, environmental conditions, the duration of the habilitation, and material and organizational factors.[10]

Modification of the current curriculum seems necessary, since it puts little emphasis on the needs of children with impaired hearing. More stress needs to be given to speech development in order to improve the deaf child's vocational performance and ability to survive in society.

Vocational Training

Listed below are the different types of special secondary schools for children with hearing defects:

- vocational schools for the deaf
- vocational schools for the mentally handicapped deaf
- comprehensive vocational schools for the deaf
- technical vocational schools for the deaf

These vocational schools differ by the length of the instructional program and by what the student is qualified to do at the completion of the program.

Vocational Schools for the Deaf

The instructional program in vocational schools for the deaf lasts three years. The curriculum includes basic subjects and a practical vocational training program, usually completed in school workshops and in community enter-

prises. The special vocational school program is obligatory.

Class size ranges in number from eight to eighteen pupils. Each workshop group ranges in size from four to twelve pupils depending on the professional specialty area and the degree of the pupils' hearing impairment. School graduates receive a qualified worker certificate.

Comprehensive Vocational Schools

The comprehensive vocational school program lasts for four years and has more emphasis on general subjects. With some necessary modifications the program of studies is similar to that of a secondary school for hearing pupils. The program is obligatory. The certificate received from the Comprehensive Vocational School provides the student with the opportunity to complete professional studies and to be employed as a fully qualified worker.

Technical Vocational Schools

The technical vocational school program lasts five years and admits young people between fifteen and twenty-one years of age. A program of basic subjects is required. The hearing impaired pupil receives a technical education similar to that completed by hearing students. The graduates of the technical vocational school are qualified as technicians.

All of these vocational schools have a residential component, with the majority of pupils living on the premises. Moreover, there are special classes at the vocational schools for those with normal hearing.

The teachers in the vocational schools are required to have a university education appropriate to their teaching assignment. The university program includes subjects in general education, vocational areas, and methods of practical vocational instruction, as well as qualifications in the field of surdo-pedagogics.

The majority of the alumni of the special primary schools for the deaf and hard of hearing who are not able to successfully complete a vocational training program designed for hearing pupils, complete vocational training in the special vocational schools.

Youth with hearing defects also have a chance to learn vocational skills in vocational training establishments that are part of the program of the Polish Association of the Deaf. These manufacturing establishments admit and train hearing impaired persons from the age of sixteen to forty years to learn to follow a trade. These organizations sponsored by the Polish Association of the Deaf are for persons who have not finished primary school, do not have a trade, or who completed a vocational school program, but who for various reasons, are compelled to change their occupation. Deaf and hard of hearing persons are referred to these training and educational centers by personnel at the regional branches of the Polish Association of the Deaf, and by people at the special schools for the deaf, health care center workers, and penitentiary staff.

The aim of these production and educational establishments is to ensure that hearing impaired people who have been neglected by society have a chance to receive vocational training, earn a living, and become independent citizens. The training at these residential establishments lasts from three to five years.

Cooperatives for Disabled Persons

Cooperatives for Disabled Persons are production centers that employ and train disabled persons over the age of sixteen regardless of the type and degree of his or her disability. The aim of the Cooperative is rehabilitation through professional work. Instruction is realized through training at the workshop site, or by performing specified professional duties on the job.

The most popular occupational areas for which the deaf are trained include: locksmith, hand-operated lathe operator, joiner, tailor, upholsterer, baker, weaver, knitter, purse maker, house-painter, mechanic, type-setter, printer, bookbinder, building technician,

draftsman, and dental technician. Less common trade areas include butcher, pastry-cook, laboratory assistant, and librarian. A few take positions as painters, sculptors, teachers in special schools, and social workers.

The less severe the hearing defect, the wider the range of possible occupation areas and the greater the ability to more fully identify with a trade and to find self-realization through work.

Professional and Social Life

Shaping the personality of the student with a hearing defect in such a way that the transition from parent or teacher dependency to social independence does not cause major stresses and proceeds smoothly is a very important rehabilitation task. This development of independence is important because the majority of persons with hearing defects will be working and living among hearing people.

The rehabilitation process should be directed so that the person with a hearing defect will accept his or her impairment, changed social status, and the resulting inconveniences.

The importance of promoting a proper attitude in handicapped individuals was acknowledged by Maria Grzegorzewska (1964). She stressed the following important rehabilitation goals:

- promoting the inner dynamics of the individual
- striving to make him/her more active and independent
- integrating the individual into the community

Full vocational integration allows the persons with hearing defects to join enterprises where hearing persons are employed. This equality means that employment and promotion will occur according to the individual's qualifications and performance on the job.

The deaf worker will also have an equal opportunity to be included in various forms of inservice training.

After becoming qualified for a vocation, persons with hearing defects usually start their independent life. They are usually hired by state-owned enterprises, cooperatives, or private businesses on terms equal to those that apply to hearing employees. Many hearing impaired persons secure jobs in cooperatives for disabled persons. Some who are less capable or who have multiple defects (e.g., the deaf and mentally handicapped, deaf with motor disorders) work in sheltered workshops. At this level the responsibility for the care of persons with hearing defects shifts from the Ministry of Education to the Ministry of Health and Social Welfare, acting through its network of rehabilitation centers and social service agencies.

Some employers are reluctant to employ deaf persons. They quote possible hazards and expect diminished efficiency (Eckert, 1977). At this time, no proper legal regulations exist, as they do in other countries, to protect the rights of the person with a hearing defect from job discrimination.

Investigations carried out by surdo-pedagogical students of the School of Special Pedagogics have shown that approximately half of the hearing impaired persons investigated encountered difficulties in finding a job. They cite as problems lower wages, lack of protection from superiors and co-workers, and difficulties in communication (Eckert, 1989).

Very often poor interpersonal skills and a general atmosphere of discrimination against handicapped persons at the work site hamper the integration process. This discrimination is often a cause of vocational destabilization for persons with hearing defects. The intervention of the social assistant is often required. Sometimes the deaf individual, because of limited job possibilities, is compelled to look for a job at a cooperative of deaf workers.

Investigations indicate that employed hearing impaired persons usually find acceptance and understanding at their place of work, identify with their work, obtain good results, and find job satisfaction and improved self-esteem.

Good use of leisure time is an important aspect of life. In Poland there is a wide range of leisure activities for persons with hearing defects. Sports come first followed by watching TV and reading newspapers. Also important are the cinema, clubs, and deaf community centers (usually the day-room of the Polish Association of the Deaf). The forms of entertainment found in clubs or community centers for the hearing impaired include theatrical teams, pantomime, games (especially chess), and other activities. Many hearing impaired persons engage in the hobby areas of photography and stamp collecting, fishing, and also enjoy travel. Reading is less popular.

A large percentage of the hearing impaired population hold second jobs in order to increase their income.

The majority of persons with hearing defects do not have close social contact with hearing people. They have a tendency to limit their social contacts to other deaf persons. There are few successful mixed marriages. Sometimes people with hearing defects do not marry because they are concerned that their children might be deaf. Often hearing parents of persons with a hearing defect do not approve if their hearing daughter or son plans to marry a deaf person. The parents are concerned about the future stability of such a liaison.

The main reasons limiting closer social contacts between hearing and hearing impaired persons are difficulty in verbal communication, and insufficient public awareness of deafness and the potentials of persons with hearing defects.

The Polish Association of the Deaf enters the lives of persons with hearing defects by helping them choose a suitable vocation area, advance professionally, and use leisure time wisely. The Association, through social workers and sworn court interpreters, does its best to help its members solve their various problems.

By end of 1989 the Association had

77,200 members. The Association organizes various forms of vocational counseling and training activities, and presents courses inside and outside of the work place. These courses enable the deaf person to obtain vocational certificates (qualified worker, apprentice, foreman).

The Polish Association of the Deaf manages 7 culture clubs, 14 culture and education clubs, 75 community centers, 87 libraries, 553 artistic groups, sporting teams, and other activities.

With the goal of enriching the social life of its members, the Polish Association of the Deaf is a member of the World Federation of the Deaf (WFD), and keeps in contact with the deaf from other countries in the fields of culture and sports.

Teacher Preparation in Poland

The training of teachers of the deaf coincides with the founding of the special schools for deaf children. In the beginning the training mainly consisted of sending selected persons to existing schools for the deaf.

The visits of Zygmunt Anzelm (1804) to the school for the deaf in Vienna, and Jakub Schulc (1825) and Josef Sikorski (1829) to the institute for the deaf in Berlin (Nurowski, 1983) were the starting point of the training of Polish teachers employed by the Institute of the Deaf in Warsaw.

In 1872 the director of the Institute, Jan Paplonski, organized the first teacher training course of study. The instructional program was one year in length. Experienced teachers from the Warsaw Institute for the Deaf acted as instructors. Public school teachers and priests were admitted to the course of study. After a final examination the participants had the right to teach in schools for the deaf (Lipkowski, 1983).

After the First World War, with the establishment of more schools for the deaf, the need for trained teachers for the deaf grew. By 1920, a one-year-long course of study for teachers from special schools was launched. Maria Grzegorzewska and Janusz Korczak were among the instructors of the preparation program.

In 1922 a National Institute of Special Pedagogics (PIPS) was initiated in Warsaw. The Institute's founder was Maria Grzegorzewska. She had studied in Paris and Brussels, and was well acquainted with contemporary ideas concerning teacher training.

Maria Grzegorzewska's general ideas on teacher training were based mostly upon the system used by Paedological Faculty of Brussels, Belgium.

The PIPS envisaged the preparation of teachers who could work with deaf, blind, mentally handicapped, socially maladjusted, and crippled children.

To qualify for admission to the Institute, one either had to hold a university degree but lack pedagogical practice, or have completed several years of pedagogical practice but not hold a degree. The program lasted one year, after which the graduate received a provisional certificate. After the completion and acceptance of a thesis (which could take one to two years), the program graduate received a diploma as a special school teacher.

The first month of study at the Institute was dedicated to general information about the special education system and visits to centers for persons with various types of disabilities. After selecting an area of specialization, the student served an apprenticeship under the tutelage of a selected teacher in a school representing the area of specialization. The student attended general lectures relating to all special education areas, as well as specific lectures in the area of specialization.

All courses were connected with practical training in special establishments and with exercises in laboratories and counseling centers. Program content for each student was linked to possible future work places and social environments. For this reason much time was spent on the study of detailed methodologies, and on practicum activities. An important place was reserved for vocational education (*slojd*), music, and physical education since these subjects were of the utmost significance in the revalidation process.

During World War II, the building that housed PIPS was bombed and the library, the teaching aids, and other scientific materials were lost or burned. A majority of the professors and other workers at the Institute perished. From the very beginning of the war, the Institute ceased to function as a higher school.

Immediately after the war, May 15, 1945, the Institute resumed its activities, with M. Grzegorzewska again as its directrice. Unfortunately, the new education authorities imposed limits to the range of activities of the Institute. The years 1945–1956, the Stalinist period in Poland, were marked by special repressive measures toward all citizens' liberties and manifestations of free thinking. During those years many thousands of Poles were shot or incarcerated in Polish prisons or Soviet gulags.

During the 1950s, the name of the Institute was changed and it was deprived of its former scientific and research functions. Financial resources available for nonpedagogical activities were considerably reduced. The Institute's periodical, aimed at informing people about special pedagogics and new methods of habilitation, was discontinued. New methods of habilitation of handicapped children were also prohibited. The social and moral attitudes of society were largely devastated.

Only after 1956 and the first of the sharp outbursts of social discontent did more favorable changes in the educational system begin. These changes included the needs of the special education system. The former name, The National Institute of Pedagogics (PIPS), was also reinstituted.

In the post-war development of this higher school, we can single out the following periods:

from 1945–1955: one-year program of study in Special Pedagogics

from 1955–1970: two-year courses at the National Institute of Special Pedagogics

from 1970–1976: three-year studies of the vocational higher school type

from 1976–1981: four-year studies at a university ending with a diploma

since 1981: five-year studies at a university leading to a degree

In 1976 the National Institute of Special Pedagogics changed its name to the Higher School of Special Pedagogics (WSPS) and was given the name of Maria Grzegorzewska.

Until 1958 PIPS was the only establishment in Poland training teachers for special schools. From 1958 on, as a result of the development of the special school system and an increased demand for qualified teachers to fill those schools, new centers designed to train specialists in the various fields of the special education system were organized. In 1956 the first academy established to train special educators was developed at Warsaw University. During the following years Departments of Special Pedagogics were established in other institutions of higher education.

At present seven universities and three pedagogical colleges located in different towns in Poland train special educators. However, it is only at the Higher School of Special Pedagogics (the former PIPS) that specialists for all kinds of impairments and disorders are trained. The other colleges train teachers only for those specialty areas for which there is the greatest demand and in specialty areas where the college has suitable academic and didactic staff.

A five-year-long academic program for the training of surdo-educators able to instruct persons with hearing defects was established at the WSPS in Warsaw and at the Pedagogical College in Cracow. This training is carried out in the form of day studies for secondary school graduates, and as in-service training for professionally active teachers.

The program graduates, after submitting and defending their theses on a research topic connected with the education of a child with hearing defect, receive their M.A. degree in special pedagogics with a specialty in surdo-education.

In addition to the teacher preparation previously detailed, the universities and colleges provide postgraduate certification studies lasting three to four semesters. These studies were reserved for graduates who specialize in a subject area such as history, geography, mathematics, and others who wished to become qualified to work with handicapped children. These postgraduate studies in special pedagogics are also organized for psychologists and for judges of juvenile courts.

Apart from these certification studies, there are also various forms of professional advancement courses for teachers. Generally these courses are directed by the Center for Advanced Courses for Teachers located in Warsaw and its branches throughout the country. These institutions organize conferences, courses, and seminars aimed at improving instruction and providing up-to-date information.

Besides preparing teachers to instruct in special schools, all students enrolled in a college or university are provided with the rudiments of special pedagogics. This content provides all students with an orientation to the problems of integrating disabled students into the regular classroom and provides future public school teachers with an awareness of the developmental difficulties and possibilities of handicapped children. It also acquaints these people with the provisions of the laws that guarantee deaf or hard of hearing students the right to attend public school. The law requires that teachers in special schools for children with hearing defects have completed a full and comprehensive pedagogical training program and are graduates of higher pedagogical studies, or postgraduate studies in surdo-pedagogics. Annually 120 surdo-educa-

tors complete their studies at WSPS. This includes 80 graduates of the full five-year program of study in surdo-pedagogics, and 40 persons who have obtained their qualifications at the postgraduate level. Yet the number of persons completing training to be teachers of the deaf does not fully meet the needs of the special education system. In the special schools, fully qualified teachers constitute approximately 60 percent of the staff. The rest of the faculty of these schools have varied levels of training. Many have acquired their special qualifications through experience gained while performing their job. This situation has often impeded instructional efficiency.

At present the existing heavy demand for instructors of persons with disabilities requires that certain modifications be made in the training of these specialists (teachers, psychologists, social workers). There are proposals to shorten the period of study and to include training in counseling, and in early identification and training (zero to three years of age). It is also proposed that training be provided to persons who would become specialists in special geragogics or who would work with the elderly who are handicapped. Also, there are attempts to train special education generalists or teachers trained to work with any handicapped person. These people could not be considered "generalists" until they had completed training in an area of specialization, i.e., training as a teacher of persons with a hearing defect.

In Poland the idea of continuing professional education has been implemented. It takes the form of non-formalized, unconventional self-education, as well as formal, conventional educational activities. These professional development activities include conferences, seminars, exchanges, and other educational experiences. These in-service activities are organized by educational authorities, trade unions, social organizations, or any other group of interested people. All of these initiatives are meant to update and widen the teacher's knowledge and to raise his or her teaching competency.

These professional development efforts should ultimately result in an improved education and life preparation for students with defective hearing.

Endnotes

1. In ancient records the old Polish word *glur* denoted both "deaf" and "weak-minded" (mentally handicapped).

2. In 1807 Napoleon created the s.c. Duchy of Warsaw, and in 1815, after Napoleon's fall, at the Congress of Vienna the Kingdom of Poland was established, with its capital in Warsaw.

3. Polish special pedagogics was largely influenced by the director of the Special Pedagogics Seminar in Zurich, H. Hanselmann (1885–1960), who was author of many papers in the field of the theoretical foundations of special pedagogics.

4. Details on professional preparation can be found in the section "Teacher Preparation in Poland."

5. The author (U.E.) is a co-organizer of the first residential school for hard of hearing children in Poland.

6. L. Jenike: Jan Siestrznski. *A Diary of the Warsaw Institute for the Deaf-Mute and the Blind,* Warsaw, 1856.

7. Maria Grzegorzewska (1888–1967), founder of special pedagogics, called attention to the question of an early revalidation training (Grzegorzewska, 1932). She described the work of Emma and Mary Garret of Philadelphia, who tried to habilitate deaf children from the age of two, as well as various activities with three- to four-year-old deaf children whom she observed in France and Belgium.

8. Investigations into the degree of accomplishing the curriculum in individual subjects are being conducted within master's theses in the Higher School of Special Pedagogics under the guidance of U. Eckert.

9. Master's theses investigation results under the guidance of U. Eckert.

10. There is a need both for specialists who could help such children and also for a regular supply of didactic and audiological aids.

References

Borkowska-Gaertig, D. (1976). *Research on hearing impairments with children in Poland*. IMiDZ.

Eckert, U. (1977). Factors stimulating and delimiting the development of a small child with hearing defect in the light of the realization of UNESCO recommendations. In *Questions of diagnosis and rehabilitations of a small child with hearing defects*. PAM, Szczecin.

Eckert, U. (1983). *Possibilities and limitations in the realization of an educational programme*. WSPS.

Eckert, U. (1985). Centers of education for persons with hearing defects. In *Vergleichendes Fachworterbuch*, Teil 33, 34. Berlin, Germany: Humboldt-Universitat zu Berline.

Eckert, U. (1986). Preparing a child with hearing defects for school education. WSIP. 1986.

Eckert, U. (1989). Organization of free time for people with hearing defects. *Pedagogical Studies*, LV. Ossolineum.

Goralowna, M. (1962). *What to do? My child does not hear ...* PZWL.

Grzegorzewska, M. (1932, 1933). New trends in the teaching of the deaf mute. *Special School* No.1, 2.

Grzegorzewska, M. (1964). Selected works. PWN.

Hulek, A. (1989). *Present state and modification trends of the special education system in Poland*. PWN.

Jenike, L., Siestrzynski, J. (1856). *A diary of the Warsaw Institute for the Deaf-Mute and the Blind*. Warsaw, Poland.

Kempa, M. (1938, 1939). Sonic devices for the deaf. T.XV.

Kirejczyk, K. (1977). Beginnings of rehabilitation of a small child with a hearing defect in Portland. In *Questions of diagnosis and rehabilitation of a small child with hearing defect*. PAM, Szczecin.

Kirejczyk, K. (Ed.). (1983). *Possibilities and limitations in the realization of educational programme*. WSPS.

Lipkowski, 0. (1976). On questions of integration. *Szkola Specjalna*, 1.

Lipkowski, 0. (1983). *The High School of Special Pedagogics in Warsaw 1922–1982*. WSPS.

Nurowski, E. (1983). The Polish surdoedagogics. PWN.

Polski Zwuazek Gluchjych. (1989). *The Polish Association of the Deaf: Report on the statutory activity for the year 1989*. Warsaw, Poland.

Potocka, W. (1977). Research on the school knowledge resources of a deaf pupil. In U. Eckert, (Ed.). *From the problems of surdopedagogics*. WSPS.

Schumann, P. (1940). *Geschichte des Taubstummenwesens*, Verlag M. Diesterweg. Frankfurt/M.

Siestrzynski, J. (1820). *Theory and mechanism of speech*. Warsaw, Poland. Institute of the Deaf-Mute.

Sobieszczanska, L. (1989). Coming out of the world of silence. *KiZ, 16*.

Van Uden, A. (1970). *A world of language for deaf children*. Rotterdam, The Netherlands: University Press.

Wolfgang, A. (1825). *Professors of the Romanowski Institute*. Vilnius, Lithuania.

History of Deaf Education in Puerto Rico

Miguel A. Albarrán, Ph.D.
Physical Education Department
Recreation Program
School of Education
University of Puerto Rico
Río Piedras, Campus

Yolanda Rodríguez, B.A.
Rafael Hernández Elementary School
Río Piedras
Department of Education

Introduction

Origins of the Education of the Deaf in Puerto Rico

The study of the history of the education of the deaf is a relatively new area within the education movement in Puerto Rico. Very little information regarding the history of the Puerto Rican deaf population prior to the twentieth century is available. Puerto Rican history does not mention the existence of deaf Tainos,[1] Africans, or Spaniards. These three ethnic groups comprise what later was to become the Puerto Rican culture.

Even though the existence of a deaf community is not stated, it may be inferred that deaf individuals were part of the community. For example, when the Spaniards returned to Europe after explorations in the late 1400s and 1500s, they introduced to the Old World a disease that is known today as acute syphilis (Arrillaga-Torrens, 1985). It has long been known that deafness is a possible side effect of a syphilis infection.

It is reasonable to believe that the Taino Indians had deaf members within their community, because of the different diseases that the Europeans introduced into America. The Spaniards who settled in Puerto Rico[2] engaged in sexual activities with Taino females. These intimate relationships, as well as other contact, caused the spread of diseases.

In 1521 Fray Bartolome de las Casas arrived in Puerto Rico with slaves from Africa (Cuesta-Mendoza, 1946) and integrated them into the labor force. The Spaniards and Africans brought with them several diseases previously unknown on the island. The most serious were chicken pox and yellow fever (Arrillaga-Torrens, 1985). These diseases caused a dramatic increase in the incidence of deafness.

In 1518 and 1519 chicken pox epidemics caused the death of one-third of the Indian population in the Greater West Indies (Brau, 1966; Cuesta-Mendoza, 1946; Morán-Arce,

1985). It was likely that a number of the Taino Indian survivors of this epidemic were deaf. This assumption is based upon statistics (Best, 1943) that attribute a small portion (0.1%) of deafness in the United States to chicken pox.

Mandatory Education in the West Indies

On March 20, 1503, Fernando El Católico (Fernando the Catholic), King of Spain, ordered that every child (Spaniard or Taino) had to meet twice a day at the local church for instruction (López-Yustos, 1985). This was the beginning of mandatory education in Puerto Rico. No evidence is available regarding the education of the deaf during that century or the three following centuries. Although the education of the deaf started in Spain during the sixteenth century, it did not reach the Caribbean region until the twentieth century.

Phase One: 1903–1956

After the Spanish-American War (1898), administrative control of the island government transferred from Spain to the United States. Many social and political changes started to take place, and education was no exception to this climate of change. In 1901 Puerto Rico had 835 schools with a school-age population of 40,000 (Braumbaugh, 1904). Approximately 75 percent of the school-age population was enrolled in school. Up to 1901, no data indicating the existence of an educational program for deaf children is available.

Bishop Monsignor James F. Blenk first became aware of the lack of educational opportunities for deaf pupils. He encouraged the Mission Helpers of the Sacred Heart (MHSH) to begin an educational program for the deaf. This invitation was accepted by the MHSH, and in 1902 the first program to educate the deaf was begun (Casanova, 1986) in the town of Aguadilla (on the northwest coast).

Mission Helpers of the Sacred Heart

The MHSH main congregation was located in the state of Maryland in the United States. Although the MHSH's principal religious activity was to conduct catechism classes (Alcover-Serres, 1979), apparently they were also attentive to the special needs of the deaf population. The MHSH first arrived in Puerto Rico on November 29, 1902 (Saliva-González, 1988; De Jésus, 1988). The pioneers of this new educational movement were Josephine Smith, Larkin de Sales, Demetrias Cunningham, and a deaf woman, Xavier Wholihan (Bugden, 1987).

Alcover-Serres (1979) has reported that these pioneers lacked experience in educating the deaf. Other documents indicated that the missionaries had studied at Gallaudet College, now Gallaudet University (Bugden, 1987), and that the MHSH had established a school for the deaf in Baltimore, Maryland, in 1897. This same order also originated a school for deaf-mute children in Hawaii in 1902, which was established permanently in 1914 (Gannon, 1981). In addition, members of the MHSH group received training to teach the deaf at the Kendall School in Washington, D.C., and at the Maryland School for the Deaf.

Although the language used in Puerto Rico was Spanish, the MHSH used a combined approach that utilized sign language and English simultaneously. This religious group is given credit for initiating the first phase of the history of the education of the deaf in Puerto Rico, which lasted from 1903 to 1956.

The First Schools for Deaf-Mutes in Puerto Rico[3]

Although the staff of MHSH had limited training in the education of the deaf, no money, and little or no knowledge of Spanish, in 1903 they began to teach deaf children at their mission-house-convent (Bugden, 1987) in the town of Aguadilla.

A conflicting document suggests that the school established its first class of five students at Bishop Blenk's house in 1902. By the next year the school had 33 students (Comisión, 1969), and was moved to Aguadilla. Records also indicate that the school had to be relocated twice because of the large number of students who wanted to be educated.

El Convento de la Calle del Cristo (the Convent at Christ's Street), a school for deaf girls, was opened in Old San Juan, and another school was opened in Cayey for deaf boys. Both schools were administered by Sister Xavier Wholiham. The Cayey school soon faced financial problems and was closed. The boys were moved to the Old San Juan school.

In 1907 another school was opened in Aguadilla under the direction of Sister Josephine Smith. The school's goal was to teach the children how to read and write in English and to communicate in sign language. In 1910 the MHSH bought a piece of land in San Juan (the Santurce area) and was able to obtain the financial donations necessary to construct two wooden school buildings. This new "Asylum School for the Deaf Mute" of Santurce held its inauguration in 1911 (Best, 1943). The school continued to have financial problems that were exacerbated when a cyclone destroyed part of one of the buildings.

Saint Gabriel School for the Deaf

In 1913 the MHSH started planning the Saint Gabriel School for the Deaf (Colegio San Gabriel para Sordos) on San Jorge Street in Santurce (Alcover-Serres, 1978). Interviews with school graduates and supporters indicate that the Saint Gabriel School began operating in 1915 (De Jésus, 1988; Saliva-González, 1988).

Census of the Deaf in Puerto Rico

The first and only census of the deaf population of Puerto Rico was performed in 1944 (Departamento, 1948) by the Puerto Rico Labor Department. This study was published in 1948 under the title *Census for the Blind, Mute, Deaf and Psychotic in Puerto Rico, 1944*. The census indicated the number of blind, mute, deaf, and psychotic individuals living in Puerto Rico at the time. The study divided the deaf population into three different categories (i.e., partially deaf, totally deaf, and deaf-mutes). Tables 1, 2, and 3 summarize the number of cases related to deafness, the place of residence of deaf people, and the causes of deafness, respectively.

Table 1. Summary of Cases Related to Deafness, 1944

Category	Number	Gender Male	Female	Did Not Inform
Partially Deaf	1965	1013	951	1
Totally Deaf	601	316	283	2
Deaf-Mute	1124	645	478	1

Adapted from: Departamento del Trabajo de Puerto Rico, (1948), *Censo de Ciegos, Mudos, Sordos y Psicoticos en Puerto Rico, 1944*, San Juan, Puerto Rico.

Table 2. Summary of Place of Residence of Cases Related to Deafness, 1944

Category	Number	Area Urban	Rural	Did Not Inform
Partially Deaf	1379	524	851	4
Totally Deaf	497	211	284	2
Deaf-Mute	1049	341	707	1

Adapted from: Departamento del Trabajo de Puerto Rico, (1948), *Censo de Ciegos, Mudos, Sordos y Psicoticos en Puerto Rico, 1944*, San Juan, Puerto Rico.

The 1944 census indicated that Puerto Rico had 3,690 deaf individuals. More deaf people lived in the rural areas than in the urban areas. The major causes of deafness were found to be illness and congenital problems.

Religious Congregation of the Franciscan Sisters

In 1955 the MHSH of St. Gabriel's School informed Bishop Davis that they wanted to leave the island. Bishop Davis asked Rev. Mother Maria del Pilar Franco Martorell of the Religious Congregation of the Franciscan Sisters (RCFS) of Spain if they would assume the responsibility of working with the deaf community.

The RCFS agreed to take over the responsibility of running the school. Without the support of the RCFS, educational opportunities for deaf children in Puerto Rico would no longer have been available. A major factor in the decision of the RCFS to administer the school was the fear that the deaf children might be exposed to Protestant religious beliefs.

On October 2, 1956, the RCFS arrived in Puerto Rico (Alcover-Serres, 1978). This order had experience in educating the deaf. Their philosophy concerning the proper way to educate the deaf was different from that of the MHSH. The RCFS believed in the oral method of teaching the deaf and had established educational programs utilizing the oral method in Spain, Venezuela, Dominican Republic, Chile, and Peru.

Table 3. Summary of the Causes of Deafness, 1944

Category	Number	Sickness	Congenital	Accidental: Work	Home	Did Not Inform
Partially Deaf	1379	912	211	43	204	9
Totally Deaf	479	310	98	19	67	3
Deaf-Mute	1049	98	937	2	6	6

Adapted from: Departamento del Trabajo de Puerto Rico, (1948), *Censo de Ciegos, Mudos, Sordos y Psicoticos en Puerto Rico, 1944*, San Juan, Puerto Rico.

The MHSH left on the same day that the RCFS arrived at the St. Gabriel School. The deaf students were faced with major adjustments. After 50 years of use, sign language was forbidden. Instead of English, the students were to communicate in Spanish through the use of speechreading and speech.

All these changes occurred in a matter of days. Students of the period stated that on one day they used sign language and English, and on the next day they were required to lipread and speak in Spanish.

Phase Two: 1957–1979

The New St. Gabriel School for the Deaf

The second phase of the history of the education of the deaf in Puerto Rico began in 1957 and ended in 1979.

The educational method of teaching the deaf initiated by the RCFS was accepted by parents and the civic community of the island. It was stated that the oral method gave deaf students and their relatives an opportunity to communicate among themselves.

In order to establish the new philosophy, special equipment was needed. Civic groups like the Lions Club and the Rotary Club donated equipment for the school (Alcover-Serres, 1979). In 1960 the governor of Puerto Rico, the Hon. Luis Muñoz Marín, signed a law that allowed the Department of Public Works to sell some land to the RCSH to establish a new school (Periódico, El Mundo, 1960). The area where the school was to be built was called "The City of Silence." Three years after the Puerto Rican government sold the land to the RCSH, the new school was completed.

Evangelical School for the Deaf

Within months of the RCFS's decision to take over the administration of the St. Gabriel School, a group of North American Evangelical Missionaries from Jamaica established a school on the northeast coast of the island. They rented a farm in Yuquiyú, Luquillo, and started what was called the Evangelical School for the Deaf. The EM had difficulty finding qualified faculty and were forced to hire people who used a variety of communication systems including manual, oral, and Total Communication. All of the teachers hired taught in English (Rawlings, 1989).

When the director of the school was forced to leave for a year, the Reverend Roger Rawlings from Canada was asked to become the interim director.

Reverend Rawlings had been trained in Canada to be an oral educator of the deaf. While teaching in Canada he learned sign language. After the year was over, Rev. Rawlings returned to Canada. The original director did not return and because of the lack of leadership and qualified teaching staff, the school was forced to close (Rawlings, 1988).

In 1970 Rev. Rawlings came back to Puerto Rico and reopened the Luquillo school. The new school changed from a North American missionary school to a Canadian missionary school. The reorganized school followed a Total Communication philosophy that incorporated a coded English sign system, called Signing Exact English (Matos, 1988).

A Study of the Education for the Deaf in Puerto Rico

In 1968, the Secretary of the Public Instruction Department (PID), Dr. Angel G. Quintero-Alfaro, asked Rev. Father David Walsh to conduct a study of the education of the deaf in Puerto Rico (Comisión, 1969). At that time Father Walsh was the director of the International Catholic Association of the Deaf. As a result of his study Father Walsh made the following recommendations:

- Evaluate the St. Gabriel School

- Develop a program to prepare teachers of the deaf that would:
    Provide multiple methods of communicating with the deaf
    Develop preschool programs
    Develop programs for deaf children with multiple disabilities
    Develop adult education programs for the deaf
    Establish an audiological assessment program
- Establish new schools
- Appoint a state-wide coordinator of educational programs for the deaf

In 1969 the *Report on the Situation of People with Hearing and Speech Problems* was published (Comisión, 1969). This study established the base for public programs for the deaf in Puerto Rico. A summary of its recommendations is provided below.

1. Public and private agencies should work cooperatively to provide services for the deaf population.
2. The Medical Association, the University, the Medical School, other professionals, and the general public should become aware of the medical needs of the deaf community and provide the personnel, training, and services required to meet these needs.
3. Obtain additional financial assistance from the government in order to provide better medical assessment of deafness.
4. Seek a government mandate that would provide widespread audiological assessment.
5. Revise laws in order to permit the provision of comprehensive services for the deaf.
6. Request that the Latin American Apostolic Center establish evening academic and social programs for the deaf population.
7. Request that the government rehabilitate current facilities and supply the equipment necessary to provide

an adequate educational program for the deaf in Puerto Rico.
8. The PID should work cooperatively with the private institutions that provide educational services for the deaf.
9. The Evangelical Missionary School for the Deaf should be provided the assistance necessary to reopen the school.

Many of these recommendations have been implemented and have improved the quality of the educational services provided for the deaf in Puerto Rico. For approximately a decade, however, agencies have totally ignored other recommendations that urgently need to be implemented.

Fray Pedro Ponce De Leon School

The Fray Pedro Ponce de Leon School for the Deaf was inaugurated on October 8, 1970, at the City of Ponce (southern area), Puerto Rico. This school has become the second Catholic education center for the deaf on the island. It is an extension of St. Gabriel School for the Deaf.

This school was created to solve the need for an educational program for deaf children from the southern part of the island. Because of financial problems, the school was soon closed. The PID took over the administration of the school after it closed. The school for the deaf in Ponce then reopened.

Rafael Hernandez Elementary School Public Instruction Department

Between the years 1965 and 1969 it was estimated that there were 20,388 hearing impaired children between the ages of five and twenty-one in Puerto Rico.

Up to this time, only religious groups offered educational programs for deaf children. A proposal was written in 1969 that requested federal funds be used for the education of deaf children (Departamento, 1968). In 1971, the PID of Puerto Rico established special education classrooms for the deaf as part of the public school system. It was hoped that many of the deaf children could be mainstreamed (Departamento, 1971). The first public school with classrooms for the deaf was the Rafael Hernandez Elementary School. The school still has classes for the deaf.

Even though there has been advancement in the education of the deaf in Puerto Rico, in 1971 Father Patrick McCahill published an article that described the state of the education of the deaf in Puerto Rico as a case of national disinterest in the needs of this forgotten minority (McCahill, 1971).

Two Studies Related to the Deaf

The Pedro C. Timothee School, which was initiated by the State Vocational Rehabilitation Unit, serves as a vocational rehabilitation center for the deaf in Puerto Rico. Many deaf students have attended this center and have been rehabilitated successfully and integrated into the work force.

This center was studied by a group of students from the University of Puerto Rico (Benítez, Díaz, González, et. al., 1973). Twelve thousand and twelve deaf students who attended the center from 1968 to 1972 were interviewed. Sixty-seven percent of the individuals interviewed had jobs and thirty-three percent were unemployed.

The study revealed that with proper training deaf individuals could successfully obtain work within the community. The majority of deaf individuals in Puerto Rico receive no vocational training.

Another group of students from the University of Puerto Rico (Abreu, Arzán, Cartagena, et al., 1975) studied the rehabilitation process used with the deaf in Puerto Rico. This group studied 129 deaf individuals (66 females and 63 males) from 35 different cities on the island. They found that education for the deaf ended at the sixth grade. After the

sixth grade deaf students were integrated into regular classes for hearing children and had to wait until they were eighteen years old to receive any vocational rehabilitation services.

New Educational Organizations

The decade of the 1970s brought with it new points of view concerning the education of the deaf in Puerto Rico. The educational system was affected by federal and local laws (Vocational Act of 1973, PL94-142 Education for the Handicapped Act, Puerto Rico Special Education Act). These laws made it mandatory that basic educational services be provided for the deaf. The new laws also encouraged the formation of several advocacy groups and educational organizations. These groups are as follows:

Guayama Parents of Deaf Children Foundation

In 1973 the Guayama Parents of Deaf Children Foundation was founded. This advocacy group established a Regional School for the Deaf and Handicapped at Guayama and provided support to the deaf population of the region.

International Organization for the Orientation of the Deaf

This organization was established in 1977 to assist and support the deaf community. The group's effort was directed towards community orientation, prevention and treatment of deafness, and the education and rehabilitation of deaf individuals. In 1979 it became the first organization on the island to provide sign language courses for the deaf and the hearing populations.

Interpreter Services

In 1977 the Auxiliary Services for the Deaf Unit, which is part of the Department of Social Services, first began offering interpreter services to any deaf person seeking assistance from a public agency. Prior to the inception of this service, deaf persons had to rely on relatives and friends to provide interpreter services. For example, for many years Mr. Pedro Rodriguez, who worked at the University of Puerto Rico, served as interpreter for the deaf at the San Juan Court House.

Sign Language News

In 1978, WIPR (Government Television Network) opened a sign language news segment for the deaf. This segment was presented from 6:55 p.m. to 7:00 p.m., Monday through Friday, by Aida Luz Matos. The program is no longer transmitted. None of the local television networks currently provides signed news.

Academic Achievements of Deaf Individuals

In the late 1970s several deaf people distinguished themselves as scholars in universities in Puerto Rico, thereby breaking the barriers to higher education that had existed on the island for deaf individuals.

Antonio Rivera became the first deaf student to graduate from a private university in Puerto Rico. He graduated in 1978 with a degree in business administration. In addition to his academic prowess, Antonio distinguished himself as a member of the varsity softball team. He was the first deaf person to achieve as a student and athlete.

In 1979, Yolanda Rodríguez was admitted to the University of Puerto Rico, and in 1985 she graduated with a major in education and a minor in special education. She was the first deaf student to receive a degree from a public university in Puerto Rico.

Phase Three: 1980s to the Present

During the 1980s, Puerto Rico took the initial steps towards a truly universal educa-tional system. The decade was also the time when several educational, religious, civic, and social groups that have helped the deaf community were started. These organizations are discussed below.

Deaf Pastoral Groups

Throughout the island Catholic churches created pastoral groups for their deaf members. Eventually, Baptist and Evangelical churches created such groups for their deaf members as well. These pastoral groups have taken the lead in sign language instruction.

Deaf Club

The Deaf Club is a private organization that promotes social interaction among deaf individuals. Many of its deaf members have lived in the United States (New York, Chicago, California, Florida, or Connecticut).

Puerto Rico Association of the Deaf

The Puerto Rico Association of the Deaf was established in 1982. It provides educational, legal, and vocational services and social activities for the deaf population.

Sign Language Courses

During the 1980s higher education opportunities for the deaf at the university level were organized. Several universities now offer sign language courses. The first course was offered at the University of Puerto Rico in 1981. Interamerican University and American University of Puerto Rico also offer sign language courses as a part of their special education programs.

The University of Puerto Rico and Gallaudet University

In 1986, an agreement to establish the

Caribbean Educational Resource Center (CERC) in Puerto Rico was signed between the University of Puerto Rico and Gallaudet University. The CERC provides orientation activities, advisory services, courses, and technical assistance to other Caribbean countries attempting to initiate or improve educational programs for the deaf.

Teacher Preparation Programs

In 1986 the University of Puerto Rico created a Special Education Teacher Preparation Program and a Master's Degree Program in Special Education with an emphasis in the Education of the Deaf. Yolanda Rodríguez was accepted into the master's pro-

gram and became the first deaf student on the island to attend graduate school.

House of Representatives Project for a Public School for the Deaf

In 1987, public hearings were conducted to study the feasibility of creating a public school for the deaf. At that time the Public Instruction Department (PID) was serving 2,426 deaf and hearing impaired students. These students were attending special classes or integrated into regular classrooms. Some private institutions also provided educational services for the deaf. Some of these institutions are listed in Table 4.

Table 4. Educational Centers Providing Services to the Deaf in Puerto Rico

Institution	City	Type of School	Number of Students
St. Gabriel School	San Juan	Oral, Catholic up to 9th grade	134
Andres Grillasca School	Ponce	Total Communication	—
Evangelical School for the Deaf	Luquillo	English Total Comm. Evangelical, up to 12th grade	22
Fray Ponce de Leon School	Ponce	Total Communication	22
Rafael Hernandez School	San Juan	Elementary, Total Communication	12
Regional School for Handicapped Youth	Guayama	Pre-vocational	—
Guayama Foundation for Deaf Children	Guayama	Elementary, Total Communication	18
Domenech Education Foundation, Inc.	Carolina	——	2
University Hospital at the Medical Center	San Juan	Preschool	—
Deaf Children Project, University of Puerto Rico	San Juan	Preschool, Total Communication	10

Different advocacy groups were polled for their ideas concerning the creation of a public school for the deaf. All parties involved, including parents, educators, and students, presented their positions. No consensus could be reached concerning the proposed structure, philosophy, and location of the school. These conflicting points of view led to an impasse. A bill put forth in the legislature to create a new public school for the deaf was not approved.

Postsecondary Study

Colleges, universities, and technical schools were also assessed in the House of Representatives study to identify which services they were providing deaf individuals. It was discovered that during the 1980s, deaf students had been enrolled in programs at the University of Puerto Rico, Interamerican University, Technological Commerical Institute, Puerto Rico Junior College, Cupey Technological Institute, Metropolitan University College, and Ramirez Business College. A total of 28 deaf students had been admitted to these institutions of higher education. Fourteen of the students later dropped out of their respective institutions of higher education, and eight students continued on until they successfully completed their programs. Students who left the island and continued their higher education studies elsewhere were not considered in the House of Representatives study.

State Research Conferences on the Education of the Deaf

In 1988 and 1989, the University of Puerto Rico held conferences that focussed on the education of the deaf. These conferences became the first forum on the island to discuss current research findings in the field. Educators from several different institutions have attended these conferences to share experiences and to improve their knowledge.

First Book on Puerto Rican Sign Language

Deaf Puerto Ricans have used sign language since the establishment of the first school. Puerto Rican Sign Language is mainly a mixture of American Sign Language and Creole signs, with some influence from Spanish Sign Language, Gestuno, Canadian Sign Language, and the Signing Exact English form of signed English.

In 1988, Aida Luz Matos published the first Puerto Rican sign language book. With the help of teachers, interpreters, and deaf individuals, she compiled a book that contains 1200 signs. Each sign is stated in Spanish and in English. This book has been used in sign classes offered by the PID and the universities.

Conclusion

Educational services for the deaf in Puerto Rico are still in the developmental stage. Many advancements are still needed in order to provide an adequate educational system for deaf children in Puerto Rico.

Although the struggle to achieve a quality educational system has often led to a feeling of helplessness and to declining motivation, hope is eternal, and teachers, parents, and students continue to look positively towards the future. We have not yet reached our goal of readily available quality educational services for the deaf in Puerto Rico, but this historical account indicates that much progress has been made.

Appendix:

Historical Events in the Education of the Deaf in Puerto Rico
(Compiled from Rodríguez & Albárran, 1989)

1902   ♦ (November 29): Sacred Heart Missionaries come to Puerto Rico from Maryland to start a school

1903   ♦ School for the Deaf starts at Aguadilla
       ♦ Aguadilla school closes and the students transfer
       ♦ Schools are opened at Cayey and San Juan

1910   ♦ Cayey School closes
       ♦ School Asylum for the the Deaf and Mute is established
       ♦ Cayey School moves to Santurce
1913   ♦ Planning for the Saint Gabriel School for the Deaf is started
1915   ♦ The Saint Gabriel School for the Deaf opens

1944   ♦ The first and only census related to the deaf is initiated
1947   ♦ Puerto Rico Vocational Rehabilitation Law is signed
1948   ♦ Labor Department publishes the results of the census of the deaf

1955   ♦ Sacred Heart Missionaries plan to close St. Gabriel School for the Deaf
       ♦ Monsignor James Davis invites Franciscan Sisters to work with the deaf community
1956   ♦ (October 2): Four Franciscan Sisters (two from Spain and two from Chile) arrive at Saint Gabriel School for the Deaf
       ♦ English sign language method of teaching the deaf is changed to the Spanish oral method
1957   ♦ The Rotary Club donates an amplification system to the St. Gabriel School
       ♦ Evangelical missionaries come from Jamaica
       ♦ Evangelical School for the Deaf is established at a farm in Luquillo

1960   ♦ Deaf students and nuns visit Washington, D.C.
       ♦ Governor Luis Muñoz Marín signs a law that allows the acquisition of the land for the new St. Gabriel School for the Deaf
1962   ♦ The land where "The City of Silence" is to be constructed, is blessed
1965   ♦ (January 31): The new St. Gabriel School is inaugurated
1968   ♦ Public Instruction Department develops proposal to serve the deaf community
1969   ♦ Governor's Commission Study on the education of the deaf is concluded

1970   ♦ (October 18): Fray Pedro Ponce de Leon School is inaugurated at Ponce, Puerto Rico
1971   ♦ Public Instruction Department provides special education for deaf students
       ♦ Rafael Hernandez School at Rio Piedras is the first public school with special education for the deaf
       ♦ Father Patrick McCahill visits the island and publishes an article that profiles the critical needs of the deaf community. He concludes that the community at large is disinterested and that the deaf are a forgotten minority
1973   ♦ Guayama Parents of Deaf Children Foundation is established

1975 ◆ A master's thesis concerning the education and rehabilitation of the deaf is completed at the University of Puerto Rico, Río Piedras
1977 ◆ An Auxiliary Services Unit for the Deaf that provides interpreter services is created
     ◆ Oidos (means "ears" in Spanish) *Organizacion Internacional de Orientacion de la Sordera* (International Organization on Deafness) is founded
1978 ◆ Public Broadcasting Television network starts a signed news program
     ◆ Antonio Rivera becomes the first deaf male to graduate from a private university in Puerto Rico. He receives an undergraduate degree in Business Administration from Interamerican University, San German, Puerto Rico
     ◆ The First Regional School for the Deaf and Handicapped is opened at Guayama

1982 ◆ Puerto Rico Deaf Association, Inc. is founded
1985 ◆ Yolanda Rodríguez becomes the first deaf female to graduate from a state university in Puerto Rico. She receives an undergraduate degree in Special Education from the University of Puerto Rico, Río Piedras, Puerto Rico
1986 ◆ First program to prepare teachers of the deaf is instituted at the graduate level at the University of Puerto Rico
     ◆ University of Puerto Rico and Gallaudet University establish the Caribbean Center on Education Resources in Puerto Rico
1987 ◆ Puerto Rico Interpreters Association, Inc. is founded
     ◆ Assistant Secretariat for Adapted Recreation of the Department of Recreation and Sports starts providing recreation and leisure services for the deaf
     ◆ Program for preschool-aged deaf children is established at the University of Puerto Ric
1988 ◆ Creation of the first Public School for the Deaf is proposed
     ◆ First National Conference on Puerto Rican Education of the Deaf is held
     ◆ First Deaf Sports Encounter is conducted by Department of Recreation and Sports
     ◆ Yolanda Rodríguez is accepted into the master's program in Special Education at the University of Puerto Rico
1989 ◆ Second National Conference on Puerto Rican Education of the Deaf is held
     ◆ Second Deaf Sports Encounter sponsored by the Department of Recreation and Sports is held

---

Endnotes

1. Native population that lived in Puerto Rico when Christopher Columbus discovered the island in 1492 and mistakenly called them Indians.

2. Puerto Rico is the name that the island became known as after its colonization by the Spaniards. The island used to be called Borinquen in Taino language, which means "land where the sun rises." At one time the island was called San Juan Bautista (Saint John Baptist) and the capital was Puerto Rico (Rich Port), but the Spanish government switched the names of the capital and the island.

3. Deaf people were referred to as deaf-mutes (sordo-mudos).

References

Abreu, S.R., Arzán, C., Cartagena, C.L., et al. (1975). *La rehabilitación de sordo (tesis)*. Río Piedras, Puerto Rico: Universidad de Puerto Rico.

Alcover-Serres, E. (1979). *Singladuras: Historia de la Congregación de Religiosas Terciarias Franciscanas de la Inmaculada*. Valencia, España.

Arillaga-Torrens, R. (1985). Enfermedades enel Nuevo Mundo al principio de la colonización. In L. Moran Arce, *Historia de Puerto Rico*. San Juan, Puerto Rico: Librotex.

Benítez, O. M., Díaz, L. M., Gonz·lez, J., et al. (1973). *Factores asociados al empleo de personas sordas (tesis)*. Río Piedras, Puerto Rico: Universidad de Puerto Rico.

Best, H. (1943). *Deafness and the deaf in the United States*. New York: Macmillan.

Brau, S. (1966). *La colonización de Puerto Rico*. San Juan, Puerto Rico: Instituto de Cultura Puertorriquena.

Braumbaugh, M. (1904, 1985). Lake Monok Conference of Friends of the Indian and Other Dependent People. In A. Lopez Yusto, *Historia documental de la educacion en Puerto Rico (1503–1970)*. Puerto Rico: Sanders.

Bugden, B. M. (Ed.). (1987). Mission Helpers of the Sacred Heart. *Listening, X* (3), National Catholic Office of the Deaf.

Casanova, S.A. (1986, 1987). Historia del audioimpedido en Puerto Rico. In D.G. Matos Figueroa, *La seleccion vocacional de la poblacion audioimpedida en Puerto Rico (Tesina)*. Río Piedras, Puerto Rico: Universidad de Puerto Rico.

Comisión del Governador para el Estudio sobre Rehabilitación de Lisiados. (1969). *Informe sobre el comite a cargo de las personas con problemas de habla y en audición*. Río Piedras, Puerto Rico: Departamento de Servicios Sociales.

Cuesta-Mendoza, A. (1946). *Historia de la educación en el Puerto Rico colonial: Vol 1.* (2nd ed.) Mexico, D.F., Mexico: Impreso Manuel León S·nchez, S.C.L.

De Jésus, F. (1988). *Breve historia de la pastoral catolica de sordos en San Juan*. Conferencia, Colegio San Gabriel.

De las Casas, B. (1985). *Historia de las Indias:* Vol. III. Santo Domingo, República Dominicana: Alfa & Omega.

Departamento de Instrucción Pública. (1968). *Propuesta del programa de educación especial para niños sordos y con problemas de audición*. San Juan, Puerto Rico.

Departamento de Instrucción Pública. (1971). *Programa de educación especial para los grupos de estudiantes sordos*. San Juan, Puerto Rico.

Departamento de Instrucción Pública. (1987). *Plan estatal de educación especial para los años 1988–90*. San Juan, Puerto Rico.

Departamento del Trabajo de Puerto Rico. (1948). *Censo de ciegos, mudos, sordos y psicóticos en Puerto Rico, 1944*. San Juan, Puerto Rico.

Gannon, J.R. (1981). *Deaf heritage: A narrative history of deaf America*. Silver Spring, MD: National Association of the Deaf.

López, Yusto, A. (1985). *Historia documental de la educación en Puerto Rico, 1503–1970*. Puerto Rico: Sanders.

Matos, A.L. (1988). *Aprende señas conmigo: Lenguaje de señas en Español-Engles* [Sign language in English-Spanish]. San Juan, Puerto Rico: Editorial Raices.

McCahill, P. (1971). A case of disinterest: The deaf in Puerto Rico. *American Annals of the Deaf*.

Moran-Arce, L. (1985). *Historia de Puerto Rico*. San Juan, Puerto Rico: Librotex.

Periodico R. Mundo. (1960, Julio 16). Gobernador Firma Ley, Venderan Parcela Gobiernoa Colegio Niños Sordomudos. San Juan, Puerto Rico.

Rawlings, R. (1988). *Comunicación personal*. Hato Rey, Puerto Rico.

Rawlings, R. (1989). *Comunicación personal*. San Juan, Puerto Rico.

Resolución de la Cámara 853. (1987). Informe Conjuntoa la Camara de Representantes para la Creación de una Escuela para Niños Sordos. San Juan, Puerto Rico.

Rodríguez, Y., & Albarrán, M.A. (1989). *Historical events of deaf education in Puerto Rico*. Paper presented at The Deaf Way Conference, Gallaudet University, Washington, D.C.

Saliva-González, R.L. (1988). *Breve historia de la educacion del sordo en Puerto Rico*. Conferencia dictada en la Universidad de Puerto Rico, Hoja mimeografiada; Río Piedras, Puerto Rico.

Saliva-González, R.L. (1989, Jan-Feb). Pastoral de sordos en Puerto Rico. *Listening, XI* (6), National Catholic Office of the Deaf.

Sister Xavier Mary of St. Hubert. (1983, May-June). *Listening, VI* (3). National Catholic Office for the Deaf.

Universidad de Puerto Rico. (1988). *Programa de la Primera Conferencia Estatal de Investigación en Torno a la Educación del Sordo Puertorriqueño*. Río Piedras, Puerto Rico.

Universidad de Puerto Rico. (1989). *Programa de la Segunda Conferencia Estatal de Investigación en Torno a la Educación del Sordo Puertorriqueño*. Río Piedras, Puerto Rico.

The Extent and Kind of Educational Services for the Deaf in Saudi Arabia

by
Zaid Abdullah Al-Muslat, Ed.D.
General Secretary of Special Education
in the Ministry of Education, Riyadh, Saudi Arabia

Introduction

The focus of this paper will be on the education offered deaf individuals in the Kingdom of Saudi Arabia. The education of the deaf from its inception to the present day will be examined.

The basic principles of education in Saudi Arabia were initiated through the Educational Policy developed in 1970. This policy is the cornerstone of the development of a formal educational system in the Kingdom of Saudi Arabia. The Education Policy paper declared a special concern for the education of handicapped and gifted pupils. Since the Policy called for the creation of special programs to meet the needs of exceptional students, institutes for the education of the deaf have developed and spread throughout the country. These institutes for the education of the deaf are under the direction of the Ministry of Education.

This paper presents information about the educational development and services for the deaf and hard of hearing that exist in the country. The various supportive social and medical services provided to the deaf by the Kingdom will also be discussed. Attention will be given to the current situation and to the development of programs and institutes that reflect the latest in methodology and technology.

The concluding section looks at new issues and trends aimed at improving educational programs for the deaf in the institutes and in other types of educational settings. Scientific research aimed at determining the primary causes of hearing loss in Saudi Arabia is discussed.

Basic Principles

Educational Policy

The unification of the Kingdom of Saudi Arabia that was achieved by King Abdulaziz in 1932 paved the way for the Kingdom's concern for education. Perhaps it goes without saying that the aggressive and progressive approach taken by the government in building educational programs has been the single most important factor that has contributed to new and innovative developments.

As is true of all citizens in Saudi Arabia, the handicapped are part of our society and have rights and duties according to their capabilities. The government's deeply rooted belief that education is for everyone has enhanced the availability of educational opportunities for all handicapped persons, including the deaf.

The process of the development of educational policy in Saudi Arabia has identified three principles:

1. The Philosophy of Education springs from Islam. From Islam the nation has formulated the system of government, laws, and morals that govern its way of life.
2. The State provides free education of all types and at all levels for the citizens and residents of the country. The State establishes schools and pays the salaries of all teachers and personnel who work in the schools. All necessary materials are also purchased by the Ministry of Education.
3. The springboard to the full utilization of all of the State's resources is the development of manpower through education. The budget for education is increased by the State in accordance with the growing educational needs of the country.

In addition, several of the articles included in the Educational Policy of 1970 concerned the education of sensory, physically, and mentally handicapped individuals. The Policy indicated that diversified educational and training opportunities be set up to meet the needs of handicapped persons. An evaluation plan was to be established to assess whether or not all branches of special education have achieved their objectives. This evaluation plan would also include institutions for the deaf and hard of hearing. Several agencies now share the responsibility for these assessment, evaluation, and follow-up activities.

Governmental Agencies

A Handicapped Services Coordination Committee organizes the work of three Ministries involved in special education. Each Ministry is in charge of certain programs for different handicapped groups. These agencies are:

1. The Ministry of Education, which provides educational programs to different types of handicapped children and youth who are educable and of school age. The Secretariat-General of Special Education is in charge of these educational programs and supplies the social, technical, and welfare needs.
2. The Ministry of Labour and Social Affairs provides training and rehabilitation programs for the deaf and hard of hearing who are beyond school age. In addition, welfare programs are set up to serve children through adults who possess multiple and severe disabilities.
3. The Ministry of Health provides physical rehabilitation programs that require medical, psychological, and consulting services. Many hospitals have started audiological, speech and hearing, and physical therapy clinics.

Other Governmental agencies provide additional services. The Civil Services Bureau, for example, has a special office that is charged with the responsibility of finding employment opportunities for the handicapped with different agencies of the government.

The General Presidency of Youth Welfare provides sporting activities and recreational opportunities for the handicapped. A special club for the deaf was established in 1980. Different types of cultural, social, and sporting activities are available to deaf people at the club for the deaf. The club competes with non-deaf clubs in different sporting areas and is furnished and supported financially by the General Presidency of Youth Welfare. One of the activities supported is an annual week-long Olympics. During the Special Olympics handicapped persons compete against each other. All handicapped individuals are encouraged to become involved and to interact with society.

King Saud University has organized two important programs during the last few years. The first program, housed at the College of Education, is designed to prepare special education teachers. The second program, conducted at the College of Applied Medical Science, was established to prepare audiologists and speech and hearing specialists.

Development of the Education of the Deaf
Establishment of the Al-Amal (Hope) Institutes

The first two institutes for the education of the deaf and hard of hearing were established in 1964; one for boys and another one for girls. Only a small number of pupils (16 boys and 25 girls) were enrolled during the school's first year of existence. When the idea of teaching the deaf was first introduced, a number of educators expressed serious concern and apprehension. However, efforts by the government to raise public awareness about the potential of the deaf have succeeded. The parents of the deaf and hard of hearing children responded positively to this bold new step. By 1991 several hundred deaf and hard of hearing pupils were enrolled in these two institutes. In addition, many other institutes have been opened in different educational regions of the country. The total enrollment of deaf persons during the 1991 school year was 2,526 pupils. See Figure 1 for the location of schools for the deaf in Saudi Arabia.

Figure 1: Geographic Distribution of Institutes for the Deaf, 1991

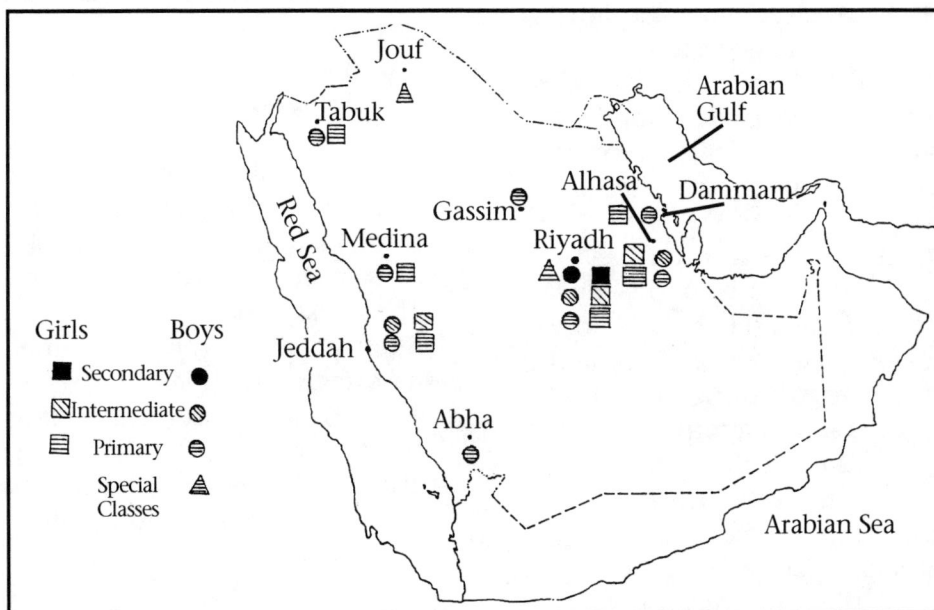

Conditions for Admission to the Hope Institutes

According to the Directorate of Special Education (1981), a child has to meet the following requirements in order to be admitted to Al-Amal Institutes:

1. The child has to be completely or partially deaf.
2. An applicant's intelligence quotient should not be less than 70.
3. He or she should have no other handicapping condition that may prevent him or her from profiting from the use of the educational services of the Al-Amal Institutes.
4. He or she should not be less than four years of age.
5. He or she has to be a Saudi citizen, or have legal residency (applied in 1991).

Administrative Development

An administrative unit called the Special Education Directorate was founded in the Ministry of Education to enhance the development of the education of the deaf and hard of hearing. The aim of the Special Education Directorate is to prepare, administer, and monitor program progress and effectiveness. It is the aim of the Special Education Directorate that the educational programs developed should be specially designed to meet the needs of the deaf and hard of hearing and to ensure that these children become independent citizens who can help serve in the development of their community and country.

The administrative unit promotes the institutes for the deaf, measures their results, and assists their employees to become more efficient and productive workers. The functions of the administrative unit are detailed in the *Directory of Special Education* (General Directorate of Special Education, 1981) and are as follows:

1. To participate in the implementation of the general goals and objectives of the General Secretariat and its areas of specialization.
2. To supervise the Hope Institutes and to follow up on the educational development of the institutes through organized visits to these institutes during each academic semester. To formulate reports about the progress of the institutes that are

shared with the educational districts, with the goal of developing solutions to any problems uncovered.

3. To develop special curricula and select textbooks that are suitable for the deaf and hard of hearing. To continuously re-evaluate the curricula and textbooks selected.

4. To participate in and encourage research studies related to the education of the deaf and hard of hearing.

5. To seek new methods of teaching the deaf and hard of hearing students and to share the information with the Hope Institute, with the goal of improving the level of teacher performance.

6. To participate jointly with the Inservice Education Department in planning workshops and courses.

7. To study the schools for the deaf's yearly need for teachers, other personnel, instructional materials, and equipment. To assess the adequacy of existing dormitory facilities.

8. To make plans for sports, recreational, and social activities in each institute and to provide follow-up on the implementation of these plans.

9. To maintain effective communication with related departments in order to exchange ideas, experiences, and information applicable to the improvement of the education of the deaf.

10. participate in public awareness activities that provide information about the abilities of the deaf to study and work successfully.

11. To suggest new programs and institutes that coincide with the government's current five-year plan and that will play a strategic role in the national development of the Kingdom.

Educational Stages and Weekly Study Plans

In Saudi Arabia there is no difference between the schools for the deaf and the public schools in terms of the number, days, and length of lessons arranged in the weekly study plan. In general, schools are open five days a week, Saturday through Wednesday. The weekly study plan includes 30 lessons (six lessons daily) at the preparatory and elementary stages. Each lesson lasts for 45 minutes. A 30-minute snack break is provided after the third lesson. According to regulations, the class size for deaf and hard of hearing people is between five and ten pupils.

There are five educational stages at the institutes for the deaf. These stages are as follows:

1. Kindergarten and Preparatory Stage

During the kindergarten and preparatory stages, deaf boys and girls between the age of four and six attend the Hope Institute for Girls and complete a special curriculum. The purpose of this stage is to prepare the deaf students for the elementary level. The curriculum in this stage concentrates on developing all aspects of the child's language, including his or her residual hearing and speech. In addition, a simple academic program is presented that includes speech therapy, written and read Arabic, science, mathematics, physical education, and art. Play therapy is commonly used. At the Al-Amal Schools and the Institutes for Boys, this stage is shortened to one school year for those from the ages of six to fifteen. See Table 1 for an analysis of the kinds of classes required in the preparatory and elementary stages.

2. Elementary Education Stage

At this level, male and female pupils study in separate schools for six years. This stage includes a special curriculum modified from the regular public school curriculum to suit the needs of deaf children. Special

Table 1. Weekly Study Plan for Al-Amal Elementary Institutes

	Preparatory	1st	2nd	3rd	4th	5th	6th
				Grade			
Islamic Education	3	3	3	3	6	6	6
Arabic Language:							
Hearing and Speech Therapy	4	4	4	3	2	1	1
Reading	4	5	5	4	2	2	2
Writing and Handwriting	2	4	3	2	1	1	1
Composition	-	-	1	2	2	2	2
Dictation	-	-	-	2	1	1	1
Grammar	-	-	-	-	2	2	2
Total	10	13	13	13	10	9	9
Mathematics	5	6	6	6	5	6	6
Geography	-	-	-	-	1	1	1
History	-	-	-	-	1	1	1
Sciences	2	2	2	2	2	2	2
Total	7	8	8	8	9	10	10
		B. G.	B. G.	B. G.	B. G.	B. G.	B. G.
Art Education	5	3 3	3 3	3 3	3 2	3 2	3 2
House Keeping	-	- -	- -	- -	- 1	- 2	- 2
Physical Education	5	3 3	3 3	3 3	2 2	2 1	2 1
Total	10	6	6	6	5	5	5
Grand Total	30	30	30	30	30	30	30

attention is given to areas such as speech development, the development of residual hearing, the use of hearing aids, and speechreading. Speechreading is considered to be the most important means of communication between deaf and hearing children. See Table 1, the weekly study plan, for more details about the subjects taught at this stage.

3. Intermediate Vocational Education Stage

Pupils at this stage are engaged in a three-year program that includes the following theoretical and vocational subjects: Islamic Education, Arabic language, science, mathematics, physical education, and social studies. Vocational education comprises almost one-third of the weekly educational plan (32 lessons per week).

Boys study typing on the Arabic typewriter, photocopying, printing, and electrical technology. The girls study typing, tailoring, and manual and machine trades. Table 2, the weekly study plan for intermediate vocational institutes for the deaf, shows the training offered to students at the intermediate stage.

Table 2. Weekly Study Plan, Al-Amal Vocational Intermediate Institutes

Subjects	Hours/Week per Grade		
	First	Second	Third
Islamic Education	3	3	3
Arabic Language	5	5	5
English Language	3	3	3
Mathematics	4	4	4
Social Studies	2	2	2
Health and Industrial Security	1	1	1
Art Education or Housekeeping (G)	1	1	1
Physical Education	2	1	1
Vocational Rules and Theories	1	2	2
Vocational Major (Field Work)	10	10	10
Total Number of Hours of Instruction	32	32	32

4. Special Vocational Training Program for Adults

A vocational training program for adults who missed the opportunity to be educated during their childhood (twelve years or older) has been developed. The program is located at the intermediate institutes. By 1991, 85 adults had completed this program. Table 3 shows the number of graduates from the intermediate program between 1975 and 1991. The Ministry of Labor and Social Affairs has established vocational rehabilitation centers for the handicapped in three cities, Riyadh, Taif, and Dammam. More than 300 deaf and hard of hearing adults have graduated from these centers. To avoid duplication of educational services, in the future these centers will service persons above the age of fifteen. Pupils below the age of fifteen will be accepted at institutes offering the elementary stage.

Table 3. Graduates from Vocational Section of Intermediate Institute for the Deaf in Riyadh, 1975–1991

School Year	1975	1976	1979	1980	1981	1983	1985	1986	1990	1991	Total
Number of Graduates	5	9	5	2	2	4	2	2	9	6	46

5. Secondary Education Stage

The secondary education stage was started in 1988 for boys only. The secondary stage for girls began in 1990. This stage includes a three-year school program that contains a theoretical and vocational curriculum. Some of the vocational areas of specialization were extended from the intermediate stage and others are new. The new areas include work in secretarial science as a library assistant, and in computer science. Table 4 shows a weekly study plan at the secondary stage.

Eighty-two percent of the deaf and hard of hearing pupils are enrolled in the preparatory and elementary stage. The vocational intermediate stage enrolls sixteen percent, and only two percent are enrolled in the secondary stage.

Table 4. Weekly Study Plan for Al-Amal Tech. Secondary Institutes

Subjects	Hours/Week per Grade		
	First	Second	Third
Islamic Education	5	3	3
Arabic Language	10	7	7
English Language	5	3	3
Mathematics	3	3	3
Social Studies	2	2	3
Pysical Education (Boys) or Domestic Education (Girls)	2	2	2
Technical Major	5	12	12
Total Number of Hours of Instruction	32	32	32

Building Facilities and Equipment

Building Facilities

The provision of adequate facilities and equipment to ensure a sound educational program for deaf and hard of hearing students is a high government priority.

To achieve this goal, large plots of land were reserved (about 50,000 square meters) for each institute for the deaf in Saudi Arabia. On each site the following facilities were built:
- an academic unit
- a residential unit (dormitory)
- an open Olympic-size swimming pool and closed gymnasium for sports and multi-purpose activities
- a health clinic
- a dining hall and kitchen

The buildings at each Institute for the Deaf have central air-conditioning and are designed to accommodate up to 300 residents.

The first two modern institutes were completed in Jeddah in 1980.

Six institutes following the plan detailed above have been completed (two in Riyadh, two in Jeddah (the Western Province), and two in Alhasa (Hofuf). The cost of these six projects totaled of more than 66 million dollars. The intermediate and secondary institutes for the deaf required special designs because of the vocational education programs.

Audio Equipment and Hearing Aids

The Ministry of Education, represented by the General Secretariat of Special Education, provides the latest audio-visual aids and assistive equipment to all Al-Amal Institutes.

Important equipment available at Al-Amal Institutes includes:

- Audiometers to measure hearing
- Individual hearing aids of three types: body aids, behind the ear aids, and eyeglass aids
- Group amplification equipment for each classroom. The sound and speech are transmitted between the teacher and the student and between the student and his or her peers.
- Audio-loop system for magnifying the sounds inside the classroom
- Equipment for speech training and audio-visual materials

Speech and Hearing Centers

Upon the approval of the Minister of Education, the first speech and hearing center was started in 1987 as a part of the Al-Amal Elementary Institute for the Deaf in Riyadh. An ear, nose, and throat specialist who also has a diploma in speech therapy was appointed to the staff of the institute. Speech therapists were also appointed to the Al-Amal Institute and the institutes for the mentally retarded. Pupils at the regular public schools who have speech and/or hearing problems are referred to these specialists at the center. Later, two speech and hearing centers were

opened in Jeddah, one for boys and one for girls. The purposes of these centers are:

1. To provide inservice education for teachers and personnel at the institutes for the deaf in the following areas: hearing diagnosis, the use of devices for speech therapy, the use of hearing aids, information about deafness, current methodology and classroom management, and the correct use of hearing assessment and amplification equipment in the classroom. These centers also work to increase public awareness about deafness and to educate new personnel, parents, and others about deafness.
2. To make ear molds for pupils who need individual hearing aids.
3. To hold and participate in seminars for and with related agencies.
4. To prepare a program to ensure that all pupils who need speech therapy in an educational region will receive the services of a speech therapist. To supervise the work of the speech therapists.
5. To provide an annual medical diagnosis of the condition of each deaf child's ears, nose, and throat. To provide those children who are referred to the centers with proper medical treatment and refer the difficult cases to the appropriate hospital.
6. To provide an assurance that the hearing level of all of deaf and hard of hearing children is measured and that the school staff is aware of the hearing status of each child.
7. To provide the results of each childís audiological assessment to his or her teachers, with recommendations for treatment.
8. To prepare evening programs for students enrolled in the public schools of an educational region who need special therapy.
9. To prepare work formats and written reports to the Secretary General of Special Education.

10. To complete field work studies on the causes of deafness and speech defects in order to develop adequate treatment plans and solutions to existing problems.

Statistical Analysis of the Present Situation

The Al-Amal Institutes for the Deaf and day schools for the deaf have been growing rapidly, especially during the 1980s. In 1964, when the first two institutes were opened in the Riyadh, there were only 41 deaf boys and girls enrolled. At present there are 2,526 deaf and hard of hearing pupils registered in the 23 educational programs for the deaf. Seven of them are located in Riyadh itself. The Riyadh area is the largest educational district in the country and enrolls 928, or more than one-third of the pupils enrolled in schools for the deaf. Of the 928 deaf pupils, 568 are boys and 360 are girls. Table 5 illustrates enrollment figures, as well as the number of pupils who are male and female, residents and non-residents.

Table 5. Pupils in Residential Institutes and Non-Residential Settings, 1991

Sex	No. of Resid.	No. of Non-Resid.	Total of Pupils	% of Resid.
Girls	257	711	968	26.5%
Boys	561	997	1558	36.0%
Total	818	1708	2526	32.4%
% of Girls	31.4%	41.6%	38.3%	

Furthermore, educational programs for deaf and hard of hearing students involving 278 classrooms are distributed throughout the nine educational regions in Saudi Arabia. Almost two-thirds of the population enrolled in classes for the deaf are boys. It is interesting to note that the institutes for girls who are deaf had more pupils than did the institutes for boys during their first six years of existence. Later, the number of boys exceeded the

number of girls. The situation continues up to the present. Figure 2 shows the percentage of deaf pupils according to educational level. Figure 3 shows the growth in classes. Figure 4 shows the difference in number of boys and girls from 1964 to 1990.

Figure 2. Percentage of Deaf Pupils According to Educational Level, 1991

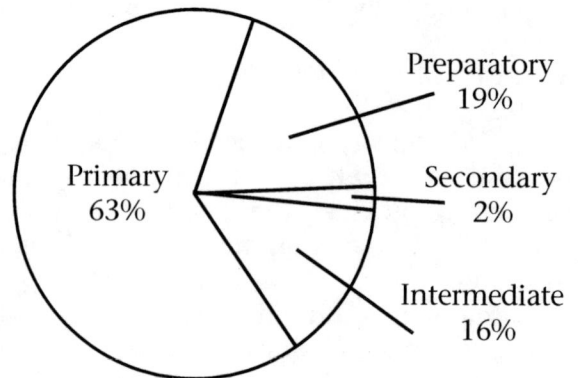

Figure 3. Growth in Number of Classes, 1970–1990

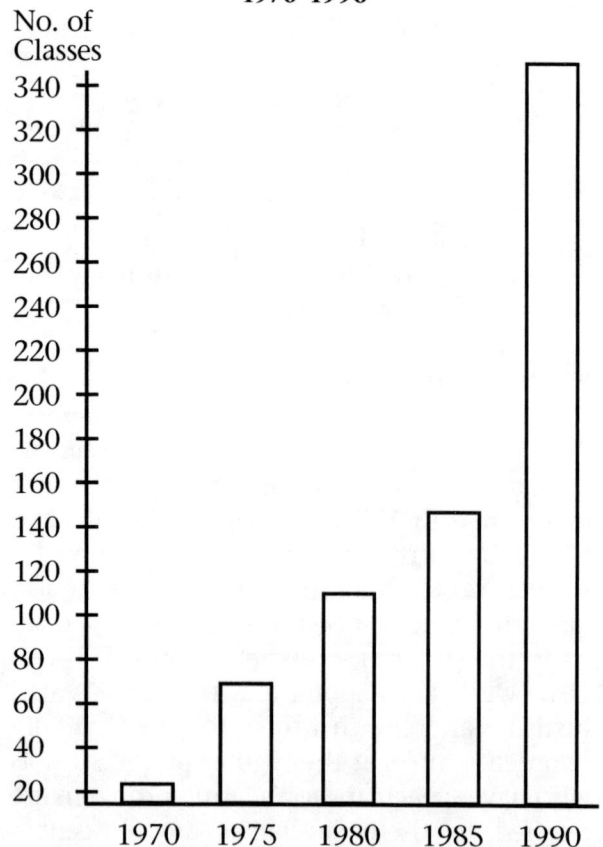

Figure 4. Number of Classes at the Institutes for the Deaf, 1991

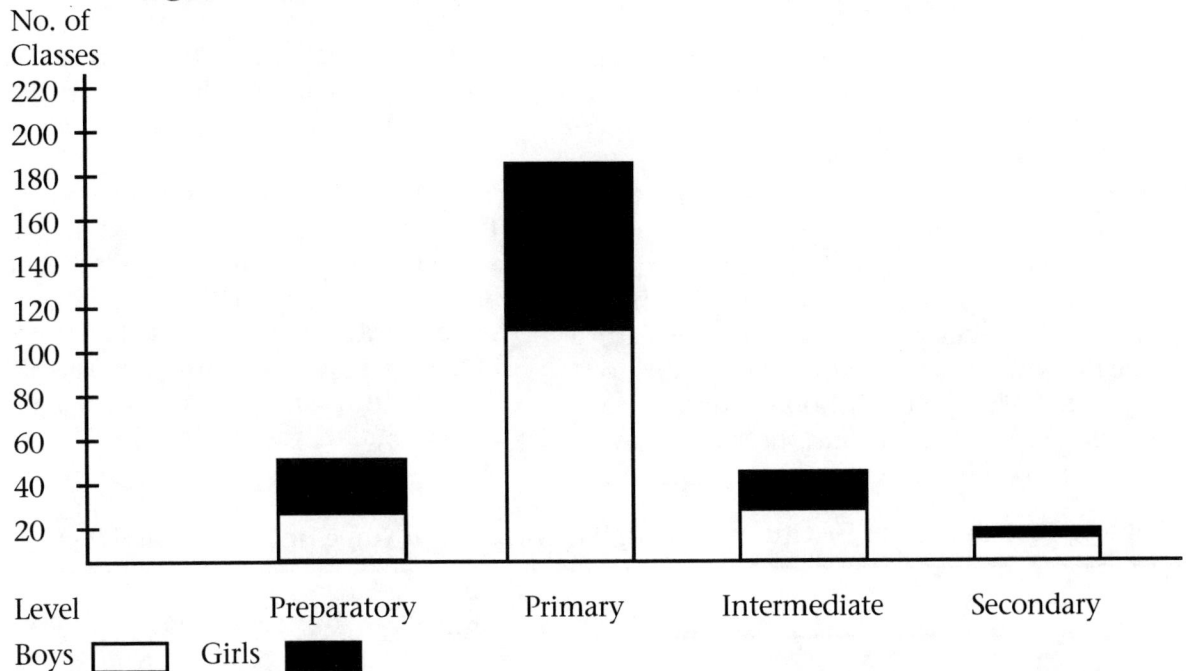

No. of
Classes

```
220
200
180
160
140
120
100
 80
 60
 40
 20
```

Level   Preparatory   Primary   Intermediate   Secondary

Boys ☐   Girls ■

Distribution of Services Across the Country

There are four types of educational options available for deaf students in the several regions: (1) residential institutes, (2) day schools, (3) special classes, and (4) evening classes. See the map earlier in the chapter for the distribution of the programs across the Kingdom of Saudi Arabia.

Residential Institutes

Most of the educational programs for deaf students in Saudi Arabia have dormitories in order that children from outside of the cities can be accommodated. Deaf children from inside the cities commute to the school daily. The residential institutes for girls found in large cities such as Riyadh, Jeddah, and Alhasa include the preparatory, elementary, and intermediate stages of education. The girls' institute located in Medina contains only the kindergarten, preparatory, and elementary stages. There are nine residential institutes for boys distributed among six

regions. More than one-third of the total number of deaf boys (36 percent) live at the institutes. About one-fourth (26.5 percent) of the deaf girls live at a residential institute.

These institutes have special health care, social, recreational, and physical education services. Deaf pupils enjoy all services free of charge.

Day Schools

Day schools for the deaf are a recent addition to the educational services for the deaf. These day schools started about fifteen years ago. Day school pupils commute between home and school each day. There are four day schools for boys and girls who are deaf. Two of the day schools are in Tabuk and two are in Dammam. The deaf and hard of hearing children in the day schools study the same curricula as do the children at the residential schools. There are 152 deaf boys and 137 girls attending these day schools.

Special Classes at Regular Elementary Schools

There are two kinds of new programs located at regular elementary schools. The first is for children who are hard of hearing and children who have speech difficulties. It is located in Riyadh. The pupils with hearing and speech difficulties attend a regular elementary school for boys. There are 58 deaf pupils who occupy five classrooms. As much as possible, the regular curriculum is followed. Some of these children have later been able to return to their original schools. Those who require special help remain in the special class until their speech problems are overcome and they have regained confidence in themselves. If a deaf student cannot profit from a special class, a special committee may recommend that he or she be enrolled at Al-Amal Institute for the Deaf in Riyadh and attend as a day student.

A second kind of program was opened in 1990–1991. It is a special class for eight deaf students enrolled in a regular elementary school in Al Jouf. This program utilizes the same curriculum that is used at the Al-Amal Institutes. More information and statistical data about the nine regions that have special class programs are provided in Table 6.

Table 6. **Distribution of Institutes and Pupils According to Stages in Educational Districts, 1991**

| District | Sex | Element. & Pre. | | Intermediate | | Second. | | Total |
		No. Inst.	No. Pupils	No. Inst.	No. Pupils	No. Inst.	No. Pupils	No. Inst.	No. Pupils
Riyadh	B	2	369	1	103	1	96	4	568
	G	1	266	1	65	1	29	3	360
		3	635	2	168	2	125	7	928
Western	B	1	337	1	122			2	459
	G	1	270	1	45			2	315
		2	607	2	167			4	774
Eastern	B	1	90					1	90
	G	1	85					1	85
		2	175					2	175
Al Hasa	B	1	75	1	42			2	117
	G	1	84	1	25			2	109
		2	159	2	67			4	226
Medina	B	1	65					1	65
	G	1	47					1	47
		2	112					2	112
Tabuk	B	1	62					1	62
	G	1	52					1	52
		2	114					2	114
Gassim	B	1	61					1	61
Abha	B	1	128					1	128
Jouf	B	Class	8					Cl.	8
Total	B	9	1195	3	267	1	96	13	1558
	G	6	884	3	135	1	29	10	968
		15	1999	6	402	2	125	23	2526

Evening Classes

Table 7 indicates that there are two educational programs offered in the evening for deaf adults. One is located in Riyadh and the other is at the Gassim Al-Amal Institute. The deaf adults of Saudi Arabia are benefiting from the evening programs.

Table 7. Evening Classes, 1991
Location of Institute

	No. of Classes	No. of Pupils
Riyadh	2	18
Gassim	2	22
Total	4	40

Comparison of the Deaf to Other Handicapped Children

In 1960, blind children became the first category of handicapped children to be provided educational services in Saudi Arabia. Educational programs for the deaf followed in 1964, and programs for the educable mentally retarded began in 1970. In 1970, blind children made up 81.4 percent of the handicapped children served. In 1975, 33.8 percent of the children served were deaf, 54.2 percent were blind, and 12 percent were mentally retarded. By 1980, the number of deaf children served reached 46.3 percent of the total, compared to 30.6 percent who were blind and 23.1 percent who were educable mentally retarded. In 1985, 61.3 percent of the handicapped students served were deaf, followed by the EMR (23.1 percent) and the blind (15.6 percent).

This pattern has continued with minor changes in the percentages for each disabled group. The percentage of the total number of handicapped children in each category in 1990 was as follows: deaf, 51 percent; mentally retarded, 37 percent; blind, 12 percent. See Figure 5 for the enrollment picture from 1965 to 1990.

Figure 5. Comparison of Deaf Pupils to Other Pupils in Special Education, 1970–1990

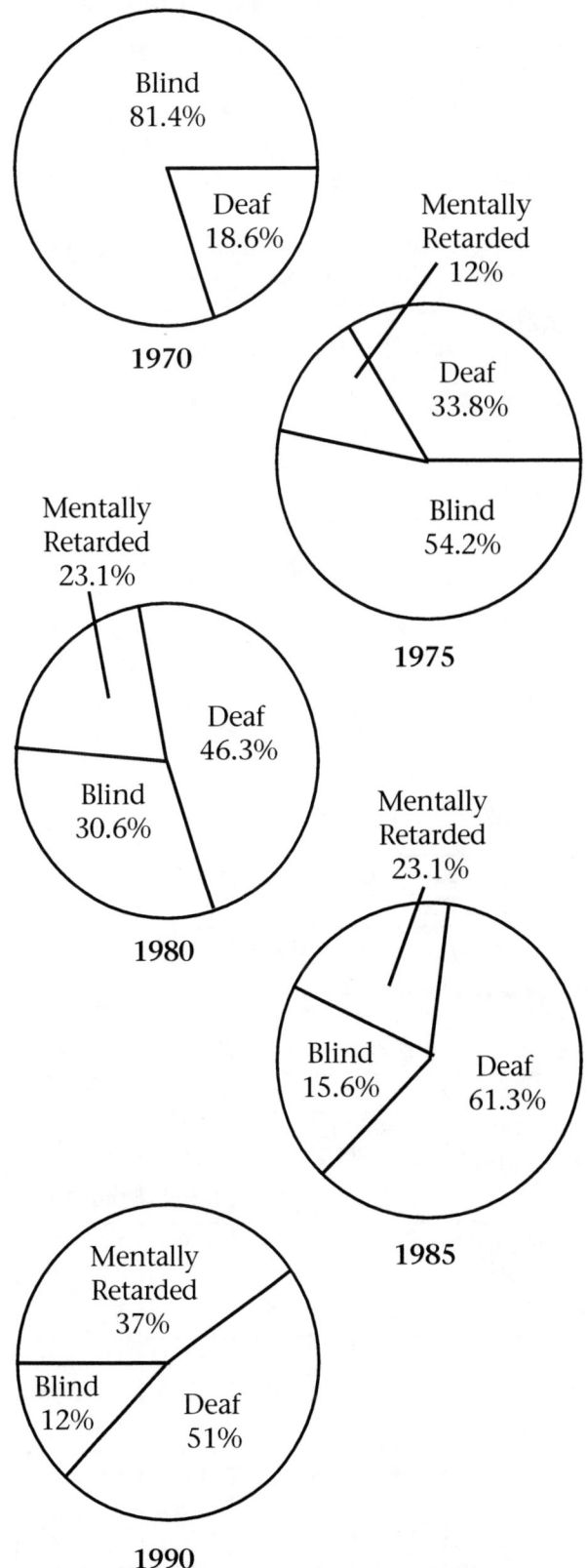

Blind 81.4%
Deaf 18.6%
1970

Mentally Retarded 12%
Deaf 33.8%
Blind 54.2%
1975

Mentally Retarded 23.1%
Deaf 46.3%
Blind 30.6%
1980

Mentally Retarded 23.1%
Blind 15.6%
Deaf 61.3%
1985

Mentally Retarded 37%
Blind 12%
Deaf 51%
1990

Figure 6 illustrates the growth in the number of deaf children receiving services. This increase may be attributed to increased public awareness and to improvements in the educational services offered by the institutes for the deaf. In the past, parents of deaf children did not bring their deaf children to the institutes at as early an age as they do today.

Figure 6. Growth of Deaf Children Receiving Services, 1965–1990

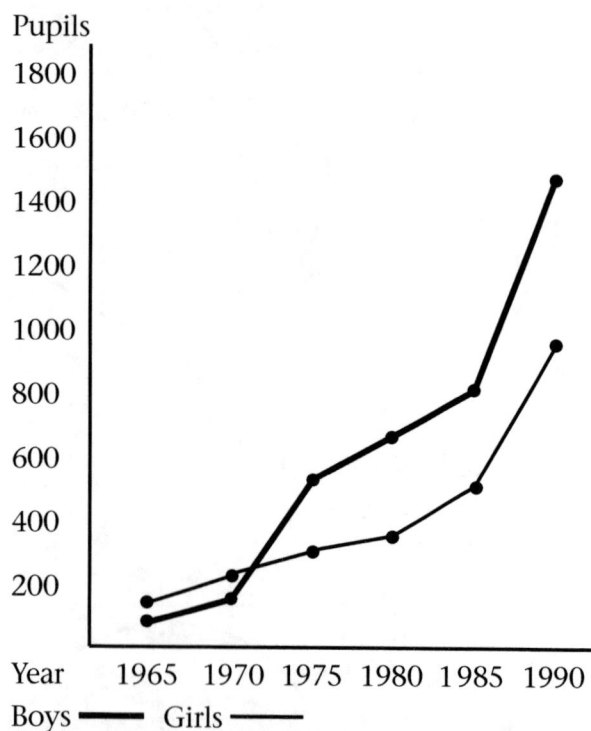

Average Age of Pupils

Table 8 shows the average ages of deaf pupils at the Hope Institutes. An examination of this data indicates several significant points. First, there is a gradual decrease in the average age of male and female students who are deaf at the preparatory stage. The table shows that the average age was six years and six months during the 1988-89 school year, but that in 1990-91 the average age had been reduced to five years and nine months. This is a positive trend. The average age for girls is lower than that for boys because the institutes for girls will accept children at the age of four years whereas the institutes for boys will not enroll boys until they are six years of age.

The average age of deaf boys and girls in the primary stage has decreased from eleven years and six months in 1988-89, to ten years and eight months in 1989-90. During the 1990-91 school year the average age went up slightly but it still was not as high as it was three years ago. During the 1990-91 school year the slight difference between the average age of boys and girls had disappeared. The average age for both was eleven years and two months. The six-year length of the primary stage makes it difficult for some pupils to complete all grade levels. This situation causes the average age of sixth graders to fluctuate. The

Table 8. Deaf Pupils' Average Ages at the Hope Institutes for the Deaf, 1988–1991

School Year	Type of Institute	Preparatory No. of Pupils	Avg. Age Yrs. Mon.		Elementary No. of Pupils	Avg. Age Yrs. Mon.		Intermediate No. of Pupils	Avg. Age Yrs. Mon.		Secondary No. of Pupils	Avg. Age Yrs. Mon.		Avg. Age of Pupils No. of Pupils	Avg. Age Yrs. Mon.	
1988/1989	Male	135	6	9	890	11	8	217	17	9	-	-	-	1242	12	-
	Female	249	6	3	530	11	4	116	16	5	-	-	-	868	11	4
	Total	384	6	6	1393	11	6	333	17	1	-	-	-	868	11	4
1989/1990	Male	198	6	7	932	10	7	242	16	9	42	19	4	1469	13	7
	Female	238	6	4	535	10	9	131	16	6	-	-	-	848	11	2
	Total	436	6	5	1467	10	8	373	16	7	42	19	4	2318	12	4
1990/1991	Male	194	6	7	1001	11	2	253	16	8	92	18	6	1558	13	4
	Female	240	5	-	564	11	2	135	16	4	29	20	7	968	13	6
	Total	434	5	9	1565	11	2	388	16	6	125	19	6	2526	13	5

decision to raise the top age of admission to the primary stage to fifteen years of age instead of twelve years of age may explain the inconsistency in the average age at elementary stage.

Third, the results of the study indicate that from 1988-1991, the average age of girls was lower than that for boys in the intermediate stage of education. The study also shows that there is a gradual decrease in the average age for both girls and boys.

The gradual decrease in the average age, especially at the preparatory stage, may have taken place as a result of parents' increased awareness of the importance of educating their deaf children. Efforts also have been made to qualify these children to hold governmental jobs at the completion of the intermediate vocational stage. This factor tends to encourage parents to seek an education for their deaf children at the Al-Amal (Hope) Institutes and to see the importance of an early education for their deaf children. The lower average age for girls at the intermediate stage may be explained as follows: Many of the older girls get married before they complete the intermediate stage; thus the total number of girls at this stage is much lower than the total number of boys.

The secondary stage was opened in 1989-90 for boys and in 1990-91 for girls. The age average is very high for both boys and girls (19 years 6 months). Most of the pupils enrolled graduated a few years ago and have been waiting for this educational opportunity. The average age for boys dropped from nineteen years and four months in 1990 to eighteen years and six months in 1991. At the time of this writing, the average age for girls was expected to drop as well.

Graduates of the Intermediate Vocational Institutes

The first group to graduate from the Riyadh Intermediate Vocational Institute in 1975 consisted of six deaf girls and eighteen deaf boys. Al-Amal Intermediate Institute in Riyadh was the only intermediate institute in existence until 1984. In 1984, seventeen boys and twelve girls graduated from the intermediate vocational institute in Jeddah. In 1986, twelve boys graduated from a similar institute in Alhasa (Hofuf). A total of 82 persons graduated from all intermediate institutes that year. In 1988, 97 pupils graduated from the six vocational institutes (two in Riyadh, two in Jeddah, and two in Alahsa). Table 9 illustrates the growing number of graduates from the intermediate institutes. During the 1991 school year, the total number enrolled in all of the intermediate institutes was more than a thousand. Of the 935 total graduates of the intermediate institutes by 1990, 685 were boys and 250 were girls.

In addition to the intermediate vocational institutes, there is another program for deaf students from the ages of twelve to fifteen. These students complete a two- or three-year-long program in certain vocational areas at the Riyadh Intermediate Vocational Institute. About 100 students have completed this program.

The Ministry of Labour and Social Affairs has also created rehabilitation centers for handicapped persons. Two are in Riyadh, one for male students and the other for female students, and two are in Taif, one each for male and female students. A fifth rehabilitation center for male students only is located in Dammam. More than 300 deaf persons have completed the two-year program and have learned vocational skills such as electronics and tailoring.

Table 9. Increase in Graduates from Intermediate Institutes for the Deaf, 1975–1991

Institute	Riyadh		Jeddah		Hofuf		Total
Sch. Year	Males	Females	Males	Females	Males	Females	
1975	18	6					24
1976	17	6					23
1977	9	3					12
1978	21	5					26
1979	10	7					17
1980	26	16					42
1981	51	2					53
1982	56	24					80
1983	53	9					62
1984	41	8	17	12			78
1985	24	5	22	10	12		82
1987	41	9	30	8	4		92
1988	28	14	29	9	8	9	97
1989	27	15	22	11	2	8	85
1990	30	15	26	9	13	8	101
1991	25	13	20	15	9	11	93
Total	504	172	187	81	48	36	1028

Special Benefits for the Deaf and Hard of Hearing

The deaf and hard of hearing enjoy special treatment whether they are studying in schools, graduates of Al-Amal Institutes, or citizens of the country. Some of the important benefits offered to the deaf in the Kingdom of Saudi Arabia include:

1. A financial allowance for deaf pupils during their school years, whether they live in a residential school or with their families. The amount of the allowance increases as the student progresses to a higher level of education (primary, intermediate, secondary). See Table 10 for the amounts of these allowances.
2. Scholarships to study abroad for gifted and talented graduates who are deaf. At the present time, graduates attend colleges in England and the United States of America. Currently there are several deaf students from Saudi Arabia at Gallaudet University.

Table 10. Deaf Students' Monthly Allowances

Educational Stage	Day School	Residential School
Primary	S.R.* 90 U.S. 24	S.R. 300 U.S. 85.3
Intermediate	S.R. 135 U.S. 33.3	S.R. 375 U.S. 100
Secondary	S.R. 300 U.S. 85.3	S.R. 450 U.S. 110
Vocational Training	S.R. 300 U.S. 85.3	S.R. 450 U.S. 110

* The Saudi Arabian unit of currency is the riyal.

3. A 50 percent discount on all air, sea, or ground transportation inside or outside of the country.
4. When appointed to a government job, deaf graduates receive a higher salary than do their hearing peers with an equivalent diploma.
5. Government-backed financial loans

to help graduates who would like to establish their own businesses.

6. Free transportation to and from the schools for the deaf for the student who lives inside or outside of the city. Free transportation at the beginning and the end of each school year for those students and their guardians who live some distance from a school for the deaf.

Preparation of Teachers and Administrative Staff

When the first two institutes for the deaf were opened in Riyadh in 1964, there were only eleven teachers of the deaf. The need to prepare additional Saudi teachers was obvious. In 1968 a special program was developed in cooperation with UNESCO to prepare 40 elementary level teachers of the deaf (20 male and 20 female). They completed six months of evening inservice classwork, which ended with an internship. Persons in Saudi Arabia interested in becoming teachers of the deaf have completed preparation programs either in Saudi Arabia or in countries such as England, Egypt, and Syria.

Recently, the College of Education of King Saud University has developed a new special education department designed to prepare teachers of the deaf, the mildly and severely handicapped, and the blind. It is an undergraduate program four years in length. However, most of the teachers of the deaf still come from neighboring Arab countries, especially from Egypt.

The number of male and female teachers of the deaf, administrators, and custodians is presented in Table 11. The number of teachers of the deaf has increased in proportion to the increase in the numbers of schools for the deaf and pupils who are deaf. A recent count indicated that there were a total of 890 personnel working at the schools for the deaf–528 teachers, 189 administrators, and 203 custodians.

The percentage of teachers and administrators who are Saudi citizens has been growing. In 1989, 18.5 percent of the teachers came from Saudi Arabia. By 1991, the number had increased to 32 percent. The same trend was evident among the administrators. The percentage of administrators who are Saudi citizens increased from 30.5 percent in 1989 to 38.9 percent in 1991. It is interesting to note that the majority of Saudi teachers of the deaf are male, while the majority of the administrative staff in the institutes for the

Table 11. Number of Teaching Staff and Personnel: 1989, 1990, 1991

School Year	Sex	Teaching Staff				Administrative Staff				Custodians			
		Saudi	Non Saudi	Total	% Saudi	Saudi	Non Saudi	Total	% Saudi	Saudi	Non Saudi	Total	% Saudi
1989	M	67	200	267	25.1	23	73	96	23.9	51	51	102	50
	F	21	134	155	13.5	24	34	58	41.4	84	35	119	70.6
	T	88	334	422	18.5	47	107	154	30.5	135	86	221	61.1
1990	M	97	192	289	33.6	11	59	70	15.7	51	51	102	50
	F	24	121	145	15.6	32	34	66	48.5	67	39	106	63.2
	T	121	313	434	21.9	43	93	136	31.6	118	90	208	56.7
1991	M	114	221	335	34	21	62	83	25.3	49	55	104	47.1
	F	55	138	193	28.5	41	35	76	53.9	59	40	99	59.6
	T	169	359	528	32	62	97	159	38.9	108	95	203	53.2

deaf are female. The percentage of the Saudi female custodians is higher than that of Saudi male custodians.

Teachers of the deaf in Saudi Arabia who have six months or more of specialized preparation enjoy an additional salary bonus of 30 percent. Those without specialized training receive a 20 percent bonus. The teaching load is also lower than that of their colleagues in the public schools (eighteen lessons per week).

Research on Deafness and Speech Defects

The earliest research study conducted in Saudi Arabia that related to the deaf was referred to in the *Report on Handicapped Persons* (Ministry of Education, 1972). The results of the study revealed that the causes of deafness were as follows:

measles–60%
associated with middle ear
   infections–25%
accidents–4%
other causes–4%
unknown–7%

Recently a team of medical doctors directed by Professor Seraj Zackzook, Ear, Nose and Throat Professor at King Saud University, investigated preschool children in the country at risk of becoming deaf or hard of hearing. The name of this study was "Survey of Hearing Impairments Among Saudi Pre-School Children in Riyadh." It is hoped that the study will lead to the development of a survey of all children in the country who are at a high risk of becoming deaf.

New Trends and the Outlook for the Future

The new trends that have taken place in the field of the education of the deaf in Saudi Arabia may be summarized as follows:

1. New programs for hard of hearing and speech impaired children, which emphasize the use of the regular public school curricula, have been started in regular public schools.
2. The general education level of deaf students has been upgraded by opening a secondary stage for boys and girls.
3. Evening classes have been provided for deaf adults.
4. Hearing and speech centers have been established to help students with speech and hearing problems, both in the special education institutes and in regular public schools.
5. Periodic accurate measurement of the hearing level of deaf and hard of hearing children and frequent check of the adequacy of the children's ear molds have been instituted.
6. The maximum entrance age for acceptance into the schools for the deaf has been raised to accommodate more school-age children.
7. The curricula found in the schools and classrooms for the deaf has been modified and improved.
8. The doors of the Hope Institutes have been opened to field training and for the preparation of teachers, psychologists, and speech and hearing majors.
9. Deaf and hearing students have been integrated and participate together in different activities such as camping, sports competitions, and art projects.
10. Local seminars and conferences on the education of the deaf and hard of hearing have been held, and participation in international conferences is encouraged.
11. Following the model of Al-Jouf School (northern part of the country), deaf and hard of hearing students have been integrated into regular public schools.
12. Research and studies related to the deaf and their education, particularly in the areas of sign language, causes

of deafness, and the attitude of the deaf students toward the subject matter taught in the intermediate and secondary institutes have been completed or are on-going.

Conclusion

This paper has presented the latest information about the education and rehabilitation of the deaf and hard of hearing in Saudi Arabia since the programs were established in 1964. The positive effects of the state educational policy developed in 1970 were discussed. A statistical analysis of the extent and kind of educational services was discussed to provide a clear picture of the 22 programs and 2,526 deaf and hard of hearing pupils served by the Ministry of Education in the Kingdom of Saudi Arabia. Other agencies involved in the rehabilitation, treatment, and education of the deaf and hard of hearing were covered.

The preservice and inservice education of teachers of the deaf and hard of hearing, and the number and personnel at the Hope Institutes for the Deaf, were discussed. The number of teachers of the deaf has increased in direct relation to the increase in the number of deaf pupils and schools and classes for the deaf and hard of hearing in the country.

In conclusion, the trends and future directions of the education of the deaf in Saudi Arabia are promising. It is hoped that the deaf and hard of hearing will be able to compete equally with hearing people in the field of education and in the world of work, not only to meet their own needs but the needs of their families and society. It is true that many deaf persons who have succeeded in school are engaged in manual labor or unskilled jobs. The road is still very long before we will see many deaf persons in our colleges and universities. If the deaf have not been equal participants in the fruits of life in Saudi Arabia in the past, it is hoped that this will change in the future with improved educational and vocational opportunities.

Finally, the intelligence and capacity of deaf and hard of hearing individuals needs to be recognized, and the opportunity to participate equally in the growth and development of the country provided.

References

Al-Muslat, Z. (1984). *Efforts of the kingdom of Saudi Arabia in the field of educating the deaf.* Paper presented at The Deaf Way Conference, an international conference and festival for the deaf, Gallaudet University, Washington, DC.

Al-Muslat, Z., & Salem, M. (1982). *Education of the deaf and hard of hearing in the kingdom of Saudi Arabia.* [Memeographed in Arabic only]. Riyadh, Saudi Arabia.

Data and Educational Documentation Center. (1986–1988,1988). *Educational development in the kingdom of Saudi Arabia.* Ministry of Education.

Data and Educational Documentation Center. (1986). *Special education.* Statistical and Documental Exhibit. Riyadh, Saudi Arabia.

Department, Ministry of Education. (1972). *Special education: Report on handicapped persons in the kingdom of Saudi Arabia.* Riyadh, Saudi Arabia.

The General Directorate of Special Education. (1981). *Directory of special education in the kingdom of Saudi Arabia.* Riyadh, Saudi Arabia: Ministry of Education.

The General Secretariat of Special Education. (1990). *Report on the achievement of special education during the fourth 5 Years Plan* (1985–1990). Riyadh, Saudi Arabia: Ministry of Education.

Higher Commission of Education. (1970). *The educational policy in the kingdom of Saudi Arabia.* Riyadh, Saudi Arabia.

The Vocational Rehabilitation Center for the Handicapped. (1988). *Vocational rehabilitation.* Riyadh, Saudi Arabia: Ministry of Labour and Social Affairs.

Education of the Deaf in Spain

Marian Valmaseda Balanzategui
and
Esther Diaz-Estebanez Leon

Historical Background

Spain is a country with a great tradition in the education of the deaf. The first data available goes back to 1555, when Fr. Pedro Ponce de Leon (1520–1584), a Benedictine monk, started teaching a deaf-mute of noble birth from Burgos.

Ponce de Leon is recognized as being the first educator of the deaf and, according to some learned researchers, for using a method not yet equaled. According to several authors who have studied his biography (Cecilia, 1980; Eguiluz, 1974), Ponce de Leon is supposed to have educated some twelve students, all of noble birth, in his 40 years as a teacher. There is documented evidence of his method of teaching in a book entitled *Doctrine for the Deaf-Mute*. Unfortunately, though, this book is no longer in existence.

According to Fortich (1987), different authors agree that Ponce's method consisted of three main stages. The first stage, called "mute graphic teaching," consisted of manual training aimed at achieving global and ideographic writing which later permitted the acquisition of an ample vocabulary. The vocabulary learned was later recorded in a notebook. Dactilology, a manual alphabet widely used by different religious communities, was probably used in this stage.

The second stage, "oral teaching," consisted of learning to pronounce the words that had been gathered in the notebook. The third stage, entitled "superior cultural preparation," was aimed at giving the students the necessary knowledge required to maintain their status as part of the nobility. Ponce de Leon stated, "I had students who were deaf-mutes from birth, and were the children of the nobility and principal people, whom I taught to speak, read and write, count, pray, help with Mass, know the Christian Doctrine, and take part in confession orally. To some I taught Latin and Greek, the Italian language, . . . natural philosophy and astrology . . . ."

Manuel Ramirez de Carrion (1570–1652) followed Ponce de Leon's teachings and educated several deaf children of the Castilian nobility. He first resided in the Province of Cordova, but later moved to Madrid in order to educate Don Luis de Velasco, son of the Lord High Constable of Castile. After four years, he returned home and left his pupil, Don Luis, in the hands of a new instructor, Juan Pablo Bonet. Periodically he returned to supervise the progress of Don Luis' education.

In his book, *Marvels of Nature*, de Carrion declared that the education of the deaf is one of the great marvels of science. He did not reveal his methods of teaching the deaf in this book and continued to keep it a secret.

Juan Pablo Bonet (1579–1633), a cultured military man and the private secretary of the Lord High Constable of Castile, offered to continue the education of the nobleman's son when de Carrion decided to return to Madrid. Apparently, Bonet had no preparation in the field of the education of the deaf except for what he had observed during his daily contact with Ramirez de Carrion. In 1620, at the end of one year of work with his pupil, he published a book, the first in the world of its kind, about the education of the deaf, *Reduction of Letters and Arts to Teach the Mute to Speak*.

Quiros and Gueler (1973) proposed that, given Bonet's lack of experience, it is perhaps the methods of Ramirez de Carrion that Bonet describes. Regrettably, both Bonet and Ramirez proclaimed themselves to be the creator of the "de-mutization method," even though both knew that the origins of the method stemmed from the work of Ponce de Leon. In conclusion, Quiros and Gueler (1973) state, "Despite all the objections to Bonet's writings that may exist, he will always have the distinction of having written the first book about the education of the deaf and be credited for first describing the demutization procedure."

In 1795 Lorenzo Hervas-Panduro wrote a book entitled *Spanish School of Deaf Mutes*. He is, according to Perello and Tortosa (1978), the first person to have used the term *deaf-mute*. The term *mute* had been used before that time. Hervas-Panduro was a man of great knowledge in various fields, and his contributions in the field of comparative linguistics is especially important.

According to Fortich (1987), "Hervas praised the simultaneous method of teaching the deaf or the use of both speech and sign concurrently." He called his point of view of the mixed or combined methods, or what would currently be called Total Communication, "somatological communication."

First Schools for the Deaf

Also in 1795 at the request of Don Manuel Godoy, the first school for the deaf, School of the Friars, *Escolapios de Avapies*, was created in Madrid. In March 1802 the name of the school became The Real School of the Deaf-Mute of Madrid. At first the school only admitted boys, but began admitting girls in 1816.

In February 1800, the municipal government of Barcelona allowed some school rooms to be used to teach the deaf. A school with 27 students was opened in Barcelona in 1836.

Article 108 of the Public Instruction Law, dated September 9, 1857, includes information about the creation of special schools for the deaf and blind in university districts. Thus schools for the deaf were created in Burgos in 1868, Santiago in 1864, Salamanca in 1868, Zaragoza in 1871, Sevilla in 1873, and Valencia in 1887. By the end of the nineteenth century, it was amply demonstrated that the deaf could be educated, and it was acknowledged at the same time that society had the moral and legal obligation to provide instructional programs for deaf children.

Educational Services for the Deaf

Until the last few years, almost all deaf and hard of hearing children have attended special schools located in all regions of Spain. Some of these centers were specifically for the deaf, while others took care of the education of children with a variety of handicapping conditions. The provincial schools enrolled students from a large geographic area. Many of the students remained at the schools for many years.

Some hard of hearing students attended special classes in regular schools. A small number of students, normally hard of hearing, attended regular classes and followed the same curriculum as their hearing classmates. (See Appendix A for a breakdown of the number of schools and students.)

Recently this situation has been greatly modified by the inception of the Educational Integration Project.

Educational Integration Project

The Law of the Social Integration of the Handicapped or Disabled (LISMI), approved in 1982, created a new legal framework that stated the right of handicapped students to be educated within the regular schools. The 1985 Royal Decree of the Order for Special Education solidified this objective and included in its articles a program that proposed to integrate from 50 to 70 percent of the students who had special education needs over the next eight years.[1]

Because of regional autonomy and decentralization of educational decision making, currently the educational programs for deaf students vary from region to region. Cataluna, the Vasc country, Galicia, Islas Canarias, Valencia, and Andalucia have total educational autonomy, while the remainder of the Autonomous Communities (Madrid, Castilla-Leon, Castilla-La Mancha, Cantabria, Baleares, Asturias, Extremadura, Aragon, Murcia, and the cities of Ceuta and Melilla) depend upon direction from the Ministry of Education and Science (MEC).

In some regions, the policy of educational integration has caused a large reduction in the enrollment of students at the special schools. Enrollment has diminished to the point that some of the special schools have been closed. In other regions, though, the special schools have been responsible for the decision about the integration of deaf students. These regional decisions are carried out by professionals who work in the special schools, and who are in charge of the education, organization of services, and whatever support the deaf students in the region may need. These schools have become the educational resource centers for the whole region.

In some geographical areas all schools are considered as potential schools for integration. Thus parents have the choice concerning which school they want their children to attend.

In other zones (especially in the autonomous communities dependent on the MEC), the integration of the deaf students must take place in the schools especially suited for that purpose.[2]

The MEC decided that the first step in the process of determining whether or not a school is to become an integration center should be made by a School Council composed of parents and teachers. Once a school reaches a decision, the school then petitions the MEC and requests to be considered as an integration site. Upon acceptance as part of the Project of Integration, the school is eligible for extra personnel and material resources from the Ministry. (See Appendix B for information on students in centers of integration.)

Mandatory Education Centers

In general, four educational options are available for deaf children.

Centers Specializing in the Education of the Deaf

The students who attend these schools have a severe hearing loss plus other handicaps in addition to deafness. These schools may be public or private, the latter being partially or totally financed by government funds. These schools have special resources, personnel, and material designed for the education of the deaf.

Regular Public Schools with Special Classrooms for the Deaf

The regular schools that have one or more classrooms for students with defective hearing contain the specific technology and specialized teachers needed to educate deaf children. In these classrooms one finds groups of deaf children of different ages.

In this school environment, the deaf students share spaces in common with their hearing schoolmates. These spaces may include the play yard, cafeteria, and classrooms for some school subjects.

Regular School Integration Centers

These are the general education schools that accept children with special educational needs. These schools provide deaf students with the possibility of integrating with their hearing schoolmates. It is rare that they may find other deaf students to communicate with in this environment. These schools have special teachers and logopaedists who provide support, as well as materials designed specifically for deaf students. These resources vary depending on the model of integration adopted by each region.[3] The preparation of the professionals assigned as well as the materials provided these schools is not always appropriate to the needs of deaf children.

Specialized Regular Integration Center

These regular education centers specialize in the integration of students with hearing impairments.

Due to the specific technical needs of some handicapped students, the Ministry of Education created some Centers of Integration with a specific preference to children with a hearing impairment or a motor deficiency. Thus, among the many schools that received the nomination of "Integration Center," some specialize in the integration of deaf children and some in the integration of students with a motor deficiency.

These centers promote a better allotment of resources and higher teacher motivation. The added advantage of these centers is that the deaf students have the opportunity to interact not only with their hearing schoolmates, but with their deaf schoolmates as well.

Deaf students in these specialized centers are not ordinarily found in special classrooms for the deaf but in the regular classroom receiving the specific support needed from the teacher and the logopaedist. These services are provided within or outside of the regular classroom, and individually or in groups, depending on the methodology used at the center. The main aim of these specialized centers is the total education of these students, rather than it being the exclusive responsibility of the special teacher.

Due to the close proximity to the deaf children's homes, parents sometimes opt for the regular schools for their deaf children. In this situation, since the school lacks the specialized teachers and materials required, when support is needed the parents must turn to private sources.

What has been said so far is only a brief explanation of each of the possible placement options. Within each option and center, considerable variation is found. Thus, for example, some special schools try to incorporate, to a greater or lesser degree, an exchange with hearing students at nearby regular schools and create "open" classrooms in which the deaf students share classroom activities with hearing classmates of the same age. The integration centers also try to incorporate deaf adults into the program to provide the deaf children with adult models. Among the existing placement options, subtle differences exist concerning available financial resources, the use and allotment of the existing physical resources, and, most important, the preservice and inservice preparation of the faculty.

Interdisciplinary Teams

Although the ultimate decision concerning the educational placement of students with special needs, including those who have a hearing loss, lies with the parent, the interdisciplinary team provides orientation and assistance. These teams are basically made up of psychologists, pedagogues, and social workers, and in some cases also include logopaedists and physicians. The team is responsible for evaluating the children's development in all areas and for providing the parents with information about the educational placement options offered by the zone or sector. Appendix C contains more data on different kinds of interdisciplinary teams.

The network of interdisciplinary teams, whose numbers have increased considerably in the last few years, includes teams that focus on early care, and most recently, specific areas of disability.

The teams for early care are responsible for the education of children between birth and age six, and for the establishment of the specific care that each child needs. An important part of the team's job is to orient schools for infants (public or private), by providing them with specific guidelines, training, and assistance in adapting certain curricular materials.

Pre-elementary education is not obligatory in Spain, although practically all students now begin their schooling at four years of age. The public relies upon both public and private schools for the education of infants from one and one-half to two years of age.

Schooling at a very early age is especially relevant in the educational development of deaf students. Once the hearing loss is detected (by the health services), these children are steered toward early child care services. Services of this type are part of the charge of the Minister of Social Matters, whose fundamental focus is to provide clinical assistance. The Ministry of Education, through the teams for early care, facilitates the schooling of deaf infants by referring them directly through a logopaedist to schools for infants.

In Spain, the tradition of itinerant home-based care does not exist, possibly due to the fact that children have recourse to direct service by educational establishments at a very early age.

Occasionally members of sector teams, both the teams for general as well as for early care, do not have the training needed to provide adequate guidance for deaf children and their families. In September 1988, to alleviate this problem, specific interdisciplinary teams for the care of the deaf were established. These teams work closely with the other existing guidance services to carry out when necessary student evaluations, school orientation activities, and family support and follow-up.

Parent Support

Parents of deaf children often receive information about possible communication and educational options from several different agencies and professionals (both public and private). At times these services are not sufficiently coordinated. Consequently the information that parents receive is often confusing and even contradictory.

The first evaluation of the child is conducted by the health system. The health system is charged with the detection and diagnosis of the hearing loss. Besides the clinical staff, some health system services include the services of psychologists and/or social workers who are the professionals responsible for informing the parents about possible available services. This may include information about hearing aids, early care options, state financial assistance, and so on. Once the child is in school, normally the school itself, together with the interdisciplinary teams, will be responsible for establishing periodic individual and group meetings for the parents. The purpose of these meetings is to inform, educate, and enlist the collaboration of the family in the process of educating their deaf son or daughter. Occasionally parent groups are

organized to provide psychological support to the families, and to assist parents in improving their oral and sign communication competency.

Parents' associations have been organized throughout the country. These associations offer information and counselling to parents and include logopaedic and pedagogical support, and information about leisure-time activities.

Communication Methodology

Spain's long tradition of oral education of the deaf was reinforced by resolutions passed at the 1880 International Congress on the Education of the Deaf. The communication and educational approach followed with deaf students in Spain has been driven primarily by the priority placed upon teaching deaf children to speak, read lips, and read the printed page. Signing, until very recently, has been rejected at the educational level, even though the use of signs has been "tolerated" among deaf students and used by some teachers during moments of leisure.

While there is a continuum of signed languages ranging from Spanish Sign Language to Signed Spanish, the sign system favored by the majority of public school programs is a sign language that parallels spoken Spanish syntax. Probably the sign system most commonly utilized is what would be called Pidgin Signed Spanish.

Cued Speech has been well received in Spain, probably because it is based on Spanish speech sounds and is easily learned by parents and educators. The Spanish system of Cued Speech is made up of eight manual configurations and three points of articulation.

Another reason why Cued Speech is widely accepted relates to research that has been conducted during the last several years at the Free University of Brussels under the direction of J. Alegria (1979, 1987, 1989). His research focuses upon the reading processes of deaf children educated with Cued Speech.

The research findings have been widely disseminated in Spain and are followed closely by educators and researchers in the field. In spite of the obvious interest in Cued Speech, its use in education programs for deaf children continues to be very limited.

Spanish Sign Language is becoming more and more popular and is accepted by the deaf community as their natural language. Sign interpreters are now a common sight at meetings, conferences, and congresses. Sign courses for teachers of the deaf are more and more common. Little research has been conducted on the effect of sign language on the education of deaf children. Currently few native signers are available as teachers of the Spanish Sign Language classes.

The introduction and use of sign systems in educational programs for deaf children has not come about at the initiation of interpreters, but rather has emerged from the professionals directly involved in the education of deaf pupils—classroom teachers, support staff, and logopaedists. This is a fact at both the special schools and at the preferential integration sites. Interpreters have been introduced into some classrooms in experimental programs, especially in non-compulsory secondary schools. The general trend, though, is for the teachers of the deaf to gain sufficient skill in the use of sign language to be able to use it effectively to educate their deaf students. In some of the Integration Centers, the entire faculty of the school has been involved in learning Spanish Sign Language.

Post-Compulsory Education

Once the General Basic Education course of study has been completed, two tracks are available for students to continue their education; the Baccalaureate and Professional Training. The students who have achieved the required objectives in the general basic education track will receive the diploma entitled "School Graduate" and will have access to higher education either in a professional training program or in the baccalaureate degree program. Those who after eight years of schooling have not acquired the diploma will receive a Certificate of Schooling and will have access to professional training but not to a baccalaureate degree program.

Deaf students who obtain the diploma of School Graduate and who desire to continue their studies for the Baccalaureate do so in ordinary colleges and universities attended by their hearing classmates. Although the opportunities are limited, five institutions of higher education have recently been incorporated into the National Integration Plan. A specified number of deaf students have been integrated into the institutions and provided with specialized support teachers.

The professional training in which the majority of deaf students enroll has at present three modes:

- Ordinary Professional Training
  Ordinary professional training is provided only at general centers of professional training. Just as in the case of Institutes for the Baccalaureate, seventeen of these centers have joined the Integration Plan and have incorporated groups of deaf students and provided the necessary support services.
- Adapted Professional Training
  Technical programs are provided for deaf students in common subject areas and the applied sciences. Three special technical training centers provide this type of program for deaf students.
- Task Teaching
  Task Teaching Centers are designed for deaf students with other handicapping conditions, especially mental retardation. Currently there are two centers that provide basic and life skill development programs.
  Vocational development programs

are available at these centers. These students also have access to other centers that offer different services.

Teacher Preparation

Initial Training

To teach at any level of education, public or private, it is necessary to have a university degree and to have completed an appropriate accredited pedagogical program. Although there are degree holders and graduates of other institutions of higher education, most of the teachers in pre-schools and in general basic education programs are graduates of the universities designed to prepare teachers for schools offering the GBE.[4]   The preparation received at the university takes three years to complete, and the curriculum consists of a series of courses whose content is related to the teaching of the general basic education program and to psycho-pedagogic subject matter.

After the General Basic Education Program is completed at the University, those teachers who want to work with deaf students must complete additional course work that specializes in subject matter dealing with problems of hearing, speech, and language. The specialized course of study takes two additional years to complete. When the course work is completed the person is granted a degree entitled Specialist in Hearing and Language Disorders. The preparation is not aimed exclusively at preparing teachers of the deaf. No such degree exists. The logopaedists prepared are able to work with students who have several kinds of learning problems.

At present fourteen universities provide this type of education. Graduates of institutions designed to prepare teachers for the GBE as well as those who have earned a Master's degree in Psychology and Pedagogy have access to the specialized preparation.

Professional Development

Research findings, innovations in education, and changes in didactic techniques call for professional development activities that will keep the teachers' knowledge base and pedagogy up-to-date and allow them to respond satisfactorily to all difficulties encountered in their professional practice.

Because of the initiatives of the universities, as well as other private agencies, the Ministry of Education and Science has created a network of teacher centers (NTC) for the preparation of non-university-level teachers. In 1989 a total of 106 NTCs were in operation, distributed among the provinces and under the management of the Ministry of Education and Science. Some of the Autonomous Communities with complete jurisdiction over education matters in their area have created their own preparation programs.

The NTCs have at their disposal provincial consultants in special education who encourage, channel, and organize training activities for teachers.

The National Resource Center for Special Education maintains connections with these teacher centers by preparing training activities and curricular materials, thus taking part indirectly in the permanent training of teachers of the deaf.

Presence of Deaf Teachers

The Law of Public Function of 1971 impeded access of handicapped persons to teaching positions. The passage of the Law of Social Integration of the Handicapped (1982), in which the social and working rights of disabled persons is affirmed, provided in 1984 a series of measures and a new law to reform and abolish the 1971 Law of Public Function.

Past laws and the system of education in place provided deaf persons with little access to higher education and subsequent degrees. Thus, it was nearly impossible for a deaf person to become a teacher of the deaf. A few hard of hearing and late-deafened persons did find employment at schools for the deaf.

At present, the Ministry of Education and Science has become more sensitive to the important role that deaf adults can play in the education of deaf students. Deaf adults act as models with whom students can identify with and as experts skilled in the use of sign language and knowledge of the deaf community. This increased sensitivity of the MES has led to the start of some pilot projects, in which deaf adults collaborate with the preferential integration centers in the task of educating deaf students and orienting their parents. Many obstacles still exist with regard to the attitudes of society, legal constraints, and educational limitations that need to be removed before the full utilization of deaf persons in the education of the deaf can be realized.

The Future

Currently, the most noteworthy developments in the education of the deaf are probably the projects designed to integrate deaf children into the public schools and the ongoing dialogue among educators, parents, and deaf people regarding the best methods of communicating with and teaching deaf students. If the education of the deaf is going to be improved in Spain, the dialogue must continue. This process, no matter how bitter, produces improved prospects for deaf persons in the future.

After several years of experience, the integration of deaf children into the regular schools is firmly established. The integration experience has led to improved academic performance by the deaf students, more positive attitudes, and a better understanding of the educational needs of deaf children, particularly in the areas of language and communication. However, general consensus is far from being achieved. The experience of integrating deaf students in the regular schools during the past few years has also provided a great amount of information concerning the difficulties found in educating deaf students in the regular classroom. The difficulties encountered stem from the lack of trained teachers, the scarcity of resources, and organizational and methodological problems. An additional drawback is society's lack of sensitivity to both the educational needs of the deaf child and the deaf community's needs for equal opportunities.

The special schools for the deaf are the subject of much controversy. Often parents of deaf children and associations of the deaf represent opposing points of view as to the future of the schools for the deaf. The debate concerning the role of the schools for the deaf has yet to be completed.

The next few years should be marked by a continuing debate concerning the optimum communication modality to be used to educate deaf students, the appropriate educational setting, and the role of teachers of the deaf. To a great extent, the answers to these questions should determine the future of the education of the deaf in Spain.

Possible changes in the education of deaf children and youths in our country in the coming years will be intimately connected with modifications experienced by the entire system of education in Spain. For several years significant changes in legislation and regulation connected with education in general have occurred. It is impossible to consider possible changes in the direction of the education of the deaf without taking into account the direction general education will take.

The Law of Education that went into effect in 1992 will present problems for the education of deaf children and youths in Spain. The problem areas caused by the new law are: the increase in the compulsory period of education by two years or until the age of sixteen, and the reorganization of teacher education programs.

The new law will possibly have positive and negative repercussions upon the education of deaf students. The presence of a curriculum designed to meet the needs of the deaf students, better training of faculty with regards to the methodological and organizational modifications needed in the schools, and more resources, both personal and material, should result in attainment of an educational system more in tune with the needs of today's society and the needs of all students, including deaf students.

Great variations in educational options for deaf students' services currently exist. These options include special education schools or centers for the deaf that try to incorporate, to a greater or lesser degree, exchanges with hearing students of nearby schools; special education "open" classrooms in regular schools in which the deaf students share many activities with hearing classmates of the same age; and integration centers that educate deaf and hearing children in the same classroom.

How existing resources will be allocated to the different educational options for deaf children and its effect upon the professional preparation of faculty is yet to be determined. The challenge is clear and so is the responsibility of all parties involved, including educators, parents, deaf persons, and educational administrators: to strive to attain an education system that will make possible greater and better personal, cultural, and social development of deaf students in Spain.

Appendices

Appendix A:

Data on Special Education Centers of the Deaf, 1986–1987

Total Number of Schools	21
Total Number of Students	3,353*

Male – 1,892   Female – 1,461

Ratio of teachers to deaf students	1/ 10–12
Ratio of teachers to deaf students with multiple disabilities	1/ 6

* This data includes students with multiple disabilities.
Source: *Teaching Statistics in Spain 1986/1987*. Madrid, Spain. MES.

Appendix B:

Students in Centers of Integration, 1989

1. EGB

Total number of students in school	984

Male – 585   Female – 399

Number of EGB Centers of Preferential Integration	36

2. Intermediate Schools

Students of Intermediate Schools in Ordinary Centers (including professional training and Baccalaureate)	275

Male – 160   Female – 115

Number of P.T. Centers of Preferential Integration	7
Number of Baccalaureate Centers of Preferential Integration	1

Source: Census in development NRCSE

Appendix C:

Interdisciplinary Teams (MES Jurisdiction)

General Interdisciplinary Teams	234
Early Care Interdisciplinary Teams	5
Specific Interdisciplinary Teams for the Deaf	8

Endnotes

1. The inception of the Project of Integration has been, among others, one of the elements that has permitted a deeper examination of the education of the disabled and its deficiencies. Many of the Centers of Integration may be considered as being innovative. The need to improve the quality of teaching, as well as the need to develop a framework in which to organize education according to the needs of the society, has driven the present Ministry of Education to propose educational reform. The legal framework for the reform has been approved.

The educational reform offers a new curricular design and new educational options for students currently in center-based educational programs.

2. Schools involved in the Integration Project since 1985 were evaluated by a research team from 1985–89. The objective of the study was to determine which variables eased the process of integration and education of students in regular schools. Only three integration centers for deaf children were studied, which accounts for the very limited data available about the students who were integrated.

3. In the area of the MEC jurisdiction, the assignment of teachers is as follows: a) for 16 unit centers, 3 support teachers and 1 logopaedist; b) for 8 to 16 unit centers, 2 support teachers and 1 logopaedist; c) for less than 8 unit centers, 1 support teacher and 1 logopaedist. These proportions are modifiable according to the peculiar needs of the center and of the students, and can be increased if necessary.

4. GBE: General Basic Education constitutes the compulsory education now in force in Spain. It continues for eight years or from the ages of six to fourteen. The new Law for the General Regulation of the Education System extends this compulsory period two more years, or from six to sixteen years of age.

References

Alegria, J., & Morais, J. (1979). The development of the ability of phonetic analysis of the word and learning to read. *Psychological Files, 47*, 251-270.

Alegria, J., & Leybaert, J. (1987). *Reading acquisition in the deaf child.* Documental Series. Madrid MES, NRCSE.

Alegria, J., Dejean, C., Acpouillez, J. M., & Leybaert, J. (1989, May). *Role played by Cued Speech in the identification of written words encountered for the first time by deaf children.* Paper presented at the Annual Meeting of the Belgium Society of Psychology. Louvain La Neuve.

Alonso, P., Diaz-Estebanez, E., Madruga, B., & Valmaseda, M. (1989). *Introduction to bimodal communication.* Training Series. Madrid MES, NRCSE.

Barbera, F. (1985). *Teaching deaf mutes by the purely oral method.* Valencia, Spain: Manuel Alufre Press.

Cecilia, A. (1980). The oral method of Ponce de Leon. *PROAS, 69*, 36-37.

Clemente, R., & Valmaseda, M. (1985). *Psycho-pedagogical bases for the early stimulation of the severely deaf child.* Unpublished document. CIDE.

Eguiluz, A. (1974). Preliminary aspects of deaf-muteness. *PROAS, 6*, 9-11.

Fortich, L. (1987). *Hearing deficiency: An interdisciplinary approach.* Valencia, Spain: Ed. Promolibro.

Hervas-Panduro, L. (1795). *Spanish school of deaf mutes.* Madrid, Spain.

Marchesi, A. (1980). *Influence of educational and linguistic social variables in the cognitive development of severely deaf children.* Fundacion General Mediterranea.

Marchesi, A. (1981). The language of signs. *Estudios de Psicologia, 5-6*, 155-184.

Marchesi, A. (1983). *Influence of the manner of early communication in the cognitive-linguistic development of severely deaf children.* Unpublished document. Madrid, Spain: CIDE.

Marchesi, A. (1987). *The linguistic and communicative development of deaf children.* Madrid, Spain: Ed. Alianza Psicologia.

Marchesi, A. (1988). *The integration of deaf children in Spain.* Paper presented at the First North-Hispanic American Meeting on the Integration of Deaf Children. April, 1988. Washington, D.C., Gallaudet University.

MES (original MED) (1989). *Statistics of teaching in Spain: 1986–87.* Madrid, Spain: MEC.

Perello, J., & Tortosa, F. (1978). *Deaf-muteness.* Barcelona. Spain: Ed. Cientifico-Medica.

Pinedo, F. J. (1989a). *Statistics of teaching in Spain: 1986–87.* Madrid, Spain: MEC.

Pinedo, F. J. (1989b). *A voice for silence.* Madrid, Spain: Ed. Fomento de Empleo Minusvalidos, S.L. [Promotion of the Employment of Handicapped People].

Pinedo, F. J. (1989c). *New Spanish dictionary of signs (gestures).* Madrid, Spain: Ed. Fomento de Empleo Minusvalidos, S.L.

Quiros, J. B., & Gueler, F. S. (1973). *Human communication and its pathology.* Buenos Aires, Argentina: CMIFA [original acronym].

Torres, S. (1988). *The complemented word.* Madrid, Spain: Ed. CEPE [original acronym].

Valmaseda, M. (1989, March). *Language as a tool for the education of the deaf child.* Paper presented at the Fifth Monographic Course on Systems of Communication, Methods. Madrid, Spain: ECODA.

Education of the Deaf in Sweden

by Kerstin Heiling

Introduction

Sweden is a small country with just over eight million inhabitants. The country has a long tradition of population registration. Thus the number of deaf and hard of hearing persons in the population is rather well known. Hearing impaired students make up 0.2 percent of the student population of the Swedish comprehensive school system. More than two-thirds of the hard of hearing children in Sweden attend regular school classes. Deaf children in Sweden attend special schools (Hammarstedt & Amcoff, 1979). During the 1989–90 school year a total of 493 pupils in grades one to ten attended schools for the deaf.

It is the responsibility of the Ministry of Education and the National Board of Education to set policy and to administer the rules and regulations of the Compulsory School Curriculum and Education Ordinance. These bodies also initiate research and development activities.

The Compulsory Education Curriculum (Lgr 80) incorporates the goals and guidelines that govern education in general, pupil welfare, and special education. When the curriculum was implemented at the beginning of the 1980s, it established a new philosophy of special education that emphasized three principles:

1. A handicap is relative to circumstances in the environment.
2. A holistic view of the pupil with special needs must be taken.
3. The principle of integration emphasizes the concepts that problems should be dealt with where they arise, and the support services needed should as far as possible be provided within the class room or working unit.

During the 1970s and 1980s, pupils with different kinds of disabilities who in the past received their education in special schools or special classes were placed with increasing frequency in regular public school class rooms.

However, for the deaf the situation is different. Profoundly deaf and severely hearing impaired pupils usually attend special schools. This is due largely to the point of view that deafness as a communication handicap is substantially reduced in a surrounding where sign language is readily available.

About 1200 hearing impaired pupils attend regular public schools. Most of these students receive special support services from an itinerant teacher or other forms of instructional assistance. Amplification systems, including wire loops or FM radio systems, are normally available to deaf children found in the regular class rooms. In the metropolitan areas, in addition to being educated in the regular class room, hearing impaired children are also taught in self-contained class rooms.

Special school or regular school placement decisions are usually based on the child's main channel of communication rather than on his or her audiogram. Total mainstreaming of children who are prelingually deaf into a regular public school class room is not advocated in Sweden today.

The Swedish Education System

In Sweden approximately 98 percent of the children and adolescents between the ages of seven and nineteen years attend free public schools. The general features of the educational system are outlined in Table 1.

Table 1. Comparison of Regular Schools and Schools for the Deaf

	Regular Schools	Schools for the Deaf
Age	Higher Education	
20		
19	Adult Education	
18		National
17	Secondary	secondary
16	school, 2 to 4 yrs.	school, to 5 yrs.
15		
14		

Regular Schools		Schools for the Deaf
Age	Higher Education	
13	Upper level (gr. 7–9)	Upper level (gr. 8–10)
12		
11		
		Intermediate (gr. 5–7) Compulsory Comprehensive School
10	Intermediate (gr. 4–6)	
9		
8		
7	Lower level (gr.1–3)	Lower level (gr. 1–4)
6		
5	Preschool	
4		
3		

Preschool education, for children under the age of seven, is not mandatory. Municipalities, however, are obliged by law to make such education available for all six-year-olds. Handicapped children as a rule are admitted to preschools from the age of three.

The Compulsory Comprehensive School (*Grundskolan*) is attended by almost all children aged seven to sixteen. It is divided into three levels: lower (grades one to three), intermediate (grades four to six), and upper (grades seven to nine). This schooling is not differentiated; all children take essentially the same courses. A few elective subjects are available at the upper level.

The Secondary School (*Gymnasieskolan*) is an integrated system of 25 different lines of study that are from two to four years in length, and that contain various theoretical and vocational orientations. At the secondary school level each student must decide his or her area of specialization. This decision will shape the student's future education and employment. Secondary school is not com-

pulsory, but about 85 percent of all youngsters attend.

Higher education is offered by the university system. The universities are required to make suitable arrangements and provide support services for handicapped students.

A variety of **Adult Education** opportunities are available for those who want to augment a limited basic education or who risk unemployment and require training in another vocational area.

The **folk high schools** represent a special kind of adult education. They provide courses that vary in length and content. Some of the courses are especially adapted for persons with special needs or disabilities.

Special School for the Deaf and Severely Hearing Impaired

There are five comprehensive schools for the deaf located in different parts of the country. Each enrolls pupils from its region. There are also two schools for deaf children with special problems. These schools recruit pupils on a national basis. One of the schools is designed for the education of mentally retarded deaf children. It is presently serving about 40 pupils. The other school, with about 25 deaf pupils, admits children with serious emotional disturbances or severe language disorders.

The special schools provide the same educational opportunities for the deaf and severely hearing impaired students that the compulsory school system provides for pupils with normal hearing. The Compulsory School Curriculum is applied to deaf children with certain amendments and additions. The course of study at the schools for the deaf continues for ten years instead of nine years, as is the case for children in the regular public schools. The extra year is added at the lower level.

A great deal of technical equipment is used in the schools for the deaf. In addition to hearing aids and amplification systems, overhead projectors are available in all class rooms. Video equipment is used widely to supply information to deaf children. Video programs are produced by the Swedish National Television System and by videograms from the Swedish Association for the Deaf. Videorecordings are also used in sign language lessons and for videogram exchanges among the schools for the deaf. Computers (PCs) are available and are used to teach Swedish, mathematics, and English.

Support service personnel located at the schools for the deaf include a full-time social worker, psychologist, nurse, and audiological engineer. Schools for the deaf also enlist the part-time services of an audiologist, pediatrician, and vocational counselor. The support services are usually of high quality.

The special schools try to include as many extra-curricular school activities as possible. Great importance is attached to contacts with the community at large. Minibuses take the pupils on outings and on visits to factories, museums, and so on. Recreation leaders organize a large number of leisure activities. Some are designed just for the deaf students and some include contact with hearing youngsters.

In most parts of Sweden, pupils enrolled in the lower grades are able to live at home and commute to school daily by taxi. If possible, public transportation is used by the older students. Some of the children, whose parents live far from the schools for the deaf, live in small groups in villas or flats in residential areas near the school or stay with private families who often have a deaf child of their own. This is especially true in the sparsely populated parts of northern Sweden. All pupils go home on the weekends and for school vacations.

Special Secondary School

Almost all of the pupils who graduate from the schools for the deaf go on to the National Secondary School for the Deaf (Riksgymnasiet for dova) at Orebro, which is in the central part of Sweden. At the secondary school they can choose from fifteen different lines of study that have either a theoretical or a vocational orientation.

The deaf pupils who attend separate classes in regular secondary schools are required to follow the same syllabus as do the hearing pupils. The aim of these educational programs is to provide the deaf pupils with the same level of preparation received by their hearing counterparts. To better meet the goal of academic parity with hearing students, the course of study for all of the deaf students enrolled in the special secondary school is extended by one year. Many of the teachers in the special secondary school are trained as teachers of the deaf and are competent in the use of sign language. Those who are not fluent in sign language are assisted by interpreters.

Employment, and Postsecondary and Adult Education

After graduation most of the deaf pupils find employment. Many are assisted by a special counselor for the deaf who is located at a regional employment office.

Those students continuing on to a university are entitled to have sign language interpreters.

There is also a folk high school for deaf people in Leksand. It is owned and organized by the Swedish Association for the Deaf. It offers theoretical courses of different length and content for the adult deaf. The school also offers a vast array of sign language courses. The folk high school offers training programs for interpreters and sign language teachers and produces video programs in sign language. The school is also the center for the study of deaf history and culture.

Method of Communication

The National Supplementary Curriculum for the Schools for the Deaf in Sweden states that the education provided deaf children should be bilingual. The goal of the curriculum is that the students will be proficient in both Swedish Sign Language and the Swedish language. Currently most deaf children become fairly fluent in sign language during the preschool years. The schools for the deaf have the responsibility to develop Swedish Sign Language as the children's primary language and to provide a thorough knowledge of written and, if possible, spoken Swedish. Beginning with the fifth grade, English is usually taught, sometimes in combination with British or American Sign Language.

Although sign language was permitted when teaching older pupils during the late 1960s, it was not until the early 1970s that it was accepted and used to teach younger students. The method of communication used in schools for the deaf still varies considerably from teacher to teacher and from class to class. A growing number of hearing teachers and school personnel have learned to use sign language.

Some form of pidgin Signed Swedish is probably the most common form of sign language used by a majority of hearing adults. The continuum of sign systems used in the schools ranges from Signed Swedish at one end of the continuum to Swedish Sign Language at the other end (Hansen, 1985). Swedish Sign Language is favored by most deaf adults.

The sign system called Signed Swedish was developed during the late 1960s. It includes symbols for verb flexions, suffixes, articles, and so on. Since it was found to be rather awkward in daily communication, Signed Swedish has not found favor and is not commonly used today.

Teachers and Teacher Training

All of the teachers who are part of the faculty of the schools for the deaf are required to be certified teachers of the deaf. In addition to training as an ordinary teacher and three years of teaching experience, teachers of the deaf must complete a special training program. Very few of the teachers in schools for the deaf are deaf themselves. The number is growing since more deaf students are completing teacher training programs. Deaf people are more frequently employed as teacher assistants or as part of the boarding staff.

The special training program that leads to certification as a teacher of the deaf is located at the School of Education, University of Stockholm. The program, which takes three full semesters of study including practicum periods to complete, was revised in 1990–1991, when a new syllabus was implemented. In addition to the academic and educational qualifications required, students must pass a sign language test or provide some proof of sign language competence in order to be admitted. A small number of other professionals who work with the deaf, including psychologists and social workers, have also been admitted to the revised program.

In order to carry out the bilingual education mandate of the state, an extensive inservice training program has been initiated. All teachers at the schools for the deaf are offered a university level, full-time one semester sign language course.

Early Intervention and Support

Once a child is diagnosed as deaf or hard of hearing, he or she is referred to an audiological guidance center. The diagnosis is usually made between the age of twelve to twenty months or earlier if the infant is considered to be at risk. High-risk infants are entered into an audiological screening program. The child is usually fitted with a hearing aid, free of charge, and the family is involved in a home visit program. A teacher visits the infant's home about once a week to show the parents techniques to use to stimulate the child's language development and to provide the parents with guidance. In most regions of the country, the parents of deaf infants are offered practical information and emotional support by a social worker and/or a psychologist. As a rule, parents of deaf and severely hard of hearing children are encouraged to learn sign language as soon as possible in order to have a means of communicating with their child.

At the age of three, the deaf or severely hard of hearing child is guaranteed access to a preschool that has special services for hearing impaired children. In some communities deaf children as young as one year of age are permitted to enroll in day care centers. Placement of children with a mild to moderate hearing impairment in local preschool programs has a high priority. In sparsely populated areas where the distances to be travelled are too great for the deaf child to attend preschool regularly, the visiting teacher continues to work with the child in the home. Most preschools in Sweden enroll both deaf and hearing children. The preschool teachers hired to work with deaf preschool children usually have completed training required to be a teacher of the deaf. Quite often deaf adults are part of the preschool staff.

Most medical care in Sweden, including audiological examinations and other medical needs that a hearing impairment might require, is supported by the state medical program at a very reduced fee.

In addition to free hearing aids, deaf and hard of hearing children and adolescents are offered a selection of technical aids free of charge. These assistive devices include visual signals for the door and the telephone, a vibrating alarm clock, and amplifying devices for the television set and the telephone. From the age of four, the deaf child is provided a teletype device by the state at the cost of an ordinary telephone.

Parent Education

Several organizations operate parent education programs throughout Sweden. During the time the deaf child is in preschool, the audiological guidance center in each county of Sweden is responsible for parent education programs. Parents of the preschool deaf child are offered introductory courses that provide medical and practical information. Other courses focusing on child development, parenting, and educational issues are also available.

Psychological support and guidance services may be informal or organized and are conducted on an individual or group basis.

At the time the deaf child transfers from preschool to compulsory school and from compulsory school to upper secondary school, the parents and student are offered the courses and guidance required to help them make the best choice possible concerning the deaf child's future education.

Sweden does not have any requirement similar to the Individual Educational Program (IEP), which is part of the United States Education of the Handicapped Act (PL 94-142). Thus parent involvement in a child's educational planning and evaluation is on a more general level than is true in the United States.

The sign language courses offered to parents are usually separate from other parent education activities and are organized as intensive courses taught over a period of several weeks, courses taught in the home by the visiting teacher, courses taught over weekends, courses taught by a part of summer camp, or courses taught in the evenings.

Academic Performance of Deaf Children

As part of a longitudinal study of the academic performance of deaf children in Sweden (Norden, 1981; Heiling, 1990), all pupils in the eighth grade of the Lund School for the Deaf were assessed yearly over a five-year period (1985–1989). The test battery consisted mainly of tests of the Swedish language and of mathematical and numerical ability.

The results were compared with results on the same test presented to eighth graders in schools for the deaf during the 1960s. At that time the oral method of teaching the deaf was widely used in Sweden.

The test results indicated that the subjects tested in the 1980s were superior to their deaf age-mates from twenty years earlier in all tests measuring ability to understand and use written Swedish. The current students also performed significantly better on tests of mathematical and numerical ability. The differences between the groups from the two decades were more pronounced, however, in the tests measuring language proficiency.

Between one-third and two-thirds of the subjects tested (depending on testing time limits) read at or above the fourth grade level, which according to the UNESCO-criterion is equal to a functional reading level. One out of ten had a reading ability comparable to that of an average hearing eighth-grader.

On tests of numerical and mathematical ability, around 40 percent of those tested had results equal to or better than the average for hearing age-mates.

On most tests, those deaf students with additional handicapping conditions performed poorly.

Tests of the Swedish language have also been administered to pupils in the lower grades. Results show a general tendency toward an improved level of academic performance.

Historical Background
Education of Deaf Pupils

The oldest school for the deaf in Sweden, the Manilla School in Stockholm, was founded in 1809 by a clerk at the Royal Chancellory, Mr. Par Aron Borg. Instruction of deaf children earlier than 1809, it if existed, took place in the home. The original aim of the Manilla School was to provide vocational training for deaf students in the areas of tailoring, shoe-making, carpentry, weaving, sewing, and other areas.

Influenced by the French or manual method of teaching the deaf, Borg and his fellow teachers, some of whom were deaf, used sign language to instruct the deaf children. Swedish was taught largely by use of the written word.

In the middle of the nineteenth century, several private or state-run institutions for the deaf were founded. Many of the schools established at that time also enrolled blind or mentally retarded pupils.

In 1889 the State introduced a law entitled "The Education of the Deaf and Dumb." The law stated that regional schools would provide an eight-year course of study for deaf students. Pupils were assigned to classes employing different methods of communication including speech, writing, or sign. Those students assigned to classes designed to focus on speech communication were exclusively oral. If writing was the assigned system of communication, written language and finger-spelling was used. Students assigned to a sign communication class utilized sign language, fingerspelling, and the written language. It was stated that "the less gifted" used sign language. The method of communication used with deaf children varied from school to school (Nystrom, 1990).

In 1938, the education of the deaf was totally reorganized and administered centrally by the Swedish National Board of Education. As part of the new organization, the value of vocational training was formally recognized and two national vocational schools were established.

With the development of hearing aids and other types of auditory equipment, oral communication became the exclusive method of instruction during the 1950s and 1960s.

The Uniform School Curriculum Act of 1969 created the uniform Swedish compulsory school system. The new act increased the length of the course of study at the schools for the deaf from nine to ten years. The Uniform School Curriculum Act of 1969 also declared that schools for the deaf should apply the regular school curriculum and syllabi as far as was feasible.

The National Special Secondary School for the Deaf was started in 1967 and gradually replaced other vocational and theoretical programs for the deaf throughout the country.

Teacher Preparation

In 1874 formal courses to prepare teachers of the deaf were begun at the Manilla School. Deaf individuals were not admitted to these courses, since disabled persons were not considered to have the ability necessary to be an adequate teacher. Deaf teachers were not allowed to teach academic subjects in schools for the deaf for nearly 100 years after the first school for the deaf was originated. There were, however, deaf teachers instructing courses in handicrafts. It was not until 1967 that the program to prepare special teachers of the deaf became part of the University of Stockholm. The first deaf students were finally admitted to formal teacher training about ten years later.

Significant Current Issues

The foremost, or priority, issue concerning the education of the deaf in Sweden today is the debate over the development of a true bilingual education for deaf pupils. Much of the discussion has focused upon the methods to be used to teach Swedish as a second language, as well as the techniques that can be used to contrast and compare Swedish and Swedish Sign Language.

Problem-oriented education that utilizes flexible grouping of students and teams of teachers are other topics of current interest.

Organizations representing young hard of hearing individuals and their parents are requesting closer coordination with education programs for deaf students. Since it has been found that many hard of hearing pupils do not function well in mainstream classes, there is a growing interest in the education of hard of hearing pupils and debate concerning how special units for the hard of hearing should best be organized.

Since the 1980s, an increasing number of immigrant children, mainly from eastern Europe and Asia, have enrolled in the schools for the deaf. This infusion of immigrant children has created issues concerning the implications of educating deaf children with different cultures and languages.

The education of the deaf in Sweden is in a state of development and change. Not only have there been changes in national educational policies, but the new generation of deaf children requires that the curriculum content be modified and existing instructional pedagogy be examined. Most of the deaf children in schools for the deaf today are rather fluent in sign language and have a general level of knowledge and social competence not common in earlier groups of deaf children. The goal for schools for the deaf in Sweden today is to learn to cope with the multidimensional challenges these children present.

References

Hammarstedt, B., & Amcoff, S. (1979). Integration of hearing impaired pupils in the Swedish comprehensive school. *Pedagogisk Forskning.* Uppsala, Sweden: Samspecprojektet, rapport nr. 10. (In Swedish)

Hansen, B. (Ed.). (1985). *Sign language research and sign language use.* Copenhagen, Denmark: Center for Total Communication. (In Danish)

Heiling, K. (1990). *Has anything happened in twenty years? Achievement level of Swedish deaf eighthgraders in the sixties and twenty years later - a comparison.* Malmo, Sweden: School of Education. (In Swedish)

The Manilla School for the Deaf. (1983). Stockholm: Team Tryck.

Norden, K. (1981). Learning processes and personality development in deaf children. American *Annals of the Deaf,* 4, 404-410.

Nystrom, A. F. (1990). *Foundations of the education for the deaf and dumb in Sweden.* Orebro, Sweden: 1900–1908. (In Swedish)

Education of Deaf People in the Kingdom of Thai

by
Charles Reilly and Sathaporn Suvannus

About the Authors

Sathaporn Suvannus was the Principal of the Sethsatian School for the Deaf in Bangkok from 1973–1983 and Secretary-General of the Foundation for the Deaf of Thailand from 1975–85. A master's level graduate of Hunter College (New York) in the education of the physically handicapped, Mrs. Suvannus has had a distinguished career of service to disabled people. She was Chief Supervisor of Special Education in Thailand from 1965–1983. Suvannus is a well-known writer, the leading chronicler of the history of efforts to help the deaf in Thailand. She wrote the piece on Thailand in *The Encyclopedia of Deafness* (McGraw-Hill, 1987).

Charles Reilly worked with deaf people in Thailand from 1978–1985. He was manager of the project Reaching the Unreached: Thailand's Deaf Community (1981–1985). He served as chief trainer during the establishment of the National Association of the Deaf, a deaf-run society with a secretariat and several clubs for the deaf in different parts of Thailand. From 1978–1981, using deaf teachers, Reilly developed a language enrichment curriculum for new pupils who were deaf at the Sethsatian School for the Deaf. He is the co-compiler of the *Thai Sign Language Dictionary, Book One* (1986). In 1991–1992 Reilly was awarded a Fulbright Scholarship to complete a dissertation on the process of self-education among deaf people in boarding schools (University of Maryland).

Acknowledgments

Expert advice was given by Dr. Owen Wrigley, University of Hawaii, and the following from the royal Thai Government: Mr. Kamoal Thitkamol; Mr. Paitoon Kongkarsuriyachai; from the Department of General Education, Ministry of Education and Statistics, Dr. Duangtip Surintatip; and from the Education Population Division, National Office, Mrs. Taweepron Tuwicharnon. Thanks to all of these people. The authors take sole responsibility for the views expressed and for any mistakes.

The Kingdom of Thailand: Introduction

Situated in Southeast Asia, the Kingdom of Thailand covers an area of 513,000 square kilometers. It is nearly the size of France. Fifty-six million people live in a country endowed with ample space and resources to allow for a decent quality of life. Although most of the people are involved in agriculture, urban growth is rapid. Ethnic groups include Thai, Chinese, Laotian, Malay, and Sino-Tibetan hill tribes. Under the pennant of His Majesty the King, the Buddhist religion, and a competent military, the Thai nation has fostered a strong national identity. Politically, Thailand (ex-Siam) has been a constitutional monarchy since 1932. His Majesty King Bhumibol Adulyadej, Rama IX, remains influential due to his popularity with the people. A bicameral parliament, a prime minister, and a large bureaucracy run the affairs of the state. Control is centralized, deriving from the capital city of Bangkok.

History of the Education of the Deaf in Thailand

Thailand has had an educational system for over 700 years, but the education of deaf people began only 40 years ago. Its nature can be better understood after a brief review of the historical and ideological roots of the country's general educational system. The three historical periods in the development of education in Thailand were noted by Watson (1980).[1] These periods are discussed below.

1. Religious Education, Thirteenth to Nineteenth Centuries

Thai education originated in monastic schools in Buddhist temples. Only boys were taught reading, writing, arithmetic, and the basic Pall language, an ancient Indian language used in prayer. The belief was that learning and educating were religious acts, a form of merit-making. Whereas parents gave life, monks imparted a way of life and knowledge that made life worth living (Watson, 1980, p. 69).

From the thirteenth to the nineteenth centuries, the content and purpose of education as moral betterment was practically unchanged. Deaf children were not offered any special education, but the monks at the temples strived to educate all.

2. Royal Initiative: Mid-Nineteenth to Early Twentieth Centuries

The royal family of Thailand began to assert state control over education in the 1870s. The West's emphasis on practical lessons, including medicine and engineering, was deemed useful to Thailand by King Mongkut (r. 1851–1868), who permitted missionary schools and sent members of the royalty abroad to study. Secular education for both boys and girls in the general society was promoted by his son, Chulalongkorn, Rama V (r.1868–1910). In a break with the past, this king intended that the new form of secular education be a public resource: "All children from my own to the poorest should have an equal chance to be educated." He established a Ministry of Public Instruction (now the Ministry of Education), and developed curriculum and imported textbooks. As head of the church, he compelled the teachers in the temples to increase the intensity and utility of their instruction (Chakrabongse, 1960, p. 224; Watson, 1980, p. 2).

3. Secular Public Schooling: Twentieth Century

Temple schools were gradually replaced by free-standing institutions, under the supervision of provincial and local officials and directly accountable to the central government. The main purposes of education were to instill loyalty to the nation and to teach the skills needed for individual and societal economic progress. A Compulsory Education Act was passed in 1921. Until 1980 the Act exempted disabled children and those living far from the schools. The main thrust of the educational system since 1980 has been to expand facilities, geographic areas served, and the number of grade levels.

The number of children in elementary and secondary schools increased from four million in 1961 to over eight million in 1981. Today almost every child lives reasonably close to a school. Boys and girls attend in equal numbers. While institutions of higher education serve much smaller numbers, Thailand has a fully developed higher education system, encompassing university, vocational, and non-formal extension programs.

The major themes of education in present day Thailand are:

- to expand services and facilities in order that more children can attend school and for longer periods of time
- to maintain a curriculum that emphasizes traditional moral and ethical values
- to serve economic goals
- to continue a school policy and practice that is centrally determined and allows only slight participation by the public

These themes have asserted a profound effect on the education of deaf people in Thailand.

Elites Initiate Education of Disabled Children

The turn-of-the-century commitment of H. J. King Rama V to provide equal access to education for all children inspired the thinking that led to the start of schooling for deaf people some 50 years later.[2] As was true of schooling for the general public, the education of the deaf was initiated by members of the elite class in response to what was happening internationally. It was the idea of M. L. Pin Malakul to initiate special education for handicapped children. In his capacity as Under-Secretary of State for Education, he attended a UNESCO meeting in 1946 and learned about the United Nations Declaration of Human Rights. The concept that schooling is a human right and that it is the duty of the state to provide education to its citizens was a convincing idea to Thai social leaders.

A grant was accepted from the United States for a Thai teacher to study special education. M. R. Sermsrl Kasemsri, an official of the Ministry of Education, subsequently studied at Hunter College in New York during the 1948–49 academic year. She helped Miss G. Caulfield, a blind woman from the United States, start Thailand's first school for the blind in 1939.

After receiving her M.A. degree she studied at Gallaudet University from 1949 to 1951. M. R. Sermsri then returned to Thailand to head an experimental center for the deaf. The center opened in Bangkok on December 10, 1951, which also happened to be the third anniversary of the Declaration of Human Rights. Initially the center had but five pupils. Within six months there were 50 children in attendance. Until December 1953, the Unit for Teaching the Deaf was allocated a room at Sommanatwiharn Temple School (Municipal # 17).

During the school's first year it had no budget from the Ministry but operated through a good number of private contributions. For many years only the efforts of committed individuals kept the education of the deaf alive. The education of the deaf was considered experimental by educational authorities, who were ambivalent about the provision of regular services for disabled people. The passage of time brought about a slow change in the attitude of the people of Thailand towards disabled people. Fortunately, disabled children are under the royal patronage of H.R.H. Princess Mahachakri Sirindhorn. The role of the royal class in the promotion of social change is a characteristic of Thai society and has benefited disabled people in the country.

Joint Private-Public Cooperation

The growth of schooling for the deaf has depended upon a joint effort between the government and the private sector. A charitable group, the Foundation for the Deaf, under the patronage of Her Majesty Queen Sirikit, has been a leading player in the raising of funds and the mustering of services of concerned people. In 1952 the Foundation for the Welfare of the Deaf was established after Mme. La-aid Pibul Songkram, wife of the Prime Minister, attended a Gallaudet University commencement and was impressed with the achievements of the deaf people there. In 1958, with the support of the Foundation and a land donation by Lady Noranet, the Ministry of Education was able to open the Dusit School for the Deaf (now Sethsatian School) in northern Bangkok. In 1955 the school's enrollment was 43 pupils, with 76 children on a waiting list. By the end of that academic year, five deaf students had completed the final exam of the Elementary Education Course (grade four) along with hearing children from the Phyathai School, Bangkok. Three boys who were deaf passed the examination. This proved that the education of the deaf people was possible and no longer needed to be considered experimental.

A Pioneer: Kamala Krairiksh

Mrs. Kamala Krairiksh, a master's degree graduate of Gallaudet University, was the major figure in Thai education of the deaf for twenty years. Starting with her appointment as Principal of Dusit School in 1954, Kamala led the way to a full-blown educational system for deaf children. She supervised the building of most of the schools for the deaf in Thailand and was instrumental in the training of teachers of the deaf. She collected signs used by Thai deaf people, invented new signs, and adopted American signs to compile the influential Sign Dictionary for Teachers, Book One. With the aid of E. Benson of Gallaudet

University, Kamala also invented the Thai manual alphabet, by using handshapes from the American manual alphabet and by combining them to represent the larger number of Thai characters. During her tenure as Principal of Dusit School, a combined approach was utilized, which stressed equal use of oral methods and manual methods of communication. Peer tutoring by older students was encouraged, and superior graduates were retained as teachers.

In 1969 Kamala founded the Center for Deaf Alumna, the predecessor of the Thailand National Association of the Deaf. Many deaf people recall how she pushed them to learn, thus assisting them to attain advanced training and good jobs. From 1981 to 1985, after her retirement, Kamala served as President of the Foundation of the Deaf. His Majesty the King bestowed upon Kamala Krairiksh the title of "Honored Lady."

Present Educational Programs and Services for the Deaf

Over the past 40 years special education in Thailand has progressed slowly but continuously. Most of the attention has been focused upon the expansion of the basic education program to outlying areas and to the addition of grade levels. Table 1 shows the number of each type of school, organization, the number and percentage of pupils enrolled in each type of school, and student/teacher ratios in each type of school for the deaf in Thailand.

For five schools the 1991 enrollments are given. The 1991 enrollment shows growth of over 2 percent from 1990 figures. One welfare institution, Pakret Home, has a ratio of 53:1; the other welfare institutions have an 11:1 ratio.

A breakdown of the total enrollment figure shows that children enrolled in the pre-primary grades comprise 17 percent of the total; primary grades one through six

Table 1: **School Enrollment of Thai Deaf and Hard of Hearing Children, 1990–1991**

	Number of Pupils	Number of Schools	% Total Enrollment	Student/Teacher Ratio
Type of School				
Special residential	2,631	6	86	10:1
Separate class in regular public school	320	9	11	11:1
Mainstreamed in a welfare institution	86	4	3	22: 1

Total Enrollment: 3,037   Total Number of Schools: 19

Source: Special Education Division, "Special Education in Thailand" (1990)

make up 68 percent; lower secondary (grades seven through nine) totals 12 percent; and higher secondary (grades ten through twelve) consist of only 3 percent of the total.[3] There is virtually no education for the deaf above the twelfth grade.

The ratio of students to teacher is 8:1 for pre-primary and 10:1 for the primary grades. By contrast, in regular primary schools the ratio is one teacher to 20-25 pupils, depending on the region (Royal Thai Government, 1984, p. 265). Both boys and girls are schooled without prejudice. Figure 1 shows the distribution of services throughout the country and the dates when the services were established.

Special Schools

Thailand has six residential institutions for the deaf,[4] one residential school for the hard of hearing, and two day schools for the deaf that board some students. Three of these nine institutions are located in the Bangkok metropolitan area. These schools are the Nonthaburi Residential School, and the Sethsatian and Tungmahamek Day Schools.

Thailand is divided into twelve educational regions. Each school for the deaf serves those who live in the region. Children who have a bilateral hearing loss of greater than 85 dB are admitted to the schools for the deaf. Those with more hearing attend the Cholburi School for hard of hearing or enroll in a main-

Figure 1. **Map of Thailand with Location, Year of Establishment, and Type of Schools for Hearing Impaired Children**

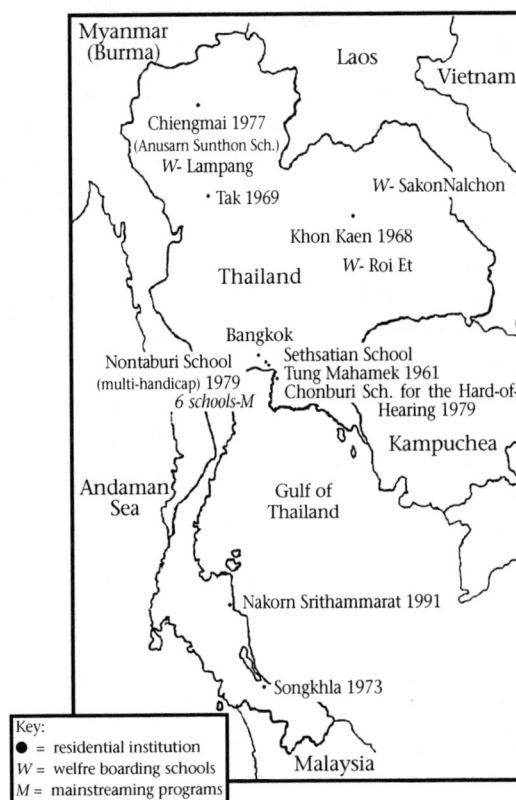

stream program. All schools accept pupils from the ages of six to fourteen. The average age of entry is eight.

In the residential schools children learn sign language from each other. All schools permit the children to use the Thai Sign

Language. Free time is provided to allow the children to develop their own social relationships. Many deaf people attribute most of their childhood learning to interactions with other deaf people at the residential schools. The special schools are often a gathering point for the adult deaf community, too. This helps to overcome the feelings of isolation common to deaf people from rural areas. However, there is no central policy that encourages the schools to welcome deaf adults.

Mainstreaming

The Thai Ministry of Education stated in 1957 that its objective was "to integrate disabled children into a normal educational setting to encourage future integration into normal society." There have been programs designed to mainstream mentally retarded children since 1956 and blind children since 1965. Experimental mainstreaming programs for deaf and hard of hearing children were begun around the mid-1970s and have grown steadily. Programs in regular day schools and boarding welfare institutions now enroll 14 percent of Thailand's deaf and hard of hearing students.

Thai parents often favor regular schooling for their deaf and hard of hearing children. The demand for these services exceeds the number of facilities and trained teachers available. Day, residential, and mainstream programs are discussed below.

Mainstreaming in Regular Schools

All six schools that mainstream deaf children are run by the central government and are located in the capital city, Bangkok. The five schools at the primary level are (1) Phyathai; (2) Samsen Kindergarten; (3) Raj Winit; (4) PraTamnak Suan Kularb; and (5) La-or Utit Demonstration School.

The first three schools above integrate one to five deaf and hard of hearing children into each regular class. The official policy states that the program is for children with a hearing level of less than 55 dB. In actuality, children with up to a 90 dB hearing level are accepted. The Phyathai School operates one or two self-contained classes at the beginning of the year for children who are not ready for full integration. Later, all are mainstreamed. At the kindergarten level, La-or Utit, run by Suan Dusit Teachers College, integrates a few deaf and hard of hearing students with hearing children. PraTamnak has a special department for profoundly deaf preschool children ages four to seven. Grade levels are parallel to those found in preschool programs for hearing children. Fourth-year pupils are integrated for some activities such as physical education and for socialization purposes. Children who finish the fourth year go on to schools for the deaf and mainstream programs.

The sixth school offers mainstreaming at the lower secondary level, the sixth through the ninth grades. For hard of hearing children, Pibun Prachasan School in Bangkok has offered mainstreaming at the secondary level since 1975. Intended primarily to serve socially disadvantaged pupils from the Bangkok slums, and under the management of the Special Education Division, this school fully integrates pupils with a 45-90 dB loss. These pupils are supported by itinerant teachers, and on some occasions an interpreter is provided.

The student/teacher ratio is 1:19. Slow learners and mildly mentally retarded pupils are integrated as well. Writes co-author Suvannus, "Children are happy in this school . . . . No teachers treated them as exceptional children. Other parents do not think that they are special children, even though some of them cannot produce understandable speech. . . ."[5]

If a regular classroom teacher has no training in special education, only one handicapped child will be placed in her classroom. Those with special education certification must have at least three to five deaf children placed in the class in order to receive the "occupational hardship" stipend given to those teachers who teach special children. This policy encourages the school to group deaf and hard of hearing children into a few classrooms. It has been demonstrated that there are advantages to having groups of special children in a mainstream classroom.[6]

The deaf and hard of hearing children tend to form a group. This seems to support their language and social growth. Grouping of deaf children into a few classes seems to make the integration process less difficult for the teacher. As for peer interaction, while there has been no research done, some teachers have said that deaf and hard of hearing children have no problems relating to hearing children in the regular schools. It is a Thai tradition to help others in need. The hearing pupils often assist the deaf and hard of hearing students enrolled in their classes.

Issues in Mainstreaming in Regular School

People in Thailand are not in agreement about the merits of mainstreaming. Some teachers feel that is unfair for deaf and hard of hearing students to use the same curriculum and the same tests as do hearing children. Others feel that it is unfair that teachers must devote more attention to the deaf children than to others in the class. Schools with the strongest administration and highest academic standards are chosen for mainstreaming. If mainstreaming is expanded nationwide, there is a fear that schools with weaker administrative and academic standards will not be able to properly handle the demands of a good integration program.

Mainstreaming in Residential Welfare Institutions

Thailand has a number of boarding schools established for children from hill tribes or from poor backgrounds. Deaf and hard of hearing children whose parents live in remote areas are enrolled in these residential welfare schools. The three welfare schools that accept deaf children are the Thawartburi at Roi-Et, Sakon Nakon, and Jit-Ari in Lampang. Mainstreaming deaf children in the welfare boarding schools is experimental. If it works well, the program will be put into action in

other welfare schools throughout the Kingdom. In addition, the Pattya Home for the Disabled Children, under the Ministry of Public Welfare, cares for abandoned and multihandicapped deaf children as well as those who hear. This school has only one teacher trained in the area of deafness. The staff has been provided training in manual communication.

Informal Programs

Throughout the nation there are good-hearted individuals, both private and government people, who have provided learning opportunities for the deaf despite the communication difficulties. The government encourages the private sector to take the initiative in helping the disabled. [7]

Multihandicapped deaf people are served by Sathaban Saeng Sawan in Bangkok and by other non-profit groups. The Pattaya Orphanage sponsors preschool and vocational training for deaf youth. In northeastern Nakhon Phanom, a deaf adult named N. Pitipat runs a basic skills program for deaf individuals from six to twenty years old. The Thailand National Association of the Deaf, with American assistance, has provided the schools for the deaf with two substantial dictionaries of Thai Sign Language.

Educational Policy and Challenges for Deaf Education

As is true in most nations, schooling in Thailand is controlled by the central government. Authorities at the capital control hiring assignments and compensation of personnel and set objectives and policies. Provincial-level officers and the provincial Governor, an appointed office, handle part of the supervisory function.

The special institutions and welfare schools are under the authority of the

Division of Special Education, which is part of the Department of General Education (DSE/DGE) and is located in the Ministry of Education. The Division of Special Education may soon be upgraded to the status of a Department of the Ministry of Education, which should provide an expanded number of personnel, increased budget, and increased visibility. The mainstream programs are under the jurisdiction of the Office of the National Primary Education Commission (NPEC), which handles education programs in Thailand. The Ministry of Public Welfare cares for children with multiple disabilities and disabled children who have been abandoned.

Important government documents include provisions for educational services to disabled people, including the deaf. These documents include the National Scheme of Education, Buddhist Era, Year 2520 (A.D. 1977); the National Curriculum for Elementary Education, B.E. 2521 (A.D. 1978); and the Elementary Education Act, B.E. 2523 (A.D. 1980). As part of the seventh five-year national plan (1991–96), the Ministry of Education has approved a Plan for The Development of Education, Culture and Religion (hereafter referred to as "the 1992–96 Development Plan"). There is no central plan that governs all activities in Thailand. As many as five ministries may share the responsibility for a single area of work. Appropriations for the education of the deaf come from the Ministry of Education, the Ministry of Interior (Department of Public Welfare), Ministry of Public Health, Office of the Prime Minister, Office of the Royal Household, Bureau of Universities, and Bangkok Metropolitan Authority.

Three major policy issues face the education of the deaf in Thailand. These issues are as follows: (1) the expansion of access to special education; (2) the relative role of boarding schools and mainstream programs; and (3) the improvement of the quality of services. This section of the chapter focuses on these issues.

Policy Issue #1: Expansion of Access to Special Education

Today most people in Thailand agree that it is important to send non-disabled children to school. It took most of the twentieth century for society to reach this consensus and to develop a national school system. Public attitudes of resistance and economic limitations were the main obstacles to growth. These same obstacles now hinder the expansion of education for the disabled. The value of sending disabled people to school is not yet widely recognized in Thai society.

No one knows how many deaf people there are in Thailand. Using the common demographic figure of a prevalence rate of 1 in 1,000 people who become deaf before reaching the age of four years, Thailand would have had 56,000 prelingually deafened people in 1991. This figure includes people of all ages. Table 2 shows the sub-set of school-age deaf people. In brackets is the percentage of this group that is now in school. The appendix at the end of the chapter explains how the calculations were arrived at.

Table 2: Estimated Prevalence and School Enrollment of Deaf Children in Thailand [8]

Deaf People 7-12 Enrolled in school		Deaf People 13-15 Enrolled in school	
Number Enrolled	% Enrolled	Number Enrolled	% Enrolled
10,161	[18%]	14,829	[15%]
1/1000 prevalence estimate			
9,632	[19%]	14,090	[16%]

Source of Estimate: Royal Thai National Statistical Office, 1970.

Of the deaf children between the ages of seven and twelve, about 18 or 19 percent are now in school. Of the deaf children from thirteen to fifteen years old, about 15 to 16 percent are now in school. Ninety-nine percent of the hearing children aged seven to twelve and 33 percent of the thirteen- to fifteen- year-olds are enrolled in school (Ministry of Education, 1987, p. 46; Office of the Prime Minister, 1984, p. 265). However, the comparison may be unfair since education for deaf people is only 40 years old. In 1940 about 60 percent of non-disabled children were enrolled in the four-year compulsory education program (Watson, 1980, p. 107). Compulsory schooling began in 1921, but disabled children were legally exempted from compulsory education until 1980. Education for the disabled in Thailand is still in its infancy and also has developed at a much slower rate.

Expansion of services is a major goal of the Special Education Division. The building of three more schools, two in the Northeast and one in the North, was planned during the 1992–1996 National Development Plan (Royal Thai Government, Planning Division, 1991). As of July 1992 funds had not yet been committed to this project. In 1991 a new school opened in the South at Nakorn Srithammarat.

Obstacles to Increased Enrollment

Some of the obstacles to the growth of schools for the disabled include a lack of public awareness of currently available services, reluctance of parents to bring their children to school, and the lack of facilities and adequate budget resources.

Lack of Information

The majority of Thailand's population lives in rural areas and is isolated from information about services for deaf children. There is no system to provide parent education and media coverage of the topic. The availability of interpreter services for the evening TV news broadcast and the development in the late 1980s of a popular comedy program have greatly raised awareness about sign language. Well-promoted annual events such as the Day of the Disabled have caused the attitude of the public to be more positive. Despite efforts to provide information, however, many people have little interest in articles or TV programs concerning the deaf or hard of hearing. Sign language is considered to be strange, and people reportedly get bored watching the sign language interpreter on the TV screen.

Attitudes Towards Deafness

Most people in Thailand believe that the disabilities in their children result from their own wrong deeds (Karma), either in this life or in the previous cycle of incarnation. By tradition and temperament, Thai people generally have a humanitarian outlook. Their sense of responsibility and guilt compels them, however poor they are, to shelter disabled children as much as is possible from any interference from the outside world (Suxvanarat, 1989). This attitude makes it very difficult for the Government or others to extend a helping hand to the disabled of Thailand.

In the rural areas deafness is not considered to be a serious handicap. Deaf children are able to help around the house, work on the farm, plant vegetables, and look after cattle. Since they can physically participate in all activities of the family and the community, they are not considered to be disabled. Although the majority of children in rural areas have completed compulsory education, most do not use the knowledge learned in school in everyday life.

In the metropolitan areas parents seem to have more disappointments and anxieties in dealing with their deaf and hard of hearing children. Because of parental attitudes, the deaf child is often rejected, over-indulged, or over-protected, thus hampering the child's development.

Economic Considerations

Economic considerations may keep deaf and hard of hearing children out of school. Sending a child to school may be at the expense of farm or factory production. While the Thai government provides the cost of educational services from central revenues, parents incur the required transportation expenses. Many parents doubt that education for their disabled children is worth the financial outlay. In Thai society it is a commonly held belief that disabled children will be unable to progress very far in society or in an occupational area with or without an education. This sentiment is echoed in the law. Education for disabled children has never been explicitly mentioned in the law as compulsory.[9] Most families are pleased to get an exemption from the mandatory education law for their disabled child, and officials usually comply.

Financial Limitations

The government has made a strong effort to enroll disabled people in school, by relieving the parents of the financial burden. Room, board, and tuition in the provincial schools is provided free of cost by the central government. Boarders at the Bangkok schools pay only for their living expenses. The federal budget amount provided to the schools includes only the bare essentials, i.e., salaries, supplies, utilities, maintenance, and the costs of board and room. The official budgeted amount per pupil, $360 (U.S.), is roughly twice that which is allocated for regular pupils (Department of General Education, 1988, p. 79). Nevertheless, in 1990 the two Bangkok schools spent more than twice the official budget amount.[10] Principals of all special programs must limit enrollment, stretch the budget to cover more children, or raise outside funds. The government provides funds only for a specific number of pupils. The number of new pupils accepted each year depends on how many leave. The authorities try to limit enrollments in the special schools by mainstreaming profoundly deaf children, using entrance exams to screen out those who are not ready for school, and providing automatic promotion to the next grade level. Each of these strategies has serious limitations. More funding is essential if the education of deaf and hard of hearing children is to be improved.

Extension of Services to More Levels

All schools offer nine years of instruction. In 1987 instruction was extended to the twelfth grade in two of the Bangkok schools for the deaf. Eventually all schools will offer a program that includes kindergarten through grade twelve. Deaf children will be in school for fourteen to fifteen years. More and more deaf children are entering school yearly, and more are staying until the full program is completed. Most of the schools for the deaf are full and several are over-crowded. A dilemma for the Ministry of Education is whether to focus on expanding basic services to more deaf children or to extend the number of levels of education currently available.

The Need for Preschool Education

New pupils typically enter the special schools between the ages of seven and nine. This is an improvement from years ago. Many eligible children are on a waiting list for one to three years. Some deaf children are never enrolled, due to the lack of budget and space. Many families give up. Increasingly, the schools accept only the younger applicants. Sometimes, however, depending upon the compassion of the school principal, children as old as fourteen are accepted to one of the schools. Several schools use screening tests to select the students who will be enrolled. Unfortunately, those who are judged "not ready to learn" are denied admission. At home, many of these children do not receive the parental and educational support needed to promote cognitive development. This unfortunate majority of deaf children in Thailand loses the opportunity to attend school.

For the lucky few who are enrolled, the first few years are a difficult period for pupils and teachers alike. The prelingually deaf pupils usually come to school with no language. These children lag far behind their hearing peers in general knowledge and social awareness. They do not adjust well to living away from home. Older deaf pupils refer to this initial period as their "know-nothing" time. As Figure 2 below indicates, this means a lack of sign communication skill, an inability to reason or act in an independent manner, and ignorance about the rules and ways of the school and the peer group.

Figure 2. **The sign that deaf Thais use for their prelingual period [know-nothing]**

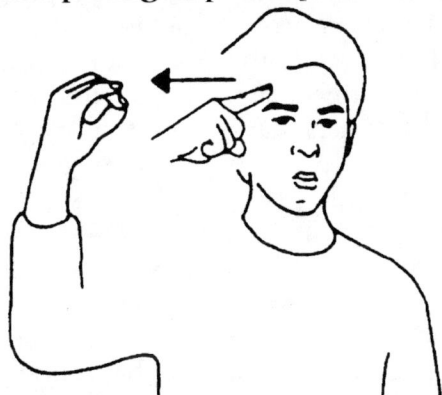

Rural Schools

In the rural schools that do not have kindergartens, the child enters at the first grade level and immediately begins to study the regular public school curriculum. Since the deaf child is not ready to handle the regular public school curriculum, this makes the teacher's job very difficult. Some teachers become so frustrated that they reduce direct instructional time. The deaf children, too, are burdened by too many challenges, including learning specific academic skills, adjusting to living away from home, being the least respected member of the student body, and learning Thai and Thai Sign Language. Most deaf pupils spend two or three years at the first level. They are held back until it is felt that they are ready to handle the curriculum at the next level. The decision to promote or fail a student is made solely by the teacher, (except at Cholburi School, which has an automatic promotion policy). The class may contain newcomers and repeating students from the ages of six to fourteen. The benefit of having different age groups in the same class is that the older pupils can help instruct the younger ones. On the other hand, those who have repeated the same level for several years are frequently bored after completing the same rudimentary lessons again and again.

The situation in schools with kindergartens is much better. For example, at the Chiengmai School, the younger children are given special lessons adapted to their skill level and are protected from the hardship of competing with older children. Thailand has made good progress in expanding preschool services for the deaf during the last decade. The government has recognized that kindergartens are very important but has not yet provided the funding necessary to have a kindergarten in all schools. All of Thailand's preschool programs have excellent student-to-teacher ratios of under 1 to 10. The special schools in Bangkok and Chiengmai offer the students the kindergarten level for a period of two to three years. Deaf children as young as three years of age are admitted. Kindergarten is also offered at two of the mainstream schools, PraTamnak and La-or Utit, both of which have separate classes for the deaf.

The central government's plan to expand and establish preschools in the rural provinces awaits expansion of the current budget and facilities. On the Eastern Seaboard there is a missionary-run kindergarten sponsored by the Pattaya Child Welfare Foundation. Free board and instruction is offered to poor deaf children between the ages of four and eight. In 1990 there were 30 children, three classrooms, and five teachers at the school.

Higher Secondary Level

Higher secondary level is now available to deaf children but the drop-out rate is high. Enrollments in educational programs in Thailand are like a pyramid. Over 99 percent of non-disabled children continue their study through the sixth grade. Only 33 percent of the fifteen-year-olds were enrolled in the ninth grade (Ministry of Information, 1987, p. 46). For deaf children exact graduation figures are not available. Less than 20 percent of Thai deaf children were attending elementary school in 1992, as estimated in Table 2. And only about 8 percent of deaf people in the twelve- to fifteen-year-old age group were enrolled in grade nine. Because of additional drop-outs before graduation, the final percentage of all deaf children who actually graduate from elementary and lower secondary level is lower than the figures provided for the current enrollment. Graduation rates will be discussed later in the chapter.

If the deaf child is part of the fortunate minority that is permitted to enroll in school, it is likely that she or he will finish the six years of the elementary level. For example, in Sethsatian School during the 1975 to 1985 period, 85 percent of those who entered the first grade finished grade six. Only 57 percent of the entrants to Sethsatian School from 1975 to 1985 completed the ninth grade. For those who do go on to the secondary level, again, most will continue until graduation. No figures are available for deaf children, but a 1988 statistical study of the entire secondary system, presumably including the schools for the deaf, revealed that 3.39 percent of lower secondary pupils dropped out (16,352 pupils) and 4.07 percent (20,077 pupils) dropped out at the upper secondary level.

By 1995 compulsory education in Thailand was extended from six to nine years for all children. Fulfilling this goal for deaf children will be difficult with the current educational system. All special schools now offer nine grades and the Bangkok schools provide instruction through the twelfth grade. As of now, pupils in rural schools need to move to costly Bangkok in order to complete the higher grades. The shortage of facilities means that students may not be encouraged to stay in school. The secondary grades often do not receive the same amount of state resources that are provided to the primary grades.

The number of school grades provided to deaf pupils has not expanded because teachers, the public, and the pupils doubt the value of additional schooling. Even for deaf children, there are pressures to join the labor force. People from rural areas are less likely to complete nine years of schooling than people living in urban areas. This indicates that the two groups have a different opinion of the value of education.

Some students assert that the courses required are too difficult. Secondary entrance exams must be passed. Some deaf people state that there is no reason to stay in school since the teachers do not provide the needed higher level skills. Many of the deaf students indicate that the teachers have poor sign language skills and that the instruction provided by the teachers is dull. Teachers in the secondary education programs for the deaf are accused of not seriously trying to prepare pupils for higher education or for vocational areas.

Those deaf students who drop out lose any chance of acquiring essential school credentials. The high drop-out rate may decrease the quality of residential life in the schools for the deaf, since so few older pupils remain behind to act as role models, to assist in language development, and to provide everyday life skills and knowledge.

Policy Issue #2: How to Improve the Quality of Services

The Ministry of Education is attempting to improve the standard of instruction in regular public schools. In special education, the focus continues to be on the expansion and extension of services. Some say that an increased budget amount that would provide funds for teacher preparation, equipment, and so on is the only way to improve the quality of instruction.

Using the Hidden Resources of Education within the Boarding Schools

In the boarding schools for the deaf there is an effective, informal process of education going on among the hundreds of pupils themselves. This occurs because the Royal Thai Government allows signs to be used during all school activities. Proof that deaf children are learning from other deaf children is found in the use of the national sign language. New pupils have no previous knowledge of sign language, but within a few years all of them have learned the Thai Sign Language, and use it far better than do their teachers. They have learned the sign language from their older peers.

Deaf people in Thailand have stated that they enter school in a state of "know-nothing" (see earlier description of the concept of "know nothing"). Usually within a period of three years the deaf children have learned enough to be in a state of mental awareness, which they call "becoming mindful." Figure 3 shows the sign for "becoming mindful."

Figure 3. **The Thai sign for [being mindful]**

Restricted Peer Education

In traditional Thai society older children take care of younger children. In the residential schools for the deaf, senior pupils accept the responsibility to look after younger pupils.

This kind of informal education is carried out by the children themselves. The older pupils teach the younger pupils about the rules of the school and the rules of the peer group during assemblies and after school hours in the dormitories. Ritually, children imitate school-time behaviors, lining up and drilling even when no teachers are around. During these interactions the older children often order younger children to do things. They usually comply. The younger subjects surrender total control over their physical movements (enforced line-ups and lock-step drills), their eyes (during meditation), and their signed expressions (arms held in positions which preclude signed communication). They are powerless to act, to communicate, and even to look.

At Sethsatian and Chiengmai, the older pupils are trained to provide formal instruction to younger students, principally during vocational and extra-curricular activities. It is believed that the older pupils are the most capable persons to communicate with the younger deaf children and to promote the children's socialization to school life.

Unrestricted Peer Education

A second kind of informal "self-education" occurs when authority is not being exercised. Given the chance, the pupils conduct a rich and unrestricted interaction among themselves. They form four kinds of groups for various activities of a voluntary nature: (1) intimate peer groups conversing (among peers of the same age), (2) games and sports (including vigilantism, victimizing), (3) signmaster and audience, and (4) older-younger meetings (welcome and voluntary instruction). Each of these activities has its own sets of rules and structure.

The usefulness of unrestricted interaction among deaf youth is demonstrated by discussing the example of the "signmaster" and his various kinds of "creative narrative." The signmasters are usually surrounded by a number of people, who attentively watch their stories, jokes, satire, and opinion. The signmasters are appreciated for their quick wit and their ability to entertain and inform.

Most importantly, these signmasters teach new vocabulary words and concepts to the younger deaf pupils. Many deaf graduates recall specific older deaf pupils who exerted a major influence in helping them gain initial (sign) language and cognitive skills (Reilly & Wannuwin, 1990). The tradition of "signmastery" is a valuable asset in Thailand's schools for the deaf. It is unrecognized by the authorities.

There are also numerous other ways that older pupils are used as a resource to improve instruction in the classroom, i.e., by tutoring, storytelling, and the assessment of readiness in youngsters. For additional details please refer to the writings of C. Reilly listed in the bibliography at the end of this paper.

Policy Issue #3: When to Mainstream Deaf Children

In 1991 the former Special Education Director of Thailand, Mr. Karnol Thitkamol, made the following remark about mainstreaming:

> There is at the moment a major argument in Thailand about whether mainstreaming or a boarding school is the appropriate placement for the deaf child. Schooling in boarding institutions will not remain the dominant policy of the Ministry, and will soon be complemented by increased use of mainstreaming. [11]

Mr. Thitkamol also noted that a disadvantage of a residential school is that it is a much more expensive place to educate a deaf child, as opposed to placing him or her in the regular school system. Mainstreaming appears to be favored by the teacher education colleges and NPED, while DSE/DGE thinks that there is a role for both boarding schools and mainstream programs. The 1991–1996 Education Plan states that there will be ten new boarding schools and 149 new mainstream sites.

Successful mainstreaming of the deaf child usually requires special support services in the form of interpreters, note takers, and itinerant teachers. These hidden costs are often overlooked in the debate about the cost of special education for deaf children. These services are not usually provided to deaf pupils enrolled in Thailand's regular schools.

Curriculum and Achievement

A National Curriculum

The same curriculum is used for both deaf and hearing students throughout Thailand. Currently, the emphasis is on literacy, numeracy, and industrial and commercial skills. A major theme is to provide children with the traditional Thai concepts of morality, virtue, and civic behavior, which are emphasized in mandatory activities such as the Boy Scouts, Red Cross Youth, and religion classes. The Department of General Education permits schools for the deaf to select subjects to replace those that deaf students are unable to perform. As an example, typing is substituted for music. Deaf students often join with hearing children for craft activities and sports.

Teachers Wish to Provide a Relevant and Simple Curriculum for the Deaf

Unlike the curriculum in regular schools, teachers in the special schools for the deaf are free to adjust the level of difficulty of the instructional program. Observations and interviews in classrooms in special schools indicate that instruction is greatly simplified for deaf children.[12] No explanation of the material is provided. Only parts of textbooks are taught. From one grade to the next the degree of difficulty increases less than is true in a regular school.[13] In some schools the actual time deaf children spend in the classroom is much shorter than is listed in the official schedule. Deaf children often complain that instruction is boring because the lessons do not challenge their abilities. Ironically, the current curriculum for the deaf is almost identical to that of the monastic schools of centuries past, having been stripped of all but the most "essential" skills. The course of study normally includes reading, writing, trades, and virtues training, and is often taught via repetitive copying of texts and through recitation.[14]

Several explanations are available as to why teachers of the deaf simplify instruction. First, there are the major language differences and difficulties between the hearing teacher and the deaf pupil. The teachers are comfortable using the Thai written and spoken language, which most deaf pupils do not know. After a few years, deaf students become fluent in the use of Thai Sign Language, but most of the teachers never learn to use the sign language well.[15] Second, many of the teachers feel that the official curriculum is not relevant to the lives of deaf children. Some teachers have low expectations of their pupils' abilities. There is an attitude that deaf people are basically unable to learn abstract knowledge and are only suited for the manual trades. Teachers and parents alike ask the question, "Why have the deaf children learn the advanced curriculum since society won't accept them anyway?" Hence, the teachers tend to teach only what they think the deaf children need to know, which includes practical work and living skills. The simplified curriculum does not provide the deaf people of Thailand with the academic foundation required for higher education and the education at a level that would lead to better jobs. A few teachers in each school do recognize the intellectual potential of their deaf pupils. These isolated pioneers are struggling to adapt teaching methods to the needs of each child. Reform in classroom methodology is an essential step towards the improvement of the education of the deaf in Thailand. The support of school administrators is needed to work against the prevailing school climate of low

expectations and failure.

The shift towards more vocational training that is now underway in the special schools highlights this attitude. After grade six the Thai education system tracks students into a general academic curriculum or into a program of vocational studies. Two models are used. In the first model the extended three years of compulsory education (grades seven to nine) will be devoted to general education. The second model provides vocational education during the three years, in the hope that the school learners will be able to earn their living from the skills learned at school.

Administrators in the schools for the deaf favor the vocational model. In fact, secondary education for the deaf has emphasized vocational training for some years, and occupies two-thirds of the pupils' time in grades ten through twelve. A few regular schools are willing to integrate hard of hearing students into academic tracks if itinerant teachers are regularly available to assist the deaf students.

Teacher-Designed Examinations

Deaf students take the same schedule of examinations as do other students at all levels. The deaf graduates earn the same certificate as do students in the regular school, but it is commonly known by higher education officials and employers that the program of study is not equal in rigor. Exams are prepared by teachers within each school. Sometimes there is an exchange of tests among schools and teachers and the establishment of a test bank. The head teacher for each subject area is responsible for setting objectives and levels of testing. The difficulty of the exams devised within the special schools is far lower than that found in ordinary schools. Since the exams are not standardized for the special school or regular school population, it is impossible to compare results or the relative effectiveness of the methods used. If the simplicity of the tests used indicates the level of academic performance of the deaf children, clearly the standards are below those used with hearing children.

Reading is a prime example. Whereas about 85 percent of the general Thai population is literate, even after nine years of schooling most deaf students are still illiterate (Royal Thai Government, 1984).   Most deaf children show little progress in written language competency from the time they enter school until the time they leave school (Bunyanuson, Tammasaeng, & Phuripricha, 1987). Perhaps if academic testing were conducted in a language that the deaf children easily understood, the national sign language, the children would demonstrate a higher level of academic proficiency. The deaf children's deficiencies in writing and reading often hide their knowledge and full potential.

Communication Methods

In the special schools the individual teachers have considerable latitude in choosing the communication system to be used in class. The Ministry of Education has been supportive of initiatives aimed at using different approaches. Most Thai administrators and teachers prefer the oral/aural method. However, most would agree with Kamala Krairiksh, who said that although all educators of the Deaf accept the value of speech training, they have found that a number of deaf students cannot entirely benefit by this kind of instruction. Since, Krairiksh said, "It is human to make man happy," she believed that manual language should be allowed for the Thai deaf.

Total Communication Philosophy

The simultaneous method, or the use of speech and some form of sign at the same time, is the most commonly used method of communication. The "Total Communication Philosophy," or the idea of meeting the communication needs of each child, is

emphasized. Signs are permitted in the classrooms of all special schools. Anusarn Sunthon in Chiengmai has moved from the use of oral method during its initial ten years of existence to the use of the simultaneous method. In 1989 H.R.H. Princess Sirindhorn advised the school staff to adjust their teaching according to the needs of each individual child and stated that those who could not profit from speech training should be taught the manual language. Cholburi School for the Hard of Hearing states that the official method of instruction is the oral system, but in practicality the school has made a gradual conversion to the use of signs. Teachers who found that they were not able to make the students understand their lessons, master the prescribed instructional objectives, or pass examinations at the end of each educational level have responded by using whatever method was needed, including sign language, to make their instruction more effective and efficient.

Slight emphasis is placed on speechreading, speech development, and auditory training for those students with usable residual hearing and those deaf children who show the potential to develop their speech and speechreading skill. Hearing aids are often provided on loan. All schools for the deaf have one to three rooms equipped with loop induction systems and group hearing aids. The use of this technology is not forced on the profoundly deaf students.

Use of Manual Languages

It is widely recognized by educators in Thailand that the manual language promotes effective communication and that deaf people themselves are more satisfied when signs are used. A confusing array of signs is used in each residential school for the deaf. The children in each school use a regional variation of the Thai Sign Language. Many educators and administrators have consistently opposed the adoption of any official invented or borrowed sign system. This has boosted the status of the indigenous sign language.

However, many of the teachers who live at a residential school for the deaf have not learned how to use the Thai Sign Language fluently. A number of the deaf students say that they have great difficulty understanding the signing of their teachers. Teachers receive very little training in the use of Thai Sign Language. In addition, the teachers do not spend much time signing with students and deaf adults who are fluent signers. Many of the teachers tend to use a combination of invented signs, signs that the children use, and signs that are found recorded in manuals prepared by the Ministry. Usually the teachers speak and sign simultaneously. The signs normally follow the syntax of the spoken Thai language. Parts of sentences that are spoken may not be signed. Different teachers communicate in different ways. Therefore, the deaf children are forced to try and understand the particular style of each teacher. Many of the deaf children do not understand much of their teachers' communication. However, there are small numbers of teachers in each school who strive to master the sign language used by the children. These people are generally held in high esteem by deaf people in Thailand.

While there has been no intensive research, it seems that the dominant form of Thai Sign Language emanates from Bangkok. It is not learned at the school for the deaf but learned by the deaf students upon graduation from school.[16] In schools that are isolated from the adult deaf community, many of the signs will be understood only by the pupils in the school.[17] In schools where contact with deaf adults is common, the children use signs readily understood in the deaf community. The government has been supportive of visits by graduates to their former schools. Since jobs are not readily available in many rural areas, most of the graduates of rural schools for the deaf move away and never return.

The Thai Sign Language has a vocabulary and grammar that is distinct from the spoken Thai Language. The Thai manual alphabet was derived from the shapes of the American manual alphabet and developed by Khunying Kamala Krairiksh in 1954. It is not used very often by deaf people or their teachers, although charts of the manual alphabet have been distributed widely. A typical signed conversation between deaf people in Thailand uses far less fingerspelling than does signing between deaf people in the United States. Most deaf people in Thailand remain primarily mono-lingual in Thai Sign Language since efforts to teach them to be fluent in the use of written and read Thai have not been successful.

While very few hearing people use the Thai Sign Language well, more and more people are becoming intrigued by the language. This rise in interest is due largely to the use of interpreters on television. Although the general quality of the interpreters is poor, it has helped raise public awareness. People are beginning to believe that signing is not a shameful, animal-like behavior. Although Thai Sign Language is now taught informally by deaf people, formal instruction is not widely available. The National Association of the Deaf in Thailand (NADT) is the leader in providing sign language instruction, thanks to grants from the Department of Public Welfare. Recently, courses in sign language have been started at Ramkamhaeng University. Since 1980 a team of deaf people and American linguists have been investigating the structure of the Thai Sign Language. Two editions of the *Thai Sign Language Dictionary* have been produced. This volume provides a solid foundation for the establishment of a curriculum for teaching signs. The *Thai Sign Language Dictionary* can help Thailand's teachers, parents, and interpreters obtain the formal training they so desperately need and should promote improved communication with the deaf people of Thailand.

The mainstream programs for the deaf and schools for the hard of hearing continue to use the oral/aural method exclusively. The Thai approach to oral education is not as strict as the classical oral model. Because some parents want their children to have an oral/aural education, they successfully pressure the oral schools to accept their profoundly deaf children. The mix of pupils with partial and profound hearing losses makes instruction more difficult. Success with the oral method is extremely difficult due to the articulation of the Thai language. Its five tones can give five different meanings to the same formation of the vocal mechanism.

Deaf People as Teachers

During the early years of the history of the education of the deaf in Thailand, graduates of the schools for the deaf took an active and important role in the education of deaf children. Deaf adults were relied upon to teach younger pupils and to help establish new provincial schools. During the first ten years, as many as 25 percent of the teaching staff of some schools were deaf. Lady Kamala Krairiksh, the head of the first two schools for the deaf, secured special training and teaching positions for a group of about a dozen deaf people. A member of the first class of graduates from Khon Kaen School (established 1968) recounts how influential these deaf people were.

> There were five deaf teachers and maybe fifteen hearing teachers. The deaf teachers taught and oversaw the dormitory. Everyone watched them to learn signs and other things. Then one deaf man got in trouble, and the administration thought all deaf teachers were troublemakers. They all had to leave. We continued to use the signs we had learned from them. (N. Wannuwin).

Using teachers who were deaf was evidently a temporary strategy since deaf adults were relegated to low level supervisory and support roles, as graduates of newly founded teacher training programs became available. Many of the original group of deaf teachers stayed on through the 1970s and 1980s as aides and as instructors in the arts and in physical education. The contributions of the best of the deaf teachers surpassed any of the contributions of the hearing teachers.

Today there are about two dozen deaf people working in the Thai schools for the deaf. Some recognition has been provided to a few outstanding deaf adult staff members who have demonstrated tremendous diligence and productivity. The positive example shown by these deaf people has helped to change attitudes about the use of deaf people as teachers. Grateful principals found ways to ensure that a handful of deaf people be appointed as government employees with accompanying job security and benefits. Currently, only two deaf persons are employed as full time teachers of the deaf in Thailand.

For three decades the most important service conducted by the Foundation for the Deaf was paying the salaries of most of the teacher assistants who at were deaf. This act has improved the lives of many deaf children in school. Deaf persons on the Foundation payroll are paid only about one-third as much as teachers and do not qualify for tenure or benefits. By 1983 even supporter Krairiksh was saying that the Foundation should not support deaf teacher assistants since it was the responsibility of the Ministry of Education. The number and the status of the deaf staff members continue to drop. It is the responsibility of the schools to propose the names of competent deaf adults to the Foundation. Often the schools do not submit any names to the Foundation and justify this lack of action by indicating that they cannot find any deaf persons who are "qualified" to teach.

It is a national priority to employ deaf adults as teacher assistants and to encourage them to act as a liaison between hearing teachers and deaf students. The deaf person's ability to communicate and develop rapport with the students is superior to that of the hearing teachers. The hearing teachers often rely on deaf staff members and older pupils to assist in the management of the younger pupils' behavior. The great potential value of utilizing deaf people to teach subject matter content has not been recognized by the Thai educational establishment.

Thus far there has been no systematic attempt to help more deaf people earn their teaching credentials. Most deaf people are unable to meet the official qualifications required to become a teacher. The major obstacles in the way of deaf people achieving teacher certification are low academic achievement and limited use of the Thai language. The lack of interpreters and support services at institutions of higher education precludes the opportunity for a deaf adult to obtain the advanced education required for teacher certification. The certification requirements do not recognize the deaf adults' strongest assets, the ability to communicate and empathize with the pupils and to provide a good role model.

Since sign language is not considered to be a worthy medium for learning, many deaf staff members feel that their contributions go unrecognized. Many of the deaf staff feel that they are treated unfairly and are intentionally saddled with many tasks that no one else wants. Because of a higher level of commitment, the deaf teacher is often in conflict with his or her hearing colleagues.

The deaf in Thailand have formed a national association that uses Thai Sign Language as the vehicle of communication. Improving the education of the deaf is the goal of the National Association of the Deaf (NADT), which was established in 1983. Thousands of copies of the two volumes of the *Thai Sign Language Dictionary* have been given to schools and parents. The sign dictionary has over 3,000 signs. The research required to develop the *Thai Sign Language Dictionary* was supported by funds from the United States, Canada and Australia.[18] American trainers and technical advisors were used.

Informally, deaf adults have a significant role in the education of children who are deaf in Thailand. Especially in the rural areas, the special schools are a gathering place for deaf adults. Through their interactions with deaf adults, the deaf children learn social rules, sign language, and knowledge of the world. Since the typical deaf adult has little interest in school affairs, and their involvement is not encouraged by hearing educators of the deaf, there is little cooperation between the deaf community and the schools for the deaf. The United Nations Decade of Disabled Persons brought about increased participation of the deaf community in discussions at the national level concerning services for disabled people in Thailand. In 1981, the International Year for Disabled Persons, the national organizing committee began drafting a rehabilitation act to be considered by the government and the parliament. Later, disabled people and parents of the mentally handicapped were involved in the revision of the act.

Community School Relations: Parental Involvement

In Thai culture it is the responsibility of teachers to take sole charge of children while they are in school. Parents assume that the teachers will do their best. Teachers are highly respected in Thai society. Ordinary people hesitate to express their opinions out of a sense of deference, and do not get directly involved in school affairs. Language differences and the lack of relationships between social classes and ethnic groups can also impede parent-teacher cooperation. Parents and the local community have no formal role in school operations. Elected school boards do not exist, nor do advocacy groups. Direct parental influence is not customary. Influence on the school usually comes from members of the elite class of Thai society who have the ability to contact high-level officials.

More parents are now becoming aware of the importance of a good education for their child's future. They request and support programs, especially mainstream programs. However, many parents are not ready to make a special effort to assist their children at home.

Some teachers insist that many of the deaf children's instructional problems stem from the fact that incoming deaf pupils are deficient in language usage and cognitively unprepared for instruction. The parents have not learned sign language or the manual alphabet. No parent education is available. Sometimes the school is considered as a place where deaf children are "dumped." The past principal of Sethsatian School, Sathaporn Suvannus, has stated that more than half of the boarders in the dorms of the special schools were neglected by their parents. The parents stated that they trusted the teachers to do the right thing and placed the entire responsibility for their children's education in the hands of the school. The schools have tried to rectify this situation by interviewing parents when they bring their children to school and by encouraging them to take an interest in their deaf children.

The special schools are the society's primary source of information about disabled children. Many teachers have been offering advice to parents for decades. In the 1980s all of the schools made an effort to improve services by starting parent-teacher associations (PTAs). The main purposes of the PTAs were to gain financial support, develop guidance programs, and promote vocational placements.

Model programs for active school-parent cooperation and collaboration are found at the Phyathai School under the leadership of the Special Education Division and at PraTamnak Suan Kularb School under the direction of H.R.H. Princess Mahachakri Sirindhorn, the third child of H. M. The King of Thailand. At the beginning of their children's attendance at these schools, parents are presented with an orientation program that includes the techniques of communicating with their deaf child and how to assist the school program. Parents regularly attend lectures and discussions. Several other schools now have programs similar to the one discussed above. Parents and educators now realize the benefits of discussion and sharing. Parent-Teacher Associations are continuing to expand. Few Parent-Teacher Associations exist in the rural schools because of the large geographic areas covered by the school and because of traditional parental attitudes.

The Vocational Status of Deaf People

Most deaf people in Thailand have never attended school, do not join the deaf community, and do not know Thai Sign Language. Most deaf people usually remain in a rural area. Little is known about their life conditions. Presumably, they engage in labor-intensive farming and small-scale manufacturing. Communication is by gesture and spoken language to the extent possible. This unreached majority of deaf people needs to be studied.

Deaf people who have been to school possess distinct advantages over their unschooled peers. They receive some degree of benefit cognitively from their experience in the classrooms for the deaf. Those who attend special schools learn Thai Sign Language and gain access to the collective knowledge of the deaf community. Membership in the deaf community influences where they will live, whom they will marry, and how they will conduct their lives. School attendance does not alleviate the tremendous difficulty that deaf people in Thailand have in finding work, as compared with hearing people. Whereas the national unemployment rate is 8 percent, a 1985 survey of 489 deaf adults found that 49 percent had no income.[19] A 1981 survey of 238 deaf people found that 29 percent were without an income. Sixty-nine percent were women.[20] Deaf women are 1.43 times more likely to be unemployed than deaf men.

Staying in school longer apparently makes no significant difference in finding work. The 1981 survey showed that 36 percent of those who had completed 7.9 years of schooling were unemployed. Twenty percent of those with one to six years of schooling were unemployed, as compared to 13 percent of those who had no schooling at all. The 1981 survey suggests that more schooling for deaf persons does not result in higher income levels.[21]

When the deaf do find work they often earn less, because of the attitude of society that non-speaking people deserve less and are less able to defend themselves against exploitation. The per capita income for people in Thailand is U.S. $1,192[22] while for deaf people it is about $936.[23] There are cases of deaf people successfully running their own enterprises in the rural areas. These enterprises include animal-raising businesses and supply stores. After farming, the chief occupations of deaf people are sewing, selling, construction, sign painting, plumbing, wood-working, and service in a beauty shop. Assembly line work is common. With rare exceptions, deaf people are not hired by the central government.[24] The National Association of the Deaf (NADT) has been a training ground for social service occupations.

Economic growth and job availability centered in Bangkok and a few other cities is the main reason why many deaf people migrate to urban centers. They seem to move to urban areas to find companionship as well as to find work. It is in the streets of Bangkok that the deaf community has found a measure of economic success. Mostly after hours, hundreds of deaf people sell handicrafts to tourists. The economic system of deaf persons is multi-layered and is comprised of merchants with many employees and many sales booths, vendors with one booth, wage-earning clerks, and commissioned suppliers. Many deaf people have left jobs because of the attraction of starting their own, hopefully profitable, business. The vernacular is the Bangkok dialect of Thai Sign Language, which may take over a year to learn.

The Curriculum of the Schools

The curriculum of all schools for the deaf provides for vocational education for children in grades seven to nine. Grades ten to twelve are devoted to providing deaf students with training in the following areas: ceramics, mechanics, electronics, painting, and printing. The subjects are selected for the students according to the current job market. The Foundation for the Deaf in Thailand has recently constructed a building at the Sethsatian School aimed at providing job training for upper secondary students. The Foundation has also secured a grant from the Danish government for the establishment of a comprehensive rehabilitation center for the deaf and hard of hearing. Some teachers have gone beyond the call of duty and offer special tutoring to those who have left school.

After leaving school, a deaf person has few vocational training choices. The Prapadaeng Vocational Center for the Disabled of the Ministry of Public Welfare admits deaf people. Very little sign language is used in instruction. No sign language interpreters are available in government and private institutions. Nevertheless, some deaf youth have successfully completed training courses due to their own perseverance and the support of concerned educators. Others have received their training in polytechnic schools run by the Adult Education Department, where about 20 subjects are offered.

In late 1991, after receiving government approval, the Ratchasuda College for the Disabled in Nakorn Pathom, under the patronage of H.R.H. Princess Sirindhorn, began planning a technically oriented training program. It is the intention of the program that university-level credit will be awarded for courses completed. This would allow the courses to be transferred to regular colleges and universities. During 1981–1983 the results of a pilot program called Reaching the Unreached, sponsored by IHAP and USAID, provided evidence that highly motivated deaf persons could succeed in regular trade schools and thereby obtain employment with higher incomes (Hochschwender, 1985). Support services provided included note takers and weekly interpreted teacher-student consultations. Currently there is no job placement service for deaf people in Thailand.

Some shops and factories have provided training for deaf graduates. Many have been hired at the completion of the training. Silent World Crafts, a factory owned by the National Association of the Deaf, trains carpenters and craft painters. The Don Bosco Vocational School offers a high-quality two-year program in graphics and printing for deaf boys. Parents of deaf students who live outside of Bangkok must use their own resources to find training or job opportunities for their children.

The Push for Higher Education

Many deaf people feel that they are capable and deserve the opportunity to receive higher education. Since the median age in Thailand is twenty-one years, there is a growing pool of eligible deaf students. Only a small percentage of people in Thailand receive a university education. There is a traditional belief in Thailand that a university education is not worth the investment of time and money since it does not guarantee a greater income. Because the economy can absorb only a limited number of university graduates, admission to the university is highly competitive. Yet higher education is now becoming more widespread because of the establishment of open universities and televised instruction. In the wake of these changes in Thai society lies the hope of higher-education opportunities for deaf people.

There is an effort underway by a group of professionals and parents to secure more opportunities for deaf students to study for a bachelor's degree. Mahidol University and Suan Dusin Teachers College are among the institutions considering the feasibility of admitting deaf students. While the educational system is gradually expanding, the deaf students' lack of literacy and fundamental academic skills threaten to frustrate plans to open additional higher-education opportunities.

Teacher Certification

The typical standard required for certification as a teacher of the deaf is the bachelor degree or four years of study beyond grade twelve. During times of teacher scarcity in particular subject areas, those who hold a diploma from a college of education, vocational institute, or technical college (five years beyond grade nine) are recruited and given special training.

There are six training sites for educators of the deaf. All are located in Bangkok. They are as follows: (1) Suan Dusit Teachers College, which has offered bachelor's degrees since 1969; (2) Srinakarinwitoj University, Prasanmitr campus, which has an M.S. degree program and a special two-year program that is the equivalent of a M.A.; (3) Chulalongkorn University; (4) Thammassat University; (5) Mahidol University, Ramadhibodi Hospital Campus, which in 1976 began a master's degree program in communication disorders in the fields of audiology and speech pathology, and in 1981 started a post-graduate program in auditory technique; and (6) Supervisory Unit of the Ministry of Education, which has been in charge of pre-service, in-service, on-the-job training, and a special course to train teachers of the deaf since 1955.

The Supervisory Unit of the Ministry of Education provides strong support to teachers by conducting supervisory visits, and arranging meetings and seminars throughout the year. The Ministry of Education supervisors also help teachers develop teaching techniques, prepare special lessons, and conduct extra-curricular activities. Chulalongkorn University and Thammassat University have offered many courses in special education and the rehabilitation of disabled persons. After the completion of the special training offered by the Special Education Supervisory Unit and a practicum of one year, graduates are eligible to teach in schools for the deaf. Administrators report that most of their teachers had no intention of teaching deaf children but just happened to be assigned to a school for the deaf. Many of these teachers hope to transfer to regular schools.[25]

Teachers' salaries are very low in Thailand when compared to the salaries of persons in private sector jobs. A special stipend is given to teachers of the disabled. This stipend is equal to 20 to 25 percent of the monthly base salary of a regular classroom teacher. This special stipend is provided to alleviate the "hardship" of teaching disabled people. The government does not use the stipend as an incentive for teachers to improve their communication skills or ability to teach deaf children.

Future Directions

There has been great deal of expansion in educational services provided for deaf students in Thailand during the past 40 years. In spite of this expansion, the education of the deaf in Thailand is still under-developed at present. Those who work with the deaf are not pleased with the current situation. The major problems include:

Funds for buildings, equipment, and maintenance are insufficient.

The nation has made improved educational opportunities a high priority. Over 20 percent of the national budget is committed to education. The private sector has also supported the deaf population with funds and opportunities but at a lower rate than for other categories of disabled people. The demand for quality services is increasing. The sustained growth of the Thai economy has permitted an increase in the support for education. Increases in the amount provided for special education will depend upon national priorities.

Schools bear the burden for nearly all services provided for deaf people, from cradle to grave.

There is a need for other agencies to carry some of the burden for the delivery of effective services. There is a need to expand services beyond the basic school program and include preschools, parental services, mental health counseling, and vocational training. People with multiple handicaps are in dire need of services. The rural populations need far more attention and emphasis.

The provision of vocational education and training opportunities is not sufficient.

Although they are successful when working with family and friends, trained deaf workers have difficulty in securing jobs in open competition. Deaf adults and older pupils are in need of improved vocational education to enable them to make a good living. Construction, design, photography, sewing, and advertising design are areas in which deaf people have been successfully trained. Deaf people prefer to work for organizations that employ other deaf people. A campaign is needed to educate employers about the merits of hiring deaf workers.

Summary and Conclusions

- As part of the national vocational model, the education of deaf pupils will focus on vocational training for one-half of their school years (the last three years of compulsory education and the first three years of upper secondary education).

- A mainstream program may become the only alternative for a deaf student who wishes to complete the general education tract required to continue on to an institution of higher education. Most profoundly deaf people will not be able to study academic subjects at the secondary level or above because of inadequate language use, academic preparation, and needed support services including interpreters and note takers. Instruction at the special schools needs to be upgraded and a curriculum provided that emphasizes academic areas as well as vocational education.

- There is currently a lack of trained personnel including competent administrators and teachers. Reform in teacher training is needed.
- There is a lack of agreement on the proper communication methodology to use to teach deaf children. A forum where an exchange of perspectives and pedagogy can occur is needed.
- Teachers and parents lack information on the development and education of deaf and hard of hearing children.
- Little systematic cooperation between medical and educational personnel is evident. The awareness of medical personnel concerning the prevalence of childhood deafness and the importance of auditory screening and early diagnosis needs to be increased. Medical personnel need lists of schools for the deaf so that they can refer parents to the proper educational resources. The centralization of medical and educational administration and delivery services in Thailand might ease logistic obstacles.
- The schools fail to recognize the contribution and valuable role deaf adults and the deaf community play in the education of deaf and hard of hearing children. Policies that impede the access of the deaf community to the children in schools for the deaf should be eliminated. Obstacles to the certification of deaf individuals as teachers of the deaf should be removed.
- Deaf people are not fully accepted as equal citizens in the Thai society. Some teachers and communities still treat deaf people as second-class citizens. Although deaf individuals receive some charitable assistance, it is not the kind of assistance that will enable them to become independent and contributing members of the nation. Primarily in the capital city, deaf people with access to interpreters are becoming more accepted by society and are invited to participate in various activities. The TV stations now offer a few interpreted programs.
- The acceptance of Thai Sign Language as a recognized language of Thailand is needed and is one of the main goals of the Thailand Association of the Deaf. The Thailand Association of the Deaf feels that the use of the Thai Sign Language can be an effective way of improving the education of deaf students in the country. Although Thailand has restricted the use by ethnic minorities of other languages, Thai Sign Language acceptance is not opposed since the deaf population poses no political threat. The need for sign language interpreters is critical. Sign classes and interpreter training programs are urgently needed.
- Access to foreign research and developments is restricted. Opportunities to meet and visit with foreign professionals, attend conferences, and receive assistance from other countries would broaden the scope of ideas and knowledge of workers in this special field and would assist in the growth and development of the deaf and hard of hearing population of Thailand.

Appendix:

Estimating the Deaf Population's Involvement in Education

Estimating the Participation Rate in Schooling by Deaf People in a Developing Nation[26]

The percentage of deaf children in Thailand who are receiving an education is estimated at by dividing the total enrollment of schools for the deaf into an estimated total school population, as shown in Table 2. In 1991 the total enrollment of deaf children in grades one through nine in Thailand was 2,213. Of this number 1,870 were in grades one through six, which corresponds to ages seven to twelve, and 343 deaf pupils were in grades six through nine, which corresponds to ages thirteen to fifteen.

The figures were arrived at by subtracting the number of pupils in mainstream programs for hard of hearing from the total enrollment of hearing impaired children reported in Table 1. (The figure includes all special and welfare schools, including the Cholburi School for the Hard of Hearing, since many pupils at that school have more than an 85 dB average hearing loss.)

Dividing the enrollment figures above into estimates of the size of the school-age deaf population gives a rough idea of the enrollment rate.

Estimating the school-age deaf population can be done either by using census/survey figures or by using the prevalence of rate of deafness.

Estimate Using Census/Survey Figures

Estimate 1: A census completed in 1970 in Thailand found 47,477 people to be "deaf or mute" or deaf with other handicaps (Royal Thai National Statistical Office, 1970). By extrapolating from this figure, the current number would now be 59,080 since the national population has grown by 24 percent. About 17.2 percent of the Thai population is between the ages of seven the twelve years (Office of the Prime Minister, 1984, p. 281). By this estimate Thailand has 10, 161 deaf children aged seven to twelve, including some with additional handicaps (.172 x 59,080), and 14,829 deaf children aged seven to fifteen (.251 x 59,080).

Alternatively, the Summary of Disabled Persons survey of 1986 found 76,100 "deaf and/or mute people" in Thailand. An adjusted total figure of 86,100 is probably more accurate because as many as 10,000 deaf people who do not live in private homes were not counted. Only people living in private household were included. Residents of the boarding schools for the deaf and adults who had already left home were not counted (personal communication with the Head of Education Statistics Unit, Ms. Taweeporn Tuwicharanon, Chief of Education Population Division, 12/12/91).

The 1990 census in Thailand asked citizens to tell if any of their family members were disabled and provide their ages.

Estimate Using Prevalence of Rate of Deafness

Estimate 2: Agencies like the UN use a prevalence estimate of one prelingually deaf person in every thousand people. This has been verified by actual counts in the United States (Reis, 1982). Applying the following formula (.001 x 56 million = 56,000) indicates that there are approximately 56,000 prelingually deaf people of all ages in Thailand. A high prevalence of serious health conditions in developing nations may indicate that this figure underestimates the true number.

To estimate the number of deaf persons of school age, multiply the all-age figure by the percentage of the nation's population that is of school-age. That calculation would indicate that there would be 9,632 prelingually deaf children ages seven to twelve (.172 x 56,000) and 14,090 deaf children ages seven to fifteen.

Estimate 3: The prevalence rate found in nations with similar health and economic conditions may be applied. Published rates of deafness for developing nations are very low (Nepal found .43/1000 and Pakistan .59/1000). According to Scott Brown, Ph.D., Center for Assessment and Demographic Study, Gallaudet University, these rates should not be used because they are inaccurate and seriously under-count the true number.

Endnotes

1. The account of general education relies on the work of Keith Watson, *Educational Development in Thailand* (1980). His contributions provide the reader with a much fuller understanding of the context of deaf education.

2. The year 1898 is usually said to be the starting point of regular state schooling. In that year the Organization of Provincial Education decreed a steady effort at providing schooling to both sexes throughout the nation. Efforts to establish a state school system during the three prior decades were extremely active, but limited in scope and marked by opposition and the search for a conception of Thai education. See Watson, *op. cit.*, chapter 6.

3. Pupils not included here are those enrolled in regular local schools in rural areas; their numbers are unknown. Many deaf adults have stated that their parents sent them to regular school first and later moved them to a special school program when they failed to learn.

4. Boarding schools are here defined as schools in which more than one-half of the pupils live at the school.

5. Personal communication, Sathaporn Suvannus, 1992.

6. Erting, C., & Johnson, R. (1989). Ethnicity and socialization in a classroom for deaf children. In C. Lucas (Ed.), *The sociolinguistics of the deaf community* (pp. 41-83). New York: Academic Press. Also see the work of Claire Ramsey at the University of Washington.

7. Most education for disabled people in Thailand is handled by the private sector, often with personnel provided by the government. Before 1976 only the schools for the deaf were run by the Ministry of Education, while people with other disabilities were educated by other agencies or private groups. Some officials have stated that because deafness is an invisible disability and not a sympathy-arousing condition in the mind of the public, the Ministry of Education has had to take full financial responsibility for the education of the deaf.

8. The estimate of enrollment is based on an assumed correspondence between age and grade level (enter at age seven and add one year of age for each grade level, so a fifteen-year-old is in grade nine). Actually this does not fit the situation of Thai deaf students well, since the average age at admission is over eight years old and the wastage rate (repetition of grades) is high. Many pupils are seventeen or older before graduating from the ninth grade.

9. In 1980, the 1921 law was amended to make education compulsory for all children, but because disabled children had not been explicitly mentioned, there has been little shift in public or official attitudes.

10. At Sethsatian in 1990, operating costs were $650 (U.S.) per pupil and at Tungmahemek School they were $1,000 (U.S.) per pupil.

11. Conversation with Mr. Karnol Thitkamol, Ministry of Education, Bangkok, December 11, 1991. Mr. Karnol Thitkamol was Director of the Special Education Division in Thailand and in 1992 moved to an oversight capacity as the Deputy Director-General of the Department of General Education, Ministry of Education, Bangkok.

12. The welfare schools, comprised mostly of schools for hill tribes, also simplify the curricula using the same arguments. These are administered by the Special Education Division, as are the schools for the deaf.

13. Reilly. C. (1983). *Survey of conditions in the deaf community.* Unpublished manuscript. Available from P.0. Box 29531, Washington, DC 20017.

14. The teaching of Buddhist monks is still closed to deaf people. This is a reflection of the lack of interpreters and also the general attitude that deaf people are less capable of abstract thought and language. Deaf men may not become monks because of the code that requires the person to be in full possession of sensory faculties necessary for advancement towards Enlightenment. The schools do have their deaf pupils engage in short prayers and meditation, although without explanation of the significance.

15. Statement is based on interviews with many deaf children and adults reported in Reilly, C. (forthcoming), *Self-education of deaf children in boarding schools,* Doctoral dissertation in progress, University of Maryland.

16. Chiengmai, Sethsatian, Tungmahamek.

17. Especially Tak.

18. Aid program of the International Human Assistance Programs, Inc. Funded by USAID/Thailand and other donors, 1981 1989.

19. Wright, J. (Ed.). (1990). *The universal almanac.* Kansas City: Andrews & McMeel.

20. National unemployment figures exclude those who are not actively seeking work. The estimate for deaf adults counts all jobless people as unemployed. Thus, the unemployment rate may be overstated for deaf people. Survey data from the National Association for the Deaf in Thailand. (1985). [Statistics on deaf adults in Thailand]. Unpublished raw data. Bangkok, Thailand; Toosetarat, S., & Reilly, C. (1981). *Facts and figures on members of the Center for Deaf Alumni in Thailand.* Unpublished manuscript. Bangkok, Thailand: Center for Deaf Alumni.

21. These findings may be challenged on the grounds that the mean age of respondents was 28 years, and only 30 percent were over age 30, thus in their peak earning period. On the other hand, the sample is drawn primarily from Bangkok, where unemployment and salary levels are the highest in the country.

22. Royal Thai Embassy. (1990). *Economy of Thailand.* Public distribution handout. Washington, DC.

23. Based on self-reported data from a 1985 survey. Excludes those who reported no income.

24. There are a few deaf people on the staff of the schools for the deaf and the public welfare department.

25. Sae Diinoo and Prayat Thongkham, Chiengmai School. Personal communication, September, 1991.

26. Thanks to Scott Brown, Ph. D., Center for Assessment and Demographic Study, Gallaudet University, for advice on the appendix.

References

Board of National Education. (1981). Education for the disabled. (Special issue). *National Education Periodical*, 15, 2 (December 1980 January 1981). Bangkok, Thailand: Roongreungsan Press.

Bunyanuson, S., Tammasaeng, M., & Phuripricha, P. (1987). *The written language ability of deaf students*. Bangkok, Thailand: Foundation for the Deaf (In Thai language and available from 135 Praram Road, Bangkok, Thailand).

Chakrabongse, H. R. R. Prince Chula. (1960). *Lords of life: A history of the kings of Thailand*. London: Redman.

Department of General Education, Ministry of Education. (1988). *Educational statistics*, Abridged Version (Academic Year Buddhist Era 2531).

Department of Teacher Training, Ministry of Education. (1981). International year of the disabled 1981. (Special issue). *Kurupritas* [a Thai-language teachers' education periodical].

Dusit School for the Deaf. (1955). *Report on services for the deaf*. Dhonburi, Thailand: Wudhisuksa Technical School.

ENT Department, Ramadhibodi Hospital, Mahidol University. (1988). *Program of postgraduate education, audiology, speech pathology and audio-technique*. Unpublished manuscript. Bangkok, Thailand: Author.

Foundation for the Deaf in Thailand. (1976). *Twenty-five years of education for the deaf in Thailand, 25th anniversary report*. Bangkok, Thailand: Chareonkij Printing House.

Foundation for the Deaf in Thailand. (1983). *Thirty years of services for the deaf, 30th anniversary report*. Bangkok, Thailand: Thammasart University Printing Press.

Hochschwender, J. (1985, September). *Final evaluation: IHAP Reaching the Unreached program*. (To USAID/Thailand for OPG# AID 493-0296-G-SS-1035). Bangkok, Thailand: Partnership for Productivity, Inc.

Kaleidoscope Current World Data. *Thailand*. Santa Barbara, CA: ABC Clio.

National Association for the Deaf in Thailand. (1985). *Statistics on deaf adults in Thailand*. Unpublished raw data. Bangkok, Thailand: Author. (Available from 11/3 Soi Pikul, Sathorn Road, Bangkok, Thailand 11010).

Panyacheewin, S. (1991, December 9). A little hearing can go a long way. *Bangkok Post, XLVI*, No.343.

Post-Graduate Department. (1989). *Work and program in special education in Srinakarinwiroj University*. Unpublished manuscript. Bangkok, Thailand: Srinakarinwiroj University.

Reilly, C. (1992, June). *Outstanding in the field: Making good choices in data collection: Examples from fieldwork in a Thai boarding school for the deaf*. Paper presented at the 1992 Forum on Ethnography in Education, School of Education, University of Pennsylvania, Philadelphia. Available from the university's Center on Urban Ethnography, 3700 Walnut St., Philadelphia, PA 19104-6216.

Reilly, C. (forthcoming). *Self-education of deaf children in boarding schools*. Doctoral dissertation in progress, University of Maryland.

Reilly, C., & Wannuwin, N. (1990, November). *Self-education in the boarding institution for the deaf in Thailand*. Paper presented at the American Anthropological Association, New Orleans, LA. Available from P.O. Box 29531, Washington, DC 20017 USA.

Reis, Peter. (1982). *Hearing ability of persons by sociodemographic and health characteristics: US. Series 10* (140). DHS Publication (PHS) 82-1568. Dept. of Health and Human Services.

Royal Thai Government, Office of the Prime Minister, National Statistical Office. (1970). *National census of the kingdom of Thailand*. (Available from National Statistical Office. Lam Luang Road, Bangkok 10100, Thailand).

Royal Thai Government, Office of the Prime Minister. (1984). *Thailand in the 80's*. Bangkok, Thailand.

Royal Thai Government, Office of the Prime Minister, National Statistical Office. (1986). *Summary of disabled persons from sample survey, 1986*. Bangkok, Thailand: Author.

Royal Thai Government, Ministry of Education. (1987). *Annual report of the ministry of education, 1987*. Bangkok, Thailand.

Royal Thai Government, Planning Division of the Department of General Education, Ministry of Education. (1991). *Summary overview of the education, seventh plan for the development of education, culture and religion, 1992–96*. Bangkok, Thailand: Author.

Suan Dusit Teachers College. (1989). *Twenty years of special education at Suan Dusit Teachers College, 1969–1989*. Bangkok, Thailand: Author.

Suvannus,S. (1987). Education of the deaf in Thailand. In J. Van Cleve (Ed.), *The encyclopedia on deafness*, (Vol. 3). (pp. 282-284). NewYork: McGraw-Hill.

Suwanarat, M., Reilly, C., Ratanasint, A., Anderson, L., Rungsrithong, V., Yen-Klao, S., Buathong, W., & Wrigley, 0. (1986). *Thai Sign Language dictionary: Book one*. Bangkok, Thailand: Thai Wattana Phanich Press.

Suwanarat, M., Wrigley, 0., Ratanasint, A., Anderson, L., & Rungsrithong, V. (1991). *Thai Sign Language dictionary*, Revised and Expanded Edition. Bangkok, Thailand: Thai Wattana Phanich Press.

Suxvanarat, K. (1989). *Land of smiles? The deaf culture in Thailand*. Plenary address to The Deaf Way Conference, Gallaudet University, Washington, DC.

Tooserarat, S., & Reilly, C. (1981). *Facts and figures on members of the Center for Deaf Alumni in Thailand*. Unpublished manuscript. Bangkok, Thailand: Center for Deaf Alumni.

Watson, K. (1980). *Educational development in Thailand*. Hong Kong: Heinemann Asia.

Wrigley, 0. (1985). *Progress reports on Reaching the Unreached project, 1981–85*. (Reports to USAID/Thailand for OPG# AID 493-0296-G-SS-1035). Bangkok, Thailand: IHAP.

Training Teachers of the Deaf in Zimbabwe

by
Albert Rickie Gwitimah
Lecturer, United College of Education, Bulawayo, Zimbabwe

Basic to any system of education is a dynamic teacher education program. The successful educational treatment of the hearing impaired is dependent to a great extent on the availability of qualified teachers. While efficient organization, modern equipment, and suitably designed boarding accommodations are necessary if progress is to be made in what is considered one of the most challenging fields of education, it is true to say that the teacher is the key figure. The education of the hearing impaired child depends in great measure on the trained teacher's ability to help the child to communicate and live with the "cruel" speaking society.

History of Teacher Education of the Hearing Impaired in Zimbabwe

In Zimbabwe, the training of teachers of the hearing impaired was started at United College of Education in 1986, three years after the setting up of the Department of Special Education, which initially catered to the visually handicapped (blind). This department had been established by the Ministry of Education and Culture to provide in-service training for qualified teachers in specialized areas of teacher education. Now, this department is charged to supply "responsible, creative, dedicated, well-informed, disciplined teachers of the hearing impaired." Before the establishment of the department, teachers of the hearing impaired were trained in the country of Malawi (at Montfort College in quite a big number) and overseas, especially in England, specifically at Manchester, Birmingham, and Newcastle Universities respectively. These teachers formed the nucleus of a system of training within the country itself. This training was instrumental in satisfying the needs of the country.

Many arguments can be advanced against the scheme of training teachers of the deaf overseas. As a permanent method it would be ruled out on the score of expenses alone, especially in terms of foreign currency, which is in short supply in third-world countries. Moreover, it is questionable whether it is sound for teachers to undergo their specialized training in an environment so different from the one in which they would be absorbed in. However, as a temporary expedient, it had been satisfactory, giving the country breathing space in which to plan for her own resources by making use of the services of Zimbabwean teachers who had obtained certificates, diplomas, and degrees from overseas countries.

The initial course for teachers of the deaf was thus modeled on the Mount Gravat Course in Australia and the Certificate Course for Teachers of the Deaf at the Department of Audiology and Education of the Deaf, Manchester University. But the present course is not a direct copy of the existing ones in western countries. It has been adapted to meet local needs and conditions. The adaptations in the Zimbabwean Training Program have been made through a needs analysis and have been influenced by the philosophies of education enunciated by the country's policy makers.

The training program aims for quality, for introducing classroom specialists and not hearing aid technologists. Teachers of the deaf are, of course, specialist teachers, but firstly, they must be good general teachers. Teachers in our Zimbabwean program must first have completed a basic teacher training course—but why is this necessary? The reason is simple. The deaf child is first of all a child, then secondly he or she is deaf; that is, he or she has all the needs and problems of the non-handicapped child, with the added complication of deafness. So from that note, teachers of the deaf must have a thorough knowledge of general teaching on which to build the specific knowledge of teaching deaf children.

For our course, the first few batches of teachers were required to have taught in a special school for at least two years, or have at least two years of qualified teaching experience in regular schools. With the passage of time, however, there is a likelihood that the minimum length of teaching experience could be increased to four years for those without experience in special schools. Still, whether teachers should have experience with teaching ordinary children before training to teach hearing impaired children is controversial. Here is the situation: This course was set up as a result of a needs analysis, first to in-service those teachers who were trained ordinarily but who were teaching in special schools, which in our case counted for almost all teachers in special schools. This presents a formidable problem because of the numbers involved. Secondly, most of the teachers in special schools at present would not meet the university requirement that they should have obtained at least five ordinary level subjects, before being enrolled in this program. The ages of some of these teachers also present a problem. It would seem therefore, that a mixture (as it is at present) of teachers straight from initial training and two years teaching and those who have had several years of teaching experience is necessary.

Candidates are selected on the basis of their academic qualifications. They should have at least a certificate in education offered by the Department of Teacher Education of the University of Zimbabwe, and five ordinary level subjects, including English language.

Admission Procedure

United College of Education, under the Ministry of Higher Education, advertises in all local papers in June and July of each year, calling for applications for various specialist courses offered by the College. Interested teachers apply and prescribed forms are sent to them by the College. Completed forms are sent back to the Principal of the College, who sits down with the Head of the Department of Special Education for shortlisting of students. Those on the short list are invited for the interview around November of every year. The interview is there to assess the suitability of the cadres to be enrolled in the intensive one-year course. The leading team on the interviews consists of specialist lecturers from the Special Education Department, assisted by senior lecturers of the College's establishment. This Committee, which then selects prospective candidates, looks for:

- Reality of the students' choice. This is an issue of motivation, for some candidates are only interested in future prospects
- Dedication to the teaching service
- Attitude towards the handicapped
- Right temperament and personality for this kind of work
- Academic and professional qualifications

Considering the highly demanding nature of the work that the specialist teacher has before him, it is extremely important that the candidate possess certain personal qualities and traits necessary in meeting stresses and strains inherent in the job. Thus the teacher-to-be should be physically fit, emotionally stable, creative, resourceful, patient, persevering, and above all dedicated to the work. To achieve this, though it is not the case now, rigid screening has to be adopted as a policy.

Successful candidates are informed in mid-December and are required to report for the course in mid-January. Those teachers selected should inform the responsible authorities in their regions and should make their own arrangements for study leave. Also, teachers who are selected for specialist training are also required to sign an agreement to serve for a period of four years in any part of the country after the completion of the course, as directed by the Ministry of Education and Culture, a consumer Ministry.

All teachers attending the one-year, in-service course receive their full salary and live in boarding hostels free of charge.

Objectives of the Course in the Teaching of the Deaf

Our main objective in the designing of this course is the study focus "on total development and particular needs of the hearing impaired child. It also examines the opportunities that are available for their development."

As a result of the above, the course content is made up of the following components:

- **The Principles of Educational Treatment of Hearing Impairment.** This subject aims to introduce the students to the problems and issues of the deaf.

- **Historical Developments and Contemporary Provisions in the Education of the Hearing Impaired Child.** The students are expected to understand the developments in the education of the deaf and relate how the history of Zimbabwe has influenced the philosophy and methodology of the education of the hearing impaired.

- **Audiology, Anatomy, and Physiology of the Ear.** In this area, students acquire a knowledge of the cause and nature of hearing loss and methods of assessing it, including sensori-neural and conductive hearing losses and higher order hearing disabilities. This subject also discusses the basic anatomy and physiology of the ear, the disorders that affect it, and the cause of these disorders in relation to the learning problems of the hearing impaired. It also considers instrumentation for teachers of the deaf, including amplification devices.

- **Curriculum and Special Methods in Teaching.** This area considers the methodologies and settings employed in the education of hearing impaired children. In this area, students are

exposed as well to the complex controversies regarding communication with the deaf.

- **Language, Speech, and Speechreading.** This subject addresses the language development of normal hearing and hearing impaired children. It discusses the techniques employed to evaluate and promote the linguistic development of hearing impaired children. The students should be able to communicate expressively and be able to impart the basic principles governing either the Shona or the Ndebele language, and/or the English language. Shona and Ndebele are two major languages used in Zimbabwe respectively, depending on which part of the country one is residing in.

The subject also deals with the basic sciences of speech reception and production, the stages of speech development and production, and with the principles and methods of teaching speech to hearing impaired children at various ages.

The reader will notice that the Zimbabwean Syllabus, as described above, is based on that of reputable institutions abroad (e.g., Manchester, Birmingham, Newcastle, Mount Gravat, and Sint-Michielsgestel) but is specially adapted to Zimbabwean needs. The Zimbabwean teacher training program provides the student with a broad liberal education, a strong professional foundation, and an adequate knowledge in the field of specialization. To make our syllabus authentic, it is ratified and approved by (1) the Department of Teacher Education of the University of Zimbabwe, which certificates our teachers, (2) the Ministries of Higher Education, and (3) the Ministries of Education and Culture respectively. Our syllabus also calls for exposure of our teachers-in-training to present trends and needs, and thus elicits from each student a high degree of professional competence. Our syllabus is also revised from time to time so as not to fall behind the dynamism of changing training modes.

In the training course itself, the department tries to provide a balanced program of lectures, lecture-cum-discussions, library assignments, seminars, films, slides, peer-teaching, demonstration lessons, periodic tests, and visits to special schools and units. Handouts to augment students' notes are also issued during the course.

Teaching Practice

This is a practical element of the course that every student should undertake in order to be certificated. Properly organized, teaching practice is recognized as an important ingredient in the in-service as well as in the pre-service version of training in the institutions. Teaching practice for the Department of Special Education at the United College of Education is organized and supervised primarily by the staff of the department. It is understood in the College that each specialist department will devise arrangements to meet the needs of its own teachers. At present the teachers follow a six-week teaching practicum around the country. Throughout their teaching practice, all students are constantly supervised by the lecturing staff, the headmasters of the special schools, and other specially experienced teachers.

Also during the students' six-week teaching practicum, they are evaluated practically by an assessor sent by the University's Department of Teacher Education. This department of the University is the one responsible for the certification of these teachers.

United College of Education students carry out their teaching practice in five institutions, two of which are missionary centers, one which is administered by an association, and the final two, which are joint ventures of the government and charitable organizations. The missionary-related centers are Emerald Hill and Henry Murray School for the Deaf; Jairas Jiri Naran Center is an association-administered center; and King George VI and St. Giles are government-cum-charitable organization rehabilitation centers. Table 1 provides further information about these sites.

Table 1. Practicum Sites for Teacher Training in Zimbabwe

Name of Institution	Date Established	Type of Disability	Responsible Authority	Enrollment	Total Number of Teachers	Teachers Qualified to Teach H/Ican
Emerald Hill, Harare	1947	Hearing impaired only	Dominican Sisters (Catholic)	206	29	11
Henry Murray, Masvingo	1947	Hearing impaired only	Dutch Reformed Church	308	45	13
Jairos Jiri, Gweru	1968	Hearing impaired only	Jairos Jiri Association	290	53	10
St. Giles, Harare	1956	Children of different disabilities	Charitable organisation with Government	66	7	3
King George VI, Bulawayo	1953	Children of different disabilities	Charitable organisation with Government	60	8	4

All five institutions that offer educational programs to hearing impaired children cater to this type of disability, but the last two provide for a variety of disabilities, one of which is hearing handicap.

These institutions were established by private organizations without any centrally coordinated planning. This led to remarkable differences in many areas of their development, especially the absence of a standard manual communication system and the prevalence of different localized gestures and signs in the schools. That situation has caused quite a number of problems, especially to our students from some different institutions. For example, if a student-teacher from Henry Murray goes to practice at Emerald Hill, that teacher will have problems in signing, for the communication modes are diametrically different. Officials from the Ministry of Education and Culture and lecturers from the Ministry of Higher Education (the writer included) have sat down and started researching ways of standardizing sign language in Zimbabwe. This research is still in progress, but it is envisaged that after its completion it will enhance our special education system, especially education for the hearing impaired.

Conclusion

Zimbabwe, a third-world country and newly independent, is fortunate to have initiated professional training for teachers of the deaf. But how successful our training is can only be judged by the work our teachers do when they leave us. With great confidence in the ones we have already trained, I feel certain that they will bring continued credit to their College.

Whatever success we have been able to achieve has been due to the unstinted support given by the Department of Teacher Education of the University of Zimbabwe and the Ministry of Higher Education and to the loyal and enthusiastic lecturing staff, and the magnificent way in which heads and teachers in the practicing schools have shouldered responsibility.

References

Gwitimah, A.R., & Chimedza R.M. (1980). *Constraints in training teachers of the deaf in Zimbabwe.* Seminar paper given at the Commonwealth Society for the Deaf, University of Sussex, Brighton, England.

Singh, S. (1980). *Training teachers of the deaf in Malaysia.* Seminar paper given at the Commonwealth Society for the Deaf, University of Sussex, Brighton, England.

Summary and Conclusions

The education of the deaf has a long and illustrious history. In most of the 27 countries in this book, this history has followed common patterns. These highly significant and characteristic patterns provide a common thread to follow throughout this text.

Founding of Schools

Although no single overriding factor influenced the founding of schools for the deaf, perusal of Table 1, "Founding of Schools for the Deaf," indicates that schools in several countries were established by missionaries, monks, and other religious leaders whose aim was to assist the deaf in finding salvation. This proved to be the major goal of the education of the deaf during much of its history. In several countries, including the United States, deaf persons were instrumental in the creation of schools for the deaf. The good works, influence, and initiation of kings and queens, nobles, and wealthy philanthropists also led to the formation of schools in other nations.

The powerful influence of the "French" or manual system of teaching the deaf of Abbé de l'Épée and his successors and the "German" or "oral" system of Samuel Heinicke led many individuals to visit the schools of these pioneers and return to their respective countries and establish schools that reflect those of these giants in the field.

Table 1. Founding of Schools for the Deaf

Country	Year Founded	Founder	Background of Founder	Name of School	City
Australia	1860	Thomas Palteson, Fred Rose	deaf, deaf	New South Wales Victorian School	Sydney Melbourne
Canada	1831	Ronald McDonald	Trained by Gallaudet & Clerc		Champlain, Quebec
Czech Republic and Slovakia	1886	Kaspar Herman	nobleman	Prague Institution for the Deaf and Dumb	Prague
	1835	Liplovsky Mikulas	charitable institution		
Denmark	1806	Peter Castberg	physician for the deaf	Royal Institute	Copenhagen
France	1760	Abbé de l'Épée	monk	National Institute of Rue Saint Jacques	Paris
Germany	1770	Samuel Heinicke	cantor		Leipzig
Ghana	1957	Dr. Andrew Foster from the U.S.	educator, minister	Ghana Mission School for the Deaf	Osu
Greece	1937	Helen Patalidou	teacher sent to Clark School in U.S.	National Institute for the Protection of Deaf Mutes	Athens

cont.

Country	Year Founded	Founder	Background of Founder	Name of School	City
Hungary	1802		rich nobleman		Vac
India	1885	Dr. Leon Meurin M.R. T.H. Walsh	missionaries	The Bombay Institute for the Deaf	Bombay
Israel	1932	Mr. J.B. Hexter	teacher of the deaf from Berlin	Hebrew School for the Deaf	Jerusalem
Japan	1878	Taishiro Furukawa	teacher		Kyoto
Lebanon	1956		charitable institutions	Lebanon School for the Blind and Deaf	Baabda
Nepal	1966				Kathmandu
The Netherlands	1790	Henri Daniel Guyot	studied at de l'Épée's school in Paris	Institute for the Deaf	at Haren near Groningen
Nigeria	1958	Lagos Society for the Care of the Deaf	missionaries	Wesley Methodist School for the Deaf	Lagos
Norway	1825	Andreas Christian Moller	deaf		Trondheim
Poland	1816	Jakup Falkowski	priest		Szczuczn
Puerto Rico	1902	James F. Blenk	Mission Helpers of the Sacred Heart		Aquadilla
Saudi Arabia	1964		government	Al-Amal Institutes	Jeddah
Spain	1555	Dr. Pedro Ponce de Leon	priest	Class of deaf children	Burgos
	1795	Dr. Manuel Godoy	priest	The Royal School of the Deaf and Mute	Madrid
Sweden	1809	Par Aron Borg		Manilla School for the Deaf	Stockholm
Thailand	1958	M.R. Sermsri Kasemsri		Dusit School for the Deaf	Bangkok

Significant Events

Governmental and parliamentary action have played an integral part in the development of the education of the deaf in almost all of the countries included in this book. The influence of these governing bodies has led to mandatory education for deaf children. This mandatory education policy often included the number of years of education required, the location of schools, the curriculum to be used, the qualifications of teachers, and the required allocation of financial resources. In some nations the laws and policies agreed upon were not put into action, and the governmental structures created did not function. Pressure groups, advocacy groups, political action groups, and coalitions made up of parents, deaf individuals, concerned citizens, friends, and teachers have also played a major role in shaping the education of the deaf and the attitude of society towards the deaf. Wars, civil strife, and revolutions have been key factors. To a lesser extent, religion and the pronouncements of philosophers have played a part.

Educational Services and Placement Options

The scope of educational services provided to deaf individuals in the 27 countries included in this book range from a few years of elementary or primary education with a vocational focus to a full complement of educational services, beginning with infants who are deaf and their parents and ending with a comprehensive, academically oriented high school or postsecondary program. See Table 2 for classification of the educational services for the hearing impaired in these countries.

Table 2. **Educational Services for the Deaf and Hard of Hearing**

Country	Infant Ed. Deaf	Infant Ed. H.H.	Preschool Deaf	Preschool H.H.	Kindergarten Deaf	Kindergarten H.H.	Primary/Elementary Deaf	Primary/Elementary H.H.	Middle School Deaf	Middle School H.H.	Secondary Vocational Deaf	Secondary Vocational H.H.	Secondary Academic Deaf	Secondary Academic H.H.
Australia	X	X	X	X	X	X	X	X	X	X	X	X	X	X
Canada	X	X	X	X	X	X	X	X	X	X	X	X	X	X
Czech Republic and Slovakia			X	X	X	X	X	X	X	X	X			X
Denmark	X	X	X	X	X	X	X	X	X	X	X	X	X	X
Egypt							X	X						
El Salvador			X	X	X	X	X	X	X	X				
France	X	X	X	X	X	X	X	X	X	X	X	X	X	X
Germany			X	X	X	X	X	X	X	X	very	few	very	few
Ghana					X	X	X	X	very	few	very	few		
Greece			X	X	X	X	X	X	X	X	X	X	X	
Hungary			X	X	X	X	X	X	X	X	X	X	X	X
India			X	X	X	X	X	X	X	X	very	few	very	few
Israel					X	X	X	X	X	X	most	voc.		
Japan			X	X	X	X	X	X	X	X	X	X	X	X
Lebanon			X	X	X	X	X	X	very	few				
Nepal					X	X	X	X						
The Netherlands			X	X	X	X	X	X	X	X	X	X		
Nigeria					X	X	X	X	X	X	X	X		
Norway			X	X	X	X	X	X	X	X	X	X		
Poland					X	X	X	X	X	X	prim.	voc.		
Puerto Rico					X	X	X	X	X	X	X	X		
Saudi Arabia					X	X	X	X	X	X	X	very few	very	few
Spain			X	X	X	X	X	X	X	X	X	X		
Sweden			X	X	X	X	X	X	X	X	X	X		
Thailand			X	X	X	X	X	X	X	X	very	few		

Table 3. Educational Placement Options for Deaf and Hard of Hearing Students

Country	Residential Schools Deaf	H.H.	Self-Contained Day Schools Deaf	H.H.	Public School Classes Deaf	H.H.	Resource Rooms Deaf	H.H.	Integrated Itinerant Services Deaf	H.H.	Fully Integrated Deaf	H.H.
Australia	X	X	X	X	X	X	X	X	X	X	X	X
Canada	X	X	X	X	X	X	X	X	X	X	X	X
Czech Republic and Slovakia	X	X									X	
Denmark	X	X	X	X	X	X	X	X	X	X	X	X
Egypt			X	X								
El Salvador			X	X	X	X	X	X	X	X		
France	X	X	X	X	X	X	X	X	X	X	X	X
Germany	X	X			X	X	X	X	X	X	X	X
Ghana	X	X	X	X								
Greece	X	X	X	X	X	X						
Hungary	X	X				X			X		X	
India	X	X	X	X							very little	
Israel	X		X		X		X		X	X		
Japan	X	X	X	X	X	X			X	X	X	some
Lebanon	X	X							very few		very few	
Nepal	X											
The Netherlands	X		X						very few			
Nigeria	X		X									
Norway	X				X		X		X		X	
Poland	X		very few						very few		very few	
Puerto Rico	X		X						X		X	
Saudi Arabia	X		X		X		X		X		X very few	
Spain	X		X		X		X		X		X growing	
Sweden	X				X		X		X		X**	
Thailand	X				X		X		X		X 14%	

*Many have returned to schools for the deaf
** Depends upon individual merit.

Table 3 provides a picture of the educational placement options available for deaf and hard of hearing children. Placement options may be very limited or may provide a comprehensive array and combination of educational placement options.

Heavily populated urban areas tend to have a much broader choice of placement options than are available in isolated and rural areas. Material, financial, and personnel resources are usually very scarce and difficult to obtain in sparsely populated regions.

Hard of hearing children are educated in the same facilities as deaf children or in separate residential schools, self-contained classes in a public school, or they may be integrated into regular public school classrooms.

Curriculum

In some nations, educational programs for the deaf use the curriculum designated for the regular public school system. In others, the curriculum used is especially designed for children who are deaf. A third option is the use of a modified state-prescribed curriculum that adds content in those areas specific to the education of the deaf: auditory training, speech development, speechreading, and modified language development. Table 4 compares the curriculum of schools for hearing impaired students in 26 countries.

The percentage of deaf children who are integrated or mainstreamed into the regular

Table 4. Comparison of Curricula for Hearing Impaired Students Across 26 Countries

Country	Number of Schools	Students	Use Regular Public School Curriculum	Use Special Curriculum	Combined	No. of Years of Education	% Integrated into Regular Classes
Australia		6,000			x	5 or 6 to 14 or 16	50%
Canada	7, res.			x		12 years	signif. number
Czech Rep. and Slovakia	20, res.	2,500				9 years	very few
Denmark				x	10 years	signif. number	
Egypt	35, day school	5,144	x			10 years	very few
El Salvador	2	200				Preschool –age 18	very few
France	1	14,088					signif. number
Germany	77	14,000				10 years	signif. number
Ghana	12	485					12 years
Greece	6, res.	712			x	12 years	very few
Hungary	6, res.	1,426			x	10 years	H.H. only
India	436 sh	30,000				12 yrs., 10 levels	very few
Israel		42,000			x	9 years	deaf - few; H.H. - many
Japan	107 sh					9 years	Some*
Lebanon		409	x		8 years	none	
Nepal	6	383					
The Netherlands	5	1,200					
Nigeria	43						
Norway	1, res.	1,100					
Poland	22, res.	4,5002	x			14 years	
Puerto Rico	10 sh	2,426			12 years		small number
Saudi Arabia	83	2,526		x			
Spain							8 years
Sweden	8	493	x		10 years		
Thailand	9	3,0		x	9 years;	many K–12	14%, growing

public school system varies from country to country and ranges from no integration to over 50 percent. Integration may connote a comprehensive array of support services including sign language interpreters, notetakers, assistive listening devices, and real time captioning or no support services at all.

A significant percentage of deaf children are enrolled in special education programs specifically designed for their needs in highly industrialized countries such as Australia, Canada, France, Japan, Germany, Denmark, Sweden, and Norway. In many of the less developed countries, the percentage of deaf students provided an adequate education is very low. It is as low as 1.0 to 1.5 percent in Egypt and 30 percent or lower in several other countries.

Worldwide, the trend is moving away from educating children with a hearing loss in residential schools and towards educating them in regular public schools. This is especially true of hard of hearing children. These students may be partially or fully mainstreamed and may or may not receive the support of a resource room or itinerant teacher. One country, Norway, passed a decree in 1987 declaring that it would no longer support residential schools for the handicapped after a phase-out period.

On the other hand, other nations have attempted to integrate deaf students into regular public school classes with little success. This lack of success has led to a movement by many of the mainstreamed students back to the schools for the deaf. Prime examples of this outcome are Japan and Poland.

Many residential schools have become regional or national resource centers that provide the public school classes and integrated settings with support services and consultation. The services usually include audiological, communication, psychological, counseling, educational, and curricular support. These residential centers may provide the services of audiologists, speech pathologists, pedagogists, psychologists, physical therapists, occupational therapists, and social workers.

Wars and revolutions have curtailed or abolished educational services for deaf children in several countries in Europe, Africa, and the Middle East. Poland, Germany, and Lebanon are prime examples. In Poland during World War II, persons found teaching the deaf could be executed. In Germany during World War II, the deaf were considered as defective by the Nazi government and were sterilized or eliminated. Internal conflicts in Lebanon have caused education of the deaf to stop and start on a number of occasions.

Communication Philosophies

In the majority of nations, the communication philosophy or methodology that guides the education of the deaf has followed a predictable evolution. Those countries that began educating the deaf between the late 1700s and the mid-1800s usually followed the pioneering philosophy of the "French" or "manual" philosophy developed and promoted by Abbé de l' Épée at his school in Paris, or the "German" or "oral" philosophy created by Samuel Heinicke at his Leipzig school. Some took a middle ground and followed a communication methodology that used a combi-

nation of signs and speech. With a few switches from one camp to the other, the situation stayed constant until the second half of the 1800s.

The first International Congress on the Education of the Deaf, held in Milan, Italy, in 1880 marked the end of an era and the beginning of a new direction in the education of the deaf worldwide. At the Congress, resolutions were proposed and passed stating that the oral method of educating the deaf was preferable and that the use of signs was detrimental academically and socially and should be discouraged. From that time on, nearly all nations switched to the oral approach. This pattern continued unabated for nearly a century. Countries that initiated educational programs for the deaf between 1880 and the early 1970s almost unanimously adopted oral communication as the method of choice.

In the 1960s American Sign Language and the native sign languages of other countries became the object of study of several prominent researchers. This research indicated that American Sign Language and other native sign languages were full and complete visual language systems, equal to established verbal languages in their ability to be used as vehicles for effective communication.

Dissatisfaction with the academic performance of deaf children utilizing the prevailing communication systems (Babbidge, 1967)* coupled with new research on native sign languages, federal and state laws, and the development of "new" sign systems that followed the syntax of the spoken language of the country, set the stage for a change and welcomed in a new communication philosophy to the scene: Total Communication.

The phrase Total Communication was coined by Roy Holcomb, an American educator who was deaf, and advocated by David Denton, past superintendent of the Maryland School for the Deaf, and others. This philosophy

* Babbidge, H. D. (1965). Education of the deaf: A report to the Secretary of Health, Education, and Welfare by his advisory committee on the education of the deaf. Washington, DC: U. S. Dept. of Health, Education, and Welfare.

proposed that any and all expressive and receptive communication modalities, including signs and speech, would be utilized to achieve full communication efficiency. The child's individual needs would be the determining factor. The conversion to this approach began in the 1970s, and by the 1990s Total Communication had become one of the most prominent philosophies guiding the education of the deaf worldwide.

As we approach the third millennium, a new philosophical direction and communication methodology, the "bilingual, bicultural approach," is slowly gaining support. In this communication system the deaf are considered to be a cultural group with their own language—the native sign language of the country—and not a group with a disability or a defect that needs to be rectified. The native sign language of the country is used as the language of instruction, and the spoken and written language of the country is learned as a second language.

Cued speech, tactile approaches, systems using the manual alphabet, and coded sign systems that follow the syntax of the spoken language of the country are additional communication methodologies that have small but loyal followings.

A few countries have continued to follow primarily an oral approach (Czech Republic and Slovakia, Hungary, Saudi Arabia). Others continue to be primarily oral in communication philosophy but are moving slowly towards Total Communication (Germany, Greece, India, Lebanon, Spain). Another group of nations, although still using the oral approach to some extent, advocates Total Communication (Australia, Egypt, France, Israel, Japan, Nepal, Nigeria, Puerto Rico, Thailand). The following countries use a combination of both communication systems: Denmark, El Salvador, Ghana, Poland. Canada, The Netherlands, Norway, and the United States are primarily following the Total Communication philosophy but are moving slowly towards a bilingual, bicultural approach. In one country, Sweden, the bilingual, bicultural approach has become the most common system.

Technological advances in the form of improved hearing aids and other listening devices and expanded use of improved cochlear implants may result in a resurgence of the oral-aural communication methodology in programs for deaf and hard of hearing children. This trend should continue in future years.

The bilingual-bicultural movement should also continue to attract new advocates as the millennium approaches. What additional new communication methodologies may emerge or old ones resurface in the coming years is anyone's guess.

Sign Communication

The three sign systems most commonly used for instruction in schools for the deaf are the native sign language of the country, a sign language system that parallels the syntax of the verbal language, and a "pidgin" sign language system that is a combination of the other two.

The First International Congress on the Education of the Deaf ushered in a period of nearly a century when sign language was discredited. The poor academic performance of deaf children with all current communication methods and research on sign language has brought renewed interest in the use of a visual communication system to educate deaf children.

Countries that have followed the oral tradition are now researching their native sign systems (Germany, India, Lebanon) or have or are developing native sign language dictionaries (Australia, 1975; India, 1980; Lebanon, in the works; Nepal, 1987; Thailand, 1980s; Puerto Rico, 1988). In some nations several native sign languages are in use, and no one system has been adopted as the standard for the country (Nigeria, Ghana, Thailand, Zimbabwe).

Whether to use the native sign language or a sign system that parallels the verbal language of the country is an argument that has continued from the inception of the education of the deaf until today. Of the countries surveyed, the controversy continues in the following countries: Czech Republic and Slovakia, France, The Netherlands, and Spain. Teachers, parents, and other professionals tend to support the use of a sign system patterned after the spoken language, whereas deaf adults, some teachers, and parents tend to support the use of the native sign language as the language of instruction. Most likely this controversy will not be resolved in the foreseeable future. Definitive research must be produced to indicate that children who are deaf have significantly improved academic performance with one sign system or the other.

Academic Performance

Most chapter authors did not provide definitive statistics covering the academic performance of deaf and hard of hearing students in their respective countries. Yet the statistics and commentaries that were provided uniformly indicate that deaf children were significantly behind their hearing counterparts in almost all academic areas, and especially in the use of the common spoken and written language or languages of the country.

Comments indicated that in some nations, those deaf and hard of hearing children who were integrated into the regular education system seemed to be performing better academically than those at the residential schools. It was noted by the authors that the mainstreamed students tended to have more usable hearing and come from a higher socioeconomic strata. In other countries the opposite was true. Many students had left the integrated classrooms and returned to the residential schools.

Some promising reports of improved academic performance were received from Sweden and other nations that have introduced the native sign language of the country at a very early age. Early identification, enrollment in early intervention programs, and use of advanced hearing aids and cochlear implants hold significant promise for improved academic performance.

Parent Education, Early Identification, and Early Intervention Services

Parent education, early intervention, and early childhood programs vary widely from no services for deaf infants and their parents to an extensive and comprehensive array of services. Table 2 provides evidence of which countries have services for this age group. As more countries realize the importance of early identification, intervention, and educational services for deaf and hard of hearing infants, toddlers, and their parents, these vital services should become more widespread.

Vocational and Career Education

Vocational education and training opportunities for students who are deaf ranged from none provided (Nepal), to little (Greece, India, Lebanon, Nigeria, El Salvador), to extensive (Germany, Hungary, Poland, Sweden, Saudi Arabia).

Very few nations indicated that career education, job placement, and follow-up services were provided (Australia, Hungary, Israel, Saudi Arabia).

Vocational training is included as part of the curriculum in almost all of the residential schools for the deaf. In several it made up a substantial part of the curriculum (Thailand, India, Saudi Arabia). Traineeships and apprenticeships are mentioned as available in Australia, the Czech Republic and Slovakia, Denmark, Germany, and Thailand. In Australia, Hungary, Poland, and Thailand the adult deaf organization of the country provides vocational education, apprenticeships, career education, and job placement services and follow-up.

A majority of the countries also provide special trade schools for the deaf or permit deaf students to attend trade schools established for those who can hear normally. Students who are hard of hearing usually attend the trade schools set up for hearing students. Very few trade schools provided the needed support services, including interpreters, notetakers, and listening devices.

Several nations (Australia, Denmark, Israel, Saudi Arabia, Sweden, Thailand) have created a governmental agency that is similar to the vocational rehabilitation agencies found in the United States. These agencies are responsible for career assessment, vocational education, job training, job placement, and follow-up.

Underemployment and unemployment were reported as major problems among the deaf population in a number of countries. Jobs for deaf people are virtually nonexistent in Nepal. Australia cited an unemployment rate of 37 percent and Puerto Rico 33 percent. Thailand indicated that 49 percent of the deaf population had never been employed and that the percentage among women was substantially higher.

For those who did find work, jobs were concentrated in a limited number of semi-skilled occupational areas (shoemaker, tailor, dressmaker, housepainter, power machine operator, printer, farm worker). In Australia, only 1 percent of the deaf population was employed in the professions, as administrators or supervisors. This situation was found to be common in most countries. Laws have been passed by the parliaments of Egypt, India, Sweden, and a few more nations that require a certain percentage of all available jobs be set aside for the disabled citizens of the country. In Egypt it is 5 percent, and in India, 3 percent.

Laws passed by governing bodies and the general attitude of the citizens towards the disabled have made employment opportunities plentiful in the following countries:

Denmark, Egypt, Hungary, Saudi Arabia, and Sweden.

Postsecondary Opportunities for the Deaf

The enrollment of students who are deaf in institutions of higher education ranges from no enrollment in some nations to a special technical college developed specifically for the deaf. Table 5 compares postsecondary opportunities for deaf students among the nations listed.

Currently no deaf students, or very few, are enrolled in colleges or universities in the countries of Egypt, El Salvador, Lebanon, and Nepal. A very small number are found enrolled in Greece, India, Puerto Rico, Saudi Arabia, and Thailand. The nations of Australia, France, Germany, Hungary, Israel, Nigeria, and Poland provide an open door enrollment policy, but few deaf students can master the required entrance exams or have the required educational background for admission.

The nations listed above that do permit deaf students to enroll usually provide inadequate support services. Adequate support services including sign language interpreters, notetakers, and assistive listening devices, are available only in Denmark, Japan (Tsukaba Technical College only), Spain, and Sweden, and to a limited degree in France and Germany.

In general, higher education opportunities for hard of hearing students are far greater than those for deaf students in most of the nations represented. In a few countries (Hungary, The Netherlands, Nigeria) enrollment in colleges or universities is limited to the areas of special education or teacher preparation. In Denmark all universities are open to the deaf.

A number of students who are deaf are enrolled in Griffith University in Australia and at the University of Alberta, University of

Table 5. Overview of Teacher Preparation and Postsecondary Opportunities for Deaf Students

Country	Program Length	Number of Programs	Program Level	Date of Origin	Communication Philosophy	Certification	Deaf Teachers	Deaf Students in Higher Education
Australia	3 years or post BA	5	BA or Masters	early	Oral TC	yes	few	few who are academ. qualified
Canada	1 year	4	Masters	1983	TC	yes	several	open
Czech. Republic and Slovakia	*	several	Post BA	*	Oral/Aural	no	none	hard of hearing or late deafened
Denmark	4-year program + 2 year intern	several	BA + Post BA Internship	*	Oral TC	yes	few, but improving	gifted deaf student at Gallaudet
Egypt	1 year BA program	2	BA/Post BA	*	Oral	no	none	none
El Salvador		0	0	0	Oral TC	no	one	very few
France	*	*	*	*	Oral TC	*	few	few
Germany	4 or 5 yr. BA	2 yr grad prog.	5	BA or Grad level	Oral	yes	few	few
Ghana	3 years	1	BA	1967	Col oral Sch TC	no	few	none
Greece	1 year inservice	1	inservice	*	Oral	no	few	few
Hungary	4 years	4	BA	*	Oral , TC	yes	several	several
India	1 year and 4 years	13	diploma (12)BA, Post BA, (1) and MA (1)	1983	Oral , TC	no	few	few
Israel	4 years	1	BA and post BA	1964	Oral , TC	yes	very few	very few
Japan	4 year +	8	BA (6) MA (2)	*	Oral	no	few	few
Lebanon	1 year	1	*	1986	Oral	no	very few	none
The Netherlands	4 year+	0	BA + 1 year	*	Oral, TC	yes	one	very few
Nepal	*	*	*	*	Oral , TC	no	none	none
Nigeria	3 year and 4 year	4	BA ,MA , Ph.D.	1974	Oral, TC	yes	few	several
Norway	2 years	10	Post grad, Ph.D.	1976	TC	yes	several	*
Poland	2 year and five year	10	BA and Post BA	1872	Oral , TC	no	few	few

cont.

Country	Program Length	Number of Programs	Program Level	Date of Origin	Communication Philosophy	Certification	Deaf Teachers	Deaf Students in Higher Education
Puerto Rico	2 years	1	MA	1986	Oral, TC	no	few	few
Saudi Arabia	6 months or 4 years	2	inservice, BA	1978	*	*	*	*
Spain	3 years	2	BA	*	Oral , TC	yes	no	no
Sweden	1 year Post BA	1	Post BA	*	Bilingual	yes	few but growing	few but growing
Thailand	4 years	6	BA, Post Grad and MA	1969	Oral , TC		very few	very few
Zimbabwe	2 year 4 year	1	Inservice, BA	1986	Oral , TC	yes	few	few

*information not supplied

Western Ontario, and Nova Scotia's St. Mary's College in Canada. In Spain and Sweden, students who are deaf are admitted to a number of institutions of higher education.

Of all of the nations only Tsukaba Technical College in Japan, which has been patterned after the National Technical Institute for the Deaf in the United States, was developed to service deaf students.

The major stumbling blocks that must be overcome in order to increase enrollment in colleges and universities are: the continuing attitude among the citizenry of some countries that deaf individuals are not capable of successfully completing a college or university education, and the unavailability of elementary and secondary education opportunities of a sufficiently high quality to provide students who are deaf with the knowledge, concepts and skills needed to pass the required entrance exams. The lack of adequate support services for those students who do manage to be enrolled is another major hindrance.

Globally, college and university opportunities for students who are deaf are improving slowly but are still far from being adequate or acceptable.

Teachers of the Deaf Who Are Deaf

During the early history of the education of the deaf, teachers of the deaf who were deaf themselves made up a significant percentage of school faculties. In fact, deaf persons are responsible for the development of the first schools for the deaf in several countries. Dr. Andrew Foster, an educator and minister from the United States, who started the education of the deaf in several African countries in the 1950s, is a notable example.

The First International Congress on the Education of the Deaf, held in Milan, Italy, in 1880, marked a worldwide change in the communication methodology used to teach deaf children. With the change from the manual method of Abbé Charles de l'Épée to the oral system of Samuel Heinicke came the demise of the careers of most deaf teachers of the deaf. From that period on, persons who were deaf were either fired or moved to lowly nonacademic positions such as dormitory counselor, arts and crafts instructor, or teacher assistant. No new deaf teachers were hired. This situation continued for nearly a century and did not begin to change until recent years. In some nations persons who are deaf are still not eligible to be teachers of the deaf (Czech Republic and Slovakia, Egypt, Nepal, Saudi Arabia).

The absence of adequate academic preparation at the elementary and secondary level including needed language competencies, medical reasons including the provision that one must hear normally, the absence of necessary support services, the oral tradition of the country, and the continuing attitude of society that views a person who is deaf as not capable of achieving a college education are the major barriers to employment as a teacher.

In some countries these barriers have been broken down, and teachers who are deaf are considered to be a critical and needed part of the faculty of schools for the deaf. It is argued that only a person who is deaf can provide an appropriate role model or teach the native sign language of the country effectively. New antidiscrimination and fair employment legislation and governmental decrees have cleared away obstacles and permitted persons who are deaf to compete for teaching positions on an equal basis. The change in communication philosophy away from the oral method to a Total communication or bilingual philosophy has provided job opportunities for deaf teachers of the deaf. Table 5 indicates the employment status of individuals who are deaf in each nation.

Currently, the number of countries that hire deaf teachers of the deaf is small. As the obstacles that now impede the employment of qualified individuals are eliminated, the number of nations that hire persons who are deaf should increase markedly.

Teacher Preparation

The teacher preparation programs in the 27 countries represented in this book cover the full range of possibilities, from those that are fully able to prepare teachers who can provide quality instruction to deaf and hard of hearing students to those that offer little or no preparation. Effective programs are found in Australia, Canada, the Czech Republic and Slovakia, Denmark, Germany, Hungary, Israel, The Netherlands, Norway, Nigeria, France, Spain, and Sweden. Those countries that provide teacher education programs that fall somewhere between effective and ineffective include Egypt, Ghana, Greece, India, Japan, Poland, Puerto Rico, Saudi Arabia, and Thailand. El Salvador, Lebanon, and Nepal bring up the low end of the teacher preparation spectrum, providing little or no opportunity for a person to become a teacher of the deaf.

During the early period of the history of education of the deaf, teachers of the deaf from Australia, Greece, Lebanon, Nigeria, and Saudi Arabia received their teacher preparation in foreign countries. Great Britain, France, and Germany were the nations most responsible for the preparation of these individuals. Middle Eastern countries looked to Egypt as a place where people could receive the preparation necessary to become a teacher of the deaf. Ghana served the same function for several African nations.

Immigrants and missionaries, as well as citizens who traveled to other countries to learn the craft, were often instrumental in the establishment of new teacher preparation programs. These people brought with them the educational philosophy, communication methodology, and pedagogy learned in other nations (Egypt, Israel, Poland, Saudi Arabia).

Table 5 and the chapters included from each nation clearly indicate that the configuration of teacher preparation programs varies greatly from country to country. This is particularly true in the areas of program length, course of study, course sequence, prerequisites, balance between theory and practice, amount and availability of practicum, and required prerequisite academic level.

There is a significant correlation between the level of economic development in each country and the development of teacher preparation opportunities. Developing countries often have limited financial, material, and manpower resources and have higher and more basic needs and priorities than the establishment of special education and the development of programs to prepare teachers of the deaf (Egypt, El Salvador, India, Lebanon, Nepal).

Changes in communication methods from an oral approach to Total Communication (Ghana, India, Israel) or a bilingual approach (Sweden) has had a major effect upon the curriculum of teacher education programs. In general, but not in all cases, preparation programs reflect the communication philosophy of the educational programs for students who are deaf in the nation.

The goal in some countries of integrating children who are deaf into the regular public school system has a significant impact upon the content of teacher preparation programs (Norway). The role of the teacher has changed from one in which the person is in charge of a self-contained classroom of children to that of an itinerant or consultant teacher who has much less direct contact with students. The competencies required to consult, collaborate, tutor, and be a member of an instructional team are vastly different than those required of a self-contained classroom teacher. This modification in teacher roles has resulted in major changes in the curriculum of teacher education programs.

Some teacher preparation programs have been and are still being restricted because of political interference and wars. During World War II in Poland and other European countries, teacher education programs ceased to operate. Civil strife in several Middle Eastern and African countries has also curtailed the preparation of teachers of the deaf.

Internal problems in the form of faculty members' lack of motivation, commitment, or proper training have restricted the establishment of suitable practicum experiences and adequate practicum supervision (Japan). The lack of balance between theory and practice, with theory far in excess of practice, has also hindered the development of adequate teacher education programs (Egypt, Japan).

Often, those who do complete a training program have little interest or commitment to the field and transfer at the first opportunity from a classroom for children who are deaf to a classroom for children who hear (Japan, Thailand).

In Ghana and other countries, the pedagogy and communication philosophy that underpins the curriculum of the preparation program is out of step or has no relationship to that used in the schools for the deaf. The graduates of these teacher education programs are unable to provide adequate educational services.

Another common drawback to the preparation of quality teachers is the lack of a standardized sign language (Ghana, India, Lebanon, Zimbabwe). Since the sign system varies from school to school, it is impossible for training centers to provide the instruction and practicum required for sign communication competency.

In Egypt, Greece, India, Japan, Lebanon, Nepal, Poland, Saudi Arabia, and several other countries, the number of teachers produced each year by the existing teacher education institutions is far less than that needed to meet the growing demand.

Although the preparation of teachers of the deaf has far to go before the quality and quantity of the teachers produced is adequate to meet world needs, several countries are successfully meeting the challenge and more should follow in future years. A promising note is that persons who are deaf make up part of the teacher education faculty in Canada, the United States, and a few other countries.

Needs

All 27 nations included in this book indicated needs that must be met before the quality of educational services for deaf and hard of hearing children and adults can be improved. Listed below in descending order are the major needs that were expressed:

- Provide enough well-trained teachers who can supply quality instruction to

deaf and hard of hearing children.
(12 countries)

- Improve the quality of teacher preparation. (10 countries)
- Provide an adequate supply of hearing aids, and proper hearing aid evaluation, fitting, and service. (10 countries)
- Change societal attitudes to one that views the deaf as capable of learning and contributing positively to society. (9 countries)
- Provide improved quality educational services. (9 countries)
- Develop an early identification program. (9 countries)
- Develop or improve support services and support personnel; i.e., interpreters, speech pathologists, audiologists, psychologists, and so on. (9 countries)
- Develop or improve vocational education, career development, apprenticeships, job placement services. (9 countries)
- Improve academic performance. (9 countries)
- Provide modern equipment and technology. (8 countries)
- Develop or improve parent education, parent counseling, and create parent organizations. (8 countries)
- Develop or improve curriculum for deaf and hard of hearing students. (7 countries)
- Provide improved quality and quantity of instructional materials. (6 countries)
- Create or improve employment possibilities. (6 countries)
- Develop appropriate assessment tools. (6 countries)
- Provide or improve facilities. (6 countries)
- Overcome the problem of multiple languages spoken, read, and signed. (6 countries)
- Create or improve early identification/intervention/early childhood programs. (6 countries)
- Develop or improve postsecondary opportunities. (5 countries)
- Develop or improve adult education opportunities. (5 countries)
- Provide adequate funding. (5 countries)
- Create or improve secondary school opportunities. (4 countries)
- Increase the number of deaf and hard of hearing children served. (4 countries)
- Develop or improve educational services to sparsely populated rural regions. (4 countries)
- Develop services for deaf and hard of hearing children who possess multiple disabilities. (3 countries)
- Develop or improve research on deafness. (3 countries)
- Provide assistive devices, i.e., captioned television, teletype devices, and signal systems. (3 countries)
- Develop resource rooms, itinerant services, and improved opportunities for integration into the regular public school system. (2 countries)
- Provide higher salaries to teachers and support personnel. (2 countries)
- Provide additional sign language classes. (2 countries)
- Improve services for a country's native population. (2 countries)
- Establish a stable government. (1 country)
- Provide improved services for hard of hearing students. (1 country)
- Develop a program for gifted deaf and hard of hearing students. (1 country)

Current Issues and Directions

As the world approaches the new millennium, the major issues that face the 27 countries included in this text are strikingly similar. The directions countries are taking to confront these issues are discussed below:

1. The Proper Placement of Deaf and Hard of Hearing Students. For most of the history of the education of the deaf, students were educated in residential schools. In recent years enrollments in many residential schools have declined. Special classes in public school districts, or integration into classes for normally hearing children, have become popular placement options. This trend is escalating and more deaf children are being mainstreamed for all or part of the school day.

Because of enrollment declines, the future of residential schools has become a topic of public debate. In Norway, for example, most of the schools for the deaf have either closed or are scheduled to close in the near future. Residential schools for the deaf have also closed in Australia, Canada, Spain, and the United States. In coming years the disposition of residential schools for the deaf and the merits of full- or part-time integration will continue to be major topics of discussion.

2. The Optimum Communication System. Although the "methods" controversy continues in many nations, several trends are emerging. A number of countries that followed the oral tradition for nearly a century are moving towards the use of the Total Communication philosophy. Other nations are continuing to staunchly support oral-aural methodology. Some countries that have advocated the use of the Total Communication philosophy in the past, are moving towards increased use of the bilingual, bicultural model of educating the deaf.

A controversy common among advocates of the Total Communication philosophy is whether to use the native sign language or an invented sign system that follows the word order of the common spoken and written language of the nation. This controversy, which traces its origin back to the time of Abbé de l'Épée, has gained new vigor and strong supporters on both sides of the issue. With the lack of clear and convincing evidence of the superiority of one position over the other, the methodology controversy will continue to generate heated debates in years to come.

The rise in the use of cochlear implants and their continued improvement may have significant implications for future methodology of choice and may precipitate a rebirth of the popularity of the oral-aural method of educating the deaf.

3. Attitude of Society. Although attitudes tend to change slowly, the general direction worldwide is towards greater acceptance of deaf individuals and recognition that they are capable of achieving academically and vocationally and deserve equal rights and opportunities.

Political pressure applied by parents and deaf adults has forced the passage of legislation that has helped ensure improved equal rights and opportunities in education and employment. This pressure has led to increased budgets, new and improved facilities, curriculum, educational services, equipment, materials, and more qualified teachers. This trend should continue and spread.

This direction is not universal, however. In some countries children who are deaf are still considered to be a reflection of the sins of the parents, generators of bad Karma, and human beings who are incapable of learning or meaningful employment.

4. Sign Language, Deaf Culture. Research, change in attitude, advocacy of deaf adults, and changes in the communication systems used to teach the deaf have led to renewed interest in the native sign language and culture of the deaf community. Byproducts of this new interest are the creation of sign classes and sign language dictionaries in countries where they did not exist, and the hiring of deaf adults as teachers and teacher assistants. This trend should grow stronger in future years as the appreciation of the strengths, qualities and potential of the deaf population is fully recognized.

5. Early Intervention/Early Childhood. The critical value of early diagnosis, intervention, and education to the academic and linguistic progress of deaf children is almost universally recognized. Early intervention and early education services are improving, and more and more countries are developing new or improved services for deaf infants and their parents. This is a key element in the general worldwide improvement of educational services for children who are deaf.

6. Support Services, Assistive Devices. The majority of countries discussed in this book have some distance to go before the provision of adequate support personnel, including well-qualified interpreters, speech pathologists, audiologists, and psychologists, is realized. The general availability of assistive devices such as teletype devices and captioned television is another area of great need. Currently, few nations have an adequate supply of assistive devices. Increased public awareness and continued advocacy on the part of parents and the deaf community will be great assets in meeting these needs in the future.

7. Teacher Preparation. An adequate supply of well-qualified teachers was noted as the most common concern among the nations included in this book. Very few countries have enough teachers to meet current needs and do not provide prospective teachers with the preparation necessary to present a quality education to deaf and hard of hearing children.

The recruitment of qualified deaf and hard of hearing people to become teachers of the deaf is finally being recognized as a priority need. Currently very few deaf people are engaged in teacher education because of legal, academic, and attitudinal roadblocks. These barriers to the acceptance of deaf individuals as teachers are slowly being eliminated and the future looks positive.

Conclusion

The education of the deaf has made much progress during its 400-year history but still has a long road to follow before optimum educational opportunities are available. Hopefully, this book will provide a resource, a tool, and a perspective that can assist nations of the world in continuing this progress towards the goal of a quality education for all deaf and hard of hearing children on this planet.